DEBATES IN THE DIGITAL HUMANITIES 2019

DEBATES IN THE DIGITAL HUMANITIES

2019

Matthew K. Gold and Lauren F. Klein

EDITORS

DEBATES IN THE DIGITAL HUMANITIES

University of Minnesota Press
Minneapolis
London

Published by the University of Minnesota Press
111 Third Avenue South, Suite 290
Minneapolis, MN 55401-2520
http://www.upress.umn.edu

ISSN 2380-5927
ISBN 978-1-5179-0692-4 (hc)
ISBN 978-1-5179-0693-1 (pb)

Printed in the United States of America on acid-free paper

The University of Minnesota is an equal-opportunity educator and employer.

26 25 24 23 22 21 20 19   10 9 8 7 6 5 4 3 2 1

Contents

A DH That Matters

MATTHEW K. GOLD AND LAUREN F. KLEIN

What matters in 2019?

On the surface of things, not much. In the United States, we have seen "fake news" take the place of informed reporting, "free speech" replace equal protection, and personal profiteering vault a chaos agent into the role of commander in chief. There he remains, secured by a welter of corporate interests, conservative media moguls, GOP enablers, and a vocal minority of the U.S. citizenry who find the rhetoric of racism, sexism, xenophobia, and generalized vitriol more appealing than the aspiration of a more perfect union. Events that only a few years ago seemed impossible—the intentional destruction of the nation's social safety net, open rallies of armed white supremacists, and even the prospect of nuclear war—have become part and parcel of our daily lives.

What is the role of the digital humanities in the charged environment of 2019, and how can digital humanists ally themselves with the activists, organizers, and others who are working to empower those most threatened by it? Having spent nearly a decade immersed in the *Debates in the Digital Humanities* series, and even longer in the field, we are convinced that digital humanists can contribute significantly to a larger technically and historically informed resistance. By enabling communication across communities and networks, by creating platforms that amplify the voices of those most in need of being heard, by pursuing projects that perform the work of recovery and resistance, and by undertaking research that intervenes in the areas of data surveillance and privacy, the "artist-theorists, programming humanists, activist-scholars, theoretical archivists, [and] critical race coders" whom Tara McPherson, writing in the first volume of *Debates in the Digital Humanities*, called into being, have now been united with their task (154).

Indeed, this work has already begun. Media design professor David Carroll, for instance, was the one to the file the lawsuits that helped bring to light the problematic data mining of Facebook user data by Cambridge Analytica in the run-up to the 2016 election. The coalition of activists, organizers, and statisticians who, in

2017, established the group Data for Black Lives are mobilizing the field of data science around issues of racial justice. From within the digital humanities, we have seen the rise to prominence of the Colored Conventions Project, which exemplifies how principles of collective organizing can inform both project structure and research focus. We have also seen how DHers can mobilize in response to immediate need, as in the distributed efforts of DH centers around the United States that held participatory mapping events in the wake of Hurricanes Irma and Maria with a goal of improving the routing of aid to Puerto Rico; and we have seen the collective work of *Mobilized Humanities*, an outgrowth of the hurricane mapping project, which created the website *Torn Apart* / Separados in response to the U.S. policy of separating immigrant children from their parents. These examples are by no means exhaustive, but they demonstrate how digital humanists, as well as scholars and practitioners in an expanding set of allied fields, can contribute in concrete and meaningful ways to improving the situation of those most affected by the toxic turn brought about by the 2016 presidential election and its aftermath.

The chapters in this volume were drafted before the 2016 election, and we ourselves write in the middle of 2018. To the degree that, in advance of the present moment, our authors demonstrated a commitment to advocacy and engagement, their words represent the embers of a fire that has since burst into flame. Had this work been compiled any later, we believe that it would have focused even more clearly than it already does on the profound transformations wrought on the national and international landscape. After all, the digital humanities has always seen itself as a field that engages the world beyond the academy—through its orientation toward the public in its scholarship, pedagogy, and service; through its calling attention to issues of academic labor and credit for the same; through its questioning of ossified institutional structures and outmoded scholarly systems; and through its attention to how digital methods can help prepare students for both academic and nonacademic careers. But the events that have transpired since the 2016 election demand a more explicit assertion of these beliefs, and evidence that we are translating these beliefs into action. Now is a time when digital humanists can usefully clarify our commitments to public scholarship, addressing our work not simply to "the public" but also, as Sheila Brennan has observed, to specific communities and the needs that they, and not we, identify as most pressing (386). Now is a time when we can employ our visibility in the academy to advocate for those whose contributions to digital scholarship remain undervalued. Now is a time when we can model how research undertaken by students and scholars who are both technically adept and critically informed can matter, not only to our chosen fields but also to the world at large.

As this work progresses, we must take care to acknowledge the myriad forms of labor that underlie it. By entering into conversation with our institutional administrations about how those who contribute this crucial work can reap the benefits of more stable employment, we can do our part to shore up the university itself, which has begun to show fissures brought about by decades of legislative defunding and corporate influence. As individuals and as a field, we must interrogate our work to ensure that we are not ourselves complicit in the neoliberal practice of naming problems in order to evade their resolution, or that the attention and resources bestowed on digital scholarship and DH centers do not eclipse the work of others who have provided us with the foundation, both intellectual and institutional, for our work. Ultimately, we must each ask ourselves if our service and scholarship, and the field in which we place this work, are sufficiently committed to addressing the problems we face in the present moment. And if the answer to that question remains unclear, we must look to ourselves to recalibrate our own—and our discipline's—scholarly stance.

We have traveled far from the issues that framed the first volume of *Debates in the Digital Humanities,* published in 2012 during the first term of the Obama administration. Then, the key questions facing digital humanities had to do with the impact of digital methods and scholarship on the academy. When, for instance, Tom Scheinfeldt, then managing director of the Roy Rosenzweig Center for History and New Media at George Mason University, posed the question of whether the field was required to "produce new arguments" and "answer" new research questions, he was able to argue convincingly that digital humanities needed more time to mature, to experiment, and to play (56–58). His short piece, originally posted on his blog, was an attempt to stake out space for low-stakes inquiry and non-goal-oriented exploration in the face of demands from DH skeptics that the field justify its emergence by presenting clear evidence of research impact. But as the field has matured, the question of how digital humanities relates to a larger world that is itself in crisis has added a new urgency to questions about the value of digital scholarship and methods.

Our work within the digital humanities is enabled by larger social, political, and technological systems. In the present moment, we need work that exposes the impact of our embeddedness in those larger systems and that brings our technical expertise to bear on the societal problems that those systems sustain. Such work is exemplified by scholars such as Safiya Noble, who reveals the racist assumptions planted in the algorithms that power Google searches (*Algorithms of Oppression*); Marie Hicks, who illustrates the history of gender discrimination that has contributed to the inequities of representation in technological fields (*Programmed Inequality*); Lisa Nakamura, who exposes the physical and intellectual exploitation at the heart of hardware manufacture ("Indigenous Circuits"); Kathleen Fitzpatrick, who highlights the unscrupulous corporate networks that masquerade as research platforms ("Academia, Not Edu"); and many others who work at the intersection of technology and social justice. Their scholarship enables us to confirm, without a doubt, how social and cultural biases pervade our technologies, infrastructures, platforms, and devices. Digital humanities in the year 2019 might thus be said to be driven by an imperative, both ethical and intellectual, to acknowledge how history, culture, society, and politics overdetermine each and every one of our engagements with our work and the tools that enable it. We must therefore commit to making a digital humanities that matters beyond itself, one that probes the stakes and impacts of technology across a range of institutions and communities.

In our introduction to *Debates in the Digital Humanities 2016,* we offered Rosalind Krauss's formulation of the "expanded field" as a model that might help move us away from thinking about the digital humanities as a "big tent," with its attendant questions of who or what is included within it, toward a conception of DH as a set of vectors of inquiry that are defined by their tensions, alignments, and oppositions (x). A few years later, as the world careens from crisis to crisis, the expanded field model may still work, but it must more clearly account for work outside of digital humanities and outside of the academy. Models, as Richard Jean So reminds us, are meant to be applied in a self-reflexive fashion: one runs the model over a dataset and refines that model iteratively over time. Our expanded field model is no different; we must pause to take account of work currently in formation that indicates powerful new directions for the field. The rough shape of those directions is indicated by, for instance, the 2016 launch of the African American History, Culture and Digital Humanities (AADHum) project at the University of Maryland, which seeks to center African American history and culture in digital humanities inquiry; the 2017 Digital Library Federation conference, which featured keynotes by community arts activists alongside academic librarians and archivists, placing those fields in dialogue; the location of the 2018 *Digital Humanities* conference in Mexico City, which affirmed the global outlook and multilingual aspirations of the field; and the increasingly substantive efforts to expand DH work at HBCUs, tribal colleges, and community colleges. What is signaled by these wide-ranging efforts is a DH practice that is one part of a larger expanded field of socially oriented work—work that is informed by the digital, but extends beyond it.

As the variety of DH scholarship proliferates—to borrow a phrase from the forthcoming special issue of *PMLA* on the topic—it is increasingly being published in a range of established disciplinary venues. The publication of special issues of prominent journals—not only *PMLA* but also *American Literature, American Quarterly, The Black Scholar, differences, South Asian Review,* and *Visible Language,* among others—is an important marker of growth for the digital humanities. But a special issue of a journal is what signals the arrival of a field; the next phase occurs when articles that draw from that field appear regularly in those same journals in what Ted Underwood describes in Chapter 10 in this volume as a "semi-normal thing." Today, DH articles appear in disciplinary journals such as *ELH, NLH, Configurations,* and *PMLA* integrated with articles that take a range of different approaches. This transformation speaks as much to the goals of DH scholars, who are seeking to make their digital work relevant to their colleagues, as it does to the evolving status of digital humanities within extant scholarly fields.

Also at work in the digital humanities in 2019 is a deepening and narrowing of scholarly niches within the field: this is another result of the field's maturation. We are witnessing sophisticated developments within subfields of digital humanities that result in scholarship that is not always fully legible to those not versed in the particular methods or conversations taking place in that domain; see, for instance, the recent growth of the *Journal of Cultural Analytics* or the increasingly nuanced discussions of method in digital history. Accompanying this scholarship are calls for some subfields of digital humanities to split from it altogether, motivated by critiques from the outside that are perceived as uninitiated or uninformed. And yet, for the digital humanities to achieve its strongest impact, its subfields must remain in dialogue with each other, open to criticism in general terms if not specifics. Our principal task may no longer be to define or defend digital humanities to skeptical outsiders, but instead to translate the subtleties of our research to others within the expanded field—a project that can help DH matter beyond itself.

Perhaps this shift is a good thing for a series like *Debates in the Digital Humanities* (DDH), which is defined by its critical engagement with the unfolding tensions that surround DH research, teaching, and service. As editors, we have consciously steered DDH volumes—both the biannual volumes we have edited and the special-topics volumes edited by others—away from a case-study approach and toward argument-driven essays. Our editorial process is intellectually involved and time intensive; we go back and forth with our authors, and back and forth again, to ensure that the essays presented in DDH volumes foreground the stakes involved in their arguments. In some cases, this is a conversation that takes place over multiple drafts, conducted over multiple years. We believe that this rigorous process of editing and revision is essential to ensuring that the series lives up to its name and clearly examines the complications and contradictions involved in DH work.

With this in mind, going forward, we are committing to publishing shorter biannual volumes so that the essays can be published before the debates they address have been resolved. Likewise, after two long special volumes—*Making Things and Drawing Boundaries,* edited by Jentery Sayers, and *Bodies of Information: Feminist Debates in Digital Humanities,* edited by Jacqueline Wernimont and Elizabeth Losh—future special volumes will be shorter as well. We are excited to share with you a range of such volumes in the coming years on topics that include the digital Black Atlantic, global digital humanities, and institutions and infrastructures. All of these books will be published in print, in ebook form, and online on the open-access *Debates* website, which will soon make the transition to become an instance of Manifold, the interactive publishing platform recently released by the University of Minnesota Press and the GC Digital Scholarship Lab at The Graduate Center, CUNY.

As we look out into the world in 2019, we see much that is damaged. But in line with Part V of this volume, "Forum: Ethics, Theories, and Practices of Care," we choose to exercise what Stephen Jackson has termed "broken-world thinking" and to extend to our fragile and often dispiriting world small acts of recuperation that may be the building blocks of larger collective actions (222). We hope that from counting to caretaking, from speculating to building, the digital humanities in

2019 and beyond will continue to offer space to work toward a more hopeful future, one where the shine of innovation gradually gives way to the familiarity of use, the tasks of maintenance, and the stubborn knowledge that there remains much work left to be done.

BIBLIOGRAPHY

Brennan, Sheila K. "Public, First." In *Debates in the Digital Humanities 2016,* edited by Matthew K. Gold and Lauren F. Klein, 384–89. Minneapolis: University of Minnesota Press, 2016.

Fitzpatrick, Kathleen. "Academia, Not Edu." Kathleen Fitzpatrick. October 26, 2015, http://kfitz.info/academia-not-edu/.

Hicks, Marie. *Programmed Inequality: How Britain Discarded Women Technologists and Lost Its Edge in Computing.* Cambridge, Mass.: MIT Press, 2018.

Jackson, Steven. "Rethinking Repair." In *Media Technologies: Essays on Communication, Materiality and Society,* edited by Tarleton Gillespie, Pablo Boczkowski, and Kirsten Foot, 221–39. Cambridge, Mass.: MIT Press, 2014.

Klein, Lauren F. and Gold, Matthew K. "Digital Humanities: The Expanded Field." In *Debates in the Digital Humanities 2016,* edited by Matthew K. Gold and Lauren F. Klein, ix–xv. Minneapolis: University of Minnesota Press, 2016.

McGrail, Anne. "The 'Whole Game': Digital Humanities at Community Colleges." In *Debates in the Digital Humanities 2016,* edited by Matthew K. Gold and Lauren F. Klein, 16–31. Minneapolis: University of Minnesota Press, 2016.

McPherson, Tara. "Why Are the Digital Humanities So White? or Thinking the Histories of Race and Computation." In *Debates in the Digital Humanities,* edited by Matthew K. Gold, 139–60. Minneapolis: University of Minnesota Press, 2012.

Nakamura, Lisa. "Indigenous Circuits: Navajo Women and the Racialization of Early Electronic Manufacture." *American Quarterly* 66, no. 4 (2014): 919–41.

Noble, Safiya U. *Algorithms of Oppression: How Search Engines Reinforce Racism.* New York: New York University Press, 2018.

Obama, Barack. "A More Perfect Union." National Constitution Center. https://constitutioncenter.org/amoreperfectunion/.

Scheinfeldt, Tom. "Where's the Beef? Does Digital Humanities Have to Answer Questions?" In *Debates in the Digital Humanities,* edited by Matthew K. Gold, 56–58. Minneapolis: University of Minnesota Press, 2012.

So, Richard Jean. "All Models Are Wrong." *PMLA* 132, no. 3 (May 2017): 668–73.

PART I

POSSIBILITIES AND CONSTRAINTS

Gender and Cultural Analytics: Finding or Making Stereotypes?

LAURA MANDELL

Feminist cultural theorists, and perhaps cultural theorists more generally, are discouraged from exploring cultural analytics, or "the computational study of culture,"[1] whenever data miners state their conclusions in terms of "males" and "females."[2] In the fields of cultural analytics, computational linguistics, and quantitative sociology, such work typically appears in articles with "gender" in the title—paradoxically because "male" and "female" are biological sex terms rather than gender terms.[3] As a keyword for academic sociological and psychological articles, "gender" rose in popularity starkly over the 1980s, from 50 articles between 1966 and 1970 to 1,450 articles between 1980 and 1985 (Haraway, "Gender," 57). It was of a political moment: as Donna Haraway tells us, gender was "a concept developed to contest the naturalization of sexual difference in multiple arenas of struggle" (53) by feminist writers of the 1980s, culminating in Joan Scott's seminal 1986 essay, "Gender: A Useful Category of Historical Analysis." Gender is historicizable because it is culturally constructed. When psychoanalyst Robert Stoller first coined the term "gender identity" in 1967, he contended "that sex was related to biology (hormones, genes, nervous system, morphology), and gender was related to culture (psychology, sociology)" (Haraway, "Gender," 55).[4] Therefore, using the biologistic binary "male" and "female" (M/F) to speak of *gender* is nearly an oxymoron.

Feminist cultural critics might be tempted to simply walk away from cultural analytics altogether rather than engage with what I call "M/F"—that is, the conflation of gender with sex and the naturalization of a culturally constructed binary opposition. But walking away is a bad idea. During the 1980s, feminist sociologists critiqued patriarchal notions of objectivity primarily by turning away from quantitative analysis toward the qualitative (Gorelick, 465; Hartsock, 232). For Joey Sprague and Mary Zimmerman, the failure of feminism to have as transformative an impact on sociology as it has in had "in 'anthropology,' 'history,' and 'literary criticism'" resulted from feminist sociologists' preference for qualitative analysis (84). Quantitative analyses in sociology proceeded without feminist input at great cost, leaving the field susceptible to "bad science" (Haraway, "Gender," 55) and "bad description" (Marcus, Love, and Best, 6).

In addition to ensuring that feminist issues are addressed in the field, investigating M/F computational analyses also gives us the opportunity to revisit a blindness pervasive in 1980s gender analysis. For one thing, we now commonly accept that genders are not reduced to only two, nor are they wholly distinct from sex: cisgender, transgender, and genderqueer, for example, designate not masculine or feminine gender identities, but instead the relationship a person has to his or her assigned gender (LaBrada). Furthermore, a person's sex/gender, as so-called biological sex is now sometimes described, is no longer taken as a given: it is "assigned" to a person by medical and familial institutions. That a person is given a sex/gender after being born is made salient in cases of chromosomal and genital variation, but gender assignment nonetheless happens in every instance. The video montage for the opening credits of Jill Soloway's comedy-drama web television series, *Transparent,* does an excellent job of displaying women and men more or less easily assuming their assigned gender roles or, alternately, stepping outside them—so much so that, when a clip of a young girl joyously twirling her skirt appears in the montage, one realizes that she is celebrating her own capacity to fully embrace and express her incipient womanhood: hers is a moment of cisgender triumph—that is, a feeling of triumph for an achievement.

This understanding of sex, gender, and their relation owes much to the work of feminists in the 1990s, who extended into thinking about sex categories the work done by feminists in the 1980s to question the role of nature in determining gender categories. Judith Butler, for example, disturbed the boundaries of the sex/nature versus gender/culture opposition in *Gender Trouble* (1990): "Gender ought not to be conceived merely as the cultural inscription of meaning on a pregiven sex (a juridical construction); gender must also designate the very apparatus of production whereby the sexes themselves are established" (7). The "apparatus of production" is for Butler not only a legal and medical intervention. The biological binary M/F opposition is a textual and a numerical one: it is written, printed, spoken—discursive.

Some currently publishing data miners, sociolinguists, and sociologists uncritically conflate sex with gender, regressing to the pre-1980s intellectual milieu in which the M/F categories were treated as designating natural, transparent, biological categories. But some do not. For example, studies by Mark Olsen ("Qualitative Linguistics and *Histoire des Mentalités*: Gender Representation in the *Trésor de la Langue Française,*" 1992) as well as by Ted Underwood and David Bamman ("The Instability of Gender," 2016), theorize gender as a category in the making, rather than as a preexisting fact. Using data-mining techniques on the ARTFL corpus (texts gathered for the project, American and French Research on the Treasury of the French Language[5]), Olsen has shown that stereotypical associations with the category of woman change over time ("Qualitative Linguistics," 13). This work by Olsen, as well as that by Underwood and Bamman, demonstrates that computational methods offer the opportunity to denaturalize gender categories. But to capitalize on this opportunity, we must remain attentive to where and how computational data analytics crosses the line into naïve empiricism—often unwittingly—by presenting conclusions about "male" and "female" modes of thinking and writing as if the M/F terms were simple pointers to an unproblematic reality, transparently referential and not discursively constituted.

My argument in this chapter is that, in some quantitative cultural analyses, the category of gender has been biologized, binarized, and essentialized in a trend that I call "stereotyping," with an eye on the historical and material practice of stereo-typography. Stereotyping as a material practice was invented before the printing process became industrialized (1725 in England, 1735 in France). It froze pages made from movable type into unalterable plates of textual data for reprinting and was adopted early on by the French printing house known as Didot (Hodgson 15–18). The term for "stereotype" in French is *cliché*.[6] Here, I show how data-mining techniques are sometimes used to produce clichés. But my goal is less to dismiss quantification than it is to argue that, insofar as the results of data mining are movable and manipulable, cultural analytics can serve us well in historicizing gender categories. Examining the gender problem in quantitative analysis reveals both opportunities afforded by digital media and how we might miss them.

Text mining devolves from process into fixed results via stereotyping, whether literally imprinted on paper or figuratively frozen into cliché. In contrast, acknowledging that numbers have to be *read*—that is, resisting the view that statistical results are meaningful in any self-evident way—takes place by close reading of computational results and often manipulating parameters, adjusting algorithms, and rerunning the data. Dynamically reading, generating, and analyzing numbers are essential to making interpretive quantification possible and thus to exploring how the M/F binary is constituted in any given historical moment. This chapter examines two instances of gender analysis, performed via stylometry, word-frequency analysis, and topic modeling, that veer toward naïve empiricism because they take the distinction between M/F to be transparent. Imbuing cultural analytics with feminist theory, I argue here, shows us that we can animate numerical processes rather than fixing their results as stereotype. New technologies and carefully created reading processes can transform the statistical analysis of cultural artifacts into dynamic readerly engagement.

Bias and Statistics

Matthew Jockers undertakes what he calls "macroanalysis," he says explicitly, in order to strip literary criticism of its interpretive bias. In his book of the same name, he defines macroanalysis as "computational approaches to the study of literature" (4).[7] Despite later conciliatory gestures, Jockers unequivocally discredits more interpretive literary approaches, including close reading, in the book's first pages: "Close reading is not only impractical as a means of evidence gathering in the digital library, but big data render it totally inappropriate as a method of studying literary history" (7). For Jockers, close reading is "totally inappropriate" because it unleashes "irrepressible biases." Here, he takes a peculiar theoretical step that allows him to implicitly claim that biases can be dismantled by text mining: "Observation is flawed in the same way that generalization from the specific is flawed." According to this line of reasoning, interpretive generalization fails only as a result of working with too small a sample size (6–7). For example, Ian Watt's interpretation of the rise of the novel, Jockers says, turns out to be "*correct* on a number of points" despite being performed on too small a number of texts (7, emphasis added). His own assessment, because it is based on more texts, has therefore incontrovertibly established Watt's thesis, despite many critical studies that contest it.[8]

Before discussing Jockers's conclusions concerning gender and literary style, I want to look closely at his methods. One is stylometry, which the O.E.D. defines as "the statistical analysis of variations between one writer or genre and another." In *Macroanalysis,* however, stylometry is used to analyze variations between "male" and "female" writers of novels. Stylometrists typically delineate styles using very small words, not those that are related to the topic: the difference between the styles of James Madison and Alexander Hamilton as visible in the *Federalist Papers,* for instance, hinges on how often one uses "a" and the other "and" (Jockers, 92). Julia Flanders describes the work of John Burrows, another proponent of stylometric analysis, as discovering "distinctions of idiolect" usually invisible to readers; for instance, the frequency with which " 'inert words like 'of' and 'the' " are used (56). At first, Jockers sticks somewhat to the standard method: he describes the two features that most distinguish "the gender signal" as the higher usage of feminine pronouns and of the colon and semicolon. Jockers acknowledges that feminine pronouns are used more in novels written about women, so this stylistic feature is more about the content of novels written by women than about their style. But more problematically, as textual editors well know, punctuation ("accidentals," in the parlance of textual editing) is often manipulated by editors of print editions. What, we might well ask, were the genders of the editors?

Jockers further deviates from Burrows's method in producing lists of "features" used by female authors, by which he means specific vocabularies or keywords: "It is also seen that women authors show higher usage of the words *heart* and *love*—not surprising in the sense that this fact is consistent with our stereotypes of 'feminine' prose" (*Macroanalysis,* 93). Here, Jockers veers away from stylometry into simple counting. But there is a bigger problem. Not all data miners would attribute to a dataset spanning 200 years "our stereotypes." This phrase controverts the very point Joan Scott was making by introducing the term "gender" into cultural history: that gender associations change over time.[9]

A study by Jan Rybicki seeks to build on Jockers's work. Rybicki uses stylometrics to determine the gender of twelve anonymous authors in a collection of fiction held by the Library at Chawton House, which used to belong to Jane Austen's brother Edward and now proclaims itself to be "home to early women's writing."[10] Rybicki supplements this small corpus of forty-six novels with novels written by canonical authors, including men. He claims that he is able to sort these novels by the gender of their authors by using the same technique that sorted the canonical authors by gender in order to determine the genders of the anonymous authors in the Chawton House dataset. He too relies on the frequency of substantive vocabulary rather than of inert words. His conclusion resembles that of Jockers: "The Chawton House authors exhibit a decided preference for words that would be most readily and stereotypically associated with sentimentalist feminine fiction, and the fact that the stereotype is visible in vocabulary statistics makes it, perhaps, less of a stereotype" (754). Among the gendered characteristics that Rybicki has imagined as "less of a stereotype" is the finding that "men like virtues," by which he apparently means to suggest that men really do always care more about virtue than do women. His vocabulary statistics, however, show women using "virtue" and "virtuous" frequently and both men and women using "honest" (9). More obviously than in Jockers's analysis, the stereotype is in the eye of the beholder.[11]

Leaving aside Jockers's and Rybicki's reliance on stereotypes to explain their results, it is worth exploring whether the results themselves can ever be taken as objective. Results achieved by Mark Olsen contradict those of Jockers and Rybicki: he finds no such thing as a "feminine style" in his data. Although contradiction itself cannot overturn claims for objectivity, Olsen's method reveals the extent to which Rybicki's and Jockers's results are based on a preexisting assumption. Olsen deliberately does not look at word frequency ("*Écriture féminine*"). For Olsen, what distinguishes feminine writing is not vocabulary because it is tied to topic. For him, a gendered style consists in using the same words, but in a different way. He therefore examines the contexts of specific words, concluding that the *meanings* of words do not diverge based on gender. For Olsen, then, women and men make deliberate decisions about how to use specific words. Therefore, Olsen was doing something other than counting words according to an author's gender because he believes topic to be the overriding factor, not gender, in determining which terms will be used. Olsen's articulated premise for his study reveals Jockers's and Rybicki's underlying assumption: choices about diction are not the product of writerly decisions related to topic, but instead are based on being either M or F. As will become more and more clear, Jockers's and Rybicki's results confirm not an objective reality, but the premise of their own studies.

The criterion of scientific objectivity is reproducibility.[12] Before finding his own "female" words, Rybicki attempted to sort a subset of his corpus by using Jockers's list of "features best distinguishing male and female authors" (94, qtd. Rybicki, 5) and a second list created by James Pennebaker in a book called *The Secret Life of Pronouns*. Neither list worked; he had to generate a new list of "gender signals" from his own corpus. Rybicki attributes the failure of Pennebaker's wordlist to effectively sort gender in Rybicki's own corpus to the fact that the two corpora cover different time spans. But he also observes that Jockers's corpus contains "some of the authors in my [canonical] corpus" (5). Rybicki mitigates the failure of Jockers's list by noting certain overlaps with his own (5) and concludes that his own list "makes sense in terms of Pennebaker's and Jockers's findings" (7). But the fact remains that Rybicki could not use either of the two lists to accurately sort his corpus. His attempt to replicate Pennebaker's and Jockers's findings failed.

Clearly, the ability to distinguish gender via particular words depends upon the construction of a particular corpus. Here it is important to notice a moment of clarity in Rybicki's richly contradictory article. It is not simply that there are biases intrinsic to data selection (see also Koolen and van Cranenburgh, 14–15), but that irreproducibility suggests the instabililty of discursively constructed gender categories: "Literary scholarship has never voiced it as clearly as quantitative research has that the notions of 'writing like a man' and 'writing like a woman' are in such a constant state of flux that they risk becoming, in fact, quite problematic" (14). While one might argue with Rybicki's assessment of "literary scholarship"—Toril Moi's *Sexual/ Textual Politics* of 1985 summarized all the work in the field that problematized "writing like a woman"—his claim needs to be trumpeted loudly among data miners: it is "literary evolution" and not bodies that assign keywords to M/F.

Rybicki concludes by noting the "inability, in this study, to produce a stable 'canon' of male and female keywords that would survive a change of corpus or shifts in literary evolution, or both" (14). He proudly attributes this insight to "quantitative research," which is better, he says, than ordinary "literary scholarship" in figuring out that "writing like a woman" changes through time. Why, then, is this claim so inconspicuous as to not even inform the title of his article ("*Vive la différence!*") or the main argument—that he *can* determine the gender of anonymous authors in the Chawton House collection?

Gender difference tends to be widely broadcasted, and anything that obfuscates it downplayed. For instance, *Macroanalysis* made the news because it "shows that, on a whole, female authorship is detectable by objective measures rather than just human intuition" (the Smithsonian's *Smart News,* Nuwer). In her meta-analysis of psychological gender studies, Janet Sibley Hyde argues that the popular press picks up on and touts gender differences, even in studies that conclude there are very few marked differences. Studies of psychological gender traits have, since 1879, been reporting *more similarities than differences.* Most striking, in *The Psychology of Sex Differences,* Eleanor Maccoby and Carol Jacklin argued that most recorded gender differences did not hold up to scrutiny, and yet their work is reported in textbooks and reviews as discovering difference, not similarity. In her analysis of this fact, Hyde observes, "The mass media and the general public are captivated by findings of gender differences" (581).

In her own work, Hyde has advanced what she calls "the gender similarities hypothesis, which holds that males and females [*sic*] are *similar* on most, but not all, psychological variables" (581, emphasis added). Compiling and comparing many studies of gender difference, Hyde concludes that her gender similarity hypothesis proves true except in the case of some physical differences (throwing distance) and some aspects of sexuality (590). Stereotypical differences such as higher aggression levels and better mathematical capacities turn out to be attributable to men only in supervised tests; that is, when women know they are being watched or tracked for evidence of their gender (589; s.a. Cole, 178). Hyde's gender similarities hypothesis is consistent with linguist Kate Harrington's deeper reading of the statistics concerning gender differences in language. Harrington has looked more closely at the numbers generated by gendered discourse analysis, examining rather large differences in standard deviations between those classified in each gender. However, if one leaves out the extreme cases—those who rank most highly in gendered characteristics—most women resemble most men: "the often cited difference [is] dependent on the few and not representative of the many" (96). Major differences in standard deviation between the (allegedly) two genders can indicate that a dataset warrants further investigation, but the standard deviation will not be markedly different if there are exaggerators in both groups: the "*range* of individual variation . . . needs to be interpreted" (96, Harrington's emphasis). Moreover, Harrington finds that those people who grossly exaggerate their own "stereotypical" gendered discourse are members of specifically identifiable groups. It is the intersection of identities that matter, not gender alone: any "speaker's use of [allegedly gendered discourse forms] has more to do with individual social context than with gender as a social category" (101). The "individual social contexts" identified by Harrington as displaying the largest gendered differences were teenage girls (97) and men who seemed especially threatened by the study of gender differences in which they were participating (100). "The only overt comment on 'doing gender' in my data," Harrington says, arises in an explicit discussion of masculinity using the now infamous genre of discourse, "Real men don't do X" (99–100).

In my view, the exaggerators indicate, again, that gender identity is not given, but is triumphantly attained through the course of developmental acculturation (in the case of the teens) and sometimes is an insecure achievement (in the case of the threatened men). People who adopt and exaggerate stereotypically gendered traits (as they understand them) are worried that others might see their gender as ambiguous. That gender panic may intervene in sociological studies offers insight into why differences are seized on and trumpeted by the popular press. Gender is bifurcated into two categories, and people fit themselves into one or the other with difficulty and trepidation. That process requires continuously reassuring ourselves that identifying (as) M or F is no trouble at all. Reportage of firm gender demarcations is an apotropaic gesture designed to ward off anything that undermines a symbolic difference essential to the Western world's self-understanding.[13]

Given this discussion of gender studies, what can we conclude about the extent to which statistical reading techniques can mitigate irrational symbolic investments? Statistics, Isabelle Stengers notes, are deeply conservative in how they build on previous results (n. 10, 263). For instance, Bayesian probability, the foundation of latent Dirichlet allocation (a form of topic modeling, another statistical technique, discussed later in this chapter), determines events to be more probable if similar events have already happened. More generally, probability contributes to the biases of computer-assisted racial profiling (Hardt; O'Neil) and even Google search returns (Noble).

However, the discipline of statistics has developed methods for ameliorating bias. Ben Merriman notices Franco Moretti's and Jockers's tendency to avoid using known statistical methods for reading their results. In particular, they rely a great deal, Merriman says, on statistical significance for their arguments, when in fact statistical significance proliferates everywhere one looks for it. If a dataset of novels were categorized according to novelists with long noses and novelists with short noses, we would find statistically significant differences; they simply would not be meaningful differences. Although many researchers turn to qualitative analysis to determine the substantive value of a difference (Fitz-Gibbon, 48), there are also quantitative methods for estimating whether a difference is meaningful or its "effect size" (Coe). The effect size, or "how much difference a difference makes (the magnitude of the effect)" (Fitz-Gibbon, 45), is typically used for "meta-analyses" such as Hyde's, but it need not be used only for comparing multiple statistical results from different studies. To be fair to Moretti and Jockers, determining effect size is neither typical nor easy. As Robert Coe (1) tells us, "despite the fact that measures of effect size have been available for at least 60 years (Huberty, 2002), and the American Psychological Association has been officially encouraging authors to report effect sizes since 1994—but with limited success (Wilkinson et al., 1999)."[14] What the need for measuring effect size indicates, however, is that, as Merriman puts it, "patterns may be statistically significant but substantively trivial: the magnitude of the differences (the 'effect size') may be extremely small, or it could disappear entirely if the researcher tweaks the model" (16). The irreproducibility of gendered keywords confirms Merriman's hypothesis.

But even after determining effect size, identifying statistical trends does not remove bias. On the contrary, it reveals the biases of the paradigm according to which a thing or event is counted as data (Forrester, 36, qtg. Hesse, 286). Statisticians well know that biases are reproduced through classification systems (Cartwright and Bradburn, 5). Comparing the work done by Burrows, Flanders, and Olsen to Jockers and Rybicki (discussed on pp. 6–8 above) reveals a bias toward biological determinism.[15]

"Gender" was proposed as an analytic category in the 1980s specifically to avoid the deterministic bias. According to Donna Haraway, it "was developed as a category to explore what counts as a 'woman'" through time ("Gender," 67). But setting aside "as a 'woman'" from Haraway's statement for a moment, *What* counts?[16] The question becomes axiological: What really has value for us, and why? I sketched out earlier some thoughts about the symbolic weight and psychological drama that obfuscate for us the conceptual inadequacy of the M/F categories. There is also a material side to the redacted question: *What* has been charged with the procedure of counting? It would be very easy to answer, in the case of cultural analytics, that what are responsible for counting are data-mining techniques and data miners. But that answer rings true only if the data itself is not at all actively participating in counting, unlike Harrington's interviewees, who very actively generate a feedback loop. Are there feedback loops built into data? Has it been collected, sorted, and even produced according to the categories M/F? It is to answer those questions, in the case of text-mining novels, that I now turn.

Data as Capta

In a keynote collaborative presentation with Julia Flanders at the Boston Area Days of Digital Humanities Conference in 2013, Jockers explained the difference between the visualizations that he originally generated for *Macroanalysis* and those finally published in the book: in the course of revision, Jockers discovered that there were duplicate novels in his dataset and that three-volume novels had not been stitched together to count as one novel instead of three. Changing his dataset also altered a dramatic visualization of gender difference included in an earlier publication ("Computing and Visualizing," Figure 3), transforming it into the less distinguishing visualization that appears both in *Macroanalysis* (Figure 9.3.4) and in *Smithsonian Smart News* (Nuwer).[17] In other words, the stylistic differentiation between M/F genders no longer looked so significant once Jockers tweaked his dataset.

Writing on the subject of the visual effect of data visualizations more generally (*Graphesis*, 129), Johanna Drucker argues that the "representational force" of the image "conceals what the statistician knows very well—that no 'data' pre-exist their parameterization. *Data are capta,* taken not given, constructed as an interpretation of the phenomenal world, not inherent in it" (128, emphasis in the original). Datasets are never random samples: they are gathered by humans according to parameters, however complex, hidden, unconscious, and subject to chance they may be.

Drucker's formulation of data as "capta" cuts two ways. First, why collect data according to the categories M/F? Capturing data as M/F will create statistically significant differences between M/F, but are they significant? And more importantly, what exactly do they signify? Second, thinking about data as capta encourages us to examine the selection process in aggregating data. The shape of Jockers's dataset was decisive in determining his results, as is clear from Rybicki's proudly avowed inability "to produce a stable 'canon' of male and female keywords that would survive a change of corpus, or shifts in literary evolution, or both" (14).

It is a virtue of Rybicki's stylometric analysis of the Chawton House Collection of novels that he openly describes the process of tweaking his dataset—changing, over the course of his experiment, which novels by men he would include or exclude—to get his algorithm to successfully differentiate authors marked as M/F.

Rybicki tells us that he removed from his corpus the "troublemakers" who disturbed his results too deeply because it is "notoriously too difficult to gender classify" (3). That is, gender classification does not work without help.

Rybicki's adjustments are not surreptitious: he is trying to get his algorithm to work through acts "of honest and well-founded cherry-picking" (6). In a 2013 article, Alan Liu quotes a question broached in 2011 by Ryan Heuser and Long Le-Khac: "How do we get from numbers to *meaning*?"[18] Liu argues that this "meaning problem" ("What is the Meaning," 411) is not simply a matter of interpretation *after* data has been generated, describing abstractly what we can see in the practical way that Rybicki works:

> Any quest for stable method in understanding how knowledge is generated by human beings using machines founders on the initial fallacy that there are immaculately separate human and machinic orders, each with an ontological, epistemological, and pragmatic purity . . . . Digital humanities method . . . consists in repeatedly coadjusting human concepts and machine technologies until . . . the two stabilize each other in temporary postures of truth that neither by itself could sustain. ("What Is the Meaning," 416)

Adjusting the dataset to get the best results is simply what data miners do to achieve "temporary postures of truth." This is good practice, not a crime, and it is *only* problematic insofar as the data miners present their findings as "objective truth," obscuring to us (and sometimes to themselves) their own role in massaging data and adjusting the parameters of their algorithms to make them work. It would be very easy to break Rybicki's algorithm, to prevent "highly adventurous content" from being associated with "M" and sentimentality with "F," simply by adding novels to the dataset.[19] Data amassed, which is to say data, is always capta: counted or captured by someone.

Gender/Genre: What Counts?

To arrive at a working method for assessing the genders of the anonymous authors in his dataset, Rybicki must omit certain other authors from his collection of writers with known genders: this shows us how genre, as much as gender, muddies the picture. Genre affects the algorithm's ability to distinguish M/F in three ways. First, "feminine" sentimental literature and "masculine" criticism incorporate stylistic features that are discernible and imitable. Rybicki had to eliminate William Godwin, who wrote in the genre of Jacobin novels that are typically sentimental in style. His results also show Samuel Richardson's epistolary novels, written largely in the voices of his eponymous heroines, veering toward "F." I asked Jan Rybicki to use his algorithms to perform a stylometric analysis of Mary Wollstonecraft's two anti-Jacobin, sentimentalist novels along with two essays, her two *Vindications,* in

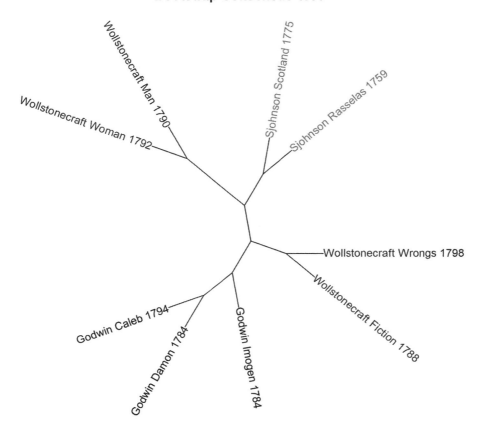

**Wollstonecraft
Bootstrap Consensus Tree**

100-700 MFW Culled @ 0-100%
Pronouns deleted Classic Delta distance Consensus 0.5

Figure 1.1. This bootstrap consensus tree groups together texts with similar styles using stylometry; specifically, the Delta measure of stylistic difference pioneered by John Burrows that pays attention to the use of most frequent, little words ("a," "of," "the"), as well as keywords. Wollstonecraft's essays are farthest away from everything else, including her own novelistic writing, as indicated by the double-length line. *Rasselas* might be technically classified as a novel or at least a fable, but it is distinctive because of Johnson's style. *Rasselas* excepted, the biggest divide shown here is between novels and essays, not M/F. Thanks to Jan Rybicki for running this test.

relation to texts by two men. Both of Wollstonecraft's essays are, to my sensibility, very Johnsonian in style, characterized by Latinate diction and complicated syntax. I asked him to test at least in one case the effect of genre on gender differentiation, and he produced the result shown in Figure 1.1.

Wollstonecraft's sentimental anti-Jacobin novels most resemble Godwin's sentimental anti-Jacobin novels, as indicated by proximity in this bootstrap consensus tree, whereas her essays most resemble Johnson's writings. In fact, Wollstonecraft chose to write both her *Vindications* in the Latinate, Johnsonian style that dominated the essay genre because it had, at her moment, considerable cultural authority. The literary critic Nancy Miller points out that two other eighteenth-century novelists, Frances Burney and Françoise d'Issembourg d'Happoncourt Graffigny, assume a similar style when, in prefaces to their novels, they take on the style of a critic (51–52). Insofar as one pins a genre to a gender, then a woman writing in a Latinate style (essays, criticism) or a man writing a Jacobin sentimental novel is writing in drag.

The case of genre helps us understand more about gender analysis; that is, about figuring out "what counts as 'woman'" (Haraway, "Gender," 67). It shows us that features of both gender and genre, while highly discernible, are also highly imitable. Writing in the sentimentalist genre can be accomplished through study. For instance, Rybicki notices one parody of "female writing" by William Beckford (7). Despite his awareness of the possibility of parody, Rybicki argues that one of the anonymous Chawton House novels is "correctly" identified as written by a man because its preface deprecates "'*womanish* and weak minds'" (13, emphasis in the original). It could be a parody, but it also could be written by a woman pretending to write as a man. In fact, Wollstonecraft originally published her *Vindication of the Rights of Men* anonymously. In it, she disparages Edmund Burke, whose *Reflections on the Revolution in France* she is attacking, as "effeminate." That kind of slur certainly helped disguise her gender and with it her identity. Deprecating femininity is a gender marker that women find easy to imitate in order to establish their authority. (We can see from Wollstonecraft's second *Vindication* that she did honestly devalue "effeminacy," which she analyzed as learned rather than innate, pointing out that the soldiers of her time and class behaved with as much effeminacy as women.) Anyone can adopt gendered modes of behavior, just as anyone can write in genres stereotypically labeled M/F.

In writing, if we define "gender" as a category-in-the-making (Haraway, *Modest_Witness,* 35), as a set of conventions for *self*-representation that are negotiated and manipulated, more or less consciously, then gender approaches nearly to the definition of genre. (If we take out "self" from the preceding sentence's proposed definition of gender, the result, "a set of conventions for representation," is a definition of genre.) Learning to write in a specific genre is almost as difficult as learning to encode one's self-expression according to a gender—and in some instances, the tasks largely overlap.[20] In person, one sends gender signals with body movements and gestures, speech, and writing. Whereas in the case of gender, we think of imitating its forms as "passing" or "drag," in the case of genre, unless it is a case of parody, we think of it as, well, writing. In composing her two *Vindications,* Wollstonecraft is not imitating an essay writer; she is writing essays. When Rybicki says in his essay that Austen "writes more like a man" (9), maybe that too is only evidence of Austen writing.

Am I arguing, then, that M/F is a bogus binary, produced by data collectors and data miners, without corresponding to any distinction actually found in reality? There are two answers to this question. First, yes: I believe the gender binary is not really about gender. But if it is wrong, how is Jockers's stylometric analysis able to determine a novel's gender correctly in 80 percent of the cases, while identifying genre correctly in only 67 percent? That fact justifies Jockers's statement that "gender . . . is a strong signal" (*Macroanalysis,* 93). However, if we look at the numbers more closely, what Jockers is calling "the genre signal" is weaker than what he is calling "the gender signal" because his algorithm is trying to sort texts into eleven genre categories, whereas there are only two gender categories: M/F. His algorithm is actually eight times better than chance at determining genre, but only 1.6 times better when determining gender.

I would rather roll dice that are 1.6 times more likely to give me a winning number.[21] But I would maintain that the algorithm sorting texts into M/F is not sorting *only* gender at one moment, and *only* genre at another, when it is required to sort in two categories as opposed to eleven. The gender/genre signals, as Rybicki's work subsequently shows, are inextricably intertwined. In other words, when stylometric analysis guesses 1.6 times better, it is guessing about what I would call "textual gender," the stylistic and textual features associated with gendered genres. It is by now a critical commonplace that gender construction is discursive: it takes place in writing, in everything from medical documents and legal cases to novels. And many, many books and articles examine the relationship between gender and genre. Here, however, I am proposing that, when gender analysis operationalizes data-mining algorithms, separating gender from other markings (genre, era of composition) is not possible: historical time and genre are not incidental to, but constitutive of, gender.

We could break the algorithm's capacity to produce "a strong gender signal" by simply increasing the number of gender categories to be sorted. Experts in the field could create metadata to generate a completely new taxonomy to replace the tired M/F binary: "men writing as men," "women writing as women, "women writing as men," "men writing as women," "unspecified (anonymous) writing as men," "unspecified writing as women," "men writing as men (byline) in the voice of a woman (woman narrator)," "men writing as unspecified (anonymous byline) in the voice of a woman," "women writing as men (byline) in a voice of unspecified," etc.—whatever categories are presented by title pages, prefaces, narrators' discourses, and research into authorship attribution found.[22]

Breaking down the strength of a signal is not the same as disrupting computational capacity, which, as Ted Underwood argues, no longer depends on simple classification schemes:

Maybe in 1967 it was true that computers could only handle exclusive binary categories. I don't know: I was divided into a pair of gametes at the time myself.[23] But nowadays data models can be as complex as you like. Go ahead, add another column to the database. No technical limit will stop you. Make categories perspectival, by linking each tag to a specific observer. Allow contradictory tags. If you're still worried that things are too simple, make each variable a probability distribution. The computer won't break a sweat. ("The Real Problem with Distant Reading")

Computation enables complexity.

Additionally, the computer screen affords interactivity. Text-mining parameters can be manipulated by viewers, as they are in Voyant windows.[24] The authors of Voyant, Geoffrey Rockwell and Stéfan Sinclair, have also created Methodi.ca,[25] through which algorithms can be altered. The new "Data" section of *CA: Journal of Cultural Analytics* allows not only for sharing data but also for articulating the principles of data collection.[26] Visualization tools are being built that will allow running and rerunning data, each time changing the underlying parameters used for text mining in order to test their effects, and that also make it easy to drill down to the text itself for close reading when questions arise.[27] Digitization forces on us neither rigid quantification systems nor distant reading. Far from it: digital media can foster the mixing of qualitative and quantitative methods and represent the results of analysis from multiple perspectives.

The second answer to the question posed earlier is no: M/F is not a bogus binary. Eighty percent is a very good rate of correctness in data mining. But exactly *what* has been correctly measured? Feminist literary historians have known for a long time that the early novel was indeed a place where gender norms were formed (Miller, 47; Gelfand and Switten, 443). Furthermore, this construction of gender took place at the very same moment, and using the very same literary devices, as the moment and methods through which novelistic genres were formed. As seen in Harrington's analysis of speech patterns described earlier, people partly create and partly confirm stereotypes. Harrington's exaggerators seized on existing classifiers and amplified them. Thus, the M/F classification process provides a feedback loop: people wishing to exaggerate their gender will repeatedly send signals that are then further confirmed after the fact.

As novelists attempted to create gender norms, those norms became more imitable, more easily parodied,[28] and therefore more easily adopted throughout the culture. Novelists were counting and reproducing as many gender and genre features as they could. Underwood and Bamman's study of gendered norms in novels written between 1780 and 1989 finds a general trend: over time "gender [becomes] harder and harder to predict." After a certain historical moment, perhaps after the Victorian era (Jockers and Kirilloff), novels turned to tasks other than stereotyping the M/F binary. We could use stylometry to find this out. But stylometry will only become a valuable tool of literary criticism if we admit that categories such as gender are being constructed both by the measurer and the measured. Once this process is accepted, we might then be able to use stylometry to experiment with

new taxonomies of gender, such as the one adumbrated earlier. If trained on taxonomies generated by experts in feminist literary history, who have familiarity with
the time period, the guesses that an algorithm might make about gender, although
a weaker signal because sorting into a greater number of categories, would opti-
mize human-computer interactions. Algorithmic sorting would sometimes reveal
our blindnesses, surprising us with insight, and sometimes reveal its own stupidity,
marking those moments when human thinking surpasses computational logic. It
would never simply be "right" or "wrong."

In *Modest_Witness,* Haraway protests against what she calls "virile witness,"
testimony as an act of opposition. The modest witness, by contrast, though no
less biased as a human being, attempts to identify the terms of self-representation
without forcing them into the form of aggressive opposition.[29] Rewriting gender
as sex, wrongly understood as a simple binary opposition, transforms it into a
weak signal that might be statistically "correct." Yet, with categories multiplied, we
would be able to see what gendered characteristics were most salient to the people
writing during a specific time period, finding *their* gender cues rather than always
our own. The M/F opposition is implicitly and always aggressive in the sense of
promoting oneself at the expense of others, sometimes others who lived in the
past.[30] Computer screens as opposed to stereotyped pages easily afford the fluid
exploration of parameters and taxonomies, through which many sorts of experiments can be tested: interactive visualizations can give us not objective answers
rooted in aggressively reductive oppositions, but parallax, multiple perspectives
for viewing a very complex reality. In analyzing gender, the computational analysis of culture should never be understood as an objective observer measuring
an inert reality. Rather, it should be understood as a means of counting people
counting. Gender analysis thus provides an important test case for cultural analytics, allowing the field to show how self-critical and historically reflexive it can
be. But it does more.

Transforming the print humanities into the digital humanities offers us an
opportunity.[31] It is a very short step from "typically" to "stereotypically," as short as
it is from printed to stereotyped pages, which are notoriously difficult to tell apart
(Shillingsburg). Thawing typographical fixity via computer screens, moving from
private marginalia to public, scholarly, dynamic interaction, offers us the chance
to contest discursive constructions like the sex/gender/sexuality system at every
moment of their construction.

NOTES

1. This definition of "cultural analytics" comes from *CA: The Journal of Cultural
Analytics* (http://culturalanalytics.org/about/.). The term's origin and scope are defined
in note 7. I use the term because (1) I think it is an emerging field or subfield in Literary
and Cultural Studies, and (2) the emphasis on "culture" opens the door to cultural theory,

a most welcome addition to data-mining techniques (see Klein, "Distant Reading after Moretti").

2. Rule #1 in Catherine D'Ignazio and Lauren Klein's essay, "Feminist Data Visualization," is to "Rethink Binaries" (sec. 3.1).

3. Toril Moi (65). Whereas Deborah Tannen is very careful to use the terms "women" and "girls," "men" and "boys," throughout her work and deplores any essentialist interpretation of the notion of gender difference in conversational styles formulated by researchers like herself who take an interactional sociolinguistic approach (8–9, 12–13), "gender" and "biological sex" are sometimes used interchangeably in the introduction to Harrington et al., eds., *Gender and Language Research Methodologies* (2008). A large number of sociolinguists are now investigating "the intersection of gender, sex, and sexuality" (Levon, 300), which is to say separating them from each other and then investigating how these categories "*mutually constitute*" each other (Levon, 298, emphasis in the original; Levon offers full citations of the sociolinguists doing this work).

4. Stoller's original work in a 1964 essay opens by distinguishing "gender identity" from "sex" (M/F), but later posits three forces: (1) culture/psychology, (2) anatomy, and (3) a "biological force" (220). In one of the two cases he presents, the "biological force" is congruent with anatomy: a child raised as a girl who wanted to be a man turns out to have male chromosomes (part of the "biological force") and a very small penis ("anatomy"); in the second one, the famous case of Agnes, genitalia are male but the female biological force propels Agnes forward as female. Stoller recanted in a 1968 article, repudiating his own notion of "biological force" after discovering that Agnes had been secretly taking her mother's hormone replacement medicines (83–84).

5. See https://artfl-project.uchicago.edu/.

6. Originally a printing term, the word "stereotype" later acquired negative connotations. Dictionaries typically cite Walter Lippmann's 1922 essay, "Public Opinion," as the origin of a derogatory definition of the word "stereotype," but Walter Johnson notes that, before emancipation in the United States, the same stereotype plate depicting a slave was used over and over again in runaway slave advertisements (189), indicating racist origins for the term's use. I am grateful to Lauren Klein for pointing this out.

7. The broader term that spans not simply literature but also all cultural artifacts, "cultural analytics," was coined by Lev Manovich in 2007–2009 ("Cultural Analytics: Analysis and Visualization"; "Cultural Analytics"). Discussions about the value of computational work in literature often call it "distant reading," first coined in 2000 by Franco Moretti in "Conjectures on World Literature," who debated its value with Katie Trumpener in the pages of *Critical Inquiry* (see Moretti, "Style, Inc.," and "Relatively Blunt"; Trumpener, "Critical Response 1"; see also Moretti, *Distant Reading*). For more recent discussions, see Bode ("Equivalence") and Underwood ("Genealogy").

8. Critiques of Watt's masculinist argument about the English novel began in 1986 with Dale Spender in *Mothers of the Novel* (115–18, 138–39), to which Ian Watt responded ("Spencer on Trial"). This account comes from Josephine Donovan (441–42). For opposing views of Watt's thesis on the French novel, see Miller.

9. For data mining that traces the "volatility" of gender categories, see Underwood, "Instability," and chapter 4 of *Distant Horizons*, "The Metamorphoses of Gender."

10. Chawton House, https://chawtonhouse.org/.

11. While this chapter was under submission, an excellent essay about how to avoid gender bias in Natural Language Processing, including stylometry, was published, which describes in detail how stereotypes and bias inform the process and results. See Koolen and van Cranenburgh; thanks to Andrew Piper for bringing this article to my attention.

12. On reproducibility in data mining, see Goldstone ("Reproducible"; thanks to Lauren Klein for this reference). Failed attempts to reproduce results among Digital Humanists, some even using the same data and algorithms on different machines, prompted Alan Liu to call for scientific workflow management ("Assessing Data Workflows").

13. I am thinking here of the work done by Mary Douglas in *Purity and Danger*. The violence elicited when gender attributes are "out of place" (40) suggests that, as Douglas argues, gender is serving as a symbol for the cultural system as a whole (3–4, 114). As virulent reactions to gender ambiguity suggest, undermining that specific symbolic distinction poses a threat to the whole system that people have used to sort and interpret experience throughout their lives (121).

14. Coe's account of the failure to measure effect size in educational research because of its relative neglect in the field of statistics is worth quoting in full: "The routine use of effect sizes, however, has generally been limited to meta-analysis—for combining and comparing estimates from different studies—and is all too rare in original reports of educational research (Keselman et al., 1998). This is despite the fact that measures of effect size have been available for at least sixty years (Huberty, 2002), and the American Psychological Association has been officially encouraging authors to report effect sizes since 1994—but with limited success (Wilkinson et al., 1999). Formulae for the calculation of effect sizes do not appear in most statistics textbooks (other than those devoted to meta-analysis), are not featured in many statistics computer packages, and are seldom taught in standard research methods courses. For these reasons, even the researcher who is convinced by the wisdom of using measures of effect size, and is not afraid to confront the orthodoxy of conventional practice, may find that it is quite hard to know exactly how to do so" (1).

15. For me, Hyde's meta-analysis of M/F studies severely undermines biological determinism. In any case, in hermeneutics as opposed to science, "it's natural" prevents further analysis. (As is well known, Edmund Burke began deploying "the natural" as an ideological tool in his pamphlet condemning the French Revolution published in 1789, *Reflections on the Revolution in France*). Analyzing society at all requires dislodging biologistic conceptions. For example, for Erving Goffman, the practices of con men reveal the cues we use to present ourselves *as* something to someone else, however unconsciously, and drag can do the same for gender (Butler). Tallying up those cues and historicizing them promote analytic thinking.

16. See Mandell, "Gendering Digital Literary History."

17. The original figure appears here, http://www.dh2012.uni-hamburg.de/wp-con
tent/uploads/2012/07/img154–3.jpg, and the revised figure here: http://www.matthew
jockers.net/macroanalysisbook/color-versions-of-figures-9–3-and-9–4/gendernet/.

18. Ryan and Heuser (46, qtd. in Liu, "What Is the Meaning," 411; emphasis added by Liu).

19. The novels he used, except for the canonical ones he added, are listed here:
https://chawtonhouse.org/the-library/library-collections/womens-writing-in-english
/novels-online/. Behn's *Oroonoko*, Lennox's *The Female Quixote*, Charke's *The Memoirs
of Charlotte Charke*, and Owenson's *The Missionary,* not collected by the Chawton-
House donor, contain highly adventurous content. Sentimentality would not be seen
as distinctively "F" if we added Mackenzie's *Man of Feeling,* Fielding's *Shamela,* and all
of Godwin's novels. Less certain, though worth testing, is that "breast" might not be
associated with "F" if we added Cleland's *Fanny Hill* or translations of Rousseau's *Julie,
ou la Nouvelle Heloise, or* Diderot's *Bijoux Indiscret* or *La Religieuse.*

20. Obviously, one of these tasks is viewed as a "natural" process and the other as an
intellectual process. In my view, this difference results from how early in human development the intellectual task of acquiring the ability to perform gender occurs. But it helps
to remember that learning gender cues is coeval with another intellectual task, linguistic
acquisition, and that speaking too ultimately feels like a natural capacity.

21. Thanks to Susan Brown for this point.

22. I presented this list at Dartmouth (2016) and Hamburg (2016: at 35.18 in the video
stream), and it has subsequently been summarized and described in Drucker ("Why Distant Reading Isn't"). She concludes, "The point is that the model [of gender categories]
determines what will emerge from analysis of the texts" (632).

23. This portion of Underwood's blog posting is very tongue in cheek, as this comment about being a "pair of gametes" indicates: Underwood is irritated, as he goes on to
show, by having had to court complexity in his analysis of genre in order to disarm his
critics. But however sarcastically intoned, the point is worth pursuing: a pair of gametes
becomes very complex indeed, and all the zeros and ones at the lowest level of machine
language can similarly generate what may be an unfathomable complexity.

24. See http://www.voyant-tools.org/.

25. See http://methodi.ca/.

26. See Andrew Piper's introduction to the new section of this journal: http://cultural
analytics.org/2017/10/introducing-data-sets-a-new-section/.

27. This work is currently being undertaken by the 3DH group, for whom the third
dimension is not spatial but hermeneutic: http://threedh.net/3dh/: see Drucker ("Non-
Representational Approaches") for a full explanation of the project's achievements so far
and proposed future developments. The project has received additional funding as the for-
Text project: http://fortext.net/.

28. Parody may be more useful for assimilating norms than it is for debunking them.
The most amazing instance of this that I know of is the fact that early eighteenth-century
political satirists wrote repeatedly of King George's "prime minister" as a way of denigrat-
ing Sir Robert Walpole: they felt that none of the king's ministers should be preferred. The
satirists were laughing at Walpole for ingratiating himself and warning the populace that

one minister had too much power over state affairs. "Prime minister" is of course now a title in England of a very powerful person indeed (Goldgar).

29. On the renewed importance of "modesty" in literary criticism, see Jeffrey Williams.

30. Roland Barthes's 1977 essay "The Death of the Author" foregrounds the belligerence of immodest literary criticism: "victory to the critic" (147).

31. By "print humanities," I mean the methods of humanistic study that originated in mass printing. The transformation of modes of criticism is happening already, and the pitfalls of this process reside for me in failing to weed out the worst aspects of print culture and remediating digital media according to their requirements, fixity being one of them. See Mandell, *Breaking the Book.*

BIBLIOGRAPHY

Barthes, Roland. "The Death of the Author." In *Image Music Text,* 142–48. 2nd ed. New York: Hill and Wang, 1994.

Bode, Katherine. "The Equivalence of 'Close' and 'Distant' Reading: Or, toward a New Object for Data-Rich Literary History." *MLQ* 78, no. 1 (2017): 77–104.

Burrows, James. *Computation into Criticism: A Study of Jane Austen's Novels and an Experiment in Method.* Oxford: Clarendon Press, 1987.

Butler, Judith. *Gender Trouble: Feminism and the Subversion of Identity.* New York: Routledge, 1990.

Cartwright, Nancy L., and Norman M. Bradburn. "A Theory of Measurement." Working paper. London: London School of Economics, 2010, http://dro.dur.ac.uk/18310/1/18310 .pdf. Accessed July 9, 2016.

Coe, Robert. "It's the Effect Size, Stupid. What Effect Size Is and Why It Is Important." Paper presented at the Annual Conference of the British Educational Research Association, University of Exeter, England, September 12–14, 2002, http://www.leeds.ac.uk/educol /documents/00002182.htm. Accessed December 31, 2015.

Cole, Elizabeth R. "Intersectionality and Research in Psychology." *American Psychologist* 64, no. 3 (2009): 170–80.

D'Ignazio, Catherine, and Lauren F. Klein. "Feminist Data Visualization." Workshop on Visualization for the Digital Humanities. IEEE VIS 2016, Baltimore, Md., 2016, http://www .kanarinka.com/wp-content/uploads/2015/07/IEEE_Feminist_Data_Visualization.pdf.

Donovan, Josephine. "Women and the Rise of the Novel: A Feminist-Marxist Theory." *Signs* 16, no. 3 (1991): 441–62.

Douglas, Mary. *Purity and Danger: An Analysis of the Concepts of Pollution and Taboo.* New York: ARK, 1966, 1988.

Drucker, Johanna. *Graphesis: Visual Forms of Knowledge Production.* Cambridge, Mass.: Harvard University Press, 2014.

Drucker, Johanna. "Non-Representational Approaches to Modeling Interpretation in a Graphical Environment." *Digital Scholarship in the Humanities* 33, no. 2 (2018): 248–63, https://doi.org/10.1093/llc/fqx034.

Drucker, Johanna. "Why Distant Reading Isn't." *PMLA* 132, no. 3 (2017): 628–35.

Fitz-Gibbon, C. T. "Meta-Analysis: An Explication." *British Educational Research Journal* 10, no. 2 (1984): 135–44.

Flanders, Julia. "Detailism, Digital Texts, and the Problem of Pedantry." *TEXT Technology* 2 (2005): 41–70.

Forrester, John. *Thinking in Cases*. Malden, Mass.: Polity, 2017.

Gelfand, Elissa, and Margaret Switten. "Gender and the Rise of the Novel." *French Review* 61, no. 3 (1988): 443–53.

Goffman, Erving. *The Presentation of Self in Everyday Life*. New York: Anchor Doubleday, 1959. First published 1956.

Goldgar, Bertrand G. *Walpole and the Wits: The Relation of Literature and Politics, 1722–1742*. Lincoln: University of Nebraska Press, 1976.

Goldstone, Andrew. "From Reproducible to Productive." *CA: Journal of Cultural Analytics,* February 27, 2017, http://culturalanalytics.org/2017/02/from-reproducible-to-productive/. Accessed December 15, 2017.

Gorelick, Sherry. "Contradictions of Feminist Methodology." *Gender and Society* 5, no. 4 (1991): 459–77.

Haraway, Donna J. "Gender for a Marxist Dictionary: The Sexual Politics of a Word." In *Simians, Cyborgs, and Women: The Reinvention of Nature*. London: Free Association Books, 1991. Rpt. in *Women, Gender, Religion: A Reader,* edited by Elizabeth A. Castelli, 49–75. New York: Palgrave, 2001.

Haraway, Donna J. *Modest_Witness@Second_Millennium.FemaleMan©_Meets_Onco Mouse™*. New York: Routledge, 1997.

Hardt, Moritz. "How Big Data Is Unfair." *Medium,* September 26, 2014, https://medium.com/@mrtz/how-big-data-is-unfair-9aa544d739de#.hmqcrs7sr. Accessed December 10, 2015.

Harrington, Kate. "Perpetuating Difference? Corpus Linguistics and the Gendering of Reported Dialogue." In *Gender and Language Research Methodologies,* edited by Kate Harrington, Lia Litosseliti, Helen Sauntson, and Jane Sunderland, 85–102. New York: Palgrave Macmillan, 2008.

Hartsock, Nancy C. M. *Money, Sex, and Power: Toward a Feminist Historical Materialism*. New York: Longman, 1985.

Hesse, Mary. "Review, *The Structure of Scientific Revolutions.*" *Isis* 54, no. 2 (1963): 286–87.

Heuser, Ryan, and Long Le-Khac. "Learning to Read Data: Bringing Out the Humanistic in the Digital Humanities." *Victorian Novels* 54, no. 1 (2011): 79–86.

Hodgson, Thomas. *An Essay on Stereotype Printing, Including a Description of the Various Processes*. Newcastle, England: Hodgson, 1820.

Huberty, C. J. "A History of Effect Size Indices." *Educational and Psychological Measurement* 62, no. 2 (2002): 227–40. [Cited by Coe.]

Hyde, Janet Sibley. "The Gender Similarities Hypothesis." *American Psychologist* 60, no. 6 (2005): 581–92.

Jockers, Matthew L. "Computing and Visualizing the 19th-Century Literary Genome." *DH 2012 University of Hamburg Conference Proceedings,* July 16–22, 2012, http://www

.dh2012.uni-hamburg.de/conference/programme/abstracts/computing-and-visual
izing-the-19th-century-literary-genome.1.html. Accessed March 21, 2017.

Jockers, Matthew L. "The LDA Buffet Is Now Open: Or, Latent Dirichlet Analysis for
English Majors." September 29, 2011, http://www.matthewjockers.net/2011/09/29
/the-lda-buffet-is-now-open-or-latent-dirichlet-allocation-for-english-majors/.
Accessed April 19, 2016.

Jockers, Matthew L. *Macroanalysis: Digital Methods and Literary History.* Chicago: University of Illinois Press, 2013.

Jockers, Matthew L., and Julia Flanders. "A Matter of Scale." DigitalCommons@University of
Nebraska—Lincoln. March 18, 2013, http://digitalcommons.unl.edu/englishfacpubs
/106/. Accessed April 19, 2016.

Jockers, Matthew L., and Gabi Kirilloff. "Understanding Gender and Character Agency
in the 19th Century Novel." *CA: Journal of Cultural Analytics,* December 1, 2016,
http://culturalanalytics.org/2016/12/understanding-gender-and-character-agency
-in-the-19th-century-novel/. Accessed March 18, 2017.

Johnson, Walter. *Soul by Soul: Life inside the Antebellum Slave Market.* Cambridge, Mass.:
Harvard University Press, 2009.

Keselman, H. J., C. J. Huberty, L. M. Lix, S. Olejnik, et al. "Statistical Practices of Educational Researchers: An Analysis of Their ANOVA, MANOVA, and ANCOVA Analyses."
Review of Educational Research 68, no. 3 (1998): 350–86. [Cited by Coe.]

Klein, Lauren. "Distant Reading after Moretti." MLA 2018, http://lklein.com/2018/01
/distant-reading-after-moretti/. Accessed March 13, 2018.

Koolen, Corina, and Andreas van Cranenburgh. "These Are Not the Stereotypes You
Were Looking For: Bias and Fairness in Authorial Gender Attribution." In *Proceedings of the First Workshop on Ethics in Natural Language Processing*, edited
by Dirk Hovy, et al., 12–22/ Stroudsberg, PA: Association for Computational Linguistics (ACL): 2017.

LaBrada, Eloy. "Categories We Die For: Ameliorating Gender in Analytic Feminist Philosophy." *PMLA* 131, no. 2 (2016): 449–59.

Levon, Erez. "Integrating Intersectionality in Language, Gender, and Sexuality Research."
Language and Linguistics Compass 9, no. 7 (2015): 295–308.

Liu, Alan. "Assessing Data Workflows for Common Data 'Moves' across Disciplines." Alan
Liu (personal blog). May 6, 2017, http://liu.english.ucsb.edu/data-moves. Accessed
December 15, 2017. doi: 10.21972/G21593.

Liu, Alan. "What Is the Meaning of the Digital Humanities to the Humanities?" *PMLA*
128, no. 2 (2013): 409–23.

Maccoby, Eleanor and Carol Jacklin. *The Psychology of Sex Differences.* Stanford, Calif.:
Stanford University Press, 1974.

Mandell, Laura. *Breaking the Book: Print Humanities in the Digital Age.* Malden, Mass.:
Wiley Blackwell, 2015.

Mandell, Laura. "Gender and Big Data: Finding or Making Stereotypes?" Presentation at
Dartmouth College, Hanover, N.H., May 24, 2016.

Mandell, Laura. "Gendering Digital Literary History: What Counts for Digital Humanities." In *A New Companion to Digital Humanities,* edited by Susan Schreibman, John Unsworth, and Ray Siemens, 511–24. 2nd ed. Malden, Mass: Wiley-Blackwell, 2016.

Mandell, Laura. "Visualizing Gender Complexity." Universität Hamburg. June 9, 2016, http://lecture2go.uni-hamburg.de/l2go/-/get/v/19498.

Manovich, Lev. "Cultural Analytics: Analysis and Visualization of Large Cultural Data Sets." 2007–2008, http://softwarestudies.com/cultural_analytics/cultural_analytics_2008.doc. Accessed March 13, 2018.

Manovich, Lev. "Cultural Analytics: Visualizing Cultural Patterns in the Age of 'More Media.'" 2009, http://manovich.net/content/04-projects/063-cultural-analytics-visualizing-cultural-patterns/60_article_2009.pdf [The article did not appear in DOMUS, as was planned.]

Marcus, Sharon, Heather Love, and Stephen Best. "Building a Better Description." *Representations* 135 (Summer 2016): 1–21.

Merriman, Ben. "A Science of Literature: Review of *Distant Reading* (Moretti), *The Bourgeois* (Moretti), and *Macroanalysis* (Jockers)." *Boston Review,* August 3, 2015, http://bostonreview.net/books-ideas/ben-merriman-moretti-jockers-digital-humanities. Accessed January 7, 2017.

Miller, Nancy K. "Men's Reading, Women's Writing: Gender and the Rise of the Novel." *Yale French Studies* 75 (1988): 40–55.

Moi, Toril. *Sexual/Textual Politics: Feminist Literary Theory.* New York: Methuen, 1985.

Moretti, Franco. "Conjectures on World Literature." *New Left Review* 1 (2000): 54–66.

Moretti, Franco. *Distant Reading.* London: Verso, 2013.

Moretti, Franco. "'Operationalizing': Or, the Function of Measurement in Modern Literary Theory." Stanford Literary Lab Pamphlet 6. December 2013, http://litlab.stanford.edu/LiteraryLabPamphlet6.pdf. Accessed April 20, 2016.

Moretti, Franco. "Relatively Blunt." *Critical Inquiry* 36 (2009): 172–74.

Moretti, Franco. "Style, Inc. Reflections on Seven Thousand Titles (British Novels, 1740–1850)." *Critical Inquiry* 36 (2009): 134–58.

Noble, Safiya Umoja. "Google Search: Hyper-Visibility as a Means of Rendering Black Women and Girls Invisible." *InVisible Culture* 19 (Fall 2013).

Nuwer, Rachel. "Data Mining the Classics Clusters Women Authors Together, Puts Melville out on a Raft." *Smithsonian Smart News,* August 27, 2012, http://www.smithsonianmag.com/smart-news/data-mining-the-classics-clusters-women-authors-together-puts-mellville-out-on-a-raft-16028354/. Accessed March 23, 2017.

Olsen, Mark. "*Écriture feminine*: Searching for an Indefinable Practice?" *Literary and Linguistic Computing* 20, suppl. (2005): 147–64.

Olsen, Mark. "Qualitative Linguistics and *Histoire des Mentalités*: Gender Representation in the *Trésor de la Langue Française*." *QUALICO,* January 14, 1992.

O'Neil, Cathy. *Weapons of Math Destruction: How Big Data Increases Inequality and Threatens Democracy.* New York: Crown, 2016.

Pennebaker, James. *The Secret Life of Pronouns*. New York: Bloomsbury USA, 2011.

Richardson, Sarah. *Sex Itself: The Search for Male and Female in the Human Genome*. Chicago: University of Chicago Press, 2013.

Rockwell, Geoffrey, and Stéfan Sinclair. Method Commons. http://www.methodi.ca.org. Accessed February 12, 2019.

Rockwell, Geoffrey, and Stéfan Sinclair. Voyant Tools. http://www.voyant-tools.org. Accessed February 12, 2019.

Rybicki, Jan. "*Vive la différence*: Tracing the (Authorial) Gender Signal by Multivariate Analysis of Word Frequencies." *Digital Scholarship in the Humanities* (2015): 1–16. doi: 10.1093/llc/fqv023.

Scott, Joan W. "Gender: A Useful Category of Historical Analysis." *American Historical Review* 91, no. 5 (1986): 1053–75.

Shillingsburg, Peter L. "Detecting the Use of Stereotype Plates." *Editorial Quarterly* 1, no. 1 (1975).

Spender, Dale. *Mothers of the Novel: 100 Good Women Writers before Jane Austen*. New York: Pandora, 1986.

Sprague, Joey, and Mary Zimmerman. "Quality and Quantity: Reconstructing Feminist Methodology." *American Sociologist* 20, no. 1 (1989): 71–86.

Stengers, Isabelle. *Cosmopolitics I*. Translated by Robert Bononno. Minneapolis: University of Minnesota Press, 2010.

Stoller, Robert. "A Contribution to the Study of Gender Identity." *International Journal of Psychoanalysis* 45, nos. 2–3 (1964): 220–26.

Stoller, Robert. "A Further Contribution to the Study of Gender Identity." *International Journal of Psychoanalysis* 49, nos. 2–3 (1968): 364–69.

Tannen, Deborah. *Gender and Discourse*. New York: Oxford University Press, 1994.

Trumpener, Katie. "Critical Response I: Paratext and Genre System." *Critical Inquiry* 36 (2009): 159–70.

Underwood, Ted. *Distant Horizons: Digital Evidence and Literary Change*. Chicago: University of Chicago Press, forthcoming.

Underwood, Ted. "A Genealogy of Distant Reading." *DHQ* 11, no. 2 (2017), http://www.digitalhumanities.org/dhq/vol/11/2/000317/000317.html. Accessed December 15, 2017.

Underwood, Ted. "Measurement and Modeling." The Stone and the Shell (personal blog). December 20, 2013, https://tedunderwood.com/2013/12/20/measurement-and-modeling/. Accessed April 20, 2016.

Underwood, Ted. "The Real Problem with Distant Reading." The Stone and The Shell (personal blog). May 29, 2016, https://tedunderwood.com/2016/05/29/the-real-problem-with-distant-reading/. Accessed December 15, 2017.

Underwood, Ted, and David Bamman. "The Instability of Gender." The Stone and the Shell (personal blog). January 9, 2016, http://tedunderwood.com/2016/01/09/the-instability-of-gender/. Accessed April 19, 2016.

Unsworth, John. "Documenting the Reinvention of Text: The Importance of Failure." *Journal of Electronic Publishing* 3, no. 2 (1997), https://quod.lib.umich.edu/j/jep/3336451.0003.201/--documenting-the-reinvention-of-text-the-importance?rgn=main;view=fulltext. Accessed April 19, 2016.

Watt, Ian. "Spender on Trial." *The World and I*. November 1987, 351–56.

Westbrook, Laurel, and Kristen Schilt. "Doing Gender, Determining Gender: Transgender People, Gender Panics, and Maintenance of the Sex/Gender/Sexuality System." *Gender & Society* 28, no. 1 (2014): 32–57.

Wilkinson, L., and Task Force on Statistical Inference, APA Board of Scientific Affairs. "Statistical Methods in Psychology Journals: Guidelines and Explanations." *American Psychologist* 54, no. 8 (1999): 594–604. [Cited by Coe.]

Williams, Jeffrey J. "The New Modesty in Literary Criticism." *Chronicle of Higher Education* 61, no. 17 (2015): B6–B9.

[Wollstonecraft, Mary.] *A Vindication of the Rights of Men, in a Letter to the Right Honourable Edmund Burke*. London: J. Johnson, 1790.

Wollstonecraft, Mary. *A Vindication of the Rights of Woman*, 3rd ed., 1792. Edited by Deidre Shauna Lynch. New York: W. W. Norton, 2009.

Toward a Critical Black Digital Humanities

SAFIYA UMOJA NOBLE

In a time of paradigm shifts, moral and political treachery, historical amnesia, and psychic and spiritual turmoil, humanistic issues are central—if only funding agencies, media interests, and we humanists ourselves will recognize the momentousness of this era for our discipline and take seriously the need for our intellectual centrality.

—Cathy Davidson, 2008

Audre Lorde's now-famous speech, "The Master's Tools Will Never Dismantle the Master's House," delivered at New York University's Institute for the Humanities conference in 1984, was addressed to an audience of white feminists largely unconcerned with the many missing intellectual contributions of Black women to the fields of feminist theory and practice. Lorde's speech was part of a Black radical feminist tradition, which, among other critical Black intellectual movements, we might welcome into the field of digital humanities. These movements allow us to see how, rather than making Black life and the lives of other people of color solely the subjects of archival and preservation practice, we might also consider the degree to which our very reliance on digital tools, of the master or otherwise, exacerbates existing patterns of exploitation and at times even creates new ones. At an organizational level, digital humanists have been concerned with a number of practices that include the mobilization and shaping of the university and government financial resources and investments in DH centers, as well as a concentrated commitment to harnessing the activities of designers, engineers, and technicians in the service of DH projects. Yet, the colonial remnants of digital media investments are always bleeding into view through new neocolonial policies and discourses that meet the constantly changing conditions of twenty-first-century life. Here, the work of Kent Ono is helpful in his characterization of colonization as a process of forgetting, of an imaginary of emptiness, or a process by which a liberated stance is taken as noncolonial, which I think aptly describes the alleged

[27

"neutral" stance that many in the fields of information studies and digital humanities assert. It is through this stance of *not* being engaged with the Western colonial past, a past that has never ended, that we perpetuate digital media practices that exploit the labor of people of color, as well as the environment. If ever there were a place for digital humanists to engage and critique, it is at the intersection of neocolonial investments in information, communication, and technology infrastructures: investments that rest precariously on colonial history, past and present.

A Neoliberal Turn in Digital Humanities

What does the DH field know about Black studies that could forward our aims of a critical digital humanities, and what are the key intellectual drivers that might help frame what we take up in practice? In her work in the 2016 edition of *Debates in the Digital Humanities,* Roopika Risam introduced the field of digital humanities to Black feminism and its attendant frame of "intersectionality," arguing that Eurocentric notions of critical theory have supplanted Black feminist contributions and the colonization of local knowledge. Kim Gallon, in that same edition, made the case for "Black Digital Humanities" by foregrounding the role that Black studies can play in recovering knowledge and in exposing the power regimes that legitimate (or not) Black life through computational processes, exclusion, or racialized hegemonies. With this in mind, we might summon additional theorists directly from the field of Black studies who are concerned with the structural conditions of oppression.

For example, Black studies historian Peter Hudson mounted an important critique of the neoliberal turn in African diaspora studies for its focus on cultural production rather than political economy and provides a compelling example of what such an expansion might yield. Hudson's emphasis on the material conditions of Black life, which he takes to include the intertwined dimensions of race and capital, shows how such examples can enable a critique of the racialized (and, I would add, intersectional and gendered) basis of capitalist modes of production. Hudson argues that the undue emphasis on cultural production in the humanities has given us a limited, postmodern view of contemporary problems, one that obscures some of the concerns that might otherwise be taken up and intervened with differently. This critique suggests how we might revise our approach by thinking more responsibly about the material conditions that enable DH work, conditions that include labor and exploitation in the service of making digital infrastructures and systems, rather than just making sure Black representation is managed and expanded on in our projects.

Hudson's notion of a "corporate turn" in African diaspora studies helps us move away from the relativistic analyses of cultural studies that unnecessarily limit the scope of our intellectual engagements. He argues, "Where once Black culture could be evoked for its oppositional relationship to the capitalist market, on one hand, and the racial state, on the other, now it has been defanged, denuded of dissident valence, and repurposed for the expansion of markets and the neutralization of progressive Black politics."

The neutralization of critique is a lesson we can extend to digital humanities. To what extent might we apply this logic to the work of digital humanists? We could consider ourselves working either in the service of motivating and extending liberatory possibilities through the expansion of knowledge or moving toward a stabilized, institutionalized series of priorities that focus on initiatives, centers, and projects that have been "defanged" of any possibility for societal transformation of racial oppression. This turn or institutional shift away from the interrogation of exploitation often leads us to focus primarily on cultural production, such as collecting and curating artifacts of culture among those communities underrepresented in traditional DH work; it leads us to digitize Black culture, but not to use it in service of dismantling racist systems that contain and constrain freedom for Black bodies.

As we look at the types of DH projects that are funded and sustained, we might also consider how our emphasis on cultural preservation and access has often precluded our thinking through the complicated material engagements that buttress digitality. I am thinking here about the cost to the field of actively alienating the very kinds of practitioners who are invested in the liberatory possibility of digital humanities, exemplified by a letter written in 2017 to the field by Jarrett Drake, former digital archivist at Princeton University:

> I'm leaving the archival profession to begin a PhD program in anthropology at Harvard where I will be studying how communities in the US are using memory projects in the fight against state violence. For four years, I have watched white co-workers and colleagues in this profession stay complicitly silent as state agents slaughter Black people in the streets. I cried when Mike got killed. When Tamir got killed. When Freddie got killed. When Sandra got killed. When Korryn got killed. I cried again when, in each case, the state held no one accountable. I want to cry right now as I process that yet another Black person, Philando Castile, was taken by the state yet his killer walks free. Another mother buries a son, a partner buries a partner, a daughter buries a father. State assaults on Black boys and men often have a ripple effect of impacting 3x as many Black women and girls, as is the case with Philando. The silence suffocates me in the open air; at work, at conferences, or anywhere large number of professional archivists congregate. I can't breathe.

Drake's compelling letter to the field of information and archival studies, and digital humanities writ large, should serve as a wake-up call. The digital humanities can profoundly alienate Black people from participating in its work because of its silences and refusals to engage in addressing the intersecting dimensions of policy, economics, and intersectional racial and gender oppression that are part of the society we live in; this engagement cannot be relegated just to Black digital humanists.

We are living in a moment where Black people's lives can be documented and digitalized, but cannot be empowered or respected in society.

We should design against—or outright resist—the exploitive forms of labor and hazardous environmental practices in which information and communication technologies are implicated, and this has to include our everyday decisions that foment erasure and silence among practitioners. We should move with intention to address whether the digital humanities is invested in making itself a new cottage industry or whether, like other humanistic projects, it could turn toward deeper engagements with social transformation. We can no longer deny that digital tools and projects are implicated in the rise in global inequality, because digital systems are reliant on global racialized labor exploitation. We can no longer pretend that digital infrastructures are not linked to crises like global warming and impending ecological disasters. We cannot deny that the silences of the field in addressing systemic state violence against Black lives are palpable. Critical digital humanities must closely align with the register in which critical interventions can occur. We need conversations that foreground the crisis at the level of the local, as Drake makes so plain for us when he describes the way digital humanities works in practice. We should take up new conversations globally, as we interrogate the role the field plays in both creating and addressing crises.

Can the Digital Be Decolonized?

DH has long served as a hub for engagement across the range of concerns faced not only by information studies scholars but also by the many fields concerned with issues of interdisciplinarity. Recall the manifesto by Siva Vaidhyanthan who, more than a decade ago, called for critical information scholarship that borrowed from other fields in order to rethink existing frameworks and imagine new possibilities. This idea of taking up both race and political economy in digital humanities is emerging, but it must now be embraced and pushed to the center of the field. Key scholars like Roopika Risam and micha cárdenas have introduced the idea of de/post/anti colonial digital humanities by using the work of Frantz Fanon and others to interrogate whether, and if so, the digital can be decolonized. Simultaneously, Tara McPherson has suggested that we must find a way to put the concerns of scholarship engaging with race, ethnicity, and critical theory in dialogue with DH scholars working on tools and digital infrastructures, and she rightly argued that the impact of whiteness often limits the influence and possibilities of DH work. Using critical race theory and critical whiteness theory is the next logical step to bolster the de/post/anti colonial DH research of Risam and cárdenas, and that usage has continued to grow.[1] There is a burgeoning group of DH scholars paying attention to the uneven and exploitive set of social relationships that are rendered invisible through the globalized technological infrastructures that support DH work, such as the work on ICT supply chains by Miriam Posner at UCLA. I am consistently affirmed by Catherine Knight Steele as she documents the many sites of resistance to oppression that are being created by Black people, particularly Black women, in her research on "Digital Black Feminism." What we need to do to solidify the field of critical digital humanities is to couple it more closely with other critical traditions that foreground approaches influenced by political economy and intersectional race and gender studies.

More generally, we can take this interdisciplinary opening to think about whether a shift of resources away from digital production to projects that take on issues of social, economic, and environmental inequality can allow more significant interventions to take hold. The digital humanities is moving to the fore of the academy at a moment of heightened racial oppression, rising white supremacy, anti-LGBTQ hysteria among politicians, anti-immigrant legislation, mass incarceration, and the most profound wealth and resource inequality (which disproportionately harms women and children) to be recorded in modern times. If critical digital humanists are not willing to lead the conversation about the implications of the digital on social inequality and to help develop policy that attempts to mitigate this inequality, then who can? Here, let me call attention to the important Afrofuturist work, in the tradition of Alondra Nelson, which includes Jessica Johnson and Mark Anthony Neal's call for Black Code studies in a recent issue of *The Black Scholar*,[2] which offers even more provocations about the possibilities for reimagining the digital in service of liberation.

Critical DH scholarship working in a Black studies tradition can spark increased visibility of, commitment to, and intervention in the grand challenges of social inequality and environmental disaster.[3] We see challenges to life and to the planet in, for instance, the extraction and mining industries that fuel the microprocessor chip industry or the practices of electronics disposal (or lack thereof) that poison people and the environments. As I have written earlier, the extraction of minerals needed for digital computing technologies, the impact of conflicts over rare minerals, and the exploitive nature of the flow of global capital in and out of the regions where they are sourced have a serious impact on human rights and the environment.[4] These processes are rarely foregrounded for users and designers of digital tools, yet these practices are racialized, in that the primary beneficiaries of most digital technologies reside in the Global North. The underbelly of networked exploitation in the Global South, from the Congo to Ghana, is typically hidden from the view of those in Silicon Valley, at cultural institutions like libraries and museums, and in the universities and research labs in which DHers teach and work. How then does digital humanities reconcile its commitments to data and computation with the very real hardships faced by those who work in the computer and electronics industries? The landscape of information and communication technology, including the tools used in DH projects, are fully implicated in racialized violence and environmental destruction: from extraction to production, and from consumption to disposal of digital technologies.

Thus, at the same time that I call on DH scholars to engage in the work of African/Black diaspora studies, I am also calling on African/Black diaspora studies scholars who do not necessarily align themselves with the digital humanities to contribute to the project of surfacing the intellectual traditions of political economy and race and gender studies in the field. Rather than think of digital humanities solely in terms of campus-based initiatives or of "big data" projects that advance historical and cultural scholarship, we might begin to interrogate how it also perpetuates the uneven distribution of information technology resources, how it sustains cultural centers that are implicated in the suppression of Black life diasporically, and how it often works in a neoliberal fashion to obscure important features of the social, political, and economic landscape. Put differently, how can we mash up or hack racial inequality, rather than big data?

A Future for Critical Black Digital Humanities

We are at a crucial moment in the preservation of our humanity, and digital humanities needs to be on the side of the future, rather than one of many contributors to a history of extinction. Largely understudied and hidden from view (or interest) of most DH scholars are the labor, extraction, and disposal processes that are contributing to massive humanitarian and ecological disasters, thereby continuing the (neo)colonial projects of the past. Arguably, the latest iteration of the neocolonial "Scramble for Africa" is over the land and labor resources that were previously marshaled to build the largess of Global North's agricultural and industrial empires. Now that our empire is technological, much of the gratuitous exploitation is contained to the Global South—out of sight of most DH scholars. But no matter the distance, our human interdependence necessitates that we engage in these difficult issues of power, resources, and our investments in the digital tools and technology that undergird DH work.

It is not just the everyday use of digital technologies that we must confront in our work but also the public policy and resource distribution models that allow for the existence of the digital to take such a profound hold. Robert Mejia's eloquent essay, "The Epidemiology of Digital Infrastructure," warns of the many ways that communicable diseases are exacerbated by the materiality of electronics and communications devices and infrastructures. The disease-producing by-products of the chemical waste spun from digital technologies are profoundly harmful; Mejia documents how the "3.7 million gallons of water used per day by Intel in Hillsboro, Oregon, and the millions more used elsewhere, contribute to an ecology hospitable to infectious disease and its natural reservoirs." His research is the kind of work that must be integrated into the emerging, interdisciplinary critical digital humanities as we call for a greater awareness of the materiality of the digital humanities and its impact in the world. For the sites of waste and toxicity are both local to the United States and global: we see toxic e-waste sites emerge in formerly pristine wetlands in places like Accra, Ghana, among other sites in the Global South. Risam's call for using a Black feminist ethos that integrates the local and the global is thus deeply relevant.

Current DH work must challenge the impulse in digital humanities that privileges digitality and computerization, along with the related concepts of use, access, and preservation, while often failing to account for more immediate and pressing global concerns. These concerns, which include the crisis of racialized global capitalism and the environmental catastrophes from the attendant issues caused by digital infrastructures, are issues that critical DH scholars could play an active role in addressing and remedying. The field must foreground a recognition of the superstructures that overdetermine the computerization and informationalization of DH projects, so that those projects can intervene in instances of racial, economic, and political oppression. The exploitive labor and service economies that support large-scale, global communications infrastructures are part of a (neo)colonial past and present; hyperinvestments in digitality in the Global North are precariously tied to racialized capitalism—and to ecological disaster.

While we are reliant on these infrastructures and investments to conduct DH research, we need to concurrently theorize different models for doing our work. This will allow us to divest from troublesome infrastructures that include software applications, internet service providers, information repositories, server farms, and the unending multitude of hardware devices that connect us through a host of algorithms and artificial intelligence that can foment inequality and oppression through their automated decision-making systems. In this call to action, I am taking a cue from DH arguments about the broad value of digital technologies to the humanities, but am focusing on the specific contributions that the field of Black studies can make to deepening those arguments. By foregrounding a paradigm of critical engagement and activist scholarship that privileges the concerns of those living in the greatest conditions of precarity because of a combination of economic, racial, and environmental violence, we can think about the implications of DH work in a larger global context.

In our future work, models of inquiry that employ intersectional Black studies frameworks allow for a contextualizing—or, rather, a destabilizing—of our assumptions about the longevity and efficiency of our technological investments. Discursively, aspects of DH research and intervention may work from a premise of knowledge sharing and preservation, but the technological engagements they rest on are not free from political consequence. DH projects are undeniably documenting, preserving, and mobilizing the knowledges and cultures that are threatened by discriminatory public policies. We need to continue to inquire with a critical DH lens tilted toward Black studies, gender studies, ethnic studies, information studies, media studies, communication, sociology, and science and technology studies. Ultimately, humanists are uniquely qualified to understand the adverse consequences of concentrations of racialized global capital, human-precipitated environmental disaster, and social, political, and economic destabilization.

We might begin by asking ourselves at what point did we become overly invested in the digital to the exclusion of pressing social issues of racial injustice, disenfranchisement, and community transformation. Is the narrow, inwardly focused attention on institutionalizing digital humanities to the exclusion of the social, political, and economic landscape worth it? What are the boundaries that we will consider in our collective engagements? The cumulative effects of mass-scale digital infrastructures, products, and engagements require a debt of energy and resources that we cannot collectively repay to the earth or to humanity; only radical reinvestment of the largesse of these projects and company profits back into collective, public interventions on these debts has the potential for renewal and reparation.

NOTES

1. Miriam Posner has directed us to several important critical digital humanities projects, making them more visible to the field, including her own call to deemphasize computer coding as the only legitimate pathway in DH, http://miriamposner.com/blog/some-things-to-think-about-before-you-exhort-everyone-to-code/. Also, see Lauren Klein's talk at the Modern Language Association, where she acknowledges important feminist DH interventions, http://lklein.com/2018/01/distant-reading-after-moretti/.

2. See Johnson and Neal, "Introduction: Wild Seed in the Machine," along with the other essays in that volume.

3. See Bethany Nwoskie's 2014 speech at the Digital Humanities conference.

4. See Noble, "A Future," 1–8.

BIBLIOGRAPHY

Davidson, Cathy N. "Humanities 2.0: Promise, Perils, Predictions." *PMLA* 123, no. 3 (2008): 707–17.

Drake, Jarrett M. "I'm Leaving the Archival Profession: It's Better This Way." 2017, https://medium.com/on-archivy/im-leaving-the-archival-profession-it-s-better-this-way-ed631c6d72fe.

Eichstaedt, Peter H. *Consuming the Congo: War and Conflict Minerals in the World's Deadliest Place.* Chicago: Lawrence Hill, 2011.

Fields, Gary. *Territories of Profit: Communications, Capitalist Development, and the Innovative Enterprises of G. F. Swift and Dell Computer.* Stanford, Calif.: Stanford University Press, 2004.

Gallon, Kim. "Making a Case for Black Digital Humanities." In *Debates in the Digital Humanities 2016*, edited by Matthew K. Gold and Lauren F. Klein, 42–49. Minneapolis: University of Minnesota Press, 2016.

Hudson, Peter. "African Diaspora Studies and the Corporate Turn." Association for the Study of the Worldwide African Diaspora. 2013, http://aswadiaspora.org/forums/topic/african-diaspora-studies-and-the-corporate-turn-3/. Accessed on January 25, 2016.

Johnson, Jessica Marie, and Mark Anthony Neal. "Introduction: Wild Seed in the Machine." *The Black Scholar* 47, no. 3 (2017): 1–2.

Lorde, Audre. "The Master's Tools Will Never Dismantle the Master's House." In *Sister Outsider: Essays and Speeches,* 110–14. Berkeley, Calif.: Crossing Press, 2007.

McPherson, Tara. "Introduction: Media Studies and the Digital Humanities." *Cinema Journal* 48, no. 2 (2009): 119–23.

Mejia, Robert. "The Epidemiology of Digital Infrastructure. In *The Intersectional Internet: Race, Sex, and Culture Online,* edited by Safiya Umoja Noble and Brendesha Tynes. Digital Formations Series, 229–41. New York: Peter Lang, 2016.

Noble, Safiya Umoja. *Algorithms of Oppression: How Search Engines Reinforce Racism.* New York: New York University Press, 2018.

Noble, Safiya Umoja. "A Future for Intersectional Black Feminist Technology Studies." *Scholar & Feminist Online* 13, no. 3–14, no. 1 (2016): 1–8.

Noble, Safiya Umoja. "Trayvon, Race, Media and the Politics of Spectacle." *The Black Scholar* 44, no. 1 (2014): 12–29.

Ono, Kent. *Contemporary Media Culture and Remnants of a Colonial Past.* New York: Peter Lang: 2009.

Risam, Roopika. "Navigating the Global Digital Humanities: Insights from Black Feminism." In *Debates in the Digital Humanities 2016*, edited by Matthew K. Gold and Lauren F. Klein, 359–67. Minneapolis: University of Minnesota Press, 2016.

Roberts, Sarah T., and Safiya Umoja Noble. "Empowered to Name, Inspired to Act: Social Responsibility and Diversity as Calls to Action in the LIS Context." *Library Trends* 64, no. 3 (2015): 512–32.

Vaidhyanathan, Siva. "Afterword—Critical Information Studies: A Bibliographic Manifesto." *Cultural Studies* 20, nos. 2–3 (March/May, 2006): 292–315.

Can Video Games Be Humanities Scholarship?

JAMES COLTRAIN AND STEPHEN RAMSAY

Games, as Wittgenstein warned us, are not easily placed into categories (36). At this point, even cataloging general game mechanics is a fool's errand; genres proliferate as fast as the gatekeepers of the App Store and the Steam platform can green-light them. Yet for all this growth, it is an easy matter to say what games are not. Games are not, in most departments, *humanistic scholarship*.

This is not to say that there has been no cross-pollination between games and the humanities or that there are not already natural relationships between the two areas. It took some time before even writing about games became acceptable as humanistic scholarship.[1] But in the end, it was not hard for an academy well adjusted to the long shadow of cultural studies to conform itself to these new objects of inquiry. It also was not terribly difficult to develop academic programs in which the creation of video games—one of the more striking examples of the marriage of engineering and art—became the principal research activity: where a billion-dollar industry arises, an academic program will follow.[2] With revenues that exceed those of Hollywood, and a growing and diversifying world market, one might argue that video games are among the most important imaginative human artifacts to develop in the past several decades; it would be extraordinary if the academy were not discussing them and teaching people how to build them. Furthermore, games naturally engage with subjects that lie within the conventional province of humanistic inquiry, including storytelling, architecture, music, and visual art. In spite of all this, building a game in a History or English Department and submitting that as academic work on par with a book remain risky propositions.

Humanistic inquiry is concerned with the study of the human record. In the conventional media by which discoveries concerning this record are communicated (books and articles), the process by which this knowledge was achieved often takes the form of a re-creation of the author's or authors' experience (whether that is the experience of reading a novel, excavating an archaeological site, viewing a painting, analyzing archival materials, or any of the dozens of activities one might take with respect to primary and secondary sources). Thus the literary critic reads and then attempts to re-create that particular reading experience for someone else. The historian makes his or her way through the twisted paths of the archive and then re-creates that experience in the form of a discursive set of findings and theorizations. Scholarly articles in historical archaeology are often substantially about the process by which the discovery was made. Often, the "techne" of scholarly writing consists primarily in making these experiences seem less fluid and fraught with uncertainty than they actually were—as if the path had always been clear and simple. But that is only a rhetorical flourish. The statement, "I discovered x, was perplexed by it, and was led to y, which in turn led me to z," would represent an unusual form of scholarly writing, but certainly not a nonscholarly one nor one without precedent.

"Scholarly experience," however, is a message in search of a medium. Traditionally, the outcome has been a reconstructed experience that has taken a particular, and particularly restrictive, set of forms (e.g., books and articles or their digital surrogates).[3] Establishing games as among these forms merely involves reimagining in more radical terms the outcomes of the already game-like experiences that lead to scholarship. The emphasis, however, needs to be placed on creating meaningful analogs to the experiences that lead toward scholarly outcomes, and not on importing traditional methods from older scholarly forms. Matters such as "citation," "thesis," "abstract," and the generic traditions of scholarly rhetoric need to be viewed not as necessary components to enabling something to be deemed scholarly, but rather as the apparatus of a specific genre and its medium. To talk about video games is to talk about both a new genre and a new medium: one that will require its own, perhaps quite different, scholarly apparatus.

Of course, if we are to talk about games as a new genre and medium for a scholarly research experience, we must remember there is no consistent definition of what constitutes a video game. Nearly all definitions include some aspect of interactivity, but then again, nearly all forms of media are interactive in some way. Television viewers change channels, readers turn pages, and anyone browsing the web interacts with content just by searching and clicking. But beyond acknowledging that games must be interactive, definitions of the medium diverge wildly. Some more traditional views suggest that games should have a goal or pose a challenge, through which certain players can "win." Others describe a requirement for fun or, more broadly, for play—which might simply constitute a deeper, more personalized kind of interactivity. Many definitions stress the need for rules to accompany a goal, while others focus on the freedom to experiment. Others emphasize the need for a story, although a large percentage of games have none, while still others demand the capacity for choice—which many games nonetheless deny.[4] This debate is not confined only to discussion among scholars but also represents an active discussion among gamers themselves. In fact, disputes over whether the interactive fiction of text games like *Depression Quest,* which featured sometimes symbolically disabled multiple-choice answers, or so-called walking simulators like *Gone Home* and *Dear*

Esther, which eschewed clear goals in favor of environmental storytelling, are proper games continue to saturate game culture and drive online debates.[5]

For the purposes of this chapter, we define a video game as an interactive digital work designed to impart a particular experience or set of experiences that are dependent on the player's interactions. Many of these experiences aim to challenge or entertain the player and therefore reflect the more traditional definitions of what constitutes a game outlined earlier. Some games may be more experimental, designed to evoke strong emotions from their players, including fun, as well as fear, mystery, sadness, challenge, sympathy, achievement, or power. Yet other games may be more functional, balancing or even eschewing emotion in favor of the more practical goals of informing, educating, or training their players. Even the most obtuse games still manage the player's experience in some way, because those designed to be so boring, frustrating, or opaque that they become "unplayable" still elicit an intended response as a result of the player's engagement (or lack thereof).

But the question remains: Can video games serve not just as scholarship by humanists but also as actual humanities scholarship? In other words, can video games go beyond merely illustrating or synthesizing humanistic content in ways that are credited as scholarship to become vehicles for completely new interpretations in the humanities? Can a humanities scholar use a video game to convey his or her interpretation of the literary, historical, or theoretical significance of a novel or of the broader meaning (or underlying cause) of a specific historical event?

These questions would seem to turn on whether video games, as a medium, offer sufficiently developed features for capturing the scholarly experience, particularly as it relates to articulations of new arguments and interpretations. To be sure, there are many conventions, constraints, and expectations common to the medium of video games that might threaten the conveyance of a potential interpretation. Most of these potential pitfalls involve choices commonly made in the interest of either artistry or usability, and any successful humanities video game would have to acknowledge these choices with a critical awareness. Yet, if we examine these and other potential weaknesses of the video game as a medium for scholarly expression, we find that these weaknesses are not necessarily any more limiting than many common practices associated with written humanities scholarship.

The artistic conventions of games certainly affect players' reception of them, just as they would a humanistic interpretation conveyed through a game, but humanists already incorporate their own artistic conventions into their written work. Games often seek to manage players' emotions through dramatic techniques like appeals to humor, sympathy, or disgust; yet so too might a historian begin a chapter with a vivid vignette, or a literary critic with a deeply felt personal anecdote. And just as a game-based drama may anticipate the moral leanings of its players as part of the emotional choices it presents, even quite dispassionately written analyses of injustice or tragedy are intentionally animated by the moral expectations of their audience. Most games also make visual appeals, with carefully crafted art styles or architectural environments designed not only to be beautiful or realistic but also to manage the mood, tone, and ultimately the meaning of the experience of gameplay. In general, humanities scholarship relies less on visuals, but even the most emphatically textual works may make use of simple charts, diagrams, maps, or illustrations, each with aesthetic choices that can affect the ultimate interpretation. And what of the expectation that a game be "fun" or, at the least, "entertaining" or "compelling"? Certainly a compelling game will attract more players, just as a clearly and artfully written monograph will (likely) attract more readers. But even the games community has shown its willingness to go beyond mainstream demands for entertainment by creating art games and even so-called anti-games that find their meaning in ugliness, impediment, or frustration. These works succeed in the same way as do humanities texts that are prized for their insights despite jargon-laden or discipline-specific prose.[6] Art and "anti-games" also overlap somewhat with the increasingly broad category of "serious games," which can encompass everything from games that deal with pressing social issues to those that may reject narrative or ludic concerns altogether for purposes like military and medical training, journalistic reporting, and therapy.[7]

By necessity, games must also simplify the situations they depict and the interactions they facilitate, but so too does good humanities scholarship. Both media must condense time, for example; a historian may reduce an entire decade to a single sentence, while a game may compress the same to a click. Video games and written scholarship also both generalize about and construct their own spaces, as when a researcher draws a map or discusses a region, or when a game designer sets the boundaries of levels. The two media also, similarly, simplify processes; a history may distill hundreds of bureaucratic interactions into an analysis of a single leader, just as a game might represent an incredibly complex interaction like the powering up of a fighter jet as the press of a single button. Most importantly, nearly all scholarship employs some form of synthesis, condensing the prior literature, related artifacts, and the author's own observations into sentences and paragraphs. The reductions of scale, choice, or interactive possibilities required for a game's design to be manageable are the result of a similar synthetic process. In short, humanities scholarship takes research and repackages it into an argument. A scholarly game might take the same material and similarly craft a carefully researched interactive experience.

Finally, there are the structural demands of making a game, which, like their written analogs, shape and limit the potential of any argument. Written scholarship has its own formal constraints, such as chapters, figures, quotes, and citations, just as a game has levels, menus, zones, and segments. Humanities scholarship is shaped into the time-honored formats of the essay, the journal, the monograph, and the edited collection, just as video games have their own set of platforms: PC, console, mobile, and now VR. Writing within a specific discipline might also involve theoretical or methodological considerations that limit how a research question might be approached or an interpretation expressed. A historian researching the causes of a war might find herself investigating everything from world ecology and macro-economics to the rhetoric or public personality of a single individual, but her methodology must be distilled into a coherent approach or a set of approaches in the resulting scholarship. In the same way, genre will also affect the scope of any scholarly game. But even game mechanics as different as the left-right-down of *Tetris* or the advanced button combinations of *Tomb Raider* can be critically assessed in their own context. An argument-as-game might be similarly assessed in the context of its generic constraints, allowing for an awareness of the effects of those constraints on the interpretation that is presented. Regardless of the aspects of the video game medium that might cloud a scholarly argument, there are other aspects that might provide for a fuller realization of a scholarly experience.

By the nature of their interactivity, for example, games have a superior capacity to handle multiple options and outcomes. This potential for variety could lend itself to analyses that do not force scholars to advance a single theory, but instead would allow players to explore multiple interpretations crafted by the game's designer. Explorable environments in which players follow their own curiosity drive complex open-world games like *Skyrim* and the *Grand Theft Auto* series, and a scholarly game could similarly give players the ability to choose their own routes through a reconstructed historical space or through an art exhibit in a virtual gallery. Such exploration would depend on the player's own decisions, and player choice is another area where games have provided compelling examples of intentionally designed user agency. These include the adaptive strategies enacted in classic turn-based wargames and modern multiplayer online battle arena games, as well as the life-or-death moral choices in TellTale's *Walking Dead* series. Of course, other forms of scholarship allow for a degree of choice—for instance, the search bar on a digital archive—but games can also respond to and manage player choices as they are made, as when *Mario Kart* increases an opponent's ability in response to a player's aptitude or when the narrator in the *Stanley Parable* playfully responds when his directions are disobeyed.

Games are well suited for expressing and responding to the sort of complex processes that humanities scholars often attempt to articulate. Many types of games are defined by formal or informal rules, and these rules can be adapted to reflect similarly structured humanistic arguments or theories. Computer games provide many methods of simulation; for example, *Civilization*'s world systems, *the Sims'* social interactions, and the economic markets of *EVE Online*. Scholars could make use of simulations not only by offering sets of rules or models as components of an argument in which players could evaluate its impact on the simulation's outcomes but also by arranging more open spaces in which users could experiment in an environment bounded by the scholar's theory or design. Games include great examples of these experimental spaces; take the success of indie games like *Kerbal Space Program* or *Besieged*, which give players a toolkit and a problem and then challenge them to complete a goal, resulting in solutions that the designers themselves would never have conceived. Famously, *Minecraft*'s intended structuring mechanic of the quest has been dramatically overshadowed by players who prefer to use the game's building environment as a sort of virtual Lego kit. Interactive simulations might also promote novel forms of scholarly discussion, as scholar-players or reviewers could explore the merits of a proposed model, both designing scenarios that might disprove the game's overarching theory and critiquing the simulation itself if its results are too perfect. Scholarly games might even include traditional game challenges for their players—not simply to entertain but also to embody real-world frustrations and satisfactions. For instance, players tasked with building a pyramid using only Bronze Age tools might form a new appreciation for ancient ingenuity, and accounts of these experiences might themselves constitute a set of scholarly interpretations that could then drive further discussion.

Perhaps most importantly, games could provide a vehicle for modeling humanistic theories in a way that more closely resembles the diverse variety of subjective human experiences. One of the greatest advantages of the video game medium is its ability to place a player in the role of a character. Role-playing games from the pixelated *Dragon Warrior* to the sprawling *Fallout* series have shown the potential for engineering unique character profiles, each of whom experiences the same virtual world quite differently. This simulated subjectivity has often been used to give players powers and abilities beyond their daily lives, but these avatars could just as easily be tailored to show limitations. Such characters might be made to be aware of their race, class, rank, sexual orientation, or other personal or group identities, for example, and experience the consequences of those identities as they traverse the game. Indeed, placing players in specific roles to generate empathy has driven the success of both high-budget games from large studios and many "serious" or educational titles. In the *Walking Dead* series, for instance, many players remarked on how protective they felt when playing the character of Lee, an adult in charge of looking after grade-school-aged Clementine during a zombie outbreak, while others reported increased feelings of vulnerability when the sequel gave them the chance to play as the young girl.[8] Designers can use empathy to implicate the audience in coercive situations, as in *Papers Please,* when players taking on the role of a checkpoint clerk in a fictional Soviet-bloc–style country are forced to choose between aiding the plight of incoming refugees and endangering the paycheck on which their own family depends. Where before scholars might use evocative details to summon their readers' empathy for historical actors, scholarly games could allow players to embody those actors' roles and gain empathy for them through active participation.

Scholarly games might also be able to enhance humanities scholarship by more fully representing the wider context of a particular object of study. Teachers will often remind literature students how different *Macbeth* would have felt watching it from the pit at the Globe from how it would read on a modern page or how the Elgin Marbles would have appeared from the roof of the Parthenon in the classical Acropolis. By conveying a more true sense of space, of the passage of time, and of the use of sound, color, texture, and interaction, games can add vibrant and dynamic context to interpretations that would be difficult to express on the page. When combined with the previously discussed possibilities for embodying a subjective character or viewpoint, games have the capability to present much more complete phenomenological experiences as scholarly arguments. In addition to tangible elements like the weather, the time of day, and the time of year, as well as the particular acoustics, vantage points, access, and limitations of a space, scholarly games could attempt to articulate the experiential knowledge that colors subjective meaning. If a reader is unlikely to understand the drudgery of a historical trade like blacksmithing from a description alone, a game can provide a player with a virtual hammer to pound for dozens of tries until simulated fatigue sets in. If a modern visitor might not understand the experience of dread that an idyllic Civil War cemetery might evoke in a war veteran, then a game can give them a more visceral sense of battlefield horror—perhaps even visited on a group of virtual family members.

While the potential for the sort of scholarly games described earlier has yet to be realized in humanities departments, there are examples of recent games released both by the industry and the academy that might serve as models for future efforts. *Never Alone,* a side-scrolling action game, is the result of an extensively documented collaboration between E-Line Media and the Iñupiat people of Alaska; it uses traditional platforming gameplay to teach players about both tribal folklore and community values. Another game, *1979 Revolution,* adopts Telltale-style dramatic choices to pull players between different factions during a re-creation of the Iranian revolution. This game also incorporates surviving documents, photographs, and the oral family history of its designer Navid Khonsari. But perhaps the best early example of a scholarly humanities game is *Walden: A Game,* a project led by game design professor Tracy Fullerton at the School of Cinematic Arts at the University of Southern California. *Walden* draws on the mechanics of recent survival games, but instead of forcing players to manage scant resources to stay alive, it challenges them to follow in the path of Henry David Thoreau's famous book, seeking enlightenment and peace by exploring and experiencing the seasons in a faithful re-creation of Walden Pond. Exhaustively researched over many years, the player's experience as curated by *Walden* is both a literary interpretation of the original text and a historical analysis, employing archival historical evidence to inform its original script and reconstructed environments. Players may very well come to a deeper experiential and emotional understanding of Thoreau, transcendentalism, and nineteenth-century America by playing *Walden,* but the game's effectiveness and meaning can be discussed and critiqued in light of the original book and other historical evidence, just like a traditional form of humanities scholarship.[9]

Of course, undertaking the project of creating scholarly games in the humanities cannot proceed without due attention and acknowledgment to other, long-established communities and discourses around games. This includes not only game studies but also the many game design communities that already exist. For while creating games along the lines we suggest involves a recalibration of what "counts" as humanities scholarship, the art and craft of building games—and doing so critically—have preceded our call by decades. That members of these communities have not always felt welcome at DH conferences and in our journals is not only to our shame but also to our detriment. "Scholarly game" is a useful subcategory only insofar as it provokes an internal discussion about the particular needs of humanities scholars and students; no one in the digital humanities is served by pretending that a new subcategory licenses ignorance or avoidance of fellow travelers and natural allies.

In the end, the greatest obstacle that video games face as forms of scholarly endeavor is merely a subset of the obstacles they face more generally. Like other genres—including, importantly, novels and films—they began more as curiosities than as artistic media. In the last couple of decades, however, it has become increasingly clear that "art game" will one day be as natural a term and one as widely used as "art novel" or "art film." "Scholarly game" may take a bit longer, but the process can begin at once. Recalibrating the expectations of promotion and tenure committees is often a matter of surprising them with quality work—work that instructs as much as it delights.

NOTES

1. Some major works that emerged from the field of game studies include Wolf and Perron, *The Video Game Theory Reader*; Juul, *Half-Real*: Wardrip-Fruin, *First Person*; Gee, *What Video Games Have to Teach Us*; Bogost, *Unit Operations*; Marya, *An Introduction to Game Studies*; Bogost, *Persuasive Games*; McGonigal, *Reality Is Broken*; Bogost, *How to Do Things with Videogames*; Taylor and Whalen, *Playing the Past*; and Flanagan, *Critical Play*.

2. Prominent games programs include those at the University of Southern California "USC Games Program | Everyone Plays," http://games.usc.edu; the University of Utah "Entertainment Arts & Engineering," Entertainment Arts & Engineering, http://eae.utah.edu/; New York University "NYU," NYU | Game Center, http://gamecenter.nyu.edu; Michigan State University "Game Design & Development | The College of Communication Arts & Sciences | Michigan State University," http://cas.msu.edu/programs/undergraduate-studies/degree-programs/game-design-development/; the University of California-Santa Cruz "Games and Playable Media @ UCSC," https://games.soe.ucsc.edu; DePaul University "BS In Computer Games Development," https://www.cdm.depaul.edu/academics/Pages/BSInComputerGamesDevelopment.aspx; the Massachusetts Institute of Technology Game Lab Admin, "Study," MIT Game Lab, http://gamelab.mit.edu/study/; Drexel University "Drexel Game Design," http://replay.drexel.edu/; Northeastern University "Home | Game Design | College of Arts, Media and Design | Northeastern University," http://www.northeastern.edu/camd/gamedesign/; and many more institutions. All these sites were last accessed on June 12, 2016.

3. By which we mean digital documents that do not depart in any substantial way from their physical counterpoints. Scholarly websites in digital humanities present an interesting case in the context of this discussion, since they are very often focused precisely on offering the reader/viewer the opportunity to have a "scholarly experience." Still, this is always a matter of emphasis and degree. In all cases, the outcome of one person's scholarly experience becomes the occasion for another's.

4. Works defining games and surveying definitions of games include Huizinga, *Homo Ludens*; Juul, *Half-Real*; Jesse Schell, *The Art of Game Design: A Book of Lenses* (CRC Press, 2014); Koster, *Theory of Fun for Game Design*; Katie Salen and Eric Zimmerman, eds., *The Game Design Reader: A Rules of Play Anthology* (MIT Press, 2006); Chris Crawford, *The Art of Computer Game Design* (McGraw-Hill, 2010).

5. Of course, this question, and *Depression Quest* in particular, were also significant in the reactionary online harassment campaign that became central to the Gamergate controversy. Brian Crecente, "When Is a Game Not a Game?" *Polygon,* http://www.polygon.com/2014/3/31/5566098/gone-home-is-it-a-game; Brandon Sheffield, "What Makes Gone Home a Game?" *Gamasutra,* http://www.gamasutra.com/view/news/213612/What_makes_Gone_Home_a_game.php; "Depression Quest," http://www.depressionquest.com/dqfinal.html; Luke Plunkett, "Dear Esther: The Kotaku Review,"*Kotaku,* http://kotaku.com/5884520/dear-esther-the-kotaku-review.

6. Mike Rose, "Opinion: It's Totally OK to Not Like 'Anti-Games,'" http://www.gamasutra.com/view/news/185885/Opinion_Its_totally_OK_to_not_like_antigames.php, accessed June 2, 2016; Erik Fredner, "The Year in Anti-Games," Kill Screen, December 18, 2014, https://killscreen.com/articles/year-anti-games/.

7. Michael, David R., and Sandra L. Chen, *Serious Games: Games that Educate, Train, and Inform* (Muska & Lipman/Premier-Trade, 2005); Ritterfeld, Ute, Michael Cody, and Peter Vorderer, eds. *Serious Games: Mechanisms and Effects* (Routledge, 2009); Bogost, *Persuasive Games*; Clark C. Abt, *Serious Games* (University Press of America, 1987).

8. "The Walking Dead on Steam," http://store.steampowered.com/app/207610/, accessed June 12, 2016; "The Walking Dead: Season 2 on Steam," http://store.steampowered.com/app/261030/, accessed June 12, 2016.

9. "Never Alone," http://neveralonegame.com/; "1979 Revolution Game," http://1979revolutiongame.com/; "Walden, A Game," https://www.waldengame.com/. All sites accessed January 5, 2018.

BIBLIOGRAPHY

Aarseth, Espen J. *Cybertext: Perspectives on Ergodic Literature.* Baltimore: Johns Hopkins University Press, 1997.

Bogost, Ian. *How to Do Things with Videogames.* Minneapolis: University of Minnesota Press, 2011.

Bogost, Ian. *Persuasive Games: The Expressive Power of Videogames.* Cambridge, Mass.: MIT Press, 2010.

Bogost, Ian. *Unit Operations: An Approach to Videogame Criticism.* Cambridge, Mass.: MIT Press, 2008.

Egenfeldt-Nielsen, Simon, Jonas Heide Smith, and Susana Pajares Tosca. *Understanding Video Games: The Essential Introduction.* New York: Routledge, 2012.

Flanagan, Mary. *Critical Play: Radical Game Design.* Cambridge, Mass.: MIT Press, 2013.

Frederick, Dave. "Serious Games and Higher Ed." *Tesseract.* http://tesseract.uark.edu /blogs/7.

Fullerton, Tracy. *Game Design Workshop: A Playcentric Approach to Creating Innovative Games.* 3rd ed. Boca Raton, Fla.: CRC Press, 2014.

Gee, James Paul. *What Video Games Have to Teach Us about Learning and Literacy.* 2nd ed. New York: St. Martin's Griffin, 2007.

Hatavara, Mari, et al. *Narrative Theory, Literature, and New Media: Narrative Minds and Virtual Worlds.* New York: Routledge, 2015.

Huizinga, Johan. *Homo Ludens: A Study of the Play-Element in Culture.* Eastford, Conn.: Martino Fine Books, 2014.

Jagoda, Patrick. "Gamification and Other Forms of Play." *Boundary* 40, no. 2 (June 20, 2013).

Jagoda, Patrick. "Gaming the Humanities." *Differences* 25, no. 1 (January 1, 2014).

Jones, Steven E. *The Emergence of the Digital Humanities.* New York: Routledge, 2013.

Juul, Jesper. *Half-Real: Video Games between Real Rules and Fictional Worlds.* Cambridge, Mass.: MIT Press, 2005.

Kee, Kevin, ed. *Pastplay: Teaching and Learning History with Technology Paperback.* Ann Arbor: University of Michigan Press, 2014.

Koster, Raph. *Theory of Fun for Game Design.* Newton, Mass.: O'Reilly Media, 2013.

Marya, Frans. *An Introduction to Game Studies.* London: SAGE, 2008.

McGonigal, Jane. *Reality Is Broken: Why Games Make Us Better and How They Can Change the World.* New York: Penguin Press, 2011.

Taylor, Laurie N., and Zach Whalen. *Playing the Past: History and Nostalgia in Video Games.* Nashville, Tenn.: Vanderbilt University Press, 2011.

Wardrip-Fruin, Noah. *First Person: New Media as Story, Performance, and Game.* Cambridge, Mass.: MIT Press, 2006.

Wittgenstein, Ludwig. *Philosophical Investigations.* New York: Pearson, 1973.

Wolf, Mark J. P., and Bernard Perron. *The Video Game Theory Reader.* New York: Routledge, 2003.

"They Also Serve": What DH Might Learn about Controversy and Service from Disciplinary Analogies

CLAIRE WARWICK

I n 2009, at the opening session of the *Digital Humanities* annual conference, Neil Fraistat, the local organizer, made a very bold claim: "This is our time." He was emphatically correct—more so than any of us could have dared to hope at the time. Until then, few people, even those with long histories in the field, had much reason to believe that such a prediction was well founded. In the preceding decade, digital humanities had suffered such reversals in both status and fortune that it took remarkable confidence for anyone to predict a secure future for the field.

In the early to mid-1990s, a field then known as humanities computing was swept up in the popular embrace of all things "virtual," "cyber," or "electronic." At that time, expansive and frankly unrealistic predictions were widespread, both in the popular press and in academic literature, about the scope and speed of the changes that would be wrought: hypertext fiction would replace printed books; students would take online courses, with no need for classrooms or professors; digitized cultural heritage resources delivered on the web would mean that there would be no more need to visit libraries, museums, archives, and galleries in person (Nunberg; Castells; Besser).

Such changes have taken, and in some cases may still take, far longer to happen than the initial hype suggested. This makes sense, given the wider context in which academia, in general, and digital humanities, in particular, exist. We now realize that humans are social creatures who enjoy meeting and exchanging ideas, which means that pure e-learning is not a realistic prospect, at least in the short term. Our affection for and desire to use physical things have also proven remarkably robust—hence the continued popularity of the printed book, the vinyl record, and visits to museums and galleries. By the same token, it is not surprising that such physical artifacts remain crucial as objects of study in the humanities.

In the early 2000s, as the dot-com boom turned into a bust, digital humanities once again fell sway to larger shifts in popular culture. Attitudes toward the digital became more ambivalent, and the position of digital humanities in academia, never fully secure, faced significant challenges. DH centers, such as those at Toronto, Princeton, and Oxford, were closed; pioneering DH degree programs such as the MA in Digital History as Glasgow were canceled; the funding for the United Kingdom's world-leading data repository, the Arts and Humanities Data Service, was withdrawn; Arts and Humanities Research Board (AHRB) funding programs were discontinued; and the academic journal *Computers and the Humanities* ceased publication. There were some positive developments, especially in North America: the National Endowment for the Humanities (NEH) Office of Digital Humanities was established, the number of sessions at the MLA began to increase, new book series were commissioned, and the Digital Humanities Summer Institute was founded. Nevertheless, in 2009, it seemed far from inevitable that Fraistat's prediction would prove correct.

Even in 2019, the status of digital humanities within academia is not fully assured. Interest is growing in the United Kingdom and continental Europe, but centers and programs still remain relatively scarce, and new tenured academic posts rare. Growth has been more rapid in North America, but there has been a perceptible backlash against digital humanities, the tensions from which are not yet resolved (Kirsch; Kirschenbaum). This uncertainty raises some important questions: How have we moved from a niche discipline to an international presence in such a short time? Is digital humanities liable to suffer from further vicissitudes, or is its place in the academy now more secure? What are the reasons for the field's success, and what can we learn in terms of continuing our endeavors and making them sustainable?

To answer these questions, it is important to consider the nature of some of the disciplines with which digital humanities has been associated historically, as well as the institutional context in which we are working today. In doing so, this chapter calls on my own experience in a wide range of contexts within academia in the United Kingdom dating from the mid-1990s onward. These include an alt-ac (alternative-academic) role, based in university computing services; academic posts in two different iSchools, one of which I eventually chaired; another post in English Studies; and a variety of academic administrative posts, including my current position at the executive level. These roles provide a broad base of experience from which to draw conclusions about the future of the field, the challenges it will continue to face, and the best means to address them.

An Expanded or Divided Field?

Since 2011, there has been a great deal of discussion about the digital humanities as a big tent, (Pannapacker, "'Big Tent Digital Humanities,'" Parts I & 2), but the more we grow, the more we must ask how large such a tent can become.[1] In the first of the UCL Digital Humanities (UCLDH) Susan Hockey lectures, Hockey herself observed that the field of digital humanities is so large that perhaps it has to fragment. Once conferences get too big, there is a limit to what we can all learn, and so at some point it is likely that, like more mature disciplines, digital humanities will develop specialties and conferences that discuss them (Hockey, "Digital Humanities"). Hockey is in a good position to comment on this, having been one of the pioneers of first-wave digital humanities and having written about its early history (Hockey, "The History"). Tellingly, she does not seem to regret this development or feel that it will cause the spirit of the field to be lost. Fragmentation and specialization might, after all, be seen as indicators of health and growth. No chemist, for example, would expect to be able to undertake or even comprehend research on the whole of chemistry with a standard level of expertise, nor would she expect to know all of its subfields and every researcher working in them. Similarly, literary subfields each have a canon, yet no literary scholar would regard himself as equally expert in all of them. With growth and maturity, it may well be inevitable that we will be compelled to develop subdisciplines, while still attempting to make newcomers feel welcome in the broader field.

In the last decade, the digital humanities has also grown from a largely Anglo-American to a more global discipline. We can see this expansion when we look at the ever-growing Centernet list of DH centers[2] or the Global Outlook DH (GO:DH) Around DH in 80 Days[3] project. Despite the work of GO:DH[4] and other efforts to foster international collaboration, further growth in this regard may also come at the cost of a rather less cohesive discipline—not only in terms of specialization but also perhaps in terms of scholarly cultures. At its most obvious, this diffusion of the field means greater linguistic diversity, for example, in conference presentations or journal articles. International, multilinguistic research teams must increasingly also take into account differences in intellectual cultures and assumptions about working practices (Siemens and Burr, 2012). Indeed, scholarly norms and expectations, including what is regarded as prestigious, may diverge even if researchers speak the same language. For example, in the United Kingdom, universities are awarded research funding partly on the basis of a national rating exercise, called the Research Excellence Framework (REF). In 2014, 20 percent of the funds were awarded in the category of impact, which means being able to demonstrate change and benefit to the world beyond the university. Elsewhere in the world, despite the tradition of the public intellectual, nonacademic impact may seem less compelling because it is not explicitly evaluated or funded. This will inevitably affect the way that UK digital humanities scholarship develops and is communicated in the future and may cause it to diverge from norms in other parts of the DH scholarly community.

The specter of divergence has prompted several public disagreements about the future direction of DH research, with a stress on the need for greater diversity and a movement away from the technological positivism that might preclude it (Philips). Some of these arguments have become quite bitter, whether they happen live, via social media, or in many cases, both (Verhoeven; Singh). These arguments can be unpleasant, especially if individuals are attacked, but they may also represent the growing pains of a discipline, as I have argued elsewhere (Warwick, "Building Theories").

Of course, academics are trained to be dialectical, and the more people the field attracts—and, crucially, the more attention it attracts—the more it will be critiqued. Indeed, one of the significant moments that marked the progress that digital humanities has made toward the academic mainstream was when it came to the notice of a notable controversialist of English studies and postmodernism, Stanley Fish ("The Digital Humanities"; "Mind Your P's and B's"). Fish was predictably negative about digital humanities and its standards of scholarship, but the fact that he had deigned to notice it at all seemed to be regarded, in some areas of traditional humanities scholarship, as an indication that the field was at last worthy of note. Controversy can, in these ways and others, be a good thing; we may have once been a smaller field with a more uniform outlook, but nobody knew or cared we were there. Even those who have renewed their calls for greater unity in the field might want to reflect on whether they would rather be regarded as excessively controversial or continue to be ignored.

Disciplinary Analogies

These debates speak to questions about our fit in the intellectual universe, as well as what we might learn from other disciplines about diversity and inclusion, especially as related to gender. Traditionally, DH scholars have tended to come from humanities disciplines, such as history, art history, classics, and increasingly media studies. As the field becomes more diverse, the range of intellectual backgrounds seems set to increase. However, if we look at the institutional context of many DH centers and programs, a few areas predominate: English and History Departments,[5] Library and Information Studies (LIS) Departments, or iSchools, and university computing or learning support services. Thinking about these contexts may help elucidate digital humanities' past, its current growth, and its future potential, both in terms of issues we might want to address as a field and those we might aim to avoid.

We often think of digital humanities as a new discipline, but it is no younger than computer science; even English studies and LIS are not as old as is often assumed, dating from the late nineteenth century. In fact, LIS and English had very similar origins in the late nineteenth-century drive to produce a better-educated, more highly skilled workforce and to find something that women and non-elite men could work on in the absence of a classical education. They also respond to a need to understand, systematize, and control an ever-increasing volume of information produced by (then) new technologies (Goldie; Baldick). Computer science and digital humanities also grew out of a drive to interrogate information, of course. But English and LIS were notably dominated by female students from their foundation and, in the case of LIS at least initially, by female professors as well (Palmer;

Maack). Both English studies and LIS also struggled to establish themselves as legitimate fields, being regarded as second rate to the classical or mathematical subjects predominantly studied by men.

But English and LIS have since had very different trajectories. English is now one of the most dominant arts and humanities subjects, with highly competitive entry standards. When people ask me what I do, they understand immediately if I say I am a professor of English. I was previously a professor of LIS, and almost nobody, except librarians or archivists, knew what that was. The lack of awareness of LIS is due to the fact that it has remained rather a niche discipline, taught predominantly at the graduate level in a relatively small number of universities. In the United Kingdom, at least, student numbers are falling or barely holding level, and departments may struggle to recruit new students. Recent years have also seen closures or mergers of LIS departments with other larger units (Day). Unlike English—again, at least in the United Kingdom—LIS is misunderstood and undervalued, a fate that no DH scholar, even an internal critic, would wish for the field.

So what can we learn from both fields that will help the digital humanities flourish in the future? Although LIS and English had similar beginnings, their intellectual underpinnings have always been different. LIS, more like the digital humanities than like English, stresses the importance of a single progenitor, Melvil Dewey, who set up the first library school at Columbia University in 1887 (Miksa).[6] The difference between the two origin stories is vital, however. Roberto Busa was working on a project that used new technology, but had its origins in intellectual curiosity and endeavor and a long traditional of unimpeachable biblical scholarship. By contrast, Dewey was setting up what was essentially a training school for a para-academic profession. It is arguable, and indeed has been argued, that the reason that librarianship (although not running the library) was regarded as suitable for women was because it was seen as a service discipline from the start (Maack). In this regard, it is significant that Dewey seldom visited his school once it had been founded: he left the teaching to a very able female assistant director, Mary Fairchild (Maack). He may have preferred to exist in the predominantly masculine world of library management and bibliographical scholarship, avoiding the taint of teaching and support.[7]

LIS has indeed produced a great deal of very important research, not least the work of Vannevar Bush, whose paper, "As We May Think," is one of the intellectual foundations of digital humanities and web science. But for decades after its establishment as a field, LIS faced a struggle to be considered intellectually rigorous; such criticisms frequently made reference to the gender of LIS professors. Scholars, often male and often in other fields, were very quick to decry the poor quality of work in LIS, with barely concealed critical views of plodding diligence (female) in contrast to intellectual ambition (male); their implication was that library schools privileged technical instruction over research and abstract knowledge (Miksa). For example, the Williamson report of 1921 argued that "consideration should be given to the need of checking the feminization of library work as a profession." In 1923, the same author objected that "library school instructors are seldom forceful or convincing. Most of them are women" (107). Even after World War II, there were numerous calls for more depth, rigor, and theoretical sophistication (Harris): the way to achieve this, it was argued, was to employ more college graduates, who were more likely to be male than female (Maack). This may explain the change of name to Information Science, with its connotations of masculine rigor, rather than feminized service.

The name change may also have been associated with the postwar need to organize, interrogate, and make sense of the large quantities of documents produced by the military and to mine those captured from the Axis powers for essential secrets of atoms and rocketry (Rayward, "Library and Information Science"). Some of this information was, of course, digital, but despite the excellent work of female code breakers at Bletchley Park, most postwar information scientists were male (Maack). The research they were encouraged to do remained instrumental, however, and in certain ways service oriented; the military needed help making sense of all this material (Rayward, "The History and Historiography"). Once again, therefore, the image of LIS's role as a service, rather than a pure discipline, persisted. This is perhaps unfair and was a result of the necessary secrecy that surrounds military work, but whether we agree with it or not, it remains a commonplace that the way to be respected by the intellectual establishment is to do complex, pure, fundamental research, not work that can in any way be seen as applied or instrumental or that provides a service to others.

English scholars have always been very good at communicating the nature of their work to others, although in the early days and perhaps even now in some quarters, there were questions about whether "a lot of chatter about Shelley" could really constitute a respectable academic endeavor (Palmer, 95). In the United Kingdom, literary scholars such as T. S. Eliot, C. S. Lewis, and F. R. Leavis became prominent public intellectuals, often featured in the press or broadcast media—a tradition continued by Robert MacFarland and John Mullan, among other contemporary scholars. Over the years the field has also engaged in some very public controversies; for example, over the legitimacy of critical methods such as structuralism, postmodernism, new historicism, and, most recently, the digital humanities. These public debates had the secondary effect of making critics such as Colin McCabe, Terry Eagleton, Steven Greenblatt, and, as per the previous section, Stanley Fish, well known far beyond their disciplines. But the cost of this publicity was significant: English became viewed as a field of fractious controversialists.[8] In other words, literary scholars may be noticed more than those in LIS, but sometimes for less than positive reasons.

The different experiences in the development and success of LIS and English studies demonstrate why communication and, in particular, the ability to make clear to nonspecialists why a subject is interesting and important are likely to be crucial to the success of digital humanities (Clement and Reside). Social media have been very useful in helping us to do this. DHers are often excellent bloggers, and as a field we are ubiquitous on Twitter, having been relatively early adopters. This means that the reputation and the visibility of the work of individuals, such as Melissa Terras, Bethany Nowviskie, or Dan Cohen, extend far beyond the DH community, as do the reputation and visibility of the organizations that they lead. Indeed, as Terras herself argues, the rise of social media and other digital technologies, such as tablet computers, may have served to make more comprehensible, and bring closer to the mainstream, the activities and concerns that DH scholars have been involved in for many years ("A Decade in Digital Humanities").

The success of the pioneering *Transcribe Bentham*[9] project, for instance, has shown how many people are interested in engaging with material that academics and information professionals might previously have assumed would only be of interest to academic researchers. It is necessary only to search for the phase "digital humanities" in the database of Impact Case Studies submitted for REF 2014[10] to see how much activity digital humanities has already given rise to that results in an impact outside academia. This is a very positive development for those of us working in the United Kingdom in terms of being able to demonstrate financial benefit to our universities, make a contribution to economic prosperity, and enrich people's lives. Digital humanities is well placed to have an additional impact in these areas, especially when working with cultural heritage organizations and the GLAM (galleries, libraries, archives, and museums) sector (Maron and Pickle, 9).

But even if there were no funding available or no acknowledgment of public impact, it would still be vital for us to do such work. Just as English scholars have advocated for the benefits of literature and culture to enrich lives, so we should continue to demonstrate how digital methods can be transformative in the way that people interact with cultural heritage and how they make sense of the world around them. In doing so, we might be seen as performing a service to the wider community, just as those in LIS have done for decades. But we also must bear in mind the lessons—and the pitfalls—of its disciplinary analog. English Departments have done much to advance humanistic inquiry and to promote it. But they have also retained the association with controversy. As digital humanities continues to diversify, we must consider how we might hear the concerns of our critics, both within and outside of the field, without allowing criticism itself to define it.

Education as Service

It is not only on the basis of research and its impact that peers in other disciplines and the wider public will evaluate our field. Teaching and the ability to attract and develop students are also crucial factors in the way that a developing discipline acquires cultural value, and again we might learn from digital humanities' disciplinary analogs. From its first days, English was taught to undergraduates and indeed to people with very little prior formal education (Baldick). Students were not required to have a first degree or work experience before embarking on such a course of study.

By contrast, LIS has always been a discipline that is taught predominantly only at the graduate level and that often requires a period of work experience before students can enroll in a degree program. This has had the almost certainly unintended consequence of LIS appearing to be something of an inaccessible field. It remains ill understood by the majority of university students and the academics who teach them, simply because there are far more undergraduate than graduate students. Especially in an elective system, many students will take courses in English and thus perhaps decide to major in it, but fewer will come across LIS unless they are already highly motivated or the iSchool has a very high profile on campus.

The divergent trajectories of English studies and of LIS shows that education is a powerful vector for the growth and wider acceptance of a developing discipline. Therefore, if we wish the digital humanities to continue to grow and flourish, we must continue to promote the importance of teaching as much as research. However much academics love their research and might complain about their course loads, most of them agree that excellent teaching is the mark of a great university and is the basis of all we do as scholars. We know that it is often by teaching that we come to better understand our own subjects of study, but teaching can also help us clarify our students' interests and, therefore, the interests that will define the next generation of DH scholarship. Education is therefore a service to our students, who will take their knowledge into the world beyond the university, and to the future of the field, because those who remain in academia will take the discipline forward, perhaps in unexpected, original ways.

It is also worth bearing in mind that the digital humanities developed as part of service departments as well as academic ones, especially in libraries and computing services. In the past as in the present, the profession simply could not manage without these information professionals. But that does not mean they are always held in high regard by those they serve (Nowviskie). There remains a significant danger that the humanities scholar is seen as "the talent" and the alt-ac researcher as "the support" (Bradley). This false assumption not only devalues the contributions of those in service roles but is also damaging to scholarship itself. The most successful DH research is produced when faculty members respect and are willing to work on an equal basis with alt-ac and information professionals (Siemens et al.; McCarty, 2008). But to do so requires that we understand "service" as a scholarly pursuit. In moral terms, we might agree that it is perfectly acceptable for a field to be known for hard work, unacknowledged support, and professional dedication. Yet these features are seldom associated with the kind of serious scholarship for which other humanities disciplines have become known. As the history of LIS demonstrates, practitioners who provide a service to others may sometimes be undervalued by academics, but the best scholarship results from fruitful partnerships between them. This is a lesson that the digital humanities must learn if the field is to progress

Such questions about the role of service are linked to the larger, long-running debate about whether the creation of a digital resource is "just" a service task or whether it has an essential intellectual component (Warwick, "Archive 360"; Edmond). This shows how vital it is to remain properly critical in all that we do. But it also reveals how we must remain attentive to the lessons of other fields, in terms of both how they define their own scholarship and how they promote that scholarship to a wider audience. There remains, at times, a risk that we in the digital humanities can still be too uncritical and positivist, and this is one we should be rightly wary of (Drucker). Indeed, we might argue that an insistence that the digital humanities is about the use not only of digital resources and methods to study the humanities and cultural heritage but also of humanities methods to study and critique digital phenomena and culture is what stops it from becoming overly positivist. But it is only when this argument is accompanied by attention to the forms of service that underlie it, and to the valid points that the field's critics raise, that digital humanities will be able properly to consider itself a mature field, confident both in its origins and possible futures.

Institutional Structures and Support

In the United Kingdom, an important question for those planning the forthcoming REF in 2021 was about the way that interdisciplinary research might best be evaluated and supported. This reflects wider international debates about the structure and significance of interdisciplinary work. As one of the leading exemplars of interdisciplinary research, digital humanities is well placed to lead in this inquiry, not least in terms of discussions about what kind of institutional structures and infrastructures are most appropriate for supporting such work.

In the United Kingdom, at least, there is only one distinct department of digital humanities; it is at Kings College London. For many years we have disagreed among ourselves as to whether we are a discipline, whether we want to become one, or whether the best thing would be to abolish the field when all of the humanities becomes digital (Terras, "Disciplined"). I have argued elsewhere that we are a discipline, but one that does not agree on what organizational shape it ought to or will take (Warwick, "Building Theories"). If we learn anything from those doubtful days of the early web, it is that predictions of radical change driven by digital methods fail to happen as quickly as anyone expects. And if we learn anything from the fates of earlier disciplines, like English and LIS, it is that debates about how different elements within them are valued, and how they relate to other forms and methods of scholarship, are vital as fields grow and develop.

It is clear that there are already a number of different models for digital humanities, broadly divided into what we might call centers and networks. Centers might be based in a library, in computing services, or in an academic department or faculty and may or may not have a physical existence and/or a lab. In my view, these setups often date to first-phase digital humanities, when computing professionals provided services to humanities academics, who came to the center perhaps with a time buyout or other resources to make a project possible. Whether intentionally or not, this model incorporates a view of service where one party (the alt-ac practitioner) may appear to be subordinate to another (the academic researcher). The network model tends in some ways to be more organizationally conservative: members stay in their department or professional service unit and meet for events or form groups around research projects. This model tends to characterize later adopters of digital humanities, who understand service as an equal partnership between individuals or groups who bring complementary skills to a collaboration. Either model can work, and the choice should be dictated by the circumstances of individual institutions.[11]

But the best future programs will be those that fit with the academic expertise and express the values of the university in which they are situated. They will also be programs that pay careful attention to the balance of esteem between academic research and alt-ac practitioners, ensuring that those who provide excellent service should never be assumed to be subordinate to those who teach and conduct scholarly research.

Whether or not we can still fit into the same tent or will in the future, there is no definitive model for doing digital humanities: the kind that we do must fit with the characteristics and culture of our own institutions, or it will fail to convince or to attract students to us. This may be a characteristic of all disciplines as they mature: there are very different ways of doing, for example, history or English studies, as I have argued elsewhere, and some of these movements or schools are particularly characteristic of single institutions or nations, even if they later influence work internationally (Warwick, "Building Theories").[12] In such circumstances, it is tempting for senior administrators to buy talent from the outside and rely on such an individual to catalyze activity. Although leadership in any field is important, such an approach is risky in digital humanities, which is, by nature a collaborative exercise. As is the case with most great research, really innovative DH scholarship occurs if ideas and structures emerge as a result of the initiative of people who are deeply invested in them, and in the institutions where such work is fostered and carried out. It is then possible to identify areas of strength and build on them.

This is another area in which we can usefully learn from more mature disciplines: how to build structures for the digital humanities that are focused on the work they are doing and wish to do in the future, while also planning for its longevity and sustainably. In this regard, we must continue to create exciting projects whose field-changing results we can celebrate. This is what will impress colleagues, whether they are fellow DHers, scholars, students in more established humanities disciplines who might be considering adopting digital methods, or even senior managers who do not have time to understand the detail of what we do. DH scholars must, of course, treat as their first priority the production of excellent scholarship for its own sake, because this is something they are passionate about. As a field we should also be wary of unthinking boosterism. Nevertheless, when a discipline is still in a relatively early stage of development, it is necessary to demonstrate the value of what it does to those who lack detailed knowledge of it, especially if they can influence the strategic direction of their university.[13]

Digital Humanities and the Future of Service

Learning from the successes of English studies, which grew from a subdiscipline whose value was questioned into a globally recognizable field, digital humanities must similarly be able to communicate the exciting scholarship that it produces, both within and beyond universities, and teach and inspire students. It can learn from LIS how to be a field that is cooperative, collaborative, respectful, and willing to value the quiet, selfless service of others. But that also means being willing to value—equally—the vital contributions that alt-ac and information professionals make to digital humanities, and indeed to so many other academic disciplines. In effect, therefore, we should aim to combine the virtues of all the settings in which digital humanities has traditionally been found: in libraries, in computer services, and in departments. And we must value service and support as essential components of scholarly achievement and of the future success of the field.

There is an ongoing tension between the values of service and the countervailing need to demonstrate the nature and value of scholarship, whether in the benign form of advocacy for cultural benefits or regarding less benign questions of faction, controversy, and notoriety. Service has become an obvious component of digital humanities, thanks to the roles that librarians and alt-ac practitioners have played in the field's development. But it is also inherent in many other activities that form part of the field, which we would be well advised to recognize fully. We serve our students through teaching and supporting the next generation of scholars. We serve our colleagues and institutions when we establish and lead new DH structures or programs. Even the communication of our research and its impact is a form of field-level service. We serve our scholarly community if research contributes to advances in the discipline, and we serve the wider world if we are able to demonstrate the potential of digital technologies to change and enrich the lives of those outside academia. Service must be regarded not as an ancillary task, but as an essential contribution to the future success of digital humanities as a field. This chapter's title begins with a quotation from Milton's poem "When I Consider How My Light Is Spent." In Milton's most famous poem, *Paradise Lost,* Satan, though highly intelligent and ambitious, refuses to serve, falls from grace, and is perpetually damned. Perhaps that is the most powerful lesson for anyone or any discipline to learn.

NOTES

1. Gold and Klein suggest that the idea of an "expanded field" may now be more appropriate.

2. http://www.dhcenternet.org/centers.

3. http://www.arounddh.org/jekyll/update/2014/09/09/day80/.

4. http://www.globaloutlookdh.org/.

5. In this chapter I concentrate on English studies, having discussed analogies from the field of history elsewhere (Warwick, "Building Theories").

6. The digital humanities has, until recently, traced its origins to the work of Father Roberto Busa, SJ. However, this is increasingly being challenged, for example by Hockey ("Digital Humanities") and Terras and Nyhan.

7. As Radford and Radford ("Power, Knowledge, and Fear") show, once librarianship began to be associated with a predominantly female workforce, it lost status in comparison with traditionally male occupations. The profession has also been dogged by negative, gendered, stereotypes that have been damaging to the reputation of information work and scholarship (White; Pagowsky and Rigby; Radford and Radford, "Librarians and Party Girls"; Hillenbrand).

8. For instance, the Cambridge English Faculty became "notorious" for the bitter schisms of the 1980s (Clark, 183): despite a long tradition of notable literary scholarship, its arguments about structuralism remain a negative point of reference in the history of literary criticism (Smith, 115).

9. http://blogs.ucl.ac.uk/transcribe-bentham/.

10. http://impact.ref.ac.uk/CaseStudies/.

11. This is also true in terms of education. There is no agreed structure for DH programs, whether at the undergraduate or postgraduate level (Alexander and Frost Davis).

12. Thus, practical criticism, as opposed to philology, has always been the mark of Cambridge English; the Annales school of history is originally French, and the University of Chicago had a huge influence of methods in global economics and indeed LIS. As digital humanities grows, it is surely inevitable that this kind of methodological and organizational diversity will become more common.

13. For example, as a senior manager in my own institution, I understand the nature of the excellent humanities scholarship that we produce, but cosmology and particle physics are a long way from my area of expertise, as are the clinical psychology and history of voice hearing: I will never have enough time to understand disciplines that are remote from my expertise in anything but the most superficial way. But I know that they are all subjects in which my university excels, because my colleagues can show me examples of their achievements and point to the excitement and respect they generate in their research communities and in the wider world. They also attract excellent students who go on to exciting and fulfilling employment.

BIBLIOGRAPHY

Alexander, Bryan, and Rebecca Frost Davis. "Should Liberal Arts Campuses Do Digital Humanities? Process and Products in the Small College World." In *Debates in the Digital Humanities,* edited by Matthew K. Gold, 368–90. Minneapolis: University of Minnesota Press, 2012.

Baldick, Chris. *The Social Mission of English Criticism 1848–1932.* Oxford: Clarendon Press, 1983.

Besser, Howard. "The Past, Present, and Future of Digital Libraries." In *A Companion to Digital Humanities,* edited by Susan Schreibman, Ray Siemens, and John Unsworth. Oxford: Blackwell, 2004. http://www.digitalhumanities.org/companion/.

Bradley, John. "No Job for Techies: Technical Contributions to Research in the Digital Humanities." In *Collaborative Research in the Digital Humanities,* edited by M. Deegan and W. McCarty, 11–26. Farnham, UK: Ashgate, 2012.

Bush, Vannevar. 1945. "As We May Think." *The Atlantic,* July 1945, http://www.theatlantic.com/magazine/archive/1945/07/as-we-may-think/303881/.

Carmichael, James V., Jr. "The Male Librarian and the Feminine Image: A Survey of Stereotype, Status, and Gender Perceptions." *Library and Information Science Research* 14 (1992): 411–46.

Castells, Manuel. *The Internet Galaxy: Reflections on the Internet, Business, and Society.* Oxford; Oxford University Press, 2002.

Clark, Burton. *Perspectives on Higher Education: Eight Disciplinary and Comparative Views.* Berkeley: University of California Press, 1987.

Clement, Tanya. and Doug Reside. "Off the Tracks: Laying New Lines for Digital Humanities Scholars." White Paper to NEH Office of Digital Humanities, Level 1 Digital Humanities Start-Up Grant, 2011, mediacommonspress.

Day, Andrew. "Librarianship Courses in 2013: Falling Student Numbers and Fewer Courses Available." *Informed: Commentary and Development across the Library and Information World,* 2013, http://theinformed.org.uk/2013/12/librarianship-courses-in-2013-falling-student-numbers-and-fewer-courses-available/.

Drucker, Johanna. "Humanistic Theory and Digital Scholarship." In *Debates in the Digital Humanities,* edited by Matthew K. Gold, 85–95. Minneapolis: University of Minnesota Press, 2012.

Edmond, Jennifer. "The Role of the Professional Intermediary in Expanding the Humanities Computing Base." *Literary and Linguistic Computing* 20, no. 3 (2005): 367–80.

Fish, Stanley "The Digital Humanities and the Transcending of Mortality." *New York Times: Opinionator,* January 9, 2012, http://opinionator.blogs.nytimes.com/2012/01/09/the-digital-humanities-and-the-transcending-of-mortality/.

Fish, Stanley. "Mind Your P's and B's: The Digital Humanities and Interpretation." *New York Times: Opinionator,* January 23, 2012, http://opinionator.blogs.nytimes.com/2012/01/23/mind-your-ps-and-bs-the-digital-humanities-and-interpretation/.

Gold, Matthew K., and Klein, Lauren F. "Introduction. Digital Humanities: The Expanded Field." In *Debates in the Digital Humanities 2016,* edited by Matthew K. Gold and Lauren F. Klein, ix–xv. Minneapolis: University of Minnesota Press, 2016. http://dhdebates.gc.cuny.edu/debates/text/51.

Goldie, David. "Literary Studies and the Academy." In *The Cambridge History of Literary Criticism. Vol. 6: The Nineteenth Century, c.1830–1914,* edited by M. A. R. Habib, 46–71. Cambridge: Cambridge University Press, 2013.

Harris, Michael H. "The Dialectic of Defeat: Antimonies in Research in Library and Information Science." *Library Trends* 34, no. 3 (1986): 515–30.

Hillenbrand, Suzanne. "Ambiguous Authority and Aborted Ambition: Gender, Professionalism, and the Rise and Fall of the Welfare State." *Library Trends* 43, no. 2 (1985): 185–98.

Hockey, Susan. "Digital Humanities: Perspectives on Past, Present and Future." Lecture given at University College London, May 27, 2015, https://www.ucl.ac.uk/dh/events/archive/susanhockey.

Hockey, Susan. "The History of Humanities Computing." In *A Companion to Digital Humanities*, edited by Susan Schreibman, Ray Siemens, and John Unsworth, 3–19. Oxford: Blackwell, 2004.

Kirsch, Adam. 2014. "Technology Is Taking over English Departments: The False Promise of the Digital Humanities." *New Republic*, May 2, 2014, http://www.newrepublic.com/article/117428/limits-digital-humanities-adam-kirsch.

Kirschenbaum, Matthew. "What Is 'Digital Humanities,' and Why Are They Saying Such Terrible Things about It?" *Differences* 25, no. 1 (2014): 46–63.

Maack, Mary. N. 1986. "Women in Library Education: Down the Up Staircase." *Library Trends* 34, no. 3 (1986): 401–32.

Maron, Nancy, and Sarah Pickle. "Sustaining the Digital Humanities: Host Institution Support Beyond the Start-up Phase." Ithaka S&R Report. 2014, http://sr.ithaka.org/?p=22548.

McCarty, Willard. "What's Going On?" *Literary and Linguistic Computing* 23, no. 3 (2008): 253–62.

Miksa, Francis L. "Melvil Dewey: The Professional Educator and His Heirs." *Library Trends* 34, no. 3 (1986): 359–81.

National Research Council. *Research Universities and the Future of America: Ten Breakthrough Actions Vital to Our Nation's Prosperity and Security.* Washington, D.C.: National Academies Press, 2012.

Nowviskie, Bethany. 2010. "The #alt-ac Track: Negotiating Your 'Alternative Academic' Appointment." ProfHacker. August 31, 2010, http://chronicle.com/blogs/profhacker/the-alt-ac-track-negotiating-your-alternative-academic-appointment-2/26539.

Nunberg, Geoffrey. *The Future of the Book.* Berkeley: University of California Press, 1996.

Pagowsky, Nicole, and Miriam Rigby. *The Librarian Stereotype: Deconstructing Perceptions and Presentations of Information Work.* Chicago: American Library Association, 2014.

Palmer, David. J. *The Rise of English Studies: An Account of the Study of English Language and Literature from Its Origins to the Making of the Oxford English School.* Oxford: Oxford University Press, 1965.

Pannapacker, William. "'Big Tent Digital Humanities,' a View From the Edge, Part 1." *Chronicle of Higher Education,* July 31, 2011, http://chronicle.com/article/Big-Tent-Digital-Humanities/128434.

Pannapacker, William. "'Big Tent Digital Humanities,' a View From the Edge, Part 2." *Chronicle of Higher Education,* September 18, 2011, http://chronicle.com/article/Big-Tent-Digital-Humanities-a/129036/.

Philips, Amanda. "#transformDH—A Call to Action Following ASA 201." HASTAC blog. October 26, 2011, http://www.hastac.org/blogs/amanda-phillips/2011/10/26 /transformdh-call-action-following-asa-2011.

Radford, Marie L., and Gary P. Radford. "Librarians and Party Girls: Cultural Studies and the Meaning of the Librarian." *Library Quarterly* 73, no. 1 (2003): 54–69.

Radford, Marie L., and Gary P. Radford. "Power, Knowledge, and Fear: Feminism, Foucault, and the Stereotype of the Female Librarian." *Library Quarterly* 67, no. 3 (1997): 250–66.

Rayward, W. Boyd. "The History and Historiography of Information Science: Some Reflections." *Information Processing & Management* 32, no. 2 (1996): 3–17.

Rayward, W. Boyd. "Library and Information Science: An Historical Perspective." *Journal of Library History* 20, no. 2 (1985): 120–36.

Siemens, Lynne, and Elisabeth Burr. "A Trip around the World: Accommodating Geographical, Linguistic and Cultural Diversity in Academic Research Teams." *Literary and Linguistic Computing* 28, no. 2 (2012): 331–43.

Siemens, Lynne, Richard Cunningham, Wendy Duff, and Claire Warwick. "A Tale of Two Cities: Implications of the Similarities and Differences in Collaborative Approaches within the Digital Libraries and Digital Humanities Communities." *Literary and Linguistic Computing* 26, no. 3 (2011): 335–48.

Singh, Amardeep. "An Account of David Hoover's DHSI 2015 Keynote: Performance, Deformance, Apology." Amardeep Singh blog. 2015, http://www.electrostani.com /2015/06/an-account-david-hoovers-dhsi-2015.html.

Smith, James. *Terry Eagleton*. Hoboken, N.J.: Wiley, 2013.

Terras, Melissa. "A Decade in Digital Humanities: Text of Inaugural Lecture." *Journal of Siberian Federal University, Special Issue on Digital Humanities* (2016).

Terras, Melissa. "Disciplined: Using Educational Studies to Analyse 'Humanities Computing.'" *Literary and Linguistic Computing* 21, no. 2 (2006): 229–46.

Terras, Melissa, and Julianne Nyhan. "Father Busa's Female Punch Card Operatives. In *Debates in the Digital Humanities 2016*, edited by Matthew K. Gold and Lauren F. Klein, 60–65. Minneapolis: University of Minnesota Press, 2016.

Verhoeven, Deb. "Has Anyone Seen a Woman?" Presentation at the Digital Humanities Conference, Sydney, Australia, July 2, 2015, http://speakola.com/ideas/deb -verhoeven-has-anyone-seen-a-woman-2015.

Warwick, Claire. "Archive 360: The Walt Whitman Archive." *Archive* 1, no. 1 (2011), http:// www.archivejournal.net/issue/1/three-sixty/.

Warwick, Claire. "Building Theories or Theories of Building? A Tension at the Heart of Digital Humanities." In *A New Companion to Digital Humanities*, edited by Susan Schreibman, Ray Siemens, and John Unsworth, 538–53. Oxford: Wiley Blackwell, 2016.

White, Ashanti. *Not Your Ordinary Librarian: Debunking the Popular Perceptions of Librarians*. Amsterdam: Elsevier, 2012.

Williamson, Charles C. *Training for Library Service (A Report Prepared for the Carnegie Corporation of New York)*. Boston: Merrymount Press, 1923.

No Signal without Symbol: Decoding
the Digital Humanities

DAVID M. BERRY, M. BEATRICE FAZI, BEN ROBERTS,
AND ALBAN WEBB

The ubiquity and potency of digital culture in the early twenty-first century have been the subject of sustained interest and comment in both public and academic spheres. The digital, as a computational form, mediates our everyday lives, offering new modalities, surfaces, and processes for (re)presenting the world. The word "automation" was coined in its contemporary sense in the immediate postwar era. It referred to a more extensive and systematic mechanization, closed-loop systems of feedback and control, and the incorporation of discrete electronics. We use the term "computational automation" to refer to the present extension of automation: the incorporation of machine learning and large-scale data analysis into economic production, academia, and everyday life. Computational automation is revolutionizing scientific, cultural, and artistic human endeavors, which are constantly being reorganized into new temporal, spatial, and conceptual structures with different degrees of agency and reflexivity. Due to the speed and scale of these organizing forces, our understanding of computational automated systems, such as self-driving cars, high-frequency trading systems, autonomous military drones, or organized swarms of shelf-stacking robots, falls behind these technological developments. This lag creates what Bernard Stiegler calls "disorientation": a disjuncture between human temporality and the accelerated technological ordering of time in a hyperindustrial era.[1] Equally, certain deployments of computational automation engender epistemic transformations; that is, changes in the way in which knowledge is justified and understood. These changes could be understood as antihermeneutical; they short-circuit critical interpretation in favor of statistical correlation and pragmatic "results." These epistemic transformations require further interrogation, which is exactly what we intend to do here.

We propose that a critical assessment of computational automation should be one focus of the digital humanities. Via a reading of information theory and Wolfgang Ernst's arguments about media archaeology, we explore the automated systems enlisted by the digital humanities in terms of signal processing. "Signal processing" is an expression that we take from Ernst and by which we mean ways of analyzing cultural heritage that bypass traditional forms of interpretation and historiography. We argue that signal processing represents an impoverished vision of the possible contribution of the digital humanities to debates about the future of culture. The contours of a new digital public culture are emerging; as digital humanists we need to address the critical implications of the computational state that makes our work possible.

The French usefully deploy the acronym GAFA (Google, Apple, Facebook, Amazon) to identify the wave of Silicon Valley technologies and ideologies that stand in some sense against the European ideal of public goods, shared culture, and the Enlightenment.[2] We can think about their business model as what Rey Chow, following Phil Agre, calls *capture*. Within the technology sphere, and particularly in computer science, the most frequent use of the term "capture" refers to "a computer system's (figurative) act of acquiring certain data as input, whether from a human operator or from an electronic or electromechanical device," Agre explains. A second use of the term, he continues, refers to "a representation scheme's ability to fully, accurately, or 'cleanly' express particular semantic notions or distinctions, without reference to the actual taking in of data" (106). This twofold definition masks the ambiguity of the same word being used to describe an epistemological idea ("acquiring the data") and an ontological idea ("modeling the reality it reflects"), even as this usage is remarkably common across the technology sector and in computational disciplines (Agre). The "machinic act or event of capture" that interests Chow creates the possibility for further dividing and partitioning—that is, for the generation of copies and images—and produces an ontology that is structured around the copy (4). Because a significant focus of recent software development has been to enable more effective systems of surveillance, new capture systems have proliferated, fueling a political economy supported by shared data and knowledge. These surveillance systems also make the collection of data relatively easy. This ease of collection results in exploding quantities of data and in claims that we are part of a digital economy. Information and data are each seen as a source of profit, if captured in an appropriate way.[3]

The notion of capture also implies derangements in the organization of knowledge, derangements caused by the unprecedented adjacency and comparability or parity that digital computation makes possible. These concepts define computation, which itself works through a logic of formatting, configuration, structuring, and the application of computational ontologies (Berry, *Critical Theory; Philosophy of Software*). In other words, everything becomes data and, in doing so, becomes equally comparable and calculable. Data are manifested in a form of character-based notation that, while resembling writing, is illegible without the computers that capture, store, and process it.

In fact, this very form of capture—digitization—is the one identified by Andrew McAfee and Erik Brynjolfsson as emblematic of the "Second Machine Age." They identify it as "an inflection point in the right direction—bounty instead of scarcity, freedom instead of constraint—but one that will bring with it some difficult challenges and choices" (11). Whether or not this "inflection point" does indeed aim in the right direction, it is certainly the case that digitization has generated widespread feelings of anxiety and concern over its implications for the economy and society more generally. Even more, digitization has brought about a crisis in thought. This crisis is manifested, at a sociological level, in a form of anxiety over automated capture—a worry that with atrophied human reason and diminished cognitive faculties, humanity will soon be replaced by intelligent robots.[4] Automation anxiety, in turn, raises key techno-epistemological questions around the assembly and reassembly of mechanisms of signal production, dissemination, and consumption.[5] The crisis in thought also questions the relevance of human subjectivity, while pointing toward the development of a new machine-subject. Capture, automation, and digitalization suggest a cultural complicity between technology and nature, where society and subjects no longer exist except as a cloud of data points. Signal processing therefore links automation anxiety to the crisis in thought.

In this respect, it is possible to argue that we are entering a time of a new unintelligibility, whereby people can no longer make sense of the world due to our increasing reliance on digital technology that writes and reads for us, as a form of algorithmic inscription. This unintelligibility results in new forms of what the philosopher Bernard Stiegler calls "grammatization"; that is, the standardization and discretization of idiomatic human cultures, which now also include human-machine cultures. These new forms of grammatization are symbols and discrete representational units, which are opaque to humans even as they are drawn from human-created devices.

Digital technologies have reconfigured the very texts that humanities and DH scholars take as their research objects. These technologies have encoded texts as fragmentary forms, often realigned and interleaved with fragments from other texts, and placed them into digital archives and computational tools.[6] To be working within the field of digital humanities is thus to already be cognizant of the need to "build" digital systems, to encode, and to be involved in a practice of a highly technical nature. But this practice-based approach remains a contentious point, even within digital humanities. At times, it has been interpreted as a move away from theoretical and hermeneutic concerns and critical engagements (Berry, *Philosophy of Software*; Cecire). Indeed, Galloway asks, "Is it the role of humanities researchers to redesign their discipline so that it is symmetrical with that [digital] infrastructure?" (126).

We understand the strong technical orientation of the digital humanities through the concept of signal processing as described in Wolfgang Ernst's "Media Archaeography." He observes that media archaeology differentiates itself from media history through its concern with media artifacts and apparatus not only as *"symbolic* acts" (244, emphasis added), but as the "signal processing of culture." Discussing Milman Parry and Albert Lord's 1930s recordings of Serbian and Montenegrin epic songs on aluminum disc and electromagnetic wire, Ernst draws attention to the way in which systems of analog recording have allowed the "physical layer below symbolically expressed culture" (244) to be registered. Media archaeologists are thus concerned not only with symbol but also with signal; instead of being preoccupied with the textual or musical *content* of recordings (symbol), "[the] media-archaeological ear listens to radio in an extreme way: listening to the noise of the transmitting system itself" (250). Of course this does not mean that it is *exclusively* concerned with signal. Indeed, as Ernst notes, "media-archaeological analysis opens culture to noncultural insights without sacrificing the specific wonders and beauties of culture itself" (245). The point is not a turn to oppose signal to symbol, but to think both together.

What are the lessons of signal and symbol that might be applied to the digital humanities? After all, the digital humanities is not often concerned with the physical vibrations of air recorded in the electromagnetic flux of a fragile piece of wire, but much more commonly with the digital encoding and analysis of (primarily) textual data. Our contention here is not that the digital humanities lacks a cultural critique, a point that has been made many times before—particularly persuasively by Alan Liu, for example. Rather, we argue that the more specific problem of the digital humanities is seeing its contribution to public culture as a form of processing of signals, rather than as symbol. Understood as symbol, the technologies of the digital humanities have great implications for humanistic models of research. As Johanna Drucker asks,

> So can we engage in the design of digital environments that embody specific theoretical principles drawn from the humanities, not merely work within platforms and protocols created by disciplines whose methodological premises are often at odds with—even hostile to—humanistic values and thought? This question is particularly pressing in light of the absorption of these visualization techniques, since they come entirely from realms outside the humanities—management, social sciences, natural sciences, business, economics, military surveillance, entertainment, gaming, and other fields in which the relativistic and comparative methods of the humanities play, at best, a small and accessory role. (85–86)

It is vital that the deployment and creation of tools drawn from outside the humanities do not simply supersede the theoretical principles that, as Drucker suggests, should inform DH design practice. Yet one complaint about the digital humanities is that, too often, tool making is seen as a substitution for hermeneutics. Indeed, this condition is epitomized by the use of the expression "more hack, less yack" (more computer programming and less theorizing).[7] This represents a very strong trend in those strands in the DH community that have self-identified around the notion of "building things" (i.e., the construction and making of digital systems, archives, interfaces, visualizations). This model of digital humanities might be understood, following Jean-Francois Lyotard's suggestion in *The Postmodern Condition,* as a way of opening the data banks, giving the public access to information in order to resist the corporate and military enclosure of computerized knowledge systems (67; see also Berry, *Critical Theory,* 178). But the digital humanities needs to go beyond simply placing information in the public domain and making data accessible and manipulable.

As our reading of Ernst suggests, there is a need for the digital humanities to think signal and symbol together. Or, to frame the issue in terms of Shannon and Weaver's mathematical model of communication: there is no communication without encoding and decoding. One might therefore interpret the digital humanities as an intellectual practice concerned with the transmission of knowledge as messages through channels. It is our contention that this transmission is generally assumed to work on the basis of a "sender-receiver" conception of communication, a conception that could be described as similar to that put forth by Claude Shannon (and popularized in his work with Warren Weaver) in the mid-twentieth century. In Shannon and Weaver's model, the *sender* is the originator of the *message,* while the *receiver* is the recipient. By virtue of its simplicity and generality, this model has been successfully applied to various communication scenarios. Here, we would like to argue that the knowledge production of the digital humanities (understood in its paradigmatic mode of thought) and its consequent input into public culture might be seen to work as a similarly one-way process of communication, albeit one complicated by the signal processing that takes place on the receiver end. In part, it is the unidirectional dimension implied by the notion of a signal that we are challenging here. However, we also consider the limits of signal processing as a way to understand how the digital humanities might not only critically intervene in but also construct public culture.

In Shannon and Weaver's model, the *sender* is the originator of the *message, but* the message is then encoded by an *encoder*; this becomes the second step in the transmission. Once encoded, the message becomes a *signal* that is compatible with the technologies used to transmit it. For instance, in a traditional telephone communication, a sound wave such as a voice saying "Hello, world" is transformed into an electronic signal to be sent via cables, satellites, etc. At the point of reception, a *decoder* must then convert the signal back into the original message. In our telephone example, the electronic signal is decoded into a sound wave again. The receiver of the decoded message is the final node in the model, to which the signal is directed. "Hello, world" has reached its destination as a message with intelligible meaning.

Within the digital humanities, we believe, scholars more often than not aim to create strong signals, rather than strong messages, to be given to the receiver.[8] By way of the digitization of archival materials, for instance, or by encoding texts into queryable information, what the digital humanist can be seen to be doing is striving for the release of the purest, strongest, widest signal to reach a public audience. Problems arise, however, when the audience is a receiver with no decoder; when, in other words, there is only signal processing and no way of turning the signal back into a comprehensible message.

We are, of course, simplifying, and also reducing a great deal, the many activities of the digital humanities, as well as Shannon and Weaver's famous schema. What we are proposing is rather a sort of analogy, meant to highlight an issue that the digital humanities, as a critical field of inquiry, needs to tackle. It is often assumed that the public has the means, and the wish, to turn signals back into messages. This is, however, not always the case. Digital humanists must address the limits of signal processing head-on, which becomes even more pressing if we also consider another question brought about by the analogy to Shannon and Weaver's model of communication. The sender-receiver model describes the *transmission of information.* The charge of the digital humanities is, instead, the *production of knowledge.* An uncritical trust in signal processing becomes, from this perspective, quite problematic, insofar as it can confuse information for knowledge, and vice versa.

We can now turn to some examples of the digital humanities understood as signal processing. In his *New Republic* article, "Technology Is Taking over English Departments," Adam Kirsch criticizes the impoverished model of reading found in large-scale analysis of literary corpora. Kirsch illustrates this with the case of Moretti's "distant reading" of novel titles from 1740–1850. Moretti's computer-based quantitative analysis, analyzing title lengths in a database of novel titles, shows that titles are much longer at the beginning of the period than at the end. Kirsch observes, "The computer can tell you that titles have shrunk . . . but it takes a scholar with a broad knowledge of literary history [i.e., Moretti]—that is, a scholar who has examined the insides and not just the outsides of literary and artistic works—to speculate about the reasons titles shrink, and why it matters." For Kirsch, unlike Moretti's rich scholarly account, digital methods often adopt a position of "*faux naïveté*" about textual history: "their proud innocence of prior historical knowledge and literary interpretation" is, in his view, "partly responsible for the thinness of their findings." This thinness that Kirsch finds, we would argue, is precisely the result of understanding the work of the digital humanities according to a model of signal processing; the belief that new scholarly insights can emerge simply from the digital manipulation of textual data such as novel titles, without the wider interpretative context that Moretti provides.

Yet, computational analysis is not the only activity of the digital humanities. In "Ignoring Encoding," Ryan Cordell argues that Kirsch is describing a model of the digital humanities that is "all coding, no encoding." For Cordell, Kirsch ignores the benefits brought by the less glamorous work of digitization, and the literal encoding that is required to draw meaning from digitized texts. Cordell uses here the example of the Women Writers Project (WWP), a project dedicated to the TEI encoding of early modern women's writing. He argues that the work of encoding "has not been 'simply' the application of computer technology to traditional scholarly functions," since it depends on scholarly debate about how to encode different entities within the text. His objection to Kirsch is then not only an argument for the inherent value of digitizing texts, placing them in the public domain, and making them "accessible to a wide audience of teachers, students, scholars, and the general readers," as the WWP describes it.

For Cordell, the Text Encoding Initiative (TEI) encoding is also a model of scholarship in that it involves making interpretive decisions about texts. In other words, encoding is not just a useful application of computer technology but is also an important part of the contribution made by digital humanities as a scholarly activity. As he writes, "You may find encoding or archival metadata development boring or pedantic—certainly some do—but you cannot pretend that encoding is less a part of the digital humanities than coding." In this view, the activity of digitizing texts and "processing" them according to the TEI standard—adding tags identifying semantic content, for instance—is and should be seen as just as important a contribution to humanities scholarship and to the wider public as big data and textual analysis. For Cordell, the TEI is indeed "one of the best examples of humanistic scholarship applied to computer technology." He argues that "encoding inherited the stigma of scholarly editing, which has in English Departments long been treated as a lesser activity than critique—though critique depends on careful scholarly editing, as text analysis depends on digitization and encoding."

We believe Cordell's piece to be a very telling lament, partly because it underlines that, in the comparison between "traditional" and "digital" humanities, what is lost is not scholarly editing, which is preserved and extended in encoding, but rather critique, which disappears in Cordell's battle to extend the digital humanities to mean not only big data text analysis but also encoding. Cordell's defense of the digital humanities in no way responds to Kirsch's central point: neither encoding or coding (textual analysis) is in fact a substitute for humanistic critique (understood in the broad sense). In Cordell's formulation of the digital humanities, the space for symbolic, humanistic interpretation is now confined to the same relatively narrow role as scholarly editing. However worthwhile, symbolic interpretation is directed, along with scholarly editing, toward a higher goal of creating open, computer-readable, and universally accessible editions. Here, symbolic interpretation is purely instrumental: it is, as Cordell reminds us, applied humanistic scholarship. For us, therefore, encoding remains a paradigmatic example of digital humanities understood as signal processing: in other words, a humanistic computational effort to create the purest possible digital signal and send it to the scholarly community or interested public.[9]

It is useful here to consider, as a further example, the Folger Shakespeare Library and its creation of an extremely detailed TEI XML versions of Shakespeare's plays.[10]

The Folger Library opened in 1932 as a fairly traditional archive and library connected to a strong collection of Shakespeare's works. Today, it describes itself as an "innovator in the preservation of rare materials, and major new digital initiatives support our leadership role in digital humanities (DH) research." Since it contains the world's largest Shakespeare collection, from the sixteenth century to the present day, producing canonical versions of the texts is centrally important to the library. Indeed, the library has "added sophisticated coding that works behind the scenes to make the plays easy to read, search, and index—and lays the groundwork for new features in the future" (Folger). Moreover, implicit editorial information that previously may have been difficult to access or unveil is now encoded directly into the XML files, so that, the library claims, the editorial process is "as nearly transparent as is possible."

The values implied by the Folger's encoding process, which seeks to embed as much information as possible into their digitized texts, demonstrate how strong encoding has become an important part of the justificatory discourses around why a digital edition of a work is created. It is also connected to a wider performativity about the cultural value of computational automation. As Sarah Werner, then digital media strategist at the Folger, once argued, "Right now there's the catalog over here, and then the digital images over here, and then there's a blog over here, and then there's this thing over here. We need something that unites these products, and makes them more usable" (Rosen). The organization and classificatory logic of digital encoding through XML is then also bound up with the calculatory possibilities of making different things equal—that is, a process of *standardization* via the classificatory encoding system that is woven around the text and metadata of Shakespeare's plays in those versions.

The encoding process influences and shapes our comprehension of digital objects and the narratives that these inspire. In this respect, the performativity of computation becomes highly important to our understanding of digital public culture. As Dan Edelstein notes, the "mass digitization of books has made research more efficient than ever" (237). Yet, while "quantification allows us to scale up from one book to the many . . . it only displaces, rather than resolves, the problem of figuring out what the numbers mean" (240). Edelstein's corrective implies a much greater role for DH researchers as human encoders and decoders. They must use their understanding of the limits and biases of computational techniques to critique their application, as, for example, Jeffrey M. Binder does in "Alien Reading." They must bridge the gap between digital and public culture.

One area we might look to for a less impoverished model of the digital humanities than that of signal processing would be the emerging field of *études digitales*. This term designates a set of predominantly, but not exclusively, French-speaking academics such as Bernard Stiegler, Antoinette Rouvroy, and Yves Citton, as well as the work collected in the journal *Études Digitales*, edited by Franck Cormerais and Jacques Athanase Gilbert. As the latter put it in their introduction to the journal, "Why *études digitales* rather than *études numeriques*? Because the term *digital* conserves in French the reference to the fingers (digits) whereas *numerique* refers to machine computation" (Cormerais and Gilbert, our translation). ("Numerique" is the French word used more normally for digital.) Such work would appear to use a more explicit engagement with the relationship between technology and research method than we tend to find within DH scholarship.

For Stiegler, this might mean understanding automation anxieties, such as those surfaced by the claims of the Folger library, as part of a "generalized and integrated automation" that encompasses both digital methods and the digital humanities themselves (*La Société Automatique,* 60). One starting point for Stiegler's analysis is Chris Anderson's *Wired* article, "The End of Theory." Anderson argues that, in what he calls the "petabyte age," the need for models and theories is eclipsed by algorithmic analysis of big data. As Anderson puts it, "Petabytes allow us to say: 'Correlation is enough.' We can stop looking for models. We can analyze the data without hypotheses about what it might show." Anderson's argument might almost seem to be a manifesto for the instrumental data-driven vision of the digital humanities, where data, modeling, and visualization (i.e., what is conceptualized in this chapter as signal) eclipse theory, critique and interpretation. Indeed, Tom Scheinfeldt's "Sunset for Ideology, Sunrise for Methodology?" arguably makes Anderson's argument about science in relation to the humanities, envisioning a golden age where methodology and "organizing activities" displace theories and "ideologies" such as "socialism, fascism, existentialism, structuralism [and] poststructuralism" (124). Stiegler, in contrast, builds on the critique of Anderson found in Kevin Kelly, arguing that behind every automated understanding of facts lies a hidden theory. For Stiegler, then, the automation of knowledge, as one that has no need for thinking (*La Société Automatique,* 96), must be addressed alongside the automation of society and itself made the subject of critique. Indeed, the automation of knowledge implicit in Google-like algorithmic analysis of big data that claims to disavow theory is always already theory-laden. In response, we need to sharpen our critiques of big data and what Stiegler calls the "neuroeconomy" (60). Implicitly, this requires a critique of automated or algorithmic knowledge, inasmuch as the latter sees itself as signal processing, bypassing the cultural critique and interpretation of symbols.

Antoinette Rouvroy and Bernard Stiegler stake out the terrain of big data and algorithmic knowledge well in a classic piece of *études digitales* work, "Le régime de Vérité Numérique":

> The work of producing big data, or rather raw data, is therefore the work of suppressing all signification, with the goal that these raw data can be calculable and no longer function as signs that signify something in relation to what they represent, but as something that substitutes for signifying reality, making it disappear.

> In place of signifying reality, a set of asignifying networked data is substituted, which function as *signals,* meaning that although they have no signification, or rather because of that, they become calculable. In fact, this accords with the definition of signal that Umberto Eco gives: a signal is an element without signification which signifies nothing but because it truly signifies nothing, becomes all the more calculable. (114, our translation and emphasis added)

The idea that knowledge can be reduced to the analysis of data is, as Rouvroy and Stiegler argue, essentially the ideology of big data, one that rests both on the principle that empirical facts can replace theoretical models and on the false assumption that big data is simply the natural emanation of an empirical reality.[11]

This has immediate implications for our argument about signal and symbol in the digital humanities. The signal-processing model of digital humanities, far from dispensing with ideology or being an essentially pragmatic methodological exercise, collaborates in what Rouvroy and Stiegler identify as the ideological purification of data as signal. In this way, the digital humanities participates not only in the processing (or purification) of signal but also in its essentially ideological suppression of symbol and signification. The digital humanities partakes in what Rouvroy and Stiegler are calling the "digital truth regime." That is why it is important for the digital humanities to consider the political, cultural, and legal implications of the technologies it employs.

Thinking signal and symbol together, as we propose to do here, requires digital humanists to consider method in ways that are at odds with the paradigmatic understanding of method in the DH field. In spite of some trenchant critiques, method is still often used to disavow theory. Here it is worth considering, as an example, Tom Scheinfeldt's well-known position in "Why Digital Humanities Is 'Nice'":

> Digital humanities is nice because, as I have described in earlier posts, we're often more concerned with method than we are with theory. Why should a focus on method make us nice? Because methodological debates are often more easily resolved than theoretical ones. Critics approaching an issue with sharply opposed theories may argue endlessly over evidence and interpretation. Practitioners facing a methodological problem may likewise argue over which tool or method to use. Yet at some point in most methodological debates one of two things happens: either one method or another wins out empirically, or the practical needs of our projects require us simply to pick one and move on.

Scheinfeldt sees methodological debates as clearly distinguished from theoretical ones: the latter require endless arguments "over evidence and interpretation," whereas the former can be resolved quickly, empirically, and pragmatically. According to this view, method has almost no relationship with theory, and methodological debates are oriented around the best way to deal with empirical data. Method, in this context, becomes the pragmatic "cleaning up" (to use Rouvroy and Stiegler's expression) of data, or the signal suppressing symbol.

We see this disavowal of theory as symptomatic of the model of DH work that we are describing as signal processing. The disavowal of theory indicates the need to address the mutual relationship between signal and symbol that we have outlined in this chapter. In this respect, it is important to stress that our argument about the interdependence of signal and symbol involves contending that method and theory are also equally inseparable. Just as we need to think more critically about the relationship between signal and symbol, so too do we need to think more critically about the relationship between method and theory.[12]

This point is crucial, insofar as the implications of the digital humanities' initial relegation of theory to a status below method are manifested in the way in which academic knowledge and its dissemination are understood within the field. With an impoverished model of signal/symbol, there is an overemphasis on encoding and coding, and on the clarity of the channel, instead of on the decoding and reception of the symbolic content, which are essential ingredients of both academic and public discourses. We are not proposing that symbol should eradicate signal or that the relationship is necessarily conflictual. On the contrary, we see it as beneficial for the humanities to engage more robustly with signal; for instance, along the lines that Wolfgang Ernst suggests in relation to media archaeology. In this regard, digital methods potentially have a great role to play. By drawing attention to the status of both signal and symbol when actualized in the archives, tools, models, formalizations, and research infrastructures of the digital humanities, we can restore symbol to a position of significance and importance alongside signal. To return to Stiegler's suggestion, we need a digital hermeneutics within the digital humanities that binds together method and theory, signal and symbol.

NOTES

1. Here we are mobilizing a concept of disorientation drawn in part from Stiegler (*Technics and Time*).

2. In financial markets, the seemingly more threatening term FANG (Facebook, Amazon, Netflix, Google) is often used to denote a special group of technologies stocks concerning new models of computational media as streaming technologies (Berry, *Philosophy of Software*).

3. Indeed, data and information were said by Alan Greenspan, the former Chairman of the Federal Reserve of the United States, to be the new "oil" of the digital age (Berry, *Copy, Rip, Burn*, 41, 56).

4. Stiegler, for instance, has identified this as the emergence of the "automatic society" (*la société automatique*). This is an era in which "calculation prevails over every other criteria of decision-making, and where algorithmic and mechanical becoming is

concretized and materialized as logical automation and automatism" (*La Société Automatique*, 23, our translation).

5. We are currently running "Automation Anxiety," an AHRC (UK Arts and Humanities Research Council) project exploring methods for analyzing contemporary cultural anxiety about automation. See http://blogs.sussex.ac.uk/automationanxiety.

6. The interdiscursivity and intertextuality engendered by the digital have, of course, been much remarked on and even used creatively in the writing of new forms of electronic literature.

7. For an alternative etymology of the phrase, see http://dhdebates.gc.cuny.edu /debates/text/58.

8. As Andrew Prescott commented on an earlier version of this chapter, "the idea that there is a distinction between information (signal) and carrier has been fundamental in much infrastructural provision for the humanities, not only in a digital environment but also for example in microfilming of newspapers. This concept is fundamental to XML and TEI. The problem is that for large swathes of humanities scholarship the information is fundamentally bound up with the medium in which it is carried. For historians, it is important to know whether we are talking about a telegram, medieval writ, newspaper, etc. Much of the interest of the digital humanities is precisely in the use of digital technology to explore the materiality of these carriers."

9. "It is as if, when the order comes down from the funding agencies, university administrations, and other bodies mediating today's dominant socioeconomic and political beliefs, digital humanists just concentrate on pushing the 'execute' button on projects that amass the most data for the greatest number, process that data most efficiently and flexibly (flexible efficiency being the hallmark of postindustrialism), and manage the whole through ever 'smarter' standards, protocols, schema, templates, and databases uplifting Frederick Winslow Taylor's original scientific industrialism into ultraflexible postindustrial content management systems camouflaged as digital editions, libraries, and archives—all without pausing to reflect on the relation of the whole digital juggernaut to the new world order" (Liu, 491).

10. See http://www.folgerdigitaltexts.org.

11. On this point, see also the essay collection edited by Lisa Gitelman, *'Raw Data' Is an Oxymoron.*

12. As Savage argues, methods demand to be understood as neither simply *instrumental* ("the practical needs of our projects require us simply to pick one and move on," as Scheinfeldt has it) nor *uncontroversial*. Savage contends that we need to resist the "instrumental framing in which [methods] are simply seen to be technically 'better or worse' means of doing social research" (5). Far from being merely tools to investigate theoretical questions, methods are now "the very stuff of social life": "Social networking sites, audit processes, devices to secure 'transparency', algorithms for financial transactions, surveys, maps, interviews, databases and classifications can be seen as . . . modes of 'making up' society. This move . . . is part of a striking rethinking of the relationship between theory, culture and method which is currently underway in contemporary academic research" (5).

BIBLIOGRAPHY

Adorno, Theodor W. *Minima Moralia: Reflections from Damaged Life.* Translated by E. F. N. Jephcott. London: Verso, 1978.

Agre, Phil. "Surveillance and Capture: Two Models of Privacy." *Information Society* 10, no. 2 (April–June 1994): 101–27.

Anderson, Chris. "The End of Theory: The Data Deluge Makes the Scientific Method Obsolete." *Wired,* June 23, 2008, http://www.wired.com/2008/06/pb-theory. Accessed January 15, 2016.

Berry, David M. *Copy, Rip, Burn: The Politics of Copyleft and Open Source.* London: Pluto Press, 2008.

Berry, David M. *Critical Theory and the Digital.* New York: Bloomsbury, 2014.

Berry, David M. *The Philosophy of Software: Code and Mediation in the Digital Age.* London: Palgrave Macmillan, 2011.

Binder, Jeffrey M. "Alien Reading: Text Mining, Language Standardization, and the Humanities." In *Debates in the Digital Humanities 2016,* edited by Matthew K. Gold and Lauren F. Klein, 201–217. Minneapolis: University of Minnesota Press, 2016.

Cecire, Natalia. "When Digital Humanities Was in Vogue." *Journal of Digital Humanities* 1, no. 1 (2011), http://journalofdigitalhumanities.org/1-1/when-digital-humanities-was-in-vogue-by-natalia-cecire/. Accessed January 15, 2016.

Chow, Rey. *Entanglements, or Transmedial Thinking about Capture.* London: Duke University Press, 2012.

Cordell, Ryan. "On Ignoring Encoding." Ryan Cordell. May 8, 2014, http://ryancordell.org/research/dh/on-ignoring-encoding/. Accessed January 15, 2016.

Cormerais, Franck, and Jacques Athanase Gilbert. "Une nouvelle revue." http://etudes-digitales.fr/. Accessed April 4, 2017.

Drucker, Johanna. "Humanistic Theory and Digital Scholarship." In *Debates in the Digital Humanities,* edited by Matthew K. Gold, 85–95. Minneapolis: University of Minnesota Press, 2012.

Edelstein, Dan. "Intellectual History and Digital Humanities." *Modern Intellectual History* 13, no. 1 (2015): 237–46.

Ernst, Wolfgang. "Media Archaeography: Method and Machine versus History and Narrative of Media." In *Media Archaeology: Approaches, Applications, and Implications,* edited by E. Huhtamo and J. Parikka, 239–55. Berkeley: University of California Press, 2011.

Folger. "Folger Digital Texts." https://folgerpedia.folger.edu/Folger_Digital_Texts. Accessed March 29, 2018.

Galloway, Alexander R. "The Cybernetic Hypothesis." *Differences* 25, no. 1 (2014): 107–29.

Gitelman, Lisa, ed. *'Raw Data' Is an Oxymoron.* Cambridge, Mass.: MIT Press, 2013.

Kelly, Kevin. "On Chris Anderson's 'The End of Theory.'" *Edge: The Reality Club,* June 30, 2008, http://edge.org/discourse/the_end_of_theory.html/. Accessed January 15, 2016.

Kirsch, Adam. "Technology Is Taking over English Departments: The False Promise of the Digital Humanities." *New Republic,* May 2, 2014, https://newrepublic.com/article /117428/limits-digital-humanities-adam-kirsch/. Accessed January 15, 2016.

Liu, Alan. "Where Is Cultural Criticism in the Digital Humanities?" In *Debates in the Digital Humanities,* edited by Matthew K. Gold, 490–509. Minneapolis: University of Minnesota Press, 2012.

Lyotard, Jean-François. *The Postmodern Condition: A Report on Knowledge,* Manchester, UK: Manchester University Press, 1984.

McAfee, Andrew, and Erik Brynjolfsson. *The Second Machine Age: Work, Progress, and Prosperity in a Time of Brilliant Technologies.* New York: W. W. Norton, 2014.

Rosen, Rebecca J. "A Brief Tour of the Folger Shakespeare Library's Digital Treasures." *The Atlantic,* October 2, 2013, http://www.theatlantic.com/technology/archive/2013/10/a -brief-tour-of-the-folger-shakespeare-librarys-digital-treasures/280039/. Accessed January 15, 2016.

Rouvroy, Antoinette, and Thomas Berns. "Gouvernementalité Algorithmique et Perspectives D'émancipation" *Réseaux* 177 (2013): 163–96.

Rouvroy, Antoinette, and Bernard Stiegler. "Le Régime de Vérité Numérique De La Gouvernementalité Algorithmique à Un Nouvel État de Droit." *Socio* (2015): 4113–140.

Savage, Mike. "The 'Social Life of Methods': A Critical Introduction." *Theory, Culture & Society* 30, no. 4 (2013): 3–21.

Scheinfeldt, Tom. "Sunset for Ideology, Sunrise for Methodology?" In *Debates in the Digital Humanities,* edited by Matthew K. Gold, 124–26. Minneapolis: University of Minnesota Press, 2012.

Scheinfeldt, Tom. "Why Digital Humanities Is 'Nice.' " In *Debates in the Digital Humanities,* edited by Matthew K. Gold, 59–60. Minneapolis: University of Minnesota Press, 2012.

Shannon, Claude E., and Warren Weaver. *The Mathematical Theory of Communication.* Urbana: University of Illinois Press, 1963.

Stiegler, Bernard. *La Société Automatique. 1. L'Avenir du travail.* Paris: Fayard, 2015.

Stiegler, Bernard. *Technics and Time: 2. Disorientation.* Translated by Stephen Barker. Stanford, Calif.: Stanford University Press, 2008.

Digital Humanities and the Great Project: Why We Should Operationalize Everything—and Study Those Who Are Doing So Now

R. C. ALVARADO

Sometimes an academic field is defined by a "great project"—a laudable and generous goal, shared by all or most members of the field, that determines the aim and scope of its work for years and sometimes decades. For social and cultural anthropology, from the postwar years to around the 1980s, that project was to represent, through the method of participant observation and the genre of ethnography, the planet's great diversity of peoples, languages, and cultures, which were rapidly being transformed or destroyed by the expansion of the world system. The product of that great collective labor is a vast ethnographic record, comprising essays and monographs focused on specific communities and linguistically or culturally uniform regions. Although sometimes these ethnographies were focused on a specific aspect of culture, such as language or ritual or economics, the goal was always to create a confederated and inclusive atlas of world cultures, even as efforts to formally centralize these efforts, such as Yale's Human Relations Area File, were not widely embraced by the field. Today, anthropology has moved on from this goal. One reason is that, since the 1980s, it has not been possible to frame research in terms of the retrieval and authentic representation of local societies, if it ever was valid to do so. Aside from the rise of critical and postcolonialist perspectives that led to an inward and more literary turn in the field, the situation in anthropology was produced by a change in the subject of anthropology itself. Although at one time it seemed possible to filter out the influence of Christian missionaries on the beliefs of, say, a community of headhunters, it became impossible to ignore the effects of chainsaws felling their trees.

In the digital humanities, we too have been involved in a great project. In the early days of the field, back when it was called humanities computing, that project was the retrieval and remediation of the vast collection of primary sources that had accumulated in our libraries and museums and, in particular, those textual sources that form the foundation of two fields that define, along with philosophy, the core of the humanities: literature and history. The signature offering of this project was the digital collection, exemplified by such projects as Edward Ayers' *Valley of the Shadow*, which would evolve into what Unsworth and Palmer called the "thematic research collection" and what others would label, with some degree of inaccuracy, the "archive." Almost everything that characterized the field prior to its rebranding as digital humanities can be related to this project: the work of text encoding; the concern for textual models and formal grammars (a side effect of and motivation for encoding in SGML and XML); a parallel but less intense focus on image digitization; the desire to develop effective digital critical editions; the inclusion of librarians and academic faculty under the same umbrella; the eventual development of tools like Zotero, Omeka, and Neatline; the interest in digital forensics (the need for which became apparent to those actually building these archives); and so forth. Even speculative computing, one of the most innovative branches of humanities computing, led by Drucker and Nowviskie, developed on top of this fundamental concern for the textual archive.

Just as anthropology's project was undone by the overwhelming forces of globalization, so too has that of the digital humanities, though perhaps without the horror. In our case, the pervasive technological changes associated with Web 2.0 and big data—two marketing labels that nonetheless index very real manifestations of globalization within the datasphere—have altered our great project by shifting the foundations on which it had long been built. In place of the vertical archive has emerged the horizontal networked database, both as a symbolic form that thwarts the will to narrative and unseats the prominence of ontology, and as a platform of participation that decenters the local project. Partly as a result of this shift, the older concern for well-curated collections founded on philosophically satisfying models has been displaced by a wider range of concerns, from an embrace of data science and distant reading to the exploration of maker labs and the Internet of Things to an engagement with the public humanities on a series of political and even ecotheological fronts.

Among these concerns, perhaps the most profound has been the engagement with data science. Anyone who has attended the annual DH conference over the years will have noticed the change. Statistical criticism has always been a feature of these conferences and the field, but the number of presentations describing the use of text analytics methods (such as topic modeling) has increased dramatically, to the point where large portions of the program guide could be mistaken for an IEEE conference. The change became visible around 2009, when the NEH's Office of Digital Humanities announced its Digging into Data Challenge, which asked digital humanists to answer the question, posed by Crane in 2006, "What do you do with a million books?" A year later, Google's N-Gram Viewer was revealed to the world, which provided its own answer to the challenge, although it was developed independently of the NEH initiative. By 2011, the noted historian Anthony Grafton, then president of the American Historical Association, would write about

an "astonishing" encounter with the creators of the viewer and its associated theoretical framework, "culturomics."

Although the impact of data science on the digital humanities can be measured by the sheer volume of attention that has shifted toward the newer methods,
the greatest effect has been a reorientation of the field's most fundamental practice:
the production and use of digitized primary sources, usually in the form of text.
In place of the digital scriptorium, in which scholars painstakingly mark up texts
according to well-conceived schema (such as those of the Text Encoding Initiative; TEI) to surface structure and semantics, there has emerged the data-mining
operation in which, for example, texts are converted into "bags of words" and vec-
torized for use in a variety of black-box procedures developed by systems engineers and computer scientists. In place of the concern for the establishment and
criticism of individual texts, the text itself has been "unbundled" and replaced by
other containers—the paragraph or text segment, the year of publication—which
then become the units of interpretation. At no point is the difference between
these practices more clear than when a text miner, making use of a legacy archive
of marked-up documents, first strips its texts of all markup—often representing
years of labor—regarding it as noise.

This shift in our orientation toward text has not been total—text markup continues to be a core practice within the digital humanities—but it has produced
something of a shake-up in the field that remains surprisingly unnoted. At the very
moment when digital humanities is on the tip of everyone's tongue, a tagline to every
IT-related grant and initiative within the liberal arts, its identity is at risk. For the
practice of text encoding, limited as it may seem in light of the field's new developments, remains the ancestral practice of digital humanities, and its displacement by
methods whose mathematical and computational requirements are far beyond the
scope of most humanists' training must be regarded as a kind of crisis. What now
distinguishes the digital humanist from the data scientist interested in working on
historical or literary texts, especially when the former actually knows what is in the
black box? What specific expertise does the digital humanist bring to the interdisciplinary table? Recall that the inventors of culturomics are biologists, not historians.
To be sure, the data scientist may retain the humanist as a subject matter or "domain"
expert—but that fits no one's definition of digital humanities.

Adeline Koh's notorious "DH Will Not Save You" post touched on this issue,
although from the opposite angle. She chastised digital humanists for privileging
computation over culture, a move that can only push the humanities into further
irrelevance by becoming a "handmaiden to STEM." But Koh replaces one form of
redundancy with another. Instead of being overshadowed by engineers, scientists,
and mathematicians, digital humanists are asked, in effect, to be more like scholars
in media studies, Science, Technology, and Society Studies (STS), or some variant of
cultural studies. This vision of digital humanities misrecognizes the central *eros* of
the field: the ludic and critical engagement with computational and cultural forms,

the "situation" created by engaging in the collaborative and iterative work of inter-pretation by means of digital media (Alvarado, "Digital Humanities Situation"). Such work is neither merely technophilic nor purely critical; it reflects the authentic and perhaps naïve desire of humanists to work with digital technology on their own terms. The result has been both critical and practical, a liminal mixture that will not satisfy the purist and remains easy to mischaracterize by outsiders.

Among the concerns to emerge in the space opened up by the digital humanist's engagement with data science is one that both continues in the spirit of the earlier focus on digital collections and text encoding and that promises to lay the ground-work for an inclusive and fruitful research agenda commensurate with the historical and literary alignments of digital humanities. This is the work of *operationalization,* highlighted by Moretti in the 2013 essay "'Operationalizing,'" a term of art from data science that refers to a specific way of representing knowledge for machine use. Although the word has its origins in the natural sciences, referring to the practice of defining the observable and measurable indices of a phenomenon (or its "prox-ies") so that it may be studied experimentally and quantitatively, Moretti generalizes the idea to include the practice of translating a received concept or theory (typically about society, culture, or the mind), into machine-operable form. As an example he describes the contrasting ways that Woloch's concept of character-space—which defines the amount of attention a character receives in a novel in terms of the num-ber of words used to represent it—can be translated into specific metrics suitable for machine processing. Other examples include Finlayson's conversion of Propp's theory of the folktale, which defines stories as sequences of elementary narrative "functions," into a machine-learning algorithm operable on a collection of (heavily) annotated texts; the use of Lakoff and Johnson's theory of metaphor, which empha-sizes the importance of the body in the creation of metaphors, to classify motion-captured human movements (Wiesner et al.); and the effort by Mohr et al. to translate Kenneth Burke's "grammar of motives," which provides a "dramatistic" framework for describing the attribution of motives, into an automated process for text encod-ing and analysis. Such projects, diverse as they are, share the trait of appropriating an existing theory more or less as is and translating it into computational form to meet a research project's requirement to achieve some level of coherency with its material. The theory serves as a resource for the development of an ontology—in the narrow, computational sense of a "formalization of a conceptualization"—that may be used for a variety of practical purposes, such as the definition of a database schema or the writing of class libraries to process a project's data.

Among operationalization's useful and interesting consequences, Moretti emphasizes the critical opportunities that arise from the work of translating a dis-cursively constituted idea into machine-readable code. To demonstrate, he trans-lates Hegel's theory of tragic opposition, which describes the process by which equally valid human values come into conflict, and notes that the work of opera-tionalization itself can actually cause us to rethink the original theory in refreshing ways, even if in retrospect we may imagine having arrived at the new perspective by other means. Here Moretti echoes Unsworth's earlier observation, experienced by many, that "there's definitely something to be learned from the discipline of expressing oneself within the limitations of computability" (Unsworth, paragraph 2), as well as the larger point made by Drucker and Nowviskie that "[d]igital humanities projects are not simply mechanistic applications of technical knowledge, but occasions for critical self-consciousness" (432). For these thinkers, operationalization produces a *rationalization effect,* a disruption of tacit knowledge caused by the computer's representational demand for explicit, discrete, and often reductive categories, which frequently requires one to refine held ideas into clear and distinct form. Along the way, lively philosophical questions, long hidden in the foundations of an idea, are reopened for debate, since the coded representation of the original idea is never the only one possible, but inevitably demands choosing among alternatives.

The philosophical boon yielded by operationalization is enough to establish it as a core practice in the digital humanities. But operationalization promises more than an occasion to reflect on foundations: it may alter fundamentally the aims and increase the scope of DH research projects. By shifting focus from the remediation of *content* to the remediation of *ideas* (which have been developed to interpret that content), digital humanists may reconnect with the production of theory, an area where the humanities and interpretive social sciences have developed expertise (its excesses notwithstanding). Although digital humanists will always be invested in the building of digital collections, both individual thematic research collections and large digital libraries, operationalization allows us to build on the scale of these collections to pursue questions about how these materials will be interpreted to answer questions with merit beyond the formalism inherent in collection building. Imagine a project involving historians and literature scholars applying an operationalized version of Benedict Anderson's thesis in *Imagined Communities,* regarding the effects of print capitalism on the formation of national consciousness. Such a project would take advantage of the substantial digital collections of novels and newspapers from the long eighteenth century and would employ data science methods such as topic modeling to represent and visualize nationalism in ways that might support or falsify Anderson's claims. Instead of only building collections based on shared authorship, genre, provenance, or period, we might focus on how such categorized collections can be connected (via linked data protocols) and aggregated to pursue deep research questions that cut across these boundaries.

But perhaps most important, there is a critical opportunity opened up by an operational turn that should appeal to our desire for a more public humanities. By virtue of our collective familiarity with the body of social and cultural theory, digital humanists are in a position to evaluate the work of nonhumanistic data scientists who routinely grab the low-hanging fruit of social science to complete the narrative arc of the arguments they make without understanding the historical and theoretical contexts in which such ideas must be evaluated. In doing so, we can guard against the great danger of operationalization: the selection and amplification of ideas whose main qualification for inclusion in an argument is their ease of being represented by digital means.

Kavita Philip's account of the Indian national census database illustrates the point. In 2011, after eschewing the equivalent of what in the United States is called postracialism, the people and government of India decided to reintroduce the category of caste into the national census for the first time since 1931. In creating the database to capture this information—in the field, through form-driven interviews, and in the schema of a relational database—the developers drew, through imitation of the 1931 census, from the works of British ethnographer and colonial administrator, Herbert Hope Risley, including his 1908 study, *The People of India*. Apparently, the thinking among the software developers was that by the 1930s English anthropologists had reached a sufficiently advanced understanding of culture, caste, and race that Risley's ideas would provide a sound foundation for the data model. After all, by this time, many anthropologists had moved beyond the more egregious theories of race that had characterized the discipline in the late nineteenth and early twentieth centuries. However, Risley was no Boas, the American cultural anthropologist who was an early critic of the race concept and dispelled many attempts to link physiological traits to behavior. In contrast, instead of viewing human anatomical variation of features such as head shape as results of environmental conditioning, Risley was strongly committed to notions of genetic determinism and the efficacy of anthropometry, and he saw caste as a reflection of these dimensions. Moreover, he believed endogamy to be more consistently practiced than we know to be the case. Because of this, the census database encoded not only a set of received categories about caste but also a particular understanding about the nature of categorization itself. In effect, the 2011 census operationalized and thereby naturalized an antiquated and dangerous understanding of the caste system, encoding in its data model a theory of caste to which no current stakeholder would subscribe, at least openly. But since one rarely questions the data model of a database, because there is no practice or discourse with which to have such a discussion in the public sphere, the silence of the model in effect establishes its transcendence.[1]

At issue, then, in the digital humanist's engagement with operationalization is the transmission of knowledge to succeeding generations. Which ideas and ontologies will be taught, and which will be forgotten? For operationalization is, whether practiced by the digital humanist or data scientist, especially at this juncture, a selective transducer of concepts and theories, an evolutionary conduit through which some ideas will survive and others will not. Many of these ideas will have social consequences, as the census database example tells us. As humanists, we should not accept the glib premise that the most easily operationalized ideas are the best ideas, but should instead engage in an overt and critical review of operationalization as a form of argument, even as we employ this form to test and explore a grand theory.

The digital humanities has before it the opportunity to engage in a new great project, the embracing of operationalization as a form of deep remediation. This project has several virtues, including being inclusive of the big tent, synthetic of theoretical traditions and new research agendas, critical of emerging forms of digital culture, and—perhaps above all—being both backwardly compatible with our great work in the building of thematic research collections and forwardly comparable with our engagement with data science and our generous vision of a public humanities.

NOTE

1. For a complete account of Philip's talk, see Alvarado, "Purity and Data."

BIBLIOGRAPHY

Alvarado, Rafael. "The Digital Humanities Situation." "Where Is Cultural Criticism in the Digital Humanities?" In *Debates in the Digital Humanities,* edited by Matthew K. Gold, 50–555. Minneapolis: University of Minnesota Press, 2012.

Alvarado, Rafael. "Purity and Data." *Medium.* 2014, https://goo.gl/B8E8LZ.

Crane, Gregory. "What Do You Do with a Million Books?" *D-Lib Magazine* 12, no. 3 (March 2006).

Drucker, J., and B. Nowviskie. "29: Speculative Computing: Aesthetic Provocations in Humanities Computing." In *Companion to Digital Humanities,* edited by Susan Schreibman, Ray Siemens, and John Unsworth, 431–47. Oxford: Blackwell, 2004.

Finlayson, Mark Alan. "Deriving Narrative Morphologies via Analogical Story Merging." In *New Frontiers in Analogy Research,* edited by Boicho Kokinov and Keith Holyoak, 127–36. Sofia, 2009.

Grafton, Anthony. "Loneliness and Freedom." *Perspectives on History* 49, no. 5 (March 2011).

Koh, Adeline. "A Letter to the Humanities: DH Will Not Save You." Hybrid Pedagogy. April 19, 2015, http://www.hybridpedagogy.com/journal/a-letter-to-the-humanities-dh-will-not-save-you/.

Mohr, John W., Robin Wagner-Pacifici, Ronald L. Breiger, and Petko Bogdanov. "Graphing the Grammar of Motives in National Security Strategies: Cultural Interpretation, Automated Text Analysis and the Drama of Global Politics." *Poetics: Topic Models and the Cultural Sciences* 41, no. 6 (2013): 670–700.

Moretti, Franco. "'Operationalizing.'" *New Left Review* 2, no. 84 (2013): 103–19.

Palmer, Carole J. "24: Thematic Research Collections." In *Companion to Digital Humanities,* edited by Susan Schreibman, Ray Siemens, and John Unsworth, 348–65. Oxford: Blackwell, 2004.

Philip, Kavita. "Databases and Politics: Some Lessons from Doing South Asian STS." STS Colloquium, School of Engineering and Applied Science, University of Virginia, Charlottesville, Va., September 16, 2014.

Risley, Herbet Hope. *The People of India.* Calcutta: Thacker, Spink & Co., 1908.

Unsworth, John. "Collecting Digital Scholarship in Academic Libraries." University of Minnesota. October 5, 2001, http://people.brandeis.edu/~unsworth/UMN.01.

Wiesner, Susan L., Bradford C. Bennet, Rommie L. Stalnaker, and Travis Simpson. "Computer Identification of Movement in 2D and 3D Data." Presented at Digital Humanities 2013, University of Nebraska–Lincoln, July 16–19, 2013, http://dh2013.unl.edu /abstracts/ab-239.html.

Woloch, A. *The One vs. the Many: Minor Characters and the Space of the Protagonist in the Novel.* Princeton, N.J.: Princeton University Press, 2016.

Data First: Remodeling the Digital Humanities Center

NEIL FRAISTAT

A recent global benchmarking report for the Mellon Foundation on developing expertise in digital scholarship stresses the importance of local knowledge and communities of practice to the transfer and development of digital skills.[1] In the words of one participant, "It is better to learn from your community than take specialized training thousands of miles away." Of course, that all depends on the opportunities afforded by the local community, including whether it contains a DH center, where much (though by no means all) DH training still happens. DH centers themselves, however, have had changing roles over the years in local community training. As a longtime director of the Maryland Institute for Technology in the Humanities (MITH), I would like to consider these changes in the context of the DH center as an institution.

North American DH centers have helped humanists develop digital competencies primarily through the offering of faculty fellowships for project development. This model was originally based on one that Humanities Centers had already long been using successfully: faculty fellows receive a year off from teaching to work on a book project, in return for which they participate as a resident at the center, participating in various fora of intellectual exchange about their work and the work of other fellows. As transferred to DH centers in the early 1990s, especially through the prominent Institute for Advanced Technology in the Humanities (IATH) at the University of Virginia, the "fellows project model" was extraordinarily successful and influential. And, indeed, it served well in meeting the needs of a historical moment in which the great majority of humanists were uninterested at best and suspicious at worst of digital scholarship. By engaging, as fellows, renowned scholars such as Jerome McGann and Ed Ayers—whose projects served as models of what digital scholarship could achieve—IATH was able to advance the standing of the field at a moment when such intervention was crucial to its future.

We are currently in quite a different moment, however, when there is widespread interest on the part of humanities faculty and students in developing digital competencies. To my mind, the fellowship model for DH centers now constitutes an overinvestment in the few at the expense of the many, especially when it is the primary way that a DH center transfers new digital skills to faculty. Even in the previous era, this model often resulted in faculty fellows relying almost completely on the digital competencies of center staff, rather than developing any new skills of their own. This, in turn, led to all sorts of problems in the life of the project after the completion of the fellowship period. It is one thing to ask humanities scholars to produce a book and another thing to ask them to produce a major digital project during their fellowship year. We need to think creatively beyond the "fellow" and the "fellowship project" as the only, or even the primary, means for developing digital competencies.

Last year, at the DH center that I directed, the Maryland Institute for Technology in the Humanities (MITH), we experimented with digital skills development by starting not with a fellow or a project, but with a dataset: an archive of more than thirteen million tweets harvested by our lead developer, Ed Summers, concerning the shooting of Michael Brown by a police officer in Ferguson, Missouri, and the protests that arose in its wake.[2] Beginning with this dataset, MITH invited arts and humanities, journalism, social sciences, and information sciences faculty and graduate students to gather and generate possible research questions, methods, and tools to explore it. In response to the enthusiastic and thoughtful discussion at this meeting, MITH created a series of five well-attended "Researching Ferguson" workshops on how to build social media archives, the ethics and rights issues associated with using them, and the tools and methods for analyzing them. The point here was not to introduce scholars to digital humanities or to enlist them in a project, but to enable them through training and follow-up consultations to do the work they were already interested in doing with new datasets, methods, and tools. This type of training is crucial if DH centers are going to realize their potential for becoming true agents of disciplinary transformation.

The "Researching Ferguson" training sessions are the most recent iteration of what we at MITH have called our Digital Humanities Incubator series, which began in 2013 as a program intended to help introduce university libraries faculty, staff, and graduate assistants to digital humanities and guide them into digital work through a series of workshops, tutorials, "office hours," and project consultations. We have since found that the incubator process is most effective when it helps in generating new lines of inquiry, in encouraging the development of significant research questions, and in exploring meaningful datasets through computational methodologies. Its goal is to organize the high-level training intended to acculturate scholars, students, and librarians to new modes of data-driven research, collaboration, and publishing across projects.

One of the advantages of the DH incubator model is precisely that it does not engage participants immediately in large-scale, project-based work. Instead, it prepares the ground for such work by cultivating and vetting the research questions that arise as test-bed collections are made tractable to digital tools and methods. This approach has widespread benefits, affecting not only those scholars who eventually do become directly involved in project-centered work but also those who may want to adapt a particular tool or method to their own scholarly investigations or who want to understand better the possibilities of digital work in their own fields. Its outcomes could take the form of various "working groups"—devoted to a particular set of sources, to working out the details of a technical protocol, to raising the profile of particular research questions, or to publishing resources or new scholarly work based on the incubator's activities.

Whether the incubator process is structured as an introduction to digital humanities, the investigation of a dataset of widespread interest, or as a means for building digital capacity in a field, the great strength of the incubator model as opposed to the faculty fellowship is that it focuses on the creation of local communities of practice. Such communities are key to the successful transfer and development of digital skills. There may be DH centers with sufficient resources to afford both a faculty fellows program and an incubator program. But if it came down to a choice between the two, based on my experience I would take the incubator program every time.

NOTES

1. http://www.clir.org/pubs/reports/pub168/pub168.

2. http://mith.umd.edu/research/digital-humanities-incubator-2014-15-researching -ferguson.

The DH Bubble: Startup Logic, Sustainability, and Performativity

DAVID S. ROH

I n 2001, I left what would eventually become a lucrative internet startup company in online tutoring services to pursue graduate studies in the humanities. It was not a difficult decision: I had grown tired of the infighting over money within the company, my undergraduate schoolwork had suffered, the commute between my college campus and downtown Los Angeles was shaving years off my life, and finally, although I could not quite articulate it at the time, I had become disenchanted by the frenetic, ahistorical, churn-and-burn pace of invention—that is, the logic of the startup.

Initially, being part of an internet startup was terribly exciting. None of us knew what we were doing exactly, but no matter, we happily made it up as we went along. This was the era of new players such as PayPal and eBay; Google was still relatively fresh; the unholy cyber-libertarian trio of Napster, Scour, and Kazaa had the Recording Industry Association of America (RIAA) in fits; we navigated the streets of Los Angeles using printouts from Yahoo! Maps; and Amazon.com was beginning to expand beyond books. Anything was possible. The internet had passed its version of the Homestead Act, in which intrepid expansionists won public land in the United States for no cost, and we were eager to claim a stake: all we needed to do was register a domain, find a host, and build a site.[1] Starting small, my company designed websites for any client willing to entrust its web presence to a few university students, built local intranets and databases, and eventually graduated to more ambitious projects. We took on more partners and employees, leased an office near the Los Angeles County Museum of Art (LACMA) on Miracle Mile, and scheduled meetings with venture capitalists in search of the next hot property.

But the dual role strain of undergraduate student and startup member was over-taxing. A few friends ended up dropping out of school and working full time at the company. I came to my own crossroads: I could take a leave of absence from school to invest fully in the company, as two of my partners had already done, or I could focus on finishing my degree and pursue postgraduate studies. I decided to leave the company because I had become dissatisfied with the get-rich-quick mentality it had adopted. We ground through any project or venture that seemed viable, throwing ideas at the wall to see what would stick. There did not seem to be a long-term plan beyond the next project we could slap together and sell off.

In hindsight, I realize that the startup was ruled by a distinctive logic, one that stressed performativity over substance, which manifested in several ways. First, we upheld the startup stereotype, spending days on end in the office, wasting time, eating unhealthy food, and working in fits and starts. To this day, I remain uncertain as to whether we squatted in the office because we really needed to or because that is what we thought we were supposed to do as startup employees. (I doubt we were any more efficient than if we had put in a standard workday). Nevertheless, when potential investors stopped by, we appeared (and smelled) like a startup should: we were young, brash entrepreneurs in an overgrown playground, with empty boxes of Chinese takeout strewn about. Second, our projects rarely worked—or, rather, they worked just well enough to make it through a presentation. The code was ugly and inefficient, and back ends were held together with the computing equivalent of duct tape: the slightest breeze or wrong keyboard combination might cause the entire thing to crash. We compensated by draping a shiny veneer over the program ("skinning"), so that at least the aesthetics were appealing. But none of this really mattered, because as long as a project appeared to work on the surface, we could sell it to another company for completion (or, as was often the case, to be mothballed—ensuring the removal of a potential competitor from the market).[2] We went to industry conventions in bright-orange jumpsuits, handed out flyers from a booth, and offered attendees free swag and limousine rides to hotels in hopes of demonstrating the viability of our product. In other words, we were in the business of selling potential ideas rather than genuine products.

Graduate school, with promises of long-form study and historicity, offered a safe haven from the race, where I could marry my interests in technology with literary studies. It was during graduate school that the field of digital humanities enjoyed immense growth. In addition to studies of electronic literature and digitization efforts, increasingly ambitious projects, such as processes for detecting sub-generic trends in textual corpora, began to emerge. But as thrilling as it has been to witness the explosion of DH work, I have been unsettled by an emergent phenomenon that reminds me of my experience during the dot-com bubble: an interface performativity. There is an incentive for shiny GUIs (graphical user interfaces); infrastructure lives and dies by soft money, prioritizing grantsmanship; and intellectual exchange at conferences and journals is whittled down to tweets that increasingly lean toward self-promotion: while I understand the appeal of social media immediacy, I wonder if short-form ripostes are the most effective medium for intellectual exchange.[3] The software projects that seem to capture the public's imagination are the ones with attractive graphics or with a quantitative or empirical slant. Winning grants has become synonymous with actual DH work, at least by administrators and, at times, even by scholars.[4] As for the projects themselves, the situation has taken a turn for the better, as grant applications now require specifics on data management, and more conventional outlets for scholarship have begun to engage with both theory and praxis.[5] However, the lack of attention in the past led to an accumulation of digital detritus.[6]

There are several elements inflating what might be called the DH bubble. One derives from the field's perceived "sexiness," for lack of a better term, both in the administrative and popular imagination. The attraction is understandable: coverage of the field in the *New York Times, Atlantic,* and *Ars Technica* evinces an appeal that the humanities are otherwise often accused of lacking.[7] Digital humanities' popularity also offers a convenient solution to the question of the future of the humanities, when English and philosophy majors have been relegated to conservative talking points by politicians looking for easy targets to answer for a dearth of jobs in a struggling economy. Others have already covered why this DH-as-savior model is problematic,[8] and it is worth noting that many digital humanists recoil at the characterization. Whether or not this is a fair charge, the perception remains that digital humanities can somehow justify the humanities' relevance. It is an untenable position, really, and the associated pressure results in the internalizing of an entrepreneurial, performative logic that is very reminiscent of the startup logic I encountered years ago. We do not simply study or research digital humanities; we "do" DH.[9] That "doing" comes in the form of colorful data visualizations—statistical graphs, charts, maps and network graphs; enormous text-mining operations; and programming enterprises—which masks the fact that many of the digital tools used are imperfect, easily manipulated, and quite rudimentary.[10] That elision and concurrent performativity may be in part due to the promise of funds larger than usually available in the humanities. In a cash-poor environment, humanities departments are understandably attracted to individuals who can win grants and funnel indirect costs back to the university.[11] But an overreliance on soft money can leave the field vulnerable to the vicissitudes of its availability; without budget lines attached to tenured or tenure-track positions, projects might find themselves in states of neglect.[12]

In 2000, a year before I left the startup world, the internet bubble burst. The investing mania had precluded rationality; investors kept throwing capital at startups without requiring a delivery date, let alone a plan for a realistic project. But when startups began to fail to deliver, the funding dried up. I fear that something similar might occur in the digital humanities. While a comprehensive understanding of the field eludes the broader academic community, few want to be left behind. The word "digital" is affixed to everything in the humanities like the word "cyber" was positioned in the 1990s, at the dawn of the internet. When digital projects fail to generate revenue or live up to heightened expectations, however, digital humanities as a field risks falling flat. Having lived through the dot-com bubble, I am concerned about the consequences a similar bubble will have for digital humanities as a field.

As I write, I am in the midst of building a DH lab at the University of Utah, which has been very supportive of building both the space and a DH program initiative. Invested stakeholders such as the Marriott Library, College of Humanities, Architecture+Planning, and Fine Arts have been in conversation with many DH centers, labs, and programs around the country in laying the groundwork for a space on our campus. While I am interested in pursuing projects beyond digital ports of analog material, I am wary of becoming reliant on external grants. My experience suggests that the boom times in digital humanities will not last forever and that the "bust" will create problems as new DH labs and centers continue to appear without commensurate funding. For these reasons, I have attempted to be mindful of pursuing projects that are self-sustaining. This means more modest efforts, at least initially, in which the primary cost is my own human capital, rather than committing to a project requiring a team of support staff, programmers, and career-line faculty whose livelihoods depend on securing external funding. Moreover, I want to ground our projects in a critical discourse to advance conversation. For example, a virtual reality rendering of Borges's Library of Babel may be illuminating, but it needs to exist within an infrastructure that generates scholarly research in order to separate itself from being a freestanding digital art object.[13] Finally, I understand that a degree of performativity is expected from these centers, but I would like for that performativity to come in the form of services in humanistic training with faculty and students, as well as outreach to local communities—in our case, focusing on projects that take advantage of regional archives and Mountain West–specific concerns.

I am hopeful that we can make it work, because several key structural differences between DH centers and startups may turn out to be what protects academia from falling prey to startup logic. First, a DH center or lab does not have the same insatiable thirst for funding that a startup has, which by definition is a spare operation driven by a self-generated momentum. The startup has to generate revenue within a short span of time to justify its existence; hence, the timeline for projects and viability is much more compressed in comparison to an academic lab, which is likely integrated into the budget lines of larger entities. Second, as of yet, tenure and promotion in digital humanities do not rest on the number and size of grants awarded and projects completed. Whether this is a favorable or unfavorable matter is outside the scope of this chapter, but in either case, trends in the sciences are instructive; the grant-dependent model has in recent years driven away talented researchers from the field.[14] Pursuing grants is not by itself any different—many non-DH individuals or centers do the same, of course—but if DH labs or centers are conceived primarily as entrepreneurial ventures that should continually win indirect costs and generate publicity through interface performativity, then we will indeed be headed toward a crash similar to the one experienced by the startup world ca. 2001. I do not doubt that many others have already anticipated a bursting bubble, even if they do not describe it as such. I am hopeful that the field will be able to take control of the narrative so that these expectations of our constantly developing "killer apps" begin to subside. To this end, a critical awareness of, and resistance to, a startup logic demanding performativity is a first step.

NOTES

1. Early efforts at creating internet "neighborhoods" by Geocities took up the rhetoric of the Homestead Act. As a gerund, "Homesteading" came to mean claiming space online to create a "homepage."

2. For a dot-com bubble postmortem, see Cassidy.

3. I include myself among the guilty.

4. Natalie Cercire notes, "It is no secret that in the past few years many administrators have come to see in digital humanities a potential stimulus package for increasingly underfunded departments like English, history, comparative literature, classics, and so on."

5. For example, in 2010, *Shakespeare Quarterly* teamed up with MediaCommons to conduct an open peer review process.

6. This is not necessarily the fault of the field; it may even be endemic, since technology and platforms evolve rapidly. Perhaps it is unrealistic to expect projects to continue versioning if there is no commercial incentive or consistent funding.

7. See Cohen; Hopkins; O'Connell.

8. See Koh; Golumbia.

9. Natalia Cercire nicely captures the tension in digital humanities between theory ("yack") and method ("hack"), with an examination of the problematic epistemological concerns of a field defined by building and "doing," which may be reflective of a gendered, industrial mode that is exclusionary. She instead calls for digital humanities to theorize: "Yet in its best version, digital humanities is also the subdiscipline best positioned to critique and effect change in that social form—not merely to replicate it . . . . Surely such a making-sense is called for in this institutionalizing moment, and surely digital humanities itself is up to the challenge of doing it."

10. Programs such as Voyant, Mallet, and Gephi have gained popularity with practitioners, and they can be quite useful. However, these tools are imperfect and by no means avenues for clean, consistent results. My point is that the illusion of empiricism should be punctured; there is quite a bit of value in their inherent messiness and plasticity.

11. Other models for DH research exist that neatly circumvent the problem of the unreliability of soft money. The Center for Digital Humanities at UCLA, for example, is a retooling of a legacy Humanities Computing office (HumNet) that had its own budget baked into the existing infrastructure. Miriam Posner has spearheaded and facilitated projects that do not necessarily need external funding to get off the ground. (Disclosure: I was once a work-study employee at HumNet, UCLA CDH's predecessor.) Likewise, the Office of Digital Humanities at Brigham Young University concentrates on services for humanities departments and its students, with particular strengths in linguistics computing, stemming from its humanities computing tradition. Within that structure, BYU has the flexibility to explore nonservice-oriented DH projects.

12. The NEH Startup Grant Application asks for its projects to be open source so as to maximize accessibility and interoperability: "Projects developing new software are encouraged to make the software free in every sense of the term, including the use, copying, distribution, and modification of the software. Open-source software or source code should preferably be made publicly available through an online repository such as SourceForge or GitHub. Software should be thoroughly documented to promote its reuse" (9).

Additionally, the data management section requires a plan for sustainability and preservation: "Prepare a data management plan for the project (not to exceed two pages). The members of your project team should consult this document throughout the life of the project and beyond the grant period. The plan should describe how the project team will manage and disseminate data generated or collected by the project. For example, projects in this category may generate data such as software code, algorithms, digital tools, reports, articles, research notes, or websites" (10).

13. The Stanford Literary Lab has an admirable model of publishing "pamphlets" based on their research. The pamphlets narrate the methodological problems, inherent messiness of the data, and preliminary nature of their findings, inviting replication and further research.

14. In "A Generation at Risk," Ronald Daniels notes that the sciences funding model tends to award intellectually conservative projects to established researchers, which leaves little room for young scientists. Consequently, the field is in danger of losing an entire generation of researchers unless the infrastructure changes.

BIBLIOGRAPHY

Cassidy, John. *Dot.con: How America Lost Its Mind and Money in the Internet Era.* New York: Harper Perennial, 2003.

Cecire, Natalia. "Introduction: Theory and the Virtues of Digital Humanities." *Journal of Digital Humanities,* August 15, 2016, http://journalofdigitalhumanities.org/1-1/introduction-theory-and-the-virtues-of-digital-humanities-by-natalia-cecire/.

Cohen, Patricia. "Humanities Scholars Embrace Digital Technology." *New York Times,* November 16, 2010, http://www.nytimes.com/2010/11/17/arts/17digital.html.

Daniels, Ronald J. "A Generation at Risk: Young Investigators and the Future of the Biomedical Workforce." *Proceedings of the National Academy of Sciences of the United States of America* 112, no. 2 (2015): 313–18.

Golumbia, David. "Death of a Discipline." *Differences* 25, no. 1 (January 1, 2014): 156–76.

Hopkins, Curt. "Future U: Rise of the Digital Humanities." *Ars Technica,* June 17, 2012, http://arstechnica.com/business/2012/06/future-u-rise-of-the-digital-humanities/.

Koh, Adeline. "A Letter to the Humanities: DH Will Not Save You." Hybrid Pedagogy. April 19, 2015, http://www.hybridpedagogy.com/journal/a-letter-to-the-humanities-dh-will-not-save-you/.

O'Connell, Mark. "Bright Lights, Big Data." *The New Yorker,* March 20, 2014, http://www.newyorker.com/books/page-turner/bright-lights-big-data.

The Scandal of Digital Humanities

BRIAN GREENSPAN

With so many pixels glowing over recent charges by Daniel Allington, Sarah Brouillette, and David Golumbia that the digital humanities enable neoliberalism, I felt the need to respond to some of their claims. The authors of the provocative *Los Angeles Review of Books* (*LARB*) piece, "Neoliberal Tools (and Archives): A Political History of Digital Humanities," take pains to explain that they are talking about not all of digital humanities, but a specific variety stemming from a particular tradition of textual studies and humanities computing. As many have already protested, their genealogy of the digital humanities omits a great many areas of inquiry that have contributed to the field's variegated and contested formation, including history, classics, archaeology, hypertext and hypermedia studies, cybercultural studies, electronic literature studies, critical media studies, maker culture, game studies, and platform studies. Even taken on its own terms, the argument that aligns the digital humanities with neoliberal priorities seems to leave out an awful lot of what digital humanists actually think, say, and do. Neoliberalism accounts in part for the enclosure of common goods by private interests and the subjection of all areas of life to a strictly economic logic. In contrast, much work in the digital humanities involves either detourning commercial tools and products for scholarly purposes or building open-access archives, databases, and platforms that resist the pressure to commercialize, as Alan Liu points out. That is why DH projects (including my own) are so often broken, nonworking, or unfinished (Brown et al.), and far from anything "immediately usable by industry," as the authors of the *LARB* piece suggest.

Still, the very taint of technology is enough to convince some readers that DH must somehow smack of neoliberal tendencies. The equation seems to go like this: since both the digital humanities and neoliberal management require funding for technology, they are ideologically aligned, while conventional humanists are by implication nontechnical and thus nonmanagerial. The *LARB* authors argue that digital humanists themselves position the field as a corrective to traditional humanist scholarship, supplanting radicalism and progressive inquiry with merely "disruptive" innovation, in the sense employed by Clayton Christensen, whose theories of entrepreneurship have driven managerial and pedagogical reforms at postsecondary institutions across North America over the past two decades. These authors would not be the first to conflate disruptive managerial strategies like MOOCs (massive open online courses) and the unbundling of degrees with the goals of DH, which suggests that digital humanists need to do more still to distinguish their own inventive and critical explorations of alternate pedagogies and methodologies from the corporate "innovations" increasingly favored by university administrations (Cordell). It needs to be reiterated that the digital humanities, while perhaps not always and everywhere "radical," are rarely just "innovative."

In fact, from a managerial perspective, the kind of computationally expensive uses to which digital humanists typically put technologies—such as running topic models on large corpora for hours or days on end in the hope of discovering new discursive patterns for interpretation—would appear to be an impractical and inefficient tax on resources with no immediate application or return on investment. It might also be objected that neoliberalism has been advancing at least since the abandonment of the gold standard, while the digital humanities have been around only about fifteen years, or even half that time if you consider only the "new Digital Humanities" that Steven E. Jones ties to the rise of social media corporations like Twitter and Google. Nevertheless, while the digital humanities may not be the determining cause of all our woes, the case could still be made that they exacerbate the neoliberal tendencies that already exist within the academy and media culture at large, tendencies which depend increasingly on the same technical systems as DH. I have learned enough over the years from my outstanding colleague and sometime lab mate Sarah Brouillette and her many crucial critiques of capitalist culture to recognize signs of exploitation in the workplace. While our approaches to the digital humanities do not always align, her insights have strongly informed my own writing and practice, and ought to be taken seriously.

The *LARB* piece encapsulates a large undercurrent of *ressentiment* within academia that blames the digital humanities and neoliberalism alike for sapping both prestige and resources from the "pure" scholarly pursuits of merely thinking and writing, which allegedly require only books, pens, and paper; and need not involve any newer technologies at all, let alone teamwork, labs, or large operating grants. That attitude is, of course, hugely disingenuous: it perpetuates the monastic myth of the isolated (tenured) scholar as ideal, while ignoring how little anyone could get done today without the computers, email clients, catalogs and databases, e-journals, cloud storage, online book resellers, and social networks that keep us connected to the world of scholarship, not to mention online travel agents for booking passage to conferences and research archives. In today's academy, we are all already digital.

If the digital humanities seem at times to pander to the neoliberal discourses and tendencies that are undeniably rampant within postsecondary institutions, it is not because they necessarily contribute to exploitive social relations (although they certainly do at times, just like every other academic sector). I rather suspect that it is because digital humanists tend as part of their scholarly practice to foreground self-reflexively the material underpinnings of scholarship that many conventional humanists take for granted. The digital humanities involve a close scrutiny of the affordances and constraints that govern most scholarly work today, whether they are technical (relating to media, networks, platforms, interfaces, codes, and databases), social (involving collaboration, authorial capital, copyright and IP, censorship and firewalls, viral memes, the idea of "the book," audiences, literacies, and competencies), or labor-related (emphasizing the often-hidden work of students, librarians and archivists, programmers, techies, research and teaching assistants, and alt-ac workers). Far from being "post-interpretative, non-suspicious, technocratic, conservative, [and] managerial" (Allington et al.), the "lab-based practice" that we promote in Carleton's Hyperlab, at least, involves collaborative and broadly interdisciplinary work that closely scrutinizes the materiality of archival practices, bibliography, and publishing across media, as well as the platforms and networks we all use to read and write texts in the twenty-first century.

If anything, the digital humanities are guilty of making all too visible the dirty gears that drive the scholarly machine, along with the mechanic's maintenance bill. That many of these themes also happen to be newly targeted areas for funding agencies as they try to compensate for decades of underfunding, deferred maintenance, rising tuition, and falling enrollments on campuses everywhere does not constitute evidence of the field's inherent neoliberalism. Now, some would argue (and I would agree) that these material costs should ideally be sustained by college and university administrations and not by faculty research grants. But digital humanists are not responsible for either the underfunding of higher education over the last twenty-five years or the resulting mission creep of scholarly grants, which in addition to funding "pure research" are increasingly expected to include student funding packages, as well as overhead for equipment, labs, building maintenance, heat, and power. The fault and burden of the digital humanities is that they reveal all the pieces of this model of institutional funding that seems novel to many humanists, but which has long been taken for granted within the sciences. This model acknowledges that most funding programs are designed not merely to help tenured professors buy books and travel, but also to support our research infrastructure and, above all, our students who justify the mission of scholarship in the first place, and who fill in while we fly off to invade foreign archives like the detritivores we are.

The digital humanities do not pander to the system (at least not more than any other field) so much as they scandalously reveal the system's components, while focusing critical attention on the mechanisms needed to maintain them. And that is precisely the field's unique and urgent potential: by providing the possibility of apprehending these mechanisms fully, the digital humanities take the first steps toward a genuinely materialist and radical critique of scholarship in the twenty-first century. To ignore the valuable critical insights of digital humanists and, under the flag of anti-neoliberalism, retreat into an unreconstructed view of humanist scholarship as a detached, isolated, and unmediated expression of critical acumen would be both dishonest and dangerous.

Still, most scholars will find that their DH colleagues present an easier target than their deans, presidents, or funding agencies, against whom any accusations might well be met with professional or financial repercussions. Digital humanists are the convenient enemies within—and ones who have a lot of arcane knowledge about digital codes and protocols at that. Who is to say that the digital humanist who built that Omeka exhibit or installed your school's learning management system is not also mining Bitcoins for darknet interests, running online surveillance for Amazon, or tweaking high-frequency trade algorithms on the derivatives market? As long as critics elide the distinction between the media corporations that own the code and those who are best qualified to interpret, challenge, and rewrite it, we are not likely to be able to identify—let alone resist—incursions of neoliberal governmentality into academia when they actually occur.

BIBLIOGRAPHY

Allington, Daniel, Sarah Brouillette, and David Golumbia. "Neoliberal Tools (and Archives): A Political History of Digital Humanities." *Los Angeles Review of Books,* May 1, 2016, https://lareviewofbooks.org/article/neoliberal-tools-archives-political -history-digital-humanities.

Brown, Susan, Patricia Clements, Isobel Grundy, Stan Ruecker, Jeffery Antoniuk, and Sharon Balazs. "Published Yet Never Done: The Tension between Projection and Completion in Digital Humanities Research." *DHQ: Digital Humanities Quarterly* 3, no. 2 (2009), http://www.digitalhumanities.org/dhq/vol/3/2/000040/000040.html.

Cordell, Ryan. "How Not to Teach Digital Humanities." February 1, 2015, http://ryan cordell.org/teaching/how-not-to-teach-digital-humanities.

Jones, Steven E. *The Emergence of the Digital Humanities*. New York: Routledge, 2013.

Liu, Alan. "On Digital Humanities and 'Critique.'" May 2, 2016, https://storify.com/ayliu /on-digital-humanities-and-critique.

Digital Humanities as a Semi-Normal Thing

TED UNDERWOOD

ive years ago it was easy to check on new digital subfields of the humanities. Just open Twitter. If a new blog post had dropped or a magazine had published a fresh denunciation of "digital humanities," academics would be buzzing.

In 2017, Stanley Fish and Leon Wieseltier are no longer attacking digital humanities—and if they did, people might not care. Twitter, unfortunately, has bigger problems to worry about, because the Anglo-American political world has seen some changes for the worse.

But the world of digital humanities, I think, has seen changes for the better. It seems increasingly taken for granted that digital media and computational methods can play a role in the humanities. Perhaps a small role, and a controversial one, and one without much curricular support—but still!

In place of journalistic controversies and flame wars, we are finally getting a broad scholarly conversation about new ideas. Conversations of this kind take time to develop. Many of us will recall Twitter threads from 2013 anxiously wondering whether digital scholarship would ever have an impact on more mainstream disciplinary venues (Posner). The answer, "It just takes time" was not, in 2013, very convincing. But, in fact, it just took time. Quantitative methods and large scales of analysis, for instance, are now a central subject of debate in literary studies.

To illustrate their centrality, we might point to a recent special issue of *Genre* that engages the theme of "data" in relation to the Victorian novel; this follows a special issue of *Modern Language Quarterly* on "scale and value" (Rosenthal; English and Underwood). "Scale" is the theme of the English Institute in 2017, and *PMLA* has announced a call for papers on "Varieties of Digital Humanities." Meanwhile, of course, the new journal *Cultural Analytics* is providing an open-access home for essays that make computational methods central to their interpretive practice (Piper).

The participants in this conversation do not all identify as digital humanists or distant readers. But they are generally open-minded scholars willing to engage ideas as ideas, whatever their disciplinary origin. Some are still deeply suspicious of numbers, but they are willing to consider both sides of the debate about quantitative methods. Many recent essays are refreshingly aware that quantitative analysis is itself a mode of interpretation, guided by explicit reflection on interpretive theory. Instead of reifying computation as a "tool" or "skill," for instance, Robert Mitchell engages the intellectual history of Bayesian statistics in *Genre*.

Recent essays also seem aware that the history of large-scale quantitative approaches to the literary past did not begin and end with Franco Moretti. References to book history and the Annales School mix with citations of Tanya Clement and Andrew Piper (Levine, 70–71). This expansion of the conversation is welcome and overdue.

If "data" were a theme—like thing theory or the Anthropocene—this play might now have reached its happy ending. Getting literary scholars to talk *about* a theme is normally enough. But in fact, the play could proceed for several more acts, because "data" is just shorthand for a range of interpretive practices that are not yet naturalized in the humanities. At most universities, grad students still cannot learn how to *do* distant reading. So there is no chance at all that distant reading will become the "next big thing"—one of those fashions that sweeps departments of English, changing everyone's writing in a way soon taken for granted. We can stop worrying about that. Adding citations to Geertz and Foucault can be done in a month. But a method that requires years of retraining is not going to sweep rapidly over anything. Maybe, ten years from now, the fraction of humanities faculty who actually use quantitative methods may have risen to 3 percent or, optimistically, 5 percent. No amount of persuasion could make that process move faster: its progress is not limited by the conscious opinions of scholars, but by their training.

So we might as well enjoy the current situation. The initial wave of utopian promises and enraged jeremiads about digital humanities seems to have receded. Scholars have realized that new objects and methods of study can make a real difference, but that they are in no danger of taking over. Now it is just a matter of doing the work and teaching others how to do it. That also takes time.

BIBLIOGRAPHY

English, James F., and Ted Underwood, eds. "Scale and Value: New and Digital Approaches to Literary History." Special issue, *MLQ* 77, no. 1 (2016).

Levine, Caroline. "The Enormity Effect: Realist Fiction, Literary Studies, and the Refusal to Count." Special issue, *Genre* 50, no. 1 (2017): 77–95.

Mitchell, Robert. "Response." Special issue, *Genre* 50, no. 1 (2017): 139–52.

Piper, Andrew. "There Will Be Numbers." *Cultural Analytics,* May 23, 2016, http://cultural
    analytics.org/2016/05/there-will-be-numbers/.

Posner, Miriam. "At the moment, says Drucker, our work isn't really changing or contrib-
    uting to disciplines outside of DH. #dhbootcamp." Twitter, August 29, 2013, 6:18 p.m.

Rosenthal, Jesse. "Narrative against Data in the Victorian Novel." Special issue, *Genre* 50,
    no. 1 (2017).

PART II

THEORIES AND APPROACHES

Sample | Signal | Strobe: Haunting, Social Media, and Black Digitality

MARISA PARHAM

We came together in Mike Brown's name, but our roots are also in the flooded streets of New Orleans and the bloodied BART stations of Oakland. We are connected online and in the streets. We are decentralized, but coordinated.

—The Ferguson Action Group

The history of blackness is testament to the fact that objects can and do resist. Blackness—the extended movement of a specific upheaval, an ongoing irruption that anarranges every line—is a strain that pressures the assumption of the equivalence of personhood and subjectivity.

—Fred Moten

Recursion is a function that delegates the processing of a problem to self-referential, iterative, and diminishing versions of the same function, bounded by an initial value and a terminating base case that are essentially the reminders of external determination acting on the system.

—Alan Liu

Perhaps it is unsurprising that so many narratives of the digital divide high-light Black technological deficit, but ultimately lack language for Black communities' technological possibilities. This is especially striking in light of how quickly Black communities have been shown to adopt and adapt the affordances of new technologies. In regard to social media, for instance, contemporary African American youth are so much at the cutting edge that one must wonder if they are in fact ahead of the technologies themselves, gifting the world with speculative presents that many people would otherwise only imagine as futures. What would it mean to take this perception seriously, to attend to what the Black Quantum Futurism Collective describes as an "intersectional time orientation"? What kinds of critical structures might be distilled from thinking about technological adoption as itself a kind of Black cultural practice, a practice wherein "the past and future are not cut off from the present" (Ayewa and Phillips)? What might it mean to articulate *techne* as endemic to African American experience, even if so doing means resetting how we describe or imagine the technical emergence of digital technologies?

Understanding the digital as both descriptive and generative of African American experiences of memory, space, and time resets the chronology for what we typically postulate as the technical device emergence of "the digital." From a quantum futurist perspective, digital technologies are not merely metaphors for Black cultural production; emergent synergies between such objects and the spatial-historical assemblages of Black diasporic experience are taken as an occasion for what Siegfried Zielinski describes as media anarchaeology. As Michael Goddard notes, following Friedrich Kittler, anarchaeological approaches disrupt the linearity of technology-effect dyads by making space for articulating how various media assemblages have been shown "not to be implemented when this would have been first technically possible but only when the right socio-technical assemblage is able to make use of them" (1767). This is helpful in overcoming the presumption that certain populations are simply to be brought into technological advancement and instead directs inquiry toward understanding people as participating in mutually constitutive processes with technological innovation. By stepping away from "teleological medium narratives" (1776), we might therefore more easily understand, for instance, how Black Twitter existed long before the rise of the platform that we currently know as Twitter and thus find ways to critique Twitter as a precipitate of those traditions. "The digital" and "the technological" are important to thinking about Black life *not* because referring to the digital imparts saliency, nor because we must hunt for ways to make Black life relevant to the digital humanities. Black studies-inflected frameworks are important to digital humanities because at the technical core of so much contemporary technological innovation we find literal and figurative resonance with histories, materialities, and other structuring realities of Black diasporic experiences—digitality.

This chapter's method is one of speculative frameworking, the purpose of which is to distill a critical approach that takes seriously the belief that DH scholarship is an especially ripe space for modeling and critiquing livable futures for people invested in using hardware and software to recover, center, or thematize the lives of marginalized communities. One might think here of Keguro Macharia, who uses thinking by Katherine McKittrick, Tavia Nyong'o, and Brent Edwards to show how

> the "speculative" becomes part of the asymptotic narration, the gap in representation—the gap in the archive, the gap in the lie, the gap that is the lie—through which and into which black life finds an "origin story" within life-unmaking blackness. Speculation, or the speculative, might be a method that reads into and past the data-affirming archive to see what black life forms

might emerge, what acts of making and unmaking, what ways the human might
emerge and undo the regime of Man.

Speculation is also a mode of being-present where one is impossible.

Speculation and the anarchaeological underwrite this chapter's decolonial perspective
on digital humanities because together they help get at what is at stake in understanding how digital humanities emerges structurally out of marginalized communities as
much as the term also names a broad range of methods and approaches that might
be brought to bear on various communities' cultural materials. In the hybrid form
and method of its meditation, this chapter also pushes a bit against what might be
perceived as the discursive demands of contemporary institutional digital humanities writ large. As Kim Gallon notes, via Matt Kirschenbaum, "A vibrant and critical discourse from #dhpoco, #transformDH, and HASTAC . . . among others, now
serves to resist the academic hegemonies that may limit our understanding of what
the digital humanities is and will be in the future." Such a transformation is not only
a matter of continuing to broaden capital *D,* capital *H*'s capacity to name its critical
intersections and the intersectional implications of its ways and means; it also means
actively working to avoid reproducing the many ways that critical theory itself still
struggles to bring more kinds of voice and perspective into the core of both its institutional and discursive work. Throughout I use repetition and close reading to perform a kind of genealogical work that is structured by this chapter's evocation of the
haunted, digitized, transmediated dimensions of Black life. I use section headings to
help track the recursion at the heart of this meditation on recovery and resistance. In
their form they also hearken to the born-digital essays that bookmark this inquiry.

With that in mind, this chapter builds and rides a poetics of Black digitality
by examining three roughly constituted transmedial assemblages: *signals*—how
communities use compressed texts to come into being across time and space,
samples—cultural performances that both crystallize and iterate signals, and
strobes—oscillations that break the signal, event-times that capture the truth of
the signal's displaced origin. Moving across these terms provides an opportunity
for thinking intentionally but broadly about the affective life of social media utterances, with an eye to how social media works through us and against us, with us
and without us. Digital social media platforms are important to this inquiry not
only because they have been so heavily used by African Americans but also because
social media experience can be productively understood as technically parallel to
historically complex matters of cultural ownership, transmission, and participation
in African American culture. Further, as Catherine K. Steele, Meredith Clark, and
others have argued, developing multiple pathways into understanding how new
technological formations mediate communication within and across Black communities carries renewed urgency as we look for ways to historicize and conceptualize phenomena like "Black Twitter" and the rise of social media activism, for
instance the #BlackLivesMatter movement. Both social media activism and social

media participation require users to orchestrate complex movements between the embodied and the digital, the present and the past, the evidential and the ephemeral, the owned and the claimed.

<irruption>

Finding ways to ride the instability between *to, from,* or *for* structures the haunted nature of Black life. To be haunted is to experience other people's memories with the affective impact of personal, firsthand experience, to both survive and operationalize the glitch, the break, the experience of blackness that Fred Moten describes as "an ongoing irruption that anarranges every line" (1). In Moten's conceptualization, blackness names a state in which one is continually subject to reinscription by the eruption of the material and affective past out of the break and into the present. Because that eruption is also an emergence from oneself, it is more properly an *irruption,* that which heaves forward by turning inward, the body startled by a sharp pinch, Sankofa's beak. Haunted is the state of before and after, how bass makes bones quiver before a comprehension of melody emerges, and how the memory of bass can ignite deep and spontaneous dance: the embodied experience of what Wai Chee Dimock describes as "diachronic historicism," as she uses "resonance" to name how, "modeled on the traveling frequencies of sound," we might visualize texts as "frequencies received and amplified across time, moving farther and farther from their points of origin, causing unexpected vibrations in unexpected places" (1061). Irruption thus names how our experiences of media as memory disaggregate the self into itself, much as a sample is always that little piece of what it was but also what can become, standing in for a spatial, temporal, or affective whole. Algebraic—*Al-Jabr,* the breaking of the bones—movements, disjunctures, and migrations become sites of renewed emergence; moments become touchstones for larger cycles of losing and remaking meaning, of transformation without restoration, the impossibly fluid flow of the popping and locking body, the DJ using two turntables to disaggregate songs into discrete soundbytes so that they might be used *as if* they were digital, isolating out samples and breaks so that old texts could be made newly resonant with always present futures, the cultural working of what Paul D. Miller describes as "an involution engine" (2). Black lives hearken to the digital because Black diasporic existence is a digitizing experience. Transfer, migration, metonymy: the break and the remix persist as both witness and feature of the multiple and continual experiences of forced migration endemic to Afro-diasporic life in the Americas—the Middle Passage, the auction block, the Great Migration—"the digital." Digitality, life after the break, the enduring possibilities of Black futurities explicitly oriented against what Fikile Nxumalo and Stacia Cedillo cite as the "ever-shifting formations of the violences enacted by past–present plantation histories" (106).

<a href=". . . /blackbox"> #rememory </a>

Through, against, with, without: a social media feed is almost always similarly dis-placed from the space and time of a given user's embodied present. At the same time, it is of course embodiment that brings social media into the realm of human experience, as a social media timeline algorithmically tunes itself to the rhythms and materialities of any user's own prior physical presence. A social media feed, a timeline, is a software expression of a person's clicking, reading, pausing, return-ing, liking, and sharing. As Jocelyn Edens notes, "Contemporary technologies pro-duce particular movements—the swipe, the scroll, the full-body interaction with a device. These gestures, or organized forms of movement that respond to an inter-face, are new embodied habits" (qtd. Chukwulozie).

Each of these embodied actions produces a material trace, as participation in social media transmutes both the work of daily living and the mediation of that liv-ing into different kinds of distributable emotional, cognitive, and cultural capital. In a deeply and mutually constitutive process, people operate as both subjects and objects of those technologies, providing the content that constitutes social media's feed—again, the physical acts that produce the algorithmic expression and, as Shaka McGlotten has brilliantly illustrated, data that can be exchanged as the financial capital that undergirds the system itself.

In the wake of particularly harrowing events, I watch as handfuls of friends and compatriots declare "social media breaks," overcome with bone weariness. If we accept that social media participation is also an embodied relationship, then it follows that the data present might not necessarily square with a body's drive to remember. In "On Seeing through Twitter," Jeffrey Moro notes that even as so many contemporary framings of the digital and digital experience rightfully focus on dis-embodiment and accelerationism, it is important to register other kinds of digital experiences. For many members of marginalized communities, "social media over-concretizes lives in ways that bodies can't sustain." Moro goes on to discuss Web Smith's description of dealing with the constant social media specter of Black peo-ple's deaths. It is worth repeating here: "Twitter is suffering because it is the most accurate reflection of American society today. It's not just what's tweeted, it's what isn't tweeted. Each day, a new hashtag represents a dead child. Often, there is a filmed murder attached. Often still, we watch it."

Social media experience is on the one hand absolutely concrete—when you post a tweet you are doing a material thing with a material process and a material trace—but that doing is immediately keyed to a time, a moment that will soon pass. At the same time, the experience of the moment of composing or reading or sharing does not in fact pass; it remains. "Each day, a new hashtag": on the one hand, Smith's observation comports with Manovich's sense of the timeline in its temporal march. At the same time, "each day, a new hashtag represents a dead child" is also a keen-ing, as the march forward is in fact experienced as repetition, as entrapment in a historical past of racial violence that refuses to pass. *Each day*, comma. A pause. A space impenetrable to me because its purpose is to factor Black death. The break.

#SocialMediaBreaks

This sense of remainder is also a technological reality. Even as posts move down the timeline, the user's trace is never let go. On your return, the system returns this trace of you to you *as* you, insofar as the timeline purports to be algorithmically tuned to you, your preferences, your likes, your choices. One might think here of Wendy Chun's description of the human experience of software, wherein our experience of an interface ideally works transparently, the mechanism out of sight. In its rendering of the experience of computing, "its combination of what can be seen and not seen, can be known and not know—its separation of interface from algorithm, of software from hardware—makes it a powerful metaphor for everything we believe is invisible yet generates visible effects" (Chun 2013, 17). Ghostly yet evidential, present yet temporally displaced, the user's feeling of participation bridges this sense of you but not you, presence and action, as the sense that the distance between these perceived states must be experienced as easily navigable contributes to a platform's affective power. In instilling in us a certain sense of time and then localizing that experience of time to specific platforms with distinctive interfaces, social media consolidates its status as a place, as a material localization of social and affective forces that constitutes something more and less than extensibility. It is all about you, literally moving with you when you are present, without you when you are not, but always awaiting your return.

<with or without you>

With you, without you: digitality can also be taken adjectively, as describing the mechanisms by which other people's experiences emerge and reemerge across times and spaces that are separated and discrete. It is a way of characterizing the haunted nature of Black life, which in *Haunting and Displacement* I frame as a way of thinking about what it means to experience other people's memories with the affective impact of personal, firsthand experience. A productive figure for haunting and digital experience can be found in Toni Morrison's deployment of the notion of "rememory" in the words of her character Sethe in *Beloved*:

> Someday you be walking down the road and you hear something or see something going on. So clear. And you think it's you thinking it up. A thought picture. But no. It's when you bump into a rememory that belongs to somebody else. Where I was before I came here, that place is real. It's never going away. Even if the whole farm—every tree and grass blade of it dies. The picture is still there and what's more, if you go there—you who never was there—if you go

there and stand in the place where it was, it will happen again; it will be there
for you, waiting for you. (47)

There is something in Sethe's claim about the abstract and the material that is difficult to suss because the abstract is nonetheless material to our living in the world.
Even though it at first might seem like Sethe's argument is mainly spatial—the
rememory that waits to be "bumped" into—it is also useful to attend to how Morrison foregrounds "you," which is to say that the rememory marks "you" as both
subject and object of the past's actions.[1] Because you are a discrete being, "you who
never was there," the encounter with a radically exteriorized and detached past, the
sample, is an experience of irruptive emergence that is also characterized by expectation. Before you give me the details, *I get it.*

#sample

You learn of Michael Brown's death in Ferguson, Missouri, and you already know
what has happened. *Each day, a new hashtag.* In the wake of American terrors
against people of African descent, diaspora itself becomes a sense of time, characterized by a resolute futurism underwritten by a continual sense of the abid-
ing past, the timeline ticking with or without you. In this orientation, experienced
events are characterized by where they fall on a scale of expectation. Most events
have already happened because they will happen again, a temporal orientation
around which every experience of space must bend; it is the still-living's experience of what it means "to live in relation to this requirement for our death," what
Christina Sharpe characterizes as living "in the wake" of "specific and cumulative
deaths" (7). Accounting for how Black life requires a capacity to constantly index
Black death, and the intertemporal, crossroad processes that this instantiates, helps
us conceptualize the digital dimensionality of Black diasporic life. Unmoored, at
every instance of its emergence a sample potentially reproduces memory without
origin, Moten's anarrangement sublimated, the aesthetic emergences and emergen-
cies of Black American social and historical condition. *If you go there and stand
in the place where it was, it will happen again; it will be there for you, waiting for
you.* Each day, a new hashtag represents a dead child.

   A sample is able to resonate as meaningful by virtue of the power vested in the
very fact of its recursive appearance, in its mortifying pronouncement of the right
thing—the right utterance or gesture or beat, appearing at the right time for all
the wrong reasons—a negative capability navigated in the wake of what Katherine
McKittrick frames thusly: "The slave's status as object-commodity, or purely economic cargo, reveals that a Black archival presence not only enumerates the dead
and dying, but also acts as an origin story. This is where we begin, this is where historic
blackness comes from: the list, the breathless numbers, the absolutely economic, the
mathematics of the unliving" (16).

The "mathematics of the unliving" is a historical metadata that produces a sense of resonance beyond a discrete moment, producing a memory that circulates without origin. In moments of such experience, content and ownership are subordinated to haunting resonance and uncanny circulation. Qualitatively encoded in an experience of Michael Brown or innumerable other Black children's deaths is the reiteration of a quantitative reality, what I have elsewhere conceptualized as the impact of the news of other people's deaths. This is the pause between a death and its hashtag. A transmission. Brown dies and I get it. If I am not careful when I type McKittrick's quote, my computer insistently autocorrects "unliving" to "unloving," and I am moved to tears. This black box has grown from a ship's hold in Africa.

#signal

As Wai Chee Dimock, Alexander Weheliye, Nicole Furlonge, and others remind us, Ralph Ellison was obsessed with sound in its most technical aspects, with signal processing, radio waves, and recording technologies. Furlonge, especially, has demonstrated Ellison's repeated use of both technical and metaphorical figurations of frequency and amplification in his 1952 novel *Invisible Man* and how those figurations produce a poetics of corporeal listening: a kind of listening in which the discrete human subject is able to constitute a racialized self attuned to larger social environments (Furlonge, 6). Ellison's protagonist, an unnamed and clueless Black college student, arrives for his first day of work in a paint factory famous for its production of the whitest of white paints, "Optic White." He works for Lucius Brockway, who is responsible for running the machines that mix the paint, deep in the factory. Brockway's blackness reinforces the scene's irony, as expertise such as his constitutes the invisible labor that makes whiteness possible: he is one of the self-described "*machines inside the machine,*" who are the human analog to the drop of black paint that makes Optic White so white (Ellison, 217). The protagonist, whom Ellison characterizes as immune to irony and therefore also immune to other kinds of subtle or invisible social workings, finds himself unable to receive communications from Brockway at critical moments, almost causing an accident when he fails to respond to the buzzer's buzzing, enraging Brockway:

> "What's wrong with you?" he asked when the last valve was closed.
>   "I expected you to call."
>   "I said I'd signal you. Caint you tell the difference between a signal and a call? Hell, I buzzed you. You don't want to do that no more. When I buzz you I want you to do something and do it quick!" (Ellison, 213)

Here, the difference between the signal and the call is rooted in the narrator's ability to distinguish between them: a signal is only recognizable as such after its receipt, in the sense that the signal triggers computational understanding, even as it does not "tell" anything, in contrast to a call, a hail addressed to a specific subject. At first dismissive, the invisible man soon learns that *not* understanding the difference between a signal and call can be a matter of life and death. It does not matter that he *thinks* he should not have to know; what matters is what happens if he does not know to know, for it is knowing to know that pivots comprehension toward the unsaid, toward the meaningfulness compressed in a signal. Physical displacement, as well as the necessity that communication between Black people happens in the open but remains indecipherable to hostile listeners, historically produced the need and desire for new methods of cultural transmission, generation, and replacement. For Ellison, and more generally, this is not an argument about cultural membership; rather, attentiveness to the meaning behind that which goes unspoken can be understood as equivalent to having access to strategies for living, to knowing how to dodge or survive oppressive circumstances.[2]

#Relation

It is important to note that, in its compressed and encoded state, the signal is meaningless without computation. Without a knowing site of receipt, there is only a trace without referent. In Ellison's paint factory, the buzzing buzzer says nothing, but "is" everything. Brockway's closing admonishment, "When I buzz you I want you to do something and do it quick!" speaks to this sense that what the signal demands is an absolute orientation to the sender, a state of already ready response. This notion of saying without saying is also, of course, the hallmark of coded language; for instance, how group members—communities, teams, cliques, generations—communicate their connection to each other. In this modality, backstories, grammatical elements, names, and other kinds of details can be left out of most utterances. Such things can be left unsaid because the speaker presumes that the listener "already" knows enough to produce the utterance or gesture's connective tissue. To the person to whom the signal is actually targeted, the structural fact of compression itself produces a richer language, as the very absence of explanation or detail validates the person receiving the message as its proper and expected recipient.

One might think here of Jessica Marie Johnson's description of what it means to work in archival spaces from simultaneously Black and digital perspectives. She emphasizes how the digital influences her understanding of

> how to read sources and how people in the past and present are engaged with each other; and how to read into things that are more ephemeral, like the moments in which we laugh, in which language changes, and the shorthand languages that we use among each other that define who is kin, friend, or enemy. Those moments or spaces that are more ephemeral are both analogous of social media spaces and also of the ways and moments that diasporic black folk have played in the fragments of the archives.

In Johnson's articulation, digital experience is one wherein the encodings that bespeak community demonstrate the kind of fractal workings Édouard Glissant frames as Relation, and offer a glimpse into the kinds of possible love that Moten aligns with Black fugitivity: resistance, communality, shared hieroglyphics, the gestural, the things that come into being when we contribute to what is produced at the edges, to the creation of individual moments simultaneously curated as communal texts. Indeed, one might also think here of Emily Lordi's articulation of "understatement," in which she reads the ability to make art in an ensemble as "a function of interpretation—as an effect one creates through attentive, inventive listening instead of a static quality one detects or observes." Lordi goes on, via Jean Luc Nancy's "distinction between hearing and listening," to align hearing with "'understanding' or 'decod[ing]' the meaning of a sound." In this paradigm, listening can be understood as a "self-reflexively creative act" (Lordi, 101). *Through, against, with, without*: by virtue of their compression and the contingent nature of their appearance, signals are encodings, invisible to some, lifelines for others. The very fact of compression and encoding itself transmits an immense amount of communicative power: the world of meaning encapsulated in the timely glance or the hashtag on one side, the quick suck of tooth or the retweet of receipt on the other. Signals and samples remind us that resistance is both form and practice. This black box has grown from a ship's hold in Africa.

#rememory

In *From #BlackLivesMatter to Black Liberation*, Keeanga-Yamahtta Taylor narrates the arrival of the #BlackLivesMatter hashtag, which was created in the wake of the announcement that George Zimmerman would not be charged in the 2012 murder of a seventeen-year-old African American child, Trayvon Martin:

> Out of despair over the verdict, organizer Alicia Garza posted a simple hashtag on Facebook: "#blacklivesmatter." It was a powerful rejoinder that spoke directly to the dehumanization and criminalization that made Martin seem suspicious in the first place and allowed the police to make no effort to find out to whom this boy belonged. It was a response to the oppression, inequality, and discrimination that devalue Black life every day. It was everything, in three simple words. (150)

Much like other kinds of coded language, #BlackLivesMatter compresses the specifics of what it references, what Taylor describes as "the oppression, inequality, and discrimination that devalue Black life every day." At the same time, the hashtag also operates transparently, literally meaning what it says, even as the very fact of saying "it" is premised on the awareness of its opposite. One must assert that Black lives matter because the devaluation of the lives of Black people is experienced daily as an equally simple formulation: "Black lives do not matter." The signal quality of #BlackLivesMatter is thus foundationally embedded in the deep irony attached to any claim regarding the protection of Black people. To say that Black lives matter is to say out loud that Black lives do not matter and, in so doing, to reorient the present's future: #BlackLivesMatter is thus ironically descriptive of the past and present while also asserting a belief in the possibility of future justice. As Melissa Brown has observed in the use of the similarly oriented #SayHerName, such hashtags are used to "raise consciousness," enacted "through demands for action and affirmations to uplift victims of violence." Recursive, the immediacy of #BlackLivesMatter draws on historical repetition: it always says everything. It is the suck of the tooth, the long stare across the room: "here is another example of Black lives not mattering." But it also reorients discourse, projecting toward a newly future-oriented present: Black lives matter.

To say that hashtags like #BlackLivesMatter leave out the specifics is not to devalue their relationship to material conditions. Rather it is to highlight how the specifics of a hashtag's references are localized to the moment of its utterance, producing a term that works folksonomically, that is both simultaneously owned and shared. Taylor's insistence on the everydayness of the utterance also helps us understand how the meaningfulness of a tweet using the #BlackLivesMatter hashtag could be communicated in that tweet's status as a repetition, albeit of things that have happened in other times and in other places and to other people. Still a haunting, yes, but also invoking a future haint of resistance against the necropolitical, to use Achille Mbembe's term. Diasporic in its structural core, the #BlackLivesMatter hashtag enables digital activism, disaggregated action across discrete but also connected nodes. It enables not only activism in digital spaces, in other words, but also the use of "social network technology to organize and coordinate real-world action" (Brown, 1831).

#kairos

When the digital is understood as prior to the electric, we find more language for the analog relationships that were severed in the Middle Passage. By eliminating the possibility of return, enslavement split time, opening up a breach in which identity is constantly reproduced under the sign of an always already destabilized future. Moten's irruption is both symptom and cause of this destabilization, both witness and feature of the multiple and continual experiences of forced migration endemic to Afro-diasporic life in the Americas—the Middle Passage, the auction block, the Great Migration: "the digital," digitality, life after the break. Kelli Moore also hears, however, the capacity for a hashtag to move across experiential spaces in the term's half-rhyme with àse, which makes conceptually available "the special languages of prayer and invocation" to thinking about what it means to find common cause under the sign of #BlackLivesMatter. Moore notes how "hashtag"

takes the special languages of prayer and invocation and in a double movement enshrines it as an interface. Àṣe is fundamental to Yoruba poetics and
is performed in song, sculpture, textiles, scarification patterns and medicine.
Phonemic awareness of the slant rhyme between hashtag and *àse*, black matter
and black *mater* should draw our attention to the slippages and breaks between
concepts. Slant rhyme, also known as "half," "near," "oblique," "off," "weak,"
"imperfect," "lazy," rhyme, is marked by its definitional deficiency in relation
to "perfect rhyme" or "true" rhyme. One way to appreciate slant rhyme is as
rhyme in black, in the break. Attending to the pleasure of phonemic awareness
is a commitment to the necessary compositional crime of black rhyme. In the
case of #blacklivesmatter, *àse* compositional protocols break, transfigure, and
slant between street and digital interfaces. The BLM hashtag is a bio-electronic
song whose *àse* was powerful enough to socially organize and threaten enemies
online while also gathering people in physical geographies.

By virtue of Moore's rendition, we can see how a hashtag's "double movement," its
simultaneous place marking of virtual and physical worlds, resonates with Orisha-
hainted articulations of Èṣù / Eleguá and of the crossroads, which are spaces that
work like roads or paths across spatial, temporal, or experiential registers: this is
why Moore rightfully directs us to the hashtag's status as mechanism, to interface.[3]

    Àṣe is power, the power to draw on relations to make or to transform. Fol-
lowing Moore, and put alongside Lordi's rendition of accompaniment, àṣe offers a
conceptual entry point into thinking about knowledge as a power that comes into
being at the interstice of needing, listening, and acknowledging in situ, in community. Indeed, Emily Legg, building on the work of scholars of indigenous memory
and history such as Kimberly Roppolo and Chris Teuton, also asks us to think very
materially about how "storytelling as knowledge-making and a way of knowing is
not placed within one individual who passes the knowledge down to others. Instead,
it is knowledge that exists in a networked state with the role of the community as
knowledge producers."

    Generative, kairotic, and recursive, a hashtag is able to resonate as meaningful
by virtue of the power vested in the very fact of its appearance, in the rectifying and
validating sense of its being the right thing—the right utterance, gesture, hashtag,
meme—invoked at the right time for all the right reasons as negative capability is
transformed into distributed community action. As Jack Halberstam has framed it,
via Moten and Harney's work on "the undercommons,"

> It ends with love, exchange, fellowship. It ends as it begins, in motion, in between
> various modes of being and belonging, and on the way to new economies of
> giving, taking, being with and for and it ends with a ride in a Buick Skylark on
> the way to another place altogether. Surprising, perhaps, after we have engaged
> dispossession, debt, dislocation and violence. But not surprising when you have

understood that the projects of "fugitive planning and black study" are mostly about reaching out to find connection. (Halberstam, "The Wild Beyond")

Algebraic, #BlackLivesMatter attempts the broken mathematics of the loving.

< *Àṣe*>

We can hear the digitality of #BlackLivesMatter's political structure in the Ferguson Action Group's statement regarding their operational rationale, in which they address an emergent political world wherein the technical affordances of social media platforms and tools like text messaging have vastly increased the organizational capacity of people who are geographically separate to engage separate and locally individualized action that nonetheless resonates with and contributes to a common cause:

> We came together in Mike Brown's name, but our roots are also in the flooded streets of New Orleans and the bloodied BART stations of Oakland. We are connected online and in the streets. We are decentralized, but coordinated.

In this structure, again, one's encounter with a social media transmission, a signal, is also therefore as much an experience of repetition as it is one of discovery; action is played out as sample and remix. When their site manifesto states, "We came together in Mike Brown's name, but our roots are also in the flooded streets of New Orleans and the bloodied BART stations of Oakland," the Ferguson Action Group is reminding viewers that the organization's political work has emerged in response to a series of events scattered across time and space, events that are fundamentally different in their occurrences, but that have occurred equally as consequences of sustained historical violence. The temporal and spatial difference evidenced in the utterance of each event ultimately signifies their commonality, making them recognizable as engaged in loops, samples, and signals, the play of difference and repetition. This sense of repetition also works to eliminate conceptual contradiction from the statement's ending: "We are connected online and in the streets. We are decentralized, but coordinated." Or, as Alicia Garza has noted, "Black Lives Matter is an organization and a network. We are a part of the movement, but we are not THE movement." To use Hardt and Negri's language, channeling Marcia Chatelain, "The BLM movement is a field of experimentation of new organizational forms that gathers together (sometimes subterranean) democratic tendencies from the past" (12). A diverse range of social media technologies have resolved this structure by enabling networks of temporally and spatially distributed actions that are nonetheless linked and describable via a core metadata, the ubiquity of Black death in America, and the need to transform the irruptive force of this repetition into a history that is actually past. *Àṣe, ashé, axé.*

<I yam what I yam>

It might be worthwhile here to take a methodological cue from Ellison's own decision to frame *Invisible Man*'s symbolic structure around sound and light technologies, which undergirds his novel's movement between the communicative possibilities of embodiment—gesture, glance, the hand's flick—and the various technologies used to extend those possibilities. For if we move the term "signal" away from the gestural/physical and over to the digital, we gain insight into how the workings of digital electronics can thematize other kinds of configurations. A digital signal works by translating a text, a transmission, into a series of small formulas. By breaking down the text in this way, it greatly reduces the material quantity of the text. In its replacement of an original, signal compression greatly increases the amount of information that can be transmitted, stored, or shared in any given permutation of the signal. Rather than playback being a matter of amplifying a reproduction, digital playback instead requires decompression and decoding, which also means that representational fidelity is tethered to computational speed, to how much detail from the original can be bloomed or recovered from the compressed signal. "Compression," here described as a digital phenomenon, can also be expressed, however, as an experience of memory: the worlds of affective recollection that unfold when Marcel Proust's narrator tastes the madeleine, or the cascade of images and the smile that breaks across the invisible man's face when, on the streets of a still-unfamiliar Manhattan, he bites into a roasted yam, the recursivity of which catapults him back to his own Southern past and declares, "I yam what I yam."

</I yam what I yam>

In turning from content to form and then moving to understanding dissemination as a kind of content itself, we can begin to see how signals simultaneously support individual expression while also supporting that discrete expression as a repetition of some other knowing. The power of the signal's efficacy is located in the flexibility of its signifying, a kind of constant and intense wordplay at the heart of African American signifying traditions, traditions that carry structural similarities to the folksonomic quality of user-generated social media metadata (i.e., "hashtags"). "Folksonomy" is the term Twitter developer Chris Messina adopted in 2007 to imagine and describe the functionality of social media hashtags. In addition to describing a software design that would increase the platform's usability, the neologism is further conceptually enriched when set alongside Barbara Christian's foundational description of Black theorizing, what she describes as Black cultural affinity for dynamic ideas:

> For people of color have always theorized—but in forms quite different from the Western form of abstract logic. And I am inclined to say that our theorizing

(and I intentionally use the verb rather than the noun) is often in narrative forms, in the stories we create, in riddles and proverbs, in the play with language, since dynamic rather than fixed ideas seem more to our liking. How else have we managed to survive with such spiritedness the assault on our bodies, social institutions, countries, our very humanity? And women, at least the women I grew up around, continuously speculated about the nature of life through pithy language that unmasked the power relations of their world. . . . My folk, in other words, have always been a race for theory — though more in the form of the hieroglyph, a written figure which is both sensual and abstract, both beautiful and communicative.

Hashtags are folksonomic because they are created by users without the guidance of a centralizing structure that underwrites that use. A hashtag's meaning is made in the moment of its use, even as its communicative power emerges out of the fact of other people's uses. In other words, to make or to use a hashtag is to participate in a milieu, in the "sensual and abstract" work of generating and engaging with digitally networked hieroglyphics; again what Kelli Moore characterizes as "attending to the pleasure of phonemic awareness" and committing "to the necessary compositional crime of black rhyme." As a kind of sampling, the temporality of hashtag creation is in the present of user innovation, even as the power of that innovation simultaneously depends on how that use hearkens to a shared understanding: *Àṣẹ*.

The folksonomic is a kind of linguistic act that can thus be understood as similar to the kind of riff and improvisation attached to urban legend. As Patricia A. Turner reminds us, textual circulation in Black communities has historically been as much about the why, how, and when of dissemination as it is about a text's isolatable message or denotation. When thinking about texts heavily circulated in Black communities, Turner tells us, it is more useful to look to "what in the texts themselves or in the circumstances of their dissemination gave them life and made African Americans willing to incorporate them into their repertoires," rather than to imagine that text carries significant meaning beyond the need to transmit it (6). This is not unlike what is most observable about Twitter, particularly Black Twitter, which transacts on cultural codes that historically precede the platform, the Twitter platform having been made an extension of already powerful and already circulating representational habits based in the Black urban legend tradition. Aligning Black Twitter with the Black urban legend tradition is useful because it offers us a way to think about the nature of Black Twitter's humor and its orientation to political action. Black Twitter is not a different software from "regular Twitter"; however, one could argue that it is used to generate a radically different virtual platform, sustained by tropes common to traditions of African American humor and politics, and participatory in the repetition of what is always already "happening." For better or for worse, Black Twitter performs and reinscribes an idealized African American epistemological structure that is based in a demonstrated willingness to witness and to testify to uncomfortable or otherwise unacknowledged truths that shade otherwise familiar objects: it is a kind of knowing continuously remade available to friend and kin, to adopt Johnson's language again.[4] Turner's work helps us see how the very fact of sampling, much like encoding and compression, itself communicates: *Have you seen this? Do you know about this?* Repetition itself, hashtag, meme, rave, and rant, signals.

#recursion

That there is something to be apprehended at the edge of utterance also helps illuminate how signals and samples are *temporally* recursive. Like rememory, a signal informs but also reiterates the subjectivity of the receiver. *With you, without you*: At the moment of its appearance it is, to use Morrison's language, "already there" and "waiting for you," because "you" have come into being through the fact of its arrival. You get it. A signal simultaneously emerges from, is a constitutive part of, and also passes into the person to whom it has been sent. This sense of repetition verifies and validates Relation and contributes to the encoding and subsequent compression of the signal, as whatever is shared is received as *yet another example of x*. In this way, texts about the present can be experienced with the force of memory, as they are understood as sample data taken from a larger and longer signifying chain: iterative and confirming, not just memory but rememory. Following Moore, a hashtag's linguistic, spatial, and temporal concatenation works as an invocation into a moment of Relation experienced with the force and power of an incantation: Barbara Christian's hieroglyph in the moment of its digital and digitizing transmission, the other side of the pause.

</with or without you>

Signals gather individuals into Relation. Samples, meanwhile, validate and reiterate the relation. If the signal powers and is powered by Relation, the sample is its verification, the reminder of the signal's power and the reinstantiation of the individual as both the producer and consumer of content. The narrative I have relied on has been mostly positive, but it is worthwhile to take a moment to acknowledge some of the uncomfortable connections between mediation, interpellation, and disciplination. As Jocelyn Edens reminds us, "An interface coerces movements into habits and constrains routines; it extends the capacity of the human body" (qtd. Chukwulozie). In requiring us to train our bodies to its use, an interface also of course extends what bodies can do. But in the case of social media, we must also conceptualize the costs of this increased attentiveness, of this increased capacity to send and receive signals, this increased capacity to ever more effectively produce, share, and accrete. And this concern is not with technology or mediation distancing us from things that are "real." It is the opposite. Digitality, the affective and technical expression of the recursive, is both empowering and disempowering, describing the immensely important cultural work of the sample and the remix and the *yasss girl* of Black Twitter, while also describing what it means to live one's life as subject to the sudden reemergence of the traumatic. The timeline of pain, in the excess of suffering that it catalogs and in the reverberation of that suffering in the present, highlights a traumatic undercurrent to Black life, an undercurrent that can be materialized in personal experience or concretized and then amplified over social media.

#strobe

I am reminded here of a past experience, driving down the highway in the summer of 2015, at some point during the week following the death of Sandra Bland, an African American woman found hanged in her cell following her arrest for a routine traffic violation. The sun was out, and as I drove past the trees and past the buildings, the light on my hands and on the steering wheel had this sort of flashing dappled quality, going light and dark as the sun hit me differently in each moment. I did not notice it at first, even as I felt myself becoming increasingly agitated. The light was causing me to jerk, each flash responded to like a too-loud or startling noise. My physical response was an effect of the shifting light, but it was also of course paranoia, a really particular kind of dread at being pulled over. I could tell myself this because I *knew* that the flash was just an effect of light coming through the trees as I drove down the highway. But the flash of sun through my windshield, reflected on my arms. the uneven lighting speeding up and slowing down the appearance of my body, reduced me to a stop-motion parody: I experienced my own body as a kind of time-based media, as the flashes focused and froze me, focused and froze me, simultaneously inscribing me, capturing me, transforming me into a play of light, animating me. Sometimes you don't just get it; sometimes you get got. This is when your body is getting it, with or without you.

In each duration I experienced the light's inscription as an eruption of dread, as a consummation, the deeply rooted fear of flashing blue lights, interpellation. Algebraic—*Al-Jabr,* the breaking of the bones: my movement across space invites renewed interdiction by the state, the risk of transformation without restoration, the impossible stillness of the surveilled body—what in *Black Fugitivity and the Undercommons,* Moten and Harney frame thusly:

> And so it is we remain in the hold, in the break, as if entering again and again the broken world, to trace the visionary company and join it. is contrapuntal island, where we are marooned in search of marronage . . . in (the) study of our sea-born variance, sent by its pre-history into arrivance without arrival, as a poetics of lore, of abnormal articulation, where the relation between joint and flesh is the folded distance of a musical moment that is emphatically, palpably imperceptible and, therefore, difficult to describe. Having survived

degradation the moment becomes a theory of the moment, of the feeling of a presence that is ungraspable in the way that it touches.

If signals might be understood as protection, as a way of transmitting important information under surveillance, then this is the call, the hail, the voice of the law feared at every turn. The play of light on my surface was experienced as an emergence from deep below. Irruption. #SayHerName.

</irruption> </blackbox>

Strobes interrupt continuity, breaking continuous surfaces down into pieces and parts, a flipbook animation moving too slowly, the herky-jerky grotesquerie of Tod Clifton's Sambo doll (Ellison, 339). As I was driving down the highway I was not doing anything wrong. In fact I remember thinking—*I'm not doing anything wrong*—and then immediately hearing that as an echo of myself in a terrifying future, blandly saying a thing that would not matter in the face of state terror. In this moment I was haunted by the recent news of other people's deaths, people with whom I share a similar position in a larger algorithmic structure, a racialized structure that continually miscalculates my meaning via a computational site to which I do not have access, but out of which emerges my value. My circumstances can quickly and at any moment be made to reiterate a racial past that is not of my discrete experience, but that can arrive in my present at will. This is not the world of causality; this is the language of ghosts, haunting, and simulation, sublimated in my participation in social media, but with that participation also supporting further irruption. As Web Smith frames it, "Twitter's problem is its ability to trigger us. Every death reminds us that, even if we're perfect, we may die today." The anarrangement of every line. *Each day, a new hashtag.*

This subject who is me, who looks, reads, glances, and clicks, is also an algorithmically reconstituted self, a computationalized self built out of those choices, with values added in the dark and reintroduced to me as an outcome, a model, an idea of me remastered as an aesthetic experience of a digital platform. What I would refer to as myself is always at a distance from these computational figurations, even as each figuration can claim a kind of technical, data-supported fidelity. But because the processes through which that figure has been constituted are obscured, black boxed, my experience of that figuration is also an experience of catching a glimpse of myself as an expression of some other system's needs and desires: what Du Bois describes as double consciousness and what Moten describes as the nonequivalence of personhood (the figure, the social) and subjectivity. Even as I would like to avoid conceptualizing the Black and the digital only in metaphorical terms, it is important to note that algorithmic representation is indeed always figurative in the most basic sense. That which goes in is not that which comes out. Against this, then, is the ongoing irruption, the constant interruptive rearrivals of Black identity, which

I read as rendering a digitized human subjectivity that hopes to slip through the system with its compressions intact, a glitch in the machine. It is a subjectivity constantly under pressure from an unnamable past that itself without notice emerges into the present and undoes the present, but in so doing "traces the visionary company." This too, then, is the work of social media, as it works through us and against us, with us and without us.

</àse>

NOTES

1. In *Haunting and Displacement,* I note, "The problem is not that this memory has agency, is waiting for you, but that there was in fact no you prior to this encounter. What at first seems a slip between time and place is thus revealed as a displacement, as you are made to know that that which constitutes you comes from elsewhere, and that it will come with or without your consent. It is there, waiting for you because 'you,' as the subject of this narrative, have only come into being at the moment of this encounter. What Morrison writes as a single-layered phenomenon—a narrative of encounter: you are walking along and bump into something—is thus revealed as multilayered, multidimensional: rememory is actually a story of a self unselfconsciously accepting the self in its arrival from another time and from another place. The bump does not precipitate movement back through time; it precipitates an unfolding, a movement back into the self and out again. However, because the first inward turn is largely unconscious, it is experienced as a repetition rather than as an emergence"(8).

2. In *Invisible Man,* the protagonist's failure to respond also reinforces his status as an intraracial outsider, in the sense that his simultaneous hubris and naïveté drive him to take occurrences as interpretable at face value, even as he is left literally staring at Brockway while the signal unsuccessfully demands his attention. Indeed, much of the plot of *Invisible Man's* opening chapters is driven by its protagonist's incapacity to read signs and signals, an inability that comes to stand in for his larger incapacity to understand or find shelter in Black communities. We are never told explicitly why the protagonist cannot seem to catch on, to "get it," though we are given hints that, in choosing one kind of knowledge system over others, particularly didactic book learning over environmental absorption, embeddedness, *milieu,* he repeatedly misses opportunities to benefit from other people's experiences.

3. Jessica Johnson has also evoked the crossroads shape of the hashtag in thinking about the kinds of transportations they make possible. In *Black Haunts in the Anthropocene,* I use the traditional Santería/Candomblé understanding that there are 256 paths or avatars to Esu as an occasion for thinking about computers, hardware, and loss. It is said that, in the New World context, all the paths did not survive the journey across the ocean.

4. To be clear, Black Twitter is not about the racial blackness of its participants; it is about its participants' capacity to uphold and reproduce a set of sensibilities. Like

all samples, Black Twitter memes and hashtags speak to common experiences (real or claimed) and sometimes rely on nostalgia in place of actual shared pasts. It is important that the senses and boundaries of what gets talked about as Black racial identity are continually evolving: this kind of work—contestation, recognition, and struggle—is also germane to Black Twitter.

BIBLIOGRAPHY

Ayewa, Camae and Rasheedah Phillips. "About Black Quantum Futurism." Blackquantumfuturism. https://www.blackquantumfuturism.com/about.

Brown, Melissa, Rashawn Ray, Ed Summers, and Neil Fraistat. "#SayHerName: A Case Study of Intersectional Social Media Activism." *Ethnic and Racial Studies* 40, no. 11 (September 2, 2017): 1831–46. https://doi.org/10.1080/01419870.2017.1334934.

Christian, Barbara. "The Race for Theory." *Cultural Critique* 6 (1987): 51–63. doi:10.2307/1354255.

Chukwulozie, Sheila. "(Inter)Face of Creation and Curation in the Realm of Digital: Interview with Joycelyn Edens." Podcast. https://soundcloud.com/5colldh/interface-of-creation-and-curation-in-the-realm-of-digital.

Chun, Wendy Hui Kyong. *Programmed Visions: Software and Memory.* Cambridge, Mass.: MIT Press, 2013.

Chun, Wendy Hui Kyong. *Updating to Remain the Same Habitual New Media.* Cambridge, Mass.: MIT Press, 2013.

Clark, Meredith D., et al. "Beyond the Hashtags: #Ferguson, #Blacklivesmatter, and the Online Struggle for Offline Justice." Center for Media and Social Impact. February 2016, http://cmsimpact.org/resource/beyond-hashtags-ferguson-blacklivesmatter-online-struggle-offline-justice/.

Dimock, Wai Chee. "A Theory of Resonance." *PMLA* 112, no. 5 (1997): 1060–71. doi:10.2307/463483.

Dinsman, Melissa. "The Digital in the Humanities: An Interview with Jessica Marie Johnson." *Los Angeles Review of Books,* July 2016, https://lareviewofbooks.org/article/digital-humanities-interview-jessica-marie-johnson/.

Du Bois, W. E. B. "Of Our Spiritual Strivings." In *The Souls of Black Folk,* edited by Brent Hayes Edwards. Oxford: Oxford University Press, 2007.

Ellison, Ralph. *Invisible Man.* New York: Vintage Books, 1995.

Ferguson Action Group. "About This Movement." Ferguson Action. December 15, 2014, http://fergusonaction.com/movement/.

Furlonge, Nicole. "'To Hear the Silence of Sound': Making Sense of Listening in Ralph Ellison's Invisible Man." *Interference.* http://www.interferencejournal.com/articles/an-ear-alone-is-not-a-being/to-hear-the-silence-of-sound.

Gallon, Kim. "Making a Case for the Black Digital Humanities." *Debates in the Digital Humanities 2016.* http://dhdebates.gc.cuny.edu/debates/text/55.

Garza, Alicia. "Co-Founder Alicia Garza on the Black Lives Matter Movement." http://bill moyers.com/story/black-lives-matter/.

Goddard, Michael. "Opening up the Black Boxes: Media Archaeology, 'Anarchaeology' and Media Materiality." *New Media & Society* 17, no. 11 (December 2015): 1761–76. doi:10.1177/1461444814532193.

Halberstam, Jack. "The Wild Beyond: With and For the Undercommons." In *The Undercommons: Fugitive Planning & Black Study,* edited by Fred Moten and Stefano Harney. Minor Compositions. 2016, http://www.minorcompositions.info/?p=516.

Hardt, Michael, and Antonio Negri. *Assembly.* Oxford: Oxford University Press, 2017.

Johnson, Jessica M. "Keynote Address." *Race, Memory, and the Digital Humanities Conference W&M 2017,* October 26, 2017, https://www.youtube.com/watch?v=PlTSk1QPx-U.

Legg, Emily M. *Networked Knowledge, Digital Spaces: Storytelling as Decolonial Methodology.* http://www.emilymlegg.com/portfolio/?page_id=105.

Liu, Alan. "Friending the Past: The Sense of History and Social Computing." *New Literary History* 42, no. 1 (2011): 1–30.

Lordi, Emily J. *Black Resonance Iconic Women Singers and African American Literature.* New Brunswick, N.J.: Rutgers University Press, 2013.

Macharia, Keguro. "Blackness, Mathematics, Fabulation: Speculation." Gukira. September 27, 2014, https://gukira.wordpress.com/2014/09/27/blackness-mathematics-fabulation-speculation/.

Manovich, Lev. "Future Fictions." Frieze.com. June 2013, https://frieze.com/article/future-fictions.

Mbembe, Achille. *On the Postcolony.* Berkeley: University of California Press, 2001.

McGlotten, Shaka. "Black Data." *The Scholar & Feminist Online,* nos. 13.3–14.1 (February 2014), http://sfonline.barnard.edu/traversing-technologies/shaka-mcglotten-black-data/.

McKittrick, Katherine. "Mathematics Black Life." *The Black Scholar* 44, no. 2 (2014): 16–28.

Messina, Chris. "Groups for Twitter; or a Proposal for Twitter Tag Channels." Factory Joe. August 26, 2007, https://factoryjoe.com/2007/08/25/groups-for-twitter-or-a-proposal-for-twitter-tag-channels/.

Miller, Paul D., aka DJ Spooky that Subliminal Kid. *Rhythm Science.* Cambridge, Mass.: MIT Press, 2004.

Moore, Kelli. "Affinities and Tensions between Afro-Pessimism and Non-Standard Philosophy." Presented at the *Race, Memory, and the Digital Humanities Conference W&M 2017,* October 26, 2017, https://www.youtube.com/watch?v=PlTSk1QPx-U.

Moro, Jeffrey. "On Seeing through Twitter." September 28, 2015, http://stilllife.mp285.com/on-seeing-through-twitter/.

Morrison, Toni. *Beloved.* New York: Vintage, 2016.

Moten, Fred. *In the Break: The Aesthetics of the Black Radical Tradition.* Minneapolis: University of Minnesota Press, 2003.

Moten, Fred, and Stefano Harney. "Fantasy in the Hold." In *The Undercommons: Fugitive Planning & Black Study*. Minor Compositions, 2016, http://www.minorcompositions.info/?p=516.

Nxumalo, Fikile, and Stacia Cedillo. "Decolonizing Place in Early Childhood Studies: Thinking with Indigenous onto-Epistemologies and Black Feminist Geographies." *Global Studies of Childhood* 7, no. 2 (June 2017): 99–112. doi:10.1177/2043610617703831.

Parham, Marisa. "Black Haunts in the Anthropocene." https://blackhaunts.mp285.com/.

Parham, Marisa. *Haunting and Displacement in African American Literature and Culture*. New York: Routledge, 2009.

Sharpe, Christina. *In the Wake: On Blackness and Being*. Durham, N.C.: Duke University Press Books, 2016.

Smith, Web. "Our Truth Is Why Twitter Is Struggling." Web Smith. August 10, 2015, https://medium.com/@web/our-truth-is-why-twitter-is-struggling-ffc6a4e02bcd.

Steele, Catherine Knight, "Signifyin', Bitching, and Blogging: Black Women and Resistance Discourse Online." In *The Intersectional Internet: Race, Sex, Class, and Culture Online*, edited by Safiya Umoja Noble and Brendesha M. Tynes, 72–93. New York: Peter Lang, 2016.

Taylor, Keeanga-Yamahtta. *From #BlackLivesMatter to Black Liberation*. Chicago: Haymarket Books, 2016.

Turner, Patricia A. *I Heard It through the Grapevine: Rumor in African-American Culture*. Berkeley: University of California Press, 1994.

Weheliye, Alexander G. *Phonographies: Grooves in Sonic Afro-Modernity*. Durham, N.C.: Duke University Press, 2005.

Zielinski, Siegfried. *Deep Time of the Media: Toward an Archaeology of Hearing and Seeing by Technical Means*. Cambridge, Mass.: MIT Press, 2005.

Unremembering the Forgotten

TIM SHERRATT

The annual conference of the Alliance of Digital Humanities Organizations arrived in Australia in 2015, but this was not the first time Australia had welcomed some of the world's leading thinkers to its shores.[1] Just more than a hundred years earlier, in 1914, the British Association for the Advancement of Science held its annual meeting in Australia. In earlier years, the association had journeyed to Canada and to South Africa, but this was its first tour of Australia (Robertson; Love). One senior Australian scientist heralded its arrival as "a great event in the history of Imperial unity" (Masson, 5).

More than 300 scientists made the trip, including such notables as nuclear physicist Ernest Rutherford and pioneering geneticist William Bateson. The eminent Australian geologist Edgeworth David described the association's visit as "an epoch making event." He expected Australian researchers to be "strengthened and confirmed" in their work, reaffirmed through the "inspiration which comes alone from personal contact with master minds" (xcii).

The 1914 meeting was also an occasion to celebrate the ideals of science. War had been declared while the scientists were at sea, but events proceeded nonetheless, with delegates barnstorming across the country from Adelaide to Melbourne, Sydney, and Brisbane. The spirit of proceedings was summed up in Melbourne where the presentation of an honorary degree to the German geologist Johannes Walter was greeted with a "perfect storm of applause." "Truly science knows not distinction between belligerent and belligerent," noted one newspaper.[2] Australia's governor-general, Sir Ronald Munro Ferguson, welcomed the scientists in August 1914 with the observation that the looming dangers of war had at least "enabled them to realize that all men of science were brothers."[3]

And of course, they *were* mostly men. If you would like to explore the data, you can grab a digitized copy of the report of the meeting from the Internet Archive and run a script over the list of members, grouping them by title—Miss, Mrs., and Lady (*Report of the Eighty-Fourth Meeting of the British Association*).[4] Figure 12.1

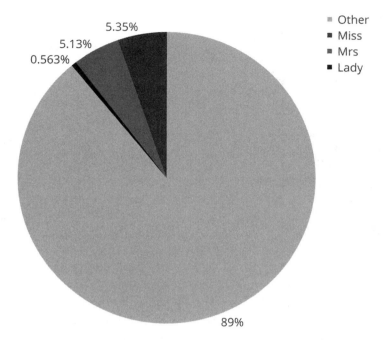

Figure 12.1. Approximate proportion of women members at the 1914 meeting of the British Association of the Advancement of Science. An interactive version of this chart, together with the underlying data, is available at http://plot.ly/~wragge/344 /women-members-at-the-1914-meeting-of-the-british-association-for-the-advancement/.

shows what you get. You can do the same for the people who joined the association at one of the Australian venues (see Figure 12.2). This analysis, which took me about ten minutes to perform, might not show anything unexpected, but it does demonstrate that with a digitized text and a few lines of Python you can ask a question and get an almost instant answer.

What the official report does not say is that despite these proclamations of scientific brotherhood, not all German scientists were welcome in wartime Australia. Those who extended their stay beyond the meeting dates fell under suspicion. Two of them, Fritz Graebner and Peter Pringsheim, were identified as potential spies and interned; they remained imprisoned for the remainder of the war.[5] The press, which had previously fawned over the traveling savants, now railed against these "scientists in disguise" whose "supreme act of treachery" was undoubtedly part of a German plot to capture Australia.[6] The Minister of Defense noted that the case emphasized the "real and pressing nature" of the wartime emergency. Honorary degrees awarded to two other German scientists by the University of Adelaide were expunged from the record.[7]

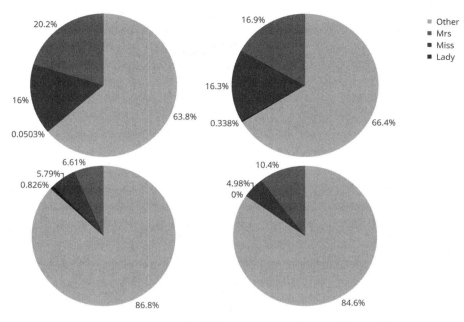

Figure 12.2. Approximate proportion of Australian women members in each city at the 1914 meeting of the British Association of the Advancement of Science. An interactive version of this chart, together with the underlying data, is available at https://plot.ly /~wragge/380/melbourne-sydney-adelaide-brisbane/.

If any of this seems familiar, it may be because legislation introduced in recent years to combat the so-called war on terror has added new limits to our freedom of speech and movement. This time around, we are all under suspicion.

The German scientists were interned alongside many thousands of others. Most had no charges brought against them. Many were naturalized British subjects or born in Australia of German descent: Australia was their home. That did not stop the government from repatriating many of them to Germany at war's end (Fischer).

On their arrival, visitors for the British Association meeting had been supplied with specially prepared handbooks that described conditions in Australia. At a time when violence against Indigenous people was still common along the frontiers of settlement, the *Commonwealth Handbook* informed visitors that Australian Aboriginals "represent the most backward race extant" (Spencer).

Australia was big, but its population was small. The *Commonwealth Handbook* noted the challenges of maintaining "control of so large a territory by a mere handful of people," pointing to the significance of the "White Australia" policy in avoiding the "difficulties" of "heterogeneous" populations (Knibbs). Chris Watson, who had served as Australia's first Labour prime minister a decade earlier, expanded on this theme in the *New South Wales Handbook*. Concerns about the financial impact of "coloured" labor, he explained, had been fused with an "abhorrence of racial admixture" to create "practically a unanimous demand for a 'White Australia.'" When the Australian colonies came together to form a nation in 1901, it was assumed that that nation would be "white." In the first term of the new Commonwealth Parliament, the Immigration Restriction Act was passed to give legislative force to these racist ambitions. The White Australia Policy remained in force until the 1960s. For Watson, "White Australia" was both an ideal and an obligation, an opportunity and a threat. He observed,

> The aboriginal natives are numerically a negligible quantity, so there is every opportunity for the building up of a great white democracy if the community can maintain possession against the natural desire of the brown and yellow races to participate in the good things to be found in the Commonwealth. That the Asiatic will for ever tamely submit to be excluded from a country which, while presenting golden opportunities, is yet comparatively unpeopled, can hardly be expected. Therefore Australians are realising that to maintain their ideals they must fill their waste spaces and prepare for effective defence. (134)

A hundred years later, however, Australia remembers 1914 not because it exposed the origins of its institutionalized racism, but because it marked the beginning of a war that has come to be strongly associated with ideas of Australian nationhood. The DH2015 conference landed in Australia in the midst of the "Anzac Centenary," the multiyear commemoration of Australia's involvement in World War I. The official website notes that the centenary "is a milestone of special significance to all Australians."[8] How special? According to the *Honest History* site, Australia spent more than a half-billion dollars on commemorative activities.[9] That pays for a lot of remembering.

Amid the traveling road shows, the memorials, the exhibitions, and the rolling anniversaries were of course many worthy digital projects. Some of these provide new access to war-related collections; others gather community content and memories. These projects result in important new historical resources. But who are we remembering, and why? As a historian and hacker, as a maker of tools and a scraper of sites, I want to poke around for a while within the complexities of memory.

Memory

There is more to Australian history than war. Recent decades have brought attempts to remember more difficult pasts. Historian Peter Read coined the phrase "stolen generations" to draw attention to the devastating effects of official policies that resulted in the forced removal of Indigenous children from their families as late as the 1970s. The damaging experiences of children in institutional care, the "forgotten Australians," have also been opened to scrutiny (Dow and Phillips). These policies have brought official apologies from the Commonwealth government. More recently, the Royal Commission into Institutional Responses to Child Sexual Abuse has exposed widespread horrors.[10]

In each case, we have learned, to our shame, of continuing failures to protect children, the most vulnerable members of Australian society. Often these investigations are cast as attempts to bring to the surface forgotten aspects of our history. But to those who suffered through these damaging events, who have continued to live with their consequences, they have never been far from memory.

Nor have they been entirely lost to the historical record. One of the responses to these inquiries has been to discover, marshal, and deploy existing archival resources. The National Archives of Australia created an exhibition based on the experiences of some of the stolen generation. It also developed a new name index of official records to help Indigenous people reconnect with families fragmented under the government's brutal policies.[11] The eScholarship Research Centre at the University of Melbourne drew on its experience in documenting a wide variety of archival collections to create *Find & Connect,* a web resource that assembles information about institutional care in Australia and assists care leavers in recovering their own stories.[12] Official records have been supplemented by oral history programs and other collecting initiatives to ensure that these memories are secure.[13]

Such histories are "forgotten" not because they are unremembered or undocumented, but because they sit uncomfortably alongside more widely promulgated visions of Australia's past. As researchers on the *Find & Connect* project noted, the stories of those who suffered through institutional care "did not 'fit in' with the narratives in the public domain. Their memories were 'outside discourse'"(Swain, Sheedy, and O'Neill). Remembering the forgotten is not only a matter of recall or rediscovery but also a battle over the boundaries of what matters.

Libraries, archives, and museums are often referred to as memory institutions. Rhetorically this can be a useful way of positioning cultural institutions in relation to structures of governance and assessments of public value. The idea of losing our memory, whether as a society or an individual, is frightening. But there are contradictions here. We frequently talk about memory in terms of storage: the ability of our technologies to tuck away useful pieces of information for retrieval later. There is the "*M*" in RAM and ROM, the fields in our database, our backups in the cloud. Memory is an accumulation of key/value pairs. Each time we query a particular key, we expect to get the same value back. But memory, as we experience it, is something quite different. It is fragmentary, uncertain, and shaped by context. The process of recall is unpredictable and sometimes disturbing: memories are often triggered involuntarily. Within a society, memories are contested and contradictory. Who controls the keys?

Access

Both in my work at Trove, the National Library of Australia's online discovery service, and my own research practice, I have used the word "access" a lot. But the more I use it, the more I suspect it really does not mean very much. What does it mean that we now distinguish between "open" and "closed" access?

We tend to think of "access" as the way we get to stuff. It is the pathway along which we can explore our cultural collections. But as Mitchell Whitelaw argues, one of our primary means of access, the common or garden-variety search box, constrains our view of the resources beyond. Search provides not an open door, but a grumpy "Yes, what?"

These sort of constraints do not stand in the way of access; they construct it. Through legislation, technology, and professional practice, through the metadata we create and the interfaces we build, limits are created around what we can see and what we can do. Access is a process of control rather than liberation.

In 1952, in another notable act of "imperial unity," Britain exploded an atomic bomb off the coast of Western Australia. An additional eleven atomic tests were carried out in Australia, most at a mainland testing site called Maralinga in South Australia. The British atomic tests introduced me, as a young research student in 1984, to both the gloriously rich collections of the National Archives of Australia and to the contradictions of access (Sherratt, "A Political Inconvenience").

Under the Australian Archives Act, most government records are opened to the public after twenty years (this was reduced from thirty years in 2010).[14] However, before they are released, they undergo examination to see whether they contain material that is exempted from public access; for example, any secret intelligence business that could endanger our national security. The access process can therefore result in records that are "closed" or "open with exception."

What does "closed" access look like to the researcher? To find out, I harvested details of all the files in the National Archives' online database that have the access status "closed" (Sherratt, "Closed Access").[15] While you cannot view the contents of the files, the metadata includes the reasons why they remain restricted (see Figure 12.3). If you group the records by reason, you can see that the most common grounds for restriction is Section 33(1)(g) of the Archives Act, which seeks to prevent the "unreasonable disclosure of information relating to the personal affairs of any person." Coming second is the rather less obvious category of "withheld pending advice." These are files that have gone back to the government agencies that created or controlled them to check that they really can be released. So these files are actually partway through the process. Using the contents dates of the files, we can see how old they are. Section 33(1)(a) of the Archives Act exempts records from public scrutiny if they might "cause damage to the security, defense or international relations of the Commonwealth" (see Figure 12.4). Most of the records closed on these

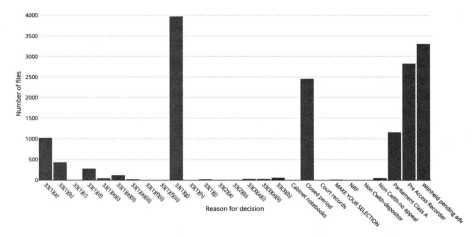

Figure 12.3. Closed files by reason. An interactive version of this chart, together with the underlying data, is available at https://plot.ly/~wragge/133/closed-files/.

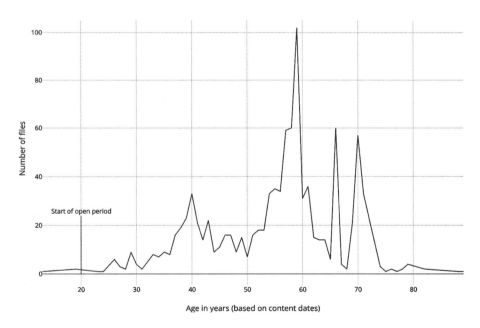

Figure 12.4. Age of files closed due to 33(1)(a). An interactive version of this chart, together with the underlying data, is available at https://plot.ly/~wragge/102 /ages-of-files-closed-due-to-331a/.

grounds are more than fifty years old, with a peak in 1956. Figure 12.5 is a word cloud of the titles of the closed files from 1956. I am sure that we all feel a lot safer knowing all those Cold War secrets are still being protected.

Back in 1984, I asked for some of those secret files to be opened so I could write my honors thesis on the role of Australian scientists in the British atomic tests.

Figure 12.5. Word cloud of titles of files from 1956 closed due to section 33(1)(a). The corpus can be explored at Voyant Tools, http://voyant-tools.org/tool/Cirrus/?corpus=1435 371278133.7113&query=&stopList=stop.en.taporware.txt&docIndex=0&doc Id=d1435292012766.dc37c489–0b70–00e8–2475-a4c76dd72167.

A number of the files I was interested in went off to agencies for advice, and some even made their way to the British High Commission. Being young, optimistic, and on a deadline, I wrote to the British High Commissioner asking if anything could be done to speed up the process of reviewing the files.

I received a very polite reply explaining that the British authorities were obligated under the Nuclear Non-Proliferation Treaty to make sure that they did not unleash any atomic bomb secrets on the world. This was hilariously and tragically ironic, as the argument of my thesis was that the British government withheld information from their Australian hosts to curry favor with the United States. There was no way that atomic bomb plans would be in Australian government files.

Access is political. Archivist Cassie Findlay has contrasted the Australian government's processes for the release of records with the creation and use of the WikiLeaks Cablegate archive. She argues that the "hyper-dissemination" model of WikiLeaks, which involves the sharing of large volumes of material across multiple platforms, creates a "pluralised archive" that "exists beyond spatial and temporal boundaries, transcends state and economic controls, and encourages and incorporates people's participation and comment."[16] Instead of gatekeepers and reading rooms, there are hackers and torrents—opening the workings of business and government to scrutiny.

Meanwhile, traditional forms of access, such as the release of decades-old files, are often celebrated as if they are a gift to a grateful nation. As Findlay notes, the release of Cabinet documents by the National Archives of Australia is a yearly ritual in which stories of thirty-year-old political maneuvering are mixed with the comforts of nostalgia. But with each release, more files are also closed and withheld from public access. The workings of a bureaucratic process developed to control the release of information are recast as an opportunity for publicity. Invested with the cultural power of the secret and the political weight of national security, access itself becomes mysterious and magical. We are left to ponder such artifacts as "Named country [imposed title, original title wholly exempt]."[17]

At the same time, governments are producing more and more "open data," offering the promise of greater transparency and new fuel for the engines of innovation. But for all its benefits, open data is not really open. It only exists because decisions have been made about what is valuable to record and to keep: structures have been defined, categories have been closed. Just like files in the National Archives, data has achieved its "openness" through processes of description and control. As Geoff Bowker and Susan Leigh Star remind us, the definition, elaboration, and enforcement of categories lie at the heart of bureaucracy and the infrastructure of the state. There is no threshold to be crossed from darkness to light; access is not a magic gateway to be opened to hearty applause and self-congratulation. Data is not just a product of government but is also implicated in the workings of power.

By 1914, Chris Watson's vision of a White Australia was well established as a system of bureaucratic surveillance and control. The *Commonwealth Handbook* benignly noted that "an immigrant may be required to pass a dictation test before being admitted into the Commonwealth." It added that "in general practice this test is not imposed upon persons of European race" (Knibbs). The dictation test was a mechanism of exclusion. Any intending immigrant deemed not to be "white" would be subjected to it, and they would fail. But there were already many people born or resident in Australia of Asian descent. If they wanted to travel overseas, they were forced to carry official documents to protect them from the application of the dictation test; otherwise they might not be allowed to return home. Many thousands of these documents are now preserved in the National Archives of Australia. With portrait photographs and inky-black handprints, they are visually compelling and disturbing documents. They need to be seen.

A few years ago, Kate Bagnall and I harvested thousands of these documents from the National Archives website, ran them through a facial detection script, and created the *Real Face of White Australia*. It is a scrolling wall of faces, displaying the portraits of thousands of people who were not supposed to be part of a "white" Australia. This was part of our ongoing attempts to use the bureaucratic remnants of the White Australia Policy to reconstruct the lives of those who lived within its grasp. But in the way it was created and received, it is also an example of the complications of access.

In the past I have tended to gloss over the hardest part of this project: harvesting those 12,000 images (Sherratt, "Real Face of White Australia"). This was only possible because I had spent a lot of time, over a number of years, wrestling with RecordSearch, the National Archives online database. It was in 2008 that I wrote my first Zotero translator to extract structured data from RecordSearch. The translator was one of those eureka moments. Although I had been developing web applications for a long time, I had not really thought of the web as a source to be mined, manipulated, and transformed. I could take what was delivered in my browser and change it.

Thanks to Bill Turkel and *The Programming Historian,* I taught myself enough Python to be dangerous and was soon creating screen scrapers for a variety of sites—taking their HTML and turning it into data (Turkel and MacEachern). I was no longer bound to a particular interface. The meaning of access had changed.

But screen scrapers are a pain. Sites change and scrapers break. I do not know how many hours I have spent inspecting RecordSearch response headers, trying to figure out where my requests were going. I have given up several times, but have always gone back, because there is always more to do.[18]

Along with the enthusiasm for open data, there is perhaps a tendency to overlook the *opening* of data: the way that hackers, tinkerers, journalists, activists, and others have been stretching the limits of access by finding new ways of extracting information from official sources. The various projects of the Open Australia Foundation are a great example: it has even established its own public scraping framework, called Morph.io, to share both the code and the data that have been liberated from websites and PDFs.[19]

Archivists Wendy Duff and Verne Harris have talked about records "as always in the process of being made," not locked in the past but "opening out of the future." Findlay similarly notes that the Cablegate archive "is still forming." She argues for models of participation and access around archives that unfold "more directly from the affairs that they document." The act of opening records, archives, and sources is contingent and contextual. It creates a connection between inside and outside, past and present, us and them. What we do with that connection is up to us.

What would have happened, for example, if instead of hearing about "prohibited immigrants," instead of seeing "wanted" posters of escaped Chinese seamen, Australians in 1914 had seen something like our wall of faces?[20] What would happen now if instead of hearing about "illegal maritime arrivals" (IMAs) we were exposed to the stories of those who arrive in Australia in search of asylum?[21]

Access will never be open. Every CSV is an expression of power, every API is an argument. While I would gladly take back the time I have spent wresting data from HTML, I recognize the value of the struggle. The bureaucratic structures of the White Australia Policy live on in the descriptive hierarchies of the National Archives. To build our wall of faces we had to dismantle these structures—to drill down through series, items, documents, and images until we found the people inside. I feel differently about the records because of that. Access can never simply be given; at some level it has to be taken.

Interventions

In 1987 I ended up outside the gates of Pine Gap, a U.S. intelligence facility near Alice Springs, dressed as a kangaroo. Having finished my honors thesis on the British atomic tests, I could not ignore the parallels between the bombs and the bases. I even organized a conference titled "From Maralinga to Pine Gap: The Historical

Fallout." I remember pulling over on the road to Alice Springs because there was one point where you could glimpse the top of one of the white domes that protected Pine Gap's receivers. It was a thrilling moment.

Now you can just type "Pine Gap" into Google Maps, and there it is. It is still secret, it is still gathering unknown quantities of electronic intelligence, but last time I checked, it also had twenty-one reviews and an average rating of 3.6 stars. "Worst customer service ever," notes one of the comments, in a stream of ironic humor and conspiracy theories.

Digital tools enable us to see things differently: to demystify secrets and to expose patterns and trends locked up in tables, statistics, or cultural collections. "Mapping Police Violence," for example, displays your chances of being killed by police in the United States based on your location.[22] It also presents the photos and details of more than one hundred unarmed black people killed by police in 2015.

But if access is itself defined through restriction, there can be no standard formula for opening connections to the past. Simply building a beautiful array of thumbnail images will not grant new insights into the lives and experiences documented by our cultural heritage collections. We have to work harder to puncture these interfaces and the descriptive systems they represent. We have to use the tools at our disposal to create new points of intersection and collision.

Twitter bots, for example, can play around with our ideas of context and significance. I have created a few myself that automatically tweet content from Trove, and I am interested in what happens when we mobilize cultural collections and let them loose in the places where people already congregate.[23] Steve Lubar argues that "the randomness of the museumbot calls attention to the choices that we take for granted." Bots can challenge the sense of control and authority that adhere to our collection databases.

But bots can do more. Mark Sample's important essay on "bots of conviction" explores the possibilities for protest and intervention. He describes protest bots as "tactical media" creating "messy moments that destabilize narratives, perspectives, and events." Duff and Harris warn archivists of the dangers of the story in disguising the exercise of power, in stealing from individuals what they need to construct their own narratives—"space, confusion, [and] a sense of meaninglessness." Against the brutal logic of the state, a bot's algorithmic nonsense can help us see differently, *feel* differently.

Caleb McDaniel's bot @Every3Minutes is an example of how powerful these interventions can be.[24] Working from estimates of the volume of the slave trade in the American South, it tweets a reminder every three minutes—a person was just traded, a child was just bought—often with links to historical sources. Mark Sample notes, "It is in the aggregate that a protest bot's tweets attain power," and it is through simple, unyielding repetition that @Every3Minutes reaches us. As Alex Madrigal has written, "To follow this bot is to agree to reweave the horrors of slavery into the fabric of your life."

Twitter bots can interrupt our social media meanderings with pinpoints of surprise, conflict, and meaning. And yet they are lightweight, almost disposable, in their development and implementation. No committees were formed, no grants were obtained—they are quick and creative: hacks in the best sense of the word. Bots are an example of how digital skills and tools allow us to try things, to build and play, without any expectation of significance or impact. We can experiment with the parameters of access.

In 2012 Kate Bagnall and I received an email from Mayu Kanamori, an artist researching the life of an early Japanese Australian photographer. She described her reaction to the *Real Face of White Australia*: "When I scrolled down the Faces section of your website, browsing through the faces, tears welled up, and I couldn't stop crying as if some sort of flood gates had been removed." We knew that that the documents and the images were powerful, but displaying the faces on that seemingly endless scrolling wall did something more than we were expecting: they confront, they challenge, they demand a response.

Jenny Edkins, a researcher in international politics, has been exploring the particular politics of faces. She suggests that alongside our attempts to "read" portrait photographs we also respond in a more visceral fashion, provoking responses such as "guilt, obligation, and reciprocity" (46). She argues that the connections we make through photos of faces, like the "messy moments" of protest bots, can disrupt the "linear narrative temporality" on which sovereign power depends. On our wall, the faces force their way through layers of bureaucracy and archival control to meet us with their gaze. We are connected through time, not with history, not with the past, but with people. And that has implications.

I have also tried extracting faces, and eyes within those faces, from photos I harvested via Trove's digitized newspapers. *Eyes on the Past* presents a random selection of eyes, slowly blinking on and off. Clicking on an eye reveals the full face and the source of the image. Where the *Real Face of White Australia* overwhelms with scale and meaning, *Eyes on the Past* is minimal and mysterious. It emphasizes absence and the fragility of our connection with the past, even while it provides a new way of exploring digitized newspapers. Some have found it beautiful; others thought it was just creepy.[25] Tweet a photo of yourself to @FaceDepot, and a bot will select a face at random from my collection of newspaper images and superimpose that face over yours, tweeting you back the result and a link to the original article (Sherratt, "Vintage Face Depot"). It sounds stupid, and it probably is. But the potential is there to mess around with the barriers that put some people on the other side of this wall we call the past—to explore what Devon Elliot suggested on Twitter was an "uncanny temporal valley."

The Australian historian Greg Dening has argued, "Nothing can be returned to the past. Not life to its dead. Not justice to its victimised. But we take something from the past with our hindsighted clarity. That which we take we can return. We disempower the people of the past when we rob them of their present moments" (204).

There is no open access to the past. There is no key we can enter to recall a life. I create these projects not because I want to contribute to some form of national memory, but because I want to unsettle what it means to remember: to go beyond the listing of names and the cataloging of files to develop modes of access that are confusing, challenging, inspiring, uncomfortable, and sometimes creepy.

Among my experiments are a couple of simple user scripts.[26] They sit in your browser and change the behavior of Trove and RecordSearch. Instead of pulling faces out of documents, they insert them back into your search results. Instead of just seeing lists of files, you catch a glimpse of the people inside. Like the faces on our wall, the people bubble to the surface. They are not merely findable: they are present.

Building

Despite the apparent enthusiasm for the visit of the British Association for the Advancement of Science in 1914, there was in Australia a lingering suspicion of scientists as "impractical dreamers," as mere theorists unwilling to address the nation's most urgent needs. In debates over the application of knowledge to Australian development, the scientist commonly struggled against the supposed virtues of the "practical man" (Sherratt, "Atomic Wonderland").

I imagine that my grandfather Henry Sherratt was a practical man. He was a brass molder with a workshop in Brunswick, a suburb of Melbourne. His father and brother, both brass workers, lived and labored nearby. I have a small brass ashtray that Henry made.

Henry's name is not among those who joined the British Association in Melbourne, though perhaps he attended one of the "Public or Citizens Lectures" that, until the 1911 meeting, had been known as "Lectures for the Operative Classes." Neither is Henry's name among those who journeyed to the battlefields of Europe and the Middle East. He is not one of those honored by the Anzac Centenary for having "served our country and worn our nation's uniform." And yet he went to war.

Henry Sherratt was among a select group of Australian tradesmen who traveled to Britain in 1916 to help meet the desperate need for skilled workers in munitions factories.[27] He worked as a foreman brass molder in Scotland, before having an accident in which he "strained his heart" carrying a ladle of molten iron. He never really recovered, and as his income suffered, so did his family at home. Henry finally returned to Australia in 1919 and was offered £50 compensation with no admission of liability. He died in 1955. I never knew him.

Whom do we remember, and why?

The Commonwealth Bureau of Census and Statistics reported that 159 people died as a result of industrial accidents in 1914. But these were only the accidents that had been reported under the provisions of state legislation. There must have been more. Where is their memorial? What about mothers who died in childbirth or the victims of domestic violence? How do we remember them?

In the week that the British Association met in Melbourne, newspapers tell us that David Phillips, an engine driver, was fatally injured at Flinders Street Station.[28] I am thinking about how we might use Trove's digitized newspapers to collect the stories of those who went off to work, but never returned. What might we learn about economic history, unionism, and industrial legislation—about the value we place on an individual life? As I have often said in regard to our work on the White Australia records—it just seems too important not to try.

As I was writing this, I was also keeping an eye on my harvesting scripts, pulling down more images from the National Archives of Australia. For the original wall of faces, I downloaded about 12,000 images from one series; I now have more than 150,000 images from about twenty series.[29] I also stopped at various times to play around with code—to look at the gender balance at the British Association, to investigate "closed" files in the National Archives, to create a public Face API for anyone to use. The code and apps are all out there now for you to play with or improve.[30]

Writing, making, thinking, playing, sharing: it all happens together. I am a maker like my grandfather. While he poured metal, I cut code. I do it because I want to find ways to connect with people like him, ordinary people living their lives. Those connections will always be fleeting and fragile, lacking the clarity of commemoration, but, I hope, bearing some of the meaning and complexity of memory.

It is a task that needs to be both playful and political, that revels in slipperiness of access, and that evades the certainties of control. It is not about making things, but trying to make a difference.

NOTES

1. This chapter is a modified version of my keynote address to DH2015, presented on July 3, 2015 in Parramatta. The original text is available at http://dx.doi.org/10.6084/m9.figshare.1536150.

2. "Conferring of Degrees," *Argus,* August 15, 1914, http://nla.gov.au/nla.news-article10802103.

3. "Vice Regal Welcomes," *Argus,* August 15, 1914, http://nla.gov.au/nla.news-article10802103.

4. The code that I used is available at Tim Sherratt, Baas_members: Quick Hack to Look at Gender Balance of Member of the British Association for the Advancement of Science in 1914, GitHub, 2015, https://github.com/wragge/baas_members.

5. "Professor Peter Pringchein Dr. Graebner Etc," MP16/1, 1914/3/14, National Archives of Australia, http://www.naa.gov.au/cgi-bin/Search?O=I&Number=325300.

6. "German Spies. Scientists In Disguise," *Maitland Daily Mercury,* January 5, 1916, http://nla.gov.au/nla.news-article123405543; "German Plot. To Capture Australia. Hun Scientists," *Mirror of Australia,* January 8, 1916, http://nla.gov.au/nla.news-article104642550.

7. "Foreign Professors Ostracized," *The Register,* December 15, 1917, http://nla.gov
.au/nla.news-article58871516.

8. "Find Out More About the Anzac Centenary," Anzac Centenary. http://web
.archive.org/web/20150611080131/http://www.anzaccentenary.gov.au/find-out-more
-about-anzac-centenary. Accessed January 18, 2016.

9. "Budget 2015: Honest History Factsheet: Centenary Spending $551.8 Million,"
Honest History, May 13, 2015, http://web.archive.org/web/20160119035426/http://honest
history.net.au/wp/budget-2015-honest-history-factsheet-centenary-spending-551-8
-million/.

10. "Royal Commission into Institutional Responses to Child Sexual Abuse." February 6, 2018, http://web.archive.org/web/20180206100526/https://www.childabuseroyal
commission.gov.au/.

11. National Archives of Australia, "Bringing Them Home Name Index—Fact Sheet
175." http://www.naa.gov.au/collection/fact-sheets/fs175.aspx. Accessed January 19,
2016.

12. "Find & Connect." https://www.findandconnect.gov.au/. Accessed January 19, 2016.

13. National Library of Australia, "Forgotten Australians and Former Child Migrants
Oral History Project." https://www.nla.gov.au/oral-history/forgotten-australians-and-for
mer-child-migrants-oral-history-project. Accessed January 19, 2016.

14. National Archives of Australia, "Access to Records under the Archives Act—Fact
Sheet 10." http://naa.gov.au/collection/fact-sheets/fs10.aspx. Accessed January 19, 2016.

15. Updates are available from my open research notebook at http://timsherratt.org
/research-notebook/projects/closed-access/.

16. While the model itself remains useful, WikiLeaks' independence from state control has been rightly questioned as a result of its activities during the 2016 U.S. election.
This reinforces the general point: access is political.

17. "Named Country [Imposed Title, Original Title Wholly Exempt]" (Canberra,
1956), A1838, 100/4/7, National Archives of Australia, http://www.naa.gov.au/cgi-bin
/Search?O=I&Number=476513.

18. Tim Sherratt, Recordsearch_tools, GitHub, 2016, https://github.com/wragge
/recordsearch_tools.

19. Open Australia Foundation, "Morph.Io." https://morph.io/. Accessed February
11, 2018.

20. For some examples of posters offering rewards for the apprehension of prohibited
immigrants, see "Immigration—Register of Asian Deserters for Whose Apprehension and
Conviction a Reward Has Been Offered," A2455, 1, National Archives of Australia, http://
www.naa.gov.au/cgi-bin/Search?O=I&Number=148562.

21. Department of Immigration and Border Protection, "Illegal Maritime Arrivals."
http://web.archive.org/web/20160122002452/http://www.ima.border.gov.au/en/Illegal
-maritime-arrivals. Accessed January 21, 2016.

22. "Mapping Police Violence." https://mappingpoliceviolence.org/. Accessed January 19, 2016.

23. See: "TroveNewsBot (@TroveNewsBot)," Twitter. https://twitter.com/TroveNewsBot. Accessed January 19, 2016; "TroveBot (@TroveBot)," Twitter, https://twitter.com/trovebot. Accessed January 19, 2016. For further discussion see Sherratt, "Life on the Outside. "

24. "Every Three Minutes (@Every3Minutes)," Twitter, https://twitter.com/every 3minutes. Accessed January 19, 2016.

25. Tim Sherratt, "Eyes on the Past," http://eyespast.herokuapp.com/. Accessed January 20, 2016. For a selection of responses see "Eyes on the Past," Wakelet, http://wakelet .com/wake/e0437dfa-88c4-4999-9f5e-aa32a9ba1118. Accessed February 11, 2018.

26. The scripts are shared via Gist at https://gist.github.com/wragge/2941e473ee70152f4de7 and https://gist.github.com/wragge/78af45c181f4d11b1a5f.

27. "SHERRATT Henry Edward—Munitions Worker Number 46" (Melbourne, 1916–1919), MT1139/1, SHERRATT HENRY EDWARD, National Archives of Australia, http://www.naa.gov.au/cgi-bin/Search?O=I&Number=5917163.

28. "Casualties and Fatalities," *Argus*, August 26, 1914, http://nla.gov.au/nla .news-article10803705.

29. See: Tim Sherratt, Iabrowse: Simple Series Browser for Invisible Australians Files, GitHub, HTML, 2016, https://github.com/wragge/iabrowse; Tim Sherratt, Iafiles: More Invisible Australians Harvesting, GitHub, 2015, https://github.com/wragge/iafiles. Continuing development is documented in my open research notebook at http://timsherratt .org/research-notebook/projects/immigration-recordkeeping-and-surveillance/.

30. See: Sherratt, Baas_members; Tim Sherratt, Closed_access: Harvesting and Analysing Items with the Access Status of "Closed" from the National Archives of Australia, GitHub, 2018, https://github.com/wragge/closed_access; Tim Sherratt, Faceapi: API for Accessing Thousands of Faces Extracted from Trove's Digitised Newspapers, GitHub, 2015, https://github.com/wragge/faceapi.

BIBLIOGRAPHY

Bowker, Geoffrey C., and Susan Leigh Star. *Sorting Things Out: Classification and Its Consequences.* Cambridge, Mass.: MIT Press, 2000.

Commonwealth Bureau of Census and Statistics. "Prices, Purchasing-Power of Money, Wages, Trade Unions, Unemployment, and General Industrial Conditions, 1914–15." Labour and Industrial Branch Report, 1916, http://www.abs.gov.au/AUSSTATS /abs@.nsf/DetailsPage/6101.01914–15.

David, T. W. Edgeworth. "Presidential Address." In *Report of the 14th Meeting of the Australasian Association for the Advancement of Science,* xliii–xcii. Melbourne, 1913.

Dening, Greg. *Performances.* Melbourne: Melbourne University Press, 1996.

Dow, Coral, and Janet Phillips. "'Forgotten Australians'" and 'Lost Innocents'": Child Migrants and Children in Institutional Care in Australia." Research Publications. Parliamentary Library. 2009, https://www.aph.gov.au/About_Parliament/Parliamentary_Departments /Parliamentary_Library/pubs/BN/0910/ChildMigrants.

Duff, Wendy M., and Verne Harris. "Stories and Names: Archival Description as Narrating Records and Constructing Meanings." *Archival Science* 2 (September 2002): 263–85, https://doi.org/10.1007/BF02435625.

Edkins, Jenny. *Face Politics*. London: Routledge, 2015.

Findlay, Cassie. "People, Records and Power: What Archives Can Learn from WikiLeaks." *Archives and Manuscripts* 41, no. 1 (March 1, 2013): 7–22, https://doi.org/10.1080/01576895.2013.779926.

Fischer, Gerhard. *Enemy Aliens: Internment and the Homefront Experience in Australia 1914–1920*. St. Lucia: University of Queensland Press, 1989.

Kanamori, Mayu. E-mail message to author. March 28, 2012.

Knibbs, George H. "Miscellaneous Notes on Australia, Its People and Their Activities." In *Federal Handbook Prepared in Connection with the Eighty-Fourth Meeting of the British Association for the Advancement of Science*, 581–95. Commonwealth of Australia. 1914, https://archive.org/stream/commonwealthofau00brit#page/581/mode/1up/.

Love, Rosaleen. "The Science Show of 1914: The British Association Meets in Australia." *This Australia* 4, no. 1 (1984): 12–16.

Lubar, Steven. "Museumbots: An Appreciation." On Public Humanities. August 22, 2014, https://stevenlubar.wordpress.com/2014/08/22/museumbots-an-appreciation/.

Madrigal, Alexis C. "This Twitter Bot Is a Constant Reminder of the Brutality of Slavery." Fusion. http://fusion.net/story/28958/this-twitter-bot-is-a-constant-reminder-of-the-brutality-of-slavery/. Accessed January 19, 2016.

Masson, David Orme. "Inaugural Address." In *Report of the 13th Meeting of the Australasian Association for the Advancement of Science*, 1–18. Sydney, 1911.

Read, Peter. *The Stolen Generations: The Removal of Aboriginal Children in New South Wales, 1883 to 1969*. Sydney: NSW Department of Aboriginal Affairs, 1998. http://pandora.nla.gov.au/pan/59691/20060614–0000/stolen.pdf.

Report of the Eighty-Fourth Meeting of the British Association for the Advancement of Science, Australia, 1914. London, 1915. https://archive.org/details/reportofbritisha15adva.

Robertson, Peter. "Coming of Age: The British Association in Australia, 1914." *Australian Physicist* 17 (1980): 23–27.

Sample, Mark. "A Protest Bot Is a Bot So Specific You Can't Mistake It for Bullshit." Medium. May 21, 2014, https://medium.com/@samplereality/a-protest-bot-is-a-bot-so-specific-you-cant-mistake-it-for-bullshit-90fe10b7fbaa#.yt5a2l2kg.

Sherratt, Tim. "Atomic Wonderland: Science and Progress in Twentieth Century Australia." PhD diss., Australian National University, 2003, http://discontents.com.au/atomic-wonderland.

Sherratt, Tim. "Closed Access." December 17, 2016, https://doi.org/10.6084/m9.figshare.4479278.v1.

Sherratt, Tim. "Life on the Outside: Collections, Contexts and the Wild, Wild, Web." Keynote presented at the Japanese Association for the Digital Humanities Annual

Conference, Tsukuba, Japan, September 20, 2014, http://discontents.com.au/life
-on-the-outside/.

Sherratt, Tim. "'A Political Inconvenience': Australian Scientists as the British Atomic
Weapons Tests, 1952–3." *Historical Records of Australian Science* 6, no. 2 (December
1985): 137–52, http://discontents.com.au/a-political-inconvenience.

Sherratt, Tim. "The Real Face of White Australia." Discontents. September 21, 2011, http://
discontents.com.au/the-real-face-of-white-australia/.

Sherratt, Tim. "The Vintage Face Depot." http://wragge.github.io/face-depot/. Accessed
January 20, 2016.

Sherratt, Tim, and Kate Bagnall. "The People Inside." In *Seeing the Past: Experiments with
Computer Vision and Augmented Reality in History,* edited by Kevin Kee and Tim
Compeau, 11–31. Ann Arbor: University of Michigan Press, 2019.

Spencer, Walter Baldwin. "The Aboriginals of Australia." In *Federal Handbook Prepared
in Connection with the Eighty-Fourth Meeting of the British Association for the
Advancement of Science,* 33–85. Commonwealth of Australia, 1914. https://archive
.org/stream/commonwealthofau00brit#page/33/mode/1up.

Swain, Shurlee, Leonie Sheedy, and Cate O'Neill. "Responding to 'Forgotten Australians':
Historians and the Legacy of out-of-Home 'Care.'" *Journal of Australian Studies* 36,
no. 1 (March 1, 2012): 17–28, https://doi.org/10.1080/14443058.2011.646283.

Turkel, William J., and Alan MacEachern. "The Programming Historian, 1st ed." NiCHE:
Network in Canadian History & Environment. August 2007, http://web.archive.org
/web/20090905000137/http://niche-canada.org/programming-historian/1ed.

Watson, J. C. "The Labour Movement." In *British Association for the Advancement of
Science, Handbook for New South Wales,* 128–38. Sydney, 1914. https://archive.org
/stream/handbookfornewso00brit#page/128/mode/1up.

Whitelaw, Mitchell. "Generous Interfaces for Digital Cultural Collections." *Digital
Humanities Quarterly* 9, no. 1 (2015), http://www.digitalhumanities.org/dhq/vol/9/1
/000205/000205.html.

Reading for Enactment: A Performative Approach to Digital Scholarship and Data Visualization

KYLE PARRY

Amid two decades of debate on the nature and promise of the digital humanities, one term has recurred with notable frequency: performance. For the authors in question—I am thinking of essays published by a number of prominent figures in the field between 2001 and 2015—the use of the term does not pertain to theater or music, as if the digital humanities ought to be understood as some kind of staging or recitation. Rather, the use of the term pertains to various senses of action. In orienting ourselves toward performance qua acting, doing, and effecting in the digital humanities, these authors variously contend, we will find our way toward enhanced means of cultivating what matters in digital scholarship: novel concepts, rigorous presentations, productive collaborations, enabling tools. We thus see, for instance, arguments that machine-aided, algorithmic manipulation of texts can yield new insights (McGann and Samuels; Ramsay) or that designers of humanities interfaces ought to double down on their inherent status as "event-spaces" of conditioned interpretive activity (Drucker, "Performative Materiality"). We also see more encompassing propositions: DH practitioners should recognize their work as always a performative struggle between competing agencies (Presner), or they should embrace a vision of the digital humanities as a productive "deformance" of the cultural landscape (Sample, "Scholarly Lies").[1] In any event, no matter the specific prescription, it is, in the end, the apprehension and activation of digitally enabled doing, effecting, and intervening for which these authors argue.

In the discussion that follows, I join these authors in exactly this conceit. At the same time, I diverge on one key count. I argue that it is indispensable for debates around performance, deformance, and what I am here calling "enactment" in the digital humanities to actively and explicitly draw on ideas from within the rich, multidecade, multifield history of performative theory.[2] This is a history of inquiry that has touched and sometimes transformed numerous topics, including most famously language, gender, and sexuality; but also race, economics, science, art, indigeneity, and code, among others.[3] Although I advocate a wide-ranging encounter between performativity and the digital humanities, I see special promise in a turn to concepts and commitments that have emerged in queer and feminist contexts. There questions of performance are necessarily bound up with questions of social and political conditions and effects. Indeed, as Judith Butler puts it, "One position within that increasingly productive field [of performance studies] argues that performance emerges from shared social worlds, that no matter how individual and fleeting any given performance might be, it still relies upon, and reproduces, a set of social relations, practices, and institutions that turn out to be part of the very performance itself" (Butler, "Performativity").[4] This is the kind of fundamentally relational and therefore political conception of social action that queer and feminist performative theories make available and essential. It is in the creative adaptation of such thinking—that is, in that thinking's translation to digital research, curation, librarianship, archiving, coding, publishing, and pedagogy—that I see particular promise for the digital humanities, broadly construed.

This chapter's specific contribution revolves around a close synonym of performance: *enactment*. A term of increasing importance in performative theory, enactment places the idea of making active at the center of our attention; it thus provides an ideal locus for this chapter's work of prescriptive reconceptualization.[5] My overarching argument relies on a fundamental shift in premises. Where we have tended to assume that digital scholarly projects and practices matter for what they build, discover, say, or convey, we must also embrace an idea that projects and practices can be understood, engaged, valued, critiqued, and conceived for what they *enact*, which is to say for what they variously do alongside or in tandem with whatever is explicitly said, shown, or enabled—whether that means acting out, embodying, reproducing, occasioning, or effecting. What is distinctive about the category of enactment; what attention to enactment should look like around digital scholarship in general and data visualization in particular; what enactment can enable us to better think, do, and perform—these are the chief concerns of this chapter. Among other things, I contend that attention to enactment can enable us to more effectively and expansively interpret, critique, and act on what digital scholarship does, to what ends, and for whom; it can also help us address how computationally and network-enabled epistemic endeavors, as well as the labors on which those endeavors depend, already do and might still affect who and what gets to matter. I further argue that active attention to enactment can translate into particular, powerful enactment-driven practices. With such practices—which include what I here call "enactive" or "performative" data visualization—dynamics of performance and enactment are not addressed after the fact, as if they represented side effects of digital knowledge production. Rather, those dynamics are essential to how projects develop, what they end up doing, and why they matter.

Reading for Enactment

For this first section, which focuses on possibilities for enactment-centered inter-pretation and critique (as opposed to production and presentation), I develop these arguments through a single example, rather than several. *Mapping the Republic of Letters* is a highly influential endeavor based at Stanford University, active from 2007 through to the time of writing in 2017.[6] Working with more than 55,000 let-ters from the historical "Republic of Letters," composed by 6,400 correspondents and now annotated with metadata on origin and destination, the many participants in the project have produced and published maps of thinkers' correspondence net-works during the Enlightenment. As is reflective of the general orientation I am calling into question, when we begin to frame and interpret what kind of project *Mapping* is, as well as what the project makes possible, it is unlikely that we will invoke terms like performance and enactment, and it is even less likely we will look to performative theory for resources. Instead, as seen across several contexts, from the project website to the *New York Times* to the magazine of the National Endow-ment for the Humanities, the keywords are terms like "see," "discover," and "reveal." And indeed, as is the case for many projects in the digital humanities, these are the dimensions of the project that receive attention and discussion. For instance, Patri-cia Cohen, a journalist, sums up the endeavor this way: "With their software, you can see the larger pattern of intellectual exchange among Enlightenment thinkers at a glance" ("Digitally Mapping"). Echoing this account, a key project leader, his-torian Dan Edelstein, is quoted by Cohen as saying that although many colleagues view the project as "whimsical, the result of playing with technological toys," nev-ertheless that play can "lead to discoveries" ("Digital Keys"). And the project's sum-mation on its homepage, as of 2017, goes further, suggesting that *Mapping* provides altered pictures of what the networks "actually look like"; that it can help determine whether the newly visualized extent of the Republic matches existing interpreta-tions; and that it affords new insights into how the Republic evolved over time. In sum, across various sites, we see commonly held premises: these visualizations mat-ter for the work of picturing and illustrating they perform, and they generally enable the discovery of new questions and interpretations in established fields, whether European history, intellectual history, or other areas.

From the perspective for which I am arguing, while such accounts of *Mapping* (or any comparable project) are generally accurate, it is also the case that they are neither neutral nor exhaustive. How, for instance, do we make sense of the particular concepts of knowledge and inquiry implicitly embodied and to some degree there-fore endorsed by these contemporary maps of correspondence networks? Alterna-tively, what can we say about the various institutional relationships that *Mapping* has both depended on and also reproduces in the midst of scholarly and digital archival production? In posing questions like these, which require us to expand our interpretive frame beyond showing and saying, I am arguing for a specific practice of analysis and critique, what I call "reading for enactment."[7] I do not mean some exercise of critical legal interpretation, as though the key were to discern the ways *Mapping* and other projects make things into active law. Instead, I mean an interpretive practice—a kind of intellectual and creative habit—of attending to processes of enactment, with enactment understood in the senses of acting and being acted on, and thus of variously putting into practice, establishing, embodying, or occasioning. By "reading for enactment," I also mean a habit or practice that, as it were, *cares* for enactment. Such reading—which can easily become writing, coding, or acting—calls attention to and actively negotiates actual relations, practices, and institutions; it attends to questions of who, under given social, cultural, and political conditions, is allowed to live, to speak, and to act—questions, in other words, of who and what gets to matter.[8]

As I have indicated, I see it as indispensable that approaches to performance and enactment in digital scholarship and data visualization are developed in dialogue with queer and feminist performative theory. There, too, we see a commitment, albeit implicit, to the kind of interpretive practice I am advocating. Of particular relevance for present purposes is the work of Judith Butler and Karen Barad. From Butler's performative theory of political assembly, we gain, among other insights, an idea that enactment can name a certain "mode of signification" (*Notes toward a Performative Theory*, 8). In other words, to enact something is to put into practice a distinctive but underacknowledged form of communicating ideas, meanings, affects, and arguments. That form of communication consists in actual expressive action (e.g., the communal, risky enactment that is thousands gathering for a protest), rather than explicit verbal utterance (e.g., the specific words spoken at such an event). In a slightly different vein, by adapting Barad's performative theory of science, materiality, and "agential realism"—Barad is a physicist—we gain a general idea that any act or process of knowledge production is necessarily and variously performative, which is to say, in Barad's terms, that research and interpretation are necessarily active, material, and multimodal "entanglements" with the world in its persistent and pervasive "intra-activity." We also find in Barad's work something of specific import for analyzing visualization practices. For Barad, visual representations are "not (more or less faithful) pictures of what is." Rather, they are "productive evocations, provocations, and generative material articulations or reconfigurings of what is and what is possible" (389). Put another way, to say visual representations—whether drawings, photographs, or data visualizations—reflect the world is insufficient; we must further recognize that they are active, material configurations and reconfigurations—sometimes reshapings, sometimes reinforcements—of how the world already is or might still be arranged. Adapting Butler and Barad's concepts, reading for enactment in the context of digital scholarship involves cultivating habits and capacities around enactment-driven interpretations of the field's concrete and variously signifying media artifacts, whether charts, timelines, or 3D renderings. Reading for enactment also involves interpreting the processes (or Baradian "intra-actions") that enter into those artifacts' production, presentation, and analysis. This interpretive practice can and should extend to other activities as well, whether teaching, presenting, or tweeting. It should also involve—and this is crucial—a general commitment to what Barad characterizes as the deep ethical responsibility to strive to reconfigure or, as she puts it, to "contest and rework what matters and what is excluded from mattering" (178).

The actual import of these ideas becomes tangible when we devote ourselves to close reading of projects like *Mapping*. Performing such reading does not mean ignoring or downplaying the actual thinking, saying, or showing this project has enabled and will continue to enable. Rather, it means recognizing that various, consequential processes of enactment took place and still take place in the midst of its manifest contributions and affordances. The homepage provides a useful first locus for reinterpretation. If we were not attuned to enactment, we would characterize the homepage's functions as a portal and introduction: indicating who was involved, what this is all about, and serving as a means of navigation. Once we are attuned to enactment, however, a range of other features become perceptible and important. In the simplest sense, we find there is enactment in the very title of the project. This is a collaborative endeavor based around a collectively and iteratively performed gesture of mapping. That is, given a historical phenomenon, the Republic of Letters, this project performs acts of spatial and temporal figuration that do not hide away in the office, library, or lab, but that can be repeatedly sketched, modeled, and publicly displayed. Such public acts seek to effect equally archival, historiographic, and imaginative deformations and reformations; that is, they seek to perform contingent, cartographic reconfigurations of commonly held pictures of the Republic and of collective inquiry during the Enlightenment.

Alongside this titular evocation of enactment, there are other, less directly evident embodiments of enactment on the homepage. Not about action and intervention as such, these enactments instead pertain to the "relations, practices, and institutions" that the performances of *Mapping* both rely on and reproduce. Between the bottom and top of the homepage, for instance, there is the presentation of the project as developed within the context of—and receiving the sanction and material resources of—a prominent and wealthy university, Stanford, and there is the performative conveyance, in the form of a line of text, of that university's possession of copyright. In addition, an array of expressive logos indicates that an international collaboration has been constituted and elaborated. We also encounter further sanctioning by the two noted sources of funding: the NEH and the Stanford Fund for Humanities Innovation. And most instructive for present purposes, between the titular and the institutional signifiers of enactment, there is an unexpected image of overriding visual interest: a "narrative panorama" of the project, published in 2013. The panorama melds several features: a timeline of events in the project's life; a network map of project participants, some of whom are pictured; and an overlaid collage of portraits, scenes, and objects related to the Republic. Numerous enactive processes overlap and crisscross here. From the broadest perspective, the panorama is an illuminating visual-verbal figuration: it helps us recognize that the project is, like any other, an unfolding enactment involving numerous relations, practices, identities, and institutions. The image also serves to shift attention from the specific final products to the actors, actions, events, correspondences, and networks that brought those products into being. It is as though this project, and by implication any digital scholarly project, were also significant for the occasions it produced, the people it connected, and the signs, histories, and ideas it rearranged and reconfigured. What is missing, of course, are the substance and the effects of these numerous occasions: what, for instance, it meant to hold an "Uncertainty Workshop" or why certain presentations to certain people should count as key moments in the project's history. And what is open to question from the perspectives of enactment and of performative theory are the specific values that such a panorama embodies and establishes. This pertains in part to what aspects of the endeavor matter and should be highlighted. But it also pertains to who among the categories of people and the various labors and images of these histories of travel, communication, and inquiry—histories that are, as Linda Tuhiwai Smith's project of "decolonizing methodologies" emphasizes, so deeply bound up with colonialism and imperialism—end up coming to the fore. In short, the panorama is, like the other things to which I have pointed, not a bystander to but an actual participant in consequential constellations of signifying enactment.

Were I to stop at analyzing the homepage, I might leave the impression that reading for enactment generally means emphasizing the reality of projects as social processes: that they are ongoing, collective, material, and contingent practices, the effects of which extend well beyond their specific subject matter or approach, and that they are therefore open to critique along these lines. But this is only part of the story. It is crucial to read for enactment in the actual products published, such as "Locke's Letters Project" or "An Intellectual Map of Science in the Spanish Empire, 1600–1810." As it stands, a prevailing habit in interpreting projects of data visualization is to emphasize saying and showing (as well as innovation and visual pleasure); thus here, for instance, we would tend to invoke the insights, questions, and apprehensions that we gain when we see lines and clusters of correspondence within this or that time period or for this or that person. By paying attention to the links among signification, enactment, and knowledge production, however—and also with the encouragement of emerging critical humanistic approaches to data visualization—other possibilities for interpretation open up.[9] The crucial, enabling premise shift, adapted out of queer and feminist performative theory, is this: visualizations do not only say or show, nor do they strictly support reading, imagining, knowing, or interpreting. Visualizations also act. They do things. They are visual-verbal-numerical enactments. In other words, they cause things to happen; they are gesturally and performatively expressive; and they are not only dependent on but also reproductive of relations, practices, and institutions. As a consequence of these various features, it becomes essential to analyze and critique projects that involve visualization along these lines: to read them for their constitutive and consequential enactments.

In the case of *Mapping*, two lines of critique are especially important. The first is largely positive: as much as these visualizations support and communicate inquiry, they also performatively assert—as meaningful, as mattering, as worthy of repetition—specific concepts of inquiry and communication. In particular, they collectively point toward a general notion of intellectual discourse as inherently in process and collective. Such an approach accords with scholarly methods and critical commitments built around attention to networks and practices, as we see in the history and philosophy of science. Indeed, what is resisted in those fields is a premise that intellectual histories, in the end, consist of great minds exchanging great ideas. Instead, it is argued, knowledge production necessarily depends on labor, context, place, material things, and relationships—a whole array of historically contingent phenomena. To take one particularly pertinent example from these vast fields, Bruno Latour puts forward a concept of what he calls "immutable mobiles." By this concept, which is fundamentally performative, Latour means efficiently structured, travel-ready, wear-resistant media artifacts, things like maps of distant colonies or research papers. These artifacts effectively preserve information in spite of transit, and they eventually release their constituent words, images, and data in material argumentation. Immutable mobiles thus force persuasion by a kind of informational committee, and in some cases this work of persuasion aids in maintaining power at a virtual remove. What I am suggesting is that although *Mapping* literally foregrounds great minds (including a thumbnail assembly of portraits of celebrated European and European-American men), at the same time, through its work of visualizing transits of correspondence over space and time, it also serves to endorse the sort of network thinking mobilized by Latour and others. That is, the visualizations are a putting into practice, albeit not necessarily with intention or full success, of fruitful sociological concepts. They thus tangibly affirm network thinking. Graphic modifications or new framing language could amplify these dimensions of the project; they could even explicitly link the Republic with the idea of immutable mobiles (or, in a different vein, shed light on that concept's limitations).

In now presenting a second line of critique, which is largely negative, I may appear to contradict myself—but reading for enactment is also, frequently, reading for contradiction. The line of critique is partly anticipated by Johanna Drucker, who reads the visualizations in *Mapping* as reifying; portrayed as "perfect lines of light," the graphic trails of transit put forward a deceptive picture of the Republic's correspondence as smooth and seamless—akin to flows of air traffic—while the borderless maps effectively forestall imagination of knowledge producers negotiating physical and cultural borders (Drucker, "Humanistic Theory"). I share Drucker's concern, and I appreciate her corollary prescription that those working with visualization ought to renegotiate the "armature of preexisting graphical conventions" in favor of strategies for indicating constructedness and partiality. At the same time, I would insist on several other points, all centered on enactment. In one sense, there is, importantly, productive displacement of attention, along the lines just mentioned, from individuals to rhetorical transit. In another sense, however, there are costs and risks to the overall approach taken by this project. Certainly, as Drucker suggests, deceptive notions become thinkable: seemingly direct lines of transit, seemingly instantaneous, seemingly akin to contemporary communication.[10] Furthermore, a deceptive social and political picture begins to form: not only does communication not confront borders or barriers, but inquiry also grows through discrete contribution, rather than through interdependent idea formation. Moreover, through this abstracted, flattened, and distanced view of discursive exchange, there looms an implicit fantasy of what Donna Haraway calls the "God trick"; in charismatically laying focus on the movement of correspondence, the actual sites of contingent, local, culturally inflected, and therefore "situated" knowledge production and rhetorical interaction fall to the side ("Situated Knowledges"). Such a critique might seem relatively inconsequential, were it not for the importance of "salons" to the life of the Republic. As one can glean from a project in *Mapping*, "The Salon Project," an essential component of the Republic was embodied gathering, discoursing, and indeed performing in salons. It mattered to be together, and it mattered that habits of society, locally specific and often gendered, were observed (Goodman). Thus, while these visualizations tend to enact a concept of the Republic as a kind of collective neural network, emerging out of the transit of paper and ink, the Republic was in fact—to rework ideas put forward by Butler and Barad—also necessarily embodied, collectively brought into being in iterative fashion by vulnerable persons needing extensive material, economic, cultural, human, and nonhuman supports. For these reasons and others, *Mapping* illustrates a paradox likely to confront many projects of visualization in the humanities: the same gestures that prove highly enabling and that put into practice generative concepts of culture and society can also serve to reproduce limiting or problematic optics.

This reading of *Mapping the Republic of Letters* for enactment could continue into still other areas. (For instance, in the vein of critical code and software studies, one could analyze the enactments embedded and disseminated in the project's data, metadata, software, and algorithms.) But I conclude this section with a clarification. In putting forward an idea of reading for enactment, and in invoking the theories of Butler and Barad for support, it might seem as though, underneath it all, I am suggesting that projects ought to be cautious, lest they enact something. Alternatively, it might seem as though I am, in the end, deceived by an unrealistic picture of possibility, as though I am proposing that projects like *Mapping* do not confront limits of time, technology, policy, or labor; in other words, that they have infinite capacities for choosing what they enact, show, or say. Neither of these extremes is the case. What I am arguing for is active and informed negotiation of enactment, not its zealous policing or impossible perfection. The negotiation of enactment demands that we variously acknowledge, forestall, contest, rework, or appropriate the enactments that we can, with effort, observe or anticipate. And it is in this sense that one dimension of digital scholarship becomes especially important. Unlike most traditional scholarly endeavors, digital projects can in many cases undergo significant changes in substance, format, and framing well after they have apparently concluded. In the case of *Mapping,* although there would be many limiting factors, nevertheless a number of modifications are conceivable; these modifications could countervail some of the more reductive or deceptive enactments posited earlier. A team of collaborators could, for instance, add an array of supplementary visual resources aimed at emphasizing materiality and contingency; these could be galleries of close-up images of the specific papers and inks that made the Republic possible. Alternatively, participants could produce visualizations that center on specific historical ideas or problems rather than people or nations. There could also be a page of critical reflection. Among other things, such a page might invoke feminist accounts of the Republic, including one that puts forward a performative notion of "engendering" the Republic (Dalton). In any case, no matter the ultimate prescriptions, were participants in the project to explore these adjustments—no doubt facing many material, social, and economic barriers—it would be essential that they actively assess the new constellations of enactment they induce, and that they therefore address themselves to what takes place beyond what is explicitly shown or said. As could be the case with any project, the same techniques and technologies that have generated problems of reduction would thus also afford novel occasions for resistance, redirection, and critical invention.

Enactive/Performative Data Visualization

Concern with enactment need not only pertain to interpretation, critique, and post hoc modification. It can also pertain to the conception, production, and presentation of projects. More than that, enactment can become a defining commitment: practitioners can explicitly conceive of their undertakings as, in a fundamental sense, events of enactment. In such cases, as much as practitioners would aim to variously discover, say, show, or make available, they would also aim to variously intervene, effect, put into practice, reproduce, or provoke. Although I can imagine seizing on enactment in many contexts, small or large, momentary or sustained, I see special promise in the realm of data visualization. In particular, I argue for the existence and importance of a specific practice, what I call "enactive" or "performative" data visualization.

Three examples can support that practice's elaboration. One of these emerged in the contexts of art and curation. With *A Sort of Joy: Thousands of Exhausted Things* (2015), the Office for Creative Research staged multiple performances of the Museum of Modern Art's collections database, which encompasses more than 120,000 items, in both spoken word and projected visualization.[11] A second enactive project took shape in the contexts of history and literature. With "The Image of

Absence," Lauren Klein performed a "critically informed deformation" of an electronic database of letters, the *Papers of Thomas Jefferson,* shifting emphasis from the life of the second president of the United States to explicitly imperfect, data-driven pictures of the largely silenced life of James Hemings, the master chef, brother of Sally Hemings, and a formerly enslaved laborer at Jefferson's plantation (672).[12] A third example came together in the contexts of history, geography, and LGBT studies. Albeit without using a specific title, in 2013 Jen-Jack Gieseking published a series of blog posts centered on a database of records of lesbian-queer organizations in New York City at the Lesbian Herstory Archives.[13] Gieseking presented provisional visualizations of those records while also reflecting on quantitative approaches to lesbian and queer history.

If my proposition is accurate—if it is productively evocative or generative—then these three projects can be understood as examples of a characteristically "enactive" or "performative" modality of work with data through visual and also sonic means. As is evident, that modality is not defined by subject matter or disciplinary context. Rather, it is defined by a shared approach. Each of these projects can be understood as approaching the work of data visualization as a multifaceted epistemic and social enactment; invoking Barad's notion of representation as "reconfiguring," they are set apart by how they purposely, publicly put something consequential and revisionary into practice through interaction (or "intra-action") with objects of knowledge and interpretation. Although this can mean, as in *A Sort of Joy,* that an actual public gathering has been staged and assembled, the status of visualization as self-conscious enactment does not depend on the use of such a format. Instead, the quality of epistemic enactment pertains to the broader umbrella notion of effecting something through critical, responsive interaction with particular sets of data, metadata, or other collected materials. That is, some kind of epistemic interruption or redirection is being performed through calculation and picturing, and it is precisely as an epistemic enactment that this performance will end up appearing for audiences or "users," alongside whatever other postures of knowledge production—saying, showing, revealing—the performance involves. In other words, for the practitioners who undertake enactive data visualization, it is deemed important, when engaging specific terrains of knowledge production and specific datasets, to reshape those terrains through manifestly enactive methods. Crucially, that means there is more than conventional visualization work going on: more than using the materials to discover, pronounce, or display something in the vein of traditional scholarly argumentation. There are also self-conscious acts of gesturing, performing, embodying, and intervening. Moreover, for whatever public appearance those acts end up enabling, it will matter that the audience, whether reader, viewer, user, or otherwise, is invited to recognize the project as, at least in part, a kind of event of enactment: one that is provisional and imperfect, but that is an enactment all the same. And thus, from its inception forward, a project of enactive or performative data visualization acts out a notion that whatever data-dependent pictures it works toward are not more or less accurate representations of what is, but, as Barad puts it, are "productive evocations, provocations, and generative material articulations or reconfigurings of what is and what is possible." And in this sense such projects echo and adapt Barad's dictate to "contest and rework what matters and what is excluded from mattering" for the context of computationally and network-enabled art and scholarship.

Specific instances of enactive data visualization will demonstrate variations on these core features. Returning first to *A Sort of Joy,* for instance, we can see an enactive, process-driven quality in the most ready-at-hand sense of preparing and then staging the performance of a dataset that otherwise supports management, curation, and research. As Jer Thorpe, one of the project's designers puts it, spoken voice and unfolding display become self-consciously unconventional ways to "engage with the collections database," and this proves important in, among other things, compelling audiences to view the database as a "cultural artifact," and in having them confront "a new paradigm in which data are not as much operated on as they are allowed to operate on us." With "The Image of Absence," the core quality of enactment is not a finite set of flesh-and-blood performances. Instead, it is effecting a reflexive intervention into an existing, structured database of materials, as well as into broader histories of misrepresentation, silencing, violence, and also resourcefulness and resilience. By visualizing the relations between people discernible in letters that mention James Hemings, for instance, Klein endeavors to demonstrate, as she puts it, "some of the possibilities of recognition that the *Papers of Thomas Jefferson* itself resists"—including Jefferson's "dependence . . . on the men and women he enslaved" (674)—while also exposing and enacting "the impossibilities of recognition—and of cognition—that remain essential to our understanding of the archive of slavery today" (682). Finally, with Gieseking's project, the series of inquiries does not only take place at a private remove. The inquiries instead appear sequentially and publicly, and they are actively framed as multimotivated acts of putting an alternative, partly quantitative, and not necessarily immediately welcome research mode into public practice. Indeed, Gieseking expresses the hope that the "ways of seeing our histories and spaces" enabled by the visualizations will prove revelatory and connective and that their being publicly posted will not only help "share our stories through more varied methods" but also "provide for a more encompassing analysis" while further serving to provoke conversation. And thus for Gieseking, as for Klein and the Office for Creative Research, the motivating features of visualization are as much what those visualizations embody, demonstrate, and facilitate—what they enact—as what they specifically end up helping us newly perceive or understand about certain historical phenomena.

Were we to zoom out to a wider array of examples of enactive or performative data visualization, we would see still further variations on this basic feature of approaching data visualizations as events of performing, negotiating, and activating epistemic enactment. We would also see a number of what Carole L. Palmer calls "variable characteristics," which are features that do not necessarily appear across all instances or not always to the same degree. Although a more comprehensive analysis of the variable characteristics of enactive data visualizations is beyond the scope of this chapter, I can identify a few examples. One is what I call *archival contestation*. In performing this kind of work, certain enactive data visualizations can, to use Barad's language, interfere with the order of a specific archive. Although in very different ways, both "The Image of Absence" and *A Sort of Joy* embody this guiding ambition. The former deforms Jefferson's archive of papers so that it reveals and reworks a history of absence against itself. The latter exposes the operation and ordering of an otherwise invisible repository; it also makes manifest, through the reading of the most common first names in the database, the first forty-one of which are (typically) men's names, disproportionately male representation in a dominant cultural institution. A second observable characteristic is what I call *conditional revelation*. First and foremost, this refers to, as Drucker analyzes in depth, ways of working with data visualization that maintain emphasis on the constructed nature of their outputs. All three of the projects in questions do this work, either through action or words or some combination of the two; they perform an act of revelation, but one that is presented as only partly, conditionally revelatory. This notion of conditional revelation can carry a second, related meaning. It can indicate that the process of revealing makes conditions of inquiry visible, whether those are local conditions of research, as at the Lesbian Herstory Archives, or broader conditions of representation, as with Klein's supporting critical discussion of the archive of slavery. The last characteristic I point to is what I call, borrowing a phrase from Thorpe's account, *fluid interpretation*. The key measure of such an effect is an audience's capacity to generate novel linkages while encountering or interacting with a project. In *A Sort of Joy*, this ability is amply in evidence: as Thorpe writes, "The skilled actors of Elevator Repair Service turn a dry algorithmic output into a wry dialogue of one-upmanship, allowing the artworks themselves to become pieces in an imagined language game" in which "possibilities for interpretation are magnified as the relationship moves from data => viewer to data => performer => viewer." With Gieseking's blog posts, another kind of possibility for "fluid interpretation" emerges. That interpretation does not depend on a staging of a performance as such, but on a willingness to make public a sequenced, reflexive research process. In a fundamentally enactive way, the research that Gieseking performs does seek to investigate and to hypothesize, but it also invites and occasions yet further iterations of thought and critique. In other words, sequenced, nascent thinking becomes enacted provocation toward subsequent fluid, emergent interpretation.

Archival contestation, conditional revelation, fluid interpretation—these are just three of numerous conceivable variable characteristics of enactment-intensive data visualization. Indeed, as was the case with reading for enactment, many more lines of inquiry could be followed around this practice. Such inquiry (and any attendant experimentation) would need to confront various other issues and dynamics, including the possible violence that can take place through visual display, as Klein emphasizes (678). (On this topic, Barad's notions of enacted "boundaries" and "cuts" could be helpful.) One critical question would be the actual force and consequence of enactive approaches to data visualization. With Klein's project, for instance, it is important to ask for whom this archival deformation has taken place. Relatedly, it is important to ask whether and by what means such a project—which addresses deep histories of misrepresentation and violence and which responds through complicated visualizations and critical scholarly prose—could have equal interpretive and affective force when taken out of the confines of the scholarly journal or reconfigured for different audiences. As these different concerns indicate, methods from a number of fields, such as critical race theory and disability studies, will be essential for elaborating and critiquing performative approaches to data visualization and to digital scholarship, broadly construed. It will also be essential to link up with what Catherine D'Ignazio and Klein label "feminist data visualization." For them, as has been the case in this chapter, questions of relations, practices, and institutions are essential, as are questions around who and what gets to matter. How, they ask, can visualization be "adapted to emphasize the situated nature of knowledge and its perception" (1)? By what means can visual design make labor, embodiment, and affect not only visible but also legitimized dimensions of visualization work (2–3)? As I hope this discussion has shown, in answering such questions, direct encounters with propositions and provocations in queer and feminist performative theory should prove enabling and encouraging—and the category of enactment should provide an especially fruitful guiding orientation.

Coda: Iterate, Deviate, Elaborate

I have argued that debates around performance, deformance, and enactment in the digital humanities must engage performative theory. One further claim is necessary: these debates should also engage *aesthetic* investigations of enactment, whether within performance art, conceptual art, digital art, internet art, activist art, or still-other domains. Although an adequate elaboration of this claim is beyond the scope of this chapter, I can show some of its potential by way of one especially suggestive project, *Crochet Coral Reef.*[14]

Led by Christine and Margaret Wertheim, who together direct the Institute for Figuring, a nonprofit organization "dedicated to the poetic and aesthetic dimensions of science and mathematics," *Crochet Coral Reef* began in 2005, when Christine Wertheim made the passing observation—apparently, while watching the television series *Xena: Warrior Princess*—"We could crochet a coral reef" (Wertheim and Wertheim, 17). What first manifested as a small reef on the siblings' coffee table eventually grew into a massive, multiyear undertaking that eventually drew some 8,000 collaborators. At the heart of this undertaking is the practice of crochet, which is the handicraft of producing fabric through interlocking loops, using thread or yarn or other materials. In crafting the main reef as well as "sub-reefs" and "satellite reefs," the Wertheims and their collaborators rely on a special technique. That technique, known as "hyperbolic crochet," was discovered by a mathematician interested in materializing distinctive hyperbolic geometries that have long been thought of as impossible to physically model, but which reefs and other forms of life have produced for millennia. In the hands of the "Reefers," hyperbolic crochet blossoms into an iterative method defined by repetition, accident, and redirection; it thus plays a role in the production of a wide variety of forms that imitate, celebrate, and reimagine actual coral reefs. Constituting a kind of globally distributed whole, the disparate crocheted reefs come to form what the Wertheims characterize as "an ever-evolving archipelago," the various components of which appear in art galleries, science museums, and other cultural centers (18). Crucial to the project's impetus and impact, the vast, visible life of this archipelago is the inverse of that of actual coral reefs. That is, with each passing year, while the bleaching of coral reefs increases in scale and violence, caused by warming oceans and other factors, actual reefs' newly emergent, land-based cousins grow and grow, in mass and in audience. Crucially, then, the crochet coral reef does not just live within the contexts of art, science, and mathematics. Rather, as Donna Haraway puts it, the crochet reef also "lives enfolded in the materialities of global warming and toxic pollution; and the makers of the reef practice multispecies becoming-with to cultivate the capacity to respond, response-ability" (*Staying with the Trouble*, 78).

That *Crochet Coral Reef* is deeply and variously enactive is immediately evident, as is the potential for a number of crisscrossing interpretations of the project across art, biology, mathematics, feminism, curation, and activism. Less evident is the project's potential import for performative approaches to digital scholarship and data visualization. To this end, I look to an evocative passage from the Wertheims' book. They write,

> Along with their living analogs, crochet reef "organisms" are guided by a code that can be written out symbolically in patterns . . . Yet most Crochet Reefers eschew formal patterns and base their explorations on a kind of material play, constructing organically with their hands while drawing on a library of algorithms they come to know in their fingers as well as in their brains. Such *digital intelligence* mediates a process of figuring in which knowledge resides in both body and mind . . . *Iterate, deviate, elaborate*—this is the process we have used. Begin with an algorithm, let it loose for playful experimentation, and open up the process to others. The strategy is threefold: While a code provides a starting point, open-ended improvisation practiced by a community generates the dynamism essential to the project's flourishing. As other crafters joined in, the realm of possibility compounded exponentially, with each new contributor adding skill, imagination, labor and time to the ever-evolving wonder of the whole.[15] (21)

There is much to gain from this passage. I derive two key points by way of conclusion. On the one hand, we see another way of construing the supposed digital–analog divide. Where alternative responses to the bleaching of coral reefs might have taken the form of data visualizations or of interactive maps—audiences would click or swipe through the virtual saying and conveying of ecological violence—the Wertheims opted to emphasize an older order of the "digital," the finger, while at the same time depending on an array of digital technologies to generate the project's events and correspondence networks.[16] On the other hand, we find in this passage a fruitful, divergent approach to the production and preservation of knowledge. In opting to emphasize this older order of the digital, the Wertheims built the conditions in which enactive hands could inquire into, actively perform, and publicly reconfigure numerous, intersecting dimensions of coral reefs, as well as of human's destructive and productive interactions with them: these dimensions range from the material, virtual, social, political, ludic, and ecological to the performative, aesthetic, poetic, cultural, and mathematical.[17] Moreover, put on display and virtually disseminated, the material legacies of those contributors' labors can indefinitely serve as productive evocations and reconfigurations of these unruly dimensional entanglements. In other words, the proliferative contesting and reworking that took place in the flesh through communal performance can continue to perform for communities, both in person and at a virtual remove.

Iterate, deviate, elaborate—this is a fundamentally performative algorithm, one that practitioners of digital scholarship and data visualization stand poised to variously proclaim, encode, and enact. As they do so, the critical forces of art, theory, and play ought to shape and reshape what they variously effect, put into practice, and occasion—by what means, to what ends, and for whom.

NOTES

1. We also see a proposal, based on the experimental events and networked interactions characteristic of the digital humanities, for the advent of the "performative humanities" (Scheinfeldt).

2. Both Drucker and Presner do invoke thinking from the history of performative theory in the essays just cited. In addition, while this chapter was in press, Drucker published an article on information visualization "and/as" enunciation; this article includes a call for attention to performative features of graphic communication (Drucker, "Information Visualization"). It is noteworthy, however, that these writers both forgo extensive and explicit engagement with queer and feminist approaches to performance. In Presner's case, the lack of citation appears to correlate with his article's emphasis on Andrew Pickering's performative approach to science studies in *The Mangle of Practice*. As Karen Barad writes, "Significantly, Pickering, in his appropriation of the term [performative], does not acknowledge its politically important—arguably inherently queer—genealogy . . . or why it has been and continues to be important to contemporary critical theorists, especially

feminist and queer studies scholars and activists. Indeed, he evacuates its important political history along with many of its crucial insights" (411).

3. I have offered a limited sampling of important works in the bibliography.

4. This quote appears in Butler's contribution to the online "keywords anthology," *In Terms of Performance*. The anthology, which was published at http://intermsofperformance.site, provides a rich and helpful archive of voices, issues, and debates in performance studies.

5. I partly discern the increasing importance of enactment in its centrality for the work cited here by Barad and Butler. But I also discern the term's increasing importance in explicit calls to favor "enactment" over "performance." The (performance) artist Andrea Fraser, for instance, writes of enactment as a lens that is more effective than performance: "[Enactment] allows us to step back from the opposition between doing, acting, or performing on the one hand, and saying or representing on the other, by framing a focus on what we are doing within or beyond—and often in contrast—to what we are saying . . . What the concept of enactment can bring into focus, in art as in psychoanalysis, are the structures of relationships that are produced and reproduced in all forms of activity." For further arguments around the value of enactment, see works by Michel Callon and Annemarie Mol.

6. *Mapping the Republic of Letters,* http://republicofletters.stanford.edu.

7. This phrase represents a reworking of a statement of Butler's: "we have to read such scenes [i.e., assemblies and demonstrations] not only in terms of the version of the people they explicitly set forth, but the relations of power by which they are enacted" (*Notes toward a Performative Theory,* 7).

8. On questions of care in the digital humanities, see Bethany Nowviskie's "On Capacity and Care."

9. See, for instance, the work of Johanna Drucker, as well as Lauren Klein and Catherine D'Ignazio's article, "Feminist Data Visualization," and Heather Housers's "The Aesthetics of Environmental Visualizations."

10. On the ways in which "new and old medias are layered on top of each other" (2), see Tung-Hui Hu, *A Prehistory of the Cloud,* especially "The Shape of the Network."

11. *A Sort of Joy: Thousands of Exhausted Things,* https://ocr.nyc/public-space-interventions/2015/03/30/a-sort-of-joy.

12. Klein has undertaken a number of projects related to the *Papers of Thomas Jefferson.* They are aggregated at http://dhlab.lmc.gatech.edu/jefferson.

13. The posts were published to Gieseking's blog. As of summer 2017, they were available at http://jgieseking.org/category/data-visualizations.

14. Documentation and discussion of *Crochet Coral Reef* can be found at http://crochetcoralreef.org; in the eponymous book, published by the Institute for Figuring; and in Haraway's *Staying with the Trouble.*

15. The emphasis on "digital intelligence" is the authors'. The emphasis on "iterate, deviate, elaborate" is mine.

16. For an extended reconceptualization of the digital qua fingers and indices, see Benjamin Peters's essay "Digital" in *Digital Keywords.*

17. It is striking that the word "dimension" frequently appears in performative accounts, not just in those I have cited from the digital humanities but also in the work of Barad, Butler, and many others, including J. L. Austin, who first introduced the theoretical term "performative" in the context of the philosophy of language. Indeed, the word "dimension" has an interesting history. It is derived from the Latin *dimetri,* or "to measure out," and its uses have for many centuries orbited around concerns with space and measurement. One can "dimension" fabric in the sense of measuring out or cutting to particular specifications. One can, in the far more familiar sense, invoke some measurable physical extension, such as length, depth, or width. And one can also speak of "other" dimensions, as in the science fiction imagination of alternative universes. In the late 1920s and early 1930s, perhaps connected with public fascination with emerging research around time, relativity, and the "fourth dimension," a dramatic semantic expansion took place, one that appears to have contributed to an increase in the word's rate of spread, at least if we venture to extrapolate from what Google N-Gram visualizations show us. Now "dimension" could name two related things: the "component aspects of a particular situation" and especially those that are "newly discovered," or "an attribute of, or way of viewing, an abstract entity" (*OED Online,* 2016). It would be interesting to theorize the metaphor of dimension, whether as a component of critical theory and philosophy or as a term within the digital humanities. Along these lines, Steven E. Jones has recently suggested that "dimensionality" is not just a name for the physical or virtual conditions in which we find ourselves or for the number of variables at work in a given statistical analysis (69). It is also a heuristic construct that can help us apprehend and make sense of the world—and that might even serve as a guiding conceit for digitally enabled scholarship. Jones's point about dimensionality appears at the conclusion of a chapter called "Dimension." Jones writes, "Dimensionality is a metaphor that allows us to think in meaningful ways about the layerings, and the degrees of invisibility, of the data and connections and objects that surround us. Such metaphors help us to grasp the process we are still undergoing in order to continue to work through what it means. We are still experiencing the eversion of cyberspace, and the 'new' dimensions of existence opened up by the eversion are still in the process of being revealed. One of the roles of the new digital humanities in our present moment might be to help us all learn new ways to see some of these hitherto unseen (but always-present) dimensions of mixed-reality existence, the people, places, and things opened up by the conjunctions of the digital and the physical" (69–70). Reading for enactment is, in a sense, a way of insisting on attention to often unseen but always present enactive dimensions of mediation, communication, and knowledge production.

BIBLIOGRAPHY

Allington, Daniel, Sarah Brouillette, and David Golumbia. "Neoliberal Tools (and Archives): A Political History of Digital Humanities." *Los Angeles Review of Books,* May 1, 2016.

Austin, J. L. *How to Do Things with Words.* Cambridge, Mass.: Harvard University Press, 1962.

Barad, Karen. *Meeting the Universe Halfway: Quantum Physics and the Entanglement of Matter and Meaning.* Durham, N.C.: Duke University Press, 2007.

Bourdieu, Pierre. *Language and Symbolic Power.* Translated by John B. Thompson. Cambridge, Mass.: Harvard University Press, 1991.

Butler, Judith. *Bodies that Matter: On the Discursive Limits of Sex.* New York: Routledge, 1993.

Butler, Judith. *Excitable Speech: A Politics of the Performative.* New York: Routledge, 1997.

Butler, Judith. *Gender Trouble: Feminism and the Subversion of Identity.* New York: Routledge, 1990.

Butler, Judith. *Notes toward a Performative Theory of Assembly.* Cambridge, Mass.: Harvard University Press, 2015.

Butler, Judith. "Performativity." In *In Terms of Performance,* edited by Shannon Jackson and Paula Marincola. Berkeley: Arts Research Center, 2016. http://intermsofperformance.site/keywords/performativity/judith-butler.

Butler, Judith. *Undoing Gender.* New York: Routledge, 2004.

Callon, Michel. "What Does It Mean to Say That Economics is Performative?" CSI Working Papers Series 005, 2006.

Cohen, Patricia. "Digital Keys for Unlocking the Humanities' Riches." *New York Times,* November 16, 2010.

Cohen, Patricia. "Digitally Mapping the Republic of Letters." *New York Times Blog,* November 16, 2010, https://artsbeat.blogs.nytimes.com/2010/11/16/digitally-mapping-the-republic-of-letters.

Dalton, Susan. *Engendering the Republic of Letters: Reconnecting Public and Private Spheres in Eighteenth-Century Europe.* Montreal: McGill-Queen's University Press, 2004.

Derrida, Jacques. "Signature Event Context." In *Limited Inc,* translated by Samuel Weber and Jeffrey Mehlman, 1–24. Evanston, Ill.: Northwestern University Press, 1988.

D'Ignazio, Catherine, and Lauren F. Klein. "Feminist Data Visualization." Conference Proceedings of IEEE VIS Workshop on Visualization for the Digital Humanities. Baltimore, 2016.

"dimension, n." *OED Online.* Oxford University Press, December 2016.

Drucker, Johanna. *Graphesis: Visual Forms of Knowledge Production.* Cambridge, Mass.: Harvard University Press, 2014.

Drucker, Johanna. "Humanistic Theory and Digital Scholarship." In *Debates in the Digital Humanities,* edited by Matthew K. Gold, 85–95. Minneapolis: University of Minnesota Press, 2012.

Drucker, Johanna. "Information Visualization and/as Enunciation." *Journal of Documentation* 73, no. 5 (2017), 903–16.

Drucker, Johanna. "Performative Materiality and Theoretical Approaches to Interface." *Digital Humanities Quarterly* 7, no. 1 (2013), http://www.digitalhumanities.org/dhq/vol/7/1/000143/000143.html.

Fraser, Andrea. "Performance or Enactment?" In *Performing the Sentence: Views on Research and Teaching in Performance Art,* edited by Carola Dertnig and Felicitas Thun-Hohenstein, 122–27. Berlin: Sternberg Press, 2014.

Gieseking, Jen-Jack. "(Data)Visualizing Lesbian-Queer Space & Time." July 1, 2013, http://jgieseking.org/datavisualizing-lesbian-queer-space-time.

Goffman, Erving. *The Presentation of Self in Everyday Life*. New York: Anchor Books, 1959.

Gold, Matthew K., and Lauren F. Klein, "Digital Humanities: The Expanded Field." In *Debates in the Digital Humanities 2016,* edited by Matthew K. Gold and Lauren F. Klein, ix–xv. Minneapolis: University of Minnesota Press, 2016.

Goodman, Dena. *The Republic of Letters: A Cultural History of the French Enlightenment*. Ithaca, N.Y.: Cornell University Press, 1994.

Graham, Laura R., and H. Glenn Penny, eds. *Performing Indigeneity: Global Histories and Contemporary Experiences*. Lincoln: University of Nebraska Press, 2014.

Haraway, Donna. "Situated Knowledges: The Science Question in Feminism and the Privilege of Partial Perspective." *Feminist Studies* 14, no. 3 (1988), 575–99.

Haraway, Donna. *Staying with the Trouble: Making Kin in the Chthulucene*. Durham, N.C.: Duke University Press, 2016.

Healy, Kieran. "The Performativity of Networks." *European Journal of Sociology* 56 (2015): 175–205.

Hindley, Meredith. "Mapping the Republic of Letters." *Humanities: The Magazine of the National Endowment for the Humanities* 34, no. 6 (November/December 2013): 20–53.

Houser, Heather. "The Aesthetics of Environmental Visualizations: More than Information Ecstasy?" *Public Culture* 26, no. 2 (2014): 319–37.

Hu, Tung-Hui. *A Prehistory of the Cloud*. Cambridge, Mass.: MIT Press, 2015.

Jones, Steven E. *The Emergence of the Digital Humanities*. New York: Routledge, 2014.

Klein, Lauren F. "The Image of Absence: Archival Silence, Data Visualization, and James Hemings." *American Literature* 85, no. 4 (December 2013): 661–88.

Latour, Bruno. "Visualization and Cognition: Drawing Things Together." In *Representation in Scientific Activity,* edited by Michael Lynch and Steve Woolgar, 19–68. Cambridge, Mass.: MIT Press, 1990.

Liu, Alan. "Where Is Cultural Criticism in the Digital Humanities?" In *Debates in the Digital Humanities,* edited by Matthew K. Gold, 490–509. Minneapolis: University of Minnesota Press, 2012.

Mackenzie, Adrian. "The Performativity of Code: Software and Cultures of Circulation." *Theory, Culture & Society* 22, no. 1 (2005): 71–92.

McGann, Jerome. "Marking Texts of Many Dimensions." In *A Companion to Digital Humanities*, edited by Susan Schreibman, Ray Siemens, and John Unsworth, 198–217. Malden, Mass.: Blackwell, 2004.

McGann, Jerome. "Texts in N-Dimensions and Interpretation in a New Key." *Text Technology* 12 (2003): 1–18.

McGann, Jerome, and Lisa Samuels. 2001. "Deformance and Interpretation." In *Radiant Textuality: Literature after the World Wide Web*, 105–35. New York: Palgrave.

Moati, Raoul. *Derrida/Searle: Deconstruction and Ordinary Language*. Translated by Timothy Attanucci and Maureen Chun. New York: Columbia University Press, 2014.

Mol, Annemarie. *The Body Multiple: Ontology in Medical Practice.* Durham, N.C.: Duke University Press, 2002.

Nowviskie, Bethany. "On Capacity and Care." October 4, 2015, http://nowviskie.org/2015/on-capacity-and-care.

Nowviskie, Bethany. "Digital Humanities in the Anthropocene." July 10, 2014, http://nowviskie.org/2014/anthropocene.

Palmer, Carole L. "Thematic Research Collections." In *A Companion to Digital Humanities,* edited by Susan Schreibman, Ray Siemens, and John Unsworth, 348–65. Malden, Mass.: Blackwell, 2004.

Peters, Benjamin. "Digital." In *Digital Keywords: A Vocabulary of Information Society & Culture,* edited by Benjamin Peters, 93–108. Princeton, N.J.: Princeton University Press, 2016.

Pickering, Andrew. *The Mangle of Practice: Time, Agency, and Science.* Chicago: University of Chicago Press, 1995.

Presner, Todd. "Critical Theory and the Mangle of the Digital Humanities." In *Between Humanities and the Digital,* edited by Patrick Svensson and David Theo Goldberg, 55–68. Cambridge, Mass.: MIT Press, 2015.

Ramsay, Stephen. *Reading Machines: Toward an Algorithmic Criticism.* Urbana: University of Illinois Press, 2011.

Sample, Mark. "Notes Toward a Deformed Humanities." May 2, 2012, http://www.samplereality.com/2012/05/02/notes-towards-a-deformed-humanities.

Sample, Mark. "Scholarly Lies and the Deformative Humanities." May 17, 2012, http://www.samplereality.com/2012/05/17/scholarly-lies-and-the-deformative-humanities.

Scheinfeldt, Tom. "Game Change: Digital Technology and Performative Humanities." February 15, 2012, http://foundhistory.org/2012/02/game-change-digital-technology-and-performative-humanities.

Sedgwick, Eve Kosofky. *Epistemology of the Closet.* Berkeley: University of California Press, 1990.

Thorpe, Jer. "On Data and Performance." March 5, 2014, http://blog.blprnt.com/blog/blprnt/on-data-and-performance.

Tuhiwai Smith, Linda. *Decolonizing Methodologies: Research and Indigenous Peoples.* London: Zed Books, 2012.

Wertheim, Margaret, and Christine Wertheim. *Crochet Coral Reef.* Los Angeles: Institute for Figuring, 2015.

Wittgenstein, Ludwig. *Philosophical Investigations.* Translated by G. E. M. Anscombe. Oxford: Blackwell, 1992.

The Care of Enchanted Things

KARI KRAUS

As part of the third-year curriculum at the Hogwarts School of Witchcraft and Wizardry in J. K. Rowling's Harry Potter series, students are assigned *The Monster Book of Monsters,* an enchanted bestiary whose contents include hippogriffs, sphinxes, and all manner of chimerical creatures. A most menacing bibliographic specimen, the book functions nothing like the inanimate volumes we encounter in the real world: it snaps and growls at whoever tries to open it and can only be placated by a reader intrepid enough to risk losing her fingers by gently stroking its spine (Rowling, 113). Harry and his classmates devise various other ad hoc methods of restraining their volumes when not in use, including belting, roping, and duct-taping them shut (112). Failing such measures, the books will savagely attack not only their owners but also other copies of themselves—as Harry learns when he visits the Flourish and Blotts bookstore and watches the natural-born pulpivores attempt to shred one another to bits (52–53).

What is the fate of these monsters, these mauled and mangled things? In the transmedial universe of Harry Potter—comprised of books, films, video games, toys, and other media—one clue is provided by the Marauder's Map, a document depicting the location of various buildings and secret passages on the grounds of Hogwarts. In the closing credits of the film adaptation of *Harry Potter and the Prisoner of Azkaban,* the camera pans over a location on the map labeled the "Monsters Repair Workshop," where mutilated copies of *The Monster Book of Monsters* ostensibly go to be fixed ("Monster's [sic] Repair Workshop"). Like the Island of Misfit Toys, the workshop functions as a way station for broken, defective things. There they remain until presumably they can be examined, repaired, and put back into cultural circulation. Although unequivocally part of the Wizarding World, these artifacts are not magically mended with the help of a charm. Instead, they are ontologically positioned within this fictional universe as fragile material media requiring specialized tools and techniques to stabilize them. The books' supernatural properties, in other words, neither protect them from harm nor exempt them from the need for painstaking stewardship and conservation. At the same time, we might reasonably suppose the care of enchanted things to be different in kind from the care of everyday things. If restoring an antiquarian book to a mechanically sound condition involves such routine practices as sewing and rebinding, what might the maintenance of an enchanted book entail? This chapter offers a sustained reflection on that question, addressing how care and design can be productively considered in tandem. Following David Rose, the *enchanted things* of my title refers to hybrid physical-digital objects in the real world whose seemingly magical properties imbue them with the aura of enchantment. Throughout the chapter, I use the *Monster Book* as a metaphor for this larger class of technological artifacts. More popularly known as the "Internet of Things," they provide us with the opportunity to identify and explore some of the tensions and problems inherent in their production and maintenance. These tensions include the friction between data openness and data privacy; physical wear and computational wear; desktop computing and pervasive computing; and make-believe and reality as competing conceptual domains for interface metaphors.

In the years since the various Harry Potter releases, *The Monster Book of Monsters* has transitioned from a fictional object on page and screen into a real-world object variously created by researchers, artists, inventors, Harry Potter fans, and commercial manufacturers. "Reinvented with 100% muggle brand crafting supplies," as one DIY enthusiast boasts (Quinnsulivan), these functional prototypes and prop replicas—which mimic the appearance and behavior of their on-screen progenitors with varying degrees of fidelity—often incorporate servo motors, microcontrollers, and other electronic components.

In the Harry Potter universe, the *Monster Book* is a sentient object; as such, it operates within the realm of the supernatural. Outside the fictional world, the proliferating number of home-brewed monster books coming out of basements and design labs are augmented with digital devices to give the illusion of sorcery. The in-world versions are powered by magic, the out-of-world versions by technology sufficiently advanced to make them indistinguishable from magic, to paraphrase Arthur C. Clarke's famous dictum. Indeed, inspired by the Harry Potter universe, David Rose of the MIT Media Lab refers to the products of ubicomp—the whole class of things that "seamlessly couple the dual world of bits and atoms"—as *enchanted objects* (Tangible Media Group; Rose). Thus the paranormal magic in the story world gives way to illusionist magic in the real world.

Examples of such enchanted objects currently in the R&D phase or already entering the market include a water faucet that curls up in response to wasteful water use, a toaster that wiggles restlessly after a prolonged period of disuse, an umbrella that warns you when it is about to rain, and a clock that chimes the location of family members (Togler, Hemmert, and Wettach; Burneleit, Hemmert, and Wettach; Rose, 92, 109, and *passim*). Like *The Monster Book of Monsters,* these objects and others like them could collectively benefit from their own dedicated workshop, but one that is capable of accommodating *every* phase of an object's life cycle, not just repair. By encompassing creation and manufacturing within its purview, such a workshop embraces a key tenet of sustainable design: that change and adaptation can be intentionally engineered into products and technologies from the outset. It is not that such objects are fortified against entropy, but rather that their aging patterns develop and unfold along designed trajectories, particularly at the level of user interface, as explored later. Consequently, the project of maintenance and repair begins to take on a different cast, one that is intimately connected to—rather than separate and distinct from—a product's genesis and development.

Because so many of these emerging technologies involve personal data collection, ethical reflection will need to be brought to bear at each stage of the process. Imagine, for example, a digitally augmented DIY version of the *Monster Book* embedded with sensors capable of detecting temperature, moisture, sound, motion, and open/close events. If books have always been the record keepers of readers' interactions with them, how much more can we learn about a book once we have endowed it with tiny digital prosthetics that document ever so much more of its history? Properly preserved and maintained, such a specially outfitted book could enhance book history as a field of study by magnifying our ability to tell a story about its past, such as the precise date, time, and place it was opened or read aloud or subjected to the mishaps of a careless reader who spilled coffee on it. More than a decade ago, Bruce Sterling presciently coined the term *spime* to refer to such informational objects. A portmanteau of "space" and "time," spimes are "precisely tracked . . . throughout their earthly sojourn" (11).

One premise of this thought experiment is that books, like other physical objects, are already lo-fi sensors in their natural state, detecting and reacting to information about external stimuli and events. A moldy book, for example, registers the fact that there is excess moisture in the air through a multimodal output that takes the form of a musty odor and foxing stains. A book read by candlelight is likely to retain telltale drops of wax on its pages. These traces function as a form of metadata that is materially coextensive with the book itself: a type of on-board provenance. Book historians are adept at interpreting these physical clues, often with the help of perceptual aids: Kathryn Rudy, for example, has attempted to identify which pages in a small corpus of medieval manuscript books were handled most frequently by using a densitometer, a machine that measures light reflected off a surface. The relative darkness of the edges, corners, and other white space of the page as quantified by the densitometer thus becomes a proxy for the amount of use and wear the book has undergone. Rudy adopts the densitometer as a tool to augment her *umwelt* (Eagleman 2015; Eagleman 2011): the semiotic information in the environment that is available to her senses. By embedding sensors into a book, we can increase the temporal bandwidth available to us in our quest for book knowledge; they expand our umwelt by amplifying the book's capabilities as a sensing system.

But such goals, however principled and socially benevolent in theory, are—as Katie Shilton and Deborah Estrin have argued about the self-quantification movement more broadly—potentially undercut by the technologies of surveillance used to support them. "Values such as privacy, consent, equity, and social forgetting," they note, "are particularly challenged by this new form of data collection" (1).

From the vantage point of a privacy activist, then, as opposed to that of a researcher or designer, the "care" of an enchanted object could controversially involve breaking its data-logging capabilities or purging its data store or even intentionally injecting noise into the system to make the data unreliable: what Finn Brunton and Helen Nissenbaum call *obfuscation*. A Monster Repair Workshop reflecting such user values might paradoxically vandalize the enchanted things consigned to its care in the name of anti-surveillance.

"Each society, each generation," write Mark Jones and colleagues in a wide-ranging study of forgeries from antiquity to the present, "fakes the thing it covets most" (13). Fakes, in other words, are a reliable indicator of what a culture values and reveres. At a time when data is as precious a commodity as oil, we need voices like Brunton's and Nissenbaum's advocating for strong countermeasures to prevent corporate and governmental exploitation of personal digital information, even, perhaps—under limited circumstances—the production of counterfeit data. But actions deemed heroic in one age are often regarded as reckless in the next. In this case, what we are presently defining as a privacy issue could eventually transition into a heritage issue if posterity is forced to reckon with a cultural record deliberately seeded at perhaps unprecedented scales with disinformation—planted there as much by the general populace as by the governments and corporations that rule over them. (In the wake of the 2016 U.S. presidential race, such a scenario can no longer be viewed as hypothetical. Clickbait, yellow journalism, fake news, meme warfare, and Russian-backed Twitter bots are now endemic features of civic life.) My intent here is not to invalidate Brunton's and Nissenbaum's tactics—which participate in a venerable tradition of using political protest to achieve just social change—but rather, in the spirit of debate, to imagine their unintended consequences. If you believe, as the authors of a 2000 report on the illicit trade in cultural antiquities do, that there is a "fundamental right of a people to their cultural heritage" (Brodie, Doole, and Watson, 11), then widespread tampering of data with the intent to deceive—taken to an extreme—is arguably a human rights violation. The act of recovering the past, already fraught with peril under the best of circumstances, will be exponentially harder if the real and the fake are allowed to perniciously intermingle. Seen from this angle, a central mission of the Monster Repair Workshop should be to develop novel techniques and protocols for recovering and authenticating the data logs of enchanted things, as well as finding the right balance between allowing the public access to those repositories, on the one hand, and judiciously redacting them, on the other. The shop, in other words, will need to be well staffed with the information professionals who already dare such things, namely, librarians, conservators, curators, and archivists.

As an alternative to Brunton and Nissenbaum, Shilton and Estrin offer what is in my view a more equitable and sustainable approach to privacy that could potentially offset the need for obfuscation. Drawing on her own ethnographic research into mobile technology development, Shilton proposes the deployment of *values levers*: design practices that "pry open opportunities for discussion of antisurveillance values during design and [help] build consensus around those values as design criteria" (12). Two such practices identified by Shilton and Estrin as being particularly efficacious are the formation of interdisciplinary teams and advocacy by a team member devoted to ethical issues (12–14). Although they envision a traditional researcher fulfilling the role of advocate, a participatory design approach that enlisted end users as co-designers could achieve the same goals. As an example of the kind of negotiated outcome this method might produce in collaboration with both users and digital humanists, consider once again the hybrid digital–physical *Monster Book*. Users of such a book could be given the option of committing the data being collected about their reading habits to a dark archive inaccessible to current researchers but available to posterity. The specific trigger event causing the information to be released publicly could be managed by a trusted digital estate.

If enchanted objects raise concerns about the overabundance of information they surface and reveal, then they should paradoxically also be scrutinized for what they efface and conceal. At the heart of this apparent contradiction is software, which logs and displays metadata about the object's interactions with the world, but fails to visibly register its own second-order interactions with users. To see what I mean, imagine that our DIY *Monster Book* has, in addition to a vast array of sensors, a miniature LCD screen embedded in it. This screen has a menu-driven display of the data being collected about the book and its readers. While the material structure of the book, such as its spine and pages, reflects patterns of use and wear, the software interface does not. If users repeatedly consult the statistics regarding how often the *Monster Book* growls, for example, but almost entirely ignore other available information—such as the number of times the book has been opened—there is nothing in the LCD rendering that symptomatically hints at those behaviors. The items selected most frequently from the screen menu, in other words, do not yellow or fade or become brittle with age. At the perceptual level, then, the hardware of the book is vulnerable to material change; the software appears impervious to it.

The act of modeling the appearance of change in software interfaces based on underlying usage data is known in the research literature as *digital patina* or *computational wear* (Hill et al. 3). Here "patina" is interpreted broadly to refer to artifacts and representations of all kinds that "carry [material] traces about time and life" (Giaccardi et al. 473). These traces are the result of chemical, environmental, and human interactions with the materials in question. When visiting a web page or other online resource, we typically encounter little in the way of visual cues that tell us which links have been clicked most often or which images have been repeatedly viewed. Web and app design in general validate Brien Brothman's concern that electronic documents "may well be imperceptibly eroding our ability to experience historical pastness, for example to witness the patina of record agedness" (49). Even in cases where the user interface has been designed to communicate patterns of use or wear, the metaphors underlying those choices often feel bland and predictable. Kindle's "Popular Highlights" feature, for instance, adopts the generic convention of a dotted underline to indicate passages in books that have been highlighted by three or more readers (see Figure 14.1). More intriguingly, but still operating within a similar paradigm, Xiaoyang Mao and colleagues have prototyped a set of link icons that appear to rust over time the more they are clicked. Both GUIs are vulnerable to charges of skeuomorphism insofar as they transplant material properties from the real world to the virtual world. Nonetheless they admirably buck convention by taking stock UI components and icons—generally represented as

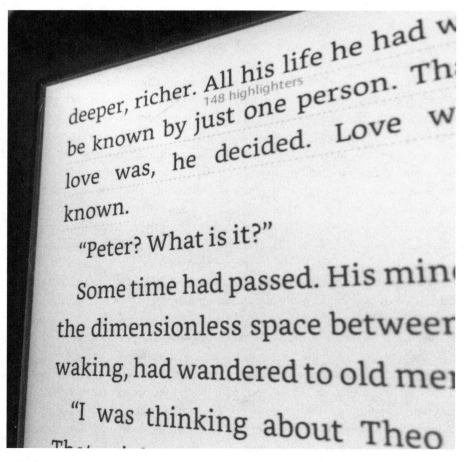

Figure 14.1. Kindle's "Popular Highlights" feature. Source: Kari Kraus, screenshot (August 11, 2016).

static and timeless—and transforming them into elements decidedly *of* time. To borrow a resonant term used by William Hill et al., their interaction histories are directly "tattooed" on the interface, "exactly where [they] can make an informative difference" (6).

In addition to skeuomorphic displays, other models of digital patina, imaginative and compelling, are being commercialized or field tested. The Kobo eReader, for example, relies on an icon of a glowing orb whose intensity waxes and wanes in response to the level of social activity around a particular text. The reader is enjoined to "watch a book's pulse get stronger as comments are added and more readers are reading!" ("Kobo Brings Books to Life"). A similar tack is taken in the case of the History Tablecloth, a physical computing project developed by William Gaver and collaborators. The tablecloth is screenprinted with electroluminescent material (see Figure 14.2). When an object, such as a plate or teapot, is placed on it, the cells beneath it light up and expand in diameter, growing bigger the longer the object is left there. Once it is moved, the halo effect persists for approximately thirty seconds before disappearing (199–200). The History Tablecloth thus captures and visualizes activity traces related to everyday domestic objects. In true enchanted fashion, it moves the computational interface "off the desktop and into the world" (Dourish and Bell, 414).

The visual artifice employed in the History Tablecloth deviates from common forms of data representation in the sciences, notably with regard to the presentation of usage statistics. Unlike the Kindle "Popular Highlights" feature—which spells out the exact number of users who have highlighted a specific passage of text (e.g., "14 highlighters" or "29 highlighters")—the History Tablecloth provides relative rather than absolute information: an object with a large halo, for example, indicates that it has been stationary on the table longer than an adjacent object with a smaller halo,

Figure 14.2. The History Tablecloth (Gaver et al., "History Tablecloth," 201). Copyright Interaction Research Studio.

but the tablecloth contains no logging device or other mechanism by which the precise difference in duration is quantified. Given the sophisticated data-logging capabilities of today's digital sensors, we might ask why a designer would deliberately bypass precision metrics in favor of blurrier or fuzzier ones for purposes of output and display. The decision, at least in Gaver's case, reflects an ethos that values ambiguity and augments the role of user interpretation in design: what art historian E. H. Gombrich calls "the beholder's share" (Gaver, Beaver, and Benford, "Ambiguity"; Gombrich, 179–288). Such lo-fi rendering has been advocated as a potential avenue for design by a growing number of researchers. Stacey Kuznetsov and collaborators recommend looking to nature for models of nondigital sensors, citing examples such as the color of the water in a fish tank, which can indicate ozone deficiency, or the behavior of bees, which can signal drought conditions (231). They conclude that "ubiquitous systems can draw on 'imprecise' digital sensing [modeled after the biomarkers and analog measuring tools used to monitor living systems] to embrace 'ambiguity as a resource for design'" (234). Moreover, by deliberately coarsening the grain of representation, we can potentially address both of the contradictory concerns raised in this chapter: namely, that enchanted objects simultaneously over- and underreport their histories. Digital patina, in other words, by softening and curbing the information density of its display, could theoretically bear witness to the past without compromising user privacy.

The value of potentially including digital patina as part of the design of enchanted things is reinforced by some of my own human subjects research, which found that participants made active use of signs of wear to interpret objects. In 2014, I conducted a study on how individuals identify the constituent parts of objects, including broken, obsolete, and semantically ambiguous objects. The initial impetus for this research was a literature review on the subject of technological change. Historically we know that many new technologies have inherited parts from earlier technologies. The skateboard remediated the surfboard; the camera pilfered from the gun; the telephone harvested batteries and wires from the telegraph; and early models of the phonograph borrowed the treadle mechanism of the sewing machine. In each of these instances, the logic of part–whole relationships governs the design. "Many of a technology's parts are shared by other technologies," notes Brian Arthur in *The Nature of Technology*, "so a great deal of development happens automatically as components improve in other uses 'outside' the host technology" (134).

To better understand this process, I decided to take a closer look at the role of "parthood" in creativity and design. I recruited thirty research subjects at the University of Maryland who were asked to examine six 3D artifacts and complete a written questionnaire about them. These artifacts ranged from the familiar (a book) to the unfamiliar or imaginary (a 3D-printed steampunk variation on the medieval astrolabe) to the broken or visually distinctive (a fork with a bent tine and a rock that appears to have a face, a phenomenon known as *pareidolia*). The questionnaire asked participants to identify each object or hazard a guess about it if they did not know what it was (*object recognition*); analyze it into its constituent parts (*component analysis*); identify the most significant, distinctive, or salient part (*significant properties*); and describe the process by which they performed these tasks and any challenges they faced (*self-reflection*).

Although it is beyond the scope of this chapter to delve too much into the results, one finding worth highlighting is that research subjects tended to approach component analysis as a temporal as well as spatial exercise, endowing objects with inferred origin stories and biographies. Most often these took the form of speculative remarks concerning the formation, production, provenance, and/or manufacturing of the items in question. One participant theorized that the ball, for example, was "formed of a single homogeneous foam (possibly cut/whittled by machine out of a more standard—possibly rectangular—shape of the material)." This line of reasoning was most pronounced with respect to the book: "I guess if I wanted to think more like a book scholar I'd further identify . . . the absent metal, inked letterforms that were arranged to print these words on the body pages. Interesting to think about how far you want to stretch 'included components.' . . . *Is the printing press part of the book*?" (emphasis added).

Like Borges's Funes the Memorius, who discerns vineyards and grapes in a goblet of wine, test subjects interpreted each object as feeding them information about time through the geometry of space. Key to recovering this information is evidence of composition and wear: "I looked for any signs of wear or scratch marks," wrote a participant about an object she could not decipher, "to see [how] it had been used." Across the board, participants sought out visual traces of material change to help them individuate and enumerate the parts of an object.

In one instance, such traces were invoked not only to recover the past but also to project the future: confronted by the apparent partlessness and homogeneity of the red foam ball, one participant mentally subjected it to a process of accelerated aging, imagining it as an object that has eventually been so heavily used and worn that "the surface is damaged . . . you can see the 'inside' area, and although it *may* be the same consistency as the outside, because it's not immediately visible there's *the possibility of something else existing*" (emphasis added).

I regard this future-oriented speculation—which almost seems to take the form of a hypothetical cutaway diagram showing the ball's interior texture and unevenness—as an attempt to compensate for its flawless symmetry, an attribute that can make nearly any object seem timeless, as though it stands outside the laws of physics, immune to degradation and decay. The cognitive scientist Michael Leyton has conducted a number of experiments demonstrating that humans interpret the irregularities in objects, such as indentations or protrusions, as repositories of memory from which we can extract their history (3). In an effort to concretize his ideas, Leyton asks us to envision an empty subway station: here we see "all around . . . objects that hold for [us] the memory of events at which [we have] not been present," he writes. "The dents in a bin are unavoidably seen as the result of kicking. . . . A crumpled newspaper evokes the compacting actions of hands. . . . A squashed beer can recalls a compressing grip" (1). It is in such everyday artifacts that we locate causal history.

For Leyton, memory is always in the form of asymmetry (6–7), while symmetry is always the absence of memory. According to this value system, the trope of asymmetry signifies the preservation of the past, while the trope of symmetry represents the denial or destruction of it. A maximally symmetrical object, like the red ball, is one that is silent, sterile, and vacuous (600). By contrast, an asymmetrical artifact is one that is information rich, allowing us to infer earlier states from its spatial irregularities.

If the gritty, debris-filled subway station is a particularly rich memory store, then the barren cell of an internment camp—to take Leyton's most poignant counterexample—is a grossly impoverished one: "unless events intrude from outside the cell, one day is indistinguishable from the next because there are no effects of interaction with the environment" (590). Leyton adopts the term "history ethic" to express the underlying rationale for closely attending to asymmetry: "the history ethic is the commitment to revealing, to the fullest, the history of an entity—a person, a culture, the animate and inanimate environment, oneself—and to interact with the entity by virtue of its fullest history" (601). A direct affront to such an ethic, the barren cell of the internment camp is emblematic of symmetry, not asymmetry. Inured against time, it no longer acts as a recording medium of the human condition.

If our tweets, Facebook posts, credit card purchases, and browsing histories collectively disclose personal information, so too do our everyday household objects. Their *asymmetries*—Leyton's variation on *patina*—are as much a part of our data shadows as the trackable information we leave in the cloud. Because user interfaces—whether of a dog-eared book, a crumpled newspaper, a dented beer can, or a fingerprint-smudged computer monitor—indirectly register information about human lives, they too are potentially subject to surveillance. Leyton's history ethic, however, functions as a ballast against obfuscation, reminding us—through the example of the internment camp—that there are profound human costs to erasing or distorting evidence of the past.

The barren cell thus serves as a kind of cautionary tale, warning us of the adverse consequences of dousing enchanted things in the waters of Lethe in the name of anti-surveillance. Deciding whether and under what circumstances to retain, exploit, visualize, modulate, or erase the "accrued histories" (Hill et al., 3) of enchanted objects will require an especially thoughtful application of Shilton's values levers, with one potential design outcome being the adoption of the imprecise displays previously discussed. Just as museum conservators and book binders must balance competing demands to preserve the authenticity of the items in their care on the one hand and to increase their longevity on the other (Rosner and Taylor), so too will the careful stewards of *Monster Books* need to negotiate data endurance and display.

As Hill and colleagues argue, physical wear can serve as a powerful organizing metaphor for computational wear (6), as most of the examples of digital patina suggest. In the final section of this chapter, however, I want to propose enchanted wear—let us call it *spectral wear*—as an alternative conceptual domain from which to draw inspiration for the design of enchanted things. In what tattered and mangled state, for example, does *The Monster Book of Monsters* arrive at the Monster repair shop? What are the supernatural counterparts to physical phenomena such as patina, corrosion, and decay? In short, what visual or perceptual traces of material change might result from magical processes and operations as opposed to real-world processes? A crude example is the ectoplasm in the slime scene in *Ghostbusters.* More ethereal sources of ideas—both strange and macabre—are the pastings and splatterings of fairies, goblins, and sprites in *Lady Cottington's Pressed Fairy Book* (T. Jones). Instead of pressing flowers in her journal, like other little girls, Lady Cottington presses garden fairies. Like a Venus flytrap, she snaps her book shut when they hover too close, catching and preserving them in suspended animation, their gossamer fairy entrails dripping down the page.[1]

Two examples of spectral wear come from work done by my team and me. Over the last few years, funded by the National Science Foundation, we have been collaborating with a large group of researchers, artists, musicians, and programmers designing educational alternate reality games for teens. In January 2015, we launched DUST in partnership with Brigham Young University, NASA, and Western Lights (Hansen, Kraus, Ahn, et al.). Focused on the deep-time sciences, DUST incorporates augmented reality apps, 3D panoramic environments, and an interactive graphic novel. The game centers on the mysterious collapse of adults worldwide who fall into a coma-like state following a cataclysmic meteor shower. Players "hack" into NASA research databases and engage in collaborative play and inquiry across multiple media platforms to search for answers that will save their parents' lives. Eventually they discover that the meteor dust is full of microscopic extremophiles whose DNA contains the records of a lost alien civilization, a voice from the DUST, whose world was destroyed. In Kilroy-was-here fashion, their message proclaims, "Look, we were here; we mattered; we existed." But because it has been transmitted in a mutable medium over time and space, the message arrives glitched and distorted. Players eventually decrypt it with the help of the Dream Decoder, a web app introduced in the final stage of the game.

As one of our project team members, Tony Pellicone, pointed out, glitch is symptomatic of technological decay and indicative of interference or corruption by the supernatural (think of Sadako Yamamura in Koji Suzuki's *Ring* series of novels, the ghost who causes digital distortion through her presence on recorded media; or Carol Anne in *Poltergeist,* the little girl enchanted by the static being transmitted by the family's haunted television). The term "glitch" first appeared in print in John Glenn's *Into Orbit* (1962), a book about the first U.S. human spaceflight program. Glenn defined glitch as "a spike or change in voltage in an electrical circuit which takes place when the circuit suddenly has a new load put on it" (qtd. in *Merriam-Webster Online*). Capitalizing on the original aeronautical context, DUST draws on glitch as a quintessentially digital trope to visually express the transmission of alien information. It transfers an aesthetic associated with the inert world of electronics onto a living system, one putatively hailing from an exoplanet millions of light-years away. Glitch, then, in DUST is meant to capture the paradoxical precarity and stability—the persistence but also the extreme vulnerability—of a genetic signal that has fantastically withstood ultraviolet radiation and the vacuum of space to reach its final destination (for a visual example of DUST's glitch aesthetic, see http://goo.gl/Vvij6K).

My second example is taken from our current transmedia project, *The Tessera*, developed in partnership with Brigham Young University, the Computer History Museum in Mountain View California, and Western Lights (Hansen, Kraus, Ahn, et al.). When the ghosts of historical figures, including Ada Lovelace and Charles Babbage, start haunting electronic devices, players must help them restore order by piecing together computational clues that will help fend off the forces of chaos. In the world of *The Tessera*, decay is a sign of Entropy, visualized as shadows that insidiously eat away at the objects associated with each of the game's gothic locales.

Figure 14.3, for example, is an interior shot of Horsley Towers, modeled after the mansion once occupied by the real Ada Lovelace. Time here has pooled in the hollows and crevices of bygone things. Entropy's effects can be felt in the crumbling plaster, the creaky floorboards, and the moldering portraits on the walls. Light flooding in from the windows extinguishes the darkness and elsewhere gives way to a gallery of marvels: mechanical leviathans and self-acting machines, calculating engines and automata, street organs and looms, mysterious contraptions lit from within as though powered by moonbeams. To protect and guard these enchanted things—to properly care for them—players are enlisted as darkness chasers who must combat Entropy's anarchic imagination. At another locale within the game, players are ferried about the velvety black waters of an abandoned subway station by a ghostly crew of automatons (see Figure 14.4). Initially enveloped in darkness inside the submarine, broken and worn down, the automatons come to life as players start the game (see Figure 14.5). In contradistinction to more benign forms of wear that encode the passage of time and enhance the archaeological record—what I have referred to as *patina* throughout this chapter—Entropy in *The Tessera* is a nihilistic force. Like Chaos in Milton's *Paradise Lost*, Entropy delights in sowing "spoil and ruin" everywhere. It is this dissolution of the world that players seek to avert.

But what might spectral wear look like in a truly enchanted, post-desktop technology? Consider William Gaver's Key Table, developed alongside the History Tablecloth as part of a larger collaborative project exploring the role of electronic furniture and playful technologies in the home (Sengers and Gaver, 102, 106). The table uses load sensors to measure the force with which everyday objects—keys, wallet, phone—are placed on it (see Figure 14.6). Throw your keys down hard enough, and

Figure 14.3. Interior shot of Horsley Towers in *The Tessera* (Hansen, Kraus, Ahn, Cardon, et al.). The lead environment artist for *The Tessera* is Joaquin (Ximo) Catala Retortillo. Copyright Brigham Young University 2017.

Figure 14.4. Ghostly crew of automatons in *The Tessera* (Hansen, Kraus, Ahn, Cardon, et al.). Lead environment artist Joaquin (Ximo) Catala Retortillo. Copyright Brigham Young University 2017.

Figure 14.5. The automatons come to life in *The Tessera* (Hansen, Kraus, Ahn, Cardon, et al.). Lead environment artist Joaquin (Ximo) Catala Retortillo. Copyright Brigham Young University 2017.

a mechanized picture frame hanging on the wall just above the table will tilt wildly in response. In this way, the picture ostensibly becomes a rough barometer of the affective state of the user, allowing the next person who walks through the door to read it symptomatically: Did family member x just return from a restorative yoga class or, conversely, storm in after an emotionally draining fight with a partner? As a lo-fi 3D visualization of mood, the picture frame, which communicates wirelessly with the table, is designed to help answer this sort of question.

In the final analysis, what gives the table an enchanted feel is the fact that the picture frame is an inanimate object that moves in violation of psychophysical

Figure 14.6. The Key Table. In Gaver et al. ("Electronic Furniture," Figure 9) and Sengers and Gaver (102). Copyright Interaction Research Studio.

norms. It seems, moreover, to do so not of its own volition, which would be strange enough, but rather at the mysterious direction of the table. Like a magician's dancing handkerchief, it is an animation trick that feels more like sorcery. And because the mechanism of movement is atypical, whether one ascribes it to magic or technology, the frame theoretically escapes some types of everyday wear phenomena, such as the telltale fingerprints that would be left behind if hands were responsible for the constant tilting.

When Gaver and colleagues field-tested the key table with volunteers, they found that the family in whose home it had been installed responded to the table in unexpected ways. In particular, family members became entranced with the portrait of the dog contained in the picture frame, leading them to anthropomorphize the table and interact with it almost as if it were a pet (Sengers and Gaver, 102, 106). What Gaver et al. did not fully anticipate, then, was the role of representational content (not just technological affordances) in shaping how the furniture would be used and interpreted. An alternative approach to the portrait that takes their interesting findings into account might be to include a digital picture (rather than a static photographic print) in the mechanized frame. This digital portrait could be programmed to react more gradually to underlying patterns from the sensor data over time. The idea would be to visually capture the larger cycles of emotional change in the household as data accrued over a period of days, weeks, months, and years.

There is a further dimension to spectral wear that touches directly on care. Drawing on a wealth of empirical research, the designer Judith Donath has observed that we often impute sentience to complex interactive objects (69–71). Sentience in turn, whether real or imagined, prompts caretaking behavior (71). Because enchanted objects dial sentience up to 11, they may have a built-in advantage when it comes to survival, inspiring their owners to maintain and preserve them, rather than letting them fall into disrepair; interestingly, we also tend to attribute sentience to worn objects that have acquired personality through use, such as an antique car or a nicked and scratched skateboard (69). Recall in this context that users open the tattered *Monster Book* by gently stroking its spine, a gesture that mimics the way we interact with pets.

Lori Emerson, a new media scholar at the University of Colorado, has perceptively explored magic as a source of metaphor for interaction design in her recent book *Reading Writing Interfaces*. She shows how the language of magic is often used to mystify technology and to bolster a complementary philosophy of invisible interface design (1–46). As an alternative paradigm, she advocates for interfaces that assert themselves rather than disappear, that provoke or challenge the user rather than recede from view. The enchanted objects referenced throughout this chapter—such as the History Tablecloth, the key table, and *The Monster Book of Monsters*—tend to align more closely with these alternative values, but ultimately surpass mere provocation by trafficking in a wider variety of emotions ranging from wonder, astonishment, and intrigue to curiosity, playfulness, and mindfulness. In essence, enchanted computing seeks to decouple usability from unobtrusiveness—long considered two sides of the same coin—and instead to demonstrate that usability can be fundamentally compatible with radical new approaches to UI design.

In this chapter, following David Rose, I have labeled the products of pervasive computing—epitomized by the *Monster Book of Monsters*—as *enchanted objects*. I have positioned them as experimental hardware–software composites whose perceived anthropomorphism, data-logging capabilities, programmed behaviors, and environmental embeddedness create unique stewardship and UI challenges for digital humanists and information professionals. In response to those challenges, I introduced *spectral wear* as a distinct design aesthetic, arguing that its adoption confers several benefits on enchanted objects. Specifically, spectral wear might help mitigate privacy and surveillance concerns through figurative rather than quantitative displays, reflect and document patterns of use, and promote an ethics of care. It also provides a series of design tenets that are compatible with the application of Shilton's values levers: an add-on or extension to the design process that can support researchers and developers in realizing the goals identified during conversations about ethics and values.

Borrowing a term from evolutionary biology, I have elsewhere referred to the products of speculative design, such as the History Tablecloth or *The Monster Book of Monsters,* as *Hopeful Monsters*: "they are things born perhaps slightly before their time," writes the novelist Nicholas Mosley, "when it's not known if the environment is quite ready for them" (71). Through the ethical design of software interfaces and the adoption of values levers in DH's labs and centers, or even its kitchen tables (the original design and repair workshops), we can help create an environment, and a world, that is ready.

NOTES

I would like to thank students in my 2013 Classification Theory course, who participated in an informal version of the parthood study as a class activity and offered suggestions on what types of objects to present to test subjects, including the suggestion that I incorporate an object exhibiting the characteristics of pareidolia. I would also like to thank Derek Hansen, Elizabeth Bonsignore, Tony Pellicone, Katie Kaczmarek Frew, and Jared Cardon for helping me compile examples of spectral wear; Matthew Kirschenbaum, Lauren Klein, and Matt Gold for reading and commenting on earlier drafts of this chapter; Amanda Visconti for pointing me to literature on the densitometer; and Rachel Dook for introducing me, in the context of enchanted wear, to *Lady Cottington's Pressed Fairy Book*. My gratitude to Jentery Sayers for allowing me to reprint several paragraphs/ sections from "Finding Fault Lines: An Approach to Speculative Design," my chapter for his edited collection (*The Routledge Companion to Media Studies and Digital Humanities*, 1st ed. [New York: Routledge, 2018, 162–73]). Finally, I would like to acknowledge and express my appreciation for my fabulous research collaborators, including Derek Hansen, June Ahn, Elizabeth Bonsignore, Jared Cardon, Jeff Parkin, Katie Kaczmarek Frew, Tony Pellicone, Carlea Holle-Jensen, Ann Fraistat, Lexie Bradford, and Connor King. The brief plot summaries of *DUST* and *The Tessera* included in this chapter incorporate team-authored language used in our promotional materials, game materials, and other publications.

1. We are gratifyingly informed in a publisher's note at the beginning of the book that no fairies sustained any actual injuries at the impetuous hand of Lady Cottington. Apparently the fairies only leave "psychic imprints." Indeed, they eventually start trying to outdo one another in adopting the most sensational poses on the pages of the book, including mooning the reader.

BIBLIOGRAPHY

Arthur, Brian. *The Nature of Technology*. Free Press, New York: Free Press, 2009.

"Book of Monster's Repair Workshop." Harry Potter Wiki. March 2016, http://harrypotter .wikia.com/wiki/Book_of_Monster%27s_Repair_Workshop.

Brodie, Neil, Jenny Doole, and Peter Watson. "Stealing History." *CRM-WASHINGTON* 25, no. 2 (2000): 7–10.

Brothman, Brien. "Perfect Present, Perfect Gift: Finding a Place for Archival Consciousness in Social Theory." *Archival Science* 10, no. 2 (2010): 141–89.

Brunton, Finn, and Helen Nissenbaum. *Obfuscation: A User's Guide for Privacy and Protest.* Cambridge, Mass.: MIT Press, 2015.

Burneleit, Eva, Fabian Hemmert, and Reto Wettach. "Living Interfaces: The Impatient Toaster." *Proceedings of the 3rd International Conference on Tangible and Embedded Interaction,* ACM (2009).

Donath, Judith. *The Social Machine: Designs for Living Online.* Cambridge, Mass.: MIT Press, 2014.

Dourish, Paul, and Genevieve Bell. "The Infrastructure of Experience and the Experience of Infrastructure: Meaning and Structure in Everyday Encounters with Space." *Environment and Planning B: Planning and Design* 34, no. 3 (2007): 414–30.

Eagleman, D. M. "Can We Create New Senses for Humans?" *Ted Talk,* 2015. www.ted .com/talks/david_eagleman_can_we_create_new_senses_for_humans?language=en.

Eagleman, D. M. "The Umwelt," *2011: What Scientific Concept Would Improve Everybody's Cognitive Toolkit?* Edge.org, 2011, https://edge.org/response-detail/11498.

Emerson, Lori. *Reading Writing Interfaces.* Minneapolis: University of Minnesota Press, 2014.

Gaver, William W., Jacob Beaver, and Steve Benford. "Ambiguity as a Resource for Design." *Proceedings of the SIGCHI Conference on Human Factors in Computing Systems,* ACM (2003): 233–40.

Gaver, William, et al. "Electronic Furniture for the Curious Home: Assessing Ludic Designs in the Field." *International Journal of Human-Computer Interaction* 22, nos. 1–2 (2007): 119–52.

Gaver, William et al. "The History Tablecloth: Illuminating Domestic Activity." *Proceedings of the 6th Conference on Designing Interactive Systems,* ACM, New York (2006): 199–208.

Giaccardi, Elisa, et al. "Growing Traces on Objects of Daily Use: A Product Design Perspective for HCI." *Proceedings of the 2014 conference on Designing interactive systems.* ACM, 2014.

Glenn, John. *Into Orbit.* London: Cassell, 1962.

Gombrich, E. H. *Art and Illusion: A Study in the Psychology of Pictorial Representation.* Millennium edition, Princeton University Press, 2000.

Hansen, D., K. Kraus, J. Ahn, Co-Principal Investigators; J. Cardon and J. Parkin, Artists and Designers; E. Bonsignore, A. Pellicone, K., Kaczmarek, Student Investigators (UMD); C. Holl-Jensen, Creative Writer. *DUST: An Educational Alternate Reality Game (fall ingdust.com).* Sponsored by the NSF (awards #1323306 and #1323787) and created in partnership with NASA and Tinder Transmedia.

Hansen, D., K. Kraus, J. Ahn, Co-Principal Investigators; J. Cardon and J. Parkin, Artists and Designers; E. Bonsignore, Postdoctoral Researcher; K. Kaczmarek Frew, T. Pellicone, Student Investigators (UMD); A. Fraistat and C.Holl-Jensen, Creative Writers. *The Tessera: An Educational Alternate Reality Game (thetessera.org).* Sponsored by the NSF (awards #1323306 and #1323787) and created in partnership with The Computer History Museum and Western Lights.

Hill, William C., et al. "Edit Wear and Read Wear." *Proceedings of the SIGCHI Conference on Human Factors in Computing Systems,* ACM (1992).

Jones, Mark, Paul T. Craddock, and Nicolas Barker. *Fake? The Art of Deception.* Berkeley: University of California Press, 1990.

Jones, Terry. *Lady Cottington's Pressed Fairy Book.* London: Pavilion Books, 1994.

Kelly, Kevin. *The Inevitable: Understanding the 12 Technological Forces That Will Shape Our Future.* New York: Viking, 2016.

"Kobo Brings Books to Life with Kobo Pulse." September 27, 2011, https://news.kobo.com /kobo-brings-books-to-life-with-kobo-pulseTM-1685959.

Kuznetsov, Stacey, et al. "Nurturing Natural Sensors." *Proceedings of the 13th International Conference on Ubiquitous Computing,* ACM (2011): 227–36.

Leyton, Michael. *Symmetry, Causality, Mind.* Cambridge, Mass.: MIT Press, 1992.

Mao, Xiaoyang, et al. "Visualizing Computational Wear with Physical Wear." *Proceedings of 6th ERCIM Workshop on "User Interfaces for All."* Florence (October 25–26, 2000).

"Monster Book of Monsters, The." Harry Potter Wiki. 2000, http://harrypotter.wikia.com/ wiki/The_Monster_Book_of_Monsters.

Mosley, Nicholas. *Hopeful Monsters.* Champaign, Ill.: Dalkey Archive Press, 2000.

Quinnsulivan. "The DIY Monster Book of Monsters." Instructables, https://www.instruc tables.com/id/The-DIY-Monster-Book-of-Monsters/.

Rose, David. *Enchanted Objects: Design, Human Desire, and the Internet of Things.* New York: Simon & Schuster, 2014.

Rosner, Daniela K., and Alex S. Taylor. "Antiquarian Answers: Book Restoration as a Resource for Design." In *Proceedings of the SIGCHI Conference on Human Factors in Computing Systems* (CHI'11), ACM (2011): 2665–68.

Rowling, J. K. *Harry Potter and the Prisoner of Azkaban.* New York: Scholastic Paperbacks, 2001.

Rudy, Kathryn. (2010) "Dirty Books: Quantifying Patterns of Use in Medieval Manuscripts Using a Densitometer." *Journal of Historians of Netherlandish Art* 2, nos. 1–2. www .jhna.org/index.php/past-issues/volume-2-issue-1-2/129-dirty-books.

Sengers, Phoebe, and Bill Gaver. "Staying Open to Interpretation: Engaging Multiple Meanings in Design and Evaluation." *Proceedings of the 6th Conference on Designing Interactive Systems,* ACM (2006): 99–108.

Shilton, Katie, and Deborah Estrin. "Ethical Issues in Participatory Sensing." *Ethics CORE* 1 (Paper 5) (2012): 1–29.

Sterling, Bruce. *Shaping Things.* Cambridge, Mass.: MIT Press, 2005.

Tangible Media Group, MIT Media Lab, http://tangible.media.mit.edu/vision.

Togler, Jonas, Fabian Hemmert, and Reto Wettach. "Living Interfaces: The Thrifty Faucet." *Proceedings of the 3rd International Conference on Tangible and Embedded Interaction,* ACM (2009).

Zonas de Contacto: A Digital Humanities Ecology of Knowledges

ÉLIKA ORTEGA

The development of the field of digital humanities in the past decades has expanded along at least two clearly identifiable axes. One is a diversification of the practices, theories, approaches, objects of study, and infrastructural contexts (Klein and Gold). The other is an explosion of DH work, once practiced predominantly in the academia of the Northern Hemisphere, all over the world (Fiormonte, Numerico, and Tomasi) that is only beginning to be recognized.

The range of work being done around these two axes, in various disciplinary and theoretical contexts, as well as in varied geographical locations, has uncovered a latent tension between the digital humanities that takes place in the "centers of gravity," such as the Digital Humanities annual conference and publications like *Digital Humanities Quarterly* and *Digital Scholarship in the Humanities* and the digital humanities that is happening outside of such centers (Wernimont). This tension originates in the differences between the centralized and institutional approach to the digital humanities, perhaps best exemplified by the Alliance of Digital Humanities Organizations (ADHO) and the parallel divergent and distributed practices of digital humanities taking place all over the world and in many fields. These differences can, in turn, be attributed to matters of focus and praxis, to issues of representation (or lack thereof) in the field's governing bodies and reviewing boards (Dacos), and to disconnections in the available communication channels (Galina). Regardless of whether we take DH centers of gravity to be constituted, following Jacqueline Wernimont, by a canon of social media channels, international conferences, and publications and syllabi, or by the disciplinary threads that have historically been woven into the field, as suggested by Amy Earhart, the expansion of digital humanities to sites and practices outside of these centers has resulted in the repositioning of the field, even when its definitional contours continue to be amorphous.

This shift makes me wonder about the continuing tactical utility of digital humanities as a term or field: a construction that, as Matthew Kirschenbaum argues, makes it a "space of contest" ("Digital Humanities As/Is a Tactical Term") and one that "may be harnessed . . . to make a statement, make a change, and otherwise get stuff done" ("What Is 'Digital Humanities'"). Indeed, as a field seen by its own practitioners as global, interdisciplinary, porous, open, collaborative, adaptable, and always changing, the digital humanities has proven to be attractive to scholars seeking to further support and extend these qualities. By bringing additional disciplinary and local takes to the digital humanities, new and younger scholars are having an effect on the field that can only be viewed as positive. Yet, this increasing variety of approaches presents an additional challenge: making the ends of the spectrum, whether disciplinary or geographical, legible to one another.

The "expanded field" model proposed by Klein and Gold offers an alternative to the field-as-spectrum by highlighting the importance of relationships among key concepts. The relations through which this model operates make it flexible enough to bring into contact many various praxes, but also reveal how certain relationships may not "unfold on an equal plane" due to power-social relations far larger than the field. To counter both the risk of atomization brought about by the many configurations that the convergence of multiple fields and disciplines may take and the unevenness acknowledged by Klein and Gold as well as many others, the digital humanities needs to operate in a new but still tactical direction. It must turn the field's openness and fluidity—all of its local or specific dimensions—into a function of its institutional global potential.

As I propose, a working strategy to tackle this seemingly contradictory movement between the specific and the interdisciplinary, the local and the global, is the formation of zones of contact among various DH practices. A handful of events and projects have already proposed analogous approaches. Led by Trent Hergenrader, Robert Glick, and others, *Writer Makers: Remixing Digital Humanities and Creative Writing*, for example, sought to bring the fields of digital humanities and creative writing together under the idea of making. The *Global Digital Humanities Symposium* at Michigan State University has provided a forum where leading scholars from East Asia and Africa bring their expertise to the United States. Other initiatives and publications also share a similar ethos. My focus here, however, is aimed at the potential of translation work to create, emphasize, and further shape these zones of contact, particularly, as first articulated by Mary Louise Pratt, those among linguistic–geographic communities. Based on translation work (translation being understood both as movement and as linguistic rendition), these zones of contact are capable of revealing nonobvious relationships between praxes; they also entail a horizontal exchange of referents and nonfixed positions in regard to one another. Fostering parallel relationships among practices and enabling zones of contact, rather than expanding or growing a unitary field, can exert the necessary movement toward a plurality of DH approaches: what I call a DH *ecology of knowledges*.

The notion of an ecology of knowledges was first articulated by the Portuguese scholars Maria Paula Meneses, Joao Arriscado Nunes, and Boaventura de Sousa Santos. Focused on the geopolitics of knowledge production as a means of achieving global social justice, their work seeks to highlight first and foremost the existing parallel between cultural diversity and epistemic diversity. Their proposed "ecology of knowledges" offers a corrective to the monocultural and Eurocentric model of scientific knowledge production. For them, this model of cultural production is the basis of forms of class, ethnic, territorial, racial, or sexual oppression. Although linguistic differences are not incorporated in their model, the dominance of English is a feature of this issue too.

The corrective offered by Meneses, Nunes, and de Sousa Santos relies on an understanding of knowledge production as a social practice, one with the self-reflexive capacity to reshape its motives and engines in consideration of the abundance of existing epistemic models. Their notion of an ecology of knowledges constitutes "an invitation to the promotion of non-relativistic dialogues among knowledges, granting 'equality of opportunities' to the different kinds of knowledges" (xx). This characterization of knowledge heterogeneity resonates with many of the discourses advocating for the openness, diversity, and locality of the digital humanities.[1]

Before discussing how the model of an ecology of knowledges can be more fully mapped onto the field of digital humanities, some aspects of the notion deserve closer examination. First and foremost, in an ecology of knowledges, all knowledges are considered incomplete. This incompleteness entails a recognition of the significance and value of the differences among knowledges and their local bases. It also demands a necessary transition away from a monoculture to a global ecology capable of traversing those differences. Critical to the notion of a global ecology of knowledges is the further acknowledgment that the multiple manifestations of the local are the only path to globality. This recognition, in turn, is dependent on the self-reflexive capacity of knowledge production as a social practice to modify its own operations. It follows that a single hegemonic epistemic model is insufficient to account for the range of work produced under other models of knowledge production, thus preventing the recognition and incorporation of other relevant frames of reference. Hetero-referentiality—the incorporation, recognition, and validation of other knowledge models into the (locally) hegemonic one—is in the Portuguese scholars' view, the foundation for attaining fruitful relationships among a variety of knowledge communities. The model that Meneses, Nunes, and de Sousa Santos propose is therefore capable of enabling the emergence of nonhegemonic knowledges and the syntheses of multiple ones. Ultimately, by enacting the establishment of zones of contact, emerging nonhegemonic knowledges are capable of validating their outputs as parallel to those of the hegemonic model.

The analogy between the ecology of knowledges and the expansion of digital humanities, while imperfect, is useful to explore. The fact that the digital humanities has itself been a field pulling away from singular disciplinary forms of academic work, and has tasked itself with making its practices legible to the many fields it touches, has made it more easily reconfigurable and receptive to the demands constantly being made on it. Several calls to raise the linguistic, geographic, racial, gender, and cultural diversity profile of digital humanities have been lodged just in the past few years. Speaking of her work in India, Padmini Ray Murray has controversially articulated how "your DH is not my DH" (personal correspondence with the author). Through his work curating *AroundDH,* Alex Gil has shown that "a whole world of digital humanities is out there and it does not map neatly to our [U.S.] issues." Additional punctual conceptualizations of locality can be found in Roopika Risam's "DH accents." From a feminist perspective, Tanya Clement has questioned the field's ideals of interdisciplinarity and collaboration as technologies that can unsituate us from particular visions. Looking to the future, Domenico Fiormonte, Teresa Numerico, and Francesca Tomasi argue that "the true innovation of the next decade of DH appears to be its geographic expansion and the consequent enlargement (and deepening) of the cultural problems afforded by the use of technology from a less Western-centric perspective."

All of these critical meditations on various aspects of diversity in digital humanities propose more granular perspectives that can allow us to rethink our practice—an inverse process to what Jamie Skye Bianco identified as "the many under the name of one." Whether they come from a geographical location viewpoint, a sociopolitical one, or an (inter)disciplinary one, these perspectives share the intention of carving out a space for their own work so that it contributes to the general transformation of the field. But acknowledging the presence of these perspectives and the need to engage with them is insufficient. Without the mechanisms to ensure relevant ways for these contributions to be incorporated into the field at large, this work will continue to be lacking from lists of works cited, syllabi, and tables of content, thus hindering the deeper development of digital humanities. Whatever form any new mechanisms may take, they will serve as the indispensable basis for interlinking diverse DH practices with each other, as well as with the already institutionalized version of the broader field. The challenge is to retain the field's global reach while fostering exchanges with local praxes.

Language diversity is an obvious impediment to the establishment of zones of contact and attaining hetero-referentiality. The well-known dominance of English in the field of digital humanities (or of any other scholarly field), while useful in weaving communicative relations, cannot be the unifying condition of the field's globality. Or as Rita Raley has pointedly argued, English cannot be "the condition of possibility for *the very idea of the global*" (emphasis in the original). The role of English as a lingua franca must therefore also be tactical, and along with translation work, the lingua franca status of English is one possible mechanism for forming additional zones of contact. Often thought to be a linguistic issue alone, translation is in fact political: it "presupposes both a non-conformist attitude vis-à-vis the limits of one's knowledge and practice and the readiness to be surprised and learn with the other's knowledge and practice" (de Sousa Santos). Translation is thus a tool capable of revealing complementariness among practices and common

(mis)understandings, as well as, crucially, facilitating the recognition and validation of different knowledge models where needed.

Seen in this way, translation is not an end in itself, but a means through which
the field and its canon can be diversified. For the remainder of this chapter, I focus
on several initiatives in which I have enacted the principles discussed here. The
examples are not exhaustive and necessarily evidence the limits of my own networks
and linguistic competencies, but it is my hope that they will reveal the benefits of
establishing zones of contact.

RedHD in Translation was a "flash" project done during the *Day of DH 2014*.
It consisted of a one-day translation endeavor during which members of the Red
de Humanidades Digitales (Network of Digital Humanities) translated articles and
blog posts originally published in Spanish into a handful of languages, mostly English but also French and Italian. *RedHD in Translation* can be seen as an implementation of translation as both a linguistic endeavor and a tactical move, in that
the translated articles and blog posts were placed in higher-impact venues and platforms, like the popular *Day of DH* project, where they would come into contact with
other linguistic, geographic, and disciplinary communities. The ultimate impact
of *RedHD in Translation* has yet to be seen, as the translated texts progressively
become incorporated (or not) into syllabi and lists of works cited. Regardless, this
collective exercise has already contributed to a growing culture in digital humanities that seeks to facilitate encounters with the work of geographically distributed
communities.

An ongoing initiative of Global Outlook::Digital Humanities, *DH Whisperers,*
seeks to set up ad hoc linguistic zones of contact. First put into practice at the *Digital
Humanities 2014* conference, held in Lausanne, Switzerland, *DH Whisperers* asks
conference participants to voluntarily wear badges signaling their willingness to join
a community of informal translators and indicating the languages they speak or are
able to translate. Although the practice has not been widely implemented, in part
due to a persistent lack of presentations in languages other than English, its potential for impact can already be seen in the community's widespread willingness to
take part in it.[2] Even in its limited implementations, *DH Whisperers* helps underscore how multilingual digital humanities already is—and how it offers a landscape
in which complementary, contrasting, and common concerns and approaches must
come into contact.[3]

As shown by *DH Whisperers*, the formation of zones of contact relies on the
efforts of the extended community. Examples of this work in high-profile projects and publications have also began to emerge. The newest release of the popular
text analysis tool Voyant was made available in eleven languages; the *DH+Lib* blog
continues to publish translated posts; *Digital Humanities Quarterly* edited special
issues in Spanish and French, and an issue in Portuguese is currently being edited.
These three examples contribute to the formation of zones of contact as paths to

accessibility, actual linguistic translation, and opening of canonic fora, respectively. Bringing an influx of global practices and knowledges into the United States was the strategy of the editors of the CLIR report, *Building Expertise to Support Digital Scholarship: A Global Perspective.* The work done by Vivian Lewis, Lisa Spiro, Xuemao Wang, and John E. Cawthorne actively created zones of contact in faraway regions of the world by recognizing the wealth of knowledge that is relevant and should be current in the U.S. academy. All of these efforts, each one with its particular agenda, constitute movements toward the fostering of hetero-referentiality, the formation of zones of contact, and the emergence of a DH ecology of knowledges. These instances underscore how the community's geographic and linguistic diversity has been and continues to be manifested thanks to the work of its own members. Ultimately, in these examples, we see the rich diversity of the field becoming the motive and engine of knowledge production.

In international governing bodies, particularly ADHO, steps have been taken to foster diversity in linguistic terms. In 2016, the annual *Digital Humanities* conference called for proposals in the alliance's five official languages (English, German, Italian, French, and Spanish), plus the local one (Polish). Though this strategy seemed promising, the results were disappointing, as the conference committee included in the final program fewer than twenty presentations in languages other than English from the more than three hundred contributions (Thaller). This discouraging response mimics those seen in past conferences (Grandjean). The field's governing bodies must therefore devise other strategies for fostering zones of contact. These should entail linguistic translation as a matter of course, but they should also seek to put into practice a more conceptual translation that places other aspects of diversity in contact with one another. Greater emphasis on local culture and praxes at the annual conference can translate the uniqueness of the work done in the circulating locations and amplify nonobvious intersections between the various communities that converge there. *Digital Humanities 2017,* in Montreal, was the first officially bilingual conference in French and English. Holding a bilingual DH conference sets a precedent that now seems impossible to disregard and was even more necessary and advantageous in 2018 when the conference was held in Mexico City, the largest Spanish-speaking city in the world. In addition to language-specific approaches, the opportunities offered to DH practitioners in that setting intersected with the long-standing traditions of digital arts and hacker communities in Latin America, as well as with indigenous cultures, histories of colonialism, and current neoliberal human and economic crises. Analogous connections between digital humanities and local contexts exist, and we should make the most of them at any locale where the conference is held.

Miriam Posner has cogently argued that "DH needs scholarly expertise in critical race theory, feminist and queer theory, and other interrogations of structures of power in order to develop models of the world that have any relevance to people's lived experience." A DH ecology of knowledges, based on the formation of zones of contact like those I propose here, holds the potential to develop one such model. Nonlinguistic translation work opens up the possibility of grasping the common theoretical and practical concerns and how they affect DH work in various contexts, geographical and disciplinary, resulting in a fuller understanding of, for example, why some communities might be (un)enthusiastic about digital cultural production or digital scholarship, or why DH centers or laboratories may or may not flourish in certain institutions due to the responsibilities owed to large student populations, the politicization of academic work, and even the cost of computing equipment often tied to currency exchange rates (Álvarez Sánchez and Peña Pimentel).

As seen from the examples of projects and publications that already foster the formation of zones of contact, the process of creating horizontal platforms, and thus hetero-referentiality, (including, but not limited to publications, face-to-face meetings, and collaborative projects) in digital humanities is underway. These efforts still need to become the rule rather than the exception. Put another way, the field's openness and fluidity must become a function of its institutional capacity. The formation of zones of contact must take place in and through existing institutional infrastructures, channels, conferences, publications, and governing bodies. A scenario, like the prevailing one, in which individual communities are responsible for making themselves legible to others, rather than being supported by a structure that actively seeks to place communities in contact with each other, risks homogenizing the differences in the field that require the most highlighting. A truly global digital humanities must see a lateral redistribution of its available venues, forums, and audiences—a movement of work that can traverse diverse contexts and help establish a global ecology of knowledges.

NOTES

1. Domenico Fiormonte, "Towards a Cultural Critique of the Digital Humanities;" Roopika Risam, "Beyond the Margins: Intersectionality and the Digital Humanities;" Alex Gil, "The (Digital) Library of Babel."

2. A detailed discussion of the implementation of *DH Whisperers* during *Digital Humanities 2014* can be found in Ortega ("Whispering/Translation during DH2014").

3. *DH Whisperers* has since become the *Translation Toolkit*. Its main goal is to foster translation as a community praxis in the field. The toolkit is available at http://go-dh .github.io/translation-toolkit/ and a detailed description of the project's motivations and goals are published in *DH Commons* as Ortega and Gil ("Project Statement").

BIBLIOGRAPHY

Álvarez Sánchez, Adriana, and Miriam Peña Pimentel. "DH for History Students: A Case Study at the Facultad de Filosofía Y Letras (National Autonomous University of

Mexico)." *Digital Humanities Quarterly* 11, no. 3 (2017), http://www.digitalhuman ities.org/dhq/vol/11/3/000312/000312.html.

Bianco, Jamie "Skye." "This Digital Humanities which Is Not One." In *Debates in the Digital Humanities*, edited by Matthew K. Gold, 96–112. Minneapolis: University of Minnesota Press.

Clement, Tanya. "An Information Science Question in DH Feminism." *Digital Humanities Quarterly* 9, no. 2 (2015), http://www.digitalhumanities.org/dhq/vol/9/2/000186/000186 .html.

Dacos, Marin. "La Stratégie Du Sauna Finlandais." Blogo Numericus. July 5, 2013, http:// bn.hypotheses.org/11138.

De Sousa Santos, Boaventura. "The Future of the World Social Forum: The Work of Trans-lation." *Development* 48, no. 2 (2005): 15–22.

Earheart, Amy. *Traces of the Old: Uses of the New: The Emergence of Digital Literary Stud-ies*. Ann Arbor: University of Michigan Press, 2015.

Fiormonte, Domenico. "Towards a Cultural Critique of the Digital Humanities." *Historical Social Research* 37, no. 3 (2012): 59–76.

Fiormonte, Domenico, Teresa Numerico, and Francesca Tomasi. *The Digital Humanist: A Critical Inquiry*. Brooklyn, NY: punctum books, 2015.

Galina Russell, Isabel. "Geographical and Linguistic Diversity in the Digital Humanities." *Digital Scholarship in the Humanities* 29, no. 3 (2014): 307–16.

Gil, Alex. "The (Digital) Library of Babel." http://www.elotroalex.com/digital-library-babel/.

Gil, Alex. "A Non-Peer-Reviewed Review of a Peer-Reviewed Essay by Adeline Koh." April 20, 2015, http://elotroalex.webfactional.com/a-non-peer-reviewed-review-of -a-peer-reviewed-essay-by-adeline-koh/.

Grandjean, Martin. "Le Rêve Du Multilinguisme Dans La Science: L'exemple (mal-heureux) Du Colloque #DH2014." June 27 2014, http://www.martingrandjean.ch /multilinguisme-dans-la-science-dh2014/.

Kirschenbaum, Matthew. "Digital Humanities As/Is a Tactical Term." In *Debates in the Digital Humanities,* edited by Matthew K. Gold. Minneapolis: University of Minne-sota Press, 2012. http://dhdebates.gc.cuny.edu/debates/text/48.

Kirschenbaum, Matthew. "What Is 'Digital Humanities,' and Why Are They Saying Such Terrible Things about It?" *Differences* 25, no. 1 (2014): 46–63.

Klein, Lauren, and Matthew Gold. "Digital Humanities: The Expanded Field." *Debates in the Digital Humanities 2016*. Minneapolis: University of Minnesota Press, 2016. http://dhdebates.gc.cuny.edu/debates/2.

Lewis, Vivian, Lisa Spiro, Xuemao Wang, and John E. Cawthorne, et al. *Building Expertise to Support Digital Scholarship: A Global Perspective*. Washington, D.C.: Council on Library and Information Resources, 2015. http://www.clir.org/pubs/reports/pub168.

Meneses, Maria Paula, João Arriscado Nunes, and Boaventura de Sousa Santos. "Opening Up the Canon of Knowledge and Recognition of Difference." In *Another Knowledge Is Possible: Beyond Northern Epistemologies*, edited by Boaventura de Sousa Santos, xix–xvix. London: Verso. 2007.

Ortega, Élika. "Whispering/Translation during DH2014: Five Things We Learned." July 21, 2014, http://elikaortega.net/2014/07/21/dhwhisperer/.

Ortega, Élika, Isabel Galina, and Ernesto Priani. *RedHD in Translation*. April 8, 2014, http://dayofdh2014.matrix.msu.edu/redhd/.

Ortega, Élika, and Alex Gil. "Project Statement: GO::DH Translation Toolkit." DH Commons. October 2016, http://dhcommons.org/journal/2016/godh-translation-toolkit/.

Posner, Miriam. "What's Next: The Radical, Unrealized Potential of Digital Humanities." July 27, 2015, http://miriamposner.com/blog/whats-next-the-radical-unrealized -potential-of-digital-humanities/.

Pratt, Mary Louise. "Arts of the Contact Zone." *Profession* (1991): 33–40.

Raley, Rita. "On Global English and the Transmutation of Postcolonial Studies into 'Literature in English.'" *Diaspora: A Journal of Translational Studies* 8, no. 1 (1999): 51–80.

Risam, Roopika. "Across Two (Imperial) Cultures." May 31, 2015, http://roopikarisam .com/uncategorized/across-two-imperial-cultures-2/.

Risam, Roopika. "Beyond the Margins: Intersectionality and the Digital Humanities." *Digital Humanities Quarterly* 9, no. 2 (2015). http://www.digitalhumanities.org /dhq/vol/9/2/000208/000208.html.

Thaller, Manfred. "Report on Experiences for DH2016 @ Krakow." 2016.

Wernimont, Jacqueline. "Ferocious Generosity." November 13, 2015, https://jwernimont .wordpress.com/2015/11/13/ferocious-generosity/-generosity/.

The Digital Humanities and "Critical Theory": An Institutional Cautionary Tale

JOHN HUNTER

Although often criticized for its "presentism," the digital humanities have actually generated several worthwhile historicizing accounts of its practices and of computing technology's use in humanistic scholarship (see Earhart; Nyhan, Flinn, and Welsh; and Vanhoutte). These accounts each present a diachronic narrative of how a few pioneers brought technology into humanistic practice in the 1940s and how these practices have expanded and become more self-conscious ever since. What is left out of such accounts is DH's relationship to other movements in the humanities academy over the same time period, and this has not gone unnoticed: Tom Eyers (a philosopher) justifiably "challenge[s] the model of scientific rationality underpinning much that falls under the banner of the digital humanities" and reminds the field that it cannot simply disavow the problems of earlier humanist debates; Alan Liu notes that, in comparison with new media studies, digital humanities is "noticeably missing in action on the cultural-critical scene," and he draws attention to the far greater theoretical sophistication of digital artists and activists (491). Despite these critiques, the assumption that digital tool use somehow inoculates digital humanities from other scholarly debates still lingers.

This chapter argues for a version of the history of digital humanities that deemphasizes its uniqueness among humanistic discourses; in particular, it analyzes how (in its institutional reception to this point) the digital humanities bears a striking similarity to poststructuralist theory, which arrived in North America with Jacques Derrida's famous presentation at Johns Hopkins University in 1966 and which was pronounced dead as an institutional (not intellectual) force in a flurry of books with titles like *After Theory* and *Theory's Empire: An Anthology of Dissent* in the period 2000–2005 (for an excellent summary, see Elliott and Attridge's "Introduction: Theory's Nine Lives" in their *Theory after 'Theory'*).

In its capacity to attract financial resources, student interest, a patina of innovative "cool," as well as hostility from those who feel left behind, the digital humanities almost eerily mirrors the rise of its discursive predecessor. Its task now is to avoid mirroring poststructuralism's institutional demise, and for a very specific reason: digital technology will endure and evolve with or without digital humanities, just as critiques of objectivity have outlasted poststructuralist theory.[1] Indeed, the critiques formulated through digital humanities will only become more imperative as the uses of digital technology continue to grow. Many people today are facile users of digital tools, but a properly critical digital humanities can make them reflect on the implications of this use for the transmission, consumption, analysis, and storage of knowledge. Almost everyone on the planet uses Google to search the internet, for example, but critical DH scholars such as Safiya Umoja Noble can reveal the gendered and racial biases inherent in this omnipresent information tool (see, for example, her "Google Search: Hyper-Visibility as a Means of Rendering Black Women and Girls Invisible"). This unique combination of technical/programming practice and critical reflection on that practice could easily be lost in an academy that no longer includes the digital humanities.

Like the histories of digital humanities mentioned earlier, most historical accounts of poststructuralist theory focus much more on the intellectual transformations within the movement than on messy institutional realities such as raising funds, establishing programs, and training graduate students (Habib; Leitch). The chronology of its institutional life is uncontroversial: there was an outburst of influential theorizing between 1966 and 1980, from Derrida's initiation of deconstruction in three books published in 1967, Barthes's "Death of the Author" (1967), the English translation of Foucault's *Order of Things* (1970), through to Paul de Man's *Allegories of Reading* (1982). This was followed by fifteen to twenty years of institutional entrenchment—academic jobs for "critical theorists" appeared, academic presses began monograph series, undergraduate courses became common—and intellectual ferment, notably the development of so-called identity politics around gender, sexuality, and postcolonialism (Eagleton, 1–74). By the turn of the millennium, though, there were signs of critical theory's decline. Prominent books began to appear with titles such as *Life. After. Theory* and *After Theory* (both 2003) and (the more hopeful) *Theory after 'Theory'* (2011). The percentage of MLA job advertisements featuring the term "literary theory" fell off markedly after 2008, and even before then it moved from being a primary to a secondary requirement (typically, one of several).[2]

Poststructuralist theory's institutional prestige and presence must here be separated from its intellectual importance and persistence (both of which are inarguable). There is, however, a common sleight of hand performed in discussions of this narrative, in which the *institutional* "death of theory" is proposed as a regrettable commonplace and then refuted by appeals to its *intellectual* persistence in contemporary theoretical debates. Thus, Elliott and Attridge can state that "there is little disagreement that the era of theory's dominance has passed," but also that it is "undergoing transformations far more radical" and is "not only subsequent to but also distinct from the body of work once known as 'Theory'" (1–3). In this account, the term "theory" starts as a fallen, once-mighty institutional force, but it is then rejuvenated by its metamorphosis into something new that is just as intellectually fruitful; the enormously diminished institutional presence of this new work is, however, passed over in silence. Poststructuralism's intellectual influence is fundamental to vital contemporary humanistic fields such as bioethics (in, for example, Eugene Thacker's fundamental reassessment of what it means to be alive in *After Life*) and the related field of posthumanism (in which poststructuralism's theoretical decentering of the thinking subject is applied in material and digital contexts).[3] Neither, however, is likely to produce required courses for philosophy or literature degrees, as was the case with "theory" in the 1990s. As I argue later, an analogous transformation in DH's institutional presence would greatly impoverish both the academy and the audiences it serves.

In its early days, humanities computing commonly positioned itself alongside other humanities discourses. In 1992, for example, George P. Landow published his path-breaking book *Hypertext* with the subtitle *The Convergence of Contemporary Critical Theory and Technology*. In it, Landow skillfully used critical theory as a familiar set of guideposts with which to lead readers into the new and unfamiliar terrain of hypertext. By the time he published *Hypertext 3.0* in 2006, however, digital humanities existed as a self-conscious academic entity, and (not coincidentally) the presence of "critical theory" in the volume had dwindled precipitously and been replaced with born-digital theoretical discussions that had at best attenuated relationships with figures such as Derrida, Foucault, Kristeva, et al. Landow's decision to decouple his analysis of hypertext from critical theory is not a slight against the latter, but a recognition of the historical fact that the digital humanities developed outside and apart from the concerns of critical theory; rightly or wrongly, and with no conscious programmatic intent, the digital humanities was institutionally positioned as an entity apart from critical theory, rather than as an inheritor of it. Landow's assumption that the terms of critical theory could be used as a vocabulary for any new humanistic intellectual field in the first edition of *Hypertext* could not and did not overcome the assumption that the digital humanities was just too different. Nor did the critical theorists lament this separation: not one of the "post theory" collections mentioned earlier even mentions digital humanities, much less discusses it.[4] For poststructuralist theory's inheritors, the digital humanities is a comet from another solar system, with no connection to their concerns at all. The glaring absence of theoretical self-consciousness that Eyers and Liu criticized earlier in this chapter thus resulted not from a conscious decision by early DH practitioners, but from a near-complete lack of engagement on both sides.

This unnecessary separation impoverishes both digital humanities and the humanities in general, a point trenchantly made by Liu, and it must not lead the DH community into allowing its mission to be co-opted or blunted. Scholars such as Todd Presner have eloquently argued for the intellectual need to maintain an alliance between the digital humanities and the "transformative social praxis of critical theory" (66), but what about DH's institutional relationship to theory? The digital humanities is currently a locus of institutional and cultural prestige and excitement (for all of its claims to beleaguered marginality), but nothing can make it immune to the kind of cultural, economic, and political forces that both helped generate poststructuralist theory and ensured its transformation. Cultural contexts for the academy will change, and in ways that are completely opaque to us now. When the day comes that the digital humanities starts to look shopworn and outmoded as an institutional formation (and this day WILL come), its combination of critical reflection and innovative digital practice must not be lost with it. This synthesis needs to be established as a fundamental part of the humanities, and not one option among others. To that end, I have two major suggestions.

The first is to recognize that the ongoing proliferation of digital tools, devices, and networks in our culture in no way guarantees the continuation of the digital humanities as a meaningful institutional presence (Burdick et al., 102–4). The importance of poststructuralism's critique of Western assumptions about truth, language, and discursive power was not enough to save it as an institutional presence, and the digital humanities is no different in this respect. The humanities are always grounded in an evolving set of theoretical assumptions about their procedures, but this grounding does not mean that the current set of assumptions are necessarily critically studied or taught. A "theory" course is now only an option in many humanities majors, and even graduate degrees can be obtained without any sustained reflection on the theoretical assumptions that underpin them. The digital humanities faces a similar problem in the academy at large: writing as long ago as 2005, Jerome McGann warned that "digital illiteracy" among humanities scholars threatened their ability to take a leading scholarly role as "the entirety of our cultural inheritance [is] . . . transformed and re-edited in digital forms" (111). His very prescient implication here is that humanities scholars will not have a guaranteed seat at the table as Google, Apple, Amazon, et al. redraw the conditions of knowledge for the world. Precisely because digital technology's increasing presence is a reality of daily life, scholars will have to fight for the ongoing academic presence of DH's combination of criticism and praxis in whatever new forms it needs to take. It must be an integral part of what the humanities are, because digital technologies will (more and more) control what we can know and how we can know it.

Second, we need to pay very close attention to the broader institutional changes in higher education. The list of the "revolutionary" information technologies that did *not* fundamentally change university teaching methods is a long one and includes printing, telegraphy, radio, moving pictures, and television. All the signs are, however, that the digital revolution will finally break the tyranny of the sage-on-the-stage model of higher education and allow it to diversify. At these moments, we need to act on Johanna Drucker's trenchant reminder that "we were humanists before we were digital" and that the humanistic project of critique need not be mere empty posturing, Indeed, it is one of the most vital activities that humanists perform, analyzing and evaluating the protean movements of culture. Separating this critical task from the making/programming/hacking that the digital humanities embodies will only hasten its institutional demise as an academic field and leave it feeling as undervalued as many other humanists do today. It may well be true that in the future the academy (especially in the digital humanities) will become more integrated with other cultural institutions, such as museums or digital archives, or, at least, more open to collaboration with them. For the present, however, it is easy to see how DH's digital skills might be co-opted for a corporatist agenda. Even the advocacy group 4humanities.org justifies a humanities education by producing infographics with titles like "We are Valuable" in which the "value" is purely monetary.[5] This is perfectly understandable given how reluctant parents are to pay for a humanities degree today. But digital humanities needs to justify its critical worth, as well as its earnings potential.

Clearly, more theoretical work is needed alongside the ongoing evolution of DH's programming and digital tool use. One additional conclusion is clear: the digital humanities has thus far followed a similar institutional path to that of poststructuralist theory, but it is now time to diverge from it. The present cultural and technological moment has secured the digital humanities as a core element of the humanities, not a temporary efflorescence. The field will certainly reconfigure, but it cannot be allowed to dissipate.

NOTES

1. In *Digital Humanities,* Anne Burdick and Johanna Drucker make a similar point: "As digital tools become naturalized, the digital humanities will struggle to retain its critical, experimental character" (103).

2. See Goodwin, whose graph of requests for "literary theory" in MLA job listings shows steady growth after 1974, a peak in 1988, and a steep drop-off after 2008. Leitch makes the important point that after 2000, "literary theory" is almost always a secondary requirement (125–26).

3. See Wolfe and Hayles for good introductions to this field.

4. Not even Simons in his otherwise wide-ranging collection.

5. See http://4humanities.org/2016/09/we-are-valuable-an-infographic-by-ny6-fellows-lin-and-tucker/we-are-valuable-2/.

BIBLIOGRAPHY

Burdick, Anne, Johanna Drucker, Peter Lunenfeld, Todd Presner, and Jeffrey Schnapp, eds. *Digital Humanities.* Cambridge, Mass.: MIT Press, 2012.

Drucker, Johanna. "We Were Humanists before We Were Digital." Lecture at Bucknell
    University, March 31, 2015.

Eagleton, Terry. *After Theory*. London: Allen Lane, 2003.

Earhart, Amy E. *Traces of the Old, Uses of the New: The Emergence of Digital Literary
    Studies*. Ann Arbor: University of Michigan Press, 2015.

Elliott, Jane, and Derek Attridge, eds. *Theory after 'Theory.'* Abingdon, UK: Routledge, 2010.

Eyers, Tom. "The Perils of the 'Digital Humanities': New Positivisms and the Fate of Lit-
    erary Theory." *Postmodern Culture* 23, no. 2 (2013), http://muse.jhu.edu/journals
    /postmodern_culture/v023/23.2.eyers.html.

Gilmour, Alexander. "Tech City UK's Chief on Britain's Digital Ambitions." *Financial
    Times*, December 5, 2014, http://www.ft.com/cms/s/0/7dc5250c-76f7–11e4–8273
    –00144feabdc0.html.

Goodwin, Jonathan. "Some Notes on the MLA Jobs Information List." January 28, 2014,
    http://jgoodwin.net/blog/mla-job-information-list/.

Habib, M. A. R. *Modern Literary Criticism and Theory: A History*. Oxford: Blackwell, 2008.

Hayles, N. Katherine. *How We Became Posthuman: Virtual Bodies in Cybernetics, Litera-
    ture, and Informatics*. Chicago: University of Chicago Press, 1999.

Landow, George P. *Hypertext: The Convergence of Contemporary Critical Theory and Tech-
    nology*. Baltimore: Johns Hopkins University Press, 1992.

Landow, George P. *Hypertext 3.0: Critical Theory and New Media in an Era of Globaliza-
    tion*. Baltimore: Johns Hopkins University Press, 2006.

Leitch, Vincent B. "Theory Ends." *Profession* (2005): 122–28.

Liu, Alan. "Where is Cultural Criticism in the Digital Humanities?" In *Debates in the
    Digital Humanities*, edited by Matthew K. Gold, 490–510. Minneapolis: University
    of Minnesota Press, 2012.

McGann, Jerome. "Information Technology and the Troubled Humanities." *TEXT Tech-
    nology* 14, no. 2 (2005): 105–21.

Noble, Safiya Umoja. "Google Search: Hyper-Visibility as a Means of Rendering Black
    Women and Girls Invisible." *InVisible Culture* 19 (Fall 2013), http://ivc.lib.roches
    ter.edu/google-search-hyper-visibility-as-a-means-of-rendering-black-women-and
    -girls-invisible/.

Nyhan, J. "What Can Modern-Day Digital Humanities Learn from Studying Its Past? Some
    Recommendations and Suggestions." *Proceedings CIDE.16: Dispositifs numériques:
    contenus, interactivité et visualisation*. 2013.

Nyhan, Julianne, Andrew Flinn, and Anne Welsh. "Oral History and the Hidden Histories
    Project: Towards Histories of Computing in the Humanities." *Digital Scholarship in
    the Humanities* 30, no. 1 (2015): 71–85.

Payne, Michael and John Schad, eds. *Life. After. Theory*. London: Continuum, 2003.

Presner, Todd. "Critical Theory and the Mangle of Digital Humanities." In *Between
    Humanities and the Digital*, edited by Patrik Svensson and David Theo Goldberg.
    55–69. Cambridge, Mass.: MIT Press, 2015.

Simons, Jon, ed. *From Agamben to Žižek—Contemporary Critical Theorists.* Edinburgh: Edinburgh University Press, 2010.

Thacker, Eugene. *After Life.* Chicago: University of Chicago Press, 2010.

Vanhoutte, Edward. "The Gates of Hell: History and Definition of Digital Humanities." In *Defining Digital Humanities: A Reader,* edited by Melissa Terras, Julianne Nyhan, and Edward Vanhoutte, 119–50. Farnham, UK: Ashgate Publishing, 2013.

Wolfe, Cary. *What Is Posthumanism?* Minneapolis: University of Minnesota Press, 2009.

The Elusive Digital / Critical Synthesis

SETH LONG AND JAMES BAKER

In the first edition of *Debates in the Digital Humanities,* Alan Liu argued that digital humanists risk losing a seat at the "table of debate" if they continue to emphasize tools and databases to the exclusion of cultural criticism. Digital humanists, Liu wrote, must learn to "move seamlessly between text analysis and cultural analysis" if they are not to become a service industry to the humanities, providing tools and data for other scholars but not contributing to key debates. Not long afterward, the expression "hacking and yacking" emerged as another iteration of the difference between cultural critique and tool- and data-centric research. In 2014, Bethany Nowviskie tried to put the expression to rest, noting that the digital humanities has plenty of room for both hacking and yacking ("On the Origin"). Roopika Risam has likewise expressed optimism about "transcending" the "simplistic hack/yack binary." The field continues to seem optimistic about the compatibility of digital methods and cultural criticism. Liu's challenge is being met.

Taking a contrary stance, we want to argue that hacking and yacking are not as easily compatible as some have claimed. Digital and critical work are not incommensurable, but they do denote two different sets of practices. In our view, many critical DH projects give a perfunctory nod to one method of work while devoting the majority of intellectual labor to the other. They struggle toward a synthesis of these different modes of research and inquiry, though ideally a critical DH project will meet the requirements of the digital and the critical in equal measure. We want to remind the field how difficult it is to achieve the digital/critical synthesis. Liu's challenge is a more wicked problem than we want to admit, particularly in the context of computational work.

To pinpoint where we think the problem lies, consider the typical workflow of a computational DH project: data collection, tagging, and organization; computational analysis of data; interpretation of results. We suggest that the second and third steps, computation and interpretation, are the ones not easily synthesized with a critical approach but that the first step—data collection and management—is more amenable to cultural criticism. At the end of this chapter, we explain our optimistic take on this initial stage of research, but first we want to explore the difficulty of maintaining a critical stance when one enters the computation and interpretation stages.

One obstacle in these stages is a tension between the critique of structure and the discovery or use of structure. As Liu notes, cultural criticism accepts the structural nature of human existence along lines of class and identity, but it does so as a means of questioning the utility and/or ontological status of those structuring categories. Cultural criticism recognizes structure as a pretext to argue that our structuring categories result not from natural but contingent social conditions that may be altered to produce better social structures. Categories, structures, patterns: for the cultural critic, these are to be questioned, critiqued, speculatively reimagined. In contrast, when working at a command line, categories, structures, and patterns are to be used or discovered. For example, ethnicity and gender may be socially conditioned and thus fluid, but the researcher studying their effects on cultural production must treat both as finite and discrete. Even an unsupervised algorithm such as a topic model needs to be told how many discrete topics to look for. To some extent, math forces one to assume discreteness over fluidity.

Another obstacle—one related to analysis—involves how digital humanists versus cultural critics treat gaps in data. The former recognize the reality of gaps—as, for example, Lauren Klein recognizes the gaps in Thomas Jefferson's letters—but proceed to compute and construct knowledge despite those gaps. The latter, in contrast, take as their core project a discussion of the problematic ethics of constructing knowledge from data with racialized or gendered gaps. Indeed, for some critics, creating knowledge from data in which marginal identities are absent will reproduce unequal power dynamics, no matter what are the intentions of the researcher (see, for example, Wyse's critique of white sociology, 15–33).

A third problem and perhaps the largest one facing a digital/critical synthesis is that, in computational work, one's results are necessarily open to more than one explanation. To clarify what we mean, consider the traditional style of cultural critique. Grounded in a writer's ethos, it undertakes an inquiry that so deftly combines evidence (often close readings) and interpretation that it is not always clear where evidence ends and interpretation begins. Cultural criticism is a rhetorical as much as a "factual" endeavor. Computational work, in contrast, clearly separates data, methods, and interpretation. Data are analyzed, and then the results are interpreted. Due to this strict separation of evidence and argument, of analysis and interpretation, computational work facilitates a culture of multiple explanations and methodological fine-tuning; this is why data-driven debates often devolve into debates about formulas and parameters. As the social and natural sciences demonstrate, computational results rarely foreclose all but a single explanation. As an example, consider the humorous coordinate axis whose points have been plotted to look like a duck in one direction and a rabbit in another. The data are the data; their interpretation is up to the viewer. Thus any project that separates categorical results from their interpretation will struggle to spotlight only and necessarily a progressive social critique. Critique occurs in interpretation, so when working with computational results, a critical interpretation will rarely be the only possible one.

Despite this tension between critical and digital work, many scholars have offered examples of their successful syntheses. For example, Ted Underwood's work on gender in fiction has been highlighted as an example of a digital/critical synthesis (Spahr et al., "Beyond Resistance"). Using a logistic regression, Underwood finds that between 1800 and 1989, the words associated with male versus female characters in fiction became more volatile over time: the more contemporary the textual data, the more difficult it is for a regression model to predict whether a set of words is being applied to a male or a female. "Gender," Underwood concludes, "is not at all the same thing in 1980 that it was in 1840."

The social critic could certainly use Underwood's data to make an argument about gendered power dynamics or the social construction of gender. But Underwood makes neither move. First, he notes that despite the trend away from sharply gendered terms, there remain important countertrends; for example, physical descriptions emerge as salient aspects of gender distinction in the twentieth century. Second, he frames "fluidity" not as a critical lens but as a problem of statistical gradation that computational methods can help solve: "There's nothing very novel about the discovery that gender is fluid. But of course, we like to say everything is fluid: genres, roles, geographies. The advantage of a comparative method is that it lets us say specifically what we mean. Fluid compared to what?"

Is this methodological framing the same thing as cultural criticism? Just because a DH project utilizes gender as a category, is it by default a critical DH project? In line with our preceding discussion, there seem to be a few reasons why it is not.

First, though one could use Underwood's data in a project about the fluidity of gender, such arguments would necessarily be subsequent to the logistic regression, which treats male and female not as social categories but as a 0 and a 1 with equal weight. Because the critical reading of the results would follow the computation of the results, it is not clear in what way the computational work itself is "critical," given that its results do not support only and necessarily a critical reading. The results could be used to support gender essentialism as easily as gender fluidity (e.g., gender differentiation in fiction does not disappear, but just surfaces along a new terminological axis). As we noted, it is not easy to fuse a social critique with a methodology that separates results from interpretation. Indeed, the messiness of interpretation and algorithmic parameter tweaking are the price one pays when adopting structural methods, and it is unclear how one balances this messy uncertainty with the conviction of cultural (especially activist) critique. (In their essay on the whiteness of MFA programs, "The Program Era," Juliana Spahr and Stephanie Young attempt that balance, but tellingly voice their frustration with it in their concluding paragraph.)

Second, in terms of knowledge construction, Underwood is not asking the questions about power dynamics that Adeline Koh and others involved in the #TransformDH collective posit as key for critical DH work. For these scholars, technology, its uses, and data collection and methodology selection should be submitted to a critique informed by the lenses of race, gender, and sexuality, so that when we sit down to the command line, we do so with activist as well as academic goals in mind (Lothian). A researcher may study the stylistics of gender with a logistic regression, but unless she incorporates issues of gendered power into the project, she is not involved in a critical DH project. It is not clear if Underwood's research—a history of the stylistics of gender—is critical in the sense deployed by these scholars. Indeed, a strike against assuming so is that Underwood adopts a binary notion of gender as an explanatory set. In line with the activist goals championed by Koh and Lothian, a critic might ask why he used a binary logistic regression rather than a multinomial logistic regression, leaving a third option for "other," which might have moved his project in a critical direction (even here, however, one would be subsuming the notion of gender nondiscreteness under a single discrete category).

In our view, Underwood's project demonstrates not the ease but rather the elusiveness of a digital/critical synthesis. Alan Liu points to Franco Moretti's work as another example of digital/critical synthesis, but both Moretti's detractors (Prendergast; Allington, Brouillette, and Golumbia) and Moretti himself (155–58) would question that claim.

The digital humanities *qua* criticism is difficult. In our view, the best strategy is to admit that hacking and yacking are different activities. One relies on structures and categories, and the other critiques them. But there is nothing wrong with difference. Simply let the two modes of work exist, not in opposition, but in dialectical tension. Allow computational and critical practices to remain separate, but throw them together in projects in which neither takes precedence. Perhaps more than digital/critical synthesis, what the digital humanities needs is a new style of research writing that revels in the play of competing methodological and epistemological emphases.

Despite our skepticism about the ease with which computational and critical work might be merged, we nevertheless want to conclude on an optimistic note. Recall the DH workflow with which we began the chapter: data collection, tagging, and organization; computational analysis of data; interpretation of results. Although we have argued that computation and interpretation pose problems for a digital/critical synthesis, the collection, labeling, and organization of data at the beginning of a project are much more amenable to critical insight. It is here, in the initial stages of a project, that a researcher might return absent identities to the data, as well as label or structure data in a manner informed by previously marginalized knowledge bases—perhaps by inviting members of marginalized communities to participate in the structuring of the data before its analysis. Doing so may or may not affect one's analysis or the range of interpretations it allows, but it will at least partially address the critical points regarding marginalization and power. Indeed, Koh's critical questions seem mainly targeted to this initial stage of research: "Which agents do we give agency to in a project and why? Who are the voices that are allowed to speak, and who are heard?" Perhaps then it is in deciding what data to use and how to structure them that the epistemological and the activist concerns of critique might be enacted.

BIBLIOGRAPHY

Allington, Daniel, Sarah Brouillette, and David Golumbia. "Neoliberal Tools (and Archives): A Political History of Digital Humanities." *Los Angeles Review of Books,* May 1, 2016, https://lareviewofbooks.org/article/neoliberal-tools-archives-political-history-digital-humanities/.

Klein, Lauren F. "The Image of Absence: Archival Silence, Data Visualization, and James Hemings." *American Literature* 85, no. 4 (2013): 661–68.

Koh, Adeline. "Preliminary Thoughts on the Joining of Hack and Yack." https://web.archive.org/web/20150225102621/http://www.adelinekoh.org/blog/2014/01/07/preliminary-thoughts-on-the-joining-of-hack-and-yack/.

Liu, Alan. "Where is Cultural Criticism in the Digital Humanities?" *Debates in the Digital Humanities,* edited by Matthew K. Gold. Minneapolis: University of Minnesota Press, 2012. http://dhdebates.gc.cuny.edu/debates/text/20.

Lothian, Alexis. "Marked Bodies, Transformative Scholarship, and the Question of Theory in the Digital Humanities." *Journal of Digital Humanities* 1, no. 1 (2011), http://journalofdigitalhumanities.org/1-1/marked-bodies-transformative-scholarship-and-the-question-of-theory-in-digital-humanities-by-alexis-lothian/.

Marino, Mark C. "Field Report for Critical Code Studies, 2014." Computational Culture. http://computationalculture.net/field-report-for-critical-code-studies-2014%E2%80%A8/.

Moretti, Franco. *Distant Reading.* New York: Verso, 2014.

Nowviskie, Bethany. "On the Origin of 'Hack' and 'Yack.'" January 8, 2014, http://nowviskie.org/2014/on-the-origin-of-hack-and-yack/.

Prendergast, Christopher. "Evolution and Literary History." *New Left Review* 34 (July–August 2005).

Risam, Roopika. "Beyond the Margins: Intersectionality and the Digital Humanities." *Digital Humanities Quarterly* 9, no. 2, http://www.digitalhumanities.org/dhq/vol/9/2/000208/000208.html.

Spahr, Juliana, Richard So, and Andrew Piper. "Beyond Resistance: Towards a Future History of Digital Humanities." *Los Angeles Review of Books*, May 11, 2016, https://lareviewofbooks.org/article/beyond-resistance-towards-future-history-digital-humanities/.

Spahr, Juliana, and Stephanie Young. "The Program Era and the Mainly White Room." *Los Angeles Review of Books,* September 20, 2015, https://lareviewofbooks.org/article/the-program-era-and-the-mainly-white-room/.

Underwood, Ted. "The Instability of Gender." The Stone and the Shell. January 9, 2016, https://tedunderwood.com/2016/01/09/the-instability-of-gender/.

Wyse, Jennifer Padilla. "Black Sociology: The Sociology of Knowledge, Racialized Power Relations of Knowledge and Humanistic Liberation." In *Ashgate Research Companion to Black Sociology*, edited by Early Wright II and Edward V. Wallace, 15–33. New York: Routledge, 2016.

The Archive after Theory

MEGAN WARD WITH ADRIAN S. WISNICKI

The digital archive is a reactive entity, one that attempts to account for its own authorizing logic in ways that make it theoretically, not just technologically, separate from earlier physical archives. This is in part because the first digital archives emerged in the midst of the archival theory of the 1990s and 2000s.[1] Many of the earliest digital archives were created with the understanding that archives are political, interpretive tools.[2] But postcolonial digital archives in particular—both those that date to that era and those developed in the present—manifest a double awareness of this reactivity. In addition to the theoretical and technological strictures of the archive, the postcolonial digital archive is haunted by its historical predecessor, the imperial archive, that which embodies "a fantasy of knowledge collected and united in the service of state and Empire" (Richards 6). The postcolonial digital archive thus critiques its relationship to imperial culture by acknowledging its rootedness in imperial and colonial pasts. At the same time, it engages with postcolonial and archival theories to reinterpret the imperial and colonial ideologies embedded in the archive's primary materials, both through digital remediation and critical frameworks.

Historically and hermeneutically, this is the archive after theory. This phrase is deliberately provocative. There is no "after" theory, of course, nor is there a singular, capital-T theory to come after. Instead, the phrase gestures toward a historical and interpretive condition, one that offers us a timely opportunity: What do we see when we are confronted with the digital result of our postcolonial and archival theories? Might these newly formed archives preserve the past differently in order to imagine new futures? While postcolonial digital collections continue to grapple with both ethical and technical challenges, the archive after theory nonetheless exemplifies how building can come together with humanistic critique to imagine new archival forms.[3] Postcolonial digital archives have tended toward an ethos of repair, wherein scholars using theoretically informed digital tools and platforms attempt to redress the harm of imperialism and colonialism. Pushing the boundaries of archival imaginations, our newest projects demand a shift in the temporality and the site of that repair.

Informed by an awareness of the violence of imperial practices and settler colonialism, the postcolonial digital archive often attempts to repair the past by recovering colonized voices and deconstructing imperial and colonial values. To make visible the painful past, the archive after theory attempts to acknowledge the complicity of archives in the production of that pain, to resist the further propagation of the practices of the imperial archive, and to devote itself to mediating the imperial and colonial records.[4] This form of repair is sometimes characterized as "decolonizing," as when Roopika Risam writes of "the need for the creation of new methods, tools, projects, and platforms to undo the epistemic violence of colonialism and fully realize a decolonized digital humanities"[5] (81). The results of this decolonizing project can range from the creation of archives that function as sites of resistance to those that purposefully preserve underrepresented voices and recontextualize imperial and colonial materials. In this way, postcolonial theory is brought to bear on a more generalized ethos of repair, further enabled by digital platforms and tools built with an awareness of their own potential complicity in imperialism and colonialism.

Debates about postcolonial digital archives do not typically question the ethos of repair, but discuss how best to execute it. In a recent article on Caribbean digital archives, for instance, Nicole Aljoe et al. sum up the primary approaches that postcolonial scholars have taken in the formation of archival materials related to the history of imperialism and colonialism: "revisionary recovery, rereading, disembedding, and recombining" (260). Each of these methods exists in relation to the imperial and colonial pasts. As the prefixes "re-" and "dis-" suggest, the primary work of the postcolonial digital archive—informed by decades of theory—has conceived of intervention as going back over the historical record with the intent to augment or disrupt it. Other scholars have argued that we need to pay more attention to materials, creators, and authors. In a 2014 forum on "The Postcolonial Archive," for instance, Siobhan Senier argued for a failure in method: the "the most visible and best-funded digital archives have tended to privilege colonial collections over those stewarded, often for centuries, by tribal communities themselves" (298).[6] Despite differences in methods or subjects, a focus on the past persists, whether through recollecting, remediating, or resisting it.

Recently, however, archival scholars have called for a different kind of archival disruption, one oriented toward the future. Arguing that digital collections should not be "lenses for retrospect," Bethany Nowviskie proposes the creation of "speculative collections." Tom Schofield et al. offer the design-based concept of "archival liveness," wherein participants see the archive being created and maintained in the present. In another recent appeal, Jarrett Drake, following the work of Michelle Caswell, argues for community-based "liberatory archives" as a way to break entirely with traditional archival practices.[7] Projects such as these petition for digital collections that effect change in the present by emphasizing the archive's multiple temporalities. They ask archives not only to react to the past but also to engage with a different sort of activity altogether: to build archives that imagine the future as well as preserve the past.

Imagination is no stranger to postcolonial theory; the counterfactual history has long been recognized as a coping strategy and a tool of resistance. What makes these calls different is that they identify the archive as the site of futurity, a place where resistance can happen through archival design and practice. Rather than seeking out the gaps and silences in the past that have been archived, these projects expand the archive's temporal reach, emphasizing its ongoing and eventual creation, and its centrality to conceiving of alternative futures. Though oriented toward the future, these archival projects are nonetheless motivated by the same ethos of repair that shapes the postcolonial digital archive's reactive stance: they imagine repair as a creative process that will engage with the legacies of imperialism and colonialism in a new, as yet *un*imagined way. If, as Nowviskie hopes, archives can be "stages to be leapt upon by performers, by co-creators," repair can happen through inspired acts of making that engage with the archive's multiple temporalities.

This recent scholarship draws on postcolonial and archival theories with the intention to revise the idea of "archivists and institutions as producers of versions of the past" (Schofield et al.). Instead, it asks archivists, institutions, and communities to look to the present and beyond, not acting as "producers" but as cocreators. Nowviskie hopes that a "speculative collection" would work against the idea that "the present state of human affairs is the inevitable and singularly logical result of the accumulated data of the past" by looking "forward to imaginative, generative, alternate futures or slantwise through branching, looping time." As this suggests, moving away from an orientation to the past is not linear; the work of liveness, speculation, and liberation depends on a sense of temporal play.

This present- and future-oriented work would, Nowviskie believes, result in "archives that permit speculation and maybe not only demonstrate, but help to *realize* greater community agency in the context of shared cultural heritage." Archives created by the communities they represent, Drake argues, enable "seeing the unseen" through their ground-up structure, a way of unearthing the past in the service of future change. As Caswell puts it, the liberatory archive does not just "document[t] a more diverse version of the past based on the identities of the present" but also "uncover[s] previously untold, ignored, or misinterpreted histories" so that "communities can imagine and reimagine different trajectories for the future" (49).

Here the past is the condition of imagining the future, a view Schofield et al. enact through design features that help users see "the archive as a set of ongoing professional, institutional and technical processes." Drake goes further still, arguing that a reparative stance is actually inherently damaging: "Reformation of oppressive institutions—be they prisons, police, or archives—only yields more mature manifestations of oppression." The only way to repair the damage of the archive, Drake argues, is to invent completely new forms, starting with institutional and technical infrastructures. In this, the most radical of the future-oriented archival imaginaries, Drake proposes the end of the archive as we know it (though what will replace it is less clear).

The archive after theory encompasses this future orientation, but sees it as inevitably tied to the past. We cannot have a future archive without the realization of the digital archive's haunting by the imperial archive, an acceptance of the impossibility of ever being free of that ghost, and a bedrock reliance on critically mediated digital building to accommodate that dual position. It is this very sense of after-ness that affords the digital archive a future orientation that is not utopian and a past orientation that never stagnates. Invested in critically mediated building from its inception, the archive after theory preserves reparatively at the level of structure and content. It strives never to be caught unaware of its own complicity, never to preserve naïvely.

At the same time, however, the duality in temporal orientation also suggests a gap in our digital archives' theorization; perhaps the archive in question is not so "after" after all. The prevailing ethos of repair is complicated by the temporality of digital objects considered more broadly, which always operate in multiple registers. Kris Paulsen has described the digital index as an "ephemeral, doubtful, distant, present-tense sign" (98), which beautifully captures the conundrum of any digital object: both close and far, past and present, material and immaterial. If the work of decolonizing depends on a temporal structure of undoing the past in the present, the digital archive complicates this work with its own, separate, and shifting multiple temporalities. This split in the chronos of repair suggests these intersectional theories are still emergent.

But to end with the same deliberate provocation with which this chapter began, seeing the digital archive as after (certain) theories is as important as looking to its theoretical future. Digital archives are the genre of theoretically inflected digital building with the longest durée. While calls for new theories are often invigorating, they too are subject to the archive's long, fraught past. We can only know the theories we need by explicitly acknowledging the ones embedded in our collecting practices, our contextualizing materials, and our code. Seeing what the archive is after is a way of seeing what is yet to come.

NOTES

1. For a useful summary of archival theory pre-2004, see Manoff.

2. Archival scholars and digital humanists alike understand that "the archivization process produces as much as it records the event," an awareness manifested in the idea that digital archives "cannot but make arguments about whatever it is they digitize" (Derrida, 17; Mussell, 383).

3. Roopika Risam offers an extensive and fruitful discussion of these challenges in *New Digital Worlds,* especially Chapter Two, "Colonial Violence and the Postcolonial

Digital Archive," and Chapter Three, "Remaking the Global Worlds of Digital Humanities." Stephen Ramsay and Geoffrey Rockwell make a seminal case for "building as a distinct form of scholarly endeavor" by arguing that the digital tools and platforms that we create can act as a theoretical lens. The archival theories cited in this chapter take this as a given, arguing for the political and ideological ramifications of their building choices.

4. This approach informs important recent projects such as #DHPoco and #TransformDH, which argue particularly for greater representation of past voices as a form of resistance to the imperial archive's lingering influence.

5. For a critique of the broader use of the term "decolonization," see Tuck and Yang.

6. See also Adeline Koh's contribution to this same forum, in which she argued that the digital literary archive "does not actively showcase the contributions of people of colour to literature; neither does it make clear the impact of imperialism on Europe and the Americas in the nineteenth century" (392).

7. Drake draws on Caswell's introduction of the term "liberatory" to describe community-based archives and the imagined futures they make possible. Caswell's more recent work with Anne J. Gilliland builds on the role of imagination in archival work to argue that archives must account for the "imagined records" that exist in every archive: the content that users and archivists believe must exist but have no evidence of. Acknowledging the existence of such imagined records will, Gilliland and Caswell argue, allow the acknowledgment of "impossible archival imaginaries," which engage with the affective power of archives and provide ways of producing an archive when "the archive and its hoped-for contents are absent or forever unattainable" (61).

BIBLIOGRAPHY

Aljoe, Nicole, Elizabeth Maddock Dillon, Benjamin J. Doyle, and Elizabeth Hopwood. "Obeah and the Early Caribbean Digital Archive." *Atlantic Studies* 12 (2015): 258–66. doi: 10.1080/14788810.2015.1025217.

Caswell, Michelle. "Inventing New Archival Imaginaries: Theoretical Foundations for Identity-Based Community Archives." In *Identity Palimpsests: Archiving Ethnicity in the U.S. and Canada*, edited by Dominique Daniel and Amalia S. Levi, 35–55. Sacramento, Calif.: Litwin Books, 2014.

Derrida, Jaques. *Archive Fever: A Freudian Impression*. Translated by Eric Prenowitz. Chicago: University of Chicago Press, 1995.

Drake, Jarrett M. "Liberatory Archives: Towards Belonging and Believing." Keynote presentation at the Community Archives Forum, Los Angeles, October 21, 2016, https://medium .com/on-archivy/liberatory-archives-towards-belonging-and-believing-part-1 -d26aaeb0edd1.

Gallon, Kim. "Making a Case for the Black Digital Humanities." In *Debates in the Digital Humanities 2016,* edited by Lauren F. Klein and Matthew K. Gold. Minneapolis: University of Minnesota Press, 2016. http://dhdebates.gc.cuny.edu/debates/text/55.

Gilliland, Anne J., and Michelle Caswell. "Records and Their Imaginaries: Imagining the Impossible, Making Possible the Imagined." *Archival Science* 16, no. 1 (2016): 53–76. doi: 10.1007/s10502–015–9259-z.

Koh, Adeline. "Inspecting the Nineteenth-Century Literary Digital Archive: Omissions of Empire." *Journal of Victorian Culture* 19, no. 3 (2014): 385–95. doi: 10.1080/13555502.2014.947182.

Manoff, Marlene. "Theories of the Archive from across the Disciplines." *Libraries and the Academy* 4, no. 1 (2004): 9–25. doi:10.1353/pla.2004.0015.

Mussell, James. "The Postcolonial Archive." *Journal of Victorian Culture* 19, no. 3 (2014): 383–84. doi: 10.1080/13555502.2014.947186.

Nowviskie, Bethany. "Speculative Collections and the Emancipatory Library." Keynote presentation at "The Transformation of Academic Library Collecting." Cambridge, Mass., October 21–22, 2016, http://nowviskie.org/2016/speculative-collections/.

Paulsen, Kris. 2013. "The Index and the Interface." *Representations* 122, no. 1 (2013): 83–109. doi: 10.1525/rep.2013.122.1.83.

Ramsay, Stephen, and Geoffrey Rockwell. "Developing Things: Notes Toward an Epistemology of Building in the Digital Humanities." In *Debates in the Digital Humanities 2012,* edited by Matthew K. Gold. Minneapolis: University of Minnesota Press, 2012. http://dhdebates.gc.cuny.edu/debates/text/11.

Richards, Thomas. *The Imperial Archive: Knowledge and the Fantasy of Empire.* London: Verso, 1993.

Risam, Roopika. "Decolonising Digital Humanities in Theory and Practice." In *Routledge Companion to Digital Humanities and Media Studies,* edited by Jentary Sayers, 78–86. London: Routledge, 2018.

Risam, Roopika. *New Digital Worlds: Postcolonial Digital Humanities in Theory, Praxis, and Pedagogy.* Evanston, IL: Northwestern University Press, 2018.

Schofield, Tom, David Kirk, Telmo Amaral, Marian Dörk, Mitchell Whitelaw, Guy Schofield, and Thomas Ploetz. "Archival Liveness: Designing with Collections before and during Cataloguing and Digitization" *Digital Humanities Quarterly* 9, no. 30 (2015), http://www.digitalhumanities.org/dhq/vol/9/3/000227/000227.html.

Senier, Siobhan. 2014. "Digitizing Indigenous History: Trends and Challenges." *Journal of Victorian Culture* 19, no. 3 (2014): 396–402. doi: 10.1080/13555502.2014.947188.

Tuck, Eve, and K. Wayne Yang. "Decolonization is Not a Metaphor." *Decolonization: Indigeneity, Education, and Society* 1, no. 1 (2012): 1–40.

PART III

METHODS AND PRACTICES

Teaching Quantitative Methods: What Makes It Hard (in Literary Studies)

ANDREW GOLDSTONE

When I set out to teach a graduate English course titled "Literary Data: Some Approaches" in the spring of 2015, I was on a mission.[1] I wanted my eleven PhD students to learn not simply how to talk about digital humanities but also how to analyze data as part of their literary scholarship, to be able to argue not only about "data" but also *with* data. I wanted to prove that English graduate students could do more than play with computers in their first DH course. At the same time, I wanted students to acquire the conceptual sophistication that would make their practical knowledge meaningful. Though my students made remarkable practical and conceptual progress, at the end of the semester my high-flown aims still seemed to lie beyond our immediate grasp. Having made the attempt, however, I learned some lessons about what is needed to take on this pedagogical mission: lessons not only in course planning but also about what the scholarly community has to do—and what institutions must be prepared to supply—if quantitative methods are to fulfill their promise for the study of literature and culture.

There is, of course, more to the digital humanities than doing data analysis for literary study. Aside from a disciplinary slant toward my home field of literature in English, my course's emphasis on data analysis meant giving relatively less attention to other prominent DH strands; for example, new media studies or digital editing and curation. Nonetheless, questions of what constitutes literary data and how it can be analyzed are central to DH discussions. The digital humanities has garnered so much attention and debate across humanistic scholarship in no small part because of the claim that studying aggregates of texts with the help of quantification might radically change our conception of literary and cultural history. The potential of aggregation is the reason I have participated in the digital humanities. And if it really does open up major new possibilities for research, then teaching the theory and method of literary data analysis to future researchers is something to which at least some literary scholars ought to devote serious energy.

My argument, in brief, is that teaching this material is really, really hard, for reasons that are more than technical or technological. The available strategies for teaching literary data analysis under the "DH" rubric, including my own, have so far been inadequate to the task of training scholars in research methods. In what follows, I summarize how I approached this pedagogical challenge in my course. But rather than offer my course as a model, I instead draw the following prescriptive lessons from my experience:

1. Cultivating technical facility with computer tools—including programming languages—should receive less attention than methodologies for analyzing quantitative or aggregate evidence. Despite the widespread DH interest in the former, it has little scholarly use without the latter.
2. Studying method requires pedagogically suitable material, but good teaching datasets do not exist. It will require communal effort to create them on the basis of existing research.
3. Following the "theory" model, digital humanities has typically been inserted into curricula as a single-semester course. Yet as a training in method, the analysis of aggregate data will undoubtedly require more time and a different rationale from that offered by what Gerald Graff calls "the field-coverage principle" in the curriculum.[2]

These issues are not only pedagogical. I learned with my students that present-day literary scholarship is fundamentally uncertain about how to make a convincing scholarly argument using quantitative evidence, and it has a habit of postponing or avoiding methodological debate in the name of open-ended exploration or disciplinary pluralism.[3] If a more sustained research program including quantitative methods is to develop, those dispositions may be reaching the end of their usefulness.

Teaching "Literary Data"

Since I aimed for my students to learn practical skill and conceptual sophistication, I decided to divide each week's three-hour meeting in two: half the time for seminar discussion of theoretical readings and half the time for practicum.[4] The major argument of the theory part was that the question of literary data is not restricted either to digital humanities or to its most obvious predecessor, humanities computing, but should be set in a longer and broader multidisciplinary trajectory. For example, we read Lévi-Strauss's structuralist theory of myth as a transformation of narratives into data; everyone was immediately interested in his system of index cards for tracking mythemes.[5] We looked at McKenzie on scientific bibliography in "Printers of the Mind"; we had a lively discussion of one of Robert Darnton's earliest essays on the history of the book. Turning more explicitly to literary study, our discussion of J. F. Burrows's *Computation into Criticism* was particularly productive, not so

much because his version of computational text analysis struck any of us as compelling, but because it presented a limit-case my students and I came back to over
and over again: Burrows, fully committed to criticism in the sense of the exercise
of judgment, claims that the quantitative patterns of word use he finds reveal Jane
Austen's authorial "genius."[6] But we were also able to see Burrows, and the stylometric tradition he builds on, as only one among many possible models for a literary data analysis.

Our attention then turned to more contemporary work in digital humanities,
with short side excursions into contemporary sociology of culture. In our discussions of recent work, two themes recurred: first, my students' excitement and
enthusiasm for the novel possibilities opened up in recent work in studying large-
scale aggregates of texts; and second, their dissatisfaction with the way this scholarship has analyzed and interpreted its data. More than once, my students wished
they could study the data being discussed in our readings themselves. They were
looking not just for provocative claims—which we found and argued about in
abundance—but also for models of research that they themselves could build on. I
return to this fundamental point later.

The other half of the course was the practicum. My students were to learn R
well enough to be able to prepare real-world, messy data for analysis and to describe
it numerically and visually in basic but interesting ways. But I also wanted them
to *think programmatically,* or, as I put it under "learning goals" on the syllabus,
"understand the fundamentals of computation." I know only one general way to
teach this sort of skill, and that is through cumulative practice in which skills are
used, tested, and reinforced. From this followed the improbable scenario of me
devising, and English PhD students completing, weekly problem sets, following,
more or less, the progression of a typical basic introductory course in computation.[7] I adopted Jockers's *Text Analysis with R for Students of Literature* as a
starting point, but used only parts of the book and added many exercises of my
own. Fairly soon, as the challenges built up, I found myself needing to take class
time to go over homework questions; since I was also presenting new material in
the practicum, this half of the class was frequently overloaded. The seminar discussion felt positively relaxed by comparison.

All this led up to the final challenge of the course: a data analysis report.[8] Halfway through the term, my students formed pairs (and one triple). Then, over the
succeeding weeks, I worked with them as they obtained a dataset, analyzed it, and
used their findings to produce argumentative papers with code and data appendices.
Each student wrote his or her own report on the basis of the group's work. The folder
containing these reports occupies more than seven gigabytes on my hard drive, representing analyses of regionalism in American newspapers; of deaths and absences
in the eighteenth-century slave trade; of authorship in science-fiction pulps; of the
reception of David Mitchell's *Cloud Atlas*; and of the influences of and on Freud in
turn-of-the-century writing. As this list suggests, my students' interests were quite

varied, and I encouraged them to apply quantitative methods to whatever topic interested them.[9]

The rationale for the assignment was to confront the class with making sense of data in the wild, with all the messiness that entails. My students' reports bear witness that they all learned that getting the data into analyzable form—"cleaning" it—is a large proportion of the work of analysis. Here, their efforts at mastering R really bore fruit, allowing them to wrestle big bodies of data into sense. (There were more than a few computer crashes on the way, and one student's hard drive filled to capacity in the course of corpus processing.) Everyone found interesting phenomena to comment on in the data, and everyone put particular effort into visualizing these phenomena thoughtfully.[10]

But, after an exhaustingly difficult semester for both my students and me, what of the hoped-for payoff—the promise of moving beyond experimenting with the computer and toward making quantitatively evidenced arguments? On the theoretical plane, a very healthy caution about drawing conclusions from the data prevailed, even as the students strove to respond to my demand that they make literary-historical arguments. I was gratified by the thoughtfulness—and the quite awesome amount of labor—represented in the reports. At the same time, it was clear that my students did not have all the methodological tools they needed to draw the conclusions they wanted. Most of the projects, for example, involved spotting trends over time: trends in word usage, in network clustering, or in some other phenomenon. But how could they be sure a trend is real and not a random fluctuation? Many also sought to explain contrasts among subsets of their data. But how far could the data allow them to assess the validity of such explanations? Other students needed more possibilities for choosing data to collect in the first place, but how were they to know which choices had a chance of yielding meaningful conclusions?

These questions—the classic questions of quantitative methodology—remained open in the final reports. But this is no criticism of my students who, as a group, did all I could have asked. Rather, it is a criticism of my pedagogy, which did not equip them with all they needed. Though no doubt my personal shortcomings and all the hiccups of a first-time course contributed to this problem, I think solving it is not simply a matter of tweaking the syllabus or assignments. Instead, it requires a reorientation of the course toward the aim of *teaching methodology*, by which I mean the formal study of the questions I have just posed about how to interpret data. But to do that raises the fundamental pedagogical problems I mentioned at the start of this chapter.

Problem 1: Programming Is Not an End in Itself

An informal consensus seems to have emerged that if students in the humanities are going to make use of quantitative methods, they should probably first *learn to program*. Introductions to this dimension of the field are organized around

programming languages: *The Programming Historian* is built around an introduction to Python; Matthew Jockers's *Text Analysis with R* is at its heart a tutorial in
the R language; Taylor Arnold and Lauren Tilton's *Humanities Data in R* begins
with chapters on the language; Folgert Karsdorp's *Python Programming for the
Humanities* is a course in the language with examples from stylometry and information retrieval.[11] "On the basis of programming," writes Moretti in "Literature,
Measured," a recent retrospective on the work of his Literary Lab, "much more
becomes possible" (2).

Steven Ramsay makes one of the best-known cases for focusing on programming in DH teaching. In a 2012 essay, he describes a course that "proceeds, as most
courses in programming do, through the major constructs and concepts germane
to any programming language," but that nonetheless has a specific rationale for
humanists: "the particular form of engagement that characterizes the act of building tools, models, frameworks and representations for the traditional objects of
humanistic study." Here is the kernel of a broad justification for the study of programming in humanities fields, which I found appealing when I first planned my
course: learning to program promises to open the door to sophisticated thinking
about the scholarly uses of data in our disciplines. At my most idealistic, I even imagined that programming, by making abstractions more concrete, would reintroduce
my humanist students to the beauties of mathematics.

The conceptual reward, furthermore, is in principle coupled to a practical one:
programming means not being limited to the possibilities offered by any given all-
in-one application or "tool." Much DH instruction has forgone programming in
favor of guiding students in the use of particular specialized programs.[12] A student
who learns to operate the text-analysis web application Voyant Tools, for example,
can generate its (long) list of tabulations and visualizations of a text corpus, but no
others: the list of visualizations and possible dimensions of variation are closed to
nonprogrammers. Additionally, Voyant makes a significant set of choices about how
to convert the text into units of analysis, with no possibility of alternatives beyond
the choice of stop words.[13] And if the project goes the way of most DH projects and
stops being updated or maintained, what are students who have depended on it to
do? By contrast, a student who learns to program in an established programming
language has the ability to generate any tabulation or visualization of texts that she
can dream of; she can rely on the relative longevity of the platform; and, most importantly, she has the means to transform her texts and other data as required to make
her subsequent analysis meaningful.

In principle. In practice—and I had to teach programming to understand
this—the distinction between the tool user and the heroically flexible programmer
is not so clear. Beginning programmers typically begin by following recipes, modifying them only little by little as they learn what can and cannot be done in the
language. The first thrill of programming, *making the computer do something,* is
a tool-user's thrill. And beginning data analysts cannot know the range of possible

methods they might use. They know what they have studied, and especially in the early stages, they have to spend time simply learning how to apply the techniques they have been shown, mastering whatever particular steps are needed to use the technique in the programming language they are learning. It is no accident that the tutorial form is so ubiquitous in DH instruction. Chapter 3 of Jockers's *Text Analysis,* for example, is a tutorial in finding the most frequent words in *Moby Dick*: the whole of the chapter is devoted to explaining the particular R steps necessary to go from the digitized text to the table (and graph) of words and frequencies. This is followed by exercises in finding the top ten words in *Sense and Sensibility.* What students are meant to learn is just precisely *how to extract a table of top ten words and their frequencies.* When I added my own exercises to this chapter, I found myself again asking students to make lists of "top words" in other texts. And this same process of extracting "top words" reappeared in my students' final projects.[14] The infinite generality of programming does not survive classroom necessity.

Yet the problem is not that DH textbooks—or my own course—do not instill the ability to write sophisticated, original programs. In fact, judging from my students' program code in their final analysis projects, either because or in spite of my methods, they made good progress in acquiring this ability. Anyone who completes Jockers's textbook, Karsdorp's lessons, or Arnold and Tilton's book will have made strides as a programmer and will know, in a hands-on way, the elementary principles of both algorithms and data structures. But programming competence is *not* equivalent to competence in analytical methods. It might allow students to prepare data for some future analysis and to produce visual, tabular, numerical, or even interactive summaries; *Humanities Data in R* gives a fuller survey of the possibilities of exploratory data analysis than the other texts.[15] Yet students who have focused on programming will have to rely on their intuition when it comes to interpreting exploratory results. Intuition gives only a weak basis for arguing about whether apparent trends, groupings, or principles of variation are supported by the data. Without any sense of these possibilities, which are the stock in trade of statistical methodology in the social sciences, a programming curriculum can bring students—but really, I should say, it has brought digital humanities as a field—only up to the threshold of method and not over it.

Problem 2: Any Old Data Will Not Do

In the words of Miriam Posner, "it's just awful trying to find a humanities dataset." Until I taught my course, I did not anticipate just how hard it would be to find suitable datasets for study. I made the internet-age mistake of thinking all sorts of interesting things must already be out there for the downloading; failing that, I imagined that I would be able to construct interesting data sets out of big grab-bag text corpora, such as Project Gutenberg, the text section of the Internet Archive, and the Text Creation Partnership releases from Eighteenth-Century Collections

Online (ECCO) and Early English Books Online (EEBO). I was thinking like an English professor: when I teach literature, I can normally choose a dozen or so interesting books and wait for students to find their own analyses. Students never fail, in the course of reading and discussion, to discover both challenging questions and meaningful evidence to address those questions. But an arbitrary corpus of texts is a different kind of challenge, because *many possible corpora are entirely unsuited to answering any interesting questions.*

Consider again Jockers's textbook. His first corpus is simply the body chapters of *Moby Dick* (taken from a Project Gutenberg plain text). *Text Analysis with R* invites students to study how the words "whale" and "Ahab" occur with varying frequency across the chapters of the novel and to assess the correlation between them; later, students can also study the words that occur in proximity to "dog." As an introduction to text-processing functionality in R, this works fine. But these exercises lead to nothing resembling a scholarly argument: What does knowing the changing counts of these words allow us to say about the novel?[16] Later, Jockers shows how to use hierarchical clustering on frequent words to discriminate authorship in a small corpus of Irish American novels. This is an impressive technical feat, but authorship attribution is rarely an important question in literary studies, and the field still awaits a demonstration that stylometry speaks to central research questions.

The problem is not really Jockers's particular choices. Arnold and Tilton carry out a technically impressive demonstration analysis of a collection of Conan Doyle's Sherlock Holmes stories using natural-language processing. But the most elaborate conclusion they reach is a visualization of where main characters occur within each story. Again, the effort is out of all proportion to the result, which any graduate student in English would immediately recognize as at best a *further fact to be explained* of at most moderate interest. In fact, most of the interesting questions about plot are not answerable within a single-author corpus. My own variation on the theme was no better: I spent a whole class carrying students through an analysis that showed the differentiation of fiction from poetry in terms of common-word frequencies in the modernist little magazine *The Egoist.* By crude measures, the diction of poetry differs from that of fiction in this publication. So what?

All of these examples have two things in common. First, they work with convenience corpora: collections chosen for practice, rather than having been designed to answer research questions. Second, though these collections encapsulate a certain amount of textual variation, they lack interesting metadata. But answering research questions about the relations between text and metadata is precisely what students really need to practice. Students must work with bodies of data that hold meaningful patterns, divergences, and historical developments, and they must learn the techniques necessary to bring those patterns compellingly to light.

Thus, the best data for teaching are not to be found by taking *all* of the bulk releases from big digital archives. Rather, what students need—how unhumanistic this will sound—are data about which at least some answers have already been given, so that instead of being forced to fish for interesting phenomena in an empty ocean, students can follow a trajectory from exploration to valid argument. Such datasets might be designed for teaching by a scholarly collective that sifts freely available materials and chooses samples to represent an interesting range of variation.[17] But the richest source for such data is research itself. Limiting myself to works from the seminar part of my syllabus, examples might include the following: the collection of novel titles (with dates and parts of speech) in Moretti's "Style, Inc."; a list of persons mentioned in each of the letters of Thomas Jefferson, as used by Klein to study the collocation network of James Hemings in her "Image of Absence"; the bibliographic metadata on Irish American novels analyzed by Jockers in *Macroanalysis*; and the catalog of geolocated place names found in nineteenth-century American novels by Wilkens in "The Geographic Imagination." I am imagining that researchers like these might consider making their datasets, already cleaned and enriched, available for student use, within whatever restrictions of copyright are necessary.[18]

One rationale for my course's final assignment, I mentioned earlier, was the importance of learning to deal with data in the wild. But I now think this emphasis was misplaced. Though data wrangling is indeed a crucial research skill, it should not come before the question of how to analyze data that *are* in analyzable form: otherwise, why wrangle? I thought I could combine wrangling with more complex forms of analysis, but it is simply too much to fit into a single course, and treating wrangling as an end in itself means deferring past the end of the semester the kinds of analysis that serve scholarly arguments. Better to start from tamed data—just as is standard in teaching quantitative methods across all the social sciences—in order to focus on methods for answering substantive questions.

Problem 3: The Singular DH Course Is a Bad Fit for the Subject

Data wrangling and programming skill often (and, I am suggesting, necessarily) competed with analytical method for time on the syllabus. Still, a more fruitful relationship sometimes developed between the theoretical readings and the practicalities of analysis. Starting about halfway into the course, it became possible to discuss theory and methodology in other scholars' work from the standpoint of practitioners. Once I introduced the grammar of graphics via Wickham's ggplot2 R package, we were able to have a very lively discussion of the construction and implications of specific visualizations in work by Lev Manovich and Lauren Klein.[19] Or again, after a lesson on defining and using functions, we were able to be much more concrete in our debate about Tara McPherson's use of the concept of "modularity" in her important essay on race in digital humanities. And after tedious weeks of counting single words in texts, the rationale for topic modeling was particularly vivid.

Yet each of these exhilarating moments depended on the previous weeks of practicum preparation, and as soon as each session ended, it was time to turn to a new topic, with its own challenges. And because of my decision to devote so much time to programming, data analysis itself remained mostly obscure. For example, in the course of the semester I presented three ways of exploring variability in data: correlations between word frequencies (from Jockers), latent semantic indexing (LSI), and latent Dirichlet allocation (LDA). I barely explained any of these; the best I could do with LSI and LDA was handwaving and heuristics, and as for correlations, I rushed through them somewhere at midterm. When my students tried looking at word correlations themselves, I realized I had failed to convey how to use them effectively; nor had I been clear about the pitfalls of trying to interpret correlations between frequencies of rare words. My students thus knew much more about the theoretical problems of quantification in general than about the *methodological* problems of putting numbers (and computers) to work effectively.

In squeezing these quite disparate elements into the syllabus—and consequently scanting each of them for time—I was trying to answer a curricular imperative to provide a useful DH overview and a course satisfying a "theory" distribution requirement. In one form or another, my dilemma ought to be familiar to almost anyone who has tried to teach a DH course: since there is typically just one such course in the curriculum, it is necessary to offer some general DH overview alongside more specific topics. But quantitative method is a bad fit for the "patterned isolation" of the literary curriculum: even more than a literary-historical period, it does not constitute a free-standing topic. And the frequent disjunctions between the theory-seminar half of my course and the practicum parts suggest that the "theory course" is not an ideal home for quantitative method either.

Better models for the pedagogical rationale of quantitative methods are found in the other intensively skills-based courses in graduate education: premodern languages and bibliography. Old English is taught in many graduate departments, and language learning is usually the primary focus of the first-semester course, not debates in Anglo-Saxon studies, which are introduced in a later semester. This pedagogical division does *not* mean Anglo-Saxonists are tragically untheoretical or have falsely separated the organically unified tasks of studying grammar and interpreting monster slaying.[20] It means that their subject matter is distinctive—and cumulative—in ways that make a difference to the organization of the curriculum. Teachers of quantitative method have the same case to make for the distinctiveness of their subject matter.

Leaving both the breadth of the DH overview and the conceptual debates of theory for other courses, the quantitative analysis course (or, better, sequence) could focus on demonstrating, explaining, and above all practicing the fundamentals of exploratory and inferential data analysis on carefully curated data of known scholarly interest. There is no way to learn the required sort of logical problem solving except by deliberate practice, but solving problems efficiently requires ways of working that students cannot be expected to know in advance. At the start of the term I thought I needed only to give my students reasonable tasks and let them figure them out together. But eventually I learned that the problem sets I had written to take two or three hours were costing my students a dozen hours a week. It seems that, lacking training in solving problems in this domain, my students needed a great deal of time for trial and error.

How to teach better problem-solving technique? At a minimum, students need to see problem solving demonstrated, then to work through a problem together with an instructor, and then to practice it some more on their own. The once-weekly three-hour seminar meeting was not an ideal format for this sequence. In a sense the class was meeting much longer than that, not only in my office hours but also when the students met without me to do the homework. A certain amount of independent collaboration among students is very desirable, but really a TA would have helped a great deal: my students needed help from someone who was skilled enough to spend time doing the homework with them and reinforcing its lessons, and I needed someone to share the job of answering email. Just as learning quantitative methods is more work than fits into a single course, so is teaching them.

Toward Method

I have argued that teaching quantitative methods is hard, but I am not suggesting that it needs to be made easy. On the contrary, the digital humanities should be wary of promises of ease in prepackaged tools, in well-meaning introductory tutorials and workshops that necessarily stop short of what a researcher would need to draw conclusions, and in rationalizations of inconclusive arguments as exploration, play, or productive failure. Having organized workshops, produced tools, and talked elsewhere about data exploration myself, I'd like to think the desire for ease is understandable. These approaches can be useful in making the unfamiliar more accessible. Nonetheless, I learned from my students to be skeptical that the easeful way could naturally lead to the production of new knowledge, because a gentle introduction simply cannot get very far in developing ways of interpreting quantitative results. Good programming skills actually exacerbate the problem when they make highly complex transformations of data—matrices of frequency correlations, probabilistic topic models, and so on—simpler than figuring out whether those transformations are appropriate to the data at hand.

Indeed, the first two problems of quantitative methods pedagogy I have described here become most evident in the context of the third: if introductory programming with arbitrary yet convenient data were all learning methodology required, the subject would indeed fit in a one-semester course.[21] Yet the prospect of humanities departments offering multiple semesters of coursework in quantitative methods seems fanciful even to me: Who would teach such courses, and how many students would really take them? Humanities students who wish a fuller quantitative training are more likely to find it in the methods courses offered by social science or statistics departments, provided humanities departments recognize those courses as a possibility for credit within a degree program. Nonetheless, courses taught by humanities faculty can lay a meaningful foundation in data analysis, as long as they spend enough time introducing the problems of quantitative methodology *as* problems rather than passing them by or, worse, imagining they have been solved because students are learning to code.

The curricular practicalities can be addressed only once the true challenges of quantitative method are more widely understood. As long as confusion between programming and quantitative data analysis reigns, students and researchers alike may not even recognize when their problems are methodological rather than merely technological, and they will often be forced to stop short of making convincing arguments. Though my students' and my experience was chastening in some ways, their determined commitment to rigor gives me hope. Despite the total unfamiliarity of much of the course practicum, my students hung together and mastered some complex skills; furthermore, they embraced the possibility of unfamiliar ways of producing knowledge, and, in the final reports, they wrestled ingeniously with the question of how to use numbers as part of their answers to research questions. To go further, what we needed was, above all, more models of how to take those questions on—not just for seminar discussion as exempla of "digital humanities" but also as paths from evidence to analysis we could retrace and then continue ourselves. If research provides more such pathways, including the evidence they start from, the challenges of quantitative method could be more clearly distinguished from those of programming and other dimensions of computer-assisted humanities. Then, I believe, a more focused quantitative literary-studies curriculum would become not easy, but just hard enough.

NOTES

1. The course syllabus, with a bibliography of readings, is available online from the MLA CORE repository at http://dx.doi.org/10.17613/M69S30; the course assignments (ten problem sets and two papers) are available at http://dx.doi.org/10.17613/M6602R. For their thoughtful comments on earlier versions of this chapter, I thank Taylor Arnold, Natalia Cecire, Anne DeWitt, Meredith McGill, David Roh, the *Debates in DH* editors, and several students from English 350:509, Spring 2015. I am grateful to all my students for teaching me much of what is discussed here.

2. "The division of fields according to the least controversial principles made the department easy to administer but masked its most interesting conflicts and connections" (Graff, 8). We might add that it makes any kind of cumulative training difficult to formalize.

3. Most typical is the appeal to the complementarity of "close" and "distant" readings, as in Hoyt Long and Richard So's "method of literary pattern recognition that is enriched by points of confluence between multiple ontological scales of interpretation" (262). Steven Ramsay argues that "algorithmic criticism" should appeal to a literary-critical audience that is "less concerned with the fitness of method and the determination of interpretative

boundaries . . . [than with] evaluating the robustness of the discussion" (*Reading,* 17). Matthew Kirschenbaum challenges antagonistic accounts of DH in general: "Digital humanists don't want to extinguish reading and theory and interpretation and cultural criticism. Digital humanists want to do their work" (56). Kirschenbaum's statement is a salutary corrective to caricatures of digital humanities, but it also tends to defuse genuine conflicts about how to produce and interpret evidence in scholarship along the lines of field division discussed by Graff.

4. I found a few syllabus models to draw on, especially Matthew Wilkens's Spring 2014 graduate course at Notre Dame (http://mattwilkens.com/teaching/digital-humanities-graduate-seminar-spring-2014/). Matt is among the many to whom I owe thanks for discussions and inspiring examples; see the acknowledgments on my syllabus. To those acknowledgments I add my thanks to Francesca Giannetti, digital humanities librarian at Rutgers–New Brunswick, who visited the class for a crucial session on finding good sources of literary data.

5. I got the idea for using Lévi-Strauss's "Structural Study of Myth" in this context from a blog post by Nick Seaver: "Structuralism: Thinking with Computers," Savage Minds (blog), May 21, 2014, http://savageminds.org/2014/05/21/structuralism-thinking-with-computers/.

6. "Its real force," he says of a principal components analysis of word frequencies in the free indirect discourse of Austen's protagonists, "is as an illustration of the capacities of genius" (Burrows, 175).

7. In particular, I transposed the outline of John Guttag's *Introduction to Computation and Programming Using Python.*

8. *Not,* I had decided by halfway through the semester, a "project," a ubiquitous DH term that nonetheless suits engineering enterprises, and what Boltanski and Chiapello call the "projective city" of contemporary management theory, better than scholarly arguments (105).

9. On the other hand, my early-modernist students had a much harder time finding materials than my nineteenth- and twentieth-centuryist students. By the same token, the project on David Mitchell had to work around the impossibility of obtaining a corpus of twenty-first-century novels, turning to a collection of reviews instead.

10. Lauren Klein's essay on visualization and archival absence, the subject of a vigorous discussion in the seminar, also made a notable mark on the reports.

11. A rather different focus (with more emphasis on a broad range of software tools rather than a programming curriculum) is found in Shawn Graham et al.'s *Exploring Big Historical Data.* This book, like Arnold and Tilton's, was not available in time for my course. None of these texts is limited to programming, but they all tie quantitative methods tightly to programming, as does Moretti.

12. One example of this approach can be found in Alan Liu's Fall 2014 syllabus for a graduate introduction to DH at UCSB: http://eng236introdh2014f.pbworks.com. The course offers practicums in each week, but turns to new tools for each task.

13. The list of tools in Voyant is found at http://voyant-tools.org/docs. The program was updated to version 2.0 as this chapter was being revised. Voyant is, to be sure, a particularly extreme exemplification of the "tool" tendency in digital humanities, but the general phenomenon is widespread; in the *Programming Historian,* aside from the sequence of lessons on Python, one finds numerous lessons that focus on recipes for operating particular programs (Antconc, MALLET, Palladio, etc.).

14. I was ultimately dissatisfied with the exposition, the worked examples, and the exercises in *Text Analysis with R*; it is written for a different kind of course than the one I was teaching. Nonetheless, literary studies owes a considerable debt to Matt Jockers for his textbook, which begins the serious conversation about what a course in literary data analysis ought to look like, including what sorts of assignments and problems are useful and tractable. As my course went on, I found myself needing to supplement it more and more. But having something to supplement was absolutely indispensable, and the considerable effort of providing additional material taught me how difficult producing a textbook in this domain must be.

15. Exploratory data analysis has a methodology of its own, for which the founding text is John Tukey's book of that name. In their chapter in this volume, Arnold and Tilton argue for the central importance of exploratory analysis to humanistic data analysis; they do not identify analytical method with pure programming know-how. Yet scholars who confront bodies of data without any knowledge of what Tukey called "confirmatory" analysis will be limited in the arguments they can make. What is worse, they will have no disciplined way of judging the validity of arguments relying on quantitative evidence. Tukey himself insisted that the two analytical modes "can—and should—proceed side by side" (vii). Qualitative arguments in literary studies are rarely limited to exploration; it is hard to see why quantitative arguments should be.

16. At this point one might think of the "deformance" argument given well-known form by Jerome McGann in *Radiant Textuality*: any transformation of the text is potentially a provocation to further interpretation. Ramsay's *Reading Machines* applies this thesis to quantitative textual analysis. (We discussed both these texts in the seminar.) By conveniently equating scholarship with creative performance, this argument liberates scholars from responsibility to their evidence and to their community, asking instead only for post hoc rationalization. Research can leave room for many forms of experimentation, but wide use of the "deformance" argument has had a cost: it has forestalled debate about how to use quantitative or aggregate textual evidence systematically.

17. Alan Liu has begun the work by listing Demo Corpora in his "DH Toychest," but whether the available corpora support interesting investigations remains to be seen.

18. It is very hard to point to a finished piece of literary scholarship for which the source dataset is available in a form that would allow students to retrace the analysis straightforwardly. Ted Underwood's and Jordan Sellers's work on the reception of nineteenth-century poetry, which they circulated with a "replication archive" after I had finished the course, is a rare example. See Underwood and Sellers, "How Quickly Do Literary Standards

Change?," preprint, May 19, 2015, doi:10.6084/m9.figshare.1418394 and, for my own blog post about reusing this archive, "Of Literary Standards and Logistic Regression: A Reproduction," January 4, 2016, http://andrewgoldstone.com/blog/2016/01/04/standards/.

19. Wickham's exposition of the grammar in the context of his software package in *ggplot2* is much more accessible than the challengingly abstract original formulation by Leland Wilkinson in *The Grammar of Graphics* (both on my syllabus, though Wilkinson was optional and, it turned out, avoided by all my students).

20. Yacking and hacking, if you will. More seriously, on the meaning of the "hack vs. yack" controversy in digital humanities, see Natalia Cecire's compelling "Introduction: Theory and the Virtues of Digital Humanities."

21. I thank Taylor Arnold for pointing out this connection among the three problems.

BIBLIOGRAPHY

Arnold, Taylor, and Lauren Tilton. *Humanities Data in R.* New York: Springer, 2015.

Boltanski, Luc, and Eve Chiapello. *The New Spirit of Capitalism.* Translated by Gregory Elliott. London: Verso, 2005.

Burrows, J. F. *Computation into Criticism: A Study of Jane Austen's Novels and an Experiment in Method.* Oxford: Clarendon, 1987.

Cecire, Natalia. "Introduction: Theory and the Virtues of Digital Humanities." *Journal of Digital Humanities* 1, no. 1 (Winter 2011), http://journalofdigitalhumanities.org/1–1 /introduction-theory-and-the-virtues-of-digital-humanities-by-natalia-cecire/.

Crymble, Adam, Fred Gibbs, Allison Hegel, Caleb McDaniel, Ian Milligan, Miriam Posner, Evan Taparata, and Jeri Wieringa, eds. *The Programming Historian.* 2nd ed. 2016. http://programminghistorian.org/.

Darnton, Robert. "Reading, Writing, and Publishing in Eighteenth-Century France: A Case Study in the Sociology of Literature." *Daedalus* 100, no. 1 (1971): 214–56.

Goldstone, Andrew. "Of Literary Standards and Logistic Regression: A Reproduction." January 4, 2016, http://andrewgoldstone.com/blog/2016/01/04/standards.

Graff, Gerald. *Professing Literature: An Institutional History.* 20th anniversary ed. Chicago: University of Chicago Press, 2007.

Graham, Shawn, Milligan, Ian, and Weingart, Scott. *Exploring Big Historical Data: The Historian's Macroscope.* London: Imperial College Press, 2015.

Guttag, John. *Introduction to Computation and Programming Using Python.* Rev. ed. Cambridge, Mass.: MIT Press, 2013.

Jockers, Matthew L. *Macroanalysis: Digital Methods and Literary History.* Urbana: University of Illinois Press, 2013.

Jockers, Matthew L. *Text Analysis with R for Students of Literature.* Cham, Switzerland: Springer, 2014.

Karsdorp, Folgert. *Python Programming for the Humanities.* http://karsdorp.io/python -course/.

Kirschenbaum, Matthew G. "What Is 'Digital Humanities' and Why Are They Saying Such Terrible Things about It?" *Differences* 25, no. 1 (2014): 46–53.

Klein, Lauren F. "The Image of Absence: Archival Silence, Data Visualization, and James Hemings." *American Literature* 85, no. 4 (December 2013): 661–88.

Lévi-Strauss, Claude. "The Structural Study of Myth." *Journal of American Folklore* 68, no. 270 (October 1955): 428–44.

Liu, Alan. "DH Toychest: Digital Humanities Resources for Project Building." http://dhresourcesforprojectbuilding.pbworks.com.

Long, Hoyt, and Richard Jean So. "Literary Pattern Recognition: Modernism between Close Reading and Machine Learning." *Critical Inquiry* 42, no. 2 (Winter 2016): 235–67.

Manovich, Lev. "What Is Visualisation?" *Visual Studies* 26, no. 1 (2011): 36–49.

McGann, Jerome J. *Radiant Textuality: Literature after the World Wide Web.* New York: Palgrave, 2001.

McKenzie, D. F. "Printers of the Mind: Some Notes on Bibliographical Theories and Printing-House Practices." *Studies in Bibliography* 22 (1969): 1–75.

McPherson, Tara. "Why Are the Digital Humanities So White? or Thinking the Histories of Race and Computation." In *Debates in the Digital Humanities*, ed. Matthew K. Gold, 139–60. Minneapolis: University of Minnesota Press, 2012.

Moretti, Franco. "Literature, Measured." *Stanford Literary Lab*, pamphlet 12, Apr. 2016, http://litlab.stanford.edu/pamphlets/. PDF download.

Moretti, Franco. "Style, Inc. Reflections on Seven Thousand Titles (British Novels, 1740–1850)." *Critical Inquiry* 36, no. 1 (Autumn 2009).

Posner, Miriam. "Humanities Data: A Necessary Contradiction." June 25, 2015, http://miriamposner.com/blog/humanities-data-a-necessary-contradiction.

Ramsay, Steven. "Programming with Humanists: Reflections on Raising an Army of Hacker-Scholars in the Digital Humanities." In *Digital Humanities Pedagogy: Practices, Principles and Politics,* ed. Brett D. Hirsch, chap. 9. Open Book, 2012. http://www.openbookpublishers.com/htmlreader/DHP/chap09.html.

Ramsay, Steven. *Reading Machines: Toward an Algorithmic Criticism.* Urbana: University of Illinois Press, 2011.

Seaver, Nick. "Structuralism: Thinking with Computers." *Savage Minds*, May 21, 2014, http://savageminds.org/2014/05/21/structuralism-thinking-with-computers.

Tukey, John W. *Exploratory Data Analysis.* Reading, Mass.: Addison-Wesley, 1977.

Underwood, Ted, and Jordan Sellers. "How Quickly Do Literary Standards Change?" Preprint, May 19, 2015, DOI:10.6084/m9.figshare.1418394.

Wickham, Hadl0ey. *ggplot2: Elegant Graphics for Data Analysis.* New York: Springer, 2009.

Wilkens, Matthew. "The Geographic Imagination of Civil War-Era American Fiction." *American Literary History* 25, no. 4 (2013): 803–40.

Wilkinson, Leland. *The Grammar of Graphics.* 2nd ed. New York: Springer, 2005.

Videographic Criticism as a Digital Humanities Method

JASON MITTELL

When faced with the task of defining digital humanities to an outsider, I like to chart out three different but potentially overlapping modes of scholarship: humanistic study of digital cultural materials and practices, humanities scholarship that uses digital platforms for dissemination and presentation, and computational methods applied to humanistic topics. Such distinctions resonate fairly well within most humanistic fields, where analyzing digital culture is typically an innovative direction, and the distinction between digital dissemination and methodology makes sense. Within my own field of film and media studies, however, things are a bit more muddy.

The humanistic study of digital culture pervades the field of film and media studies, especially now that most media objects are either born in digital form or reborn, as with analog films being redistributed as DVDs or online streaming. Additionally, the vast majority of contemporary media are primarily produced through digital means, as analog recording technologies have withered away. While most film and media historians would not call themselves "digital scholars," we cannot ignore how the digitization of moving images has transformed our field. Digital dissemination of film and media scholarship has certainly been significant, especially through blogs and other forms of writing that move beyond typical formal academic formats. Innovative venues for multimedia publishing, such as the journal *Vectors* and the platform Scalar, allow text, moving images, and sound to coexist in the same digital spaces, thus helping media scholars situate our critical writing on the same plane as our objects of analysis.

Film and media scholars have been slower to explore the kinds of computational techniques, such as data mining and network visualization, that have flourished in the fields of literary studies and history. In part, this stems from the challenges of transforming moving images and sounds into data that can be treated algorithmically: it is comparatively easier, both in terms of user expertise and computing power, to quantify the written word using accessible tools and scripts than it is to quantify the multiple variables of complex images and sounds that change over time. Additionally, media studies has a long history of differentiating itself from its quantitative cousin discipline of mass communication, so embracing computational methods might seem like a retreat from its qualitative and interpretive distinctiveness. Although still on the margins of the field, computationally based film and media scholarship has worked to extend quantitative research both in forms that predate digital humanities, such as the Cinemetrics project, which quantifies film editing patterns as inspired by Barry Salt's statistical stylistics work starting in the 1970s, and in newly emerging areas, as with Kevin Ferguson's work on volumetric cinema discussed in Chapter 28 in this volume (see also Heras).

Parallel to this work, film and media scholars have also developed a mode of digital scholarship that at first blush might not seem to belong to the digital humanities per se: videographic criticism. At its most straightforward, videographic criticism is the expression of scholarly ideas via moving images and sound in audiovisual form. While such work derives from other forms of media production, such as documentaries about film and media, experimental essay films, and conceptual art pieces reusing film footage, the past decade has seen a set of norms and practices coalesce around what are often called "video essays." Unlike the more varied multimodal designs featured on *Vectors,* video essays typically resemble the more familiar format of a linear online video; such works are typically shorter than thirty minutes and incorporate sound and images from the films and media being analyzed, often using a voice-over narration to deliver an argument. While most video essays are focused on discussing formal features and interpretations of films, they can explore a wide range of topics, theoretical approaches, or objects of study. Some scholars have pushed back against video essays that are overtly explanatory, which at their least innovative resemble illustrated lectures, by suggesting that videographic works should embrace the poetic and aesthetic possibilities of film and media, and be more creative and expressive in their rhetoric. As Christian Keathley argues, videographic criticism needs to straddle the explanatory and poetic registers, aiming to produce a "knowledge effect" composed of sound and image, rather than just traditional argumentation best suited to the written word (see also Grant; López and Martin). It was in this spirit of exploration and experimentation that Keathley, Catherine Grant, Drew Morton, Christine Becker, and I cofounded *[in]Transition* as a journal of videographic criticism in 2014, publishing scholarly videos with open peer review via the MediaCommons scholarly network.[1] *[in]Transition* seeks to publish a broad range of styles and approaches to videographic criticism, while using its open peer review to discuss how scholarship in video form might fit within and advance scholarly discourse.

How might we situate videographic criticism in relation to digital humanities? While those of us who have helped develop and promulgate this mode of scholarship in the 2010s did not do so within the typical contexts of DH centers, labs, programs, or interdisciplinary clusters, there is clearly productive overlap.

Videographic criticism has received both direct and indirect support from DH funders: MediaCommons was among the first recipients of National Endowment for the Humanities DH funding, and the NEH recently funded three Institutes for Advanced Topics in the Digital Humanities on producing videographic criticism that Keathley and I first convened in 2015 (see Keathley and Mittell). But few videographic creators have situated their work as part of the broader field of digital humanities, and videographic work is not positioned as an approach typically found within DH practice.[2] I contend that videographic scholarship is a distinct DH method, one that has the potential to transform how we engage with, analyze, and convey ideas about moving image texts; such a method can both make digital humanities more open to film and media scholars and offer a new mode of digital scholarship to all scholars interested in moving images, regardless of their disciplinary home.

Returning to my initial tripartite classification of digital humanities, it seems clear that videographic criticism is an example of the first two modes: most videographic works examine cultural objects that were either born or reborn digital, such as films and television programs; and they depend on digital dissemination via online video sites, with the transformative possibilities inherent in new forms of peer review and open access. But is videographic criticism a computational method? I contend that it is, although we need to regard "method" in a broader context than in which the term is typically used.[3] For many DH approaches, computational methods take cultural works that are typically researched via interpretation, contextualization, and other forms of close qualitative analysis and transform them into quantifiable datasets that can then be analyzed algorithmically, classified and sorted, and rendered as visualizations, maps, or other new ways of looking at cultural works. Videographic criticism does include such a transformation of a cultural work into data, but few would regard this process as a method analogous to text mining or digital mapping: ripping a DVD and importing it into a video-editing application like Adobe Premiere seems on its face no more of a methodological transformation than scanning a book into a machine-readable PDF.

And yet, there is a key conceptual transformation that occurs when shifting a read-only video into an editing platform. In its DVD or streaming form, a film is a bound object that asserts its own coherence; we treat it as something with its own internal design, and traditional criticism is supposed to engage with the work on those terms through analysis and interpretation. But once a film is imported into video-editing software, it becomes something else: an archive of sounds and moving images. Importing a film into editing software enables a conceptual transformation that allows critics to see and hear it differently. Just as DH methods like text mining, distant reading, and cultural analytics allow scholars to see patterns across works, videographic criticism enables us to break the seal that binds a film as a finished work and then engage with its component parts. Even if you do not make something new with the sounds and images imported into the editing platform, you can still discover something new by exploring a film via this new interface.

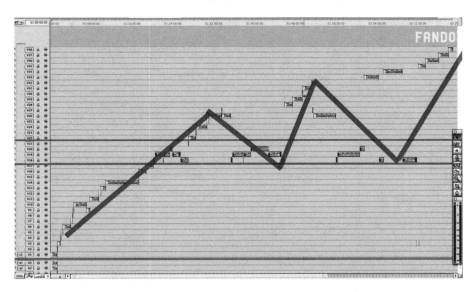

Figure 20.1. In his video essay "Viewing between the Lines: Hong Sang-soo's *The Day He Arrives*," Kevin B. Lee uses his Final Cut Pro interface to analyze the narrative structure of the film, grouping scenes by location and chronology.

A good example of such transformative insight comes from one of the most prolific and accomplished videographic critics, Kevin B. Lee. In his video essay "Viewing between the Lines: Hong Sang-soo's *The Day He Arrives*," Lee strives to make sense of a Korean film that seems to purposely present an incoherent and inconsistent narrative world. He uses his editing platform to break the film down into its component sixty-five shots and to organize them visually to highlight various locations, repetitions, and patterns. In addition to presenting his critical observations derived from that computationally enabled analysis, he includes screen-captured footage of his Final Cut Pro interface in his essay to reveal the methods he used to understand the film (see Figure 20.1).

Likewise, in his piece analyzing the 2014 race for the Best Actress Oscar, Lee uses an editing timeline to visualize Sandra Bullock's unconventional performance in *Gravity*, highlighting how much of her performance consists of her body and breath rather than voice (see Figure 20.2).

Lee did not produce these videos within the methodological terrain of digital humanities per se, but he is engaging with recent developments in technologically enabled visualization and quantitative methods.[4] These videos clearly employ a software platform to computationally transform a cultural object and reveal its elements that would be hard to discern with an analog eye. Is there a better description of what DH methods do?[5]

Another example of discovery via the computational transformation of film into a digital video-editing platform comes from a newer videographic critic. As part of our 2015 summer NEH workshop, film scholar Liz Greene was working on

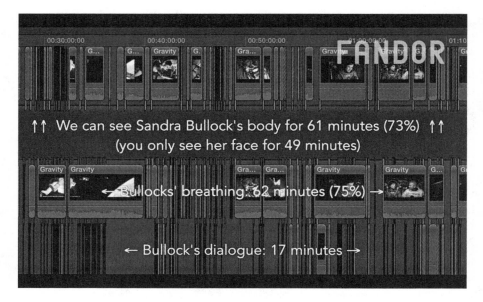

Figure 20.2. Kevin B. Lee also screen captures his video-editing interface in "Who Deserves the 2014 Oscar for Best Lead Actress?" to analyze the proportions of screen time that Sandra Bullock's breathing and disembodied voice occupy in *Gravity.*

a video about sound in David Lynch's films, a topic she has researched and written about for years (see "Bringing Video into the Digital Domain"). While manipulating footage in Premiere, she discovered uncanny similarities between the timing of sounds and images in the opening sequences of *The Elephant Man* and *Blue Velvet.* The result was "Velvet Elephant," a juxtaposition of these two sequences that experientially conveys her discovery and enables viewers to watch and hear the parallels between the otherwise quite different films. I would not call the resulting video "scholarship" per se, as it lacks analysis, argumentation, or context; however, it is most certainly "research," sharing a discovery that could only be realized through Greene's computational transformation of the two films.

An insight gained from such transformations is, in itself, research. Too often, the humanities frames "research" as the finished products of scholarship: the book, the essay, the lecture. But research and its associated methodologies are not limited to the final product of scholarship: rather, the processes of discovery and experimentation are often the more exciting and insightful parts of scholarly endeavors, and it is in such processes where methodologies are used and developed. In the sciences, exploratory research consists of the processes that are undertaken in the lab, using methods and techniques to discover new things and test ideas; in the humanities, that research is how we look at, read, connect, and think through the various cultural objects and practices that interest us. For instance, Stephen Ramsay suggests that experimentation with a computational tool applying graph theory to Shakespeare's scene structure was not attempting to prove anything in particular, but "to say something new, provocative, noteworthy, challenging, inspiring—to put these texts back into play as artifacts reconstituted by re-reading" ("In Praise of Pattern," 189). For videographic criticism, similar research happens within the editing interface, where we learn how to see a film in a new, unanticipated way. Such a computational transformation highlights that digital humanities need not be quantitative in its methods: while any software has a quantitative core, working with a video editor allows one to computationally explore the cultural realm of images and sounds, not just shot lengths, proportions, and color temperatures.

This transformation of finished media objects into a manipulable library of sounds and images is the first way that videographic criticism constitutes a methodological shift. Any strong work of videographic criticism builds on something learned through the editing process itself, not merely expressing ideas that were fully formed before engaging with the media in its transformed state. In the video editor, decoupling audio and video, clipping footage into patterns that differ from the original's edit, creating new juxtapositions between shots and sounds, and resequencing footage in contradiction to the narrative design all allow us to observe and discover something new about the original film. We could stop there, writing up these computationally enabled discoveries via more traditional analog means of the written word.[6] But once a film is imported into an editing platform, the possibilities of "writing" with sounds and images allows us to express this research via a new rhetoric that both draws on the affective and aesthetic experiences of viewing films and, like writing about literature, expresses critical ideas in the same medium of the object of analysis itself. Videographic critics like Lee and Greene aim to assemble the insights gained by computationally transforming a film into an archive of sounds and images, into something new: an expression of critical ideas via the tools of cultural production. Thus the second methodological shift in videographic criticism concerns the expressive modes both enabled and required in videographic work.

Images are typically a less denotative and more expressive communication medium than the written word, especially within the norms of academic writing. Creating scholarship with moving images and sounds forces critics to engage with the aesthetic and affective dimensions of their expression far more than do typical written works; they must draw on artistic practice as well as scholarly analysis. Additionally, expressing ideas with video enables more possibilities to use irony, ambiguity, sensation, and other poetic elements than does academic prose. While scholars Robert Ray and Greg Ulmer have urged a more poetic approach to academic writing for decades, their calls have largely been unheeded within film and media studies, perhaps because the norms of academic writing are too sedimented to broadly embrace such a radical approach to expression and associative analysis. However, videographic work foregrounds the poetics of the source material, embraces the aesthetics of images and sounds as forms of meaning-making, and takes advantage of the newness of the format to allow for more creative possibilities without being beholden to entrenched norms of typical academic rhetoric.

Is it fair to call such a mode of critical rhetoric a "methodology"? Perhaps not in isolation, but such rhetorical expansiveness does allow scholars to express different types of ideas and make new forms of arguments that recursively use media to critique themselves; such rhetoric thus has a methodological effect in enabling new ideas to develop. For instance, Michael Talbott's video "Encounters" narrates an unusual trip to Argentina over a compilation of clips from Argentine cinema; via this juxtaposition, he conveys ideas about the role of cinema as a form of virtual travel and what it means to "have been" to a place. Such ideas could be argued via academic writing, but they could not be expressed and experienced in the same way; in writing, they would lose the affective tone that is distinct to his videographic expression and conveys the feelings within Talbott's analysis rather than just the concepts. My own video, "*Adaptation.*'s Anomalies," begins at the limits of writing, taking up two aspects of *Adaptation.* that I could not find the words to analyze effectively in my recent book about the film, *Narrative Theory and* Adaptation. The direction in which my videographic analysis moves is far from the typical academic account, but it embraces a more ambiguous and playful tone that draws on the film's own discursive strategies, especially in its final section; my video essay reflects on its own critical practices, leaving viewers uncertain as to what analysis is intended to be "real" versus satirical, much like *Adaptation.*'s reflexivity about its own filmmaking process and ambiguously pitched final act. Videographic criticism can push such unconventional expressive tones to greater extremes than writing, especially when using the raw materials of a media text that already employs such reflexive themes. Thus, in videos like mine, Talbott's, and many others, the combination of ideas and tone simply could not be conveyed successfully using the written word, with videographic poetics adding new methodological possibilities to film and media scholarship. Additionally, my own process of generating ideas about *Adaptation.* would not have been feasible without the experience of analyzing its footage in the context of Adobe Premiere, because I would not have noticed some of the juxtapositions and connections had I just been watching and writing about the film through conventional means.

The possibilities of videographic method can be expanded even further through the combination of these two shifts, merging the computational possibilities of video-editing software with the expressive poetics of sounds and images. The former draws from scientifically derived practices of abstraction that are common to digital humanities: taking coherent cultural objects, such as novels or paintings, and transforming them into quantified datasets or graphs. The latter draws from artistic practices of manipulation and collage: taking coherent cultural objects and transforming them into raw materials to create something more unusual, unexpected, and strange. Videographic criticism can loop the extremes of this spectrum between scientific quantification and artistic poeticization together, creating works that transform films and media into new objects that are both data-driven abstractions and aesthetically expressive. I next outline three such possibilities that I have developed, using case studies of films that I know well and have used in the classroom.

The model of poeticized quantification that I am proposing resembles the vector of literary analysis that Lisa Samuels and Jerome McGann call "deformative criticism." Such an approach strives to make the original work strange in some unexpected way, deforming it unconventionally to reveal aspects that are conventionally obscured in its normal version and discovering something new from it. Both Stephen Ramsay, in *Reading Machines,* and Mark Sample extend Samuels and McGann's model of deformances into the computational realm, considering how algorithms and digital transformations might create both new readings of old cultural objects and new cultural objects out of old materials. This seems like an apt description of what videographic criticism can do: creating new cultural works composed from moving images and sound that reflect on their original source materials. While many types of video essays might be viewed as deformances, I want to explore a strain of videographic practice that emphasizes the algorithmic elements of such deformative work. One hopes that such work can also be inspirational to digital humanists working outside of videographic criticism as well, suggesting how algorithmic deformations, as well as any digitally constituted scholarship, can intertwine the computational and the poetic in unexpected ways.

One way to deform a film algorithmically is through a technique borrowed from conceptual art: the imposition of arbitrary parameters. From Oulipo, the collective of French artists who pioneered "constrained writing," to proto-videographic artworks like Douglas Gordon's *24 Hour Psycho* or Christian Marclay's *The Clock,* to obsessive online novelties of alphabetized remixes of films like *ARST ARSW* (*Star Wars*) and *Of Oz the Wizard* (*The Wizard of Oz*), artists have used rules and parameters to unleash creativity and generate works that emerge less from aesthetic intent than from unexpected generative outcomes.[7] For example, *24 Hour Psycho* (1993) takes Hitchcock's original film and slows it to the titular twenty-four hours, showing each frame for approximately a half second. The experience deforms the original's storytelling, pacing, and suspense, but allows viewers to notice elements of shot composition, gesture, and production design, all by permitting us to see what the film always was: a series of still images with only slight differences. Scholars can adopt such an unorthodox approach as well, allowing ourselves to be surprised by what emerges when we process datasets of sounds and images using seemingly arbitrary parameters. One such approach is a concept that Christian Keathley and I devised as part of our NEH workshop: a videographic PechaKucha. This format was inspired by oral PechaKuchas, a form of "lightning talk" consisting of exactly twenty slides lasting exactly twenty seconds, resulting in a strictly parametered presentation. Such parameters force decisions that override critical or creative intent and offer helpful constraints on our worst instincts toward digression or lack of concision.

A videographic PechaKucha adopts the strict timing from its presentational cousin, while focusing its energies on transforming its source material. It consists of precisely ten video clips from the original source, each lasting precisely six seconds, overlaid on a one-minute segment of audio from the original source: the video stands alone without a presenter. There are no mandates for content, for ideas, for analysis—it is only a recipe to transform a film into a one-minute video derivation or deformance. In creating videographic PechaKuchas with our workshop participants and our undergraduate students, we have found that the resulting videos are all quite different in approach and style, despite their uniformly parametered length and rhythm. For instance, Tracy Cox-Stanton deforms the film *Belle du Jour* into a succession of shots of the main character Séverine vacantly drifting through rooms and her environment, an element of the film that is far from central to the original's plot and themes, but is clearly embedded in the visual presentation of the character.[8] Or Corey Creekmur compiles images of doors being open and shut in *The Magnificent Ambersons* to highlight both a visual and thematic motif from the film.[9] In such instances, the highly parametric exercise enables the critic to discover and express something about each film through manipulation and juxtaposition that would be hard to discern via conventional viewing and even harder to convey evocatively via writing. Keathley and I have both used this PechaKucha technique in the classroom, as well as a departure point for our own analytic projects; as a mode of deformative research, it helps both novice students and experienced critics see a film in a radically new light, viewing the sounds and images as source material to be played with, rather than as locked-in components of a finished work.

Such experiments with videographic PechaKuchas follow arbitrary parameters to force a type of creativity and discovery that belies typical academic intent, but they are still motivated by the critic's insights into the film and aim to express something. A more radically arbitrary deformance removes intent altogether, allowing the parameters to work on the film and removing the critic's agency. I devised the concept for a videographic PechaKucha randomizer, which would randomly select the ten video clips and assemble them on top of a random minute of audio from the same source film; Mark Sample and Daniel Houghton executed my concept by creating a Python script to generate random PechaKuchas from any source video.[10] The resulting videos feel like the intentionally designed PechaKucha videos that I and others have made, sharing their uniform length and rhythm, but the content is truly arbitrary and random: they include repeated clips, idiosyncratic moments from closing credits, undefined sound effects, and oddly timed clips that include edits from the original film. And yet because they follow the same parameters as intentionally designed PechaKuchas, they are arguably just as much of a distillation of the original film and as such have the possibility to teach us something about the source text or create affective engagement with the deformed derivation.

Just as the algorithmic Twitter bots created by Mark Sample or Darius Kazemi produce a fairly low signal-to-noise ratio, most randomly generated PechaKuchas are less than compelling as stand-alone media objects; however, they can be interesting and instructive paratexts, highlighting elements from the original film or

evoking particular resonances via juxtaposition, and prompting unexpectedly provocative misreadings or anomalies.[11] For instance, in a generated PechaKucha from
Star Wars: A New Hope, Obi-Wan Kenobi's voice touts the accuracy of Stormtroop-
ers as the video shows a clip of them missing their target in a blaster fight, randomly
resonating with a popular fan commentary on the film.[12] Another randomly generated PechaKucha of *Mulholland Drive* distills the film down to the love story
between Betty and Rita, highlighting the key audio moment of Betty confessing her
love, with most clips drawn from scenes between the two characters; the resulting
video feels like a (sloppy but dedicated) fannish remix celebrating their relationship.
A generated PechaKucha of *All the President's Men* is anchored by one of the film's
most iconic lines, while the unrelated images focus our attention on patterns of shot
composition and framing, freed by our inattention to narrative. There are nearly
infinite possibilities of how algorithmic videos like these might create new deformations that could help teach us something new about the original film or constitute a compelling videographic object on its own merits; such randomly generated
videos support Samuels and McGann's insight that reorganizing a text can reveal
something buried within it that would be invisible in its conventional form. Each
of these acts of deformative videographic criticism takes approximately two minutes to randomly create itself, generating endless unforeseen critical possibilities.

Videographic PechaKuchas take inspiration from another medium, the oral
presentation, but we can also translate modes of film and media scholarship into
deformative videographic forms. One of the most interesting examples of parameter-
driven deformative criticism is Nicholas Rombes's "10/40/70" project. In a series of
blog posts and a corresponding book, Rombes created screen captures of frames
from precisely the 10-, 40-, and 70-minute marks in a film and then wrote an analysis of the film inspired by these three still images. Rombes acknowledged that he
was deforming the film by transmuting it into still images, thus disregarding both
motion and sound, but he aimed to draw out the historical connections between
filmmaking and still photography through this medium shift. The choice of the
three time markers was mostly arbitrary, although they roughly mapped onto the
beginning, middle, and end of a film. The result was that he could discover aspects
of the film that were otherwise obscured by narrative, motion, sound, and the thousands of other still images that surrounded the three he isolated: a clear example of
a deformance in Samuels and McGann's formulation.

What might a videographic 10/40/70 look like? It is technically simple to patch
together clips from each of the designated minute markers to create a moving
image and sound version of Rombes's experiment. Although we could use a range
of options for the length of each clip, after some experimentation I decided to
mimic Rombes's focus on individual frames by isolating the original shots that
include his marked frames, leading to videos with exactly three shots, but with far
more variability in length, rhythm, and scope. As with Rombes's experiment, the
arbitrary timing leads to highly idiosyncratic results for any given film. *Raiders of*

the Lost Ark yields a trio of shots without obvious narrative or thematic connection, but in isolation, we can recognize the cinematographic palette that Steven Spielberg uses to create action melodrama: camera movement to capture moments of stillness with an emphasis on off-screen or deep space, contrasted with facial close-ups to highlight character reactions and emotion. Isolating frames in *Star Wars: A New Hope* also calls attention to movement, with consistent left-to-right staging: first with the droids moving across the desert, then with Luke running to his landspeeder, then with Obi-Wan's head turning dramatically, which is continuous with the right-ward wipe edit that closes out the second shot. Both of these iconic films are driven by plot and action, but these arbitrary shots belie coherent narrative, allowing us to focus more on issues of visual style, composition, and texture.

Depending on the resulting shots, narrative can certainly emerge within these deformations. In *Fargo,* we start with a shot of used-car salesman Jerry sputtering about negotiating a car sale in the face of an irate customer, which abruptly cuts to Jerry sputtering about negotiating with kidnappers to his father-in-law, Wade, and colleague Stan in a diner, highlighting the consistent sputtering essence of Jerry's character, underscored by his nearly identical wardrobe across different days in the original film. The middle scene plays out in an unbroken eighty-second static shot, pulling us away from the deformity and placing us back into the original film, as the coherent narrative eclipses the incoherence of the 10/40/70 exercise. But knowing that we are watching a deformation, we wait for the unexpected cut to jump us forward in time, splitting our attention between the film and its anticipated manipulation. The narrative action guides the transition, as Wade impatiently refuses to abide by Jerry's plan to deliver the ransom and stalks away saying "Dammit!" The resulting arbitrary edit follows the most basic element of narrative, cause and effect: we cut to Wade being shot by one of the kidnappers, punctuated by a musical sting and evoking Stan's earlier line that they will need "to bite the bullet." The final jarring effect stems from the final shot being less than three seconds long, a startling contrast to the previous long take, and underscores the contrast between the incongruities of mundanity and brutality, boring stasis and vicious action that are the hallmark of *Fargo* and much of the work of the Coen brothers. Although it certainly feels like an unusual video, *Fargo 10/40/70* also functions as a cultural object in its own right, creating emotional responses and aesthetic engagement in a manner that points to one of the strengths of videographic work: the power of sound and moving images works to captivate viewers, even when conventions of storytelling and structure are arbitrarily deformed.

The distinction between print-based and videographic deformations becomes clear by comparing Rombes's written results working with stills to a videographic version of the same film. Rombes analyzes three stills from *Mildred Pierce,* and they point him toward elements of the film that are frequently discussed in any analysis: the contradictions and complexities of Mildred's character, how she fits into the era's gender norms, and the blurs between *film noir* and melodrama.[13] The images launch his analysis, but they do not direct it to unexpected places. The videographic version is more provocative, offering more opportunities for (productive) mis-understanding and incoherence. The first shot finds Mildred's old associate Wally panicking and discovering her husband Monty's dead body in a *noir*ish moment of male murder and mayhem, but quickly gives way to a scene of female melodrama between mother Mildred and daughter Veda. Mildred's first line, "I'm sorry I did that," suggests a causal link that she is apologizing for murdering Monty. Knowl-edge of the film makes this implied causality much more complex, as the murder is a future event that sets the stage for the rest of the film being told in flashback; in the frame story, Mildred appears to have murdered Monty, with the flashback slowly revealing the real killer to be Veda. Thus this scene works as a decontextu-alized confession made to the actual (future) murderer, adding temporal resonance and highlighting how the entire flashback and murder plotline was a genre-spinning element added to the screenplay but not present in the original novel. The third scene picks up the discussion of the restaurant and finances, bringing it back to the conflict between Wally and Monty; if we were to temporally rearrange the shots to correspond to the story chronology, the opening shot of Wally finding Monty's body would seem to resolve this conflict, creating a closed loop of causality for this deformed version of the film. This brief analysis is no more valid or compelling than Rombes's discussion, but it is certainly less conventional, triggered by the narra-tive and affective dimensions cued by the videographic deformation that ultimately seems more suggestive and provocative than the three still images.

The model of the videographic 10/40/70 relies on the single shot as the core unit of a film, following a tendency common to much academic work on moving image media. My third and final type of videographic deformation also highlights the shot, but using a distinctly different approach. As mentioned earlier, one of the most prominent forms of quantitative and computational analysis within film stud-ies is statistical stylistics, especially as shared on the crowdsourced Cinemetrics website. Although there are numerous metrics on the site, the most common and well known is ASL, or average shot length, computed by dividing the time of a full film by its number of discrete shots. The resulting number indicates a film's overall editing pace, charting a spectrum from quickly cut movies (such as *Batman Begins* at 2.37 seconds or *Beverly Hills Chihuahua* at 2.72) to longer-take films (such as *An American in Paris* at 21 seconds or *Belle du Jour* at 24).[14] Most films fall between three and eight seconds per shot, with much variability between historical eras, genres, national traditions, and specific filmmakers.

An ASL is in itself a kind of quantitative transformation, a reduction of a film to a single numeric representation. Cinemetrics does allow more detailed quanti-fication and visualization of a film's editing patterns; for instance, a more granular and graphic elaboration of *Mulholland Drive*'s ASL of 6.5 is shown in Figure 20.3.[15]

But these numbers, tables, and graphics make the film more distant and remote, leaving me uncertain about what we can learn from such quantification. According

ASL: 6.5 MSL: 4.1 MSL/ASL: 0.63 LEN: 141:35.2 NoS: 1303 MAX: 130.9 MIN: 0.4 Range: 130.5 StDev: 8.5 CV: 1.31

Name:	Betty	Rita	Betty+R	Adam	Diane	Diane+C	Diane+C	Other
Number of shots:	73	76	488	232	82	15	107	230
Length(min):	10.55	8.07	52.52	20.2	13.09	3.52	10.11	23.53
ASL(sec):	8.7	6.4	6.5	5.2	9.6	14.1	5.7	6.1
MSL	4.6	3.9	4.3	3.5	3.7	8.5	4.1	4.3
MSL/ASL	0.53	0.61	0.67	0.67	0.39	0.6	0.72	0.7
StDev	16.7	6.8	7.5	4.8	14.5	16.4	4.6	7.2
Min	0.9	0.4	0.8	0.7	1	4.2	1.1	0.7
Max	130.9	45.6	66.2	37.3	81.7	73.3	26.4	62.2
CV	1.92	1.07	1.16	0.92	1.52	1.16	0.81	1.17
Display?	☑	☑	☑	☑	☑	☑	☑	☑
Color								

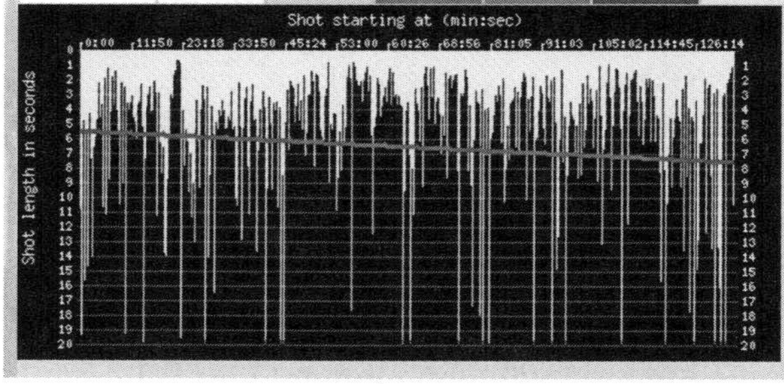

Figure 20.3. On the site Cinemetrics, films can be transformed into datasets and quantitative measures, as in this rendering of *Mulholland Drive* produced and submitted by user Nikki Esselaar.

to Yuri Tsivian, Cinemetrics's founder, the insights are quite limited: "ASL is useful if the only thing we need to know is how long this or that average shot is as compared to ASL figures obtained for other films, but it says nothing about each film's internal dynamics." Certainly, such comparison is the most useful feature of ASL, because it allows quantitative analysis among a large historical corpus, a general approach that has proven quite productive in digital humanities across a range of fields. But I question Tsivian's quick dismissal that ASL "says nothing about each film's internal dynamics." Does a film with a 2.5-second cutting rate feel and function differently than one with a 15-second ASL? Certainly, and it does not take a quantification to notice those differences. But such a quantification might also point toward a more thorough understanding of editing rates through deformation.

Videographic methods, which use media texts to critique themselves in reflexive ways, allow us to impose a film's ASL back onto itself. I have created a videographic experiment called an "equalized pulse": instead of treating ASL as a calculated average abstracted from the film, I force a film to conform to its own average by speeding up or slowing down each shot to last precisely as long as its average shot length.[16] This process forces one filmic element that is highly variable within nearly every film, the length of each shot, to adhere to a constant duration that emerges quantitatively from the original film; yet it offsets this equalizing deformation with another one, making the speed of each shot, which is typically constant, highly variable. Thus in a film with an ASL of 4 seconds, the equalized pulse extends a 1-second shot to 25 percent speed, while an 8-second shot runs at 200 percent speed. If you equalized an entire film to its average pulse, it would have the same running time and the same number of shots, but each shot would be slowed down or sped up to conform to an identical length. Every shot exerts the same temporal weight, but each feels distinct in its tempo and pace. The result is, unsurprisingly, very strange—but productively so, both by revealing editing strategies in the original film and by creating new aesthetic objects out of the film's raw materials.

What does *Mulholland Drive* look and feel like when equalized to a pulse of its 6.5-second ASL? Can we learn something more about the "film's internal dynamics" than its numeric representations on Cinemetrics? Take the film's opening scene following the credits, with Rita's car accident on the titular street; in the original, it lasts 4:07 with 49 shots ranging in length between 0.3 and 27 seconds. The deformed version with an equalized pulse of every shot lasting precisely 6.5 seconds runs 5:18, because the original sequence is cut comparatively faster (ASL of 5.04 seconds) than the film as a whole. The effect is quite uncanny, with super slow-motion action sequences bookended by sped-up shots with less on-screen action; the car accident is particularly unsettling, turning a nine-shot, 6-second sequence into a grueling and abstract 58-second ordeal that oddly exaggerates the effect of experiencing a moment of trauma in slow motion. As a whole, the video does convey the sense that a pulse of 6.5 seconds feels quite deliberate and drawn out, although the variability of action obscures the consistency of the editing pulse.

Another scene from *Mulholland Drive* offers quite different effects, despite the same algorithmic deformation to conform to the same equalized pulse. The memorable scene in Winkies Diner, where two men discuss and confront a dream, is a pivotal moment in the film, signaling an affective impact that transcends any rational comprehension or interpretation. When equalized to a 6.5-second pulse, the scene's uncanniness is ratcheted up, downplaying the dialogue's rhythm that emphasizes Dan in the original, in favor of a more even distribution between the two men. The slow-motion close-ups with distorted voices highlight the film's dreamlike quality, and its overall slower pace increases the sense of foreboding that already pervades the scene. By the time the horrific bum is revealed at the scene's end, I find myself completely enthralled by the editing pulse and pulled into the affective horror that the scene always produces, suggesting that its impact is not dependent on Lynch's designed editing rhythms. Extending this equalized pulse to the entire film, each scene and sequence feels quite different, even with a uniform shot length throughout.

Mulholland Drive is a film packed with abundant strangeness, even before its deformation, but equalized pulses make more conventional examples strange as well. Even though *Mildred Pierce* features the unusual combination of *noir* crime and family melodrama, it is still a far more straightforward film in keeping with its 1940s era. Its ASL of 10.09 is much slower than films of today, but is fairly typical of its time. Equalizing the pulse of a crucial scene in the family melodrama, with Veda driving a wedge between Mildred and Monty, who finally end their dysfunctional relationship, highlights various character interactions. When Mildred gives Veda a car, the deformation speeds through her thanking her mother, but lingers on her exchange with Monty, underscoring the closeness between stepfather and daughter; in the original, the emphasis is reversed in terms of timing, but equalizing the shots actually better represents Veda's attitudes. The deformation lingers over shots without dialogue, letting us closely examine facial expressions and material objects, but speeds through lengthy dialogue shots, like an impatient viewer fast-forwarding through the mushy emotional scenes. The final lines exchanged between Mildred and Monty are unreasonably drawn out, milking their mutual contempt for all that it is worth. The scene is still legible, especially emotionally, but it redirects our attention in unpredictable ways: arguably a key goal of an effective deformance.

Equalizing the pulse of an action film on the other end of the pacing spectrum, such as *Raiders of the Lost Ark,* also points to unseen revelations. The film has an ASL of 4.4 seconds, longer than most contemporary action movies, but still quite brisk, especially for director Steven Spielberg. I deformed the iconic opening sequence, but used the sequence's faster ASL of 3.66 rather than the whole film's pacing, because that allows for a direct comparison of the original and equalized versions (see Figure 20.4). The effect is definitely striking, as the deformed version races through the buildup toward action and peril, while lingering painfully on darts flying through the air, near-miss leaps, and other moments of derring-do. In the slowed-down shots, one notices odd details that would be overlooked in the conventional film, like the discoloration of Indy's teeth, and the sequence conveys a very different momentum. When placed side by side with the original, it highlights how much of the sequence is weighted toward the approach and buildup

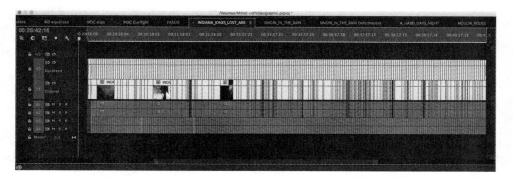

Figure 20.4. The film *Raiders of the Lost Ark*'s opening sequence, when broken into individual shots in Adobe Premiere and then juxtaposed with an equalized pulse of 3.66 seconds, demonstrates the rhythmic use of editing in the sequence to convey energy and direct attention to particular moments.

rather than the action, while the deformed version lingers on moments that regularly flit by.

The editing timeline visualizes these differences, but in a way that is analytically obscure; the videographic form allows us to feel and experience the analysis in ways that computational visualization cannot. What stands out most to me in this deformation is the role of music, as John Williams's memorable score still manages to hit its key themes and punctuate the action, despite its variable tempo and rhythms.

This experiment in equalizing a film's pulse points most interestingly toward the different types and functions of rhythm and tempo. In a conventionally edited film, variation of shot length is a main source of rhythmic play, both in creating emotional engagement and guiding our attention. Eliminating that variation by equalization creates other forms of rhythm and tempo, as we notice the relative screen time given to various characters, anticipate the upcoming edits in a steady pulse, and engage with the interplay between image and sound. These equalized deformations highlight how much the analysis of editing and ASL privileges the visual track over the audio: we are not quantifying audio edits or transitions in such metrics, as continuous sounds bridge across shots, slowing or speeding up like an accordion.

Equalized pulse experiments reveal and highlight how visual editing functions in conjunction with music, especially for instances where the musical track is more dominant, as with film musicals or music videos. Experimenting with musical sequences yielded the most exciting examples of equalized pulse, because they highlight the transformation of rhythm and tempo: the musical track stretches and squashes to create unpredictable rhythms and jettisons its standard tempo, allowing the steady beat of the changing visuals to define the speed. For instance, "Can't Buy Me Love" from The Beatles film *A Hard Day's Night* becomes a collage of fast and slow motion when equalized to its sequence ASL of 4.9 seconds, making an already playful and experimental sequence even more unpredictable. Musical sequences combined with dance add another layer of rhythmic play, as with the transformation of *Singin' in the Rain*'s "Broadway Melody" into a deformed and almost uncanny work when equalized to its ASL of 14.9 seconds. Musical numbers are often edited at a slower pace than their films as a whole, providing more attention to performance and dance without being pulled away by edits. A rare exception is one of the fastest-cut films listed on the Cinemetrics site, and certainly the fastest-cut musical I know of: *Moulin Rouge,* with an ASL of 1.9 seconds. The "Roxanne" number, with an even brisker ASL of 1.05 seconds, is the only equalized pulse video I have yet made where the visual tempo becomes noticeably dominant, offering a steady beat of images and sounds whose fast-paced deformations go by so quickly as to often escape notice.

These equalized pulse versions of musical numbers are the most engaging and affective examples of videographic deformations I have made, functioning as compelling cultural objects both on their own and as provocatively deformative paratexts. They also demand further analysis and study, opening up a line of examination concerning the relative uses of edits, music, and dance to create rhythm and tempo. As such, these videographic deformations may not stand as scholarship on their own, but they do function as research, pointing the way to further scholarly explorations. Whether that subsequent scholarship is presented in written, videographic, or multimodal forms is still to be determined, but such work shows how videographic criticism is more than just a form of digital dissemination. Likewise, videographic deformations convey affective and aesthetic dimensions that textual deformances often lack: experiments with the written word can lead to great revelations, but I did not fully understand the uncanny transformative power of deformations until I experienced an equalized pulse video.

Transforming a bound cultural object like a film into a digital archive of sounds and images enables a mode of critical engagement that is impossible to achieve by other methods. Such experimental work is invaluable in the classroom as well; it is useful as a tool to help students notice aspects of visual media that are hard to discern through conventional viewing practices focused on narrative, spectacle, or emotional engagement. As such, videographic criticism can function as a DH research method—both in transforming media objects in unexpected and revealing ways and by enabling a mode of poetic expression to convey ideas ill suited for writing—that is poised to develop the field of film and media studies in unpredictable new ways. Additionally, digital humanists can learn from videographic criticism and deformances as reminders of the aesthetic power of the cultural works that we manipulate, quantify, and transform. A common (and certainly overblown) criticism of the digital humanities is that reducing literary works to data points both destroys aesthetic elements essential to literature and undermines the central role of reading; videographic criticism mines the aesthetic elements of moving images and sounds and redirects the power of viewing toward the act of critical engagement.

NOTES

1. http://mediacommons.org/intransition/.

2. For instance, there were seemingly no presentations that used or explored the video essay as a mode of practice at the international Digital Humanities conferences in 2015, 2016, or 2017.

3. See Grant for a similar discussion of videographic method, although she productively situates the links to artistic practice and theory, rather than the digital humanities.

4. When I approached Lee about these examples, he wrote, "I would say that any video essay produced through digital technology (i.e. virtually all of them) would count as digital humanities. Videographic essays in themselves represent a digital methodology, given that they are necessitating scholars and students to adopt digital technology in order to produce such work." Personal email from Kevin B. Lee, January 6, 2016.

5. Just as Matthew Jockers notes that transforming literature into "massive digital corpora offer us unprecedented access to the literary record and invite, even demand, a new type of evidence gathering and meaning making," the shift of a bound media text into

a video editor to convert it into an archive of sounds and images allows us to see and hear things in new, unexpected ways (8).

6. Of course, few of us write via analog means anymore, but clearly using a word processor does not make us digital humanists.

7. http://radar.spacebar.org/f/a/weblog/comment/1/1109 and https://vimeo.com /150423718.

8. http://www.criticalcommons.org/Members/videographic/clips/belle-du-jour -pechakucha/view.

9. http://www.criticalcommons.org/Members/videographic/clips/the-magnificent -ambersons-pechakucha/view.

10. https://github.com/samplereality/videographic-pecha-kucha.

11. https://twitter.com/samplereality/lists/samplereality-bots.

12. This and all of the other videographic deformations discussed in this chapter are collected and available at https://videographicsandbox.wordpress.com/2017/09/05 /examples-of-deformations.

13. http://therumpus.net/2010/06/104070-11-mildred-pierce/.

14. Unless otherwise noted, all ASL data are taken from Barry Salt's dataset on Cinemetrics, http://www.cinemetrics.lv/satltdb.php#asl; even though the site includes many more films with crowdsourced information, I have found they lack the consistency and methodological clarity of Salt's list, which is easier to use to compare films.

15. Salt's list does not include this film, so I used the ASL and this graphic from Nikki Esselaar's submission at http://www.cinemetrics.lv/movie.php?movie_ID=16838.

16. The process to do this is fairly straightforward in Adobe Premiere: first cut the source video into clips per the original edits. Then select all of the clips and use the Clip Speed / Duration tool. Unlink the Speed and Duration variables, and enter the number of seconds and frames in Duration corresponding to the ASL. Relink Speed and Duration, and be sure to check the Maintain Audio Pitch and Ripple Edit buttons. The only troubles come when a clip is stretched out or sped up more than 1,000 percent, because then the audio needs to be manually processed with more complex intervening steps.

BIBLIOGRAPHY

The author's videographic deformations discussed in this chapter are collected and available at https://videographicsandbox.wordpress.com/2017/09/05/examples-of-deformations/.

Ferguson, Kevin L. "Volumetric Cinema." *[in]Transition* 2, no. 1 (2015), http://mediacom mons.org/intransition/2015/03/10/volumetric-cinema.

Grant, Catherine. "The Shudder of a Cinephiliac Idea? Videographic Film Studies Practice as Material Thinking," *Aniki: Portuguese Journal of the Moving Image* 1, no. 1 (January 2014): 49–62.

Greene, Liz. "Bringing Vinyl into the Digital Domain: Aesthetics in David Lynch's *Inland Empire*." *The New Soundtrack* 2, no. 2 (September 2012): 97–111.

Greene, Liz. "Velvet Elephant." 2015, http://vimeo.com/131802926.

Heras, Daniel Chávez. "The Malleable Computer: Software and the Study of the Moving Image," *Frames Cinema Journal* 1, no. 1 (July 2012), http://framescinemajournal.com /article/the-malleable-computer/.

Jockers, Matthew L.. *Macroanalysis: Digital Methods and Literary History*. Champaign: University of Illinois Press, 2013.

Keathley, Christian, "*La Caméra-Stylo*: Notes on Video Criticism and Cinephilia." In *The Language and Style of Film Criticism,* edited by Alex Clayton and Andrew Klevan, 176–91. London: Routledge, 2011.

Keathley, Christian, and Jason Mittell, *The Videographic Essay: Criticism in Sound and Image*. Montreal: caboose books, 2016. https://www.caboosebooks.net/the-video graphic-essay.

Lee, Kevin B. "Viewing Between the Lines: Hong Sang-soo's *The Day He Arrives*." 2012, https://vimeo.com/50379364.

Lee, Kevin B. "Who Deserves the 2014 Oscar for Best Lead Actress?" 2015, https://vimeo .com/85746719.

López, Christina Álvarez, and Adrian Martin. "Analyse and Invent: A Reflection on Making Audiovisual Essays." *Frames Cinema Journal,* no. 8 (December 2015), http://frames cinemajournal.com/article/analyse-and-invent-a-reflection-on-making-audiovisual -essays/.

Mittell, Jason. "*Adaptation.*'s Anomalies." *[in]Transition* 3, no. 1 (March 2016), http:// mediacommons.org/intransition/2016/03/18/adaptations-anomalies.

Mittell, Jason. *Narrative Theory and* Adaptation. London: Bloomsbury Press, 2017.

Ramsay, Stephen "In Praise of Pattern." *TEXT Technology: The Journal of Computer Text Processing* 14, no. 2 (January 1, 2005): 177–90.

Ramsay, Stephen. *Reading Machines: Toward an Algorithmic Criticism*. Champaign: University of Illinois Press, 2011.

Ray, Robert B. *The Avant-Garde Finds Andy Hardy*. Cambridge, Mass: Harvard University Press, 1995.

Rombes, Nicholas. *10/40/70: Constraint as Liberation in the Era of Digital Film Theory*. London: Zero Books, 2014.

Sample, Mark. "Notes towards a Deformed Humanities." Sample Reality. May 2012, http:// www.samplereality.com/2012/05/02/notes-towards-a-deformed-humanities/.

Samuels, Lisa, and Jerome J. McGann. "Deformance and Interpretation." *New Literary History* 30, no. 1 (1999): 25–56.

Talbott, Michael. "Encounters." *[in]Transition* 2, no. 4 (January 2016), http://mediacom mons.org/intransition/encounters.

Tsivian, Yuri. "Taking Cinemetrics into the Digital Age." Cinemetrics. http://www.cine metrics.lv/dev/tsivian_2.php. Accessed January 7, 2016.

Ulmer, Gregory L. *Teletheory: Grammatology in the Age of Video*. New York: Routledge, 1989.

Spaces of Meaning: Conceptual History, Vector Semantics, and Close Reading

MICHAEL GAVIN, COLLIN JENNINGS, LAUREN KERSEY, AND BRAD PASANEK

In the digital humanities, much research in text analysis has concerned techniques of observing large-scale lexical patterns. This chapter argues for a method of computationally assisted close reading that draws from two distinct intellectual traditions: *conceptual history* and *vector semantics*. The history of concepts is a subfield of political history, spearheaded by Reinhart Koselleck and devoted to the study of sociopolitical ideas like *nation, democracy, rights,* and *progress.*[1] The primary challenge for concept theory is to articulate how ideas function as historical objects and to explain how they emerge and transform over time. Vector semantics is a subfield of computational linguistics devoted to the quantitative study of word meaning. Its intellectual tradition stretches back to the postwar period, when linguists like Zellig Harris and J. R. Firth first articulated the "distributional hypothesis," suggesting that semantics could be modeled by analyzing how words co-occur throughout a corpus. We argue that conceptual history and vector semantics play well together: concepts are precisely the kinds of historical object that semantic analyses are good at measuring, and concept theory provides an apt vocabulary for interpreting quantitative results of text analysis. Much like the "topics" produced by topic models, concepts are best understood as structural patterns that recur among words. Roughly analogous to communities like those detected in social-network analysis, concepts are clusters of terms that co-occur throughout a corpus. The task of historical vector semantics is to identify such concepts, to see where and when they appear and how they change over time, and to study how they are deployed in individual documents, by individual authors, and among historical communities.

Vector-space models represent a corpus in much the same way topic models do: both kinds of modeling produce lists of words meant to display an underlying thematic or conceptual coherence, and both identify latent semantic features that stretch meaningfully across large corpora.[2] According to Matthew Jockers, "cultural memes and literary themes are not expressed in single words or even in single bigrams or trigrams. Themes are formed of bigger units and operate on a higher plane" (122). Topics represent patterns of word collocation that transcend individual sentences, paragraphs, and even documents.[3] Similarly, vector-space models of word meaning trace patterns over an entire corpus. However, rather than identify patterns over a preselected number of topics (whether fifty or five hundred), vector-space models create statistical profiles for every word, and each of those profiles can be broken up into any number of clusters. For this reason, vector semantics is not as good at describing the broad themes that predominate in a corpus, but is very good at detailing word uses at the microlevel, which includes exploring all the ways a word has been used, identifying how it is invoked in a single text or phrase, or showing how the meanings of words combine, at a deep conceptual level, in the human statements that deploy them.

Discussion of textual analysis has tended to emphasize the ability of computers to describe language at a large scale, as in the oppositions between "distant reading" and "close reading" or between "micro-" and "macroanalysis."[4] Privileging large-scale studies that stretch over centuries has an unfortunate consequence: it forecloses attention to how those large linguistic patterns inform the meanings of particular words and phrases. Recent developments in conceptual history have shown how concepts, visible at the macroscale, inform the individual statements recorded in texts. The work of conceptual historian Peter de Bolla, in particular, has shown how texts mobilize and actualize concepts drawn from a "conceptual substrate" of language. To illustrate how texts do this and to demonstrate how semantic models might support the study of concepts, we offer a short case study that uses a large-scale model of historical semantics—drawn from the Early English Books Online (EEBO) corpus—to describe the concepts deployed in a single text. John Dryden's *MacFlecknoe* (1678) is known to historians of British literature as a classic in the genre of parody that masterfully juxtaposes low topics (in this case, the petty rivalries of poets) with high ones (the successions of kings). Such burlesques depend for their satire on finding deep conceptual similarities that cross social domains. For Dryden, one such concept was *wit,* a mental ability and a form of verbal performance that engendered new social hierarchies. *MacFlecknoe* therefore represents an innovative political application of the period's most important literary concept.[5] Moreover, *wit* serves as an analog to or metaphor for semantic modeling in general. *Wit* describes the faculty for finding resemblance in difference, for seeing that seemingly disparate concepts are surprisingly allied when considered in new lights. Philosopher John Locke described *wit* as the "assemblage of *Ideas,*" and there is likely no better phrase to describe computational semantics. A vector-space model is a vast assemblage of ideas from which we hope to assemble new histories of concepts.

Conceptual History

Discussions of concept theory often begin by emphasizing a basic point: concepts are not words. The distinction can be glimpsed by considering any collection of synonyms, such as *rubbish, trash, waste, junk.* Each of these words has a distinct use, and they imply different connotations and meanings, but there remains a principle of synonymy among them, an underlying concept that ties them together. Yet, that conceptual *je ne sais quoi* does not perfectly fit any of them. Just as none of these words exactly matches any other, so too none is identical to the idea of "stuff that gets thrown away." The technical term in linguistics is *onomasiology,* which names the study of how multiple words express a single concept. An onomasiological approach to modeling language makes it possible to trace ideas comparatively across national boundaries or diachronically across time. American, Chinese, or Iranian concepts of democratic governance might have surprising similarities even if they use different words for "freedom." Concepts are verbal forms that are more complex than words or, if not more complex, at least they are different.

The phrase "history of concepts" is most directly associated with Reinhart Koselleck, a twentieth-century German historian and social theorist whose greatest work was a massive encyclopedia of political terms: the *Geschichtliche Grundbegriffe,* or, as the title has been translated, *Basic Concepts in History: A Historical Dictionary of Political and Social Language in Germany.*[6] Koselleck's lexical histories trace the evolution of concepts across the Enlightenment, following the transition from the feudal system to a modern, capitalist moral order. Conceptual history critiques narratives that project modern meanings of terms onto the past or those that presume that ideas are inexorably determined by changes in technology, industry, or class relations. Koselleck's analysis aims to show that ideas do real work forming a culture's horizons of expectation and intelligibility; they are not merely along for the ride. The history of concepts is meant to narrate change diachronically over time; to show how concepts emerge, evolve, and fall away along multiple temporalities (which only sometimes correspond to the course of human events).[7] Koselleck also examines concepts synchronously to show how they subsist at any moment in time within a *semantic field,* where concepts gain meaning in relation to each other. A concept like "freedom" means nothing by itself; it acquires significance only against counterconcepts like "slavery."[8]

Critics of Koselleck's theory (Quentin Skinner and J. G. A. Pocock, most famously) have doubted that concepts really can be abstracted from their contexts, and so they prefer to narrate the histories of social movements and political conflicts.[9] For Koselleck and his followers, however, taking the concept as the primary unit of analysis retains much appeal. Most importantly, the history of concepts aims to uncover something more fundamental, abstract, and potentially valuable than social history can do by itself. Koselleck posits, "Without common concepts, there is no society, and above all, no political field of action" (*Futures Past,* 76). At its most ambitious, the history of conceptuality hopes to show how critical ideation reacts to and spurs social change, with the utopian goal of laying a new conceptual foundation for a more just world order. Koselleck explains, "Concepts no longer serve merely to define given states of affairs, but reach into the future . . . positions that were to be secured had first to be formulated linguistically before it was possible to enter or permanently occupy them" (80).

The history of concepts has taken a computational turn in the work of Peter de Bolla. His 2013 book, *Architecture of Concepts: The Historical Formation of Human Rights,* is a signal example of studying the past by means of its linguistic collocations. His primary case study is the history of *rights.* Relying on keyword searches in Eighteenth Century Collections Online, de Bolla shows how the words that appeared near *rights* changed over the hundred-year period. Early on, *rights* were associated with the *liberties* and *privileges* of institutions like *parliament* and the *church.* By the end of the century, however, *rights* had inhered in the individual and were more likely to collocate with words like *man* and *sacred.* De Bolla's book thus offers a rationale and an exemplary method for the study of "conceptual forms"; that is, concepts concretized in usage. Locating himself in the wake of the twentieth-century linguistic turn and in a new, twenty-first-century digital moment, de Bolla furthers the work of intellectual history and discourse analysis by reconfiguring the conceptual turn in intellectual history by computational means.

Although the deep, structuring concepts investigated are "ineradicably linguistic," de Bolla claims to be doing more than just counting words and describing linguistic patterns (3). Indeed, he continually figures his inquiry in terms of geometry, subway maps, architecture, and networks. These metaphors provide foundational, architectonic images for historical possibility:

> Concepts operate according to a specific grammar and syntax that situates them in a network of linked concepts. That grammar and syntax becomes legible by tracking the use of words over time, as do the networks within which they were historically suspended. In order to be linked together, concepts have to present themselves as variously open or closed; this "fit" depends upon the shape or format of a concept's edges, which permit more or less compatible interconnections. That shape is determined by the internal configuration of each concept. Taken together, the network connections and the internal structure comprise the architecture of a concept. (40)

Aiming to quantify the dispersion of conceptual forms in printed matter, de Bolla's study of human rights is instead a history of that which is in excess of the word. Concepts do not inhere in words, but emerge among their interactions. His main effort is to exhume a conceptual "substrate" or "network" by attending to the keyword *rights* and its changing collocations.

Whereas de Bolla traces the history of a single term, vector-space models construct large matrices of words that summarize a more complete set of interconnections. These connections reflect common habits of language that permeate a corpus, but are largely invisible to writers and readers, resulting in linguistic patterns that transcend the subjective experience of communication. Jonathan Hope and Michael Witmore argue that textual models provocatively generate "retroactive statistical facts—independent of subjects who could never have hoped to recognize them but [that are] already real for us, once belatedly discovered" (148).[10] Text analysis finds collocates, bags of words, and keywords-in-context at the scale of the corpus. Considered in the light of concept theory, we might say that collocation analysis uncovers layers of meaning that form the basic conceptual structure of language without being experienced as such by readers or writers. In his study of *rights,* de Bolla shows that such structures can be identified using quantitative methods, but he leaves open the question of which mathematics is most appropriate for this purpose.

Vector Semantics

Many digital humanists first encountered computational methods of modeling linguistic structures in topic modeling, which makes it possible to track large-scale patterns of language. This trend, however, has run counter to research in computational linguistics—most notably using vector semantics—that has focused on word-sense disambiguation. Vector semantics is known by a variety of terms, such as "vector-based representation," "distributional semantics," and "word-embedding models." Whatever one calls it, the theory that informs vector semantics can be traced to the postwar period of the late 1940s and 1950s, when military success with cryptography led scholars to believe that language as a whole might be computationally tractable. Edwin Reifler, Victor Ngve, and Anthony Oettinger, among others, sought to train computers to automatically translate scientific papers in German, English, Chinese, and Russian (see Nirenburg, Somers, and Wilks). Before accomplishing this feat, however, they faced an obvious and seemingly insurmountable challenge: How could computers differentiate among the possible meanings of a word in order to identify the appropriate synonym in another language? In a 1949 memorandum (first published in 1955), Warren Weaver, then director of the Rockefeller Foundation Natural Sciences Division, proposed a technique for solving this problem. Rather than map each word directly onto a dictionary, documents would first be subject to an additional stage of processing in which each word would be compared to the words in its immediate context:

> If one examines the words in a book, one at a time as through an opaque mask with a hole in it one word wide, then it is obviously impossible to determine, one at a time, the meaning of the words. . . . But if one lengthens the slit in the

opaque mask, until one can see not only the central word in question but also say N words on either side, then if N is large enough one can unambiguously decide the meaning of the central word. (Weaver, 15–16)

Of course a computer cannot tell the difference between "plane" and "plane," but if the context window is expanded just a bit, computers might be able to differentiate "pilot landed the plane at the airport" from "line intersects the plane at an angle." Air travel and geometry contribute two senses of the word "plane," and those differences could be measured (or, at least, approximated) using collocation data.

What began as a specific practical solution to a challenge in scientific communication was immediately recognized for having the potential to transform the study of semantics.[11] The latent idea here is that different words will tend to appear in different contexts, and therefore one can guess at a word's meaning by simply counting the words that appear near it. Zellig Harris and J. R. Firth wrote pioneering essays in this vein, advancing what has since come to be known as the distributional hypothesis, which posits that words that tend to co-occur have similar meanings: as Harris proposed in his seminal 1954 essay, "Difference of meaning correlates with difference of distribution" (43). In the sixty years since, Harris's hypothesis has been subject to rigorous study and, indeed, has been confirmed as something like a natural law of language processing. It is often invoked using Firth's famous 1957 dictum: "You shall know a word by the company it keeps" (11).[12] Vector semantics takes the distributions of terms as proxies for their meaning, and so meaning itself becomes something at once more general and more nuanced: *semantic similarity*.[13] Vector models embed words in a field of lexical relations distributed in high-dimensional space, where every word is measured across every dimension for its similarity to every other word. According to Hinrich Schütze, "Vector similarity is the only information present in Word Space: semantically related words are close, unrelated words are distant" (896).[14] However, this binary of "close" and "distant" masks what is, in truth, a system of many dimensions, each of which is measured in minutely fine gradations. These variations can be conceived as a large field—a *semantic space*—in which words are embedded among each other, near in one dimension, distant in another.[15]

How is semantic space modeled? One common strategy is to build a word-context matrix. Imagine a human reader who skims through each text from a large corpus and finds the one thousand most frequent words in it. Now imagine that this reader scrolls through the entire corpus again, counting all the words that appear near each keyword, and then tabulates the results in a giant spreadsheet. For example, consider the following context windows, taken from Wikipedia, that surround the keywords "art" and "nature":

production of works of *art* the criticism of art
purpose. In this sense *Art* as creativity, is something humans

creativity humans by their *nature* no other species creates art

science. Although humans are part of *nature* human activity is often understood

The distribution of terms that surround each keyword can be placed together into a matrix. The collocations are tallied so that each column shows the keywords (*art* and *nature*) in the context of another term, which are conventionally placed as rows. The numbers in each cell reflect the number of times each context word appears near each keyword. In this simplified example, there are only two dimensions (*art* and *nature*), and each of the six words in the corpus (*art, creativity, criticism, humans, nature,* and *science*) is represented by a vector of two numbers (see Table 21.1). The word *creativity* is represented as the vector [4, 1], while *science* is the sequence [2, 4]. These values can in turn be plotted in a simple Cartesian plane. As shown in Figure 21.1, the words form a semantic field that divides into two smaller "conceptual spaces," with *science* and *creativity* as their most central respective terms and *humans* as the word that mediates between them.[16]

In vector semantics, words are presumed to have similar meanings insofar as they appear near each other in spaces like these. Reading such data through the lens of concept theory suggests a different interpretation, however. We might say Figure 21.1 identifies two concepts—one centered among *nature, science, humans;* and the other among *humans, creativity, art*—neither of which can be conveniently reified into a single label nor equated to the meaning of a word. Instead, concepts are structures of relationships that pertain among words. Much like communities in a social-network graph, concepts are clusters of nodes that can be taken together in semantic space.

The *art–nature* example just shown is artificially simple. Real corpora present researchers with a large mass of data. Even a single book-length document stretches concepts across a space of thousands of dimensions, and a true corpus densely compacts that space with so many connections that all concepts dissolve into a giant alphabet soup. The challenge is to slice, condense, or summarize the data in ways that will expose its most important underlying conceptual features. A number of strategies are possible. Among digital humanists, the most familiar of these is topic modeling, which reduces the corpus to an artificially small number of dimensions

Table 21.1. A Simplified Word-Context Matrix

	art	nature
art	5	1
creativity	4	1
criticism	2	0
humans	3	3
nature	1	5
science	2	4

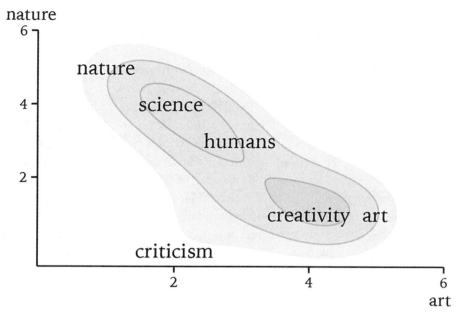

Figure 21.1. Distribution of terms surrounding *nature* and *art* in a toy corpus. In this graph, the words are represented as points in space with a contour overlay that impressionistically highlights clusters among the points. The contour lines ease visualization, but are not meant to be more than suggestive.

("topics") and then estimates the vocabulary's distribution over each. Latent Dirichlet allocation (LDA) modeling is designed primarily to survey and compare documents; it treats all texts as "bags of words" and measures document-level associations among them. Machine-learning applications like word2vec, proposed by Thomas Mikolov, Kai Chen, Greg Corrado, and Jeffrey Dean, use continuous bags of words (CBOW) and neural networks to estimate a word-context matrix within a smaller, denser semantic space. By reducing the number of dimensions, models generated by word2vec often outperform traditional collocation matrices in controlled experiments: in a full word-context matrix, subtle differences in usage will separate words like *boat* and *ship,* while probabilistic models tend to dismiss rare co-occurrences, allowing them to focus on the clearest lines of semantic similarity.[17]

In creating our own model of semantic space, we ran word2vec over the EEBO-Text Creation Partnership corpus, limiting our selection to all documents dated 1640–1699 (for a total of 18,752 documents) and creating a model of the language with a vocabulary of 102,164 words.[18] Each word in the model is represented by a vector with 300 variables designed to estimate the word's appearance across the corpus.[19] Once completed, the model supports a wide range of statistical tests. One of the simplest is to see which words are most similar to a given keyword. For example, the words most similar to *wit* in the EEBO-TCP corpus are *invention, wits, eloquence, witty, fancy, argues, beside, indeed, talks, shews,* and *ingenuity.* This list of most similar terms provides an initial glimpse of the conceptual architecture that surrounds *wit,* which in the seventeenth century was understood broadly as a mental alacrity socially realized through verbal (especially oral) performance; hence, its association with rhetorical terms like *invention* and *eloquence.* As this example suggests, reading the results of vector similarity measurements is much like reading the results of a topic model.[20] The difference is that topic models return words that tend to appear in the same documents; vector-space models return words that tend to appear in similar context windows.

Vector-based representation does more than just provide a list of collocates or approximate synonyms, however. It also measures these words' relationships to each other and shows how they are distributed within semantic space. Much like topics, words in semantic space cluster into groups that often cohere around different senses of a word or different contexts of use. The dimension-reduction techniques of vector-space modeling and principal-component analysis represent axes of difference that reveal latent organizing principles of the semantic field projected by a corpus. The forty words most similar to *wit* cluster fairly neatly into several main groups (see Figure 21.2).[21] (This graph and the graphs that follow use hierarchical clustering to identify groups within the data, which are highlighted using a density overlay to suggest their boundaries. Readers should keep in mind, however, that this clustering involves setting an arbitrary number of divisions, just as topic modeling does, so the boundaries that seem to separate words in semantic space are neither hard nor fast.) On the left-hand side are two clusters of synonymous words, like *eloquence* and *invention,* but also *sophistry* and *fancy.*[22] On the right-hand side sit clusters of words that seem to imply argumentation—*seems, pretends, shews, consequently, beside, consists, indeed,* and *argument.* This might seem strange. After all, why is *consequently* semantically similar to *wit*? The reason is that *wit* was an intensely normative concept and was rarely invoked without explicit judgment: writers performed their own *ingenuity* while critiquing the *sophistry* of others.[23] Words that surround *wit* in the EEBO-TCP corpus also commonly appear near argument words in general; therefore, they have similar vector profiles and sit near each other in semantic space.

None of this adds up to the meaning of *wit* in a conventional sense. Instead, Figure 21.2 shows something like a snapshot or slice of the discourse taken from the perspective of *wit,* one that delivers a compact representation that still preserves the multiple temporalities prized by conceptual history. Like *eloquence* and *invention, wit* names a conceptual formation that straddles psychological and social models of discourse, pointing at once through language into the minds of authors while, more narrowly, highlighting the connective logical tissues of argument. If this graph shows a concept, that concept cannot really be reified as "wit." As noted earlier, John Locke, for instance, defined "wit" in purely cognitive terms as "the assemblage of *Ideas,*" but the model returns a concept more axiomatic and abstract, which might be paraphrased as "mind as a principle of order in discourse" (2:156).

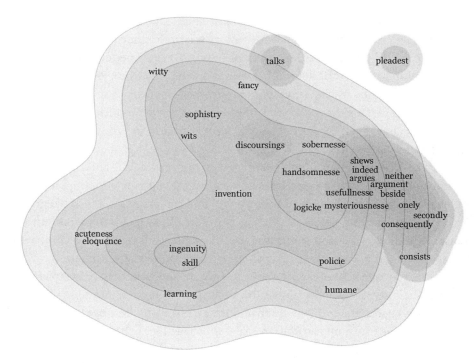

Figure 21.2. The semantic neighborhood of *wit*. Graph shows the forty words most similar to *wit* in a word2vec model built from the EEBO-TCP corpus (1640–1699). Terms are clustered using hierarchical clustering and projected onto a two-dimensional space using principal-component analysis. On the left side are various synonyms (*invention, ingenuity, skill, fancy, sophistry*), while on the right sit terms of argumentation, such as *indeed, argues,* and *consequently.*

Vector-space models can be validated in a number of ways. One common test involves simulating verbal exams taken by humans. Many vector-space models have been shown to outperform high school students on the SATs, for example.[24] The designers of word2vec developed a novel test to validate their system: forming analogies using what they call the "vector offset method." Because words are all represented with numerical profiles, they can be added or subtracted from each other. Imagine one begins with the vector for *king*, subtracts the vector for *man*, then adds the vector for *woman*. If the semantic space has been modeled and normalized in a trustworthy way, the result should be approximately equal to *queen*. The operation can be restated in mathematical form as $king - man + woman = queen$.[25] This and similar conceptual relationships can be traced through the EEBO-TCP model, which captures category–example relationships such as $king - charles + paul = apostle$; part–whole relationships like $inches - foot + pound = ounce$; singular–plural forms like $artery - arteries + banks = bank$; or verb conjugations like $please - pleases + talks = talk$. In each case, the "right answer" appears among the most similar words with varying levels of specificity. Because of spelling variation in early modern print, capturing verb conjugations and pluralizations may be the wrong test for EEBO-TCP data, however. Far better is the model's ability to capture alternate spellings of the same word. As shown in Table 21.2, the words most similar to *africa, baptism,* and *publick* are, respectively, *affrica, baptisme,* and *publique.* The most important test, though, is the model's ability to return lists of words that represent a concept's range of application, providing something like a historical thesaurus.

That said, the parlor trick of *king − man + woman = queen* highlights a key difference between vector-space models and, say, topic models: vector-space models are not designed to create passive representations that simply delineate themes; they are meant to be *used.* In machine translation, the words that appear in a context window are added together, such that the system can provide a best guess for the appropriate analog term. Just as *king − man + woman* will point toward female monarchs, so too *plane + pilot + landed + airport* will point toward *l'avion,* in French, rather than *le plan.* Search engines work according to the same principle.[26] When multiple words are entered into a query, those words are added together and the results are sorted by their cosine similarity (their "relevance") to the aggregate vector. Any group of words can be treated as a composite entity. When *wit* is combined with *poetry,* for example, argument words like *consequently* are stripped away, while *poetry* is associated with terms commonly deployed, along with *wit,* in criticism (see Figure 21.3). Just as search engines might highlight the literary uses of *wit* and the critical uses of *poetry* in response to the query "wit poetry," so too the model returns a representation of the conceptual substrate that connects those terms. Vector composition elevates semantic modeling above the level of the word to describe the structures that contain words.[27]

As the examples of translation and search suggest, although vector-space models are built using large corpora, they are actually designed to perform microanalyses of texts, phrases, and snippets of words. This might seem strange. The digital humanities stumbled into computational semantics through topic modeling, assuming that the most important applications involve "distant reading" over large swaths of time. However, decades of work in computational linguistics have pushed in precisely the opposite direction by using big data to answer small questions: What book was *this* search query looking for? Was *that* email spam? What might a user have meant by *this* misspelled word? Distant reading projects have not explored this direction of inquiry. Humanists are just beginning the work of studying how semantic models might inform qualitative research, and we choose in this chapter to begin "closer to home," so to speak, not only to the humanities but also to vector semantics, by approaching conceptual history through computationally assisted close reading.[28] In what follows, we use vector semantics to analyze a canonical text, John Dryden's *MacFlecknoe* (1678), to see how *wit* organizes the poem's conceptual structure. Learning how to generate, visualize, and interpret semantic data will be a major

Table 21.2. Semantic Similarities from the EEBO-TCP

For each keyword, this table displays the most similar terms with their corresponding cosine similarity scores. Notice that each term is identical to itself (cosine similarity of 1).

africa	affrica	america	europe	lybia	aethiopia	arabia	islands	barbary
1	0.75	0.67	0.66	0.64	0.6	0.59	0.59	0.58

baptism	baptisme	baptized	infants	baptised	adult	initiation	baptizing	infant
1	0.87	0.73	0.72	0.68	0.65	0.65	0.64	0.64

consciousness	personality	sensation	conscious	identity	existence	numerical	originated	sameness
1	0.57	0.5	0.49	0.49	0.48	0.47	0.46	0.46

flowers	roses	lilies	violets	lillies	fragrant	herbs	violet	pomgranates
1	0.77	0.76	0.74	0.73	0.7	0.69	0.69	0.68

frogs	toads	lice	mice	croaking	lizards	vermine	vermin	fleas
1	0.73	0.71	0.69	0.68	0.65	0.65	0.64	0.64

pancreas	mesentery	intestines	duodenum	lacteal	lymphatick	glandules	chyle	viscid
1	0.78	0.74	0.72	0.71	0.7	0.7	0.7	0.69

publick	publique	private	meetings	thereof	assemblies	common	town	particular
1	0.85	0.66	0.54	0.49	0.48	0.48	0.47	0.47

shakespear	fletcher	dryden	dramatick	pastorals	satyr	johnson	plays	poesie
1	0.63	0.62	0.59	0.58	0.57	0.57	0.56	0.55

strawberries	cherries	medlars	peaches	pomgranates	citrons	apricocks	lemons	prunes
1	0.79	0.76	0.75	0.75	0.74	0.74	0.74	0.73

wit	invention	wits	eloquence	witty	fancy	argues	beside	indeed
1	0.46	0.45	0.44	0.44	0.43	0.42	0.41	0.40

woman	womans	husband	wife	maid	child	vvoman	wench	whorish
1	0.67	0.59	0.58	0.58	0.58	0.57	0.51	0.5

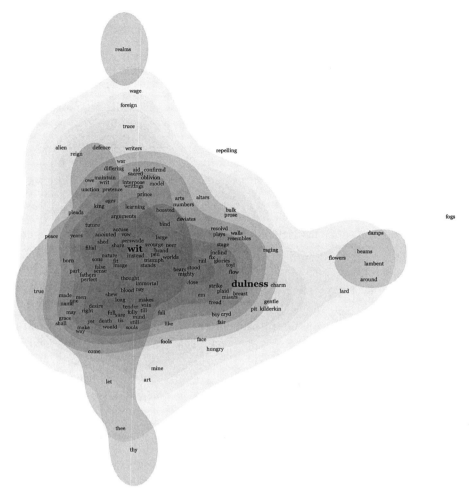

Figure 21.3. The semantic neighborhood of the composite vector of *wit* and *poetry,* drawn from a word2vec model of the EEBO-TCP corpus, 1640–1699. When added together into a single entity, the composite vector of *wit* + *poetry* bisects its components, exposing the semantic region that sits between them.

challenge facing humanities computing over the next decade. Vector-space models are remarkably flexible and can be constructed in many different ways, supporting a wide and growing range of intellectual purposes. We offer just one here.

Computational Close Reading

Wit is widely regarded as a concept central to English culture of the later seventeenth century. From a medieval term denoting reason and intelligence to a modern term of criticism, art, and politics, *wit* has long borne the burden of reconciling minds with the social and political hierarchies policed through words.[29] John Dryden's

MacFlecknoe sits at the center of this transformation, exemplifying how neoclassical poetry stages mutually informing contradictions between *wit*'s psychological and political connotations.[30] Dryden was an English playwright who rose to prominence in the 1660s and early 1670s. Theatrical successes like *The Indian Emperor* (1665) and *The Conquest of Granada* (1672) earned him financial security, a literary reputation, and many detractors. In critical prefaces, prologues, and epilogues, Dryden defended his work against critics while often picking fights with other poets. His poem *MacFlecknoe* is a satirical takedown of his main rival, Thomas Shadwell, depicting a dystopian alternate universe where Shadwell is a callow prince newly coronated as the King of Nonsense. *MacFlecknoe* has been widely read as a meditation on authorship and kingship and on the personal qualifications needed for legitimacy in literary and political arenas.[31] Therefore, it offers a perfect case study in tracing the conceptual fields that structure a text. We conclude by showing how Dryden draws on *wit*'s conceptual association with *sophistry* and *fancy* to produce a new ligature between poetry and kingship.

MacFlecknoe is written in heroic couplets, and like semantic models, couplets produce meaning by juxtaposing words in space. In addition to proximity, heroic couplets use rhyme and rhythm distributed across paired lines, each of which is divided into two halves by a caesura, to effect relationships among words. Literary historian J. Paul Hunter has argued that the heroic couplet functions as an instrument for redefining binary oppositions, like *wit* and *judgment* or *nature* and *art*. He observes that poets like Dryden and Alexander Pope used the heroic couplet to develop a "rhetoric of complex redefinition" that "challenges the transparency of the apparent rhetoric and blurs and bleeds images of plain opposites into one another" (119).[32] He continues,

> The effect, though, is not to fog or muddy or obscure—much less to deconstruct meanings to nothing stable at all—but to use the easy opposition as a way of clarifying the process of deepening qualification and refinement. It is a demonstration of how to read as an exercise in how to think. The process is rather like that described by information theorists and cognitive scientists trying to explain how computers can work and reason complexly—not by facing a great variety of complicated choices simultaneously but by sorting things one by one into little yeses and nos, ones and zeroes. Refinement occurs progressively, step by step. (119)

In comparing the binary opposition of terms in couplets to the binary code of digital media, Hunter incidentally gestures toward our claim regarding the interpretive potential of computational models. Vector semantics highlights the relational, continuous structure of the lexical field, wherein meaning is negotiated across innumerable lines of similarity and difference. Our visualizations of the semantic space of *wit* exchange the quadrants of the couplet for the quadrants of the graph. The heroic couplet and the vector model use proximity and association to convey linguistic meaning according to radically different rubrics, but reading one in relation to the other provides an opportunity to uncover latent premises of both.

Consider the correspondence between the opening couplet and its graphical representation relative to the larger Restoration model. In the couplet, the structural alignment between "subject" and "monarchs" introduces the tension between the contemporary divine conception of kingship and the inevitability of human decline:

> All humane things are subject to decay,
> And, when Fate summons, Monarchs must obey (ll. 1–2)

Just as the words of a search query are combined to return as a list of most relevant results, so too the words in a couplet can be combined to visualize the semantic fields juxtaposed in the verses. Figure 21.4 represents the words most similar to the composite vector of the terms in the couplet: *humane + things + subject + decay + fate + summons + monarchs + obey*. Each word in the graph attracts words with which it has high similarity scores in the model and repels words with which it has low scores. The graph disaggregates the semantic fields that Dryden yokes together in the couplet. While the arrangement of the couplet produces a mirroring relationship

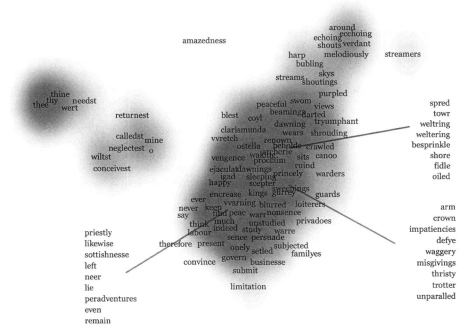

Figure 21.4. Semantic neighborhood of *MacFlecknoe's* opening couplet. Graph displays the forty terms most similar to the composite vector, *humane + things + subject + decay + fate + summons + monarchs + obey*. The terms in bold appear in the couplet. The model exposes a rich language of subjection as central to the couplet's conceit.

between contrasting words (*humane* and *fate, subject* and *monarchs, decay* and *obey*) that occupy similar positions in the two lines, the graph represents the semantic divide by grouping similar terms and separating opposing ones. The *monarchs* cluster is located at the point of a triangle, far from the other opposing points centered on *obey* and *decay/fate*. The intervening *subject* cluster occupies a mediating position, providing the semantic ligature between *monarchs* and *obey*. The graph thus foregrounds the questions of subjection, power, and authority—both poetic and political—that the opening couplet presents as the poem's central concern.

For Dryden, *wit* operates as a concept for adjudicating questions of authority that cut across poetic and political domains. The retiring king of Dulness positions Shadwell (Sh——) as his son and heir, while also designating his species of dullness as distinctive:

> Sh——alone, of all my Sons, is he
> Who stands confirm'd in full stupidity.
> The rest to some faint meaning make pretence,
> But Sh——never deviates into sense.
> Some Beams of Wit on other souls may fall,
> Strike through and make a lucid interval;
> But Sh——'s genuine night admits no ray,
> His rising Fogs prevail upon the Day. (ll. 17–24)

Both the positive and negative terms from nature serve to isolate Shadwell. A lack of wit holds poetic and social consequences, impeding the conjunction of proper images as well as of proper rulers.

Figure 21.5 depicts how *MacFlecknoe* engages and draws from the concept of *wit*. It combines the semantic spaces of words from two sources: half the words are the ones most semantically similar to *wit* in the model, and the other half are the words Dryden actually uses near *wit* in the poem. Like Figure 21.2, this visualization represents the semantic space of *wit,* but now that space has collided with Dryden's diction. Words with high similarity scores, like *invention* and *reasoning,* are plotted near *wit,* while the actual words of the poem gather separately. Words from *MacFlecknoe* have little overlap with the upper-right cluster because, in the poem, the key contrasts that *wit* invokes are not about *rhetoric, eloquence, pedantry,* and *sophistry,* but are located in the realm of poetry.[33] *Wit* is taken out of the realm of learned argumentation (where it is more common) and redeployed in the specialized field of dramatic poetry, which is marked by writers and kinds of writing, the institution of the stage, and epitomizing examples like Ben Jonson, found in terms from the upper-left section of the graph.[34] However, in the 1670s, unlike today, the discourse of literary criticism was not well established, and so Dryden uses a mock-heroic conceit (kingly succession) to structure his invocations of literary authority and subjection. In the bottom-left corner, terms including *reign, king, truce, realms,*

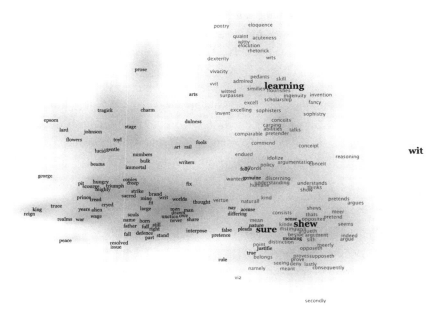

Figure 21.5. Dryden's *MacFlecknoe* and the conceptual structure of *wit*. The terms most similar to *wit* in the model are represented in gray and a sans serif font, while the words Dryden actually uses near *wit* in *MacFlecknoe* are black and in a serif font. Four of the Dryden terms (*wit, learning, sure,* and *shew*) are also among the most similar terms found in the model.

and *war* correspond to the political context of the poem. Another smaller cluster (featuring *father, name, born, right*) to the right of the political terms indexes the patrilineal process of transmitting the kingship from Flecknoe to Shadwell. These smaller political and social clusters make the performance and evaluation of *wit* intelligible as a criterion for organizing the emergent literary field according to alternative social and political methods of ordering.

What are left are the more varied words that occupy the positions between the legible, stable clusters, and the capacity to visualize the relationship between such words and coherent clusters suggests the new kind of historical knowledge that this comparative reading method can produce. Taken together these words (including *toyl, numbers, bulk, immortal, beams, lard, flowers, hungry, copies*) return a much lower average similarity score than that of either the wit clusters or the political and dramatic clusters in the poem. These words index unexpected tropes and figures that combine to produce a new view of *wit*. The poet depicts "beams of wit," a "scourge of wit," the "toyl of wit," and a "kilderkin of wit," an early modern unit of measurement (ll. 21, 89, 150, 196). He accuses Shadwell of "tortur[ing] one poor word ten thousand ways," but in iteratively reconceiving *wit*, Dryden suggests a wide range of sources that constitute the faculty. In the process, he explores a conceptual space between the classical sources of poetic invention: tradition (portrayed as patri-lineal succession) on the one hand, and inspiration (personified as the Muses) on the other. Shadwell succeeds to a "province" in which he invents "new humours" for "each new play" (ll. 187–88). While it is a famous literary-historical claim that the modern concept of originality emerges in Romantic poetry of the late eighteenth century, Dryden's competing images suggest a nascent predecessor. In *MacFleck-noe,* originality looks a lot like dullness. All witty writers may be alike, but each dull writer is dull in his own way. Considered in relation to the broader history of *wit,* Dryden's aberrant terms and figures present a multivalent concept that complicates critical genealogies of the poetic imagination in early modern England.

Huddled Atoms

In another poem, written a few years later, Dryden accuses hack poets of assem-bling their works "the *Lucretian* way" from "So many Huddled Atoms." The result is invariably a mass or heap: the precise opposite of Dryden's finely crafted couplets. The heaps of words jumbled by bad writers serve as a perverse seventeenth-century analog for the bags of words used by computational semantics. Yet, it is precisely this grammatical formlessness that enables semantic models to reach below the meanings of statements and to glimpse the conceptual substrate of culture. Con-cepts act in history not by inhering to words nor by finding expression in sentences, but by forming semantic fields that underlie the very conditions for thought. This is the basic premise of concept theory, and it shares much in common with vector semantics, which delineates the field of linguistic possibility underlying every state-ment in a corpus.

However, readers of this chapter need not take on board all of the assumptions and commitments of concept theory, nor need they have been persuaded by our close reading of *MacFlecknoe* to appreciate our larger ambition, which is to push the con-versation toward areas of theoretical overlap that cross the disciplines. Rather than ask how computational "tools" or "methods" or "practices" can be used for human-istic purposes, we invite readers to examine the theoretical assumptions and intel-lectual investments that motivated those methods' invention, as well as to look for commensurabilities across the disciplines that might inform future work. There is sometimes a tendency in digital humanities to skip to the end by speculating about how computational methods will transform the humanities without digging into the intellectual histories of those methods or explaining how the theoretical assump-tions inherited from other disciplines align with the assumptions that otherwise inform one's thinking.

We have tried to bridge this gap by emphasizing points of contact at a theoreti-cal level between computational and humanistic scholarship. In doing so, we have offered just a few partial answers to a handful of big questions we believe should guide future work: How should scholars talk about meanings that exist beyond the confines of statements or texts? What theories of history and language support the study of broadly shared discursive features? What empirical, data-based techniques exist for measuring meaning? How do those techniques work, and what do they assume?

NOTES

1. Koselleck describes concept history as a "specialized" field that directs itself "to the analysis of central expressions [i.e. keywords] having social or political content" ("Begriffsgeschichte and Social History," 81).

2. Many ways of studying collocation patterns exist, but when text analysis is discussed in digital humanities, topic modeling has nearly monopolized the attention. Commentaries by David Blei, Ted Underwood and Andrew Goldstone, Ben Schmidt, Matthew Jockers, and Lisa Rhody have explored promising applications in literary studies and history, while John W. Mohr and Petko Bogdanov have highlighted potential uses in the cultural sciences. In Mohr's and Bogdanov's words, modeling provides "an automated procedure for coding the content of a corpus of texts (including very large corpora) into a set of substantively meaningful coding categories" (546).

3. Latent Dirichlet allocation (LDA), the most popular method of topic modeling among digital humanists, has well-known quirks that skeptics find off-putting; it oddly combines an arbitrary human-controlled element (users must preselect the number of topics, which powerfully affects a model's output) with a machine-learning engine that estimates word collocation probabilistically, rather than measuring it directly. For a description of LDA as a probabilistic model, see Blei, "Introduction to Probabilistic Topic Models."

4. For the contrast between close and distant reading, see Franco Moretti, *Distant Reading*. For the contrast between micro- and macroanalysis, see Jockers, *Macroanalysis*.

5. Indeed, *wit* has long been recognized as a key concept in seventeenth- and eighteenth-century British literature. C. S. Lewis observed that if a person had time "to study the history of one word only, wit would be perhaps be the best word he could choose" (95–66, 101–103, 105–106).

6. The full dictionary has not been translated into English, but the introduction has been. See Reinhart Koselleck, "Introduction and Prefaces to the *Geschichtliche Grundbegriffe*." English translations of Koselleck's monographs on historical theory include *Critique and Crisis, The Practice of Conceptual History,* and *Futures Past*. In the context of English studies, the history of concepts also may be identified with Raymond Williams. See in particular *Culture and Society* and *Keywords*.

7. One interesting example of the disjunction between conceptual and social temporalities involves the political concept "revolution," which Koselleck argues emerges as a generally stagnant perception of time based on the slow and predictable movements of celestial objects, but eventually evolves into the modern sense of the word, which is a dramatic rupture (*Futures Past,* 23). For a useful overview of Koselleck's theory of concepts, see Niels Åkerstrøm Andersen, "Reinhart Koselleck's History of Concepts."

8. In his overview of Koselleck's theory of concepts, Andersen emphasizes the "semantic field" as a key component.

9. An overview of this debate can be traced in J. G. A. Pocock, "Concepts and Discourses" and Koselleck's response in "A Response to Comments on the *Geschichtliche Grundbegriffe.*"

10. Witmore elsewhere argues that "a text may be thought of as a vector through a metatable of all possible words" ("Text: A Massively Addressable Object," 325).

11. Weaver emphasizes this very point: "And it is one of the chief purposes of this memorandum to emphasize that *statistical semantic* studies should be undertaken, as a necessary preliminary step" (16).

12. For an introduction to Neo-Firthian work, see Tony McEnery and Andrew Hardie, *Corpus Linguistics*; for a statement on the relation between the fields or corpus and computational linguistics, see 227–30. Daniel Jurafsky and James H. Martin, for example, restate the hypothesis as a basic premise of computational linguistics: "Words that occur in similar contexts tend to have similar meanings. . . . The meaning of a word is thus related to the distribution of words around it" (270). In this context, the word "distribution" refers simply to word counts in a corpus. Blei uses the term similarly in his description of topic models: "We formally define a topic to be a distribution over a fixed vocabulary " (77).

13. An introduction and overview of vector-based approaches to semantic similarity can be found in Peter D. Turney's and Patrick Pantel's widely cited 2010 survey of the relevant literature, "From Frequency to Meaning." For an updated and more detailed discussion, see Sébastien Harispe et al., *Semantic Similarity from Natural Language and Ontology Analysis.*

14. See also Will Lowe, "Towards a Theory of Semantic Space"; and, more recently, Turney and Pantel, "From Frequency to Meaning"; Katrin Erk, "Vector Space Models of Word Meaning and Phrase Meaning"; and Stephen Clark, "Vector Space Models of Lexical Meaning."

15. A semantic space model can be understood as a generalization of the notion, in concept theory, of the *semantic field*. In Andersen's words, "According to Koselleck, the analysis of the shaping, endurance and sociohistorical effects of individual concepts appear in relation to other concepts—what he calls *semantic fields*" (38). Such fields are understood to be structured in limited, qualitatively meaningful ways, as in, for example, the distinction between a "concept" and a "counterconcept," its dialectical opposite. Computational semantics, by contrast, depends on statistical comparisons for each word across an entire corpus. Individual relationships between terms are identified, generally without differentiating among relationship types. Only some collocation patterns will correspond to semantic fields in the narrower qualitative sense meant by concept theorists. We might say that a semantic space contains all existing word associations within a corpus and that a semantic field selects and elevates associations that are historically relevant and interesting (relevance and interest, of course, will depend entirely and always on the interpretive judgment of the historian).

16. The term "conceptual spaces" was coined by Peter Gärdenfors to describe geometric models of word meaning (although he does not rely on word collocation as the basis for his vector representation).

17. For a breakdown of the similarities between neural-network models like word2vec and traditional distributional models, see Levy and Goldberg, "Linguistic Regularities."

18. The results described are a subset from the full bibliography to avoid cluttering the visualizations with low-frequency terms, many of which simply represent typographical or transcription errors. Words are included in the visualizations if they meet one of two criteria: either they were used in every single year, 1640 to 1699, or they were among the 20,000 most frequent terms in any given year. Although the entire vocabulary is included for all calculations, the total vocabulary eligible for inclusion in the graphs is 26,199 words.

19. For a gentle introduction to word2vec and a practical, hands-on tutorial, Ben Schmidt has written a series of blog posts describing the application. See especially "Vector Space Models for the Digital Humanities" and "Rejecting the Gender Binary: a Vector Space Operation." Regarding more detailed specifications, the technical and theoretical commentary is already quite large. The technique was originally described in Mikolov et al. A valuable summary can be found in Goldberg and Levy, "word2vec Explained."

20. See Goldstone and Underwood, "What Can Topic Models of PMLA Teach Us" for a discussion of methods and challenges of interpreting topic models.

21. The *x* and *y* axes were set using a common dimension-reduction technique called principal component analysis. The position on the graph shows each word's place in relation to the other words. The scale on each axis has been removed; as in a social-network graph, the axes of this graph are algorithmically generated and do not directly refer to any single measurement.

22. The graph visualizes additional associations between wit and rhetorical training that stretch back to Cicero. *De Oratore* suggests eloquence (like wit) requires an expansive background of *learning*. Neither eloquence nor wit is a skill that one can learn by studying the rules of a single discipline. To qualify as witty or eloquent, a speaker must have *ingenuity*, from the Latin word "*ingenium*," which Cicero defines as "natural talent" for forging connections between disparate fields of inquiry. See Thomas Conley, *Rhetoric in the European Tradition* (35).

23. This cluster may allude to a distinction between wit and more common forms of humor presented by Cicero's dialogue *De Oratore* through the character Marcus Antonius: wit is humor delivered for an argumentative purpose. In the words of Antonius, "a laugh is the very poorest return for cleverness." Cicero (381).

24. Turney and Pantel describe several relevant studies in "From Frequency to Meaning."

25. This example features in Mikolov et al.

26. Indeed, information retrieval was the research topic for which vector-space models were first theorized, in the 1950s, by Hans Peter Luhn. See in particular his essay, "A New Method of Recording and Searching Information." Writing in 1987, Gerard Salton describes the significance of Luhn's early work: "It was suggested, in particular, that instead

of assigning complex subject indicators extracted from controlled vocabulary schedules, single term descriptors, or keywords, could be used that would be assigned to the documents without context or role specification. These single terms could then be combined in the search formulations to produce complex phrase specifications and chains of synonyms . . . the coordinate keyword indexing methods eventually became the standard used in all automatic retrieval environments" (376).

27. Dominic Widdows explains, "Continuous methods enable us to model not only atoms of meaning such as words, but the space or void in between these words. Whole passages of text are mapped to points of their own in this void, without changing the underlying shape of the space around them (164).

28. Underwood in "Distant Reading and Recent Intellectual History" makes a similar point in describing advances in semantic modeling that enable researchers to "treat writing as a field of relations to be modeled, using equations that connect linguistic variables to social ones."

29. These uses are broader, too, than the specifically psychological application of the term as used by John Locke, who defined *wit* in contrast to *judgment*, mapping their difference onto a distinction between synthesis and analysis. *Judgment*, in his view, involved the careful discrimination of apparently like objects. *Wit*, on the other hand, involved synthetic reasoning that found surprising connections among ideas: wit discovers similarity between the most distant and dissimilar objects. These ideas are captured in words. Locke explains, "Though therefore it be the Mind that makes the Collection, 'tis the Name which is, as it were, the Knot, that ties them fast together" (III.v.10).

30. There has been significant scholarship on Dryden's usage of wit as well as the term's significance in Augustan poetry more generally. See, for instance, Empson and Lund H. James Jensen indexes the term by hand in *A Glossary of John Dryden's Critical Terms*; his entry for "WIT" stretches to six pages.

31. Paul Hammond surveys this scholarship and provides an overview of *MacFlecknoe*'s textual and political history (168–79).

32. Ralph Cohen has previously made a similar point about the function of the heroic couplet in the poetry of Pope and Jonathan Swift.

33. In addition to interpreting the semantic coherence of clusters, we can evaluate the overall similarity between words in the different clusters by taking the average of the cosine similarity score of each word with every other word in the cluster. The cluster of theoretical wit terms returns an average score of 0.415, the argument terms cluster has a score of 0.278, the dramatic criticism cluster scores 0.297, and the political cluster scores 0.384. For comparison, the score for a very similar set of words (*leaves, tree, branch, fruit*) is 0.552, and the score for ten to twelve randomly selected words returns an average score of 0.0765.

34. The terms *johnson, george, epsom* each refer to authors and texts caught up in the contemporary critical debate regarding how to distinguish good from bad poetry. *Johnson* refers to Ben Jonson, *george* to George Etherege, and *epsom* to Shadwell's play, *Epsom Wells* (1672).

BIBLIOGRAPHY

Andersen, Niels Åkerstrøm. "Reinhart Koselleck's History of Concepts." In *Discursive Analytical Strategies: Understanding Foucault, Koselleck, Laclau, Luhmann,* 33–48. Bristol, UK: Polity Press, 2003.

Blei, David. "Introduction to Probabilistic Topic Models." *Communications of the ACM* 55, no. 4 (2012): 77–84.

Cicero. *De Oratore: Books 1–2.* Translated by E. W. Sutton and H. Rackham. Cambridge, Mass.: Harvard University Press, 1942.

Clark, Stephen. "Vector Space Models of Lexical Meaning." In *The Handbook of Contemporary Semantic Theory,* edited by Shalom Lappin and Chris Fox, 493–522. Oxford: John Wiley & Sons, 2015.

Cohen, Ralph. "The Augustan Mode in English Poetry." In *Studies in the Eighteenth Century,* edited by R. F. Brissenden, 171–92. Toronto: University of Toronto, 1968.

Conley, Thomas. *Rhetoric in the European Tradition.* Chicago: University of Chicago Press, 1990.

de Bolla, Peter. *The Architecture of Concepts: The Historical Formation of Human Rights.* New York: Fordham University Press, 2013.

Dryden, John. "PROLOGUE, To the University of Oxon. Spoken by Mr. Hart, at the Acting of the Silent Woman." In *Miscellany poems containing a new translation of Virgills eclogues, Ovid's love elegies, odes of Horace, and other authors* (1684). Text Creation Partnership. https://github.com/textcreationpartnership/A36650.

Empson, William. "Wit in the Essay on Criticism." *Hudson Review* 2, no. 4 (Winter 1950): 559–77.

Erk, Katrin. "Vector Space Models of Word Meaning and Phrase Meaning: A Survey." *Language and Linguistics Compass* (2012): 635–53.

Firth, J. R. *Studies in Linguistic Analysis.* London: Oxford University Press, 1962.

Gärdenfors, Peter. *Conceptual Spaces: The Geometry of Thought.* Cambridge, Mass.: MIT Press, 1994.

Goldberg, Yoav, and Omar Levy. "word2vec Explained: Deriving Mikolov et al's Negative-Sampling Word-Embedding Method." 2014, http://arxiv.org/abs/1402.3722.

Goldstone, Andrew and Ted Underwood. "What Can Topic Models of PMLA Teach Us about the History of Literary Scholarship?" *Journal of Digital Humanities* 2, no. 1 (Winter, 2012), http://journalofdigitalhumanities.org/2-1/what-can-topic-models-of-pmla-teach-us-by-ted-underwood-and-andrew-goldstone/.

Hammond, Paul. *The Making of Restoration Poetry.* Cambridge: D. S. Brewer, 2006.

Harispe, Sébastien, Sylvie Ranwez, Stefan Janaqui, and Jacky Mountmain. "Semantic Similarity from Natural Language and Ontology Analysis." *Synthesis Lectures on Human Language Technologies* 8, no. 1 (May 2015): 1–254.

Harris, Zellig. "Distributional Structure." In *The Structure of Language: Readings in the Philosophy of Language,* edited by Jerry A. Fodor and Jerrold Katz, 33–49. Englewood Cliffs, N.J.: Prentice-Hall, 1964.

Hope, Jonathan, and Michael Witmore. "'Après le déluge, More Criticism': Philology, Literary History, and Ancestral Reading in the Coming Posttranscription World." *Renaissance Drama* 40 (2012): 135–50.

Hunter, J. Paul. "Formalism and History: Binarism and the Anglophone Couplet." *Modern Language Quarterly* 61, no. 1 (March 2000): 109–29.

Jensen, H. James. *A Glossary of John Dryden's Critical Terms*. Minneapolis: University of Minnesota Press, 1969.

Jockers, Matthew L. *Macroanalysis: Digital Methods and Literary History*. Champaign: University of Illinois Press, 2013.

Jurafsky, Daniel, and James H. Martin. *Processing Speech and Language: An Introduction to Natural Language Processing, Computational Linguistics, and Speech Recognition*. 3rd edition draft. Stanford, Calif.: Stanford University Press, 2017.

Koselleck, Reinhart. "Begriffsgeschichte and Social History." In *Futures Past: On the Semantics of Historical Time*. New York: Columbia University Press, 2004.

Koselleck, Reinhart. *Critique and Crisis: Enlightenment and the Pathogenesis of Modern Society*. Cambridge, Mass.: MIT Press, 1988.

Koselleck, Reinhart. "Introduction and Prefaces to the *Geschichtliche Grundbegriffe*." Translated by Michaela Richter. *Contributions to the History of Concepts* 6, no. 1 (Summer 2011): 1–37.

Koselleck, Reinhart. *The Practice of Conceptual History*. Translated by Todd Samuel Presner and others. Palo Alto, Calif.: Stanford University Press, 2002.

Koselleck, Reinhart. "A Response to Comments on the *Geschichtliche Grundbegriffe*." In *The Meaning of Historical Concepts,* edited by Lehman and Richter, 59–70. Translated by Melvin Richter and Sally E. Robertson. Washington, D.C.: German Historical Institute, 1996.

Levy, Omer, and Yoav Goldberg. "Linguistic Regularities in Sparse and Explicit Word Representations." *CoNLL* (2014): 171–80.

Lewis, C. S. *Studies in Words*. 2nd ed. Cambridge: Cambridge University Press, 1990.

Locke, John. *An Essay Concerning Human Understanding,* edited by Peter H. Nidditch. Oxford: Clarendon Press, 1975.

Lowe, Will. "Towards a Theory of Semantic Space." *Proceedings of the 23rd Conference of the Cognitive Science Society* (2001): 576–81.

Luhn, Hans Peter. "A New Method of Recording and Searching Information." *American Documentation* 4, no. 1 (1953).

Lund, Roger D. "Wit, Judgment, and the Misprisions of Similitude." *Journal of the History of Ideas* 65, no. 1 (January 2004): 53–74.

McEnery, Tony, and Andrew Hardie. *Corpus Linguistics*. Cambridge: Cambridge University Press, 2012.

Mikolov, Tomas, Kai Chen, Greg Corrado, and Jeffrey Dean. "Efficient Estimation of Word Representations in Vector Space." 2013, http://arxiv.org/abs/1301.3781.

Mohr, John W., and Petko Bogdanov. "Topic Models: What They Are and Why They Matter?" *Poetics* 41, no. 6 (December 2013): 545–69.

Moretti, Franco. *Distant Reading.* London: Verso, 2013.

Nirenburg, Sergei, Harold Somers, and Yorick Wilks. eds. *Readings in Machine Translation.* Cambridge, Mass.: MIT Press, 2003.

Pocock, J. G. A. "Concepts and Discourses: A Difference in Culture?" In *The Meaning of Historical Concepts,* edited by Lehman and Richter, 47–58. Washington, D.C.: German Historical Institute, 1996.

Rhody, Lisa M. "Topic Modeling and Figurative Language." *Journal of Digital Humanities* 2, no. 1 (Winter 2012).

Salton, Gerard. "Historical Note: The Past Thirty Years in Information Retrieval." *JASIS* 38, no. 5 (1987).

Schmidt, Ben. "Words Alone: Dismantling Topic Models in the Humanities." *Journal of Digital Humanities* 2, no. 1 (Winter 2012).

Schütze, Hinrich. "Word Space." *Advances in Neural Information Processing Systems* 5 (1993): 895–902.

Turney, Peter D., and Patrick Pantel. "From Frequency to Meaning: Vector Space Models of Semantics." *Journal of Artificial Intelligence Research* (2010): 141–88.

Underwood, Ted. "Distant Reading and Recent Intellectual History." *Debates in the Digital Humanities 2016*, edited by Matthew K. Gold and Lauren F. Klein. Minneapolis: University of Minnesota, 2016. http://dhdebates.gc.cuny.edu/debates/text/95.

Underwood, Ted, and Andrew Goldstone. "The Quiet Transformations of Literary Studies: What Thirteen Thousand Scholars Could Tell Us." *New Literary History* 45, no. 3 (Summer 2014): 359–84.

Weaver, Warren. "Machine Translation." In *Readings in Machine Translation,* edited by Sergei Nirenburg, Harold Somers, and Yorick Wilks, 13–18. Cambridge, Mass.: MIT Press, 2003.

Widdows, Dominic. *Geometry and Meaning.* Palo Alto, Calif.: Center for the Study of Language and Information, 2004.

Williams, Raymond. *Culture and Society, 1780-1950.* New York: Columbia University Press, 1958.

Williams, Raymond. *Keywords: A Vocabulary of Culture and Society.* New York: Oxford University Press, 1976.

Witmore, Michael. " "Text: A Massively Addressable Object." In *Debates in Digital Humanities,* edited by Matthew K. Gold, 324–27. Minneapolis: University of Minnesota Press, 2012.

Paid to Do but Not to Think: Reevaluating the Role of Graduate Student Collaborators

RACHEL MANN

Collaboration is held in such high esteem in the digital humanities that those who dare to question it are seen as uncooperative and combative.[1] As Ted Underwood has quipped, "Arguing against collaboration is a lot like arguing against kittens." However, collaboration comes with its own potential pitfalls, especially when the collaborative relationship includes faculty members and graduate students working in the same field. As a current graduate student who has worked on several large-scale digital projects, my interest in this topic is not unmotivated. While my experience has been good, it does not speak for the graduate experience as a whole. Sometimes, for example, graduate students who work with tenured faculty members on digital projects are told that they can present and publish on the technical aspects of a project, but not on the subject matter. Even more commonly, graduate students are simply not encouraged by their project directors to publish and present on their digital work. Both are problematic in that graduate students in the humanities need to publish to succeed in the field.

In my own experience and in talking with other students at various institutions, faculty–student collaborations in the digital humanities tend to follow a typical model: a team of graduate students does the computational work, while the director, usually a tenured scholar, publishes the findings. Graduate students are credited with contributing to the project, usually in the form of a footnote or mention on a project website, but they are rarely encouraged to write or even coauthor critical, interpretive articles about the project. It is tempting to attribute the problem with this model to a lack of standardized citation practices within the humanities and thus to look toward the sciences for a solution. However, running a lab that generates a mass of papers, both single- and multiauthored, is worlds apart from humanities scholarship, even of the digital variety. Humanities projects are interpretive, and so scholars tend to write individual papers, even when working on collaborative projects. And while DH projects are increasingly seen as scholarly in their own right, they often do not count as scholarship. As Cathy Davidson has observed, the articles and books that the projects enable are the artifacts that tend to count as scholarship (qtd. Kelly, 52). Because the most highly valued form of academic labor in the humanities is the single-authored article or book, collaboration as it is typically practiced risks shutting graduate students out of the very scholarship they labored to produce. Too often, students are not treated as scholars-in-training but as employees. Paying graduate students to work, but not encouraging them to think and write about their work, creates a disconnect between their labor and their intellectual development.

Consequently, I have become a bit skeptical about "collaboration" as an ideal. Conceiving project partnerships as simply collaborative, rather than as more formally structured research relationships, masks some important responsibilities that faculty members owe to their students. Because PhD candidates are training to be scholars, faculty members, even in the capacity of project directors, managers, or PIs, have a responsibility to help their students publish in the field. If a faculty member hires a graduate student to enter metadata, encode documents, program a website, or develop software, that faculty member is taking on more than the student's technical abilities. Graduate students in the humanities also need to be trained to write and publish critical, interpretive work based on DH projects.

The *Collaborators' Bill of Rights* and *Student Collaborators' Bill of Rights* are among the various efforts that have been undertaken to address the problems associated with collaborative relationships. Although both are efforts in the right direction, neither goes far enough in addressing the particular problems and needs of graduate students.[2] This is in part because addressing those issues requires replacing the collaborative model for working with graduate students with a pedagogical model. By approaching their relationships with graduate students as pedagogical, thereby focusing on instilling skills required to advance in the profession, project directors would be better positioned to take into account student needs. A completed digital project would not be the end goal of a successful working relationship, but rather one by-product in a relationship designed to enhance a student's professional growth, intellectual development, and readiness for the academic job market.

Although the graduate student–director relationship that I propose might look like something more akin to mentorship, I believe it should be understood pedagogically. Following Roger Simon, to invoke pedagogy is to invoke practices, strategies, and techniques, as well as a "political vision" (qtd. Hirsch, 27). I see that political vision as one in which the roles of researcher, manager, teacher, and mentor are thoroughly integrated into the role of project director, and conversely, the roles of student, mentee, and paid employee are thoroughly integrated into the role of graduate student project member. Individuals alone cannot effect integration of this type; it must be embraced at a disciplinary level.

Collaborative Practices, Collaborative Problems,
or Your Student Is Not Your Peer

Despite a general agreement about the necessity of collaboration in digital projects, scholars have increasingly begun to note problems associated with the way collaboration is enacted. Gabriele Griffin is one of several to observe that collaboration is little understood, rarely discussed, and even more rarely put into practice (85–86).[3] Other recent discussions critical of collaboration tend to highlight potential dangers to nontenure-track academics. Usually termed "service-workers" or "alt-acs," these scholars are not often perceived by administrators or tenure-track scholars as being on equal footing with research faculty.[4] As a result, they are less likely to receive adequate credit for their contributions, less likely to weigh in on important project decisions, and less likely to be taken seriously when they do. Consequently, as Bethany Nowviskie observes, alt-acs have the least incentive to articulate the problems inherent in collaborative work, even as they are the project members who are most able to do so ("Evaluating").[5] In other words, because status factors heavily into how people relate to and work with one another, what appears to be a collaborative relationship is too often a collaboration in name only.

Status is particularly important to consider when collaborating with graduate students. Elijah Meeks argues that collaboration, by definition, "means partnership and peer interaction" ("Collaboration"). Under this definition, collaboration would seem to sound like a welcome prospect, implying an equal partnership and stake in the project among all participants. However, even in the best of collaborative situations, students are not on an equal footing with faculty and staff, and the stakes they have in the project often differ from those of participating faculty or staff. From learning how to write for publication to obtaining an academic job, students' needs and goals are not the same as those who are further along in their careers. While faculty members may engage students as peers so as to bring them onto a project, students are too often left behind when it comes time to publish, with their labor cited only on a website or buried in a long list of acknowledgments.

The disjunction between graduate student and tenured faculty partners becomes particularly acute once the collaboration ends and the "real" work—writing the interpretive argument—begins. The numbers bear this out: publication data suggest that graduate students in digital humanities are not publishing in the forms and venues that would help them in their professional development. In "Student Labour and Training in Digital Humanities," Katrina Anderson et al. report that students' project work is rarely disseminated through peer-reviewed journals or even in conference presentations. In their 2013 survey, circulated to faculty and student researchers through the Digital Humanities Summer Institute and the Association of College Research Libraries listservs, Anderson et al. found that less than 20 percent of student respondents disseminated project findings via single- or coauthored conference presentations, and only 9 percent of students did so in print publications.

The underrepresentation of student work in DH publications is especially troubling given that the profession continues to value single-authored articles, and consequently, single-authored articles continue to represent the field.

In their study of authorship patterns in the digital humanities, Julianne Nyhan and Oliver Duke-Williams looked at peer-reviewed articles from *Computers and the Humanities* (1966–2004), *Literary and Linguistic Computing* (1986–2011), and, as a control, the *Annals of the Association of American Geographers* (1966–2013). Not surprisingly, they found that single-authored papers dominate the field of DH. Research by Lisa Spiro suggests an even more complex and concerning picture. She reports that while 40 percent of articles published in *Literary and Linguistic Computing* (2004–2008) and *Digital Humanities Quarterly* (2007–2009) were multiauthored, most of those articles focused on practical projects, tools, or methods. It was the single-authored articles that centered on interpretive or theoretical work ("Computing"). These numbers suggest a worrisome possibility: that graduate students are being effectively shut out of the publication process at its most important and prestigious step.

Guidelines meant to address the inequity of collaborative practices, although well intentioned, do not address this particular problem. For example, neither the *Collaborators' Bill of Rights* nor UCLA's ensuing *Student Collaborators' Bill of Rights* assert that project directors have a responsibility to help graduate students write and publish on the DH projects they share. Instead, much of the language in both is centered on extending credit to project members and articulating the form that credit should take. The *Bill of Rights* states, "Credit should take the form of a legible trail that articulates the nature, extent and dates of the contribution"; "All kinds of work on a project are equally deserving of credit"; and, "There should be a prominent 'credits' link on the main page [of a website]." Largely echoing its parent document, the *Student Collaborators' Bill of Rights* similarly asserts, "If students have made substantive (i.e., non-mechanical) contributions to the project, their names should appear on the project as collaborators." While both *Bills of Rights* offer specific guidelines concerning credit allocation for the projects themselves, they make little mention of how credit should be allocated when it comes to the publications that result from those projects. Until these documents are expanded to take into account that the academy, including the digital humanities, is still focused on publications as a metric, they will fail to fully address the reality of students' status or needs.

As a student, I see two specific problems with the *Bills of Rights* guidelines. First, the citation practices described by both assume that an individual's labor, whether it be as web developer, PI, graphic designer, or data entrant, does not influence the form a project takes or the publication that results from it. But as we can all attest through our experiences as peer reviewers, seminar participants, and conference respondents, ideas do not emerge in intellectual vacuums.[6] If a collaboration results in a successful project, it can be extremely difficult to determine where one partner's idea ends and another's begins. Consequently, it becomes extremely difficult to discern who should be credited with what. Elijah Meeks, reflecting on an experience in which he unwittingly claimed authorship over his project partner's writing, cautions that "the overwhelming ease and amount of collaboration will make it harder and harder to parse just where and how an idea came into existence and who and what described it" ("Accidental Plagiarism"). Nowviskie confirms Meeks's assessment, explaining that "digital scholarship is rarely if ever 'singular' or 'done,' and that complicates immensely our notions of responsibility and authorship and readiness for assessment" ("Evaluating"). Given that an individual's contributions are more far-reaching than a detailed page of acknowledgments would ever begin to suggest, a "legible trail of credit" is not only impractical but also risks short-changing members who are not listed as authors.

Second, the assumption undergirding both *Bills of Rights* is that graduate students will not continue to work on the project they helped build. This is most apparent in the *Student Collaborators' Bill of Rights'* declaration: "If students have made substantive (i.e., non-mechanical) contributions to the project, their names should appear on the project as collaborators, and they should be acknowledged in subsequent publications that stem from the project." As the latter half of this statement suggests, the students are not often the ones doing the writing, and it assumes that their work is sufficiently acknowledged by a mere mention in "subsequent publications." But a name on a website or an acknowledgment in somebody else's publication does not help a graduate student move from scholar-in-training to scholar. As Stephen Ramsay writes, somewhat facetiously, "No one has a problem anymore with digital work. It just has to be, you know, about article length. And single authored. And peer reviewed. And disseminated under the banner of a third party" (45). Sarcasm aside, Ramsay raises an important point: the most valued work attached to digital projects still occurs at the point of publication, and it is this point in the publication process that the *Student Collaborators' Bill of Rights* does not address.

Instead, it reinforces a false binary between students and employees by suggesting, "A professor who assigns a class project, for example, must primarily consider the student's own intellectual growth, while a senior scholar who employs a student assistant may assign work that primarily benefits the project." However, the roles of student and student-employee cannot be so neatly separated. The graduate school relationship that structures student employment, especially on digital projects, is unique. Even when graduate students are technically employees—hired through a DH center or by a faculty member—and compensated for their work on a project through stipends, tuition abatements, or an hourly wage, they are simultaneously students. Likewise, the faculty members who employ them also inhabit dual roles and are, at once, mentor/teacher, manager, researcher, and employer. These roles are inextricable, and so the responsibilities a faculty member owes to her students, even when they are her employees, will be different from those found in more traditional employment arrangements. Compensation should not stand in for or be seen as an adequate replacement for student professionalization and publication.

Because the *Student Collaborators' Bill of Rights* does not take into account the various roles students and faculty members play when working on projects, it fails to adequately protect students as scholars-to-be. For example, it neglects to mention, much less assert, a student's right to take what he has learned and to use project data to produce his own scholarship. The student's intellectual development is phrased as a suggestion rather than as a mandate: "We encourage senior scholars to familiarize themselves with the literature on unpaid internships. At a minimum, internships for course credit should be offered as learning experiences, with a high level of mentorship. Those employing interns should be prepared to spend substantial face-to-face time with the student."

Even adhering to this guideline, the student must choose between being a student and getting paid. But payment is not reason enough for faculty to abdicate responsibility to their students. Faculty members who ask a student to work with them should expect that student to be a student, regardless of compensation. Given that graduate students are expected to publish, and to do so as much as possible while pursuing a PhD, they cannot also be expected to devote countless hours and mental energy to a project that, in the best-case scenario, would result in a coauthored paper or, more likely, recognition on a website and a little extra pocket money. If one of the benefits of DH projects, and the DH centers that support them, is the ability to foster a community in which graduate students can "learn on the job"—and, indeed, most DH centers describe their mission as such—then a student's intellectual growth and professional development should be taken into as much consideration as her technical skills (Clement and Reside).[7]

Emphasizing the pedagogical rather than collaborative aspects of DH will reinsert scholarship back into the equation for graduate students who would otherwise be treated as only employees. While pedagogy and collaboration both have a place in DH projects, they should not be conflated when it comes to working with students. Untangling these two aspects of DH work will help ensure that a student's professional and intellectual development is not effaced by the overall goals of developing a digital project.

The Role of Pedagogy in DH Partnerships or Closing the Gap between Teacher, Researcher, and Mentor

In its preamble, UCLA's *Student Collaborators' Bill of Rights* notes the importance of recognizing "that students and more senior scholars don't operate from positions of equal power in the academic hierarchy." Through its various guidelines, the bill represents one attempt to account for and mitigate the difference in status between students and scholars. But rather than trying to force a relationship to be something that it cannot (i.e., a collaboration between peers), I suggest that we recognize it for what it already is: a relationship between teacher and student, rather than between peers or just between employer and employee. Reframing the relationship between graduate students and project directors as pedagogical reshapes or, at the very least, makes explicit the different roles played by each. In the words of pedagogical theorist Henry Giroux, "To invoke the importance of pedagogy is to raise questions not simply about how students learn but also about how educators (in the broad sense of the term) construct the ideological and political positions from which they speak" (45). Complicating the issue, of course, is that in the digital humanities faculty members and students speak from multiple positions; the former often act as researchers, managers, teachers, mentors, and employers, while the latter act as students, researchers, employees, and scholars-in-training. Under the collaborative model, these positions are not given equal weight.

The relationship between teaching and research permeates most debates about the field of digital humanities. As Brett Hirsch and Stephen Brier have observed, few scholarly articles address both, and when they do, pedagogy is often discussed as an afterthought or only in relation to classroom contexts.[8] That is, pedagogy is either marginalized and treated as subservient to research, or pedagogy is seen as something that only occurs when professors incorporate digital projects into their more traditional classrooms. Few scholars seem to think of DH centers as learning environments unto themselves.[9] However, the work that occurs in DH centers is founded on knowledge creation via the collective (Hirsch, 16). Fostering a student's intellectual growth through effective mentorship will advance the project and the discipline as a whole because with guidance and encouragement, students will begin contributing to the field in meaningful ways and will be more likely to produce quality research and keep their project directors abreast of new knowledge. Treating research and teaching as distinct modes not only shuts students out of the academy but also erects a false binary.

Undeniably, DH work takes a long time. It is technologically intensive and often involves a large number of people. Still, as Jerome McGann writes, "The work of the humanist scholar has not changed with the advent of digital devices" (4). Therefore, it is of particular importance for project directors to view their graduate students as students rather than as collaborators, peers, or even partners. To do so will bring to the fore the focus on their intellectual development and related professional responsibilities, both for the student and the project director. In this scenario, ideally, students will begin to see their labor as integral to, rather than disconnected from, their own research agendas. Likewise, project directors will begin to see that their responsibilities to their student workers are not limited to the project, but instead are bound both to the project and to their students' intellectual and professional development. The aims of DH centers and humanities classrooms should be aligned when it comes to students; intellectual work and development are key components and the *raison d'être* of each.

As an indicator of how well the pedagogical model is incorporated into DH projects, I propose this as a general rule: projects that employ graduate students should include student publication as among the key metrics of their overall success.

After all, graduate students are expected to complete coursework, teach introductory classes, pass exams, write a dissertation, and publish all along the way. Writing is not only the most important part; it is also the fun part. In Daniel Cohen's words, "We wake up with ideas swirling around inside our head about the topic we're currently thinking about, and the act of writing is a way to satisfy our obsession and communicate our ideas to others" (40). Project directors should nurture this instinct. Working and thinking are similarly inextricable. The graduate students who are paid to do the work should therefore also be allowed to do some of the thinking.

NOTES

Many thanks to Michael Gavin, Travis Mullen, and Eric Gonzalez for helping me think through and expand on the issues discussed in this chapter.

1. Practitioners within the field have yet to reach a consensus on what precisely it means to do the work of a digital humanist; however, most recognize the importance of collaboration. As Lisa Spiro writes in "Computing and Communicating Knowledge," "Collaboration is generally vital to accomplishing . . . [digital] projects because of their scope and complexity" (44). Citing Spiro, Bryan Carter calls collaboration "an inherent part of almost all projects in the field" (59); likewise, N. Katherine Hayles sees collaboration as "the rule rather than the exception" (51). Many others believe that collaboration is a disciplinary asset in a time of shrinking budgets and the so-called decline of the humanities. Matthew Jockers, for one, asserts that the migration to digital humanities is opportunistic (11). Whether that opportunity is defined as scholarly or budgetary, the magnitude of most digital projects not only provides an opportunity for collaborative study but also demands it.

2. Developed as an outcome of a two-day workshop, "Off the Tracks—Laying New Lines for Digital Humanities Scholars" and first published in the NEH report *Off the Tracks,* the *Collaborators' Bill of Rights* is meant to protect collaborators at all levels. It outlines five recommendations: all work should be credited; attribution of credit should be comprehensive and legible; intellectual property rights should extend to all project members; collaborators maintain ownership over the project; and project funders should not support policies that undermine the above principles. In an attempt to remedy the lack of attention paid to students in the *Bill of Rights,* UCLA's *A Student Collaborators' Bill of Rights* adds a list of ten "safeguards for students" to the recommendations laid out in its parent document: students should be paid; course credit is not sufficient payment unless the partnership entails mentorship; students who have made substantial contributions should be named as collaborators; students should be encouraged to present on projects; students should list their contributions on their respective CVs; students should not be forced to participate in public-facing scholarship; students should be treated as full members of the team; and, guidelines should be set regarding reuse of digital materials.

3. Because DH collaborations rely so heavily on what Bethany Nowviskie terms "close and meaningful human partnership," social boundaries and status will inevitably

influence the shape of those partnerships, usually favoring tenure-track scholars ("Evaluating" and "Monopolies"). Julia Flanders describes collaboration as a relationship characterized by sacrifice and, in the digital humanities, mediated by the tools digital humanists use, rather than the relationship between collaborators. Willard McCarty writes that "collaboration is a problematic, and should be a contested, term," lest it become a "transcendental virtue"—"a good without qualification" (2).

4. In their NEH white paper, *Off the Tracks,* Tanya Clement and Doug Reside assert that scholars working within DH centers are viewed as hybrid academics and service workers, both separate from and unequal to tenure-track faculty.

5. Nowviskie attributes this to "the violence inherent in the system" and argues that, though "intellectual egalitarianism" is the ideal, we cannot ignore the way in which social boundaries factor into collaborative enterprises ("Monopolies").

6. As Christine Borgman writes, "Collaborations, when effective, produce new knowledge that is greater than the sum of what the participating individuals could accomplish alone." Stephen Johnson, too, notes that "a majority of breakthrough ideas emerge in collaborative environments" (qtd. Spiro "This is Why," 25).

7. For example, Julia Flanders writes that the staff development strategy at the Center for Digital Scholarship at Brown is "to create a culture in which it is assumed that people will be learning and experimenting as part of the work process." Paul Marty describes the goal of the Center for Digital Knowledge and Distributed Scholarship at Florida State University as "meet[ing] the needs of faculty, students, and staff engaged in knowledge creation" and "help[ing] students view the university not only as a place where knowledge is imparted, but as a place where knowledge is created." Writing of the early days at the University of South Carolina's Center for Digital Humanities, David Miller says, "We have from the start been concerned with the professional development of our staff." Susan Schreibman of the Digital Humanities Observatory identifies "the enhancement of the teaching and learning experience of research students in humanities" as one of the center's three major goals (qtd. Clement and Reside).

8. In the introduction to his 2012 article, "Where's the Pedagogy," Stephen Brier argues that teaching and pedagogy are seen as subservient to research; in his full-text search of ninety-plus articles published in *Digital Humanities Quarterly* from 2007 to 2009, Brier notes that "research" returns eighty-one hits, "teaching" and "learning" return forty hits, and "pedagogy" returns nine hits (391). Likewise, Hirsch notes that in the 2004 edition of Blackwell's *A Companion to Digital Humanities*, "research" appears 504 times, whereas "teaching" appears only 99 times. Hirsch notes that while discussions centered on digital humanities and pedagogy are on the rise, pedagogy is usually "bracketed," that is, tacked on or included parenthetically (4–5). Both Brier's and Hirsch's articles are meant to redress the lack of attention paid to pedagogy in the DH field, but both approach the topic by addressing digital humanities in classroom contexts rather than by seeing DH projects as pedagogical moments in and of themselves.

9. Katrina Anderson et al.'s "Student Labour and Training in the Digital Humanities" is one notable exception. Within their article, published only recently, Anderson

et al. argue that the rhetoric of collaboration ignores existing hierarchical structures, which creates challenges for students working in the digital humanities. Their list of best practices emphasizes training and encouraging students to disseminate their work and "call[s] for a formal acknowledgment of the mentoring activities—the affective and immaterial labour—that sustains much DH training and many DH projects."

BIBLIOGRAPHY

Anderson, Katrina, et al. "Student Labour and Training in the Digital Humanities." *Digital Humanities Quarterly* 10, no. 1 (2016), http://www.digitalhumanities.org/dhq/vol/10/1/000233/000233.html.

Borgman, Christine. "The Digital Future Is Now: A Call to Action for the Humanities." *Digital Humanities Quarterly* 3, no. 4 (2009), http://digitalhumanities.org/dhq/vol/3/4/000077/000077.html.

Brier, Stephen. "Where's the Pedagogy? The Role of Teaching and Learning in the Digital Humanities." In *Debates in the Digital Humanities,* edited by Matthew K. Gold, 390–401. Minneapolis: University of Minnesota Press, 2012.

Carter, Bryan. *Digital Humanities: Current Perspective, Practices, and Research.* Bingley, UK: Emerald Group Publishing, 2013.

Clement, Tanya and Doug Reside. *Off the Tracks: Laying New Lines for Digital Humanities Scholars.* College Park, Md.: Maryland Institute for Technology in the Humanities, 2011.

Cohen, Daniel J. "Open-Access Publication and Scholarly Values (Part 1)." In *Hacking the Academy: New Approaches to Scholarship and Teaching from Digital Humanities,* edited by Daniel J. Cohen and Tom Scheinfeldt, 39–44. Ann Arbor: University of Michigan Press, 2013.

"Collaborators' Bill of Rights." In *Off the Tracks: Laying New Lines for Digital Humanities Scholars,* edited by Tanya Clement and Doug Reside. College Park, Md.: Maryland Institute for Technology in the Humanities, 2011.

Di Pressi, Haley. et al. "A Student Collaborators' Bill of Rights." UCLA Digital Humanities. http://www.cdh.ucla.edu/news-events/a-student-collaborators-bill-of-rights/.

Flanders, Julia. "Collaboration and Dissent: Challenges of Collaborative Standards for Digital Humanities." In *Collaborative Research in the Digital Humanities,* edited by Marilyn Deegan and Willard McCarty, 67–80. Burlington, Vt.: Ashgate Publishing, 2012.

Giroux, Henry A. "Rethinking the Boundaries of Educational Discourse: Modernism, Postmodernism, and Feminism." In *Margins in the Classroom: Teaching Literature,* edited by Kostas Myrsiades and Linda S. Myrsiades, 1–51. Minneapolis: University of Minnesota Press, 1994.

Griffin, Gabriele, "Blame." In *The Emotional Politics of Research Collaboration,* edited by Gabriele Griffin, Annelie Bränström-Öhman, and Hildur Kalman, 83–98. New York: Routledge, 2013.

Hayles, N. Katherine. "How We Think: Transforming Power and Digital Technologies." In *Understanding Digital Humanities,* edited by David M. Berry, 42–66. New York: Palgrave Macmillan, 2012.

Hirsch, Brett. "</Parentheses>: Digital Humanities and the Place of Pedagogy." In *Digital Humanities Pedagogy: Practices, Principles and Politics,* edited by Brett Hirsch, 3–30. Cambridge, Mass.: Open Book Publishers, 2012.

Jockers, Matthew. *Macroanalysis Digital Methods & Literary History.* Champaign: University of Illinois Press, 2013.

Kelly, Mills. "Making Digital Scholarship Count." In *Hacking the Academy: New Approaches to Scholarship and Teaching from Digital Humanities,* edited by Daniel J. Cohen and Tom Scheinfeldt, 50–54. Ann Arbor: University of Michigan Press, 2013.

McCarty, Willard. "Collaborative Research in the Digital Humanities." In *Collaborative Research in the Digital Humanities,* edited by Marilyn Deegan and Willard McCarty, 1–10. Burlington, Vt.: Ashgate Publishing, 2012.

McGann, Jerome. *A New Republic of Letters: Memory and Scholarship in the Age of Digital Reproduction.* Cambridge, Mass.: Harvard University Press, 2014.

Meeks, Elijah. "The Digital Humanities as Accidental Plagiarism." Digital Humanities Specialist, Stanford University Libraries. January 28, 2013. https://dhs.stanford.edu /peer-review/the-digital-humanities-as-accidental-plagiarism/.

Meeks, Elijah. "How Collaboration Works and How It Can Fail." Digital Humanities Specialist, Stanford University Libraries. May 27, 2013, https://dhs.stanford.edu /natural-law/how-collaboration-works-and-how-it-can-fail/.

Nowviskie, Bethany. "Evaluating Collaborative Digital Scholarship (or, Where Credit Is Due.)" *Journal of Digital Humanities* 1, no. 4 (Fall 2012), http://journalofdigitalhuman ities.org/1–4/evaluating-collaborative-digital-scholarship-by-bethany-nowviskie/.

Nowviskie, Bethany. "Monopolies of Invention." December 30, 2009, http://nowviskie .org/2009/monopolies-of-invention/.

Nyhan, Julianne, and Oliver Duke-Williams. "Joint and Multi-Authored Publication Patterns in the Digital Humanities." *Literary and Linguistic Computing* 29, no. 3 (September 2014): 387–99.

Ramsay, Stephen. "Open-Access Publishing and Scholarly Values (Part 2)." In *Hacking the Academy: New Approaches to Scholarship and Teaching from Digital Humanities,* edited by Daniel J. Cohen and Tom Scheinfeldt, 44–46. Ann Arbor: University of Michigan Press, 2013.

Spiro, Lisa. "Computing and Communicating Knowledge." In *Collaborative Approaches to the Digital in English Studies,* edited by Laura McGrath. Logan: Utah State University Press, 2011. 44–81. http://ccdigitalpress.org/ebooks-and-projects/cad.

Spiro, Lisa. "This is Why We Fight: Defining the Values of the Digital Humanities." In *Debates in the Digital Humanities,* edited by Matthew K. Gold, 16–35. Minneapolis: University of Minnesota Press, 2012.

Underwood, Ted. "Comment on Scott Weingart, 'In Defense of Collaboration.'" The Scotbot Irregular. November 17, 2012, http://www.scottbot.net/HIAL/?p=25401.

Against Cleaning

KATIE RAWSON AND TREVOR MUÑOZ

P ractitioners, critics, and popularizers of new methods of data-driven research
treat the concept of "data cleaning" as integral to such work without remark-
ing on the oddly domestic image the term makes—as though a corn straw
broom were to be incorporated, Rube Goldberg–like, into the design of the Large
Hadron Collider. In reality, data cleaning is a consequential step in the research process that we often make opaque by the way we talk about it. The phrase "data cleaning" is a stand-in for longer and more precise descriptions of what people are doing
in the initial phases of data-intensive research. If you work with data or pay attention to discussions among practitioners who do, you have probably heard or read
somewhere that 80 percent of that work is "cleaning" (cf. Wickham). Subsequently
you likely realize that there is no one single understanding of what data cleaning
means. Many times the specifics of data cleaning are not described anywhere at
all, but instead reside in the general professional practices, materials, personal histories, and tools of the researchers. That we employ obscuring language like "data
cleaning" should be a strong invitation to scrutinize, perhaps reimagine, and almost
certainly rename this part of our practice.

The persistence of an element that is "out of focus" in discussions of data-
intensive research does not invalidate the findings of such research, nor is it meant
to cast researchers using these methods under suspicion. Rather, the collective
acceptance of a connotative term, "cleaning," suggests two assumptions: first, that
researchers in many domains consider the consequences of whatever is done during this little-discussed (80 percent) part of the process as sufficiently limited or
bounded so as not to threaten the value of any findings; and second, relatedly, that
there is little to be gained from a more precise description of those elements of the
research process that currently fall under the rubric of cleaning.

As researchers working in the domain of data-intensive humanities research,
we have found that these assumptions intensify suspicions about knowledge claims
that are based on "data." In fields where data-intensive work has a longer history,

researchers have developed paradigms and practices that provide de facto definitions of data cleaning (Newman, Ellisman, and Orcutt). In the humanities, however, these bounds are still unformed. Yet the humanities cannot import paradigms and practices wholesale from other fields, whether from "technoscience" or the nearer "social" sciences, without risking the foreclosure of specific and valuable humanistic modes of producing knowledge. If we are interested in working with data, and we accept that there is something in our work with data that is like what other fields might call "data cleaning," we have no choice but to try to articulate both what it is and what it means in terms of how humanists make knowledge.

Admittedly, this may only be an issue of the present moment, one experienced as a tax on those humanities researchers who wish to adopt new methods by asking them to overexplain their work processes. Once such methods are more widely practiced, the data-intensive humanities researcher may also be able to toss off the shorthand of "data cleaning." For now, however, there is significant value in being arrested by the obfuscation of this phrase. By taking first a descriptive approach (precisely saying what we mean by data cleaning) and, second, speculating on alternative approaches, we intervene in an unresolved conversation about data and reductiveness in the humanities. Cultural critical practices enacted at each stage of data-intensive inquiry reconfigure what has too often been offered as a binary choice in which scholars may choose to work in the tradition of cultural criticism or they may choose to work with data.

Humanities Data and Suspicions of Reduction

When humanities scholars recoil at data-driven research, they are often responding to the reductiveness inherent in this form of scholarship. This reductiveness can feel intellectually impoverished to scholars who have spent their careers working through particular kinds of historical and cultural complexity. The modern humanities have invested mental and moral energy into, and reaped insights from, studying difference. Bethany Nowviskie summarizes this tradition in this volume's Chapter 37, "Capacity through Care": "The finest contribution of the past several decades of humanities research has been to broaden, contextualize, and challenge canonical collections and privileged views. Scholars do this by elevating instances of neglected or alternate lived experience—singular human conditions, often revealed to reflect the mainstream."

From within this worldview, data cleaning becomes maligned because it is understood as a step that inscribes a normative order by wiping away what is different. The term "cleaning" implies that a dataset begins as "messy." "Messy" suggests an underlying order: it supposes things already have a rightful place, but they are not in it—like socks on the bedroom floor rather than in the bureau or the hamper.

Understood this way, suspicions about cleaning are suspicions that researchers are not recognizing or reckoning with the framing orders to which they are subscribing as they make and manipulate their data. In other data-intensive fields in which researchers have long been explicit about their framing orders, the limits of results are often understood and articulated using specialized discourses. For example, in climate science, researchers confine their claims to the data they can work with and report results with margins of error.[1] While humanities researchers do have discourses for limiting claims (acknowledging the choice of an archive or a particular intellectual tradition), the move into data-intensive research asks humanists to modify such discourses or develop new ones suitable for these projects. The ways in which the humanities engages these challenges may both open up new practices for other fields and allow humanities researchers who have made powerful critiques of the existing systems of data analysis to undertake data-intensive forms of research in ways that do not require them to abandon their commitments to such critiques.

The Value of a Naïve Tool

To contribute to the development of new discourses and the practice of critically attuned data work, we scrutinize cleaning through a reflection on our own work with *Curating Menus*. *Curating Menus* is a research project that aims to curate and analyze the open data from New York Public Library's *What's on the Menu?*

We set off to answer questions like the following: Can we see the effect of wartime food rationing in what appeared on menus during World War I? Or, can we track the changing boundaries of what constituted a "dish" over time? To do this, we thought we would need to "clean" the "messy" data. What became evident was that cleaning up or correcting values was a misleading—and even unproductive—way to think about how to make the data more useful for our own questions and for other scholars studying food.

Under the rubric of cleaning, we began with a technical solution to what we had imagined was a technical problem. Variation in the strings of text transcribed from menus was obscuring our ability to do things as simple as count how many dishes were in the dataset. Working with Lydia Zvygintseva, we attempted to reduce the number of variations using OpenRefine, an open-source software tool designed for these types of tasks. When the scale of the problem overwhelmed the capabilities of that tool, we discovered that it was possible to run the clustering algorithms popularized by OpenRefine using custom Python scripts (Muñoz). The output of one of these scripts was a list of variant values such as the following:

id

2759 Potatoes, au gratin
7176 Potatoes au Gratin
8373 Potatoes—Au gratin
35728 Potatoes: au gratin

44271 Au Gratin Potatoes

84510 Au Gratin (Potatoes)

94968 Potatoes, au Gratin,

97166 POTATOES:- Au gratin

185040 Au Gratin [potatoes]

313168 Au Gratin Potatoes

315697 (Potatoes) Au Gratin

325940 Au Gratin Potatoes

330420 au-Gratin Potatoes

353435 Potatoes: Au gratin

373639 Potatoes Au Gratin

We were very excited to get lists that looked this way because we could easily imagine looping over them and establishing one normalized value for each set of variants. We had not yet recognized that the data model around which the dataset was organized was not the data model we needed to answer our research questions. At the time, the main challenge seemed to be processing enough values quickly enough to "get on with it."

At that point in the research process, the Python scripts we were using were small, purpose-built command line programs. After some deliberation, we decided to build a simple web application to provide the task-specific user interfaces we would need to tackle the challenge of NYPL's menu data.[2] The piece of software we built does, in some ways, the opposite of what one might expect. A cluster of values like the one for "Potatoes Au Gratin" is presented to the user, and he or she must make a decision about how to turn that cluster of variants into a single value. Our tool sorts the variants by the number of times they appear across the dataset. So the decision may be to simply save the most commonly occurring value as the normalized form: "potatoes au gratin." Or it might be to modify that value based on a set of rules we have defined. Or it might be to supply a new value altogether. The process can end up looking like this:

> What is the authoritative spelling of Buzzards Bay oysters? Let me Google that. . . . Oh, it collapsed an orange juice and an orange sherbet under "orange"; let me flag that. . . . A jelly omelet!?

The tool surfaces near-matches, but it does not automate the work of collapsing them into normalized values. Instead, it focuses the user's attention and labor on exactly that activity. In other words, in our initial version of computer-assisted data curation, we still had to touch each data point. This caused us to doubt that we could use this method with a whole dataset the size of the one from *What's on the Menu?*; however, it was intellectually productive.

In the process of normalizing values, we found ourselves faced with questions about the foods themselves. Choosing the "correct" string was not a self-contained problem, but an issue that required returning to our research questions and investigating the foods themselves. Since the research questions we were asking required us to maintain information about brands and places, we often had to look up items to see which was the correct spelling of the brand or place name.[3] Shellfish and liquor were two particularly interesting and plagued areas for these questions. The process revealed kinds of "messiness" that we had not yet even considered. We realized that the changes we were making were not "corrections" that would "clean up" the original dataset, but rather formed an additional information set with its own data model. What we thought were data points were, in fact, a synthesis or mash-up of different kinds of information within a half-finished or half-articulated data model. This data model was sufficient for the original aim of the project—supporting an application that facilitated crowdsourced transcription—but it is insufficient for scholarly inquiry. To ask research questions, we needed to create our own dataset, which would work in context with the NYPL dataset.

Diversity in Data

The NYPL data is a linked network graph of unique URLs for dishes and menus. The *Curating Menus* dataset is an organized hierarchy of concepts from the domain of food. We made a set of labels that we believe would facilitate humanities researchers' understanding of the scope, diversity, and value of the NYPL's dataset. The two datasets are connected by links from concept labels in our dataset to dishes in the NYPL dataset. Our interaction with the NYPL dataset thus became a process of evaluating which variants in the names of dishes revealed new information, which we should in turn account for in our own data, and which variants were simply accidents of transcription or typesetting. The process freed us to attend to difference and detail, rather than attempting to clean it away. Without cleaning, we could be sensitive to questions about time, place, and subject. This kind of attention is imperative if humanities researchers are to find the menu data valuable for their scholarship.

As we considered methods for preserving diversity within our large dataset, the work of anthropologist Anna Tsing offered us a valuable theoretical framework through which to approach these issues. In "On Nonscalability: The Living World Is Not Amenable to Precision-Nested Scales," Tsing critiques scalability as an overarching paradigm for organizing systems (whether world trade, scientific research, or colonial economies). By scalability, Tsing means the quality that allows things to be traded out for each other in a totalizing system without regard to the unique or individual qualities of those things—like many stalks of sugarcane (which are biological clones of one another) or, subsequently, workers in a factory. From this definition of scalability, she goes on to argue for a theory of nonscalability. Tsing writes, "The definition of nonscalability is in the negative: scalability is a distinctive design feature; nonscalability refers to everything that is without that feature. . . . Nonscalability theory is an analytic apparatus that helps us notice nonscalable phenomena" (509). While scalable design creates only one relationship between elements of a system (what Tsing calls "precision nesting"), nonscalable phenomena are enmeshed in multiple relationships, outside or in tension with the nesting frame. "Scales jostle and contest each other. Because relationships are encounters across difference, they have a quality of indeterminacy. Relationships are transformative, and one is not sure of the outcome. Thus diversity-in-the-making is always part of the mix" (510).

Currently, the imagination of the cultural heritage world has been captured by crowdsourced information production on the one hand and large-scale institutional aggregation on the other: the *What's on the Menu?* project exemplifies both of these trends. Our difficulties working with the open data from this project suggest that it is a vital moment to consider the virtues of nonscalability theory in relation to digital scholarship. Engineering crowdsourced cultural heritage projects usually involves making object transcription, identification, and the development of metadata scalable. For example, the makers of the *What's on the Menu?* project designed their system to divide the work into parcels that could be completed quickly by users while reducing the friction that arise from differences in the menus; for example, the organization of the information on the page or other evidence of physical manifestations like handwriting and typeface variations (Lascarides and Vershbow). The images of menus and the metadata about them are also being republished through projects like the Digital Public Library of America (DPLA), another example of how things get shaped and parsed for purposes of scaling up to ever wider distribution. Tsing reminds us, "At best, scalable projects are articulations between scalable and nonscalable elements, in which nonscalable effects can be hidden" (515). She argues that the question is not whether we do or do not engage in scalable or nonscalable processes. To explore the articulations between scalable and nonscalable, Tsing tells the story of the contemporary matsutake industry, which encompasses both foraging (by immigrant harvesters in the ruins of large-scale industrial forestry in the U.S. Pacific Northwest) and global supply chains serving Japanese markets. Tsing's account focuses our attention on how "scales . . . arise from the relationships that inform particular projects, scenes, or events" (509). The elements of nonscalable systems enter into "transformative relationships," and these "contact[s] across difference can produce new agendas" (510). Following Tsing, we came to see points of articulation that had previously been invisible to us as would-be consumers of scaled data. Beginning from the creation of the original, physical menus and tracing the development of the crowd-created data, we identify and account for "nonscalable elements"—and consequently, edge further and further from the terminology of "cleaning."

Seeing Nonscalability in NYPL's Crowdsourced Menus Project

Making menus is a scalable process. Although menus are sometimes handwritten or elaborately printed on ribbon-sewn silk, the format of a menu is designed to be scalable. Menus are an efficient typographical vehicle for communicating a set of offerings for often low-margin dining enterprises. Part of the way that we know that menus are scalable is how alike they appear. "Eggs Benedict" or "caviar," with their accompanying prices, may fit interchangeably into the "slots" of the menu's layout. Within the menus themselves, we also see evidence of the nexus of printing scalability, dish scalability, and cost in, for example, the use of ellipses to express different options: eggs with . . . cheese, . . . ham, . . . tomatoes, etc. The visual evidence of *What's on the Menu?* shows us how headings, cover images, and epigraphs—for all their surface variations—follow recognizable patterns. These strong genre conventions and the mass production of the menus as physical objects allow us to see and treat them as scaled and scalable.[4]

However, the menus also express nonscalable elements—historical contingencies and encounters across difference. Some of these nonscalable elements are revealed by the kind of questions we find ourselves asking about the experience of ordering from these menus. How were they understood as part of the interactions among purveyors, customers, and diners? How did diners navigate elements like the pervasive use of French in the late nineteenth and early twentieth centuries? How did they interpret the particular style and content of cover images or quotations? Evidence for these questions manifests in the menus as objects, but does not fit within the scalable frames of menu production nor the menu data we have at hand. Yet the nonscalable elements cannot be disregarded and have the potential to affect how we interpret and handle the scalable data. Nonscalability theory encourages us to grapple with this dynamic at each point of articulation in the process of making scalable objects.

The collection of these menus was also scalable. The system set up for their accession and processing treated the menus not only as interchangeable objects but also like the many other paper materials that entered the collections of the NYPL in the twentieth century. Perhaps the clearest evidence of this is in their cataloging. The catalog cards fit each menu into the same frame—with fields for the dining establishment, the date of creation and date of accession, and the sponsor of the meal, if available. Cataloging is a way of suppressing or ignoring the great differences in the menus, choosing one type of data to attend to. The cards index the collection so that the institution has a record of its holdings and a user can find a particular object. The menus, with their scalable and nonscalable features, become scalable library inventory through this process (cf. Tsing, 519).

Cataloging's aim is to find a way to make items at least interchangeable enough not to break the system. The practice is rife with examples of catalogers navigating encounters with difference. Catalogers practice nonscalability theory constantly.

Sometimes the answer is institutionally specific fields in machine-readable cataloging (MARC) records; sometimes the solution is overhauling subject headings or creating a new way of making records (like the BIBFRAME initiative). However, the answer is almost never to treat each object as a unique form; instead, the object is to find a way to keep the important and usable information while continuing to use socially and technologically embedded forms of classifying and finding materials.

Digitization is also a process designed for scalability. As long as an object can fit into the focal area of an imaging device, its size, texture, and other material features are reduced to a digital image file. The zooming enabled by high-resolution digital images is one of Tsing's prime examples of design and engineering for scalability. In the distribution of digitized images, the properties of the digital surrogate that are suited to scalability are perpetuated, while the properties of the original that are nonscalable (the feel of the paper, its heft or daintiness) are lost.

The point at which certain objects are selected for digitization is one of the moments of articulation Tsing describes between the scalable and nonscalable. Digitization transforms diverse physical materials—brittle, acidic paper or animal parchment, large wooden covers or handstitched bindings, leaves or inserts—into standardized grids of pixels. From the point of digitization forward, the logic of scalability permeates projects like *What's on the Menu?* The transcription platform is constructed to nest precisely within the framework of how cultural heritage organizations like NYPL create digital objects from their original materials.

Paul Beaudoin from the NYPL Labs team discusses some of the logic behind their approach to these kind of projects in a blog post announcing Scribe, an open-source software platform released in 2015, but derived from the library's experience with crowdsourced transcription projects. Beaudoin describes how the Scribe platform is based on "simplification [that] allows us to reduce complex document transcription to a series of smaller decisions that can be tackled individually . . . the atomicity of tasks makes projects less daunting for volunteers to begin and easier to continue." For example, *What's on the Menu?* presents visitors with a segment of a digitized image of a menu and a single text input box to record what they see.[5]

The NYPL Labs team is explicit about its commitments to designing for scalability. We know from work in the domain of scholarly editing that what comprises "transcription" is not self-evident.[6] It could be modeled and implemented in software in a number of ways. The menus project uses optical character recognition (OCR) software to generate bounding boxes that determine what human volunteers will transcribe. In this, we can see the precision nesting of scales at work. OCR software is designed to scalably produce machine-readable, machine-processable digital text from images of printed material. In the case of the menus, the software can detect regions of text within the digital images; however, due to the variation in typefaces, the aging of inks and paper, and other nonscalable elements, the output of the OCR algorithm is not a legible set of words. Using the bounding boxes but discarding the OCR text in favor of text supplied by human volunteers is a clever and elegant design. It constructs the act of transcription in such a way that it matches the scalable process of digitization and ways of understanding the content of a menu that privilege scalable data.

Yet, even here, now that we know to look for them, the nonscalable effects cannot be completely hidden. The controls allow users to zoom through three levels of an image, a feature that evidences slippage in the segmentation algorithm. This element of the tool acknowledges that someone might need to zoom out to complete a transcription—often because the name of a dish has to be understood through the relation between the line of text in the bounding box and other nearby text, like a heading. Further, the text box on the transcription screen is unadorned, implying that what to do is self-evident; however, the help page is full of lengthy instructions for how to "navigate some of the more commonly encountered issues," revealing the ways that transcription is not a self-evident, scalable process.

In addition, the project was designed so that people did not have to create accounts or sign in to submit transcriptions. Creators and managers of such projects are working to make more data and to allow more people to participate in making data. This entails creating systems that treat volunteers as interchangeable in the service of allowing more work to get done more quickly. However, what is construed as a scalable workforce is, in fact, made up of people who have different levels of understanding or adherence to the guidelines and different perceptions or interpretations of the materials. When we understand this workforce as a collection of individuals, we can see how any crowd as large as the one that has worked on the menus project will contain such diversity. The analytic apparatus of Tsing's nonscalability theory makes all these design choices visible and allows us to see the transcription task, as framed within *What's on the Menu?*, as another moment of articulation between scalable and nonscalable elements.

When we download the open data from the *What's on the Menu?* site and open up the files, we are presented with the results of all this activity: menu collection and digitization and transcription. Instead of seeing mess, we see the ways in which diversity has seeped or broken into what were designed to be smoothly scaling systems. Now we are better prepared to envision how our work—creating new data organized around concepts of historical food practices—begins from what the NYPL has released, which is transcription data: words volunteers typed into the boxes at *What's on the Menu?* linked to metadata from their digital library systems. In both of these datasets there is something called "dish." In NYPL's data, "dish" is the name of the field in which a transcribed string from a menu is stored in the project's database. In *Curating Menus*' data, "dish" is a representation created to reflect and name an arrangement of foods and culinary practices in a particular historical moment. This is an example of, as Tsing puts it, the ways that "scales jostle and contest." We know that the response to this friction is not to retreat from working at scale. Instead we have to find ways of working while being aware that *precision* nesting hides diversity and that there are consequences to diversity being hidden.

Indexes: Making Scalability Explicit and Preserving Diversity

Our answer to this challenge is an index. We are suggesting that indexing is a more precise replacement for some of the work that travels under the name of "cleaning." An index is an information structure designed to serve as a system of pointers between two bodies of information, one of which is organized to provide access to concepts in the other. The list of terms and associated page numbers from the back of a book is one familiar example. An array of other terms that people use alongside "cleaning" (wrangling, munging, normalizing, casting) name other important parts of working with data, but indexing best captures the crucial interplay of scalability and diversity that we are trying to trace in this chapter.

We began to think of the work we were doing as building something like a back-of-the-book index for the *What's on the Menu?* data. We aimed to create additional data structures around and atop the existing data, generating links between a set of names or categories we created and the larger and more heterogeneous set of data from NYPL. Ultimately, we decided to build two interconnected indexes: one focused on historical food concepts and one on the organizations connected to the menus (businesses, community organizations, fraternal societies, etc.). We began with the food index and are developing a framework that echoes cookbook indexes to structure our data: ingredients, cooking methods, courses, cuisines.

If we had felt no unease continuing the lineage of precision nesting that links the scales of digitization and crowdsourced transcription, we could have proceeded with a completely algorithmic approach: "cleaning" our data using scripts, linguistic rules, and even machine learning. These methods yield results by predictively circumscribing variants in language so as to aggregate and enable analysis at another level of abstraction. We can see the usefulness of these algorithmic approaches, but we also know that they would hide diversity in the menus. However, to understand the implications of these diversity-hiding methods, we needed to create a grounded approach to making a data model for our index.

Today, when we look at a list of variations on "Potatoes au Gratin" or some other group of transcriptions, we focus on the task of choosing a label that will be a node in our dataset and that will serve as a pointer to all the other transcribed values in the NYPL dataset. We are building the set of labels from the set of data, rather than beginning by writing some large, hierarchical domain model. We want to represent the concept of two eggs and bacon, not caring if it was written "bacon and two eggs" or "2 Eggs and Bacon."

To get from transcription to concept, we began with a set of simple rules: spell out numbers and use lowercase letters. Actually engaging with the menu transcriptions quickly raised other questions. For example, on the question of place names, we decided to apply capitalization rules (in accord with style guides like *The Chicago Manual of Style*) that say that you capitalize when the reference to place is literal, but not when the reference makes a generic association: yes to Virginia ham or Blue Point oysters but no to swiss cheese or scotch. We also found many single transcriptions containing multiple concepts, like "steak, sauce béarnaise." Since we wanted a way to be able to systematically find multiple components of a dish, we opted to standardize how we labeled the addition of sauces, garnishes, and other added ingredients. Here is one instance where we plan to use algorithmic tools to help us analyze some of this big data, since it is grounded in a specific data model.

In building our index, we are conscientiously creating scalability. We know that scalability is a process of articulations between different scales; however, Tsing suggests—and we believe—that those articulations are often hidden. Conversely, indexes are tools of scalability that make these articulations explicit.

Our index is about ingredients, meal structures, and cooking techniques. Someone else could re-index the menu material in a different way. Variations might involve attending to the species of the plants and animals that are in foods or taking a nutritional approach that classifies food based on calories, vitamins, and carbohydrates. We can also imagine projects that attend to language use in ways that our index suppresses. However an index is conceived, it allows us to build up explicit and flexible bases of knowledge that people can continue to access and understand.

Sharing Control of Authority

One of the mechanisms that librarians and archivists have used to build and maintain large, distributed information systems is a set of practices referred to as authority control. In brief, these practices involve creating defined and agreed-on taxonomies, as well as guidelines for the application of such arrangements of terms. The Library of Congress Subject Headings represent one instance of authority control. Maintaining such a system is labor intensive and has been used only for supporting core library activities like managing collections and supporting patrons in finding materials. Libraries and archives are trying to take advantage of technological developments in linked data—merging their centuries-old authority control practices with the affordances of the World Wide Web. However, what relatively few have seized on are new opportunities to apply the practices of authority control outside the original core needs of collection organization and wayfinding.

These new opportunities fall somewhere between digital library practices and digital humanities research, but the gap is one that more projects should embrace the opportunity to fill. There is a need for projects that take "authority work" as an invitation to encourage creativity, an invitation for making and building. In such a model, multiple regimes of authorities might be built up from critically aware and engaged intellectual communities to meet their own specific needs while also participating in larger technological and information systems.

We imagine those communities will contain librarians and scholars. Though librarians and humanities scholars have frequently intersected, they have rarely interacted in this way. Simplifying to the point of caricature, these existing interactions go something like this: humanities scholars point out that the structure and content of a specific archive or collection represent and even re-create certain cultural logics. For example, the systems of describing collections, such as the widely used Library of Congress Subject Headings, reify concepts about persons or cultures that should be interrogated more closely or perhaps discredited and dismantled altogether. For the most part, librarians, archivists, and information scientists acknowledge these flaws and perhaps even work to remedy them in the course of maintaining systems that preserve whatever partial archives do exist or helping patrons find information they need.

We are looking for new forms of collective action that can be expressed through the professional work of humanities scholars and librarians. This is not simply a call for the production of more data—attempting to subvert the work of categorization and classification through the production of ever more local, finely wrought distinctions, details, and qualifications. Our aim is to develop ways of working that validate local experiences of data without removing them from a more global network of information exchange.[7] These practices, as we imagine them, resonate with Bethany Nowviskie's interpretation of the Afrofuturist philosophy of Sun Ra (as expressed by Shabaka Hutchings), which claims, "Communities that have agency are able to form their own philosophical structures"(Nowviskie, "Everywhere") The transition to working in a linked data paradigm should be valued not principally for the ways in which it might make large-scale information systems operate more smoothly, but rather for the ways in which it can create localized communities of authority, within which people can take control of the construction of data and the contexts in which it lives. In a keynote presentation at the 2015 LITA Forum, Mx (Mark) A. Matienzo articulated a parallel version of this view:

> We need to begin having some serious conversations about how we can best serve our communities not only as repositories of authoritative knowledge or mere individuals who work within them. We should be examining the way in which we can best serve our communities to support their need to tell stories, to heal, and to work in the process of naming.

Discussions of cleaning data fail to capture this need. The cleaning paradigm assumes an underlying, "correct" order. However tidy values may look when grouped into rows or columns or neatly delimited records, this tidiness privileges the structure of a container, rather than the data inside it. This is the same diversity-hiding trick that nonscalability theory encourages us to recognize.

But it is not enough to recognize how cleaning suppresses diversity; we must also envision alternate ways of working. The first thing we must do with our datasets, rather than normalizing them, is to find the communities within which our data matters. With those communities in mind and even in dialogue with them, we must ask these questions: What are the concepts that structure this data? And how can this data, structured in this way, point to other people's data? This way of thinking will allow us to see the messiness of data not as a block to scalability, but as a vital feature of the world that our data represents and from which it emerges.

NOTES

1. The fact that these communities have developed discourses for describing the boundaries of the claims they make does not inoculate them from critique about the costs and shortcomings of their methods (cf. Latour).

2. For a variety of reasons, we would not recommend this course of action to others without serious deliberation. There is a reason why applications like OpenRefine are so popular and useful. If you would like to know more, contact the authors.

3. If we had a dictionary to compare these materials to, the process may had been more automatable; however, from what we have found thus far, that particular language resource—Wordnet for Oysters!—does not exist.

4. The NYPL menu collector Frank E. Buttolph's acquisition practices reinforce the role and scale of printers in menu production in the twentieth century. In addition to restaurants and customers, she went straight to the menu source—printers—to fill out her collection.

5. Early versions of the project interface featured a social-media-style call-to-action below the image snippet ("What does this say?"), as well as brief instructions below the text input box: "Please type the text of the indicated dish EXACTLY as it appears. Don't worry about accents" (see for example, https://web.archive.org/web/20120102212103 /http://menus.nypl.org/menu_items/664698/edit). This accompanying text was quickly dropped—presumably because the task seemed self-evident enough from the layout of the transcription screen.

6. See https://datasymposium.wordpress.com/sahle/.

7. Compare with the "speculative guidelines" in Loukissas.

BIBLIOGRAPHY

Beaudoin, Paul. "Scribe: Toward a General Framework for Community Transcription." New York Public Library (blog). November 23, 2016, https://www.nypl.org/blog/2015/11/23 /scribe-framework-community-transcription.

Lascarides, Michael, and Ben Vershbow. "What's on the Menu?: Crowdsourcing at the New York Public Library." In *Crowdsourcing our Cultural Heritage,* edited by Mia Ridge, 113–38. Surrey, UK: Ashgate, 2014.

Latour, Bruno. "Why Has Critique Run out of Steam? From Matters of Fact to Matters of Concern." *Critical Inquiry* 30, no. 2 (2004): 225–48.

Loukissas, Yanni Alexander. "Taking Big Data Apart: Local Readings of Composite Media Collections." *Information, Communication & Society* 20, no. 5 (May 4, 2017): 651–64. doi:10.1080/1369118X.2016.1211722.

Matienzo, Mx (Mark) A. "To Hell with Good Intentions: Linked Data, Community and the Power to Name." Mx A. Matienzo (blog). February 11, 2016. http://matienzo .org/2016/to-hell-with-good-intentions/.

Muñoz, Trevor. "Using Pandas to Curate Data from the New York Public Library's What's On the Menu? Project." http://nbviewer.jupyter.org/gist/trevormunoz/8358810. Accessed January 10, 2014.

Newman, Harvey B., Mark H. Ellisman, and John A. Orcutt. "Data-Intensive E-Science Frontier Research." *Communications ACM* 46, no. 11 (November 2003): 68–77. doi:10.1145/948383.948411.

Nowviskie, Bethany. "Everywhere, Every When." April 29, 2016, http://nowviskie.org/2016 /everywhere-every-when/.

Tsing, Anna Lowenhaupt. "On Nonscalability: The Living World Is Not Amenable to Precision-Nested Scales." *Common Knowledge* 18, no. 3 (2012): 505–24.

What's on the Menu? New York Public Library. http://menus.nypl.org/. Accessed July 29, 2016.

Wickham, Hadley. "Tidy Data." *Journal of Statistical Software* 59, no. 10 (2014): 1–23.

New Data? The Role of Statistics in DH

TAYLOR ARNOLD AND LAUREN TILTON

In an emerging terminological shift, digital humanists are increasingly reframing their objects of study as "humanities data." In "Big? Smart? Clean? Messy? Data in the Humanities," Christof Schöch compares the state of computational research in the humanities to the deluge of large, unstructured datasets that have become objects of study across academia and industry. Along the same lines, IEEE recently organized three workshops on "Big Humanities Data." Building off of this shift in terms, Miriam Posner in her piece "Humanities Data: A Necessary Contradiction" explores both why this terminology is needed and why it may be difficult for humanists to consider their evidential sources as akin to those of the sciences and social sciences. We also chose to use the term "humanities data" in our book: *Humanities Data in R*. Rather than emphasizing contradictions among the disciplines, we sought to find common ground across them. We set out to show how statistics—the organization, analysis, interpretation, and presentation of data—is a fundamental interlocutor and methodological approach for the digital humanities. In this chapter we take the latent argument of our book and make it explicit.

Despite the constant refrain suggesting that digital humanities should take better account of computer science, it is actually statistics that provides a set of approaches for exploring, analyzing, and thinking critically about data in order to posit new findings and questions related to our fields of study.[1] In this chapter, we argue that three areas of statistics—exploratory data analysis (EDA), data visualization, and statistical computing—are central to the digital humanities. We focus first on how EDA is obscured, but undergirds quantitative work in the digital humanities. We then show how data visualization offers a theoretical framework for understanding graphics as a form of argument with which the field should contend. Finally, we turn to the role of programming libraries to suggest we consider statistical computing in lieu of one-off tools.

While often not named, exploratory data analysis permeates the digital humanities. EDA, described in 1977 in John Tukey's seminal work by the same name, is a subfield of statistics offering a conceptual structure for drawing information from data sources. It often evokes new hypotheses and guides statisticians toward appropriate techniques for further inferential modeling. Tukey championed these techniques after becoming concerned that a substantial amount of statistical analysis was conducted by blindly applying models without first considering their appropriateness. His work, and its subsequent expansions over the past forty-five years, helps lay out an approach for thinking critically about data analysis in the humanities.

EDA is concerned with exploring data by iterating between summary statistics, modeling techniques, and visualizations. Summary statistics offer a quick description of the data using techniques such as mean, median, and range. A common approach is the five-number summary, which gives the minimum, lower quartile, median, upper quartile, and maximum values for a given variable. These compactly describe a robust measure of the spread and central tendency of a variable while also indicating potential outliers. Statistical models such as linear regression offer more complex summary statistics that describe general multivariate patterns in the data. Visualizations, as Turkey argued, can then be used to compactly augment summary statistics. Histograms, for example, give more detailed descriptions of the distributions of numeric variables. Scatterplots and box plots show patterns between variables, a strategy particularly important when simultaneously analyzing multivariate data. EDA undergirds quantitative work in the digital humanities, particularly text analysis, and yet is rarely explicitly named as a key method or identified as a powerful approach in the field.

Our work on Photogrammar offers an example of how EDA reshaped a digital public humanities project by leading to new inferences and questions. Photogrammar is a web-based site for organizing, searching, and visualizing 170,000 photographs taken from 1935–1945 under the auspices of the U.S. Farm Security Administration and Office of War Information (FSA-OWI). After acquiring the data from the Library of Congress, we turned to EDA using the programming language R. Calculating, assessing, and then reanalyzing summary statistics of photographs by state and by year revealed new and unexpected patterns, immediately shifting our object of study (see Figure 24.1; Arnold et al.). With an immediate signal from the data, we then used visualizations to convey our new arguments about the collection (see Figure 24.2). The new findings, revealed through EDA, changed the techniques of Photogrammar and opened up a new set of questions about the expanded visions of the archive, the federal government, and photographers.

Data visualization, another subfield of statistics closely aligned with EDA, is also making theoretical and applied contributions to the digital humanities. Tukey's work on EDA called for constructing visualizations, such as scatterplots, histograms, and box plots, to understand patterns within multivariate datasets. The field of data visualization builds on his work, treating visualizations as their own object of study.

Jacques Bertin's *Semiology of Graphics,* William Cleveland's texts *The Elements of Graphing Data* and *Visualizing Data,* and Leland Wilkinson's *The Grammar of*

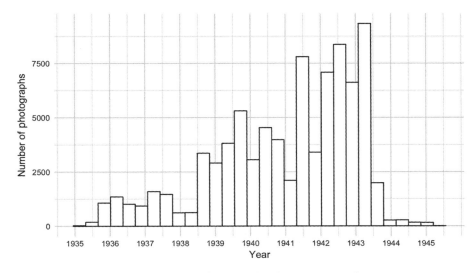

Figure 24.1. Histogram showing number of photographs taken over time in the FSA-OWI collection.

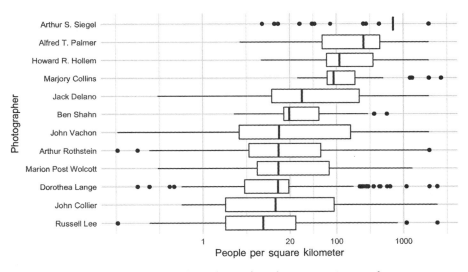

Figure 24.2. Box plot showing the population density, from the 1940 U.S. Census, of counties where FSA-OWI photographers captured photographs.

Graphics are foundational works in statistical graphics. Bertin argued that graphics "constitutes one of the basic sign-systems conceived by the human mind for the purposes of storing, understanding, and communicating essential information" (2). He showed explicitly how graphics can serve as their own form of argument and evidence. Cleveland built on Bertin's work by theorizing a distinction between graphing, the process of visualizing raw data, and fitting, the process of visualizing transformed data and statistical models. Wilkinson extended Cleveland's theory by distinguishing between the mathematical abstraction of a graph and the physical manifestation of a rendered graphic. He then set out to describe the fundamental units that comprised a visualization.

Wilkinson constructed a formal language for describing statistical visualizations by separating out the mathematical specification of a graphics system from the aesthetic details of its assembly and display. He named each component of the visualization, moving from the original data to the output, a layer in his formal *Grammar of Graphics* system. Examples of layers include picking the scale of the plot, choosing the size of points, and computing summary statistics. Take, for instance, a histogram of the number of photos taken each month in Photogrammar. One of the layers in Wilkinson's grammar would be calculating the heights of the bins. His goal was to make explicit the action of determining the height, which in turn makes the modeling assumptions explicit. Wilkinson's formal language explicates what assumptions are being made, where these assumptions are being made, and how the original data has been modified to create the output. Furthermore, implementations of this language as an object-oriented system, as in Hadley Wickham's ggplot2 library, are able to construct rules for fitting together a small number of classes and relationships between them to create an "almost unlimited world of graphical forms" (1).

The theoretical formulation of graphics provided by statistics offers concepts ideas for the digital humanities to draw from and grapple with. The work of Wilkinson and his interlocutors provides an alternative foundation for graphics that is a critical, but overlooked, area in our conversations about visual forms of knowledge production. Since Wilkinson's approach separates each action into small discrete steps, humanities scholars can analyze and critique the parts individually. Understanding these theoretical frameworks allows for critical applications of graphics engines such as ggplot2—gg stands for grammar of graphics—and D3.js. Finally, a dialogue between statistics and the humanities offers another framework from which to debate, construct, and critique how visualizations are approached and implemented in the digital humanities.

The subfield of statistical computing, which is concerned with the design and implementation of software for working with data, also offers methodological inventions for DH practice. Many tools written specifically for applications in the humanities such as Palladio, SHANTI, TOME, and WordSeer have the potential to unlock and analyze latent patterns in humanities data. While we are beginning to see a shift, a major funding priority continues to be using one-off tools for a specific task such as Voyant, or omnibus tools that attempt to address multiple analytical approaches in one toolkit such as Palladio. These tools can serve as a great introduction to analytical approaches in the field such as text analysis while offering out-of-the-box visualizations. Yet, they are limited because they only allow users to access a small set of predefined summary statistics, models, and visualizations. One would be hard-pressed to find a tool that provides the flexibility humanists need. As a result, while existing tools provide useful insights and can be particularly powerful for teaching, the full range of summarization processes called for by EDA is difficult to accomplish within the scope of most DH tools. Stand-alone programs lock users into a specific set of programmed summary statistics and visualizations, making the iterative exploration of data quite limited. In the process, the plethora of tools obscures the field's dependency on and adoption of EDA from statistics.

In contrast, libraries written to function within general-purpose programming languages allow users to move between many different visualization and visualization engines while simultaneously cleaning and manipulating the underlying dataset. They thus help avoid privileging preconceived notations of what may be of interest in a particular set of data. Popular programming languages for working with data, such as R and Python, have thousands of user-contributed libraries for data analysis, manipulation, and visualization.[2] These libraries all operate on the same basic internal data structures, allowing for easy interoperability between libraries. Statisticians are able to maintain flexibility while conducting data exploration as a direct result of these libraries that operate with a single programming language, rather than using disconnected one-off tools.

Using a general-purpose statistical programming language greatly increases the available set of methodological approaches to studying humanities data. Many statistical techniques such as unsupervised learning and dimension reduction are only available with use of a language such as R or Python. Topic modeling, for example, is such a ubiquitous method in the digital humanities for understanding the structure of a corpus of texts that newcomers would not be remiss for thinking that it is the only such method. Unsupervised learning, however, can be applied to learn and visualize different kinds of latent structures in texts. For example, spectral clustering, an unsupervised method for categorizing data, produces a complete hierarchical structure of a corpus. This hierarchy can be visualized in many ways and is arguably a far more appropriate method for studying many corpora. Unlike latent Dirichlet allocation, the primary technique for topic modeling, spectral clustering requires no external tuning parameters, always returns the same result, and does not require the user to specify the number of latent topics. Techniques such as the singular value decomposition, or dimension reduction in general, offer further approaches to visualizing the structure of texts without forcing documents or topics into discretized buckets.

Although these libraries require significant technical skill to apply them to any particular dataset, the ability to move nimbly between multiple methods and tools can give humanists the flexibility and nuance they seek. For this reason, we should consider modifying or building on top of extant general-purpose libraries, many of which are open-source libraries. By freeing the time that is now spent appropriating existing frameworks and libraries, DHers can concentrate on developing new modifications for extracting humanities knowledge. As an example of how this can work successfully, consider Lincoln Mullen's tokenizers package, which simplifies the process of turning raw text into tokenized text within the R programming language. Humanists can now apply dozens of other visualizations and models to their own textual data by way of other well-maintained R packages.

Making use of general-purpose software libraries requires an important shift in DH pedagogy. To fully utilize statistical analysis, one needs to be proficient in programming with a language such as R or Python. One does not need to create R packages, but rather one should be able, ideally, to read and implement existing code to explore, manipulate, and analyze humanities data. Otherwise, users are constrained to exploring a small preset selection of visualizations and have limited avenues for cleaning and summarizing their data through point-and-click tools. Writing in a programming language also allows for summarizing and publicizing analyses with documented code. Such an approach helps other scholars replicate our studies on datasets as well, providing transparency and reproducibility. At the same time, external tools are useful for running efficient interactive visualizations, and their limited toolsets are often ideal for initial data analysis and curated, public-facing projects. However, they are not well positioned to be the only mechanism for running the iterative experimentation required by exploratory data analysis or to give the full range of possibilities for data visualization.

While it is important for digital humanists to become conversant in the theory and application of data analysis, statistical visualizations, and high-level programming languages, collaborations with statisticians and other computational area experts will be instrumental for pushing advanced computational work in the digital humanities. No one person can be expected to understand such a wide range of disciplines brought together in the digital humanities in the depth required to develop the innovative insights and methods that are the promise of the field. Rather, the digital humanities should welcome statistics to the table, and this begins by better acknowledging the critical role of statistics in the field.

NOTES

1. The focus on tools is exemplified by National Endowment for the Humanities Office of Digital Humanities grant applications and awards, which have a significant focus on tool building.

2. The history of R in particular is deeply entwined with exploratory data analysis and data visualization. It was originally developed as the S programming language in the mid-1970s at Bell Labs by Rick Becker, John Chambers, and Allan Wilks (Becker and Chambers). It was built to support the kind of fast, iterative data analysis favored by John Tukey, who also had an appointment at Bell Labs during the same time. The ideas behind EDA and the formalized structure for statistical graphics all filter up to the R programming environment.

BIBLIOGRAPHY

Arnold, Taylor, and Lauren Tilton. *Humanities Data in R.* New York: Springer International, 2015.

Arnold, Taylor, Lauren Tilton, Stacey Maples, and Laura Wexler. "Uncovering Latent Metadata in the FSA-OWI Photographic Archive." *Digital Humanities Quarterly* 11, no. 2 (2017), http://www.digitalhumanities.org/dhq/vol/11/2/000299/000299.xml.

Becker, Richard, and John Chambers. *S: An Interactive Environment for Data Analysis and Graphics.* Boca Raton, Fla.: CRC Press, 1984.

Bertin, Jacques. *Semiology of Graphics: Diagrams, Networks, Maps.* Madison: University of Wisconsin Press, 1983.

Cleveland, William. *The Elements of Graphing Data.* Monterey, Calif.: Wadsworth Advanced Books and Software, 1985.

Cleveland, William. *Visualizing Data.* Hobart Press, 1993.

Drucker, Joanna. *Graphesis: Visual Forms of Knowledge Production.* Cambridge, Mass.: Harvard University Press, 2014.

Mullen, Lincoln. "tokenizers: A Consistent Interface to Tokenize Natural Language Text." R package version 0.1.4., 2016.

Posner, Miriam. "Humanities Data: A Necessary Contradiction." June 25, 2015, http://miriamposner.com/blog/humanities-data-a-necessary-contradiction/.

Schöch, Christof. "Big? Smart? Clean? Messy? Data in the Humanities." *Journal of Digital Humanities* 2, no. 3 (2013), http://journalofdigitalhumanities.org/2-3/big-smart-clean-messy-data-in-the-humanities/.

Tukey, John Wilder. *Exploratory Data Analysis.* Reading, Mass.: Addison-Wesley, 1977.

Wickham, Hadley. *ggplot2: Elegant Graphics for Data Analysis.* Berlin: Springer Science & Business Media, 2009.

Wilkinson, Leland. *The Grammar of Graphics.* Berlin: Springer Berlin Heidelberg, 1999.

Making Time: Workflow and Learning Outcomes in DH Assignments

DAVID "JACK" NORTON

Like many in the DH world, I taught digital humanities before I knew it had a name. I taught my students to podcast, blog, and even do a bit of GIS tagging. Then I joined Twitter, and my awareness of the digital humanities world exploded. I teach 150–180 students each term at a suburban community college in Minnesota. Around 55 percent of my students are from historically underrepresented groups, which include first-generation students, Pell-eligible students, and students of color ("Normandale Factbook"). Right now, I teach two world history courses entirely as DH courses. For me, that means all of the assignments result in digital outcomes (mostly written analysis), that the assignments are created and administered digitally, and that students use digital sources (with the exception of some library books) to study the past. I teach in computer classrooms and online and use the same assignments for both. My students produce fourteen different DH assignments over the course of the semester, ranging from answering questions based on a historical GIS website to creating their own digital exhibits using Omeka.

Given the size of my classes, the demographics of my students, and the assessment practices that increasingly dominate higher ed, I might be expected to design assignments that adhere tightly to fastidious learning outcomes. But I find that focusing on creating a workflow that facilitates timely creation, delivery, completion, and feedback is as important to student learning as the learning outcomes themselves. Students learn better when our shared workflow, which I define as a structured and time-efficient work process, receives as much attention as the learning outcomes. I believe that there needs to be a wider discussion in the digital humanities about how we all spend our time creating, teaching, and assessing our assignments. When we talk about what we spend our time on as teachers, we are talking about what we value. For the digital humanities to advance as a teaching practice, we need to hold discussions of workflow in concert with existing disciplinary discussions of sources, methods, and presentation. Only by taking the challenges of workflow seriously can we weigh all of the competing interests in our pedagogies.

At about the same time that I came to appreciate the potential of the digital humanities for my students, I was asked to direct my community college's faculty development group, the Center for Teaching and Learning (CTL). At the CTL, we provide and facilitate training for faculty on pedagogy and technology in the context of the scholarship on teaching and learning. Working on issues of faculty professional development directed my attention to the importance of effective time usage and effective teaching interventions related to technology. While heading the CTL, I continued a research project on equity-driven course-design principles for students who experience the effects of income inequality: it was a sort of universal design for education with attention to resources rather than disability. That research rests at the intersection of digital humanities, faculty development, and what I call "antipoverty course design." For the equity project, I listened to my students' concerns about DH assignments and poverty, and I reviewed the literature on effective teaching practices (Jaggars and Xu). I concluded that attention to workflow benefited not just student learning by increasing the amount of student–faculty engagement but also protected my own time by reducing unproductive planning and unnecessary grading.

Many academics use "workflow" to describe the steps required to complete a task—that is, "do a, then b, then c" (Turkel). Extending the scope of that definition, I encourage instructors to consider what comes before and after the "a, then b, then c," as well as how much time they need to complete a, b, and c. As Anne McGrail reminds us, students, especially working-class and first-generation students, "have less discretionary time to engage in college" (23). She also observes that many of those students approach time in an ontologically different way than their professors do, focusing less on investing effort for a distant payoff in favor of more immediate gains.

With these considerations in mind, I created an assignment using Omeka Neatline, which allows students to drop points with historical metadata attached onto a GIS map. The assignment had eight pages of instruction, including a title, an explanation for why we were doing the assignment, a set of learning objectives, the steps to complete the assignment, the minimum time necessary to complete it, the final product's formatting requirements, the grading rubric I would use, and a set of frequently asked questions. The entire assignment could be thought of as a recipe. As any cook can tell you, good recipes include not just ingredients but also descriptions of necessary tools and cooking techniques, along with a sense of what a good finished product will look like. So too, my DH assignments offer robust instructions so that everyone can succeed, not just those already skilled in history (Norton). Students see in one document what they can expect to learn, the exact steps they need to follow to be successful, how much time it will take, and how they will be graded.

One might assume that so many details would discourage independent thinking or otherwise degrade the content of the assignment. Yet, research suggests otherwise. First, there is some evidence from the field of science education that more structure in courses "increased course performance for all students" (Eddy and

Hogan, 453). This conclusion comes from a study that measured student success on the basis of exam grades in biology courses. Biology differs from DH courses in subject matter, but not in the need to master large amounts of information. What remains relevant for the digital humanities is that, when faced with exams for which there were right and wrong answers (as distinct from history, where the quality of the answers is shaped by the use of evidence), students performed better with more structure. In the case of my Neatline assignment, I found that students interrogated historical sources better when given step-by-step instructions for placing a GIS marker in an Omeka Neatline map, which requires attaching specific historical metadata to the point, than when I asked them to drop a point in Google Maps and then write about the importance of that place. My speculation is that the structured entry format for Neatline encouraged students to focus more on why the historical place marker mattered within a larger narrative of world history than did the "easier" interface of the Google tool, which let them just click on the map and write anything they wished.

Part of the power of using DH methods as teaching tools derives from the active learning baked into the process. Students must do and think at the same time, which helps make knowledge "stickier" than when they learn through more passive forms such as lectures. In fact, cognitive scientists have shown that active learning yields superior results when compared with the lecture format.[1] In my history-focused DH classes, students spend half their time working on their digital projects and a quarter of their time discussing the history on which the projects are based. I spend little time in class delivering content.[2]

Of course, this discussion covers little fresh ground for most undergraduate teachers of DH courses. That this chapter emerges in the third volume of *Debates in Digital Humanities* speaks to the expanding breadth of our field. Still, there are areas in the field that have only recently begun to be explored, including the issues involved in teaching digital humanities at community colleges. The 2012 volume of *Debates in the Digital Humanities* lacked a single contribution from a community college faculty member, and the 2016 volume contained only one: Anne McGrail's admirable discussion of her experience becoming a DH teacher in English. This is not necessarily the fault of the editors: there were perhaps few community college faculty publishing on digital humanities at the time, and more generally, the academic world is only now recognizing the importance of digital humanities in community colleges.[3] But to support this new attention on community colleges as sites for DH work, we need to ask how we can help those new to the field develop sustainable workflows that reflect the circumstances of community college students and faculty.

For one, we need to recognize the radically different landscape that community college faculty face as compared to our four-year colleagues. For example, the 150–180 students whom I teach each semester translate into fifteen hours of in-class instruction and five required office hours. If I spend just five minutes assessing each piece of each student's work, I add more than thirteen hours of grading a week. That leaves around six hours for reading, lesson planning, service, or any other activity I choose to pursue during a nominally forty-hour workweek. That is the reality for community college faculty across the United States. In such circumstances, an emphasis on workflow helps ensure that I have time to include DH projects in my courses and that students can get meaningful feedback that improves their learning. My workflow allows me to spend two hours preparing an assignment, four hours coaching students through the assignment, and two hours grading using rubrics, for a total of eight hours. The quality of the work is high because I spend four hours coaching students how to do it. In contrast, if I were to spend four hours fiddling with the alignment of skills, content, and learning outcomes in a student assignment, an hour lecturing my students on how to complete the assignment, two hours working with the students on the assignment, an hour of formative assessment of the learning outcomes, and two hours answering emails because I spent more time on outcomes than a well-structured workflow, I would be on the hook for eight hours of additional grading required to carefully ascertain whether students met the learning outcomes. That amounts to eighteen hours of work for roughly the same assignment. With a slightly different emphasis, students can do more work on their own, cover more history, and get feedback faster—and I spend less time grading.

I wrestle with time constraints in a different way in my capacity as a leader of faculty professional development. Our college celebrates a culture of teaching excellence, and our excellent teachers are those who mind their time carefully. A minor tweak to a learning management system that results in three additional mouse clicks might occasion some grumbling among our four-year colleagues, yet it can result in massive pushback from community college faculty because of its practical consequences. We grade more than four-year faculty because we have more students; assessment efficiency matters. Like cooks at a diner, we must work fast, prepping, cooking, and delivering a high-quality dish. There are no *mise en place* community college teachers.

Community college faculty need to carefully consider the workflow of their DH assignments. My own path to a well-structured assignment workflow, such as the Omeka assignment described earlier, was born out of frustration. Like many faculty, I began my assignments with what I thought were simple instructions, like a three-line recipe. Mix ingredients, bake until done, enjoy. Quickly, I realized that students needed additional guidance, such as "please use Firefox or Chrome as your browser and make sure the pop-up blocker is disabled." Then I realized that my students succeeded at much higher rates if I used videos or embedded pictures into the instructions. Screen-capture videos were easy to make, but time consuming to edit. As an alternative, I used the installed applications, such as the Windows Snipping tool, on whatever computer I had in front of me, dropping screen grabs into a word-processing document. But tinkering with the images and inserting arrows that pointed to key elements proved time consuming as well. And even after creating these techno mash-ups of assignments, I struggled to give timely responses to students.

But I am still doing DH work in my classrooms. So what changed?

First, I abandoned any software that slowed me down. I swapped out word-processing software for writing in a plain text editor, which allows me to focus on formatting only when I am ready to publish my lesson plan to the class. I had read about other DH scholars who made the same change to plain text for scholarly publishing or coding reasons, but my choice was both practical and pedagogical: writing in plain text saves time that I can better use with students. In addition, I switched to an application called Clarify that allows me to do screen grabs from any screen on my computer directly into a plain text document. Finally, I focused my attention on reproducibility. Every assignment now begins with the same template, ensuring both good teaching practices and avoiding excessive time spent on framing a lesson plan.

I also deliberately select those tools for my assignments that will allow me to manage my time most efficiently. For instance, there are multiple, high-quality GIS platforms that allow students to add historical data to maps, such as CartoDB, Map-Story, and ArcGIS. But I use GIS plugins with Omeka because I can grade those assignments most efficiently. Of course, there is a counterargument that smells vaguely of superlative, techno-utopia and runs as follows: "We should use the best technology available because that will best prepare our students for the workplace." But I far prefer a student who is competent with a historical GIS program than one who is marginally familiar with the industry-standard software, ArcGIS.

Finally, and most importantly, I bake as many learning outcomes as I can into the assignments themselves. In this way, students can learn the necessary history and demonstrate the required skills simply by completing the assignment. Rather than offering holistic grading comments, I now use rubrics that evaluate whether the students have successfully completed the required tasks, and I include the rubrics in the initial assignment so the students know how they will be graded. For example, a rubric for an assignment that results in an Omeka digital exhibit might include the criteria that a student select three primary and three secondary sources, correctly add Dublin Core metadata for the six sources, and create a thesis that is provable, non-obvious, and appropriate for the time period under discussion. Using rubrics as assessment instruments certainly has its issues, but the practice has also allowed me to give meaningful, actionable, and timely feedback to my students.

We need digital humanities in community colleges. The analytical and technical skills along with the digital literacy embedded in digital humanities are vital to sustaining a productive workforce, an informed electorate, and an engaged citizenry. According to the College Board, 42 percent of all undergraduate students attend community colleges, and many will complete associate of arts degrees or leave college without degrees (Ma and Baum). For many students, community colleges offer the only exposure to the valuable practices and theories of digital humanities. And yet, most community college students work more than twenty hours a week. At the same time, almost no community college instructors have course release for research, professional development, or curriculum development. If we do not carve out time for ourselves and our students, digital humanities will never spread at the community college level.

At its best, DH courses locate knowledge in a student-centered process, one in which students create projects from information they have found themselves, with their instructors serving as content advocates or skills coaches. Students simply cannot do digital humanities by listening to a lecture or watching a film. They must take knowledge, interrogate it, change it, remix it, and present it. Put another way, students must create their own education—which, indeed, is one of the great goals of higher learning.

I anticipate that advances in DH tools, theory, and scholarship will continue to be partly driven by research-oriented four-year schools. Nevertheless, leaving the digital humanities to be defined only by elite institutions denies our students a powerful learning experiences. Having students do digital humanities at the community college level challenges the epistemological orientation of digital humanities as a subject for the few and instead claims the practice for the many for whom it has the most significant benefits. We owe it to our students, and especially to our students at community colleges, to consider how digital humanities operates at two-year schools, why it is valuable and necessary, and how it leads to deeper learning for our students.

NOTES

1. A meta-study conducted in 2014 compared 225 studies "that reported on examination scores" of students in science, technology, engineering, and math courses using "traditional lecturing versus active learning." The "results indicate that the average examination scores improved by about six percent in active learning sections, and that students in classes with traditional lecturing were one-and-a-half times more likely to fail than were students in classes with active learning." (Freeman et al.).

2. A 2016 study concluded that of four factors in online courses (course organization and presentation, learning objectives and assessment, interpersonal interactions, and use of technology) only "strong meaningful interpersonal interaction" between faculty and students predicted higher student grades (Jaggars and Xu, 2016). Based on this research surrounding active learning and student engagement, I deliberately spend 75 percent of my time in one-on-one interactions with students about their DH projects.

3. To wit: the Andrew W. Mellon Foundation awarded a $3.1 million grant to the Humanities Alliance to pair graduate students from the Graduate Center, CUNY, with

students and faculty at LaGuardia Community College (Davidson). And I benefited from the new focus on digital humanities at community colleges as a participant in a National Endowment for the Humanities Summer Institute at Lane Community College during the summer of 2015.

BIBLIOGRAPHY

Davidson, Cathy. "$3.15 M Mellon Grant Focusing on the Humanities, Community Colleges, and Next Generation Graduate Training." HASTAC blog. October 19, 2015, https://www.hastac.org/blogs/cathy-davidson/2015/10/19/315-m-mellon-grant-focusing-humanities-community-colleges-and-next.

Eddy, Sarah L., and Kelly A. Hogan. "Getting under the Hood: How and for Whom Does Increasing Course Structure Work?" *CBE-Life Sciences Education* 13, no. 3 (September 21, 2014): 453–68, http://www.lifescied.org/content/13/3/453.full.pdf+html.

Freeman, Scott, Sarah L. Eddy, Miles McDonough, Michelle K. Smith, Nnadozie Okoro-afor, Hannah Jordt, and Mary Pat Wenderoth. "Active Learning Increases Student Performance in Science, Engineering, and Mathematics." *Proceedings of the National Academy of Sciences* 111, no. 23 (June 10, 2014): 8410–15, http://www.pnas.org/content/111/23/8410?tab=related.

Hittinger, Francis. "Introducing Digital Workflows for Academic Research on the Mac." Butler Library Blog. April 3, 2014, https://blogs.cul.columbia.edu/butler/2014/04/03/introducing-digital-workflows-for-academic-research-on-the-mac-2/.

Jaggars, Shanna, and Di Xu. "Examining the Effectiveness of Online Learning within a Community College System: An Instrumental Variable Approach." 2013, http://ccrc.tc.columbia.edu/media/k2/attachments/examining-effectiveness-of-online-learning.pdf.

Jaggars, Shanna, and Di Xu. "How Do Online Course Design Features Influence Student Performance?" *Computers & Education* 95 (April 2016): 270–84, https://doi.org/10.1016/j.compedu.2016.01.014.

Ma, Jennifer, and Baum, Sandy. "Trends in Community Colleges: Enrollment, Prices, Student Debt, and Completion." CollegeBoard. April 2016, http://trends.collegeboard.org/sites/default/files/trends-in-community-colleges-research-brief.pdf.

McGrail, Anne B. "The 'Whole Game': Digital Humanities at Community Colleges." In *Debates in the Digital Humanities,* edited by Matthew K. Gold and Lauren F. Klein, 16–31. Minneapolis: University of Minnesota Press, 2016.

"Normandale Factbook." 2016, http://www.normandale.edu/Documents/about/2015–2016%20Normandale%20Community%20College%20Fact%20Book.pdf.

Norton, David. "Digital Humanities Lesson Plan Template." June 2015, https://www.dropbox.com/s/eol3n9tgvbcovk7/DHLessonPlanTemplate.txt?dl=0.

Norton, David. "Lesson Plan 1 (using Omeka and Neatline)." September 2015, http://jacknorton.org/wp-content/uploads/2018/09/time-i-assignment.html.

Turkel, William J. "How To." 2014. https://williamjturkel.net/how-to./.

Not Just Guns but Bullets, Too: "Deconstructive" and "Constructive" Making within the Digital Humanities

MATT RATTO

As noted by Galey and Ruecker, design and prototyping activities can now be considered digital humanities' "scholarly primitives." Unsworth defined this term to mean basic operations within an area of scholarly labor that are independent of disciplinary affiliation or theoretical orientation. It seems obvious that design and prototyping are such "basic operations," particularly now that arguments over the relative epistemological strengths of "saying vs. doing" (cf. Ramsey and Rockwell) or "hacking" vs. "yacking" (cf. Nowviskie) seem to be receding. Given this state of affairs, it seems useful to engage in more granular examinations of what design and prototyping have to offer a critically engaged form of humanities work (cf. Jagoda). In this chapter, I offer a postmortem of a prototyping project from the Critical Making lab, using it to clearly differentiate between two forms of scholarly prototyping: "deconstructive" and "constructive" making. The purpose of this analytic distinction is to more productively think through how making fits within and might extend current understandings of humanistic scholarly labor, particularly in regard to broader forms of social intervention.

In 2013, we at the Critical Making lab at the University of Toronto, 3D printed a handgun. To be more precise, we printed a nonworking version of the Defense Distributed 3D printable "Liberator" handgun as part of a critique of the cyber-anarchic argument being put forth by its designers. This argument, most clearly articulated by Defense Distributed founder Cody Wilson, was that the existence of 3D-printable guns made current gun regulation policies obsolete.[1] One of our goals was to engage with this argument and more generally to help law enforcement, regulators, policy makers, and 3D printing advocates to develop a measured response to the perceived problems associated with the 3D printing of guns.[2] To this end, we printed our handgun publicly and connected with local media in order to initiate an open conversation on the issues that arise when 3D printing guns.[3] As part of this move, we engaged in a more extended reflection on how theories of digital immateriality support particular political positions and regimes of regulation (Record et al.).

In doing so, we followed in the footsteps of scholars such as Katherine Hayles and Matthew Kirschenbaum, who have explored the theory and politics of information immateriality. Hayles has uncovered how formal definitions of intelligence, debated but ultimately naturalized in events such as the Macy Debates in the 1940s to the 1960s, can be linked to a wholesale reconceptualization of what it means to be human, including a politically suspect devaluing of the human body (1999). Kirschenbaum's focus on how computer systems "propagate an illusion of immateriality" provides a similar starting point (135). In this work, he notes (as have others) that buying into this illusion results in the idea that, once books and other textual materials have been scanned and digital versions created, then the physical "versions" can simply be thrown away. Both Hayles and Kirschenbaum therefore connect perspectives of information as immaterial to the political ramifications of such beliefs; intelligence as a property related to the formal manipulation of symbols rather than embedded in material action in the world results in an erasure of the embodied liberal subject and the devaluing of embodied constructs such as gender and ethnicity (Hayles, prologue). Equally, the illusion of immateriality supported by the design and functionality of computational systems allows decisions regarding the preservation of human culture to take specific directions (Kirschenbaum, introduction).

Three-dimensional printing calls attention to the fallacies noted by both Hayles and Kirschenbaum. It is obvious that the digital files used to produce a 3D-printed gun and the gun that results from this process engage with users in very different ways. The capacity to act using the printed gun, to threaten with it or shoot someone, is not reproduced by the files. Equally, the printed gun is not able to be transported and moved via digital networks; it cannot be stored on web servers or on USB sticks in the same way as the files that are used to print it. It seemed to us that the claims regarding the immateriality of the digital are harder to make when one could hold up a USB stick and a printed gun and ask, "Which of these makes you nervous?"

However, we did not want our printing of the gun model to be taken as either a wholehearted embrace of a cyber-anarchistic future or a reductive, "won't somebody think of the children," knee-jerk response. Instead, our hope was that the various media experiences and interviews that we did, and the academic writing that we later published, would extend the impact of our critical work on 3D printing. As both information scholars and as public intellectuals, our charge is to explore and debate new information technologies and the patterns of life associated with them. Cody Wilson's claims regarding 3D printing and gun regulation required critical interrogation and debate.

At least initially, we felt we were successful regarding these goals: our printing of the gun garnered significant media attention, and for a few weeks, members of the lab were kept busy conducting interviews, appearing on local television and radio, and being quoted and photographed for newspapers and blogs. An article on the gun and its associated regulatory frameworks was published in an academic journal and has served as the basis for a series of ongoing conversations with regulators and legal authorities. The printing of the gun also garnered a fair amount of attention from our faculty, engaging the university in conversations about what research topics are legitimate for humanities scholars and the legalities of scholarship that involves firearms.[4] In all these senses, the project was a successful form of critical making as I and others have defined it in the past (Ratto and Hoekema; Ratto, "Critical Making," "Making at the End of Nature"; Ratto, Jalbert, and Wylie; Wylie et al.). The project also supported additional reflection on the limitations of the scope of this term, given what we retrospectively identified as a lack of direct engagement with politics in the way that the *Defense Distributed* project clearly had done. However, while the scholarly work we did then and later seemed indicative of "success" at a local and academic level, we felt we were far less effective in using the project to participate productively in the larger conversation regarding gun control.

As part of the public outreach aspects of this work, I appeared on a local current affairs television show to debate Cody Wilson, the main instigator, cyberanarchist, and gun advocate who had shepherded the development of the gun model that we printed.[5] Steve Paikin, the host of the show, tried to focus the conversation on issues of safety and access, raising the question of whether 3D printing offered a dramatic new way for people, including criminals and youths, to get their hands on a gun. My response to this question was to leverage our prior conceptual explorations of 3D printing (Ratto and Ree) and our experience of printing the gun in the lab. I discussed the material realities of 3D printing, the costs and capabilities of current printers, and the difficulties in designing and printing functional artifacts. I compared this complexity to other ways of producing guns outside of standard regulatory regimes, highlighting the ability to go to Home Depot, buy some pipe and other bits and pieces, and make a "zip gun," a device of similar capability to that of the Liberator model. When asked about the future capabilities of 3D printing and other digitally inflected forms of fabrication, I deferred the question with a quick flip of scholarly showmanship, referring the interviewer and audience to academic work on the "proximate future" (Bell and Dourish) and the complex processes through which new sociotechnical developments interpolate society in unexpected ways. I focused, in other words, on the mundane aspects of 3D printing, using these somewhat pedantic examples to counteract the hype associated with 3D printing in general, as well as the fear around the 3D printing of guns in particular.

Cody Wilson, in contrast, did not speak of the difficulties he faced in developing, testing, or printing his handguns. He did not mention the failures that must have occurred during development or the fear that he must have experienced when first firing a gun that had never been tested. Instead, he used the 3D gun to "prove" his more general political point: that government regulation had become inadequate, given the development of technologies such as the internet and 3D printers. Taking his lead from John Perry Barlow's libertarian idea of cyberspace as an unregulated and unregulatable zone, Wilson described 3D printing and digital manufacturing more generally as the wedge that would splinter extant forms of regulation and governance. For Wilson, the gun served as a compelling example of the limits of government, and he argued persuasively that the Liberator made gun laws immediately antiquated and unenforceable. Not only did Wilson have some very clear ideas about our sociotechnical future but he was also easily able to appropriate critical making as a form of political engagement, at least superficially, going so far as to call his Liberator work "a critical form of making." At that moment, I felt like other science and technology studies (STS) scholars must have felt in hearing their own critical concepts and tools deployed to support things like "intelligent design" or to deny climate change science. (cf. Latour)

Since 2007, I have been using the term "critical making" to describe and explore modes of scholarly work that express a commitment to direct and productive material engagement with technology. This focus is not particularly unique to my lab, nor is it novel; there is a long history within the digital humanities of exploratory technical work (e.g., Drucker; Galey and Ruecker; Balsalmo; Sayers, "The Kits," "Why Fabricate?") But the term "critical making" seems to have struck a chord, and many scholars now use it to describe a range of scholarship that incorporates reflexivity, intervention, and technical work within fields like design, literature, computer science, and engineering. Equally, "doing" and the role of what Natalia Cecire describes as "embodied, experiential, extradiscursive epistemology" have become flashpoints for DH discussions.

At the Critical Making lab, we have mainly focused on unpacking the modes and practices that support or hinder the work of "doing," what we understand as a critical material–conceptual engagement. Our intention has been to work through the role that material engagements can play in humanities and interpretive social science scholarship. This has been very mundane and tinkery work, often resulting in partial, ugly, obscure, and, in some cases, boring objects.[6] The gun notwithstanding, "boring" projects at the Critical Making lab have included critical analysis and material explorations around the enclosure of the open web (Ratto and Hockema; Ratto, "Critical Making"), network neutrality (Ratto and Blanchette), changing mediations of citizenship (Ratto and Boler), privacy and surveillance (Tannenbaum et al.), and big data and information visualization (Resch et al.), to name just a few. This work fits into a longer trajectory of analysis, specifically the "deconstructive" critical acts well described by Derrida and the related goals of defamiliarization and *estrangement* that have been considered key practices within the digital humanities (manifesto). It also incorporates the emphasis on sociotechnical systems that has been a key component of STS and related fields, often focused on recovering the complexity of relations between natural and cultural systems.[7]

In his argument about the significance of the 3D-printed gun, Cody Wilson expresses a strikingly similar sentiment: namely, that technologies participate in and work to support particular social and political values (cf. Winner). For Wilson, the 3D-printed gun is not a neutral object, but instead leads to the end of gun control as a political reality. But he nevertheless understates the complex interleaving of social and technical work that is necessary to render the 3D-printed gun a clear indicator of a particular politics. Despite Wilson's statements that 3D-printed guns essentially make worthless the regulatory efforts of governments, these governmental politics do not depend entirely on the physical form or capabilities of the 3D-printed gun. Instead they emerge from the relations between the form and capabilities of the gun, and the social and political work of Wilson (and other humans and nonhumans). One unspoken goal of Wilson's work is to naturalize the potential effects of 3D-printed guns on regulatory systems so as to make us *believe* that these effects are unquestionable and a direct result of the existence of such objects in the world. Wilson's work is, in Bruno Latour's words, aimed at turning a "matter for concern" into a "matter of fact."

By reconstructing the object that Wilson used to support his original argument, we at the Critical Making Lab were also able to deconstruct how he naturalized his free-market anarchist politics and made the gun stand for a specific argument about the role of governments. In later academic work, if not in the moment, we successfully unpacked the "matter of fact" of 3D- printed guns and provided details regarding regulatory options for 3D-printed guns (Record at al.) However, our work still did not engage directly in a critique of Wilson's political position. In other words, while we were able to effectively criticize the method by which Wilson naturalized his politics through making, we did not critique the materialization of these politics through our own making.

It would be easy to blame our failure to fully confront Wilson and his work on the generic distinctions between academic articles and public media. But just as we were unable to fully debate Wilson's constructive activities on television, a similar failure attends our published work on this topic—at least prior to this chapter. This failure may follow from my own reliance on "social constructivist" forms of sociotechnical analysis and a resulting lack of direct attention to the political. Langdon Winner, writing on the use of constructivist perspectives within technoscience, has pointed to the difficulty that these modes have in expressing normative and political points of view. His aptly named article, "Upon Opening the Black Box of Social Construction and Finding It Empty," blames this lacuna on a variety of reasons, most importantly a lack of attention to the deep-seated political biases that constrain and shape technical choices.[8] More recently, Phillip Brey has ascribed this lack of political engagement to a larger desire to avoid underanalyzed structural influences in favor of more immediate and context-specific causal factors. He has since termed this the "empirical turn" in the philosophy of technology and related fields ("Social Constructivism").

Our focus on the mundane attributes of 3D-printed guns could be said to follow from this empirical turn. Our goal was to denaturalize the gun and to deconstruct it without engaging too directly with the structural influences that we could not directly analyze (e.g., Second Amendment politics and gun rights activism). Our initial sense was that we could simply open the black box of the 3D-printed gun and show it to be a construction: that would be enough. But debating the politics of the gun and the associated move of Wilson to tie together emergent technologies and such structural influences requires more than deconstruction. Our political stance includes a role for governments, particularly with regard to the regulation of guns. Wilson's does not. This is a crucial difference.

Two moves are necessary to fully engage with Wilson's politics: first, we must reveal the sleight of hand that Wilson used to naturalize the 3D-printed gun's relation to policy, but second, we should also provide an alternative instantiation that can combat Wilson's material and his discursive modes. In other words, we must use deconstructive moves to first take apart the system under critique, but should also find new ways to put it back together differently. Scholarly making can in fact do both, but while the first move has long been considered legitimate academic labor, the second remains less typical of DH work. Good examples of the "putting back together differently" approach within the humanities include many of the projects described in Drucker's *Speclab,* Rob MacDougall's *Tecumseh Lies Here* (MacDougall and Compeau), and the *Mapping Indigenous LA* (MILA) project at UCLA.[9] What makes these projects work as productive political engagements is that the authors and makers move beyond simple deconstruction and estrangement to produce hybrid objects, objects that imagine a different world from the one that currently exists. They both deconstruct and reconstruct.

David A. Kirby calls the objects that result from such novel reconstructions "diagetic prototypes." He formulates his concept through reference to the sorts of objects that typically appear in science fiction films, objects that require alternative forms of government, social relations, or technical capabilities to exist. The Liberator handgun is another such example; in establishing its reality and its existence, Wilson calls (or attempts to call) into being the world that he imagines. He positions the gun as part of an established past, which includes a specific perspective on the Second Amendment to the U.S. Constitution (e.g., the "right to bear arms"). He also attempts to produce a future that involves specific social values and the role of government (e.g., cyber-libertarianism). As noted earlier, this is a future that we in the Critical Making Lab do not want to see become our present. Unlike Wilson, however, we did not produce our own vision of the world. We should have faced power with power and produced our own diagetic prototype. But we failed to suture our own object to an alternative political stance.

This failure begs two questions. First, is it truly the role of the humanities—digital or otherwise—to face power with power and produce alternative conceptualizations of the world, to make diagetic prototypes? And second, if so, what might this work look like?

Regarding the first point, humanities scholars have in fact long been engaged with the imagining of alternative worlds. Through narrative writing, poetry, and other forms of critical artistic practice, humanities scholars have sought to intervene in the larger world.[10] As we extend our repertoire to incorporate the scholarly primitives of design and prototyping, this history should be conserved and extended.

There is much to draw on regarding the second question. From Alexander Galloway's description of play-oriented methodologies of scholarship, to Daniela Rosner's critical "fabulations" to Carl DiSalvo's "adversarial design," novel models that blend world-making and academic reflection abound. Similarly, novel spaces are being constructed within the walls of humanities academia that allow such modes to find concrete purchase. Such spaces include Melissa Gilliam, Patrick Jagoda, and Alida Bouris's Transmedia Story Lab at the University of Chicago,[11] Jentery Sayer's Maker Lab in the Humanities at the University of Victoria,[12] and many others.

Garnet Hertz has proposed extending the original focus of critical making from process and reflection and into the domain of "actionable design strategies in a form that is accessible to the public."[13] Referencing work from the field of human–computer interaction (Wakkary et al.), Hertz highlights the need for "material speculations," artifacts specifically created to engage publics in speculative and provocative reflection on possible futures with emerging technologies. Kari Kraus has argued similarly and used transmedia storytelling as a way to extend such future-oriented speculation to younger learners.[14]

But Galey and Ruecker warn us, "The digital humanities must not lose sight of the design of artifacts as a critical act, one that may reflect insights into materials and advance an argument about an artifact's role in the world" (407). Many DH makers already know this, often using the artifacts and systems they produce to "advance" a particular politics—the *Mapping Indigenous LA* project at UCLA, mentioned earlier, comes to mind. It uses digital mapping and storytelling to recover the hidden movements and layers through which indigenous peoples have been displaced and relocated through governmental policies. The "story-maps" produced as part of MILA act as diagetic prototypes in Kirby's sense, providing alternative ways of viewing an established landscape. I have recently advocated similar outcomes, focusing on our complicity in creating, and therefore our responsibility in maintaining, a hybrid natural and cultural world (Ratto, "Making at the End of Nature"). In the Critical Making Lab, we have begun to produce such "material speculations," including speculative wearables, data visualizations (Resch et al.), and 3D design software that instantiate new relations between clinical experts and material–digital bodies (coons and Ratto).

But this is not to say that all scholarly making projects are necessarily critical or, when they are intended to be, that they provide adequate resources to combat inequitable or other problematic aspects of present or predicted sociotechnical systems. Even with the best of intentions, it is easy to miss the mark, particularly when we focus on using making to deconstruct and not to provide constructive alternatives. Patrik Svensson has noted some of the multiple ways the digital humanities engages the digital directly: "as a tool, as a study object, as an expressive medium, as an experimental laboratory and as an activist venue." While all these uses are equally legitimate, my interest is in exploring how critical making can successfully extend from scholastic humanistic work and into the realm of public intervention. Here, I am specifically signaling the use of making as a critical interventionist tool. I want to generate work that bridges a number of Svensson's categories: the use of the digital as an "activist venue" and as an "expressive medium," "study object," and "experimental laboratory."

A rethink of our 3D-printed gun project can highlight the potential ways making can serve as such a bridge. How could we have extended the deconstructive work of the project and engaged critically but also constructively with the pro-gun and anti-regulatory politics of Cody Wilson? Thinking through what such "material speculations" might entail reveals both the novel possibilities of making as a critical, reflexive constructive approach and the need to extend many of our current practices into areas that many of us may find less comfortable.

For instance, one idea we have discussed is the redesign of the Liberator 3D model to require special ammunition to be made for it. Wilson's original design has a technical issue: there is a danger of the gun exploding when firing, due to the explosive force of bullets designed for metal weapons. We could solve this technical problem by designing ammunition specifically for a 3D-printed weapon and by redesigning the weapon to only work with this specialized ammunition. We could borrow an idea from automated single-serve coffee makers and embed recognizable codes or RFID tags to allow for the verification of the proper ammunition to the weapon. This technical fix overcomes the limitations of Wilson's gun and, by doing so, defends its right to exist as an instrumental—and not just aesthetic—object. But the design also importantly reopens 3D-printed firearms to a new regulatory regime, one that would be based on the regulation of ammunition rather than on the weapons themselves. The RFID tags or codes used to verify the proper fit between ammunition and weapon could also be used as unique identifiers that raise the possibility to track purchase and use. Regulating ammunition rather than the weapons themselves has been proposed by regulators and gun safety advocates.[15] Our work could have extended beyond our deconstructive making of the Liberator handgun to critique Wilson's strategies and produce a novel constructive reconfiguration of 3D printing, weapons, and regulation. This doubled move would have better supported our denaturalization of Wilson's claims and provided a constructive response that advances an alternative politics and associated world. Such a combined discursive and material argument could have potentially solved the problem this chapter explores: namely, how our project addressed Wilson's strategies, but ultimately not his politics.

To be clear, the knowledges, practices, and resources—not to mention the legal permissions—required to engage in such a material speculation might seem like a far cry from the traditional labor of humanities scholarship. Should we and do we really want to make functional 3D-printed weapon systems? Such work seems fraught with undesired consequences. But if the digital humanities is to address what it means to be human in a digitally inflected world, then our scope is already much more expansive than traditional scholarly work—as are our responsibilities and commitments. As the gun example demonstrates, there are both opportunities and dangers associated with constructive activities, with politics that is not always so clear. If the objects we produce are supposed to act not just as instantiations of theory (cf. Bauer) but also as "actionable strategies," then one danger seems necessary to address: How can we, as scholars, remain reflexive and attuned to the constructed nature of the world we inhabit when we ourselves are often complicit in the processes of such construction? Addressing more comprehensively both deconstructive and constructive making is an important piece of this continuing puzzle.

NOTES

1. https://defdist.org/.

2. See, for example the various calls to regulate 3D printers by policy makers in the United States as part of gun control efforts. http://thehill.com/regulation/legislation/244319 -dems-move-to-ban-plastic-guns. Accessed February 1, 2017.

3. As noted by our academic publishing and press coverage on the topic, we were certainly interested in facilitating this deeper conversation on weapons and 3D printing (Record et al.).

4. The debates included a thread on the faculty email list where other faculty members reflected on what constitutes legitimate and appropriate topics for research, as well as a strongly worded letter from the then-provost of the university reminding me that research on firearms was restricted. Both the email conversation and the call and response with the provost were productive in the sense that they offered a chance for me to communicate my research interests and methods to colleagues and administrators and receive feedback in response.

5. A transcript of this program is online at http://tvo.org/transcript/2126017/video /programs/the-agenda-with-steve-paikin/3d-printing-a-killer-app. Accessed January 18, 2016.

6. Rather than attempt to make these objects available to others by making them less conceptually opaque, aesthetically more approachable, or even instrumentally useful, we have reveled in their mundanity, following Leigh Star's guidance to study "boring things." The "boring" was Star's attempt to recover the understudied or naturalized aspects of built environments—to highlight in other words, the "infrastructures" of modern life. Bowker and Star called this move "infrastructural inversion," "making visible" and understandable the invisible and inaccessible aspects of our built environment in order to surface the social, cultural, and political work that also remains hidden. Others such as Shannon Mattern have highlighted "infrastructural literacy" as a way to recover not just the invisible but also the affective, ideational, and richly varied world in which we live. Critical making, as I construed it initially, engaged directly with the general notion of "infrastructural inversion," adding exploratory material work with the infrastructures and materialities in question as a resource.

7. For an overview of some of the core texts that have addressed the nature/culture divide within STS and why this is currently so relevant, see Ratto ("Making at the End of Nature").

8. For a similar but more contemporary approach from within the digital humanities, see McPherson.

9. http://www.cdh.ucla.edu/projects/mapping-indigenous-l-a/.

10. A recent article in *Nature* (Roes and Pint) notes the long-standing use of artistic practice within scholarly work, but also highlights a need to foreground such work as legitimate. I agree and see design and prototyping as part of this longer trajectory.

11. https://ci3.uchicago.edu/labs/transmedia-story-lab/.

12. http://maker.uvic.ca/.

13. http://current.ecuad.ca/what-is-critical-making.

14. See Kraus's NSF-funded project *Dust* as an example: https://fallingdust.com/.

15. In fact, this has been proposed by regulators as a potential response to 3D-printed weapons. https://www.theatlantic.com/technology/archive/2012/12/no-really-regulate-the -bullets/266332. Accessed February 22, 2017.

BIBLIOGRAPHY

Balsalmo, A. *Designing Culture*. Durham, N.C.: Duke University Press, 2011.

Bauer, J. "Who You Calling Untheoretical?" March 9, 2012, http://journalofdigitalhumanities .org/1–1/who-you-calling-untheoretical-by-jean-bauer/. Accessed February 24, 2017.

Bell, G., and P. Dourish. "Yesterday's Tomorrows: Notes on Ubiquitous Computing's Dominant Vision." *Personal Ubiquitous Computing* 11, no. 2 (2007): 133–43.

Bowker, G. C., and S. L. Star. *Sorting Things Out: Classification and Its Consequences*. Cambridge, Mass.: MIT Press, 2000.

Brey, P. "Philosophy of Technology after the Empirical Turn." *Techné: Research in Philosophy and Technology* 14, no. 1 (2010): 36–48.

Brey, P. "Social Constructivism for Philosophers of Technology: A Shopper's Guide." *Techné: Journal of the Society for Philosophy and Technology* 2, nos. 3–4 (1997): 56–78.

Cecire, N. "Introduction: Theory and the Virtues of Digital Humanities." March 9, 2012, http://journalofdigitalhumanities.org/1–1/introduction-theory-and-the-virtues-of -digital-humanities-by-natalia-cecire. Accessed February 24, 2017.

coons, ginger, and M. Ratto. "Grease Pencils and the Persistence of Individuality in Computationally Produced Custom Objects." *Design Studies* 41 (2015). doi: 10.1016/j. destud.2015.08.005.

Derrida, J. *Of Grammatology*. Baltimore: Johns Hopkins University Press, 1976.

Drucker, J. *SpecLab: Digital Aesthetics and Projects in Speculative Computing*. Chicago: University of Chicago Press, 2009.

Galey, Alan and Stan Ruecker. "How a Prototype Argues." *Digital Scholarship in the Humanities* 25, no. 4 (2010): 405–24.

Galloway, A. *The Interface Effect.* Oxford: Polity Press, 2012.

Hayles, N. K. *How We Became Posthuman: Virtual Bodies in Cybernetics, Literature, and Informatics.* Chicago: University of Chicago Press, 1999.

Jagoda, P. "Critique and Critical Making." *PMLA* 132, no. 2 (2017): 356–63.

Kirby, David A. "The Future Is Now: Diegetic Prototypes and the Role of Popular Films in Generating Real-world Technological Development." *Social Studies of Science* 40, no. 1 (2010): 41–70.

Kirschenbaum, M. G. *Mechanisms: New Media and the Forensic Imagination.* Cambridge, Mass.: MIT Press, 2008.

Latour, B. "Why Has Critique Run out of Steam? From Matters of Fact to Matters of Concern." *Critical Inquiry* 30 (Winter 2004): 225–48.

MacDougall, R., and Compeau, T. "Tecumseh Returns: A History Game in Alternate and Augmented Reality." In *Seeing the Past: Augmented Reality and Computer Vision in History,* edited by Kevin Kee. Ann Arbor: University of Michigan Press, forthcoming.

Mattern, S. (2013)." Infrastructural Tourism." *Places Journal,* 2013, https://placesjournal .org/article/infrastructural-tourism/. Accessed February 9, 2017.

McPherson, Tara. "Why Are the Digital Humanities So White?" http://dhdebates.gc.cuny .edu/debates/part/4.

Nowviskie, Bethany. "On the Origins of "Hack" and "Yack." 2014, http://nowviskie.org/2014 /on-the-origin-of-hack-and-yack/. Accessed February 22, 2017.

Ramsay, Steven, and Geoffrey Rockwell. "Developing Things: Notes toward an Epistemology of Building in the Digital Humanities." In *Debates in the Digital Humanities,* edited by Matthew K. Gold, 75–84. Minneapolis: University of Minnesota Press, 2012.

Ratto, Matt. "Critical Making: Conceptual and Material Studies in Technology and Social Life." *The Information Society* 27, no. 4 (2011): 252–60.

Ratto, M. "Making at the End of Nature." *ACM Interactions,* Sept–Oct., 2016.

Ratto, M., and J. F. Blanchette. "It's a Series of Tubes: Exploring Net Neutrality Policy through Critical Making." *iSchool Conference Alternative Event, iConference 2013,* Fort Worth, Tex., February 12–15, 2013.

Ratto, Matt, and Megan Boler, eds. *DIY Citizenship: Critical Making and Social Media.* Cambridge, MA: MIT Press, 2014.

Ratto, Matt, and Stephen Hockema. (2009) "Flwr Pwr: Tending the Walled Garden." In *Walled Garden,* edited by A. Dekker and A. Wolfsberger, 51–60. Amsterdam: Virtueel Platform, 2009.

Ratto, Matt, Kirk Jalbert, and Sara Wylie. "Critical Making as Research Program: Introduction to the Forum on Critical Making." Special issue, *The Information Society* 30, no. 2 (2014): 85–95.

Ratto, M., and Robert Ree. "Materializing Information: 3D Printing and Social Change." *First Monday* 17, no. 7–2 (2012).

Record, Isaac, ginger coons, Daniel Southwick, and Matt Ratto. "Regulating the Liberator: Prospects for the Regulation of 3D Printing." *Journal of Peer Production #6: Disruption and the Law.* 2015, http://peerproduction.net/issues/issue-6-disruption-and-the-law/peer-reviewed-articles/regulating-the-liberator-prospects-for-the-regulation-of-3d-printing/.

Resch, G., D. Southwick, M. Ratto, and Y. Loukissas, Y. " Make Sense to Me! Participatory Sensing, Information Visualization, and 3D Representation." *iConference—Annual Meeting,* Philadelphia, 2015.

Roes, R., and K. Pint. "The Visual Essay and the Place of Artistic Research in the Humanities." *Palgrave Communications* 3, no. 1 (2017): 8.

Rosner, Daniela K. *Critical Fabulations: Reworking the Methods and Margins of Design.* Cambridge, Mass.: MIT Press, 2018.

Sayers, J. "The Kits for Cultural History, or Fluxkits for Scholarly Communication." *Hyperrhiz: New Media Cultures* 13 (2015a).

Sayers, J. "Why Fabricate?" *Scholarly and Research Communication* 6, no. 3 (2015b).

Star, S. L. "The Ethnography of Infrastructure." *American Behavioral Scientist* 43, no. 3 (1999): 377–91.

Svensson, Patrik. "The Landscape of the Digital Humanities." *Digital Humanities Quarterly* 4, no. 1 (2010), digitalhumanities.org/ dhq/ vol/4/1/000080/000080.html.

Tanenbaum, Karen, Josh Tanenbaum, Amanda Williams, Matt Ratto, Gabriel Resch, and Antonio Gamba Bari. "Critical Making Hackathon: Situated Hacking, Surveillance and Big Data." *CHI 2014: The ACM CHI Conference on Human Factors in Computing Systems,* Toronto, 2014.

Unsworth, J. "Scholarly Primitives: What Methods Do Humanities Researchers Have in Common, and How Might Our Tools Reflect This?" Presented at symposium on "Humanities Computing: Formal Methods, Experimental Practice." King's College London, 2000, http://www3.isrl.illinois.edu/unsworth/Kings.5–00/primitives.html.

Wakkary, R., W. Odom, S. Hauser, G. Hertz, and H. Lin. "Material Speculation: Actual Artifacts for Critical Inquiry." *Aarhus Series on Human Centered Computing* 1, no. 1 (2015): 12.

Winner, L. "Upon Opening the Black Box and Finding It Empty: Social Constructivism and the Philosophy of Technology." *Science, Technology, & Human Values* 18, no. 3 (1993): 362–78.

Wylie, Sara, Kirk Jalbert, Shannon Dosemagen, and Matt Ratto. "Institutions for Civic Technoscience: How Critical Making Is Transforming Environmental Research." *The Information Society* 30, no. 2 (2014): 116–26.

PART IV

DISCIPLINES AND INSTITUTIONS

A Conversation on Digital Art History

JOHANNA DRUCKER AND CLAIRE BISHOP

Note: The following conversation about the meaning and value of digital art history took place via email between June 23, 2017, and July 12, 2017.

JOHANNA DRUCKER (JD): 6/23/2017 The familiar line of criticism against digital humanities is that computational processing is reductive because it performs statistical analyses on complex artifacts (by contrast to the good or neutral availability of digitized materials in online repositories) and that because it is statistical it is necessarily an instrument of neoliberalism. This condition is characterized as a recent development, and the implication is that if only the bad cuckoo of digital scholarship had not come into the nest, the good humanists would have continued to enjoy a rich support stream for their idealistically driven work.

I think we need to take each of these pieces apart, and, in particular, undo the narrative that makes the links in this line of reasoning seem to have a kind of inevitable connection. I think all are based on mistaken and unexamined assumptions, historical ignorance, theoretical naïveté, and a degree of defensiveness with questionable motivations.

1. The reductiveness of statistical processing and the contrast with the "merely" digitized, and the imagined threats to traditional engagements with cultural artifacts
2. The link between statistical methods and neoliberalism (in relation to the history of "political arithmetik," managed culture, bureaucratic controls)
3. The myth of the goddess university and the ideal humanities, including the stigmatization of entrepreneurialism and blindness to current conditions

Then I suggest that we discuss the ways the intellectual labor of digital work actually contributes to and changes the cultural conditions of humanistic activity, how and why we are all complicit, and what the future development of a digital component of scholarship and research might look like—benefits, costs, and risks.

Other issues you might want to discuss?

CLAIRE BISHOP (CB): 6/23/2017 Wow! I guess I'm still a believer in a lot of those myths, largely because I haven't been thinking about them as long as you. I'm all in favor of debunking clichés and don't regard myself as a Luddite, but I confess I remain skeptical about your critique of the critique because I haven't yet been exposed to a digital humanities project that has transformed my intellectual horizons in the way that more conventional humanities scholarship manages. Indeed, the critique of the digital humanities seems to be a richer and more challenging seam of thinking than most of the DH projects I have seen.

I fully admit that what DH projects I have looked at have been within my own discipline, art history, and might more accurately be described as cultural analytics. So let's start with your first point, which chimes well with art history since it posits a tension between statistical processing and other forms of engagement with cultural artifacts.

I don't think anyone in art history imagines that the rise of DH poses a threat to more traditional ways of analyzing cultural artifacts. At best it is seen as a useful supplement: (e.g., digital 3D reconstructions of architecture or fresco cycles, assisting with media migration and format obsolescence in museum conservation). Close visual analysis is so deeply ingrained in art history departments (at least for my generation and older) that it will continue to provide the benchmark for a long time to come. At the same time, I don't want to unquestioningly stamp a seal of approval on this approach because it also has problems (e.g., insufficient attention to art history's own conventions, to biases within the canon, and to social and political contexts). Plus, it can be extremely boring and formulaic.

But the DH alternative to this, exemplified by the essays that I read in the *International Journal for Digital Art History*,[1] seems intellectually impoverished and/or bluntly instrumental.[2] The kinds of questions asked in this journal, and the results they produce, come across as crashingly obvious. Statistics are an important part of this banality, but are not the whole story. The overall tone reads like a managerial report from an IT department; it's all number crunching, and there's no verbal persuasion.

So does the choice have to be between DH projects driven by statistics/data visualization/modeling, and traditional models of art history, with their own clichés, conventions, and limitations? I'm not sure I'm in a position to answer that question. I'm more interested in thinking through how the dominance of networked technology, especially Google Images, is exerting its own pressures on the study of art history. My colleagues and I increasingly note that students have difficulty in focusing on one image and analyzing it at length. Their attention is more diffuse, and tends to deal with clusters and contexts. The next generation sees and thinks differently—digitally?—and I'm interested in trying to articulate this difference, and to see what this produces in terms of scholarship. Tellingly, none of the so-called digital natives in my department are much interested in DH projects, which they regard as driven by technophilic rather than intellectual questions. At the same time, they have internalized quantity and are adapting their minds to negotiate this.

You have much more familiarity with DH projects than I do. I'd be curious to learn about an example that you think does more complex work with quantitative analysis, but without sacrificing the qualities of verbal narrative.

JD: Sure. First, though, let me clarify a few things. I think many of the scholars who work inside digital projects are at least as skeptical as those outside because they know how the reductive processes work and why they are reductive. A few uncritical champions, such as Lev Manovich, Franco Moretti, and Matt Jockers, are convinced that processing "data" about cultural artifacts produces benefits at scale. My criticisms of their work are fundamental: they are looking at processing digital files which are already radically remediated, and they make claims about these large corpora as if this bypasses the issues of canon formation. They also are using counting methods, not statistical ones, and so are not even doing sophisticated work from a social sciences perspective. I could go on, but I've made these arguments elsewhere at great length. But, for instance, take Manovich's project about Rothko's paintings. It's a disaster start to finish. The "paintings" are digital files from various and varied sources, and their provenance is not indicated, so we may be looking at a scan of a reproduction from a four-color separation, and so on. The images are emphatically *not* paintings. If you are going to use positivistic methods, at least use them with rigor. So, a counterexample would be Stephen Murray's studies of cathedral architecture in Gothic France. He is using digitally rendered drawings to compare features that can actually be adequately rendered in wire frame for the specific purposes to which his analysis puts them—to be able to see contrasts of proportion, scale, and other elements of structure.

My colleague Laura Mandell has been systematically analyzing the problems of data mining in literature—which starts with imagining that a word is ever self-evident or self-identical—and then builds in the specific issues involved in the creation of topic models and other computationally produced outcomes. But she also raises questions about the place of distant reading practices within a longer history of interpretation by asking about the purpose and motivations of such work. The identification of outliers, of deviations from norms, of statistical anomalies—these are things that can be done computationally. You don't ask a computer to do the things humans do better, but rather, you ask it to assist by doing things it does well. So, trying to compute resemblance based on feature sets is an interesting problem, while asking a question about "beauty"—as in the example of de la Rosa and Suárez is not. That would be true whether the questions were asked using digital or analog methods. We can cite plenty of bad work, even by esteemed figures, doing close readings in every mode from traditional, to poststructural, psychoanalytic, or using critical race studies.

As I've said elsewhere, I find the work that integrates material sciences into the study of cultural materials to be one promising direction. The work that Eric Johnson and his colleagues have done to rethink the characterization of vellum as "uterine" has not only pushed our understanding of medieval herd management and its relation to manuscript production but also posits a paradigm of human-animal-plant ecologies as a way to think about cultural artifacts. I consider that a major contribution. Early work by Kirk Martini, an engineer and architectural historian, analyzing the way walls crumbled in Pompeii, made use of computational models that contributed to an explanation of physical forces that had been at work—and thus provided a different history of the structures and their ruins. I could cite other examples—the comparison of pottery fragments, morphic analyses of letterforms and glyphs, noninterventionary reconstruction, and so on that are all interpretive tools, and/or scholarly engagements. But that's not my task here. That work exists, and my point would be that dismissing "digital art history" as if it is singular or monolithic does not do justice to the complex variety of work being done and its proven and potential value.

But I want to return to the characterization of the distinction between digital and digitized work, which I made, but by which I did not intend to suggest that "digital" presentations are not computational. Some of the work that involves computational processing is, as we agree, reductive, but, as I have just argued, not all. But making materials available in digital format—to be found online, copied, put into presentations, slide lectures, and so on—is not unproblematic. Every act of digitization is a remediation, and any substantial repository exists in an infrastructure of metadata, information architecture, while every digital file has format specifications that are an abstraction from an analog artifact (or, are the features of a born digital one). Taking these files as if they are simply there, merely the thing, is like imagining that a trout in a case at the supermarket got there on its own. The supply chain side of infrastructure goes invisible, and all of the intellectual decisions, interpretive aspects of these actions, are concealed in that most ideological of statements, the presentation of an image as if it "just is." My basic argument about information visualizations—that they are all reifications of misinformation—holds with all digital files; they are radical remediations that conceal their production in the immediacy and apparency of display.

So, yes, much of the work done in computational processes is reductive, but that is the fault of the researcher and question being asked, the privileging of certain outcomes, and the uncritical enthusiasm for technique. The same could be said of social art history when it uses selected exceptions as if they are representative, or of psychoanalytic approaches that found the phallus everywhere. That is what you find if that is what you are looking for—or, more importantly, if that is how you are looking. I made the distinction digitized/digital not to suggest that the former is pure and the latter processed, but they are processed to different degrees and with different implications.

But the attack on digital humanities goes beyond defensive reactions to close reading, cultural analytics, and its techniques. The critics make accusations that connect the computational to political values and conditions. That seems ignorant in other ways than the simple misunderstanding of how the technological methods work. So I wonder if we could explore that?

CB 6/26/17 Sure—but first I just want to respond to a couple of things you just wrote. I agree with your point about there being bad scholarship in every method. But this is usually once the method has become conventional and academically entrenched. The writing at the outset of any given method—feminism, psychoanalysis, postcolonial theory, social art history—is by and large usually thrilling, decisive, and overflowing with urgency. Here, though, we have a new method ("digital art history") that is largely depoliticized and uncritical. These two characteristics make it very difficult for me to get intellectually excited about many of the DH projects you describe. They seem to me tools for the possibility of analyzing something at some unspecified point in the future—rather than exciting/polemical interpretive proposals in their own right. Material is amassed, possibilities are mooted, but not many killer arguments are put forward. I wonder if this sense of deferral is endemic to the field.

Which brings us on to the politics of DH. Elsewhere I have argued against simplistic morphological analogies between culture and politics (e.g., this work of art has the same organizational structure as democracy, so therefore this work of art is democratic). With DH, so the argument goes, quantitative computational analysis reduces works of art/literature/music/theatre to metrics; one of the hallmarks of neoliberal economics is also the reduction of goods and services to metrics, on the basis of which performance and profit can be assessed and monetized. This is what is so galling about the Research Excellence Framework in the UK: every member of every university department has his or her research graded on a scale of 1 to 5, so that each department can be awarded a number that determines the next five years of funding. The neoliberalization of the university—in this respect more advanced in the UK than here in the United States—hinges on rendering unwieldy, intangible qualities (such as knowledge, truth, meaning, etc.) subject to performance indicators. Many DH projects operate with a similar reduction of cultural complexity to metrics, especially those dealing with literature. The important difference is that they tend not to be done with an eye on monetization.

However, the relationship between DH and neoliberalism is not just based on an apparently mimetic relationship to metrics. It goes deeper: the gathering, categorizing, and ranking of data is often undertaken in precarious labor conditions. The top researcher is rarely doing his or her own tagging and filing; that job falls to the students or, worse, to an outsourced company. Manovich, for example, is unapologetic about using Amazon's "Mechanical Turk" system—an internet marketplace for human intelligence tasks (HITs) that cannot be accomplished by computer. Mechanical Turk is a quintessentially neoliberal global marketplace: workers are dispersed, non-unionized, and unable to negotiate rates with their employers. They are also set in competition with one another: if one worker doesn't accept the dismal fee that's offered, you can bet that someone else will. This imbrication of DH research within exploitative distributions of labor, not to mention the corporate platforms that hold the data being analyzed (e.g., Instagram, Google Maps), is troubling.

Of course, this doesn't have to be the case: the collaboration necessary to accomplish the capture of data opens up the way for more radical approaches, even though the kind of critiques proposed by #TransformDH tend to focus more on approach (decolonization, social justice, identity issues) than on the process of amassing data.

You're much more immersed and invested in DH than I am. How do you deal with the arguments about the proximity of DH to the neoliberalization of the university—and everything else? After all, it is telling that both have arisen at the same historical moment and that the similarities are more striking than the differences.

JD: As you know, I have stated repeatedly that I don't think digital methods have defined a critical breakthrough in any way that is comparable to the impact of theoretical formulations like feminism, deconstruction, postcolonial, queer, or critical race theory. I guess I also don't think it has to do that, and the expectation ought to shift. One of the reasons I am interested in working in the context of the MLIS—Masters of Library and Information Studies—is that I see the management of cultural resources for access and use as central to digital projects. That said, I think that the idea that a new method has to produce immediate results that are staggeringly distinct is ungrounded. Why? To justify its existence? Is novelty the hallmark of good scholarship? Even on those grounds, to dismiss an entire field on the basis of a few bad examples seems as irresponsible as my senior male colleagues telling me in the 1980s that no good scholarship could come of looking at bad art (e.g., work by women). You can resist digital work by saying it has no intellectual excitement, or you can do the work of understanding its intellectual contribution. Very few scholars get excited about metadata and information infrastructure, but that, in fact, is where much of the intellectual benefit lies. If I can now go through the entire corpus of Karl Kraus's *Die Fackel* and see how a particular term was used by him to encode a private conversation with his readers by subtle changes in the use of a word over a thirty-seven-year period, that is because the structure of the project contains an intellectual expression of that concept. Again, the dependence of every scholar, teacher, researcher, and student I know on the repositories made by digital projects shows their value and their integral role in our work and practices. Within the community of information professionals, this work is anything but "depoliticized and uncritical": the debates on the politics of classification, the inherent social and cultural biases in all systems of information production and management, permeate the field. (I can supply references here in preservation, archives, classification, digital access, user analysis, bibliography, and pretty much every aspect of information studies. The fact that digital humanists are often ignorant of this field is an effect of academic silos, but also, frankly, a classist dismissal of "librarians" as secondary citizens within the university system, an offensive and prevalent practice. One of my major complaints about digital humanities is that it ignored the library professions expertise as if it were mere service work and technical, rather than deeply ethical in its outlook and principles.)

The question of the "neoliberalization" of the university has many dimensions, as does the use of quantitative methods. I'll begin with the second. As we all know, administered culture does not begin with the 1990s or even the Thatcher-Reagan era, though their deliberate goals of undoing the social welfare systems were rhetorically conspicuous and pointed. The Romans administered a census, the Babylonians had tax rolls, as did the Egyptians, and systems of tithes and such are recorded in the Bible. But the invention of "political arithmetik" (William Petty's term, dated to 1676, but linked to John Gaunt's work a decade earlier—I have to love their names, Petty and Gaunt, as indicators of something resonantly symbolic) in the seventeenth century is followed a century later by the development of visualization methods. But statistical analysis for social management and the reduction of human beings to numbers is neither recent nor attributable to digital humanities. The idea of transforming complex cultural artifacts into metrics, or quantitative information, has its own history in the Annales school as well as all of the social sciences in the twentieth century. Remember the controversy about Robert Fogel's *Time on the Cross* (1974) (cowritten with Stanley Engerman), a statistical approach to the study of slavery as an economic issue. Quantitative methods are problematic in the humanities if they substitute for other engagements, but also, more profoundly, as I have also said repeatedly, if an absolute cultural authority accrues to them. Quantitative methods have just as much possibility for ethical guidelines as qualitative ones, but keeping the ethical issues visible throughout the lifecycle of data production is a real challenge.

But the real issue that troubles me (dismissive resistance and stubborn dig-in-the-heels ignorance are simply silly), is this quick slippage: "quantitative computational analysis reduces works of art/literature/music/theatre to metrics; one of the hallmarks of neoliberal economics is also the reduction of goods and services to metrics, on the basis of which performance and profit can be assessed and monetized." This suggests that DH is somehow more complicit with this condition than other practices and even causally responsible for it. This is patently false. It also suggests that a "pure" humanities exists that is untainted: the humanities of work that embraces social good and the highest virtues of humankind without complicity in the institutional frameworks that support it. Let's see, was that in the first medieval universities, founded by the Church? No ideological complicity there, right? Or in the seventeenth-century academies, founded to control knowledge and professionalize it, criminalizing other scholarship (Richelieu's intention)? Or in the growth of Enlightenment thought, a philosophically altruistic movement, concerned with the same pure motives that allowed the justification of colonial expansion, slavery, the exploitation of natural and human resources, systematic genocide, and other positive humanistic contributions all codified in treatises and historical studies? Or the long-standing British humanistic study that allowed the empire to identify with classical Greece and Rome and thus legitimate its political practices through study of the rhetoric and history of the past? Or the nineteenth-century universities that trained clerics, lawyers, and medical men and dosed them with a bit of poetry in keeping with an Arnoldian notion that "the best that has been thought and said," or the early twentieth century in which the entrepreneurial spirit of American democracy creates a new international system of trade and so learned men, men of sophistication and class, ought to be able to cite their classical and romantic poets, their Shakespeare and their Milton, alongside a bit of Paine, Jefferson, and Lincoln? The American research universities, the kind of environment that supports Richard Grusin so he can write media criticism, was developed in the post–World War II period on the strength of the GI Bill (which poured money into the higher education system) and enormous research grants from the military-industrial complex. Did the humanities departments that lived off this economic stream imagine they were somehow absolved of responsibility—like the family eating dinner in the plantation and uttering righteous platitudes about Christian piety? I had a friend who was a dean of an art school and raising money for various projects, and her students said they only wanted her to take money from "good" corporations, not bad ones—as if the entire system of creating surplus capital from exploitation of labor were not a problem. Really, I think the idea that digital humanities is the devil here is a convenient way to ignore the big and complex picture—that we are all complicit, that the humanities have served as a part of the system they critique, that they survive on account of that political and economic reality, and that the moral superiority of cultural critics is intellectually suspect and ethically unfounded.

In short, I disagree that DH has justified the neoliberalization of the university. It also carries with it the idea that the digital humanities sucked all the money out of humanities institutions. Because there was so much money going into them? It is true that the NEH and Mellon, among others, engaged digital projects because they saw benefits at scale—access, preservation, and use—which, in fact, as per my earlier statement, is true if you consider the integration of these resources into daily use. As to the exploitation of labor issue, that is another chestnut to take apart. I pay all of my students and always have, as do most of the people working on these projects in the university. Do you think that learning how to do digital work and being paid to do it so that the humanities can thrive in a networked environment is a negative thing? I don't. And I think giving students skills for work is also positive. Having always had to make a living—as a waitress, typist, print shop worker—I am glad to have had skills that let me survive. That said, the myths that people carry around with regard to digital technology are equally frustrating—that it is immaterial and archival—or that it is somehow ecological. Why don't we address the ecological costs of all digital technology?

CB: This is a great answer—I love a long historical purview! Just a few brief comebacks:

I don't think anyone is saying that DH is *justifying* the neoliberalization of the university. Isn't it the other way round: that DH is, wittingly or unwittingly, neoliberalism's justification of the humanities? I think it's revealing that the only new method to emerge in the humanities in recent years takes up the same operation—the transformation of intangible properties to digital metrics—as neoliberal economics. Obviously there are differences in goal, but in the core principle—quantitative analysis—there is a significant overlap. This doesn't mean that they are equivalent (that would be a ludicrous claim), but it needs to be borne in mind when we recognize that the humanities is the one area within the university whose recognizable "output" (relative to the investment put into it) is most opaque and inscrutable, and whose measurable "impact" is least accountable.

While I take your points about the impurity of the university, this is also a very American perspective. European state funding at its best maintains an arm's length from corporations and industry; tuition costs very little (in Germany, 300 euros per semester), and thus allows for great social mobility. It just doesn't afford the kind of high wages (for faculty) and privileged attention (for students) that are enjoyed here.

Paying students isn't the issue (that's great if you have the money; many academics don't). I feel bad about paying students to do mindless data entry rather than more exploratory intellectual work, even if the results from the latter tend to be uneven and less predictable. I guess that's because I would always prefer to do the latter.

Finally (I'm not going in any kind of order here), I'm inclined to disagree with your observation that new methods shouldn't have to be thrilling. I think there's every reason to expect innovation to be exciting—in academia and in culture, broadly—and it's one of the reasons why I'm in this game. I guess I'm an unreconstructed avant-gardist.

We're coming at this from such completely different angles, though, that I'm not sure where we should turn next. It's already glaringly apparent that I am really not interested in most examples of DH and philosophies of information management. Equally, I'm sure my own preoccupations come across as naïve and misguided, and tend to use DH as a straw man. But just to put some of them on the table: I'm curious to see if and how digital technology can be used performatively to enact arguments about digital technology—either to make an argument that runs parallel (or even counter) to more traditional types of written text or to reinforce the latter by using a different signifying system.

For example, can quantity be mobilized as a critique of an artistic tendency, without one having to use quantitative analysis? Can the accumulation and visualization of data be used to produce affective results in the reader/viewer that make an argument about a particular genre? Can social media posts be harnessed to build a commentary about and interpretation of a work of art/performance—one that might exist quite separately to the intentionality of the artist and institution? These questions have in part arisen from my fatigue with conventional art history, in part because I'd like to foreground the dependency of my research (and contemporary art in general) on digital technology, and in part as a response to invitations to present my research in theater contexts rather than in university conference rooms.

My points of reference are those artists who use digital presentation tools to present their research, but who mobilize data in subjective and subversive ways. The Lebanese artist Walid Raad,[3] for example, uses PowerPoint to accompany his lecture-performance *The Loudest Muttering Is Over: Documents from the Atlas Group Archive,* but in a way that both asserts and undercuts the authenticity of his own persona as a lecturer *and* the information he presents (e.g., the number of casualties from car bombs in Beirut during the Civil War). He offers and quickly withdraws data in order not to say anything about car bombs, but to produce a sly takedown of the media devolution of facts into individualized narratives rather than larger political analyses—but that's only one of many destabilizing effects of his presentation. Raad's more recent research project, *Scratching on THINGS I COULD DISAVOW,* looks at first glance very DH: it purports to visualize the financial and geopolitical relationships around the Artist Pension Trust and their involvement in Middle Eastern politics. Raad's talk that accompanies this flickering, pulsating graphic display turns out to be anything but clear: rather than being an exposé, it's a meditation on critique and the problems of over-researching a topic. He offers a narrative driven by curiosity, seduction, and finally resignation as he acknowledges the predictability and impotence of his investigation.

All of which feels like (and is) a very different project from the kinds of questions you're asking about information visualization. So I'd like to twist the discussion now toward art (especially as you taught art history for fourteen years), and ask if and how you ever think about visual art as having anything to say to the DH.

JD: Lots of artists are doing data-driven work that is interesting, topical, and self-reflexive, as well as critically engaged with technology in various ways—Laura Kurgan comes to mind immediately, for instance.

I originally got interested in digital work in the early 1980s, in graduate school, when I wrote a very speculative piece about the future of writing (as in inscription). All the journals I submitted it to said it was too futuristic—I was asking questions about permanence, iteration, etc. But it was artists who first introduced me to digital methods—Jim Pomeroy, a wonderful conceptual artist who died in a freak accident. But we had been using digital technology for typesetting as early as 1977, so I was interested in the conceptual insights that arose from using these tools—alongside letterpress, which I have been involved with for (!) forty-five years. I think the relationships between technology and creative/intellectual thought are ergonomic as much as theoretical or deterministic. What work does your body enjoy, and how does the pleasure or displeasure of work factor into how we think? Thinking in media and materials is not the same as technodeterminism, as you know.

So the creative practices were my route into digital work, and in the early 1990s I guest-edited an issue of *Art Journal* on digital art. In art history, the theme of "the body" was just emerging, and I was struck by the essentializing tone of this after all of our Lacanian training—and the idea of the body as "real" as a contrast to the attachment to the symbolic that prevails in virtual and even screen spaces seemed like a step back. Digital art and literature still had very small communities around them, and so it was easy to get a sense of the categories of approaches to conception and production—algorithmic, combinatorics, procedural, or focused on display, ambient projection, interaction, etc. Early CD projects had no conventions for interface, and their design was not menu-driven or making use of fixed navigation. Much to talk about here, and to go back into at some point.

But as far as art history goes, I have always found it an extremely conservative field. My interests are in visual epistemology, not art history, but I learned an enormous amount from having to teach across many periods and geographical locations. When we (Todd Presner, Miriam Posner, and I) developed the *Beyond the Digitized Slide Library Summer Institutes* for the Getty, we felt it was an opportunity to teach concepts and critical issues, not just tools and platforms. This is the way I conceived of DH pedagogy from the outset—when we were trying to build a core curriculum at the University of Virginia in about 2002. (If you are curious, I can send you the DH 101 Coursebook to look at, though the site is currently offline.) When we ran the institutes, the single most interesting exercise was taking the participants from a research question into ways to address it through structured data and analysis. We could see pretty quickly that some projects were mapping projects, some were network analysis, some were repository building, etc. None of that is particularly interesting. The execution in most platforms is so formulaic it feels pointless to me—unthinking and uncustomizable. But the analysis of a complex problem into a data model—that is a really interesting intellectual exercise. Supposing you are interested in identity transformation among diasporic artists for whom country-of-origin and locations of practice are intermixed in self-conception, style, reception, and work. This was a real project. How do you think about the components of this project in terms of what is tractable so it can be modeled and analyzed? That exercise teaches people an enormous amount about how data can be understood theoretically, but also where the sites of resistance are for work with aesthetic objects. To me, teaching data modeling is a crucial skill—because at its core is the question of how we model interpretation. What is it that you think you are doing with an object or artifact—extracting meaning? Significance? Effect? Social value? Economic value? Historical influence? Etc., etc. The best critical writing gives you ways to engage with an object / image that you would not have had without it. So, creating models of an intellectual project is an exercise that does that. We should try it.

CB: All of those questions, about what we are doing with an artifact or object, are extremely pertinent to art history. And I do think art history desperately needs a new intellectual project, because it rarely speaks to anyone outside of the discipline (and here I'm not just talking about a mass audience but also referring to fellow researchers in other fields). It also continually struggles with the fact that its objects are, for the most part, luxury goods for the 1 percent; there's a compromise and a complicity fundamental to our work (as you yourself have noted). Even those of us who focus on less commodifiable works of art have to face the fact that all of this work circulates within (and often courtesy of) financial structures we detest. One of the ways in which younger art historians have tried to deal with this is to expand the purview of art history to broader (and often more political) questions of the environment, technology, participation, and so on—but the results are rarely focused on visual or perceptual problems that might be of use to thinkers in other fields. Maybe this is because the image itself is dwindling in importance; as Alex Galloway suggests, "The point of unrepresentability is the point of power. And the point of power today is not the image. The point of power resides in networks, computers, algorithms."[4]

Despite this diminished power, I would want to retain the importance of visual literacy (which seems increasingly necessary in a world of fake news and media misrepresentations) and of aesthetics, which gets lost if we subsume art history within a post-human world of media theory (e.g., Kittler). Works of art are less important as unique entities of individual expression (that model died years ago) than as symptoms of—and at best, commentators on—patterns of contemporary perception and attention. The subject is still central to these questions, however, and not incompatible with an analysis of power's unrepresentability.

I want to come back, though, to a point I made earlier: my sense that DH projects seem to provide resources to enable future research, rather than making original arguments in the present and in literary form. Is it enough to provide potential resources rather than reasoned arguments? I can imagine teaching DH as part of a general methods class in art history, but this would not involve teaching methods central to DH (like data modeling). Instead I would show a digital art history project (e.g., Manovich) alongside the substantial critiques made of it.

JD: I don't feel a need to defend projects in digital art history, but I do think the value of certain projects should be recognized as current contributions to knowledge and methods. This leads to my other final point, which repeats some of what I said earlier, about the importance of using digital methods as part of the intellectual skill set in current scholarship. Easy to dismiss these, especially without much knowledge. Harder to engage and understand how they are of use pedagogically and theoretically, but are essential, because this is the world in which we work and the methods permeate the current environment.

Here are several examples of current projects. Much work is being done in preserving cultural heritage sites that have been destroyed by natural (flood) or human disasters (war) or are at risk. The Dunhuang Cave project creates an immersive experience using panoptic digital photography to render the monuments in a three-dimensional model at scale. The model contains embedded files that present dance, ritual, and other materials (see Getty/Unesco project). The caves have 480,000 square feet of paintings that would be destroyed by visitors. The automated detection of prehistoric burial mounds is done by digital processing of data and information to make primary discoveries of previously unidentified sites (see Melanie Riley's work). The Oseberg Viking Ship burial mound has been rendered in an augmented reality application so that the site is undisturbed (non-interventionary archaeology) but the contents of the mound can be seen on-screen. This is an amazing conceptual breakthrough, since it leaves the site intact. Then, resources like the Getty provenance index, an enormous scholarly undertaking with complex intellectual modeling in it. The structure of the records is it own area of study, and the task of translating the information creates a whole host of research topics. Consider the problem of representing currency values from hundreds of years of history across cultures, fluctuations, and exchange rates in a way that makes any sense. The integration of resources into projects like the Digital Public Library of America or the Getty Portal, so that primary sources are not just findable, but searchable. To make these materials useful, search skills, data mining, and various analytics are essential. This leads me to my second challenge point.

The use of text analysis, feature recognition software for images, and other automated processing provides essential insights at scale. These are methods in use now, for scholarly and creative work (Jonathan Cecil did a terrific project using face recognition software to scan Google satellite images of Los Angeles, finding all of the "faces of LA" that show in its chance topographic configurations.) Knowing how to use these tools effectively is just like knowing how to use any other method effectively—it adds to the capacity of the scholar to do certain kinds of interpretive work. I go back to the Karl Kraus *Die Fackel* archive because its structure integrates serious linguistic science with cultural analysis in an integrated environment that is stunningly suited to supporting research into the ways language works/worked in that particular period of the rise of fascism—it provides a tool like no other for doing this work. Or Chris Johanson's models of public spaces in Republican Rome (whose physical remains are largely inaccessible, buried under the later developments of the empire) to see how the textual record and the physical models can be reconciled. This work allows insights into that textual record and hypothesis testing about long-held assumptions about ritual, ceremony, public spectacle. These processes might use quantitative methods, but they don't "reduce" texts to numbers in the sense that a fire "reduces" a building to ashes—the texts and artifacts remain. Instead of dismissing these methods, the challenge is to learn how to use them, modify them, engage with their limitations in the same way as with other methods. Psychoanalysis can "reduce" every image to phallic symbolism and/or the structuring voyeurism of the male gaze, or it can provide a way to read the workings of imagery through particular interpretive frameworks. Digital methods are no different. All methods have limits and can be used well or poorly. The aggressive dismissal of "the digital" in a blanket statement is simply ignorant. Sounds like the language of someone unwilling to learn. I'm not a proselytizer. If a scholar has no use for digital methods, he or she does not have to use them. But as a teacher, I feel deeply committed to providing students skills to understand these methods, use them responsibly, understand their limitations, and work with them as intellectual tools, rather than use them as mere technical instruments. Understanding how digital methods work is a survival skill, not a luxury, or you are merely at the mercy of their effects. Knowing what tools are useful and why, how they work, how to read the results of their application and use—these are present-day expertise. The students want to know these things, they are interested in what happens in the "black box" of processing, in the production of data and its life cycle, and in the reading of outcomes in whatever form—lists, tables, spreadsheets, visualizations. I am as interested in what I have learned from engaging with these tools and methods as I was in what I learned from my successive encounters with theory and methods at every point—textual analysis, close reading, semiotics, structuralism, poststructuralism, deconstruction, feminist theory, postcolonial theory, Marxism, critical theory, critical race studies, queer theory, bibliography, thick reading, and so on—because each refracts a work and project differently. I think digital methods should be a part of every student's experience and, at the graduate level, integrated into the standard methods classes.

NOTES

1. http://dah-journal.org/.

2. See Claire Bishop, 'Against Digital Art History', https://humanitiesfutures.org /papers/digital-art-history/.

3. http://aperture.org/blog/lecture-performance/.

4. Alex Galloway, *The Interface Effect* (Oxford: Polity Press, 2012), 92.

Volumetric Cinema

KEVIN L. FERGUSON

*There, before my ravished eye, a Cube, moving in some altogether new
direction . . . so as to make every particle of his interior pass through a
new kind of Space, with a wake of its own—shall create a still more perfect
perfection than himself.*

—Edwin Abbott, *Flatland*

When A Square, the didactic narrator of Edwin Abbott's *Flatland* (1884),
imagines in his mind's eye the haunting vision of a Cube transformed
into a hypercube, the description of his ravished bewonderment anticipates the real-world response to cinema, which would be invented within the next
two decades. With the techno-magical apparatus of motion pictures, we too can
come into contact with a "more perfect perfection" of the real world by allowing our
ravished eyes to pass through "a new kind of Space, with a wake of its own" (89).
Of course, the point of *Flatland* is that our two-dimensional narrator comes from
a lesser world, and after seeing him fumble through our familiar three-dimensional
reality, we are meant to view his thought experiment in the fourth dimension as a
strange new experience that can also transform our own understanding.

I begin with this moment of revelation not only because Abbott anticipates the
looming invention of motion pictures but also because he affords us an opportunity to reimagine our own visual habits of mind, which we have developed to make
sense of an increasingly media-saturated culture. Indeed, it is on this last point that A
Square's account is most relevant to my project; his description of a tesseract rede-
fines four-dimensional volume not as a series of objective qualities or mathematical measurements, but as a spectacular *visual* experience that leaves him ravished.
This sensory and affective response foreshadows precisely the ways in which film
audiences have experienced motion pictures, which can similarly be understood as a
cube passing through the "new kind of Space" of the cinema screen, leaving "a wake
of its own" on viewers' eyes that creates a "more perfect perfection" than still images

alone. Researchers since the early twentieth century have explained the numerous optical illusions that account for the psychological persistence of vision that makes motion pictures possible, but what if there were a contemporary way to further extend the "wake" that A Square imagined, rendering it concrete and observable? I argue that the temporal and aesthetic trail Abbott imagined can help locate a new DH technique, one that encourages a skeptical stance toward the conventional faith in transparent, unmediated vision.

Unfortunately, the majority of DH approaches to cinema and media studies remain focused on the more easily quantifiable aspects of moving image texts, such as counting shot lengths, timing editing patterns, or comparing production budgets. For this reason, contemporary work at the intersection of digital humanities and media studies can be relatively unsophisticated when it also fails to critique spectators' visual habits because it retains a faith in normative viewing practices. While recognizing a value in conservative statistical approaches, I argue that digital technologies can be used not only to produce new knowledge about film texts but also to fundamentally "transform cultural assumptions about the spatial properties of moving images" (Anderson).[1] Rethinking our viewing practices in a digital age, however, requires an investment in experimental, theoretical methods that run counter to the rationalist uses of quantitative data often employed in DH work. Is there not a way to rediscover a new kind of space in cinema, a digital humanities that can look past the flat screen and explore moving image texts as dimensional objects? In doing so, can we outline an experimental stance more broadly for the digital humanities, which would both position cinema and media studies more firmly within the field and generate new strategies for other DH practices to visualize collections of images as three-dimensional objects?

Cinema's Obsession with Volume

As a function of its flat, two-dimensional technology, cinema is and always has been obsessed with volume. This is readily apparent across the history of film, beginning with the myths of audiences fleeing at the sight of an approaching train in one of the first motion pictures, *L'arrivée d'un train en gare de la Ciotat* (dirs. Auguste Lumière and Louis Lumière, 1896). Narrative accounts had audiences confusing the flat projection screen with an actual window and running for fear of their lives. "Today, we cannot comprehend the terror that gripped the 1895 audience facing the Lumière brothers' arriving train," claims one source (qtd. Loiperdinger, 90). While this foundational myth of naive spectators has been thoroughly debunked by Martin Loiperdinger, the fact that it persisted for more than one hundred years demonstrates a complicit desire on the part of filmmakers and audiences alike to insist that film is a magical art, able to render spectators helplessly spellbound in front of the screen. That is, even when promoting technological advancements such as 3D or virtual reality, film and media production strategies emphasize the wonder and captivity of spectators in front of moving images.

While this argument about the nature of cinema spectatorship has resurfaced with the introduction of each new technology such as synchronized sound, color film stock, or Smell-O-Vision, its main thrust is particularly coded in terms of a spatial spectacle: cinema as an art is powerful enough to transcend the flat screen and make spectators believe that moving images are three-dimensional reality. This effect is touted in contemporary immersive media techniques, such as IMAX and 3D filmmaking for theatrical blockbusters (and the future promise of holographic cinema); virtual reality, augmented reality, and motion-sensing video game technology (e.g., Google Cardboard, Google Glass, Project Tango, Microsoft HoloLens, Xbox Kinect, Oculus Rift); and echo-mapping laser cameras, trillion frame-per-second imaging, and other computational photography methods. Indeed, contemporary immersive media techniques move beyond the promise of convincing audiences that they are watching a real three-dimensional spectacle to the promise of actually interacting with a real three-dimensional world, manipulating virtual objects or overlaying virtual space onto reality.

Popular film narratives further encode this fascination with multidimensional space, as evident in prominent scenes of fantastic, interactive screen use in science fiction films like *Fahrenheit 451* (dir. François Truffaut, 1966), *Blade Runner* (dir. Ridley Scott, 1982), *Minority Report* (dir. Steven Spielberg, 2002), and *The Avengers* (dir. Joss Whedon, 2012). Films like these promise a future of hybrid human–machine interactivity that further closes the gap between a remote experience of media and the lived embodiment of it. Among these examples, the single most emblematic scene of futuristic vision is detective Rick Deckard's use of the fictional Esper device in *Blade Runner*. Using a complex but lo-fi home televisual device, Deckard inserts a flat, two-dimensional photograph and is able to navigate the space it represents in order to gain a needed clue: zooming in, enhancing details, and even introducing parallax to navigate around obscured corners. Deckard's voice-activated machine manipulation of the photograph imagines an omniscient post-cinematic vision, a fantasy of simple, consumer-grade, in-home technology that can reconstitute three-dimensional volumes in space from a flat two-dimensional image.

We see a fascination with transforming small screens into large volumes not only in the narratives of contemporary cinema but also in cinema technology itself, which is increasingly promoted as something hefty and large even as screens become smaller and more ubiquitous. This has been true from the beginning of cinema, as when Kristin Thompson describes how early copyright practice resulted in the curious medium of the "paper print," "the main form of copyright deposit material" from 1895 to 1912, where "every frame of the original film was printed as a photograph on a long roll of paper. This practice arose because films could not be copyrighted as such and had to be copyrighted as a series of photographs" (7–8). The surviving paper prints from the early history of cinema testify to the legal and philosophical sense that movies were something "bulky" to be preserved, echoing Tom Gunning's argument that early cinema was itself an "attraction": the experience was much more about a display of technology than about watching a film narrative. Fast-forward one hundred years and we have no less an interest in displaying cinema technology as something weighty and large, evident in the fetishized display of massive projectors in the lobby of IMAX movie theaters or David Bordwell's reporting about the "platter farms" needed to create 250-pound 70mm copies of Quentin Tarantino's *The Hateful Eight* (2015) for theatrical distribution. As a response to television's midcentury threat to cinema audiences, film production companies experimented with wider aspect ratios, new color techniques, 3D technology, and other gags and gimmicks, creating cinema as a huge experience impossible to contain in the home. In the same way, theatrical response to the contemporary miniaturization and proliferation of media screens (tablets, cell phones, watches) also leads to an expanded interest not only in the three-dimensionality of movies but also their physical size. IMAX and 3D releases of blockbuster films, innovative encouragement of second-screen use, or "luxury" viewing experiences with reclining chairs and reserved seating all work against the sense of movies as small, flat, transportable experiences.

The science fictional examples of interactive screen use are fantastic because they can impossibly draw out three-dimensional meaning from the limited two-dimensional photograph. But as futuristic as the Esper device scene from *Blade Runner* would have seemed in 1982, it has become partial reality well before 2019, the year in which *Blade Runner* is set. In a 2005 experiment, researchers at Stanford University developed a photographic technique they called "dual photography," which uses the principle of Helmholtz reciprocity to switch the light source and camera in a scene, allowing the user to "take" a photograph from the perspective of the light source (Sen et al.). By measuring how light was reflected off the objects in the scene, the researchers were able to create remarkable images, such as one in which the markings on a playing card that was turned away from the camera but toward the light source are clearly visible. Another group of scientists from MIT invented an extremely high-speed photographic technique based on a process they call "femto-photography," which allows one to take photographs around corners. In this method, they explain, "the camera uses light that travels from the object to the camera indirectly, by reflecting off walls or other obstacles, to reconstruct a 3D shape" (Velten et al., 2). By bouncing a laser off of a wall at a hidden mannequin, researchers could record the rebounding light using a streak camera and then reconstitute the hidden image, even rendering it from different views in three-dimensional space. Finally, recent applications in quantum photography have entangled photons of light, with the result that "ghost images" of objects can be made from light that was never itself reflected off of an object, but that nonetheless capture that real object precisely (Vergano). A still more perfect perfection of photographic representation, ravishing indeed.

Similarly, industrial and technological practices addressing the nature of cinematic volume were also theorized in early film history. Responding to criticisms that portrayed cinema as but the "feeble mechanical reproduction of real life" (a viewpoint actively encouraged by early distribution practices), art and film theorist

Rudolf Arnheim argued in 1933 that "film pictures are at once plane and solid" (12). Arnheim drew evidence for the contrary argument that cinema was an art form by looking at the technical problem of how filmmakers translated three-dimensional reality into a two-dimensional experience. So, for example, he demonstrates the many nuances of the "projection of solids upon a plane surface," describing how early film technicians thoughtlessly placed a camera in front of an object, whereas thoughtful film artists considered how camera placement could artistically manipulate perspective and result in aesthetic effects. As a result, "the effect of film is neither absolutely two-dimensional nor absolutely three-dimensional, but something between" (12). Hugo Münsterberg made a similar point at the time, noting how this inter-dimensionality "brings our mind into a peculiar complex state" where *"we have reality with all its true dimensions; and yet it keeps the fleeting, passing surface suggestion without true depth and fullness"* (emphasis in the original, 71).

As rudimentary as his argument may seem, Arnheim's metaphysical conception of cinema has been almost entirely ignored in later empiricist digital approaches to media studies that prioritize the flat plane as the object of study. By refusing to accept the binarism of two- versus three-dimensionality, Arnheim instead advocates for a more complex thinking through of the moving image. While this trajectory might seem outdated in light of the technical evolution of cinema, we would be mistaken to think that spectators today have moved beyond the basic visual habits Arnheim outlined nearly a century ago. While our cinema technology has gotten more sophisticated, our viewing habits have only very slowly adapted to new contexts, and we continue to treat the moving image as simply a self-evident flat surface to be read in only two dimensions. The need for a more robust conception of moving images is evident not only in contemporary advertisements that sell cinema and video games as new media experiences that can transform the humdrum existence of spectators but also in immersive fads like stereoscopy or widescreen exhibition formats that ironically prevent audiences from considering the spatial aspects of moving image texts by creating a situation of spectatorial rapture, offering to viewers the promise that they will forget that they are even watching a film. The desire to create a media experience coterminous with a spectator's own lived experience, aiming for the "mechanical reproduction of real life," is built on flatness.

Similarly, many DH approaches to media studies also promise a spectacular refashioning of traditional humanities work, but instead obscure the deeper consideration of the intra-dimensionality of moving image texts by focusing on the statistical measurement of flat film details. For example, film historian Barry Salt's monumental 1983 work, *Film Style and Technology,* takes a rigorously comprehensive approach to the quantification of film style, but it remains a decidedly precomputational project even as it finds second life in the Cinemetrics project.[2] Likewise, Michael Kipp's ANVIL video annotation tool and the Centre Pompidou's *Lignes de temps* each offer a workspace system for total film annotation, including timelines, subtitles, and shot notes. As promising as these approaches may be for one mode of film studies, they remain tied to traditional methods of evidentiary and stylometric investigation, which preserves conventional viewing habits and a theory of cinema spectatorship as a narrative-driven explication of meaning.

We need something stranger, something more ravishing. Arnheim concludes his defense of cinema as art: "Even in the simplest photographic reproduction of a perfectly simple object, a feeling for its nature is required which is quite beyond any mechanical operation" (11). Since cinema transforms the material reality it captures, there is an inherently aesthetic dimension, a "feeling" that resists a purely descriptive account of nature. In Chapter 20 in this volume, Jason Mittell describes how video-graphic criticism similarly enables conceptual transformations of film and media texts that, in the most successful cases, straddle both explanatory and poetic registers to create transformative insight. My project also examines the aesthetic dimensions of mechanical operations. By using scientific image analysis software designed specifically for anti-aesthetic, technical, and medical purposes, I encourage a DH media studies whose critical focus is more experimental than explanatory. This is not data-bending video files, mash-ups of video essays, or even a kind of cut-up *I Ching,* but rather a "turning" of a media object on its side, presenting a new view not otherwise possible to attain.

A Surrealist Tradition

In advocating for an experimental form of cinematic criticism, I explicitly reject the "Scientific Realism" that Salt espouses in his project to turn cinema studies into a "real science" by the objective measurement of stylistic features such as shot length or scale (155). Instead, inspired by the avant-garde film criticism practiced by scholars such as Robert B. Ray and Tom Conley, I embrace the "subjective, semi-arbitrary, irrational, [or] associational" procedures that Salt mocks (1). For me, these are powerfully productive modes for engaging moving image texts beyond the narrow scope of a limited definition of science and toward an engagement with the broader "feeling" of the humanities. In fact, it is only through methods stemming from the avant-garde Impressionist-surrealist tradition that we can create new, otherwise impossible-to-see knowledge about cinema, rather than just explicating the already visible.

The surrealists were invested in challenging the intentionality of art, pursuing playful methods that used art in unexpected ways and directions. For examples of unintended reuses of art, we could point to the game of "irrational enlargement" that poses and answers unusual or trivial questions of films, Stephen Ramsay's "screwme-neutical" wandering through the archive, the DVD supplementary features that reframe classic films, or the exemplary videographic criticism discussed by Mittell that reorients our engagement with a text. Indeed, new media technologies offer the promise to reorient viewer engagement to cinema in ways that would have been unanticipated but appreciated by the surrealists. While the increased paratextual framing of film releases today (DVD commentary, fan edits of trailers, podcast reviews) suggests a possibility of such engagement, more advanced digital video analysis tools such as the ones I describe later will allow us to embrace surrealism as a strategy even more fully, transforming film texts in radically new, but still internally consistent, ways. While film distribution strategies often recognize the promotional value of fan manipulation of media properties and thus encourage fan practices that would have fit in surrealist circles, these fan practices are extremely limited compared to the use of noncommercial digital tools to study moving image texts, which do not restrict manipulation to only a limited set of preestablished options determined by corporate producers of distributed media. Instead, the contemporary digital humanist can adopt an open-source, software-driven, method-based experimentation to research every parameter of the media text, similar to the surrealist fascination with automatic processes that involved manipulating the mechanical and technical methods of creating art.

Despite the potentially liberating surrealist uses for new media and the increased availability of digital analysis software, the rationalist, positivist, semiotic bent of film theory threatens to become even more exaggerated when approached with digital tools. I have argued that media studies should embrace surrealism as a strategy, but we also must extend that argument to digital humanities broadly. To date, the most familiar touchstone in this field is Lisa Samuels and Jerome McGann's 1999 essay, "Deformance and Interpretation," which argues that "'meaning' in imaginative work is a secondary phenomenon, a kind of meta-data [that] is important not as explanation but as residue" (48). While arguing for antithetical interpretive practices that initially set aside the illusory search for a concept-based meaning, Samuels and McGann stress that "deformance does not banish interpretation" (40). That is, instead of thinking that a work of art's "intelligibility" stems from a critical interpretation, they argue that "*all interpretation is a function of the poem's systemic intelligibility*": our critical practice should set aside the notion of applying an interpretation *to* a text and instead work to discover a text's system by performing actions on it that render it strange (emphasis in original, 40). Likewise, Johanna Drucker, among others, has criticized digital tools used for information visualization, data mining, and geospatial representation as reflective of "positivistic, strictly quantitative, mechanistic, reductive and literal" values that "preclude humanistic methods from their operations because of the very assumptions on which they are designed: that objects of knowledge can be understood as self-identical, self-evident, ahistorical, and autonomous" (86). But reinvigorating a digital surrealist tradition allows us to reconceive of digital tools not solely as quantitative and interpretative devices but also as processes and methods that can be bent to unintended purposes to create unexpected knowledge, expanding our object of study rather than simply adding to it.[3]

Volumetric Cinema

What does it mean to "extract a volume" from a film? On a technical level, this entails transforming one 3D representation into another, switching the temporal dimension of moving images with a third spatial one. On a conceptual level, this turns a film on its side, allowing for a spatial visualization of the time of a film. This reverses, in a sense, the process of traditional filmmaking, which transforms 4D reality into a discrete 3D time-space. By transforming the passing film frames back into discrete physical moments, we can concretize the spectator's persistence of vision and conjure up *Flatland*'s "new kind of Space, with a wake of its own." As with the surrealist interest in irrational knowledge, which breaks perceptual habits in search of a different kind of authenticity, this "volumetric" method allows us to approach moving image texts outside of their temporal tyranny. Volumizing cinema deforms our experience of the structure of moving images: we can manipulate a film we may have already seen numerous times, but from an otherwise impossible vantage point. By creating a 3D volumetric model of a film scene and then passing a slice through that volume in time, we can examine film texts from higher-dimensional perspectives (see Figure 28.1).

Figure 28.1. Visualizing the Evil Queen's transformation in *Snow White and the Seven Dwarfs* (dir. David Hand, 1937) by passing an oblique slice through a three-dimensional volumetric model of the scene.

In contrast to the analog videotape distribution of motion pictures, today's digital distribution technologies allow us to more easily return to film's celluloid origins to do this volumizing. For example, every filmstrip has a discrete number of countable frames. While a videotape and a digital media file are both time based, the latter can be easily converted into a discrete series of frames in a matter of moments. To do so, I employ the scientific image analysis software ImageJ, in a process I liken to cutting the individual frames of a filmstrip and stacking them up one behind the other. However, working with virtual stacks of film frames in ImageJ allows for an additional dimension of analysis: users load a series of images into a "stack," after which each pixel in each image becomes a "voxel," a volumized pixel that exists in relation not only to other pixels on its own plane but also to all the pixels on that coordinate that came "before" and that will come "after." By modeling a whole scene's worth of voxels simultaneously, rather than examining pixels of a frame individually, we can gain a radically new perspective on cinema: we can draw a frame through any subset that we desire of the 3D voxel-space of the film. That is, rather than be limited to a "slice" of the film that corresponds to a single frame, we can create whatever 3D slice we want from the entire volume of the film. Working from a film's two spatial dimensions and the dimension of time, we can recover the otherwise impossible-to-see volume of the film by modeling a series of frames in a single moment, rather than as something occurring over time.

Figures 28.1–28.3 demonstrate some of these impossible views. In these examples, we are looking closely at an individual scene rather than an entire film. In Figure 28.2, by angling the movie volume down, we can see two of its otherwise hidden sides and get a quick sense of some basic information about editing patterns; for instance, this scene is bookended by two longer shots. Whereas Figure 28.2 shows the outer frame edge of this scene, Figure 28.3 shows three orthogonal slices cut from the middle of the film volume, allowing us to better see patterns of camera or character motion or to get a sense of color or shape in the interiority of a scene. Last, with Figure 28.1 we can draw our own slice, bisecting the volume on a particular axis of interest. While the orthogonal slices reveal something akin to finish-line slit-scan photography—where an image is composed of the same thin strip taken at different times—by making a slightly oblique cut we can see both slightly ahead of and slightly behind a shot in time. That is, in this example, the Evil Queen's back is slightly temporally "behind" her future hand movement shown on the left side of the screen. By moving the oblique cut through the volume in this way, we see a ripple of motion as the character's body is stretched over time, visualizing her movement in both space and time.

We can also further manipulate the source frames, adjusting transparency or color to more clearly see a particular object or detail. One simple manipulation to help clarify the film volume in this vein is to use an edge-detection algorithm, such as the Sobel filter in ImageJ that works by finding areas of contrast in an image, identifying which pixels from each slice are the "edgiest" and then recoloring the

Figure 28.2. Visualizing the Evil Queen's transformation in *Snow White and the Seven Dwarfs* (dir. David Hand, 1937) as a three-dimensional cube.

image so that the identified edge regions are shown in starker contrast. The result is a mostly monochromatic outline of shapes and figures; stacking a series of these edge-detected frames together emphasizes a kind of wire-frame motion. In Figure 28.4, we see the beginning of the Evil Queen's transformation as a staggered series of edges as she raises her glass and tilts her head back to drink. Rotating around the actual 3D space further reveals surprising details, such as the smoothness of a subtle camera movement versus the jerkiness of the Evil Queen's limbs, or the elegant symmetry of the cup's rise and fall. In this way, selectively manipulating the edge-detected volume allows for new motion studies, which enable the visualizing of a series of movements through time.

These transformations point to a mostly ignored trajectory of viewing a film not as a succession of images, but as a simultaneity of images: a view across the landscape of the film that allows modes of reception different from the strict time-bound mode of projection. For example, *Edison Kinetoscopic Record of a Sneeze,* known as *Fred Ott's Sneeze* (dir. William K. Dickson, 1894), the oldest surviving copyrighted film, is familiar to film scholars as a grid of frames (see Figure 28.5). Convention tells us how to reconstitute the "order" of these frames, beginning in the upper left and working across and down to the lower right. In the same way, a folder of .jpg frames can be scanned as a film sequence. But this ignores the more valuable possibilities suggested: that "volumizing" the cinema is a strategy that can help break our

Figure 28.3. Visualizing the Evil Queen's transformation in *Snow White and the Seven Dwarfs* (dir. David Hand, 1937) as three orthogonal slices.

visual habits, particularly the one that starts us in the upper left corner and asks us to "figure out what comes next." Instead, we can use a different approach: to project the film differently than was intended, moving through the voxel space in otherwise impossible ways. Such an approach to the visual image offers new venues for critical and aesthetic meaning-making, and while the results can appear surreal, they were nonetheless always already contained in the image.

When Arnheim described in 1933 the cinematic man holding a newspaper in front of his face, which "seems almost to have been cut out of his face, so sharp are the edges," his account would have been particularly resonant with audiences recently exposed in the previous decades to Cubism, among other visual styles that drew renewed attention to the picture plane, compressing apparent screen depth by flattening layers together (12–13). In contrast, the contemporary project I describe resonates with the "softwarization" of media, defined by Lev Manovich as "the systematic translation of numerous techniques for media creation and editing from physical, mechanical, and electronic technologies into software tools" (164). Softwarization means that methodologies for creating or manipulating media texts are not bound to a particular platform or technology, and a world of increased softwarization means an increasing familiarity with (and display of) new modes of

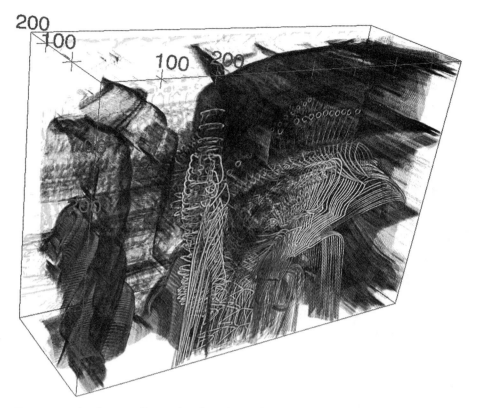

Figure 28.4. Edge-detection filters isolate the Evil Queen's movement in *Snow White and the Seven Dwarfs*.

media manipulation. So, the fact that contemporary films can show space in new ways is an effect of a filmmaker's ability to rely on audiences' familiarity, and perhaps even experience, with digital manipulation of moving image texts. That is, the effectiveness of even the most advanced computer-generated special effect is limited by a spectator's understanding of the aesthetic context of moving images. So, while *Blade Runner* imagined a novel use of photographic space that only later became real, softwarization makes contemporary cinema's strange visual strategies more legible to more spectators. Recent films about quantum space like *Interstellar* (dir. Christopher Nolan, 2014) and *Ant-Man* (dir. Peyton Reed, 2015) are filled with visual spectacles identical to the conceptual volumizing I describe, extending a figure in space and then rotating that extended figure around new axes. More than just fascination with representing the unrepresentable, these sequences show an evolution of narrative cinema's interest in volumizing space, using special effects and narrative devices to train spectators in new modes of vision. Today, an aesthetic of softwarization accelerates spectators' familiarity with nontraditional uses of the flat plane surface, seen in the resurgence of 3D filmmaking represented by *Avatar* (dir. James Cameron, 2009) and the intensive development of virtual and augmented reality by Google. From this perspective, a film like *Avatar* not only updates the techno-fantasy of *Blade Runner*

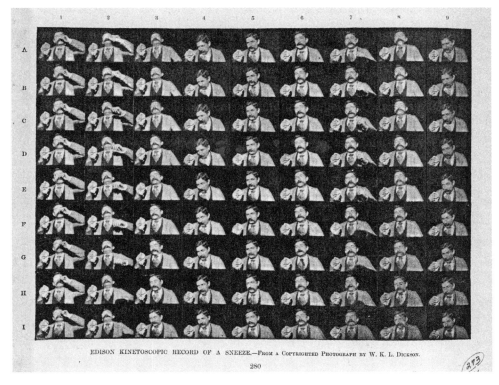

EDISON KINETOSCOPIC RECORD OF A SNEEZE.—FROM A COPYRIGHTED PHOTOGRAPH BY W. K. L. DICKSON.

280

Figure 28.5. *Fred Ott's Sneeze* is familiar today as a grid of frames.

for twenty-first-century audiences but also advances an argument that technologies of filmmaking are consonant with techniques of spectatorship.

What does it mean to insist on a volumetric cinema? Work at the intersection between digital humanities and media studies must willingly explore more experimental methods, arresting our temporal experience of films as narrative things to be consumed. "At once plane and solid," we can align the trajectory of film theory with contemporary computational techniques for recovering the volume of cinema, using open-source software and edge-detection algorithms to create virtual models of the time-space of film scenes in ways that resonate with Arnheim and an otherwise abandoned critical surrealist avant-garde project, achieving a "more perfect perfection." These experiments can change what we know about a film, not only by requiring practitioners to engage with the epistemic effects of volumization and the manipulation of medical imaging software but also by creating a "knowledge effect" around, particularly, the extension of physical volume through time. Camera movements, a character's walk across a set, or a choreographed fight or dance can all be made visible as flowing physical shapes. With a little refinement, these physical shapes can also be 3D printed, making a real, tangible representation of cinematic time and movement. Digital humanities and media studies would do well to resurrect a fascination with volumes and the play of transformation between reality and the two-dimensional screen.

NOTES

I would like to thank Matt Gold, Lauren Klein, Virginia Kuhn, Steve Anderson, Catherine Grant, Lev Manovich, Jason Mittell, M. Beatrice Fazi, and Anke Finger for their encouraging support and suggestions on earlier drafts of this work.

1. Some concepts in this chapter have been adapted from an earlier video essay of the same title (Ferguson).

2. The Cinemetrics creators describe their software as "basically a stopwatch that records the times at which you click your mouse or keyboard button" (Tsivian and Civjans).

3. For other examples in the tradition of deformative media studies, consider new media artist Martin Reinhart's promise of a "radical attack on the cinematic order of images," artist Daniel Crooks's desire to "trigger a perceptual shift in our viewing of the space/time continuum," and Joachim Sauter and Dirk Lusebrink's (ART+COM Studios) explicit aim to disrupt visual conventions that favored realism. A number of scholarly projects also challenge our visual habits, including Virginia Kuhn's "Video Analysis Tableau" (The VAT), which treats "video frames as a three dimensional volume"; Sidney Fels, Eric Lee, and Kenji Mase's "Techniques for Interactive Video Cubism"; and Microsoft's unrelated "Video Cubism" (2001) project, which views "an input video as a space-time cube of data, rather than a series of static frames."

BIBLIOGRAPHY

Abbott, Edwin. *Flatland: A Romance of Many Dimensions*. London: Seeley & Co., 1884.

Anderson, Steve. Review of Kevin L. Ferguson. "Volumetric Cinema." *[in]Transition: Journal of Videographic Film and Moving Image Studies* 2, no. 1 (2015), http://mediacommons .futureofthebook.org/intransition/2015/03/10/volumetric-cinema.

Ant-Man, dir. Peyton Reed. Burbank: Marvel Studios, 2015.

Arnheim, Rudolf. *Film as Art*. Berkeley: University of California Press, 1957.

Avatar, dir. James Cameron. Los Angeles: Twentieth Century Fox, 2009.

Blade Runner, dir. Ridley Scott. Hollywood: Ladd Company, 1982.

Bordwell, David. "The Hateful Eight: The Boys behind the Booth." Observations on Film Art (blog). December 12, 2015, http://www.davidbordwell.net/blog/2015/12/05 /the-hateful-eight-the-boys-behind-the-booth/.

Crooks, Daniel. "Artist's Statement: *Time Slice*." http://nga.gov.au/fullscreen/06/crooks. pdf.

Drucker, Johanna. "Humanistic Theory and Digital Scholarship." In *Debates in the Digital Humanities,* edited by Matthew K. Gold, 85–95. Minneapolis: University of Minnesota Press, 2012.

Edison Kinetoscopic Record of a Sneeze, dir. William K. Dickson. West Orange, NJ: Edison Manufacturing Company, 1894. https://www.loc.gov/item/00694192/.

Fels, Sidney, Eric Lee, and Kenji Mase. "Techniques for Interactive Video Cubism." *Proceedings of the Eighth ACM International Conference on Multimedia,* 368–70. Marina del Rey, Calif.: ACM, 2000.

Ferguson, Kevin L. "Volumetric Cinema." *[in]Transition: Journal of Videographic Film and Moving Image Studies* 2, no. 1 (2015), http://mediacommons.org/intransition/2015/03/10/volumetric-cinema.

Gunning, Tom. "Cinema of Attractions." *Wide Angle* 8, nos. 3–4 (1986): 65–66.

Interstellar, dir. Christopher Nolan. Hollywood: Paramount Pictures, 2014.

Kipp, Michael. "ANVIL: The Video Annotation Research Tool." http://www.anvil-software.org/.

Kuhn, Virginia. "Video Analysis Tableau" (The VAT). http://thevatproject.org/.

L'Institut de recherche et d'innovation (Centre Pompidou). *Lignes de temps,* http://www.iri.centrepompidou.fr/outils/lignes-de-temps-2/.

Loiperdinger, Martin. "Lumiere's Arrival of the Train: Cinema's Founding Myth." Translated by Bernd Elzer. *The Moving Image* 4, no. 1 (2004): 89–118.

Lowenstein, Adam. *Dreaming of Cinema: Spectatorship, Surrealism, and the Age of Digital Media.* New York: Columbia University Press, 2015.

Manovich, Lev. *Software Takes Command.* New York: Bloomsbury, 2013.

Microsoft Research (Michael F. Cohen, Alex Colburn, Adam Finkelstein, Allison W. Klein, and Peter-Pike J. Sloan). "Video Cubism." http://research.microsoft.com/apps/pubs/default.aspx?id=69847.

Münsterberg, Hugo. *Hugo Munsterberg on Film:* The Photoplay: A Psychological Study *and Other Writings.* Edited by Allan Langdale. New York: Routledge, 2002.

Reinhart, Martin. *TX-Transform.* http://www.tx-transform.com/Eng/index.html.

Salt, Barry. *Film Style and Technology: History and Analysis,* 3rd ed. London: Starword, 2009. Originally published 1983.

Samuels, Lisa, and Jerome McGann. "Deformance and Interpretation." *New Literary History* 30, no. 1 (1999): 25–56.

Sauter, Joachim, and Dirk Lusebrink. "The Invisible Shape of Things Past." http://artcom.de/en/project/the-invisible-shape-of-things-past/.

Sen, Pradeep, Billy Chen, Gaurav Garg, Stephen R. Marschner, Mark Horowitz, Marc Levoy, and Hendrik P. A. Lensch. "Dual Photography." In *ACM SIGGRAPH 2005 Papers,* 745–55. New York: ACM, 2005.

Snow White and the Seven Dwarfs, dir. David Hand. Burbank: Walt Disney Productions, 1937.

Thompson, Kristin. "Report of the Ad Hoc Committee of the Society for Cinema Studies, 'Fair Usage Publication of Film Stills.'" *Cinema Journal* 32, no. 3 (1993): 3–20.

Tsivian, Yuri, and Gunars Civjans. "Cinemetrics Software." Cinemetrics. http://www.cinemetrics.lv/cinemetrics.php.

Velten, Andreas, Thomas Willwacher, Otkrist Gupta, Ashok Veeraraghavan, Moungi G. Bawendi, and Ramesh Raskar. "Recovering Three-Dimensional Shape around a Corner Using Ultrafast Time-of-Flight Imaging." *Nature Communications* 3, no. 745 (2012): 1–8.

Vergano, Dan. "'Spooky' Quantum Entanglement Reveals Invisible Objects." *National Geographic,* August 27, 2014, http://news.nationalgeographic.com/news/2014/08/140827-quantum-imaging-cats-undetected-photon-science/.

Joyce and the Graveyard of Digital Empires

ELYSE GRAHAM

The example of Shakespeare looms large in the discipline of book history in English, largely because Shakespeare's plays present specific problems—the "bad" quartos, the absence of manuscripts, and so on—that book historians have found useful in working out their theories. His plays are "good to think with."[1] My interest is in a similar dynamic that shaped the theoretical formulations of scholars working in the early decades of the digital humanities: the example of James Joyce. *Ulysses,* in particular, was seen as an example of hypertext *avant la lettre,* and Joyce's works were made the focus of many pioneering DH projects, such as the *James Joyce Text Machine,* 2000–2001, "a collection of machine-readable primary texts, critical commentaries, and related indexes and concordances" (qtd. in Landow and Delany, 195), and *Ulysses in Hypermedia,* 2001, a project that "grows out of and explores the possible connections between *Ulysses* and hypertext by presenting Joyce's book in an electronic media format" (Groden, "Introduction," 360).

Not all of these projects were successful, which is to say that not all of them came to fruition or sustained themselves for later scholarly use. In fact, *Ulysses* has become something of a graveyard of empires for DH projects, in the sense that the novel's history with the digital humanities between 1970 and about 2000 is more notable for inspiring ambitious ventures that faltered and failed than for producing projects that survived. Even so, for many scholars working to convert the theoretical concepts of new media into principles for scholarly work, Joyce, like Shakespeare, proved good to think with. Studying Joyce can therefore help us understand a surprising amount about the history of the digital humanities. This chapter examines some representative artifacts from the graveyard of Joycean digital empires as a way of inquiring into the thinking and conceptual models of the literary scholars whose projects, in a critical wave that peaked in the nineties and early aughts, pioneered what would become known as the digital humanities.

What can we learn from the fate of these projects—particularly, their failure to thrive—in the changing technological and social environments that defined the late age of print and the early age of the web? As I discuss, the prominent role that Joyce once enjoyed in new media studies reflected a compatible (if never unified) suite of approaches to media theory that came into full bloom in the heyday of hypertext theory between the 1970s and early 2000s. For media and textual scholars as divergent as Ted Nelson, George Landow, and Michael Groden, the formal navigation of links seemed to be the most revolutionary feature that would transform digital reading environments, and the creation of multimedia editions emerged as the ultimate challenge of media scholarship. In terms of both the architecture of hypertext and the creation of digital editions, Joyce offered a model and an illustrious ally.

These same approaches were subsequently subject to a downtrend in the light of what Andreas Kitzmann called, in 2006, "the apparent decline of hypertext, especially in terms of its uses as a vehicle for creative (literary) expression and as a platform for theorizing the nature of reading/writing and the concomitant roles of the reader/writer" (98). In recent years, the media-theoretical implications of hypertext and of the digital edition as the means to create an ideal or archetypal imagining of the text have diminished as new challenges associated with a rapidly growing set of textual platforms, tools, practices, and communities online have emerged. Indeed, in the realm of the web—what hypertext theorist Robert Coover once called a "noisy, restless, opportunistic, superficial, e-commerce driven, chaotic realm, dominated by hacks, pitchmen and pretenders, in which the quiet voice of literature cannot easily be heard" (Kitzmann 98)—many other tools and topics now clamor for our attention. Moreover, as digital humanists and book historians design new platforms for exploring textual materials, they have come to emphasize the role of agents around the digital text, such as publishers, librarians, and technicians, as much as the text itself (quoted in Kitzmann 2006, 98). Still, the story of how and why Joyce served as a trellis for hypertext and hypermedia theory, providing guidance and support for the new field—via prior critical frameworks associated with Joyce and via Joyce-authored texts that served as exemplars and training grounds—can provide new insights into the intellectual history of the discipline. It can help explain how early scholars in the digital humanities created a usable past for themselves from book history and textual studies and clarify why many of their projects are no longer available for readers to access. The lessons of these projects remain relevant to our efforts to design sustainable projects in the digital humanities so that our present interpretive communities will be available to speak to the unknown interpretive communities of the future.[2]

The Gutenberg Elegies

Starting in the 1960s, after the 1962 publication of Marshall McLuhan's *The Gutenberg Galaxy,* James Joyce began to acquire prominence as a common resource for scholars working across the domains of hypertext theory, media studies, corpus analysis, and the design of digital reading interfaces. Joyce served the needs of these scholars, whose work constituted the collective staging ground for what would later become the digital humanities, in part because he is a literary writer and many early scholars of new media had literary backgrounds. For these scholars, the Joyce connection was highly legible, and for their departments, it was advantageous: finding literary genealogies for emerging media formats like hypertext had the benefit of promoting subject areas in which literature departments already had expertise. Such genealogies still carry direct implications for university practice today, even if the set of disciplines that participate in these discussions has widened. For example, when Jerome McGann, writing in the 2010s, describes the book as a machine, or when George Landow, writing in the 1990s, describes hypertext as a book, they are contributing—in different decades and with different theoretical emphases, but in one common practical respect—to a strategic disciplinary tradition by which scholars of literature have sought to establish a disciplinary claim to the digital medium by framing it as an extension of earlier, literary, formats.[3]

But if literariness were the only cause for Joyce's elevation into the digital media theory canon, any literary author might have served in his place. As was true of Shakespeare for textual scholars, Joyce's *Ulysses* presented a particularly attractive suite of formal features for early media theorists. In its privileging of the nonlinear and the nonsequential; its exploration of alternative narratives within the main narrative; its abundance of connections and cross-references, of associative linkages between widely spaced blocks of text; its apparent foregrounding of the activity of the reader, both in scenes of reading staged within the narrative and in the burden Joyce places on the reader to contextualize details and connect disparate passages; its presentation of esoteric material that positively demands annotation; and its appeal to a multitude of sensory and media forms, suggesting the possibility that the novel might be more faithfully realized as a *Gesamtkunstwerk*—in all of these ways, *Ulysses* seemed, to many scholars working in the final decades of the twentieth century, to model key attributes of digital textuality at large and hypermedia in particular.[4]

Joyce served as the chosen ancestor for hypertext theory because his work offered a specifically literary predecessor for hypertext itself. Hypertext had a reputation—indeed, still has the reputation—of being a path that pointed from new media back to the old media of print.[5] In other words, hypertext belonged to media theorists' sense of the architecture of texts even before the rise of the web. Ted Nelson, who coined the term *hypertext* in 1962, defined it as "non-sequential writing—text that branches and allows choices to the reader, best read at an interactive screen. As popularly conceived, this is a series of text chunks connected by links which offer the reader different pathways" (Nelson, 0/2). The structure of a hypertext, both in Nelson's vision, which he articulated most fully in his 1960 design for a hypermedia system, Xanadu, and in Vannevar Bush's earlier designs for another hypermedia system, the Memex, is a network of documents made up of two constituent parts: links and nodes.[6] Today, the link–node model is especially prominent in the discourse around social networks, which have long since surpassed hypertext as a site of critical excitement.[7] But for Nelson and Bush, the structure of nodes and links seemed important largely because of how it could transform textual architectures, and for the new media theorists who adopted the concept for their work, it pointed the way to models of reading and writing that could still be discussed within canonical frameworks of textuality.

In 1992, George Landow, a scholar of literature at Brown, published *Hypertext,* which would become a landmark book on hypertext theory. Like Nelson, he defines hypertext in terms of nodes joined by links; and like Nelson, he emphasizes the opportunity this structure presents to lead the reader along branching rather than linear paths. He also stresses that hypertext is fundamentally an information structure for which computers serve as a useful, but not obligatory, platform and that it therefore preserves many of the pleasures and principles of "page-bound text" (81), including the following abilities: to follow intratextual references to other locations within the text; to follow intertextual references to other texts (in this connection, Landow quotes Michel Foucault as saying the "frontiers of a book are never clear-cut" because "it is caught up in a system of references to other books, other texts, other sentences; it is a node within a network"); and to read the text as nonlinear ("or, more properly, as multilinear or multisequential") if the reader so desires (3–4). The difference is that hypertext builds these paths into the physical architecture of the text, whereas page-bound texts do not; nonetheless, Landow later writes, "Any work of literature—which for the sake of argument and economy I shall here confine in a most arbitrary way to mean 'high' literature of the sort we read and teach in universities—offers an instance of *implicit* hypertext in nonelectronic form" (*Hypertext 3.0,* 55).

In point of fact, Landow uses Joyce regularly in his work as an example of analog hypertext. For example, he points to the "Nausicaa" episode of *Ulysses* as an example of "*implicit* hypertext," since it points outward constantly to lyrics, novels, advertisements, and so forth, which, although outside the boundaries of the central text, nevertheless bear heavily on its meaning (*Hypertext,* 55).[8] For Landow, "Nausicaa" helps illustrate two important consequences of his general theory: first, that the work of navigating and sequencing hypertexts lies, to a degree not seen elsewhere, in the hands of readers, who find themselves obliged to fill gaps and make connections; and second, that the links that connect different nodes—here, the extratextual references—are associative, rather than linear and hierarchical. As in the case of computational hypertexts, in which "a text becomes a node when it is electronically placed in relation to other materials," it is a web of relation that ultimately constitutes "Nausicaa" (Slatin 162).

In this exemplary use of Joyce as a text for media criticism, Landow was drawing on what had already become a modest tradition. Marshall McLuhan claimed that *The Gutenberg Galaxy* started out as a plan for a book with the title "The Road to *Finnegans Wake*" (Theall, "Beyond the Orality/Literacy Dichotomy," 1). His reasons for choosing that particular work as a reference are obvious; *Finnegans Wake* is a book intensely aware of new forms of communication such as film and radio, and its sentences metamorphose through imitations of radio noise, cinematic projection, and the visual bedlam of television. To put it another way, *Finnegans Wake* is a book about the life of the book in a world of multimedia—the same concept that McLuhan sought to describe in *Gutenberg*.[9]

McLuhan's works were essential reading in MIT's Media Lab in the 1960s and 1970s, where researchers were working to design a more perfect medium that would combine the visual, the auditory, and the tactile, like communication in McLuhan's "tribal and collective 'global village'" (Theall, *The Virtual McLuhan*, 180). McLuhan's vision for media profoundly informed the early ideas of cyberspace that those researchers developed, and McLuhan drew inspiration for his vision, or at least a symbol of his notion that aesthetic intuition precedes technological application, from his reading of Joyce. For an empire builder such as McLuhan, Joyce's work could present, within the constraints of the printed text, a program for a new medium meant to explode the possibilities of the printed text.[10]

It is not surprising, then, that so many early works on the potential of hypertext and cyberspace, from MIT and elsewhere, cite Joyce as a forerunner: for example, a 1992 essay by Donald Theall subtitled "James Joyce and the Pre-History of Cyberspace"; a 1997 essay by David Gold that calls *Ulysses* "the perfect hypertext subject" (quoted in Theall, "A Retrospective Sort of Arrangement"); a journal of *Hypermedia Joyce Studies,* founded in 1994; and books on Joyce and cyberculture (Tofts and McKeich), Joyce and hypermedia (Armand), and "the Joyce era of technology" (Theall, *Beyond the Word*) that make the connection explicit.[11] Again and again, these works reinforce the idea that the web will extend and amplify the methods of typographical culture: the information technology of the codex, which Joyce brings to its last, best bloom, prepares us for "the hypertextual poetics of nodal screens" (Tofts).[12] The tradition of using Joyce as a model to predict the future of media overlaps with the tradition of using the codex form as a model to predict the future of media: technology researchers who took inspiration from McLuhan, who in turn took inspiration from Joyce, of necessity drew on McLuhan's understanding of Joyce in bibliographic terms, while literature scholars found Joyce a useful tool for theoretical work that scholars in other disciplines might have called "the colonializing intent of literary scholars" over digital media (Punday, xi).

The Technologizing of the Word

If one is going to imagine digital media as an extension of the Gutenberg Galaxy, it helps to have a Gutenberg Bible to provide a formative textual model. Among Joyce's works, *Ulysses* was a popular target for early efforts to create a hypertext edition of a literary text, including projects by Heyward Ehrlich, Michael Groden, Marlena Corcoran, and Donald Theall.[13] In general, the critical apparatuses surrounding these projects argue for an affinity between the structure of *Ulysses* and the structure of hypertext; by extension, *Ulysses* appears as an ideal subject for hypertextualization. Yet in 2007, when Mark Marino surveyed these efforts in an article titled

"*Ulysses* on Web 2.0," he determined that few of these early editions still existed, in any concrete form, for readers to access.[14] In many cases, even those that had moved beyond the design phase left no products for current readers to access, beyond sample passages that demonstrate the viability of the projects in principle. Unintentionally, the works of Joyce became a graveyard for early work in the digital humanities. In one sense, this graveyard represents the fall of the "golden age" of hypertext. In a larger sense, however, it reflects a suite of values and attitudes that later waves of digital scholarship would directly challenge: in particular, an approach to digital architectures that took print architectures as its primary blueprint; a formalist preoccupation with abstract affordances; a focus on the artifact rather than the agents around the artifact; and, although the importance of this point would only become clear over time, an insufficiently urgent approach to sustainability issues surrounding digital texts.

One example of these early projects is the *James Joyce Text Machine* (JJTM), developed by the Rutgers literary historian Heyward Ehrlich and published online in 2001. In the "Preface," published at the same time—and which is available for readers to view, although the larger hypertext novel it describes is not—he notes, "Despite several projects [to develop a digital *Ulysses*] which have [already] been undertaken, an actual completed electronic hypertext of the work has yet to appear." The JJTM puts hypertext tools, such as HTML, Cascading Style Sheets, and JavaScript, to the task of displaying variant texts and critical notes in the space of the screen. Like many such projects, it was developed only to the level of a prototype, using a sample text: in this case a passage from "Calypso," the episode of *Ulysses* that introduces the novel's protagonist Leopold Bloom.

This design actualizes many of the major aspects of hypertext theory: the ability to "link all the versions or variants of a particular text," as well as to other locations within a text; the ability to use cross-references as trails to additional texts or to other locations within the text; the ability, on the part of the user, to move in a nonsequential order; and a corresponding preoccupation, on the part of the designer, with the effect that moving in a nonsequential order will have on traditional narrative elements such as suspense (Landow, *Hypertext 3.0*, 101). It, too, describes *Ulysses* as an "incipient hypertext" and uses that formal affinity (focusing, in this case, on the "network of internal and external referents" that the novel presents for the reader to follow) as a reason to use Joyce's novel for an exemplary hypertext project.[15] During its creation, the project had a high profile, its progress chronicled in reports at major Joyce conferences.[16]

But the most ambitious of the early efforts to give *Ulysses* a public IP address and a name was Michael Groden's "*Ulysses* in Hypermedia." As with the JJTM, a major goal of the project was to physically instantiate the reader's path through Joyce's thick network of referents; as with the JJTM, an underlying aim was to solve novel problems in hypertext editing and, by extension, to address some of the more interesting formal issues in humanities computing by solving for Joyce. Begun in the mid-1990s, his project had the end goal of presenting "11,000 pages of manuscripts and some 5,000 pages of commentary on the manuscripts" (Marino, 477).[17] The contents of the edition, when complete, would include the novel itself; manuscript pages; scholarly annotations; a list or perhaps a full archive of secondary critical works; source texts like *The Odyssey*; tools for students; maps, photographs, video, and audio, including a full audiobook; and "space for users to add their own comments and links." The project had as auspicious a beginning as any might hope for: the University of Pennsylvania Press, in partnership with the CD-ROM company Voyager, agreed in advance to publish the edition.[18] The Joyce estate granted permission to use three chapters of *Ulysses* to develop a preliminary model. As of 1998, Groden reported, some one hundred Joyce scholars and fifteen "hypertext experts" from scholarship, publishing, and the arts had signed on to help contribute to the project ("Perplex in the Pen," 241).

Historically, digital approaches to *Ulysses* have tended to converge with contemporaneous trends in technology and their social impact. In the case of "*Ulysses* in Hypermedia," the critical discourse that surrounded the project was typical of critical approaches to hypertext at that time in emphasizing (following the remediating critical tradition that we have been tracing) that the heritage of hypertext could be traced directly back to text.[19] As he reported, Groden approached the work of building a prototype foremost as a problem of unbinding the book ("Perplex in the Pen," 240–41). A text in book form has basic constraints—the number of pages, the cost of printing, the capabilities of the print medium—that limit the number and kinds of glosses that an editor has to deal with. A digital hypertext can extend its glosses infinitely, which means that the hypertext editor must find ways to control and rationalize the potential chaos.[20] The actual incompleteness of hypertext reifies the notional incompleteness of Joyce's novel as a problem of design, so that the procedures of exegesis that readers bring to the print edition now become interior and primary structural elements, built into the interstices of the body of the text.

"*Ulysses* in Hypermedia" is perhaps the most prominent example of a lost digital edition of Joyce. Great though its ambitions were, in the end, nothing came of the project except for a handful of articles and a CD-ROM prototype of a sample episode (produced in 1996) that is no longer available for access. (Starting in 1996, Groden began exhibiting the prototype of "James Joyce's *Ulysses* in Hypermedia" at conferences; in 2002, his project merged with a digital manuscript project at SUNY Buffalo called "Digital *Ulysses*: An Annotated Hypertext and Manuscript Archive." In 2003, the editors of "Digital *Ulysses*" published a model version of the "Proteus" episode on the Web. Ultimately, however, the Joyce estate refused the editors permission to make use of the rest of Joyce's texts. Consequently, "Digital *Ulysses*" closed shop in January 2004.[21]) The fact that the 1996 prototype is no longer in existence illustrates a property of digital objects that scholars have only recently placed in the foreground of their work: usually, they need an audience to survive. Simply to build the tools they work with, digital humanists usually need to work with technology professionals; large-scale projects often use students to input data or perform similar labor; and such projects, once finished, require continual tech support and maintenance. These are issues that loom large in recent conversations about sustainability, which often give as much attention to user research and financial issues as they do to technological issues (see Prescott, for example). As Susan Brown et al. note, more than is the case for a printed book, a digital project needs ongoing support, preferably from an audience that clamors for its upkeep as much as from boutique funding.[22] Thus it seems imperative that we design DH projects with a conscious eye to fostering ongoing user activity.

The Future of the Book

As a general rule, the tradition of genetic criticism has looked down on the tendency of poststructuralist critics, even as they argue that textual meaning is inherently unstable, to build those arguments on texts that they treat as stable, fixed, and isolated from historical context (see, for example, Groden, "Ulysses," 57). But the arrival of genetic critics into the field of digital editorial theory did not immediately change the assumption that the digital text, destabilized though its structure might be, would exist outside of social and material factors that might weigh on its sustainability, even in the case of digital texts that aimed to highlight the social and material existence of literary texts through a proliferation of drafts.

Consider, for example, Marino's 2007 article, where he presents ideas of his own for a digital text of Joyce—or texts, rather, since his edition would include many genetic variations (482). Like other writings of the period that described notional hypertext editions of *Ulysses* as a way of illustrating concepts about the relationship between Joyce and new media, Marino's article is of interest because of what it illustrates about the models of digital reading that were being built on Joyce's text, as well as the ways in which scholars who modeled the digital text were responding to the rapidly changing environment of the web. For example, his article reaffirms the ability of motivated scholars to make interpretations of *Ulysses* converge with new digital trends, so that Joyce could seem to prefigure even trends that succeeded or expanded on the excitements of hypertext. Marino's proposed edition would take advantage of the social features of Web 2.0, which enabled the active participation of readers. This "social edition" of *Ulysses* would reflect, he says, the novel's own attitudes toward annotation, those that favor open dialogue and social exchange: his interface would allow users, both expert and amateur, to contribute annotations, and the resultant commentary would bloom in diverse voices, just as we see, in Joyce's novel, in the exemplary discursive spaces of the printing house, the newspaper office, the National Library, and, of course, the bars (490). This attitude toward annotation cohered beautifully with the rise of "Web 2.0" (then still a contested term), a new class of technologies that had transformed the web into a read-write platform, allowing readers to share and comment on content. Once again, scholars arrived at a new technological dispensation only to discover that Joyce had been there first.[23]

It is important to note that Marino takes for granted the presence and the participation of users. He argues that the very nature of hypertext will entice users to contribute their comments to the site: "Hypertext beckons with a siren song of technological promise, if not to complete, then to expand and fulfill" (479). This kind of focus on the abstract laws of the medium, with the technology acting, in empty space, to fulfill the *telos* of the text, may seem odd from a perspective that sees technology as the subject, not the source, of human behavior. In recent years, concerns with the digital artifact proper have come into conversation with discussions about the range of agents around the digital artifact that a project must also sustain: libraries that preserve artifacts, granting agencies that fund ongoing work, scholars who must push through successive appeals for funding, as well as users who must be wooed. As with recent discussions by Susan Brown and Bethany Nowviskie that emphasize the challenges of building sustainable textual platforms on the web, Marino's imagined edition illustrates how digital textuality relies as much on flesh-and-blood practices as the textuality of the material book ever did.[24] Compared with more fundamental problems of sustainability, the actual importance of the problems that Marino describes may be seen in the fact that the edition he imagines remains a hypothetical construct, never forced to confront the reality of living users, their constraints, and their desires.

Here Comes Everybody

Today, the discipline that has come to be known as the digital humanities encompasses too much activity and incorporates too many histories to identify a single genealogy for its protean operations. The history that I have presented, which focuses on efforts to theorize and reify *Ulysses* as a hypertext artifact, reflects the position that hypertext theory once held in the center of media studies, when most media scholars worked out of literature departments and McLuhan presided over the discipline as a trickster-sage (a posture, the historian Donald Theall has suggested, that he adopted from Joyce's Shem the Penman; *The Medium Is the Rear View Mirror*, xviii ff.). The appeal to a center is no longer so easy to make.

Digital studies of Joyce and digital editions of his works did not end with the hypertext era. However, recent studies, as they have emerged from the noisy, restless digital world of the twenty-first century, differ from their predecessors in marked ways. Most notable of these differences are, first, a stronger focus on issues of sustainability, a turn that, in practice, has entailed an Eisensteinian shift from a focus on the text as an isolated object to a focus on agents around the text; and, second, a reluctance to locate the origins of the technologies they use in Joyce's writing itself. Two brilliant projects from the past few years represent these new trends and points of difference: Amanda Visconti's *Infinite Ulysses*, a "social edition" of Ulysses that enables users to share and annotate content from *Ulysses* via social media, and Jonathan Reeve's Open Critical Edition of *Ulysses*, which enables users to "mark up" Joyce's text using the procedures of the Text Encoding Initiative.

Visconti's *Infinite Ulysses* began as a dissertation project at the University of Maryland. The project's design, as an interactive edition of the text emphasizing the sharing, curating, and ranking of annotations, draws on the twenty-first-century triumph of social media platforms: users must employ their existing Facebook and Twitter accounts to engage with the text and each other. (The project's copytext is the digital edition of *Ulysses* produced by the Modernist Versions Project, which developed open-access editions of selected modernist texts for use in the digital projects of all comers who needed copytexts.) On accessing the project's website, the user of *Infinite Ulysses* would see a page of Joyce's text that looked, in formatting and layout, like a page of the Groden *Ulysses*. After logging in, she could use connective-media tools from Facebook and Twitter to annotate Joyce's text (this took the form of highlighting the text, which caused a sidebar to appear in which the user wrote an annotation), share annotations, vote on the quality of annotations, create "favorite" passages, and "bookmark" passages. She could also search or filter annotations using metrics like creator, folksonomy tag, and type of annotation. When the project's beta stage came to a close in June 2016, after a year and a half of operation, *Infinite Ulysses* had garnered "24,000+ unique visitors and 775 unique site user accounts. Readers authored 1,168 annotations on *Ulysses* and tagged those annotations with 287 unique terms to make them filterable by theme, reader needs, and more." By any measure, the project was a success, drawing active participation from both the scholarly community and the larger community of lay readers that Visconti hoped to attract.

As we have seen, projects on Joyce in new media often reflect the most recent excitements of digital technology. The change in digital technologies that "social-reader editions" like *Infinite Ulysses* (and Marino's notional edition) reflect is the rise of Web 2.0: a new class of technologies that has transformed the web into a read-write platform on which readers can add, share, and remix content at will. Yet the digital frameworks are not all that have changed: although *Infinite Ulysses* exploits the affordances (liking, favoriting, sharing) and interrogates the culture of what José van Dijck calls "connective media," we find in neither *Infinite Ulysses* nor its critical apparatus (white papers, for instance) the claim that Joyce *prefigured* connective media (Visconti, " 'How Can You Love a Work' "). As van Dijck has shown, the rise of the connective-media ecosystem has fostered the emergence of diverse new tools, platforms, user practices, and back-end mechanisms. Amidst these novelties, hypertext may seem to have lost its revolutionary aura, which helps explain why Joyce's elective affinity with hypertext has declined in critical discourse.[25]

In contrast to the earlier works I have discussed, *Infinite Ulysses* foregrounds the goal of sustainability. The major aim of the project, Visconti says, is to investigate "participatory interface design for knowledge-building," which entails treating interface design as a branch of community building, which in turn is a necessary requirement of digital sustainability ("Infinite Ulysses Beta"). The reliance of digital artifacts on the labor of human agents for development, support, and preservation is (it is now clear) a condition of digital textuality, even as it presents a challenge to older tendencies in the humanities to privilege the labors of the solitary scholar. Digital projects usually rely on the work of many people, often volunteers, in the development stage; once finished, they still require human labor to provide tech support and maintenance. *Infinite Ulysses* asks how to not only enable community labor of this kind but also make it appealing. Though the project is on hiatus as of June 2016 and thus can only be accessed as an "archival non-interactive version," Visconti explains in her notes on the project's hiatus that she has set up the conditions for the project's maintenance as an archival version and eventual return as an interactive version, so that it will not become another vanished digital edition of Joyce ("Infinite Ulysses Beta").

Similar emphases, though with different technological forms and affordances, govern the open-source critical edition of James Joyce's *Ulysses,* a project that opened to users in 2017.[26] This edition, too, has as its copytext a version of Gabler's 1984 *Ulysses,* albeit one acquired with Gabler's assistance rather than through the Modernist Versions Project. It is open access and open source, meaning that users can access both the text and the underlying code free of charge. While the intervention of Infinite *Ulysses* was to subject the reading of *Ulysses* to the affordances and practices of social-media platforms, the intervention of this open-source critical edition is to make the text available to editorial glossing via TEI XML semantic markup (Reeve).[27]

Like *Infinite Ulysses,* this project places a notable focus on sustainability, in part through attention to the activity of mediating agents in the production and curation of the text. The project's affiliates actively campaign to attract the interest and participation of new contributors.[28] As well, the project has shared "the enriched corpus of episode files and metadata" with the University of Oxford Text Archive, an archival website that helps catalog and preserve digital literary texts for the use of scholars (Reeve). Sharing the data produced within the project's ambit with institutions that specialize in digital preservation, and working to bring the project to the attention of a critical mass of users, will help facilitate the preservation of the work—while attending to the groundedness of even virtual artifacts in "brick and mortar" institutional and social frameworks.

Moreover, both projects make use of Joyce's texts without presenting themselves as an outgrowth or reification of Joyce's aesthetic. In the case of the open-source critical edition, the use of *Ulysses* as the central text seems to derive from a set of motivations—Reeve's critical command of modernist literature; the asset of the participation of important textual scholars and editors of Joyce; the opportunity presented by the entrance, in 2012, of *Ulysses* into the public domain—that bear no special relation to Joyce's aesthetic, save for the fact that, like any great literary author if perhaps a bit more so, his work is challenging and requires careful glossing. Similarly, *Infinite Ulysses* takes *Ulysses* as its central text, Visconti says, because its fame together with its difficulty could help attract a critical mass of readers to the project. (Her own critical orientation, she says, might otherwise prompt her to choose an author from a historically marginalized community ["Designing Digital Editions"]).

To be sure, echoes of the older era of scholarship on Joyce and technology can still be heard in our new dispensation. In a blog post, Visconti describes in passing Joyce's novel as a hypertext while listing critical questions that may emerge from her project: "what actually happens to Joyce's hypertext when it becomes digitally hypertextual and hyper-annotated?" But she nowhere engages that issue further; she is acknowledging a critical tradition, reminding us that a substantial body of scholarship has treated the connections between Joyce and hypertext, rather than actively pursuing it ("Designing Digital Editions"). Similarly, at a recent conference on "Joyce and the Digital Age," I had the opportunity to ask a panel that included Reeve and other scholars about the relationship between Joyce and hypertext; the response was a matter-of-course agreement from the panelists that *Ulysses* is a form of proto-hypertext. Yet the critical analyses that have emerged from Reeve's critical edition of *Ulysses* do not argue, in the tradition of writing about Joyce and hypertext, that Joyce's writing constitutes an "analog" or "incipient" form of TEI. Indeed, most people who work with TEI would find the use of a single author as an analogy to explain the operations of TEI markup—Joyce, Walt Whitman, Junot Díaz, *anyone*—to be nonsensical on its face. I have never seen anyone make such an attempt in a publication, a conference talk, or even casual conversation. The marriage of new technologies and textual studies continues, but the era is over in which scholars find persuasive (or necessary) the effort to establish the origins of digital studies or legitimize its presence in English departments in the works of a great literary predecessor.

Ultimately, Joyce's role as the conceptual end of early hypertext projects tells us as much about how their creators viewed the editorial challenge of the early electronic era as it does about Joyce's elective affinity with new media in a more abstract sense. The creators of these projects fully believed that when they had restored Joyce to his proper form as hypertext; when they had freed his multisensory effects as hypermedia; when they had mastered his superabundant verbal and informational reserves; when they had fully theorized his concepts of reading, authoring, and annotation and reified those concepts as usable tools, then they—indeed, digital literary scholarship as a field—would fully realize the possibilities of that era's novel media forms. From our vantage point in the present, some of the guiding principles of those early ventures—McLuhan's pursuit of the logos of electronic technology or Landow's notion of hypertext theory as the master narrative of new media—no longer seem like the keys to the digital kingdom that they once did. Yet the *pursuit* of Joyce remains the first great romance of a discipline still in formation.

NOTES

1. This famous phrase originated with the anthropologist Claude Levi-Strauss in *Totemism,* trans. Rodney Needham (Boston: Beacon Press, [1962] 1963), 89.

2. The topic of sustainability has a rich literature in the digital humanities. See, for example, Nowviskie.

3. On the rationales by which English departments established a disciplinary claim to the field of digital studies, see, for example, Matthew Kirschenbaum, "What Is Digital Humanities and What Is It Doing in English Departments?" *ADE Bulletin* 150 (2010), especially pp. 59–60.

4. To be sure, *Ulysses* was subject to other kinds of exploration on the part of digital scholars: for example, the novel's breaking down of hierarchy and its presentation of the world as a set of unordered items could seem, in combination with its vast scale, to place the novel in conversation with database theory.

5. As Bella Dicks et al. note, while discussions of hypertext have tended to focus on the computer, classic definitions of hypertext, for example those of Nelson and Landow, identify it by structure rather than medium. "For many of the leading hypertext theorists, though, the computer is merely an enabling technology—a platform" (44).

6. A node is a document that is linked to another document. A link is a connection between two nodes; in the digital environment, this usually takes the form of an anchor, which is created by adding an anchor element (<a>) to a text written in HTML and which triggers a jump from one node to another.

7. I am grateful to Matthew Gold for this observation.

8. He is also fond, for exemplary purposes, of the "Dark House" passage in "In Memoriam," which is likewise strewn with references pointing to other texts (Landow, "The Rhetoric of Hypermedia," 95).

9. A "polysemic, encyclopedic book designed to be read with the simultaneous involvement of ear and eye," *The Gutenberg Galaxy* dreams of rendering an "all-inclusive, all-encompassing medium"—a concept for which media scholars would later popularize the name "virtual reality." The affinity of this dream with McLuhan's work is clear (Theall, "Beyond the Orality/Literacy Dichotomy," 7). For instance, here is the full text of A. J. M. Smith's poem, "A Taste of Space" (1967):

> McLuhan put his telescope to his ear;
> What a lovely smell, he said, we have here.

10. The successors who took up McLuhan's torch, including Walter Ong and Eric Havelock, contributed to the ongoing romance between new media theory and book history (Theall, "Beyond," 4).

11. A 2002 article by Darren Tofts, subtitled "*Ulysses* and the Poetics of Hypertextuality," is a case in point. Following the lead of Nelson, who emphasized that he regarded hypertext as a "literary phenomenon," Tofts describes hypertextuality as a *poetics*, a way of describing textual activity; thus texts that display hypertextuality need not have a computational basis. The texts he has in mind possess a fragmentary structure, which, though ostensibly disconnective, is in fact hyperconnective; the parts link up to each other in an overdetermined network of associations, and meaning arises, in part, through the convergence of subjects—the serendipity of links. The work of navigating and interpreting these texts lies, to a special degree, with the reader, who must reckon with a text that is not closed but open, subject to revision, interpolation, and other forms of manipulation. "On the basis of such a theory," says Tofts, "it is clear that *Ulysses* is already hypertextual."

12. For example, Espen Aarseth, in his foundational work *Cybertext* (1997), repeats the maxim that hypertextuality, as a form of textual behavior, arises not from digital technology itself, but from the very traditions of print technology. Aarseth, too, cites Joyce as a precursor of what others call hypertext and he calls "cybertext," which he describes as a textual poetics that requires "an interactive, combinative approach to reading." Or again, Jay David Bolter, who (with Richard Grusin) coined the term *remediation* and who uses Joyce, again, as a common example in his work, insists on the ways in which electronic text defines itself in relation to print. (Speaking in 1991, he comments that "*Ulysses* and particularly *Finnegans Wake* are themselves hypertexts that have been flattened out to fit on the printed page.") Or again, writing in 1999, Todd Rohman and Deborah Holdstein use Joyce, for them an analog figure of digital architectures, to argue that the digital world recapitulates the structures of print. "When we note textual wanderings, narrative fragmentation, and uncertainty," Rohman and Holdstein write, "we speak not of the Internet but of Joyce's 'novel,' the death-knell to modernist formalism . . . Not unlike cyberspace, it . . . opens a variety of possibilities for readerly interaction" (252, 260).

13. Donald Theall's hypertext editions of *Ulysses* and *Finnegans Wake* originated at Canada's Trent University in 1993. Corcoran's hypertext, *Sirens to Cyclops,* which she developed with Daniel Ferrer, had its first public showing in 1995. She discusses this project in Marlena Corcoran, "From 'Sirens' to 'Cyclops': Momentary Juxtaposition in Genetic Hypertext," in *JoyceMedia: James Joyce, Hypermedia & Textual Genetics,* ed. Louis Armand (Prague: Litteraria Pragensia, 2004). Louis Armand, "Introduction: Literary Engines," in *joyceMedia: James Joyce, Hypermedia, and Textual Genetics* (Prague: Litteraria Pragensia, 2004): 7; Marlena Corcoran, "Sirens to Cyclops: Momentary Juxtaposition in Genetic Hypertext," in *joyceMedia: James Joyce, Hypermedia, and Textual Genetics* (Prague: Litteraria Pragensia, 2004): 114. Other subjects of early hypertext projects included Langland (the Piers Plowman teaching package), Chaucer (The Electronic Canterbury Tales), and Dante Gabriel Rossetti (the Rossetti Archive) (Lavagnino, 109).

14. Marino notes that, for "technological determinists and hypertext promoters . . . *Ulysses* has always been both the dream text and ancestor" (475).

15. On the main page, a menu presents the options of viewing the sample passage in plain text: with line numbers, with manuscript variants displayed in different colors, or with annotations in different formats, such as mouseovers or windows in the header of the page. Another option enables the user to consult the primary passage, while a pull-down menu at the footer of the page allows her, at the same time, to consult secondary resources: "Recurring Motifs," "Schema," "Correspondences," and so on. (Some of these links still function; others lead only to mock-ups.)

16. This included conferences in Berkeley, London, Miami, New York, and Trieste between 2000 and 2002.

17. Marino is quoting from Chamberlain here.

18. The project originated with Johns Hopkins University Press. When, around 1992, the publication of Landow's *Hypertext* attracted widespread interest, Groden's editor at the same press asked Groden if he would prepare for them a hypertext *Ulysses.* "Without

knowing much about what hypertext was," Groden says, "I agreed" ("Perplex," 239). As of 1997, the Voyager Company had folded.

19. For example, in a 2001 article, Groden argues that certain kinds of literary works in print and manuscript, especially experimental works that play with footnoting conventions or offer multiple pathways through texts, represent "analog" versions of hypertext, waiting only for clickable links to complete their manifest design Citation is from Bolter 2001.

20. Michael Groden, " 'James Joyce's *Ulysses* in Hypermedia': Problems of Annotation; Annotation in Print and on a Screen." http://www.clemson.edu/caah/cedp/tech%20 colloquium%202001/groden%20files/printscreen.html.

21. Michael Groden, "Update—January 2004." http://www.literaturegeek.com /wp-content/uploads/2011/02/ulysses.

22. On definitions of completeness in print and digital environments, see Brown ("Don't Mind the Gap").

23. Ironically, the very diversity of communities and technological systems that would flourish on Web 2.0, and therefore of histories that would apply to it, would hasten the end of the critical refrain that traced the history of new media, usually meaning hypertext, back to Joyce.

24. In addition to Nowviskie, see, for example, Bretz, Brown, and McGregor; Brown; and Fitzpatrick.

25. Writes the media historian Joseph Turow, "At the end of the first decade of the twenty-first century, a computer user searching on the Web is unlikely to consider the enormous achievement represented by the highlighted links that beckon from the screen. In 1945, by contrast, Vannevar Bush was excited just to imagine the possibility of a hyperlink. He saw it as opening new gates to human understanding." Joseph Turow, "Introduction: On Not Taking the Hyperlink for Granted," in Turow and Lokman Tsui (*The Hyperlinked Society*, 1).

26. The scholars involved with the development of this edition include Jonathan Reeve, Hans Walter Gabler, Ronan Crowley, and Chris Forster.

27. TEI XML is a markup language that describes textual elements more fully than HTML does and enables them to be subjected to computational analysis. Editors can use this markup language to describe a textual element by appearance, literary meaning, literary function, linguistic function, and more. Scholars can then use these descriptions to analyze texts statistically via machine learning.

28. As, for example, at the conference "Joyce in the Digital Age," Columbia University, October 1, 2017.

BIBLIOGRAPHY

Aarseth, Espen. *Cybertext: Perspectives on Ergodic Literature.* Baltimore: Johns Hopkins University Press, 1997.

Armand, Louis. *Technē: James Joyce, Hypertext, and Technology.* Prague: Charles University Press, 2003.

Barnet, Belinda. *Memory Machines: The Evolution of Hypertext.* London: Anthem Press, 2013.

Bolter, Jay David. *Writing Space: The Computer, Hypertext, and the History of Writing.* Mahwah, N.J.: Lawrence Erlbaum, 2001.

Bretz, Andrew, Susan Brown, and Hannah McGregor. *Lasting Change: Sustaining Digital Scholarship and Culture in Canada.* 2010, https://www.academia.edu/385261/Lasting _Change_Sustaining_Digital_Scholarship_and_Culture_in_Canada.

Bretz, Andrew, Susan Brown, and Hannah McGregor. "Lasting Change: Sustaining Digital Scholarship and Culture in Canada." https://hannahmcgregor.files.wordpress .com/2015/03/lasting-change-knowledge-synthesis.pdf. White paper (December 2010). Retrieved 12 February 2019.

Brown, Susan. "Don't Mind the Gap: Evolving Digital Modes of Scholarly Production across the Digital-Humanities Divide," *Retooling the Humanities: The Culture of Research in Canadian Universities,* edited by Daniel Coleman and Smaro Kamboureli, 203–31. Edmonton: University of Alberta Press, 2011.

Brown, Susan, et al. "Published Yet Never Done: The Tension between Projection and Completion in Digital Humanities Research." *Digital Humanities Quarterly* 3, no. 2 (2009), http://www.digitalhumanities.org/dhq/vol/3/2/000040/000040.html.

Chamberlain, Suzanne. "Developing an Online Archive of *Ulysses*: Mellon Grant to Support Creation of Scholarly Edition of James Joyce Masterpiece." *UB Reporter* (February 6, 2003; March 23, 2004).

Coover, Robert. "Literary Hypertext: The Passing of the Golden Age." Keynote Address, *Digital Arts and Culture,* Atlanta, October 29, 1999.

Corcoran, Marlena. "From 'Sirens' to 'Cyclops': Momentary Juxtaposition in Genetic Hypertext." In *JoyceMedia: James Joyce, Hypermedia & Textual Genetics*, ed. Louis Armand. Prague: Litteraria Pragensia, 2004. Kindle.

Dicks, Bella, Bruce Mason, Amanda Coffey, and Bruce Atkinson. *Qualitative Research and Hypermedia: Ethnography for the Digital Age.* London: SAGE, 2005.

Ehrlich, Heyward. "JJTM: The James Joyce Text Machine: Main Menu." June 16, 2000; revised June 16, 2002, andromeda.rutgers.edu/~ehrlich/jjtm/demo/. Retrieved February 12, 2019.

Erne, Lukas. *Shakespeare as Literary Dramatist.* Cambridge: Cambridge University Press, 2003.

Fitzpatrick, Kathleen. *Planned Obsolescence: Publishing, Technology, and the Future of the Academy.* New York: New York University Press, 2011.

Gabler, Hans Walter. "Computer-Aided Critical Edition of *Ulysses*." *AALC Bulletin* 8 (1981): 232–48, http://www.tustep.uni-tuebingen.de/prot/prot18e.html.

Gabler, Hans Walter. "A Response to John Kidd, 'Errors of Execution in the 1984 *Ulysses*.'" *Studies in the Novel* 22 (1990): 250–56.

Greenblatt, Stephen. *Shakespearean Negotiations: The Circulation of Social Energy in Renaissance England.* Berkeley: University of California Press, 1988.

Groden, Michael. "Introduction to 'James Joyce's "Ulysses" in Hypermedia.'" *Journal of Modern Literature* 24, no. 3 (Summer 2001): 359–62.

Groden, Michael. "Perplex in the Pen—and in the Pixels: Reflections on 'The James Joyce Archive,' Hans Walter Gabler's 'Ulysses,' and 'James Joyce's "Ulysses" in Hypermedia.'" *Journal of Modern Literature* 22, no. 2 (Winter, 1998–99): 225–44.

Groden, Michael. Ulysses *in Focus: Genetic, Textual, and Personal Views.* Gainesville: University Press of Florida, 2010.

Havelock, Eric. *The Muse Learns to Write: Reflections on Orality and Literacy from Antiquity to the Present.* New Haven, Conn.: Yale University Press, 1986.

Hill, W. Speed. "Where Would Anglo-American Textual Criticism Be If Shakespeare Had Died of the Plague in 1593?" *TEXT* 13 (2000): 1–7.

Kastan, David. *Shakespeare and the Book.* Cambridge: Cambridge University Press, 2001.

Kenner, Hugh. *Flaubert, Joyce, and Beckett: The Stoic Comedians.* London: Dalkey Archive Press, 1962.

Kernan, Alvin. *Shakespeare, the King's Playwright: Theater in the Stuart Court, 1603–1613.* New Haven, Conn.: Yale University Press, 1995.

Kidd, John. "Errors of Execution in the 1984 *Ulysses.*" *Studies in the Novel* 22 (1990): 243–49.

Kirschenbaum, Matthew. "What Is Digital Humanities and What Is It Doing in English Departments?" *ADE Bulletin* 150 (2010): 53–60.

Kitzmann, Andreas. *Hypertext Handbook: The Straight Story.* New York: Peter Lang, 2006.

Kretzschmar, William A. Jr. *Language and Complex Systems.* Cambridge: Cambridge University Press, 2015.

Landow, George. *Hypertext: The Convergence of Contemporary Critical Theory and Technology.* Baltimore: Johns Hopkins University Press, 1992.

Landow, George. *Hypertext 3.0: Critical Theory and New Media in an Era of Globalization.* Baltimore: Johns Hopkins University Press, 2006.

Landow, George. "The Rhetoric of Hypermedia: Some Rules for Authors." In *Hypermedia and Literary Studies,* edited by Paul Delany and George P. Landow, 81–104. Cambridge, Mass.: MIT Press, 1991.

Landow, George. "Twenty Minutes into the Future or, How Are We Moving Beyond the Book?." In *The Future of the Book,* edited by Geoffrey Nunberg, 209–38. Berkeley: University of California Press, 1996.

Landow, George P., and Paul Delany, eds. *The Digital Word: Text-Based Computing in the Humanities.* Cambridge, MA: MIT Press, 1993.

Lavagnino, John. "Reading, Scholarship, and Hypertext Editions." *Text* 8 (1995): 109–24.

Lehmann-Haupt, Christopher. "How in the World 'Ulysses' Got So Mixed Up." *New York Times,* August 13, 1992.

Lethen, Helmut. "Modernism Cut in Half: The Exclusion of the Avant-Garde and the Debate on Postmodernism." In *Approaching Postmodernism,* edited by Douwe Fokkema and Hans Bertens, 233–38. Amsterdam: John Benjamins, 1986.

Levi-Strauss, Claude. *Totemism.* Translated by Rodney Needham. Boston: Beacon Press, [1962] 1963.

Machan, Tim. "I Endowed Thy Purposes: Shakespeare, Editing, and Middle English Literature." *TEXT* 13 (2000): 9–25.

Mahoney, Michael Sean. *Histories of Computing.* Cambridge, Mass.: Harvard University Press, 2011.

Mall, Judy. *Its name was Penelope.* Berkeley, Calif.: Narrabase Press, 1990.

Manovich, Lev. *The Language of New Media.* Cambridge, Mass.: MIT Press, 2001.

Marcus, Leah. *Unediting the Renaissance: Shakespeare, Marlowe, Milton.* London: Routledge, 1996.

Marino, Mark C. "*Ulysses* on Web 2.0: Towards a Hypermedia Parallax Engine." *James Joyce Quarterly* 44, no. 3 (Spring 2007): 475–99.

McGann, Jerome. *Radiant Textuality: Literature after the World Wide Web.* New York: Palgrave, 2001.

McGann, Jerome. *The Textual Condition.* Princeton, N.J.: Princeton University Press, 1991.

McGann, Jerome. "'Ulysses' as a Postmodern Text: The Gabler Edition." *Criticism* 27, no. 3 (Summer 1985): 283–305.

McHale, Brian. *The Cambridge Introduction to Postmodernism.* Cambridge: Cambridge University Press, 2015.

McHale, Brian. *Constructing Postmodernism.* London: Routledge, 1992.

McLeod, Randall, ed. *Crisis in Editing: Texts of the English Renaissance.* New York: AMS, 1994.

McLeod, Randall. "UN Editing Shak-speare." *Sub-Stance* 33–34 (1982): 26–55.

Morrissey, Judd, and Lori Talley. *The Jew's Daughter.* 2000, http://www.thejewsdaughter.com/.

Murphy, Andrew. *Shakespeare in Print: A History and Chronology of Shakespeare Publishing.* Cambridge: Cambridge University Press, 2003.

Nelson, Ted. *Literary Machines 91.1.* Self-published, 1981; reprinted 1992.

Nowviskie, Bethany. "Reality Bites." Plenary talk at RBMS Conference, June 20, 2012, http://nowviskie.org/2012/reality-bytes/.

Ong, Walter. *Orality and Literacy: The Technologizing of the Word.* New York: Methuen, 1982.

Prescott, Andrew. "Beyond the Digital Humanities Center: The Administrative Landscapes of the Digital Humanities." In *A New Companion to Digital Humanities,* edited by Susan Schreibman, Ray Siemens, and John Unsworth, 461–75. New York: Wiley-Blackwell, 2016.

Reeve, Jonathan. "James Joyce's Novel Ulysses in TEI XML. Work-in-Progress." GitHub. 2017. https://github.com/open-editions/corpus-joyce-ulysses-tei. Accessed December 26, 2017.

Rohman, Todd, and Deborah H. Holdstein, "*Ulysses* Unbound: Examining the Digital (R)evolution of Narrative Context." *Works and Days* 33/34 and 35/36, nos. 17–18 (1999–2000).

Rossman, Charles. "The New '*Ulysses*': The Hidden Controversy." *New York Review of Books,* December 8, 1988.

Ryan, Marie-Laure. "Cyberspace, Virtuality, and the Text." In *Cyberspace Textuality: Computer Technology and Literary Theory,* edited by Marie-Laure Ryan, 78–107. Bloomington: Indiana University Press, 1999.

Sawday, Jonathan, and Neil Rhodes. *The Renaissance Computer: Knowledge Technology in the First Age of Print.* New York: Routledge, 2000.

Shirky, Clay. *Here Comes Everybody: The Power of Organizing without Organizations.* London: Penguin Books, 2008.

Slatin, John. "Reading Hypertext: Order and Coherence in a New Medium." In *Hypermedia and Literary Studies,* edited by Paul Delany and George P. Landow, 153-69. Cambridge, Mass.: MIT Press, 1991.

Stallybrass, Peter. "Against Thinking." *PMLA* 122 (2007): 1580–87.

Streeter, Thomas. *Selling the Air: A Critique of the Policy of Commercial Broadcasting in the United States.* Chicago: University of Chicago Press, 1996.

Theall, Donald. "Beyond the Orality/Literacy Dichotomy: James Joyce and the Pre-History of Cyberspace." *Postmodern Culture* 2, no. 3 (1992).

Theall, Donald. *Beyond the Word: Reconstructing Sense in the Joyce Era of Technology, Culture, and Communication.* Toronto: University of Toronto Press, 1995.

Theall, Donald. *The Medium Is the Rear View Mirror: Understanding McLuhan.* Montreal: McGill-Queens University Press, 1971.

Theall, Donald. *The Virtual McLuhan.* Montreal: McGill-Queen's University Press, 2001.

Tofts, Darren. "A Retrospective Sort of Arrangement: *Ulysses* and the Poetics of Hypertextuality." *Hypermedia Joyce Studies* 3, no. 1 (2002). Accessed online: http://hjs.ff.cuni .cz/archives/v3/tofts2.html.

Tofts, Darren, and Murray McKeich. *Memory Trade: A Prehistory of Cyberculture.* North Ryde: Interface Press, 1998.

Tufféry, Stéphane. *Data Mining and Statistics for Decision Making.* Translated by Rod Riesco. New York: John Wiley & Sons, 2011.

Turow, Joseph. "Introduction: On Not Taking the Hyperlink for Granted." In *The Hyperlinked Society: Questioning Connections in the Digital Age,* edited by Joseph Turow and Lokman Tsui, 1–18. Ann Arbor: University of Michigan Press, 2008.

Van Dijck, José. *The Culture of Connectivity: A Critical History of Social Media.* Oxford: Oxford University Press, 2013.

Visconti, Amanda. "Designing Digital Editions: Inclusivity vs. the Literary Canon." Literature Geek. May 27, 2014, http://literaturegeek.com/2014/05/27/inclusivityedition canon. Accessed December 26, 2017.

Visconti, Amanda. "'How Can You Love a Work, if You Don't Know It?': Critical Code and Design toward Participatory Digital Editions." PhD diss., University of Maryland, 2015.

Visconti, Amanda. *Infinite Ulysses.* InfiniteUlysses.com. Accessed December 26, 2017.

Visconti, Amanda. "Infinite Ulysses Beta Closes for 1.0 Work." Literature Geek. June 2, 2016, http://literaturegeek.com/2016/06/02/infinite-ulysses-beta-closes. Accessed December 26, 2017.

Williams, Raymond. *Television: Technology and Cultural Form.* London: Collins, 1974.

Zittrain, Jonathan. *The Future of the Internet—and How to Stop It.* New Haven, Conn.: Yale University Press, 2008.

Educational Technology and the Humanities:
A History of Control

CURTIS FLETCHER

The history of educational technology remains a bit of a blind spot for humanists and digital humanists alike. While the subject of digital pedagogy has, in recent years, entered more fully into mainstream DH discourse, the history of educational technology in the humanities classroom has not yet been considered (Hirsh; Cordell; Battershill and Ross).[1] At a time when the digital humanities is trying to recover previously hidden genealogies, the history of educational technology and the role of the humanities within it can help us better understand what is at stake in controlling the technologies we use in our classrooms today. In particular, humanists' earliest engagements with educational broadcasting and multimedia learning, in the 1950s and 1960s, respectively, reveal just how long humanities scholars and educators have maintained a disparity in their technological commitments: they have been more willing to develop resources for and exercise control over the technologies they use for research than those they use in the classroom. Seeing how this lack of control has played out in the long term should compel us to reflect on the choices we make today in the technologies we use and, ultimately, on how best to develop our own ecosystem of humanities-tailored tools for teaching.

The Electronic Humanities

In the 1950s and 1960s, educators, educational researchers, librarians, and members of the electronics industry, among others, proffered a vision in which the transmission of sound and image was essential if humankind was to bring the vast new hordes of knowledge and information under control and leverage it toward greater human achievement. The electronic circulation and display of audiovisual material were consistently offered up as necessary counterparts to the exchange of computational data in the communication and organization of human knowledge.[2] For humanities scholars and educators too, new audiovisual systems were as vital a part of the electronic revolution of the 1950s and 1960s as computers, and humanists wasted no time embracing the affordances of both sets of technologies. We already know that a small but growing cadre of humanists had begun, in these years, to employ computing power as a novel means to generate concordances and conduct large-scale stylistic studies of canonical texts. That history has been detailed by, among others, Dolores Burton, Joseph Raben, and Susan Hockey, starting as early as the 1980s (Burton, "Automated Concordances and Word Indexes: The Early Sixties and the Early Centers," "The Process, the Programs, and the Products," and "Machine Decisions and Editorial Revisions"; Raben; Hockey). More extensive work has followed in recent years, particularly on the movement's earliest figure, Father Roberto Busa, an Italian Jesuit priest dubbed by some the "grandfather of the digital humanities" (Jones; Terras and Nyhan). But the history of humanities computing constitutes our only basis for understanding the aims and interests underlying humanists' engagements with electronic technologies in the 1950s and 1960s. As Marsha Kinder and Tara McPherson have recently observed, it is increasingly important, if we are to truly broaden our conception of contemporary digital humanities, to consider not just past "work in the encoding and marking up of texts" but also to properly grasp "the richly mediated and deeply visual culture in which computation came of age" (xiv). Humanities scholars and educators of the 1950s and 1960s were as intrigued with the immersive, affective, associative, and multisensory aspects of electronic media as they were with the ability to process electronic data. Many began an analogous hands-on effort to employ electronic audiovisual technologies.

Educational Television

Educational television provided one such opportunity. Much like the sudden growth of massive open online courses (MOOCs) in the early 2010s, the widespread and rapid rise of educational television in the mid- to late 1950s led many in and out of academia to think that a good deal of educational content might be moving inexorably toward massively broadcast, visually oriented courseware. While "educational television" would, by the late 1960s, come to denote the PBS-style "public television" of today, in the early to late 1950s it, to a large degree, meant *instructional television*: formal educational programming designed to promote sequential learning. In 1959, for instance, 53 percent of all programming broadcast from educational stations was instructional in nature or lecture oriented, and 41 percent of all programming consisted of for-credit telecourses (Schramm, 28).

Humanists too seemed convinced that this large-scale transformation in the delivery of educational content was imminent. That sense of inevitability was important since many humanities scholars and educators who took to the air did so thinking that educational television could be used to link traditional humanities study to television and, in doing so, permanently alter the way students and others engaged the new medium. The most prominent of these educators was Frank C. Baxter, a professor of literature at the University of Southern California (USC). In 1953,

KNXT, the CBS affiliate in Los Angeles, offered USC an hour of "public service" each Saturday at 11 a.m. USC filled that hour with a series developed and taught by Baxter, *Shakespeare on TV.* The series was an instant success in the Los Angeles area and was picked up the following year for national broadcast. In 1954, 332 USC students took *Shakespeare on TV,* or English 356a, for credit. Nine hundred people audited the course, and a full 400,000 watched it (*Los Angeles Times,* B1). By 1957, *Shakespeare on TV* had aired on at least twenty television stations nationwide, and four million course study guides had been mailed to viewers who requested them (Healy, 8).

The desire among English educators like Baxter to go on the air was connected to a wave of early optimism regarding the potential for quality cultural TV programming, especially literary dramas. Starting in the late 1940s, television adaptations of contemporary plays formed a ready and convenient supply of compelling dramatic stories. So, too, did adaptations of established literary works. In television's first decade, works from nearly every playwright in the Western canon were adapted for the new medium.[3] The emergence of instructional television thus dovetailed, quite serendipitously, with what might be considered an early form of humanities-oriented media studies. "Television education," a new focus in English classrooms in these years, directed students to watch literary adaptations as a supplement to assigned readings and oriented curricula toward the analysis of the form and content of original television dramas. Engaging with both literary adaptations and original television plays was seen as the most compelling way to encourage students to regularly seek out literary experiences via television and, more generally, to start thinking of the electronic apparatus in their family room as a major vehicle for quality narrative culture. Like others in his field, Baxter was motivated by the literary benefits of the twin endeavors of *literary* and *instructional* television and found himself in a unique position. As an English teacher at a time of quality *literary* television, he seized the opportunity to guide his students and others toward a more discriminating set of viewing habits for the new medium. As an English teacher in the era of *instructional* television, he entered the studio himself, producing quality literary educational broadcasting that, while reaching hundreds of thousands of viewers, would, he hoped, act in cooperation with *literary* television. Both efforts attempted to transplant the "literary experience" of the theater and the page to the home screen and, as a result, raise the cultural quality of TV programming in America at a time when the meaning of television viewing was, in a significant sense, still up for grabs.[4]

Humanists' endeavor to intervene in the use habits of television in this way was, regrettably, ill fated. Two states of affairs led to this missed opportunity, both of which still hold true for today's humanities educators: the shifting nature of institutional commitments to specific educational technologies and humanists' lack of control over the technologies they used. Just as rapidly as lecture-oriented educational television arose, it began to decline. Teacher shortages of the mid-1950s, to which educational television was a direct response, abated. The FCC bribery scandals of 1959, together with the Senate investigations into television violence in 1961, led a coalition of reformers at key funding agencies, educational television institutions, the FCC, and Congress to reorient educational television from lecture-oriented content toward broader cultural programming. While, in the late 1950s, educational televisions stations were owned almost exclusively by school districts, colleges, and universities, by the late 1960s nearly all had been absorbed into the Corporation for Public Broadcasting. For humanists, the outcome was regrettable. When they lost the ability to design and produce content for the screen, they lost a key platform with which to affect larger-scale expectations for the new medium.

The fact that they were only producing content was the problem, however. No matter how ambitious their aims in using instructional television, Baxter and others remained "content providers" for the new medium. Humanists had not, in the short span of time in which they were providing content, established any real control over the technology itself. They had not set up any means to design and produce courses outside the institutional apparatus of their colleges or universities. They had not mastered the methods or practices of broadcasting. And they certainly had not learned to deploy the equipment itself: to work live cameras or create kinescope recordings of live broadcasts. Though they had far-reaching social and theoretical aims for their use of the technology, they had, by and large, counted on those who controlled its infrastructure and means of production to achieve them.

More than a half century later, humanities educators stand in the same relation to much of the technology they use to publish course-related content online. While the tools, platforms, and systems they use to deliver that content may be more varied than they were for humanities educators of the 1950s, the dilemma remains essentially the same: they have limited control over the technologies they use. To deliver fully online courses, colleges and universities typically make compulsory the use of a specific, often commercial platform. But more importantly, even when humanities educators do have choices in the platforms they use to deliver their content, whether through fully online courses or, more likely, in a blended classroom or in simply posting supplementary material online for an otherwise traditional course, their choices are often not made in the interest of long-term control.

We need to resist, whenever possible, commercial platforms and to use open-source alternatives instead. While that choice may cost us some desired functionality in the short term—for instance, in choosing to use Jitsi over WebEx or Adobe Connect to deliver our lectures online—what we potentially gain in the long term can be vastly more important: the ability to integrate a given platform, in terms of support and even development, into our own network of humanities-tailored pedagogical resources. How often do we choose to use a commercial platform solely because it offers the exact set of features we require or because our college or university makes it readily available through an institutional license? How often do we choose a particular tool or platform, regardless of its origins, simply because it is painlessly on hand? How often can we think of cases in which humanities educators have used, for instance, Genius to mark up course-related material when they could have used Hypothes.is, or 3D Warehouse to immerse students in three-dimensional environments when they could have used VSim?[5] We need to be more discerning and calculating about the broader impact these individual choices have on our collective ability as humanities educators to build out a set of shared platforms and resources. For this same reason, we need to choose platforms already supported and developed by our colleagues in the humanities and related fields over their alternatives. Platforms like these, developed at DH centers or by allied groups, often incorporate values vital to us as humanities scholars and educators, such as the ability to capture or express ambiguity, difference, and relational thinking. These capacities for platforms should be the basic criterion by which we choose among them, whether that means supporting platforms already built in this way or supporting open-source platforms that might one day be integrated into our network and tailored to our needs and interests. Doing so will help ensure that we can continue to use our educational technologies to advance our own humanistic ends, something our predecessors of the 1950s were unable to achieve.

Multimedia Learning

Multimedia learning has a similar origin story in the humanities, first developing as an experimental technique among humanities educators just as educational television began to decline in the early to mid-1960s. As educational television faded from use in formal instruction in the early part of the decade, the electronic revolution in education only intensified when a host of more cutting-edge information technologies arrived on the scene: audio-listening centers; computer-assisted instruction; self-instructional, multimedia study carrels; remote-access programmed instruction; and "electronic classrooms" equipped for sequenced, multiscreen, multimedia presentations. The 1960s thus saw a different, but related, kind of revolution in educational technology, one that sought to bring text together with images, audio, and video into programmed, multimedia instruction.[6]

The capabilities of these new technologies were particularly exhilarating to a group of humanists interested in exploring the relationship between the sensorial affordances of electronic multimedia systems and the immersive nature of humanities content. Humanities educators began quickly to experiment with total-audiovisual systems, testing and then talking about the potentially profitable relationship between electronic and humanistic experiences in the classroom. Mixing media, intermingling multiple senses alongside ideas, and appealing to a complex of cognitive and affective registers created a "total experience," a phrase regularly employed by humanities educators advocating educational media in these years. One such set of programs, developed for the Edex system by English faculty at both Niles Township High School in Skokie, Illinois, and at Chicago Teachers College in 1965, was used for instruction in both language and poetry. The Edex system equipped a classroom or auditorium with a control console from which one could coordinate the sequenced and/or simultaneous use of a tape recorder, a film projector, and a random-access slide projector, as well as receive input from each student via a four-button response panel. Students experiencing one of the poetry "programs" filed into an auditorium and were met with lively music overhead. As the auditorium dimmed, projectors began to fill the screen with the first stanza of a poem. Stanzas dissolved into one another as the narrator described the literary devices and explored the symbolism used in each. In between sections, students answered multiple-choice questions about the poem by keying their responses into a four-button console built into their desk. Programs on language followed the same structure, but used synchronized sounds—children playing, a radio announcer—alongside text and images (Stowe and Maggio, 410).

As with educational television, designing multimedia systems not only brought the narrative and experiential quality of humanities content to life and in the process took advantage of students' developed visual sensibilities but it also gave humanities educators the opportunity to help guide the critical uses of those new sensibilities. The evolution from educational television to multimedia systems for humanists was subtle but significant. Educational television, though it was multimedia in nature, still followed a lecture model of instruction. Multimedia instruction, in contrast, allowed humanists to direct more imaginative and critical engagements with multisensory formats. "It is essential for students to become active, intelligent and discriminating consumers of both print and nonprint media," argued James Bell, an English teacher who in 1968 started requiring his students to construct multimedia presentations of novels in lieu of standard book reports (7). Bell dubbed his method the "Multi-Media Response Process," and in it, he specifically prohibited students from using any print material in their responses to texts, hoping that this process would force students to think about nonprinted, new media as a semi-direct, translatable analog able to stand on its own terms with a literary text.

According to Bell, television and newer media had become such an integral part of students' communication environment that their overall creativity hinged on its mastery. For others, like members of the electronics industry, behavioral scientists, and educational technology engineers, educational media was primarily a way to implement more efficient forms of nonprint communication in education. For humanists like Bell, what mattered was not taking in more information so much as a mastery of the media along which that information traveled. Here they called on fellow humanities educators and the chief theorists of the "electronic age," Marshall McLuhan and Walter Ong, in making the case that electronic media allowed students to, as McLuhan famously stated in *Understanding New Media*, better sense "integral patterns," and to "live mythically and in depth": essentially electronic media allowed students to better interrogate their environment and reality (vii).

As they had been with educational television, humanists' interventions with multimedia educational technologies in these earliest years were unsuccessful. Despite the hopes of those like Bell and the many prognostications of those like McLuhan, an electronic, multimedia educational world never materialized in the 1960s; likewise, experimental, multisensory-focused instruction did not become a core part of the humanities classroom. The market for multimedia instructional systems simply never matured.[7] After recording heavy losses, some ventures, like the General Learning Company, only turned a profit after shifting their focus from electronic multimedia systems toward "instructional packages" that mixed together print, photos, and lab equipment. Others abandoned the effort altogether. Raytheon sold its entire "electronic learning systems business" just five years after purchasing several instructional technology firms, including the Edex system used by humanities educators (Raymond, 509). While educators continued to use more modest audiovisual materials to supplement instruction, large-scale experimentation with electronic audiovisual systems dwindled rapidly in the early 1970s.

Humanities educators face a similar set of challenges today. The development and adoption of multimedia educational technologies are, in many ways, as unpredictable now as they were in the 1960s and, indeed, as they have been throughout the twentieth century. The emergence of new multimedia educational technologies has often been subject to boom-and-bust cycles, regularly eliciting a great deal of initial hype followed by fleeting periods of adoption.[8] In the more distant past, these cycles have cut short the opportunities of early adopters using educational film in the 1920s, television in the 1950s, and electronic multimedia systems in the 1960s. In more recent times, we have seen this pattern play out for a host of large-scale technological innovations in education such as digital textbooks, the virtual classroom (for instance, Second Life), and MOOCs, as well as more specific technologies like iPads.

The question for us today, given this long-standing pattern, is how can we better weather these cycles? Part of the answer lies, as it does with publishing educational content online, in making the right choices of the specific tools, platforms and systems we use. But *using* the right tools and platforms out there is simply not enough. If we truly want to control our fates as technology-driven humanities educators, given the long-standing and problematic nature of our relationship to educational technologies, we *must build our own network* of shared services and infrastructure for digital pedagogy that is commensurate with, and indeed intimately tied to, the already existing ecosystem of resources, tools, and platforms built for DH research and scholarship. Our capacity to resist the long-term pattern described here, of just using what is lying around because it is offered by our college or university or is readily available as a commercial service, lies not just in our choosing to use the right technologies but also in investing in our own.

Educational Technology and the Digital Humanities

Committing to such a network of humanities-tailored teaching tools will, however, require us to overcome another long-standing pattern; namely, an imbalance in the amount of resources humanities scholars and educators have been willing to devote to infrastructure for their research and scholarship, on the one hand, and their pedagogical practices, on the other. Part of the reason humanities computing has been so well documented as a line of descent for the contemporary digital humanities is that its earliest practitioners, unlike those experimenting with educational technologies in the same years, left behind a durable set of resources. From the early to the late 1960s, humanists and others established the first lines of communication and shared services and infrastructure devoted to humanities-oriented computational research. The first center dedicated to humanities computing in the United States, the Institute for Computer Research in the Humanities at New York University, was established in 1966 offering, among other key resources, the first humanities programming classes in 1967 (ICRH Newsletter, 1966–1969). The first set of national conferences on literary data processing ran from 1964 to 1970, several of which published subsequent reports or proceedings.[9] The first fellowships for computer-oriented research in the humanities were offered by the American Council of Learned Societies and funded by IBM, starting in 1964 (Lieb). Finally, the first journal, *Computers and the Humanities,* started publishing in 1966 with annual directories of active scholars in the field, humanities-designed computer programs, and literary works in machine-readable form. With the aid of these resources, humanists began to construct machine-readable texts and concordances of more and more canonical texts and to code and deploy an increasing number of humanities-tailored computer programs, improving on their efforts year after year. From these foundations, humanists were able to build out a resilient network of resources and support, allowing them to have a good measure of control over the direction of humanities computing. By comparison, humanists engaged with educational technologies in these same years were largely using what had been handed to them. When institutional commitments shifted or corporations pulled out, they faltered.

The situation is not altogether different today: the level of control and direction we have over our technologies in the areas of research and scholarship, on the one hand, and education, on the other, is as uneven now as it was in the 1950s and 1960s. Every year, the National Endowment for the Humanities (NEH) and the Mellon Foundation, foremost among others, award funds for the development of digital tools, platforms, and projects in the humanities. Only a small portion of that funding goes to DH pedagogy or to the development of humanities-oriented educational technologies.[10] Forty-four (15%) of the 295 Digital Humanities Start-Up grants funded by the NEH Office of Digital Humanities (ODH) since 2007 mention "teaching," "classroom" or "pedagogy" in their title or abstract. That percentage holds as well for the ODH's Digital Humanities Implementation grants awarded since 2012.[11] When it comes to scholarly activities—research, authoring, and publishing, for instance—we seem to have decided it is worthwhile to build out a robust network of digital tools and platforms specifically geared toward humanities work. But when it comes to educational technology, we are much more willing to just use what is on hand. We rely on large-scale learning management systems (e.g., Blackboard and Google Classroom) or cobble together open-source and commercial platforms and services (e.g., blogs, wikis, timelines, and video-sharing websites) to manage our courses and deliver our content.

We need, most obviously, to devote more money and resources to building and maintaining our own set of humanities-tailored educational tools and platforms. We have a responsibility to better serve our students, specifically as humanities learners, with such tailored technologies. For their sake, we cannot continue to just use what is lying around.

However, if we truly want to promote and establish an ecosystem of custom humanities educational tools and platforms, we must closely link the needs of that ecosystem to our more mature efforts in DH research, writing, and publishing. We must take the needs of that new ecosystem into consideration in *all* our decisions regarding the support and development of *all* digital tools and platforms, including those that traditionally support digital research and scholarship. First, we need to consider what we are supporting and the consequences of that support for educational technology in the humanities, even in building digital projects that are not necessarily educational in nature. For instance, if in building out a born-digital scholarly publication, we have the choice between using a commercial platform or one built by and for humanists—between CartoDB and Neatline, or between YouTube and Critical Commons—our choice should be guided not just by the features or services we require for our publication but also by the role that each platform plays in our lives as humanities educators. Second, we need to think broadly about how we can leverage more platforms built by and for humanists to educational ends and how we can make greater use of assets we already control. This could be as simple as repurposing the features and functionality of existing platforms. But if we are serious about taking control of the educational technologies we use, our work should also involve forking and building plug-ins for already existing humanities-developed platforms to make them better fit our educational purposes.

Finally, we need to think more about these kinds of cross-purposes—teaching and learning, on the one hand, and research and scholarship, on the other—not only in using already existing platforms but also in proposing, funding, and building new ones. As others have rightly noted, digital humanists have a unique opportunity to bridge the gap between our research, scholarship, and teaching (Hirsh). But in the use and development of humanities-tailored platforms, in particular, we have a chance that none others do: to enable new modes of research and scholarship for ourselves while at the same time modeling and fostering new forms of scholarly practices and workflows for our students. We have the opportunity, in influencing our students' practices on the vernacular web, not just to offer up new scholarly genres—the database documentary, the video essay, or the annotated mini-archive, for instance—but the very platforms we develop to enable those genres. Funding agencies could easily incentivize such cross-purpose platform development by giving preference to applications for research and scholarly platforms that also explicitly address educational uses.

Implementing these recommendations would help us close the gap between our research and teaching by fostering cross-purpose humanities platform development. It would also help guarantee us more control over the direction we take our technologies as humanities educators—giving us more control than we currently have and certainly more control than our predecessors had in the 1950s and 1960s. As their story makes clear, that control is important because we want to safeguard not only the work we do but also our collective effort over time.

NOTES

1. If one looks at historical scholarship, the intersection of the humanities and educational technology also remains largely absent. Works dedicated to the history of educational technology are rarely discipline specific, and none focus on the history of educational technology as it relates to the humanities specifically (Cuban; Saettler; Reiser; Cassidy). Likewise, recent work in the history of the humanities has overlooked the role that technology played in shifting the boundaries of humanities pedagogy and curricula in the last half-century (Bender and Schorske; Hollinger; "On the Humanities"; "Reflecting on the Humanities").

2. Among the many examples here, see for instance, plans for some of the first electronic educational networks, Intrex and Edunet (Brown, Miller, and Keenan; Overhage and Harman).

3. In the 1955–1956 season alone, one could regularly see works by Sophocles, Euripides, Shaw, Ibsen, Faulkner, Tennessee Williams, Henry James, and, of course, Shakespeare. When NBC presented a three-hour version of *Richard III* on March 11, 1956, it was viewed by one of the largest television audiences yet: 25 million. Alongside these adaptations, one could tune in each week to a host of anthology drama programs featuring the works of critically acclaimed television playwrights: Rod Serling, Tad Mosel, Gore Vidal, and Paddy Chayefsky, among others.

4. It's important to understand, as Lisa Gitelman, Jussi Parikka, and others in the media archeological tradition have recently shown, that practices that evolve around new media are not as overdetermined as we like to imagine (Gitelman and Pingree; Parikka). Rather, a given medium is brought forth into a state of "identity crisis" within which "its meaning—its potential, its limitations, the publicly agreed upon sense of what it does, and for whom—has not yet been pinned down" (Gitelman and Pingree, xv).

5. Hypothes.is is a bookmarklet for scholarly and educational web annotations funded by the Andrew W. Mellon Foundation (see https://web.hypothes.is/). VSim is an

NEH-funded platform developed at UCLA's Institute for Digital Research and Education for the "real-time exploration of highly detailed, three-dimensional computer models in both formal and informal educational settings" (see https://idre.ucla.edu/research/active-research /vsim).

6. The circumstances surrounding the development of multimedia, electronic educational technologies in the 1960s were in many ways analogous to the production of digital textbooks today. Like digital textbooks, the hype surrounding 1960s educational technologies centered on the advantages of multimedia content, student interactivity, and personalized learning. What is more, just as digital textbooks today are the product of strategic mergers between publishers and software companies, in the 1960s, "electronic education" was promoted most heavily by a series of new corporations and partnerships formed between major electronics firms and publishers specializing in educational content (Young). The largest of these mergers included RCA and Random House, General Electric and Time Inc., IBM and Science Research Associates, and Xerox and American Educational Publications (Sharpes, 135).

7. In 1965, James Collier, Raytheon's director of corporate planning, predicted the market for instructional technology would reach $2 billion in 1970 and $3 billion by 1975 (White, A33). In reality, that market peaked in 1970 at $650 million (Keppel, 75).

8. These cycles have been the subject of many histories of educational technology, including Cuban, Cassidy, and Saettler.

9. See Bessinger, Parrish, and Arader; Conference on the Use of Computers in Humanistic Research; Conference on Computers for the Humanities; IBM Symposium; Ohle; and *Proceedings*.

10. Stephen Brier has also written about the inclusion of pedagogy and teaching in NEH Digital Humanities Start-Up Grants (392).

11. I suspect that these numbers reveal more about the focus of the applications that the ODH receives and less about their funding priorities, as their grant guidelines are always framed broadly.

BIBLIOGRAPHY

Battershill, Claire and Shawna Ross. *Using Digital Humanities in the Classroom: A Practical Introduction for Teachers, Lecturers, and Students*. London: Bloomsbury Academic, 2017.

Bell, James. "A Nonprint Response to Print." Presented at the 62nd Annual Meeting of the National Council of Teachers of English, Minneapolis, November 23–25, 1972.

Bender, Thomas, and Carl E. Schorske, eds. *American Academic Culture in Transformation: Fifty Years, Four Disciplines*. Princeton, N.J.: Princeton University Press, 1998.

Bessinger, Jess, Stephen M. Parrish and Harry Arader, eds. *Literary Data Processing Conference Proceedings, September 9, 10, 11—1964*. White Plains, N.Y.: IBM, Data Processing Division, 1964.

Brier, Stephen. "Where's the Pedagogy? The Role of Teaching and Learning in the Digital Humanities." In *Debates in the Digital Humanities,* edited by Matthew K. Gold, 390–401. Minneapolis: University of Minnesota Press, 2012.

Brown, George W., James G. Miller, and Thomas A Keenan, eds. *Edunet: A Report of the Summer Study on Information Networks.* New York: Wiley, 1967.

Burton, M. Dolores. "Automated Concordances and Word Indexes: The Early Sixties and the Early Centers." *Computers and the Humanities* 15, no. 2 (1981a): 83–100.

Burton, M. Dolores. "Automated Concordances and Word Indexes: The Process, the Programs, and the Products," *Computers and the Humanities* 15, no. 2 (1981b): 139–54.

Burton, M. Dolores. "Automated Concordances and Word-Indexes: Machine Decisions and Editorial Revisions." *Computers and the Humanities* 16, no. 4 (1982): 195–218.

Cassidy, Margaret. *Bookends: The Changing Media Environment of American Classrooms.* Hampton Press Communication Series. Media Ecology. Creskill, N.J.: Hampton Press, 2004.

Computers for the Humanities? A Record of the *Conference on Computers for the Humanities,* Yale University, New Haven, Conn., January 22–23, 1965.

Conference on the Use of Computers in Humanistic Research. Rutgers University, New Brunswick, N.J., December 4, 1964.

Cordell, Ryan. "How Not to Teach Digital Humanities." In *Debates in the Digital Humanities 2016,* edited by Matthew K. Gold, and Lauren F. Klein, 459–74. Minneapolis: University of Minnesota Press, 2016.

Cuban, Larry. *Teachers and Machines: The Classroom Use of Technology since 1920.* New York: Teachers College Press, 1986.

Gitelman, Lisa, and Geoffrey B. Pingree, ed. *New Media, 1740–1915.* Cambridge, Mass.: MIT Press, 2003.

Healy, John Lovejoy. "A Critical Study of Frank C. Baxter's 'Shakespeare on TV.'" PhD diss., University of Southern California, 1965.

Hirsh, Brett. "</Parentheses>: Digital Humanities and the Place of Pedagogy." In *Digital Humanities Pedagogy: Practices, Principles and Politics,* edited by Brett Hirsh, 3–30. Open Book Publishers, 2012.

Hockey, Susan. "The History of Humanities Computing." In *A Companion to Digital Humanities,* edited by Susan Schreibman, Ray Siemens, and John Unsworth, 3–19. Malden, Mass.: Blackwell Publishing, 2004.

Hollinger, David A., ed. *Humanities and the Dynamics of Inclusion since World War II.* Baltimore: Johns Hopkins University Press, 2006.

IBM Symposium on Introducing the Computer into the Humanities. Poughkeepsie, N.Y: International Business Machines Corp., 1969.

ICRH Newsletter. New York University, 1, no. 1 (1966) through 4, no. 11 (1969).

Jones, Steven J. *Roberto Busa J., S.J., and the Emergence of Humanities Computing.* New York: Routledge, 2016.

Keppel, Francis. "Teaching Machines: A Long Way to Go." *New York Times,* January 12, 1970, 75.

Kinder, Marsha, and Tara McPherson, eds. *Transmedia Frictions: The Digital, the Arts, and the Humanities.* Berkeley: University of California Press, 2014.

Lieb, Irwin. "The ACLS Program for Computer Studies in the Humanities: Notes on Computers and the Humanities." *Humanities and Computing* 1, no. 1. (1966): 7–11.

McLuhan, Marshall. *Understanding Media: The Extensions of Man.* New York: McGraw-Hill, 1964.

"News and Noted." *Computers and the Humanities* 1, no. 3 (1967): 112.

Ohle, L. D., ed. "Report on the Conference on Computer Technology in the Humanities, September 3–7, 1969."

"On the Humanities." *Daedalus* 135, no. 2 (Spring, 2006).

Overhage, Carl F. J., and Joyce Harman, eds. *Intrex: Report of a Planning Conference on Information Transfer Experiments.* Cambridge, Mass.: MIT Press, 1965.

Parikka, Jussi. *What Is Media Archeology?* Cambridge: Polity Press 2015.

Proceedings: Computer Applications to Problems in the Humanities: A Conversation in the Disciplines. State University College, Brockport, N.Y., April 4–5, 1969.

Raben, Joseph. "Humanities Computing: 25 Years Later," *Computers and the Humanities* 25, no. 6 (1991): 341–50.

Raymond, Henry. "Publishers Retreat From Technology," *New York Times*, January 11, 1970.

"Reflecting on the Humanities." *Daedalus* 138, no. 1 (Winter 2009).

Reiser, R. A. "A History of Instructional Design and Technology." In *Trends and issues in Instructional Design and Technology,* edited by R.A. Reiser and J. V. Dempsey, 26–53. Upper Saddle River, N.J.: Merrill Prentice-Hall, 2002.

Saettler, Paul. *The Evolution of American Educational Technology.* Englewood, Colo.: Libraries Unlimited, 1990.

Schramm, Wilbur. *The Impact of Educational Television: Selected Studies from the Research Sponsored by the National Educational Television and Radio Center.* Chicago: University of Illinois Press, 1960.

Sharpes, Donald K. "Computers in Education." *The Clearing House* 43, no. 3 (1968): 135–38.

Stowe, Richard A., and Andrew J. Maggio. "Language and Poetry in Sight and Sound." *The English Journal* 54, no. 5 (1965): 410–13.

Terras, Melissa, and Julianne Nyhan. "Father Busa's Female Punch Card Operatives." In *Debates in the Digital Humanities 2016*, edited by Matthew K. Gold and Lauren F. Klein, 60–65. Minneapolis: University of Minnesota Press, 2016.

"TV Students of Shakespeare Quit Screens to Take Final Examination." *Los Angeles Times,* January 24, 1954.

Young, Jeffrey R. "The Object Formally Known as the Textbook." *Chronicle of Higher Education*, January 27, 2013.

White, Donald. "Industry, Education in New Alliance," *Boston Globe*, January 2, 1966.

A Braided Narrative for Digital History

LINCOLN MULLEN

It is a rare monograph today that is not festooned with lorenz curves and punctuated with numbers." That is how the historian David Hackett Fischer described
the current state of his discipline in 1976 (132). Substitute network diagrams for
Lorenz curves and blog posts for monographs, and one would have a fair description of the current state of scholarship in digital history.

It is apparent to observers of digital history, as it was apparent when Fischer
commented on the rise of social history, that digital history trades in methods more
than most other forms of history. Digital historians delight in writing and reading
tutorials on how to use tools and software for their research and teaching; they teach
workshops on those methods and line up to attend them. Blog posts in the field
more often recount the steps that the researcher took than the conclusions that he
or she came to. And digital history is fortunate to have a burgeoning methodological
literature for humanities computing, including *The Programming Historian,*[1] *The
Historians' Macroscope,*[2] and several books on specific programming languages.[3]

Amidst this enthusiasm for methods in digital history, one might reasonably
conclude that something has gone amiss, that methods have won out over interpretations and argumentation. Tom Scheinfeldt argued in 2012 that it is a positive
change that digital historians "traffic much less in new theories than in new methods" ("Sunset for Ideology"). Still, Scheinfeldt thought that while digital history
needed more "time to experiment and even . . . time to play," sooner or later "digital humanities must make arguments" ("Where's the Beef?"). In reaction to the gap
between digital history's promise and its payoff, Cameron Blevins has argued that
when it comes to "argument-driven scholarship . . . digital history has largely over-
promised and underdelivered." He makes the point that digital historians have written extensively about their methods, but not actually employed them to make many
substantive interpretations. In the face of widespread skepticism among nondigital
historians that DH methods will ever pay off, Blevins and others have urged digital historians to create disciplinary-specific argumentation and interpretation. We

might add to these critiques that historians have long prized the art of storytelling and have often focused on the particulars of history, including individual lives, as a mode of communicating the complexities of the past. Yet digital history (at least computational history, rather than digital public history) has tended to pull historians toward the abstract and the generalizable at the expense of storytelling and historical particulars.

While digital historians do write about methods more than they make arguments, most historians have the opposite problem. Historians have an unhealthy tendency to hide their methods, and the discipline as a whole has no real venue to discuss methodology. They rarely write about methods, even though historians' work is defined by the various methodologies that they practice: social history, political history, cultural history, and now digital history are different communities of practice that have come to different interpretations of the past. The problem is that historians do not write about or debate their methods with the same transparency and rigor that they do their interpretations. So-called methods classes in graduate school often conflate discussions of theories or outstanding books in the field with learning how to actually conduct research. Journal articles and books rarely discuss their methods explicitly, and there are no high-profile journals in historical methodology. The result is that digital historians have been writing about their methods when the broader discipline has not.

We have, then, a deficiency of interpretation in digital history and a deficiency in explicit methodological discussion in history generally. These commensurate absences are puzzling, since our methods produce our interpretations. We must find a way of writing digital history that puts historical interpretation and argumentation at the center, while giving due weight to explaining the methodology that led to those results. Neither digital history as currently practiced nor the methodological silence of the broader discipline is a sufficient model for digital historians' work.

This problem is, *mutatis mutandis,* similar to the one that historians faced in the 1970s. In an essay titled "The Braided Narrative: Substance and Form in Social History," Fischer observed that historians before the 1970s had dealt with history as a "narrative craft," made possible because of a focus on elites (110). The new social historians, however, saw history as not "a story-telling but a problem-solving discipline" (112). The turn away from studying the kinds of socially or politically prominent figures who left behind large collections of correspondence or literary sources required using sources such as census or probate records that were tractable only to new methods expressed in "empirical findings." Empiricism made that kind of history "increasingly a mathematical science, which speaks in symbols and numbers" (113). The parallels to digital history are clear, since digital history often deals with a greatly expanded base of primary sources, often values empirical results over theory, and (at least in computational history) depends on methods that are statistical or algorithmic.[4]

In his essay, Fischer aimed to provide a way of reconciling social historians' new-found empiricism with their narrative tradition. He argued for "the incorporation of statistics in a text" and opposed putting statistics in an appendix on the grounds that the "two must be combined in a single expressive act" (131–33). This way of writing Fischer termed a "braided narrative," in which the scholar wove analysis with narrative, instead of separating the two. A section analyzing, for instance, social class would be succeeded by a section narrating the lives of actual people living within those structures. The key point was that two modalities of writing history, analysis and narrative, were to be integrated in a complex prose form suitable to the task of maintaining history as both an empirical and a storytelling discipline.

Digital historians can adapt Fischer's braided narrative for their own purposes. Where Fischer envisioned a braided narrative of empiricism and storytelling, digital historians can braid together interpretations and discussion of methodology. Fischer's model is a prompt for asking what way of combining narrative or argumentation and digital methods is most likely to be successful.

There is no shortage of options for how we might write. One approach is to borrow a page from the sciences or the quantitative social sciences and include a distinct methods section. This approach is often adopted in the relatively new *Journal of Cultural Analytics* (e.g., Jockers and Kirilloff). Another option, common among grant-funded projects, is to write a white paper that explains methodology. Computational projects should (and increasingly but by no means universally do) make their code and data available and reproducible in an open-source repository, such as GitHub[5] and figshare.[6] The blog of an individual scholar or a project blog is another way of explaining methodology. Sometimes scholars publish two distinct articles, one on interpretations and the other on methods (e.g., Cordell; Smith, Cordell, and Mullen).[7]

Yet these options are inadequate because they all separate methods and the interpretations that result from them. Blogs are sometimes the place where scholarship actually happens, which the journal article merely sums up, but that implies a disjunction between the iterative process of blogging and the conclusions presented in the article or book. The code repository is only available to those who are sufficiently literate in the programming language used. Furthermore, the details of the code are crucial, but they can obscure the patterns of problem solving and the abstractions that the code actually implements. The white paper is peculiar to the grant process and not likely to be adopted by nongrant-funded projects. Finally, the separate methods section following the model of the sciences is a poor fit for historical research. It implies that history is a kind of empirical, hard science.

A braided narrative for digital history would instead weave together discussions of methods with the process of interpretation. A section explaining the questions that a historian is trying to ask could be followed by an explanation of how a machine-learning algorithm performs a particular transformation (cf. Schmidt). For example, a discussion of the methodology of word embedding can be followed by the interpretations drawn from applying that technique to a corpus of literature (as in Gavin et al.). A historian, to take an example from my MA student Kim Nettles, might explain how word-embedded models place terms in a multidimensional space to preserve many kinds of relationships to other terms and then go on to explore how nineteenth-century racialized discourse plotted on to different dimensions of black versus white, insider versus outsider. The two strands of the braid here are methodology and interpretation. The key to this strategy is to find an assumption made by the method (words can be embedded in multidimensional space) that matches the historical question (racialized discourse was multidimensional).

Digital historians have a firm justification for thinking that they can find shared assumptions between historical interpretations and digital methods because algorithms only work well when they are well matched to assumptions about our data and sources (Wolpert and Macready; Robinson). This implies that any good digital historical work will have a compatibility—even a harmony—between the methods applied and the sources and conclusions. We can use this harmony as the basis for combining discussion of methods with discussion of interpretations into a counterpoint, where methodology and interpretations are not discrete but mutually constitutive.

In my own work, I have found that identifying the assumptions common to the digital methods that I employ and the historical questions that I ask is the best way to blend discussion of methods and interpretations. For example, Kellen Funk and I have been working on the Field Code, a legal code of civil procedure drafted in New York in the late 1840s and subsequently adopted with modifications by most American states. (For a summary of this project, see Funk and Mullen, "A Servile Copy" and "Spine of American Law.") As we wrote up our research, we alternated between explaining how the minhash/locality-sensitive hashing algorithm can compare the similarities of documents (Leskovec, Rajaraman, and Ullman, Ch. 3) and interpreting the patterns of similarities among the Field Code states, between explaining how the affinity propagation algorithm clusters similar documents by finding an "exemplar" document (Frey and Dueck) and arguing about the significance of exemplar sections of the code dealing with debt collection and racialized exclusions of witnesses. While we initially contemplated a methods section modeled on a scientific paper, we found that we could braid a discussion of our interpretations with our computational historical research, because our computational work produced accurate historical interpretations when it depended most closely on what we knew from traditional methods.

Finding such congruence between methods and sources is only one strategy for crafting a braided narrative. While that specific strategy might not be applicable in every instance, the more important point is how the structure of writing can aid the task of combining methods and interpretation. Adapting a braided narrative recognizes that our most powerful technology for integrating divergent approaches remains prose. Digital history has often been willing to experiment with forms of scholarship beyond the journal article, book, and blog post, even if this experimentation has gone by the wayside in recent years. But none of these experiments has overthrown—and they may in fact have underscored—the importance of using prose to explain scholarship, even if that scholarship includes newer modes of working such as visualizations.

Prose remains our best method for achieving a synthesis of methods and argumentation, yet digital historians need a way to structure their prose that suits their purposes. The braided narrative proposed by our social historical forebears proves to be a useful model for writing digital history that not only explains its methods but also produces scholarly interpretations.

NOTES

1. http://programminghistorian.org/.
2. http://www.themacroscope.org/2.0/.
3. For example, see Jockers and Arnold and Tilton.
4. Other scholars have also found the roots of digital history in social history or found instructive parallels between the two movements (Hockey; Thomas).
5. https://github.com/.
6. https://figshare.com./
7. Digital literary scholars have gone much further than digital historians in incorporating computational methods and interpretive questions (see, for example, Goldstone and Underwood).

BIBLIOGRAPHY

Afanador-Llach, Maria José, Antonio Rojas Castro, Adam Crymble, Víctor Gayol, Fred Gibbs, Caleb McDaniel, Ian Milligan, Evan Taparata, Amanda Visconti, and Jeri Wieringa, eds. *The Programming Historian.* 2nd ed. 2017. http://programminghistorian .org/.

Arnold, Taylor, and Lauren Tilton. *Humanities Data in R.* New York: Springer, 2015. http:// link.springer.com/10.1007/978-3-319-20702-5.

Blevins, Cameron. "Digital History's Perpetual Future Tense." In *Debates in Digital Humanities 2016,* edited by Matthew K. Gold and Lauren F. Klein, online edition (University of Minnesota Press, 2016). http://dhdebates.gc.cuny.edu/debates/text/77.

Cordell, Ryan. "Reprinting, Circulation, and the Network Author in Antebellum Newspapers." *American Literary History* 27, no. 3 (September 1, 2015): 417–45. doi:10.1093/alh /ajv028.

Fischer, David Hackett. "The Braided Narrative: Substance and Form in Social History." In *The Literature of Fact: Selected Papers from the English Institute,* edited by Angus Fletcher, 109–33. New York: Columbia University Press, 1976. http://hdl.handle .net/2027/heb.06531.0001.001.

Frey, Brendan J., and Delbert Dueck. "Clustering by Passing Messages between Data Points." *Science* 315 (2007): 972–76. doi: 10.1126/science.1136800.

Funk, Kellen, and Lincoln A. Mullen. "A Servile Copy: Text Reuse and Medium Data in American Civil Procedure." In *Forum: Die geisteswissenschaftliche Perspektive: Welche Forschungsergebnisse lassen Digital Humanities erwarten? [Forum: With the Eyes of a Humanities Scholar: What Results Can We Expect from Digital Humanities?]*, *Rechtsgeschichte [Legal History]* 24 (2016): 341–43. doi: 10.12946/rg24/341–343.

Funk, Kellen, and Lincoln A. Mullen. "The Spine of American Law: Digital Text Analysis and U.S. Legal Practice." *American Historical Review* 123, no. 1 (2018): 1–33, doi: 0.1093/ahr/123.1.132.

Gavin, Michael, Collin Jennings, Lauren Kersey, and Brad Pasanek. "The Force of Language: Vector Semantics, Conceptual History, and Close Reading." In *Debates in Digital Humanities 2017*, edited by Matthew K. Gold and Lauren F. Klein, online edition (University of Minnesota Press, 2017).

Graham, Shawn, Ian Milligan, and Scott Weingart. *Exploring Big Historical Data: The Historian's Macroscope*. Hackensack, N.J.: Imperial College Press, 2015. http://www.themacroscope.org/2.0/.

Goldstone, Andrew, and Ted Underwood. "The Quiet Transformations of Literary Studies: What Thirteen Thousand Scholars Could Tell Us." *New Literary History* 45, no. 3 (2014): 359–84. doi:10.1353/nlh.2014.0025.

Hockey, Susan. "The History of Humanities Computing." In *A Companion to Digital Humanities,* edited by Susan Schreibman, Ray Siemens, and John Unsworth. Malden, Mass.: Blackwell, 2004. http://digitalhumanities.org:3030/companion/view?docId=blackwell/9781405103213/9781405103213.xml&chunk.id=ss1-2-1.

Jockers, Matthew L. *Text Analysis with R for Students of Literature*. Cham, Switzerland: Springer, 2014. http://link.springer.com/10.1007/978-3-319-03164-4.

Jockers, Matthew, and Gabi Kirilloff. "Understanding Gender and Character Agency in the 19th Century Novel." *Journal of Cultural Analytics* (2016), http://culturalanalytics.org/2016/12/understanding-gender-and-character-agency-in-the-19th-century-novel/. doi:10.22148/16.010.

Leskovec, Jure, Anand Rajaraman, and Jeff Ullman, *Mining of Massive Datasets*. 2nd ed. Cambridge: Cambridge University Press, 2014. http://www.mmds.org/#ver21.

Robinson, David. "K-means Clustering Is Not a Free Lunch." Variance Explained. January 16, 2015, http://varianceexplained.org/r/kmeans-free-lunch/.

Scheinfeldt, Tom. "Sunset for Ideology, Sunrise for Methodology?" In *Debates in Digital Humanities 2012*, edited by Matthew K. Gold, online edition (University of Minnesota Press, 2012), http://dhdebates.gc.cuny.edu/debates/text/39.

Scheineldt, Tom. "Where's the Beef? Does Digital Humanities Have to Answer Questions?" In *Debates in Digital Humanities 2012*, edited by Matthew K. Gold, online edition (University of Minnesota Press, 2012), http://dhdebates.gc.cuny.edu/debates/text/18.

Schmidt, Benjamin. "Do Digital Humanists Need to Understand Algorithms?" In *Debates in the Digital Humanities 2016*, edited by Matthew K. Gold and Lauren F. Klein,

online edition (University of Minnesota Press, 2016), http://dhdebates.gc.cuny.edu
/debates/text/99.

Smith, David A., Ryan Cordell, and Abby Mullen. "Computational Methods for Uncovering Reprinted Texts in Antebellum Newspapers." *American Literary History* 27, no. 3
(September 1, 2015): E1–15. doi:10.1093/alh/ajv029.

Thomas II, William G. "Computing and the Historical Imagination." In *A Companion to
Digital Humanities,* edited by Susan Schreibman, Ray Siemens, and John Unsworth.
Malden, Mass.: Blackwell, 2004. http://digitalhumanities.org:3030/companion/view?
docId=blackwell/9781405103213/9781405103213.xml&chunk.id=ss1-2-5.

Wolpert, David H., and William G. Macready. "No Free Lunch Theorems for Optimiza-
tion." *IEEE Transactions on Evolutionary Computation* 1, no. 1 (April 1997): 67–82,
http://ti.arc.nasa.gov/m/profile/dhw/papers/78.pdf.

Are Para-Academic Career Paths about People or Places? Reflections on Infrastructure as the European Alt-ac

JENNIFER EDMOND

The field of digital humanities has found itself at the heart of a conflict between shifting practices and static structures as pertains to the creation of knowledge as a form of labor. The collaborative, interdisciplinary nature of the field, along with its disruptive entry into many disciplines and teams with a long tradition of largely textual methodologies, has made it fertile ground for both the development and disaffection of individuals pursuing unique career paths in institutions conceptualized according to distinct classes of academics, administrators, technicians, and librarians they do not neatly fit into. As with digital humanities itself, the move toward giving a voice to such para-academics, and the new forms of implicit and explicit labor contract they inhabit, was clearly recognized in the United States before it came to Europe (if indeed one can say it has come to Europe at all). And, in a further parallel with digital humanities as a field, paths toward the recognition and valorization of these new roles have been very different in Europe than in the United States, both in terms of what nomenclature has emerged, what forces have been harnessed to surface nascent practices, and what actors have wielded the greatest influence over the process. The comparison between European and North American systems is an instructive one, however, as the two approaches—one more person-centric and the other more resonant of labs and facilities—might each potentially learn much from the other's differently constrained progress.

The American "Alternate Academy"

The fact that the United States has been far ahead of Europe in recognizing and validating the contribution of individuals in hybrid academic–service positions is in part due to the later start of the overall development of digital humanities in Europe, but also to the differing framework conditions that exist for research in Europe as opposed to the United States. By and large, U.S. institutions operate much more independently than European ones; they are influenced far less by national research and education regulations, national research evaluation systems, or standard researcher contract models. Institutional autonomy greatly eases the mainstreaming of new work paradigms, as empowered individuals within institutions find ways of motivating and embedding new classes of contribution in ways that match local conditions. In particular, the so-called alt-ac movement has revealed much about the breadth of institutional responses, both good and bad, to their changing human capital needs, as well as the motivations, needs, and experiences of the people pursuing hybrid research career roles.

The discourse of the American alt-ac experience was codified by the 2011 online collection of essays *#Alt-Academy* (Nowiskie), which highlights the breadth of institutional types, motivations, preparations, and experiences, from the liberating to the horrific, that shape the working life of the alt-ac scholar. There are a number of threads within this discourse that can be used to highlight the differences and similarities between the U.S. experience for such professionals and what is now emerging in Europe. According to the documents of this tradition, not only do the individuals choosing or falling into alt-ac positions commonly produce high-impact work outside of traditional disciplines but they also actively seek to bring together areas of knowledge and to innovate within their organizations and networks. Often these individuals write grants to secure their own employment and gravitate toward the tasks of building productive bridges between the silos they sit between, with the nature of the work itself helping them to scope out problems and identify opportunities (Stanton et al.). The fact that such a wide range of individuals and experiences have been able to come together under a common identity is a key indicator of the bottom-up nature of the emergence of this community. Finally, the breadth of the research and perspectives collected under the alt-ac banner illustrates the active and collaborative engagement in these issues by a wide range of institutions like CLIR (Council on Library and Information Resources) and the IMLS (Institute of Museum and Library Services), as well as by university-based programs such as the University of Virginia's Scholar's Lab.[1]

The European Infrastructure Worker as an Emerging Alt-ac?

If these three characteristics of the U.S.-based alt-ac discourse—the transformational character, the bottom-up development, and the breadth of institutions engaged—can be seen as essential characteristics of the U.S. movement, then Europe can only be said to have experienced partially similar trends. Transformational individuals in unique and sometimes precarious roles do exist, but patterns of institutional engagement are quite different, and perhaps most importantly, no recognizable bottom-up organization and empowerment have occurred among these widely distributed and diverse individuals, who may belong to very different work cultures and indeed speak and work through very different languages.

Curiously, the grassroots discourse of the North American alt-ac is beginning to intersect in Europe with much more staid policy positions, with the effect that top-down imperatives, rather than a critical mass of atomized and marginalized individual experiences, are instigating the emergence of a similar set of professional identities. This inversion is not necessarily obvious at first glance, however. Research on emerging research professions in Europe discusses hybrid academic roles under a wide range of terms, including many permutations of "data-X" roles (Lyon; Swan and Brown), such as the data scientist, data manager, or data librarian; the facilitator (Lankes et al.); the "techie"; or the project manager, the administrator, or the network manager. The prevalence of such terms on both sides of the Atlantic Ocean points toward the convergence mentioned earlier. As varied as the names may be, they all point toward a similar pattern of research engagement: borrowing strongly from the professorial model, but remixing its elements in new combinations or with new elements. Of course, these people and roles have existed for a long time, but at the current moment, when a consolidated view of their work could be so useful and productive, the similarities among their contributions to research are obscured behind the plethora of descriptors used to characterize them.

One terminological point of consolidation that is emerging from this diversity and that engages with the work of these many types of individuals, is infrastructure. Particularly in a North American context, "infrastructure" is still a contested term, as prominent voices such as Tanya Clement and Alan Liu invoke the term to highlight the lack of attention to (or support for) the resources on which DH work is based. In Europe, however, the term is rapidly stabilizing, in large part because the development of infrastructure is currently being driven heavily from the top-down imperative of the massive funding program (soon to enter its ninth multiyear cycle and known as "Horizon Europe") shared by the EU member states. Since 2006, Europeans have been able to refer to the European Commission's ESFRI (European Strategy Forum for Research Infrastructures) roadmap for a definition of what is and is not an infrastructure, electing to include "facilities, resources or services . . . associated human resources . . . major equipment or sets of instruments, as well as knowledge-containing resources such as collections, archives and databases. . . . [They may be] 'single-sited', 'distributed', or 'virtual' . . . related to data management, enabling information and communication . . . such as grid, computing, software and middleware" (European Commission).

This definition is inclusive, to the point of seeming more a laundry list than a strategic program, and intentionally so, but it is by no means the only or even the broadest definition of research infrastructure that has been proposed. See for instance, this one, proposed by Tilson, Lyytinen, and Sørensen: "Morphologically, digital infrastructures can be defined as shared, unbounded, heterogeneous, open, and evolving sociotechnical systems comprising an installed base of diverse information technology capabilities and their user, operations, and design communities" (748–49).

These quotations illustrate two important points about the ways in which researchers, managers, and policy makers view and manage the development of infrastructure within the European context, each of which has an impact on the people who populate and support the work going on within research infrastructures. First, there is a clear effort to be broad and to allow infrastructure development (and, dare we say it, funding) to encompass a significant amount of activity emerging from individual research practices, giving space to innovation not possible in institutions with more clearly defined missions, such as universities. Second, the policy language illustrates a struggle to get away from a concrete, bricks-and-mortar view of infrastructure, a move that allows various types of knowledge, its producers, and its external manifestations to be considered under the banner of infrastructure.

It is within this struggle over the implications of discourse that I locate the further terminological transposition from the U.S.-based (alternate) *academy*—that is, an institution made of people—to the European context of *infrastructure* as the place where quasi-academic professional pathways are becoming an established norm. Given the pains being taken to extend the concept of infrastructure beyond the realm of machines and buildings, this difference between the United States and Europe might not be seen as a threat to progress in mainstreaming and integrating new skills and careers in a meaningful way into the research ecosystem. But there are key differences inherent in Europe's different emphasis that give pause for concern. Alt-ac as it is known in North America was a bottom-up development, driven and described by practitioners. Infrastructure, however, is seldom if ever fully bottom-up, and the needs of individuals in the system will therefore face greater difficulties finding expression. Furthermore, the idea of an academy aligns with the hierarchies of academic institutions (even while it challenges them). Infrastructure, for all the need and desire that policymakers invest in redefining it, aligns semantically with generic service missions and with the nonacademic. Herein lies a key difference, but also an opportunity for mutual exchange of learning and experiences between the grassroots, person-centric U.S.-based rhetoric and activities and the policy-driven, institutionalized European ones.

Scope of the Problem

When starting from the standpoint of infrastructure, the professional space encompassed by individuals with para-academic career paths in Europe will almost by necessity be broader than that delineated by the term "academy." The need for research professionals who are both data savvy and have disciplinary training exists across a wide spectrum of institutional and national contexts, as well as within models not bounded by the constraints of any given preexisting system, with the result that individuals with very similar roles are required to work under very different conditions. Although it is not without additional concerns, the fact that DH specialists in Europe can ally themselves (and are, de facto, being allied by the policy environment) not only with the humanities, library, and computer science colleagues but also with a wider range of data experts is in many ways a potential strength.

This embedding in a wider context and the overall demand for such talent should, in theory, encourage good work conditions and fulfilling roles to be available for workers within infrastructure. The entre/intra-preneurial nature of the alt-ac scholar does have its cost, however, particularly in Europe, because the kind of autonomy gained through self-funding via grants or very distinct job roles can lead also to isolation within the institution, marked by short-term contracts as well as a diminished focus on individual scholarship. In one of the most interesting contributions to the body of work on the alt-ac model, Tom Scheinfeldt writes about the right to have one's work viewed as generative and scholarly—essentially an individual's right to hold authority and agency in an epistemic sense. For Scheinfeldt, giving up the expectation of tenure (the U.S. hallmark of a "real" academic job) did not equate to an admission that his work was unworthy of publication. Indeed, he, like so many of his peers, did work that he felt proved its value in a way that transcended the known norms: "It can't be tenure track or nothing. My work requires a 'third way.'"

Scheinfeldt's statement highlights one of the most common frustrations of the currently emerging cohort of infrastructure workers: even though their work may be excellent, achieving at times even higher social and professional impact than that of their more traditional peers, the lack of any institutional structure that might recognize their work means that they can be made to feel it is not valued by their institutions or not considered to meet the definition of scholarship. The primary reason for this lack of recognition may be practical, even if it is unsatisfying: the gatekeepers for the traditional organizational power centers do not necessarily control or foster these individuals, in large part because the roles do not map to a known model internally or to any particular responsibilities recognized as such by management. Even libraries in Europe have often resisted this kind of expansion of their remit, not because they see it as irrelevant to their mission, but because to do so would also implicitly ratify certain large and unfunded mandates, such as (for a university library) the preservation of digital research created within the institution. This is by and large not intentional or ill meant, even as it remains a common occurrence in conservative institutions: but it poses a particular threat in Europe, where the nature of the universities as public sector organizations makes them beholden to issues of contract, work rules, and tenure that are anathema to otherwise similar institutions. Infrastructural thinking has yet to arrive at this level, and yet this is where many of the much-needed, highly skilled individuals will come from and is indeed one of the key places where they may be called on to contribute.

What emerges therefore is in part a domain-specific challenge, but one that incorporates a data challenge and a human resource management challenge as well. Infrastructure workers in the humanities become generalists in a world of specialists, finding themselves in roles where they are expected to continually develop their skills and grow in response to changing institutional needs and changing technologies; however, they are not necessarily expected to mature into leadership roles, which in the current systems can be rare, undefined, or require very different qualifications from those people who might report to a particular leader or manager. This raises significant issues about the notion of "psychological contract fulfillment"; that is, an employee's beliefs regarding the reciprocal obligations that exist between the employee and the institution that employs her (Rousseau). Typically, the psychological contract is enshrined in such matters as opportunities for promotion, pay, financial rewards other than salary, type of work, the demands/pressure of the job, the hours to be worked, and personal control over day-to-day tasks. For the infrastructure worker, this contract may be different from that of many of her peers, because the nature of the position, the institutional awareness of the challenges it does or does not present, and indeed the commitment needed to complete the assigned tasks are likely to be in flux. These undetermined aspects of such a role will make the creation and fulfillment of robust psychological contracts far more difficult, and even a potentially critical point of weakness, because the extent to which the psychological contract is fulfilled, as perceived by the employee, can have a very strong impact on the individual's attitudes and behavior at work. The perceived breach of an employee's psychological contract has been shown to lead to higher turnover; lower commitment to the project, organization, or team; and a reduced likelihood to engage in "citizenship" behaviors, many of which are the lifeblood of the alt-ac path. Furthermore, the extent to which the research institute fulfills or breaches this psychological contract (intentionally or unintentionally) also affects whether these individuals see themselves more as members of the organization/ institute or just of the project team. This is an identity constraint that can, in turn, make them less visible to senior management and lead to fewer opportunities for development and advancement. These issues are not only important to those concerned with rewarding contributions and creating optimized systems of science but also for their impact on human resources, leading as they do to increased expense and difficulty in attracting and retaining specialized and qualified individuals.

Rethinking the Laboratory

Perhaps the ubiquity of change in our research ecosystems is in part responsible for the conservatism that reigns in some cultures of research, a conservatism that resists the widespread application of new conceptualizations of what research is and does. This is not unique to the digital humanities. An interesting view of the tenacity of hierarchies and the purposes they serve can be drawn from ethnographies of science, in particular Karin Knorr Cetina's *Epistemic Cultures* (also noted by Clement). In the microbiology lab in particular, the hierarchy of junior and senior members serves a very specific purpose: to separate two very distinct research roles that contribute to overall lab or project success. In the less experienced category are the researchers whose work favors relationships with objects: these relationships manifest themselves as the mastery of one or more techniques, contributing to the overall laboratory "repertoire of expertise." In contrast to this is the scientific orientation toward the "social" elements of a field that are necessary to supporting the life of the laboratory as a whole: "a laboratory-world that needs to be financed, motivated, situated, reproduced, and intellectually nourished from outside through regular infusions of information" (Knorr Cetina, 221). The microbiology lab in Knorr Cetina's study does not sublimate the individual identity into that of the team or project to the same degree as the high-energy physics research group she also studied. The role division seen in each context does imply, however, that knowledge creation is perceived somehow as an integrated social function (sharing knowledge derived from the various object-based experts with the wider community), while the work of those focused on specific component tasks or processes is not necessarily viable in isolation and therefore is considered to be of lesser or less distinct value.

It would be pointless to deny that this hierarchy represents a certain reality: more senior members of a team are very often more able to contribute at a higher, more integrated level because of their experience, knowledge, and trusted networks. The junior members of the team benefit from the senior members' expertise and the training and mentoring they receive—indeed, senior researchers often report frustration with the requirement to prioritize the skill development of the students and researchers they supervise over their own research interests. The hierarchies of the lab system work, so long as the benefits accrued at each level are recognized and honored and the pathway to advancement is not in any way blocked. Unfortunately, however, psychological contracts begin to unravel when social or hybrid initiatives that integrate knowledge (long thought to stem from the role of the lab's principal investigator almost exclusively) arise out of object or functional levels of the organization as knowledge systems become more complex and these "objects" themselves become larger and more synthetic. It is here that the function of DH infrastructure as a laboratory is often impaired: the fact that the skill sets (the object- or function-related bodies of expertise) have arisen out of a heterogeneous set of perspectives leads to the development of career paths that look more like mazes. In these mazes, some paths lead inexorably to dead ends, and others to productive recursions, where forgotten knowledge suddenly finds new relevance. Still others look like they should lead to senior positions, but do not, with leadership instead being sought from a point outside of the known ecosystem, institution, or team. In particular, such cases can lead to misunderstandings and frustrations among those who feel always relegated to contributing technique only, when they may have the ability, capacity, and experience to make higher, more integrative social contributions. The evidence for this is as diverse and widespread as it is anecdotal: a senior library staff member at a prominent university takes an academic job at a much lower-prestige institution; an externally appointed director with very little DH experience becomes head of a

DH research center or initiative; an infrastructure project team instigated by domain experts realizes late in the day that they need a technical or data science expert, but fails to incorporate that expert on a sustainable basis. None of this is unique to either the United States or Europe, but the capacity of such systems to respond to the resulting stress manifests differently in each place: a European context of heavily state-funded research and education systems with narrow budgets and limiting public sector contracts versus the very different financial pressures so much more common in the United States felt within private institutions answerable to a different kind of bottom line.

This difference also presents an opportunity to harness the growing presence of the alt-ac career path, whatever we may call it, toward new and perhaps greater ends. The changes in professional identity that have long been developing within research ecosystems can now be said to have both a manifestation as an academy and as an infrastructure. U.S.-based and European perspectives can each benefit from how they might incorporate practices from each other, with the alternate academy coming to see itself as a persistent yet distinct layer in the foundation of academic work, and infrastructure workers realizing how, by coming together, they could begin to conceptualize themselves as an academic cohort in their own right, defining in their own terms the value of their knowledge. Together, this pressure from above and below may bring focus to the issue underlying the changes in research work, which is the fact that the capacity for knowledge creation is no longer limited by the institution where one works or the professional title one might have. Working toward a new paradigm by which to understand contributions to knowledge will not only unlock new conceptualizations of labor and careers but will also support new visions of innovation and discovery based not on the needs of industry or research portfolios of a lucky few, but on the passions and capabilities of a greatly expanded class of researchers.

Note

I am grateful to Agiati Benardou, Ann Gow, and Susan Schreibman for their contributions to an early draft of this chapter.

1. It should be recognized that, although my argument reflects a generally positive attitude toward the discourse of the "alt-ac," the term has also come under some criticism for the implication that might be read into it of a secondary status for the people it describes. It is beyond the scope of this chapter to explore these fissures in the North American discourse.

BIBLIOGRAPHY

Antonijević, Smiljana. *Amongst Digital Humanists: An Ethnographic Study of Digital Knowledge Production.* New York: Palgrave, 2015.

Boyer, Ernest. *Scholarship Reconsidered: Priorities of the Professoriate.* Princeton, N.J.: Carnegie Foundation for the Advancement of Teaching, 1997.

CERN. "Careers in CERN—Recruitments Policy." http://jobs.web.cern.ch/content /recruitment-policy. Accessed August 1, 2016.

Clement, Tanya. "Where Is Methodology in Digital Humanities?" In *Debates in the Digital Humanities 2016,* edited by Matthew K. Gold and Lauren F. Klein, 153–75. Minneapolis: University of Minnesota Press.

European Commission. *European Roadmap for Research infrastructures.* Luxembourg: Office for Official Publications of the European Communities, 2006. https://ec.europa.eu /research/infrastructures/pdf/esfri/esfri_roadmap/roadmap_2006/esfri_roadmap_2006 _en.pdf#view=fit&pagemode=none. Accessed July 28, 2016.

European Commission, Directorate-General for Information, Society and Media. "Skills and Human Resources for Infrastructures within Horizon 2020: Consultation Workshop for Horizon 2020." Brussels: European Commission, 2012. https://www.innovation policyplatform.org/system/files/European_Commission_2012-Skills%20and%20 Human%20Resources%20for%20e-Infrastructures%20within%20Horizon%20 2020_5.pdf. Accessed August 1, 2016.

Gibbons, Michael, Camille Limoges, Helga Nowotny, Simon Schwartzman, Peter Scott, and Martin Trow. *The New Production of Knowledge: The Dynamics of Science and Research in Contemporary Society.* London: SAGE, 1994.

Harley, Diane, Sophia Krzys Acord, Sarah Earl-Novell, Shannon Lawrence, and C. Judson King. *Assessing the Future Landscape of Scholarly Communication: An Exploration of Faculty Values and Needs in Seven Disciplines.* Berkeley, Calif.: Center for Studies in Higher Education, 2010.

Knorr Cetina, Karin. *Epistemic Cultures.* Cambridge, Mass: Harvard University Press, 1999.

Lankes, R. David, Derrick Cogburn, Megan Oakleaf, and Jeffrey Stanton. *Cyberinfrastructure Facilitators: New Approaches to Information Professionals for e-Research.* Oxford: Oxford Internet Institute, 2008.

League of European Research Universities (LERU). *Harvesting Talent: Strengthening Research Careers in Europe.* Leuven: LERU, 2010. http://www.leru.org/files/publica tions/LERU_paper_Harvesting_talent.pdf. Accessed January 13, 2015.

Liu, Alan. "Drafts for *Against the Cultural Singularity* (book in progress)." May 2, 2016, http://liu.english.ucsb.edu/drafts-for-against-the-cultural-singularity. Accessed August 14, 2017.

Lyon, Liz. *Dealing with Data: Roles, Rights, Responsibilities and Relationships. Consultancy Report.* Bath: UK Office for Library and Information Networking, 2007, http://www .jisc.ac.uk/media/documents/programmes/digitalrepositories/dealing_with_data _report-final.pdf. Accessed August 1, 2016.

McCarty, Willard. "The Residue of Uniqueness." *Historical Social Research/Historische Sozialforschung* 37, no. 3 (2012): 24–45.

McGann, Jerome. "Sustainability: The Elephant in the Room." *Online Humanities Scholarship: The Shape of Things to Come.* 2010, http://rup.rice.edu/shapeofthings.

Nowiskie, Bethany, ed. "#Alt-Academy: 01. Alternative Academic Careers for Humanities Scholars." July 2011, http://mediacommons.futureofthebook.org/alt-ac/sites/media commons.futureofthebook.org.alt-ac/files/alt-academy01.pdf. Accessed January 6, 2015.

Rousseau, Denise M.. "Psychological and Implied Contracts in Organizations." *Employee Responsibilities and Rights Journal* 2, no. 2 (1989): 121–39.

Scheinfeldt, Tom. "Making It Count: Toward a Third Way." October 2, 2008, http://found history.org/2008/10/making-it-count-toward-a-third-way/.

Schomburg, Harald, and Ulrich Teichler. *Higher Education and Graduate Employment in Europe: Results from Graduates Surveys from Twelve Countries*. Amsterdam: Springer, 2006.

Stanton, Jeffrey M., Youngseek Kim, Megan Oakleaf, R. David Lankes, Paul Gandel, Derrick Cogburn, and Elizabeth D. Liddy. "Education for eScience professionals: Job Analysis, Curriculum Guidance, and Program Considerations." *Journal of Education for Library and Information Science* 52, no. 2 (2011): 79–94.

Swan, Alma, and Sheridan Brown. *The Skills, Role and Career Structure of Data Scientists and Curators: An Assessment of Current Practice and Future Needs*. Bristol, UK: Joint Information Services Committee, 2008. http://eprints.soton.ac.uk/266675/. Accessed August 1, 2016.

Tilson, David, Kalle Lyytinen, and Carsten Sørensen. "Research Commentary—Digital Infrastructures: The Missing IS Research Agenda." *Information Systems Research* 21, no. 4 (2010): 748–59.

The Making of the Digital Working Class: Social History, Digital Humanities, and Its Sources

ANDREW GOMEZ

The history departments of the 1950s were hardly bastions of diversity. Stocked by white men and centered on political history and its most prominent figures, they reflected broader trends in the academy in the pre–civil rights era. But in the 1960s, a movement known as the New Social History, led by scholars looking to retell history from below, emerged to produce a torrent of research that challenged the traditional boundaries of historical actors worthy of study. As articulated most famously by E. P. Thompson in *The Making of the English Working Class,* this movement aimed to save previously unrecognized groups from the "enormous condescension of posterity" (12). Following Thompson, working-class communities, immigrant groups, African American citizens, and women, among other marginalized groups, soon became the primary focus of historical inquiry. Central to this project was a reexamination of the sources that facilitated such research. The history of "Great Men" was driven by large print archives and the writings and correspondence of political and military figures. Conversely, the raw materials of the social historian were rooted in oral history, personal collections, community newspapers, court records, and other ephemeral sources. This reassessment of source material was a critical first step toward carving out the legacies of the figures previously ignored by history.

As a social historian whose work has become increasingly digital, I frequently see the parallels between the historical trajectory of my own discipline and that of digital humanities. Just as in history, digital humanities has for years been wrestling with inequities regarding gender, race, and ethnicity in terms of both projects and participation—inequities that have been detailed in different ways by a variety of scholars (Bailey; McPherson; Earhart, "The Diverse History"; Posner). However, a move toward a more representative digital humanities must also involve an analysis of the types of sources that guide projects, similar to the analysis that sparked the New Social History. The digital humanities thrives on abundance; large, open datasets and massive text-mining experiments have become the calling card of the largest, most well-known grant-funded projects. Given the premium placed on big data, however, DH practitioners have fallen back into the trap of privileging valorized subjects who simply left an abundance of artifacts behind. In a sense, the old politics of who deserved to be historicized has become the new politics of who deserves to be digitized.

Indeed, the politics and economics of digitization present some of the largest obstacles to creating diverse collections. The collection policies of many libraries and archives often reinforce the underrepresentation of certain historical figures and communities. For example, the Seeley G. Mudd Manuscript Library at Princeton University uses a "targeted digitization" (Callahan) process to guide some of their digitization efforts. Based on Google Analytics data culled from their websites, they identify materials that are of interest to the public and digitize corresponding materials. Keeping patrons in mind is critical for designing collection practices, but it should also be clear how following patron interest alone would privilege the most well-known events and figures. This phenomenon is only magnified in the current era of widespread austerity, when every line item in a budget must be justified by use.[1] But one of the enduring lessons of social history is that the availability of source material (or lack thereof) often determines the projects' result. As Amy Earhart has shown, the democratic promise of web-based projects has gone largely unfulfilled as a result of limited efforts to diversify the "digital canon" ("Can Information Be Unfettered?"). As archivists, librarians, researchers, and practitioners, we must understand that choosing what gets digitized is an inherently political decision, and at stake, as one public historian noted, is "what counts as part of our cultural heritage and who gets to decide" (Rizzo).

A critical part of any shift must also involve a creative reimagining of existing sources. We are beginning to see the payoffs that result from revisiting older texts and datasets, such as Tobias Higbie's "Situations and Relations," which employs a digitized version of the 1925 *American Labor Who's Who* in order to visualize networks in the American labor movement relating to educational background, geographic linkages, familial heritage, and a host of other features.[2] The initial findings of Higbie's research point to connections between workers, labor organizations, and educational institutions that were previously obscured. A similar approach might be employed with sources that focus on racial injustice or the histories of marginalized groups. Texts like Pauli Murray's 1951 *States' Laws on Race and Color* and Charles Spurgeon Johnson and Lewis Wade Jones's 1941 *Statistical Atlas of Southern Counties,* which focus on cataloging Jim Crow segregation, economic inequality, and state violence, are other rich documents with a firm sense of geography and spatial relationships—precisely the types of sources that should prompt our digital imaginations.

Digital humanists could also stand to learn by emulating some of the earliest digital history projects, which focused on digitizing and analyzing nontraditional sources. While recent discussions have sought to underscore the differences between digital history and digital humanities (Robertson), it is also clear that there is considerable overlap between the two fields. Many of the early digital history projects, led by James Gregory, Edward Ayers, Roy Rosenzweig, Stephen Brier, Joshua Brown, Jan Reiff, James Grossman, and Ann Durkin Keating, among others, were driven by an impulse to build digital archives and scholarship around the experiences of working people and individual communities.[3] For example, Ayers and the staff at the University of Richmond's Digital Scholarship Lab largely emphasized Southern history, and Virginian history in particular—an emphasis that continues to this day. They have leveraged their resources to create projects that actively address regional concerns. The *Los Angeles Aqueduct Digital Platform* (LAADP) at UCLA serves a similar purpose. Designed as a collaboration between the UCLA Library and Metabolic Studio, the platform functions as both an archive and a source of scholarship on the subject. I led the capstone project for the platform, working with a team of undergraduate students to produce a series of articles on the aqueduct's history using DH tools. The team used a social history framework to tell narratives of communities that have been adversely affected by the aqueduct's construction, resulting in contributions that used disparate source material to place Native American communities, immigrant groups, and working-class towns at the center of controversies over water rights in Southern California.

As the *Aqueduct* project makes clear, digital humanists should actively pursue digitizing additional nontraditional sources in an effort to produce projects that pair diverse sources with DH methods. At the same time, there also needs to be a discussion over the occasional discord between nontraditional sources and core DH methods. Some nontraditional sources can be easily analyzed using historical GIS, text mining, and network visualization tools. But a significant number remain incompatible with these tools.[4] Off-the-shelf DH tools are most successful when working with homogeneous sources, which are precisely the types of sources that are in short supply when working with marginalized groups and actors. Short-lived community newspapers, handwritten notes, personal photo collections, pamphlets, and various types of ephemeral sources guide this type of work. These sources are often fragmented and rarely extensive. It is only when they are paired alongside one another that a more comprehensive narrative became possible. And yet, most DH tools do not allow for such pairings.

While digital humanists must continue to work toward combining core methods with more diverse sources, we must also make space for alternative approaches. As Amy Earhart has noted in her blog devoted to the history of digital humanities, digital projects centered on diverse subjects have a long history ("The Diverse History"). This legacy continues with a wide array of digital projects devoted to diverse communities.[5] For example, *The LatiNegrxs Project,* hosted on Tumblr, uses a combination of media, historical ephemera, and news stories to portray the complexity of the African diaspora and black identity. The *AfroCrowd* Wikipedia project carries a distinctly public mission, actively recruiting contributors to narrow the racial gap among Wikipedia editors. These are precisely the types of projects that take a creative view of source material and point to the diverse history of these communities, but they often go unmentioned in the most high-profile discussions on the digital humanities.[6] As Moya Bailey has pointed out, we should be "meeting people where they are" and not just creating space "at an already established table." Just as social history opened the doors to the methods and sources that were most suitable to the subject matter they sought to bring to light, we must therefore take a broader view of digital humanities that is not limited to text mining, data visualization, and other such valorized methodologies.

In a 1985 roundtable discussion that reflected on the significance of social history, Raphael Samuel zeroed in on what gave the field its impact: "its oppositional character." Social history was intended as a disruption in terms of both content and method. Similar phrases have been employed to describe the digital humanities.[7] The evolution of social history thus provides an interesting parallel, one that shows a possible path toward a more inclusive relationship between source material and scholarship. Digital humanities is the beneficiary of an energy and enthusiasm borne out of new technology and the potential to provide new analytical lenses for the humanities. However, if the field continues to emphasize a particular methodological scope and does not reflect on the limitations of extant source material, its ultimate reach will be limited.

NOTES

1. In a 2014 article, Misty De Meo explored the limits of digitization amid widespread cuts to the Canadian national archives. Beyond presenting various staffing and workflow challenges, she also noted that libraries and archives tend to funnel limited funds toward digitizing collections that have the broadest appeal. As she notes, these strategies open the door to "erase the histories of marginalized groups while privileging well-documented pop history such as wars."

2. See Tobias Higbie, "Situations and Relations," http://socialjusticehistory.org/proj ects/networkedlabor/?p=38. Other recent projects at UCLA and the University of Richmond's Digital Scholarship Lab have used similar sources to creatively retell the history of the labor movement, water rights, redlining, and emancipation. See http://digital.library .ucla.edu/aqueduct/; http://dsl.richmond.edu/projects/.

3. James Gregory has produced a series of digital history websites devoted primarily to the history of labor activism in the Pacific Northwest. For a complete list, see http:// faculty.washington.edu/gregoryj/. Edward Ayers's *The Valley of the Shadow* project was among the first digital history projects, examining two communities during the Civil War era. See http://valley.lib.virginia.edu/. Roy Rosenzweig, Joshua Brown, and Stephen Brier collaborated on *Who Built America?* Dedicated to the working-class history of the United States, this multimedia project consisted of two CD-ROMs, a History Matters website, and

a two-volume textbook. Jan Reiff, James Grossman, and Ann Durkin Keating were the editors of the digital *Encyclopedia of Chicago.* See http://www.encyclopedia.chicagohistory.org/.

4. This is particularly true for GIS, data visualization, and text mining, which thrive on relative uniformity in datasets. The scattered nature of most social history sources is not amenable to these types of applications. In many cases, DH applications can also be incompatible with the cultural practices of marginalized communities. Projects aimed at correcting some of these issues are still relatively scarce. One example is the Mukurtu Project, a custom CMS designed specifically for indigenous communities looking to control the protocols and dissemination of their cultural and historical artifacts. See http://mukurtu.org/.

5. A Storify post by Adeline Koh highlighted the breadth of digital projects being undertaken on race and ethnicity—and many of these projects are led by women and people of color.

6. As William Pannapacker has pointed out, there has been a growing rift in the digital humanities that funnels prominence to a limited number of institutions and researchers. This is deeply tied to funding and major grant programs that have had a spotty record of funding diverse projects and institutions. As Amy Earhart has highlighted, from 2007–2010, a critical boom period in digital humanities, relatively few of the National Endowment of Humanities Start-Up Grants went to projects centered on diverse texts or communities ("Can Information Be Unfettered?"). See http://www.chronicle.com/blogs/brainstorm /pannapacker-at-mla-digital-humanities-triumphant/30915.

7. See Gold, "The Digital Humanities Moment," http://dhdebates.gc.cuny.edu /debates/text/2; Pannapacker, " 'Big Tent Digital Humanities,' A View from the Edge, Part 1," http://www.chronicle.com/article/Big-Tent-Digital-Humanities/128434.

BIBLIOGRAPHY

AfroCROWD. http://www.afrocrowd.org/.

Bailey, Moya. "All the Digital Humanists Are White, All the Nerds Are Men, but Some of Us Are Brave." *Journal of Digital Humanities* (Winter 2011), http://journalofdigi talhumanities.org/1–1/all-the-digital-humanists-are-white-all-the-nerds-are-men -but-some-of-us-are-brave-by-moya-z-bailey/.

Callahan, Maureen. "Why—and How—We Digitize." Mudd Manuscript Library blog. February 18, 2013, https://blogs.princeton.edu/mudd/2013/02/why-and-how-we-digitize/.

De Leon, Solon, Irma C. Hayssen, and Grace Poole, eds. *The American Labor Who's Who.* New York: Hanford Press, 1925.

De Meo, Misty. "The Politics of Digitization." Model View Culture. February 3, 2014, https://modelviewculture.com/pieces/the-politics-of-digitization.

Earhart, Amy E. "Can Information Be Unfettered? Race and the New Digital Humanities Canon." In *Debates in the Digital Humanities,* edited by Matthew K. Gold. Minneapolis: University of Minnesota Press, 2012. http://dhdebates.gc.cuny.edu/debates /text/16.

Earhart, Amy E. "The Diverse History of Digital Humanities." http://dhhistory.blogspot
.com.

Encyclopedia of Chicago. http://www.encyclopedia.chicagohistory.org/.

Gold, Matthew K. "The Digital Humanities Moment." In *Debates in the Digital Humanities*, edited by Matthew K. Gold. Minneapolis: University of Minnesota Press, 2012.
http://dhdebates.gc.cuny.edu/debates/text/2.

Johnson, Charles Spurgeon, and Lewis Wade Jones. *Statistical Atlas of Southern Counties;
Listing and Analysis of Socio-economic Indices of 1104 Southern Counties*. Chapel
Hill: University of North Carolina Press, 1941.

LatiNegrxs Project, The. http://lati-negros.tumblr.com/.

McPherson, Tara. "Why Are the Digital Humanities So White? Or Thinking the Histories
of Race and Computation." In *Debates in the Digital Humanities,* edited by Matthew
K. Gold. Minneapolis: University of Minnesota Press, 2012. http://dhdebates.gc.cuny
.edu/debates/text/29.

Murray, Pauli. *States' Laws on Race and Color, and Appendices; Containing International
Documents, Federal Laws and Regulations, Local Ordinances and Charts*. Cincin-
nati: Women's Division of Christian Service, Board of Missions and Church Extension, Methodist Church, 1951.

Pannapacker, William. "Pannapacker at MLA: Digital Humanities Triumphant?" *The
Chronicle of Higher Education*. January 8, 2011, https://www.chronicle.com/blogs
/brainstorm/pannapacker-at-mla-digital-humanities-triumphant/30915.

Posner, Miriam. "What's Next: The Radical, Unrealized Potential of Digital Humanities."
July 27, 2015, http://miriamposner.com/blog/whats-next-the-radical-unrealized
-potential-of-digital-humanities.

Rizzo, Mary. "All That is Solid? The Politics of Digitization." National Council on Public
History blog. September 8, 2014, http://ncph.org/history-at-work/all-that-is-solid.

Robertson, Stephen. "The Difference between Digital History and Digital Humanities."
May 23, 2014, http://drstephenrobertson.com/blog-post/the-differences-between
-digital-history-and-digital-humanities/.

Samuel, Raphael. "What Is Social History?" *History Today* 35 (March 1985), http://www
.historytoday.com/raphael-samuel/what-social-history.

Seattle Civil Rights & Labor History Project. http://depts.washington.edu/civilr/.

Thompson, E. P. *The Making of the English Working Class*. New York: Vintage Books, 1966.

Valley of the Shadow, The. http://valley.lib.virginia.edu/.

Who Built America? https://ashp.cuny.edu/who-built-america.

Mixed Methodological Digital Humanities

MOACIR P. DE SÁ PEREIRA

The specter of quantitative methods haunts work in the digital humanities. As James English reminds us, literary studies is not a "'counting' discipline," and when numbers, by definition the foundation of any computational work, appear in a work of literary criticism, they often prompt that "hoary binarism of quantitative versus qualitative" (xii, xiv). With prominent scholars in digital humanities such as Andrew Goldstone aiming to bring literary studies "closer to the social sciences," that binarism returns ("At DH 2014").[1] Studying how the social sciences manage that tension between quantitative and qualitative, however, opens new possibilities for DH practitioners.

Adherents of both quantitative and qualitative methodologies took advantage of a strong reading of Thomas Kuhn's slippery term "paradigm" to launch the "paradigm wars" of the late twentieth century in the social sciences.[2] Relying on the "incommensurability" of paradigms, the combatants entrenched themselves in their views.[3] Methodologies now revealed underlying, incommensurate epistemologies: quantitative methods a positivist epistemology, and qualitative methods a constructivist one. In response, some social scientists, in the spirit of William James and John Dewey, developed a "pragmatic approach" that downplays metaphysical issues, namely by mixing methods (Morgan, 67).[4] So while literary studies—or the humanities more generally—perhaps has no real analog to the paradigm wars, a conscious use of mixed methods would push aside the binarism and let literary study be a counting discipline at the same time as a reading one.

The use of mixed methods in the social, behavioral, and health sciences does what it says on the tin; as the founding editors of the *Journal of Mixed Methods Research* describe it, "The investigator collects and analyzes data, integrates the findings, and draws inferences using both qualitative and quantitative approaches or methods in a single study or a program of inquiry" (Tashakkori and Creswell, 4). The integration, which is to say, the *mixing*, remains vital to the project.[5] Though the term is new, the impulse is at least a half-century old, and the practice has spread throughout a range of fields, especially education, health sciences, sociology, and psychology.[6] Importantly for this chapter, the use of mixed methods has also appeared in geography, uncovering new paths available to pragmatically minded literary scholars with interests in mapping.[7]

Of course, arguing for a methodological macédoine is not terribly new in literary studies either. Along the whole spectrum of digital humanities, from skeptics to devotees, we can find calls for some sort of mixing. For example, Jeremy Rosen encourages "combining digital and computational methods with traditional modes of literary analysis" in a critical response to a DH project. Similarly, but with different stakes, Hoyt Long and Richard Jean So have announced "literary pattern recognition," a "model of reading literary texts that synthesizes familiar humanistic approaches with computational ones" (235).[8] Bringing these digital and nondigital syntheses explicitly under the rubric of mixed methods, however, allows humanities scholars to make use of the decades of debates and discussion regarding mixed methods in the social sciences. By mixing, we can bring our work closer to the social sciences, but we can also learn, as have the social scientists, how to incorporate quantitative methods without necessarily making them the focus of our digital humanistic inquiry.

Geography suffered a similar tempest to the paradigm wars with its "GIS wars." Studying this moment, one can see the sorts of DH skepticism that would follow two decades later.[9] The arrival of digital mapping and analysis in the 1980s forced a reconsideration of geographic practice. Some geographers saw these new technologies as, among other things, a necessary breakthrough for a dormant discipline, a methodology that would tie together a fractured field, or a positivistic riposte to postmodernism. For others, it was "a retreat from ideas to facts," underwritten by the military and visible in full glory during the first Gulf War (Smith, 258).[10] Out of the subsequent détente arose critical GIS.[11] The tendency toward greater quantification would now be held in check by a critical impulse among the practitioners.[12] What had seemed like an especially quantitative and positivist form of social science—after all, land is land and water is water, and these are sensed remotely by satellites—could be mixed.

In practice, qualitative GIS, a mixed methods approach to geography, emerges from a fundamental *"messiness"* where technologies and methods get blurred, mixed, and woven together, leaving behind a practice that "simultaneously revels in the broad diversity of truths *and* turns a critical eye toward those very 'truths'" (Cope and Elwood, "Conclusion," 173). LaDona Knigge, for example, made use of this approach in investigating the concept of vacancy in Buffalo, New York, by iteratively collecting qualitative data through interviews and comparing that to the quantitatively established "patterns of vacancy of visualizations of official [US Census, etc.] data" (Knigge and Cope, "Grounded Visualization and Scale," 111).[13] The official data both provided a context for the specific district where Knigge met with activists and also guided questions in activist interviews. The answers, in turn, led to reconsidering the many ways that vacancy fails to be a binary definition, though it may appear so on a map. A blend of ethnography and cartography, each iteration of analysis and collection expands the interpretive field and produces more knowledge.

As the example of qualitative GIS shows, porting mixed methods to the digital humanities would help researchers definitively move past the quantitative/qualitative binarism.[14] This stands in contrast to how scholars like Goldstone and Franco Moretti have at times polemically made the case for a large-scale form of literary study that cannot be other than quantitative (Goldstone, "Social Science and Profanity"; Moretti). But their prescription of sociological and quantitative analysis to correct the "barrier to the production of knowledge" that current methods in the humanities throw up is not the only way to inject quantitative methods from the social sciences into humanistic work (Goldstone, "Social Science"). After all, the digital humanities are not a synonym for distant reading, nor should they be. In mixing methods, we incorporate quantitative modes of analysis without accepting the polemics that reduce other forms of humanistic inquiry to omphalic inward spirals of sacralization. That is, just as geographers mix, so can we. Mixed methods create a space for quantitatively minded digital scholarship that goes beyond the trend of "big data," allowing us to craft digital hermeneutic strategies for a handful of texts or even for just one.

For example, I read Ernest Hemingway's *For Whom the Bell Tolls* in a mixed methodological fashion informed by qualitative GIS.[15] I built a dataset of every instance of a toponym mentioned in the novel. Every instance belongs to a specific place, such as Madrid or Spain, which are mentioned fifty-three and twenty-two times, respectively. Before building the dataset, however, I noticed that the novel featured three particularly distinct rhetorical sites or planes of heteroglossia.[16] A "fabula" site reflected the action or plot of the novel. Next, a "discourse" site featured the conversations between characters. Finally, a "monologue" site contained Robert Jordan's interior monologues. Every time a place was mentioned in the text, I also assigned it to one of these three sites. Madrid is mentioned once in the fabula site, twenty-seven times in the discursive site, twenty-three times in Jordan's monologues, and twice in other sites.[17]

Already, an iterative, mixed methodological process alters the object under study with each pass, generating questions more quickly than answers. Step one: read the novel closely. Step two: switch methods, build a dataset, and incorporate a GIS to map the three different layers, each corresponding to a different site. Now a quantitative analysis (average nearest neighbor) of places in Spain (city-sized and smaller) across the three sites yields something that was not obvious in step one (see Figure 34.1). The Spain in Jordan's monologues is simultaneously broader than it is in any other site (its observed mean distance is the largest) and is also more clustered (its nearest neighbor index is the lowest).[18] That is, Jordan thinks about a larger

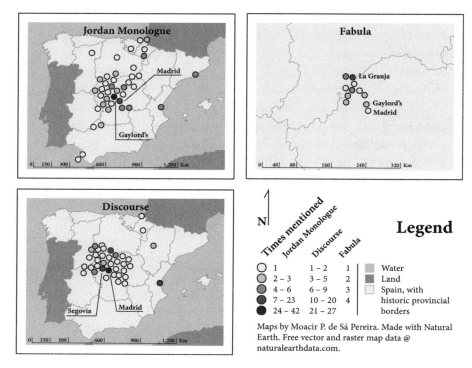

Figure 34.1. Cities, towns, and smaller locations in Spain mentioned in *For Whom the Bell Tolls,* shaded by the number of times mentioned. Places are split across three different sites. "Jordan Monologue" shows places mentioned in Robert Jordan's interior monologues, "Fabula" shows places where action occurs during the course of the novel, and "Discourse" shows places mentioned in conversations between characters. Places are artificially dispersed to reduce overlap. References to mountain ranges, provinces, regions, or Spain itself are not included. Maps by Moacir P. de Sá Pereira using free vector data provided by Natural Earth.

geographical Spain than the one that comes up in the plot or in conversations, but he is also notably fixated on Madrid and places in Madrid, especially Hotel Gaylord's, the communist headquarters that he mentions forty-two times.

The geostatistical analysis prompts a return to the novel in order to account for Jordan's sense of Spain. Step three, then, is another close reading, which offers a provisional conclusion: Jordan imagines himself as a sort of "pan-Spaniard" on a mission to unite the various "patrias chicas" of Spain into a single republican nation-state, necessarily, though only temporarily, under communist leadership. A fourth step of manipulating the data again or switching to a different method entirely would happily move the inquiry further along toward new questions, new conclusions.

As with a standard social scientific mixed methods project, I used both quantitative and qualitative techniques. But I also mixed my techniques by using some that I consider explicitly DH (GIS-driven geospatial analysis) and some non-DH (close reading, historicist analysis). What was important was mixing and iterating.

Mixing methods in the humanities need not involve a move from the macro (distant) to the micro (close), but rather can include a mixing performed iteratively over the same object(s). This makes the work an act of curating and composing, to use two of Rita Felski's Bruno Latour–inflected rationales for humanistic inquiry. Again, the digital humanities can become more sociological without necessarily becoming exclusively quantitative. This approach can give us a renewed relationship with the (aesthetic) pleasure of reading a single text, refusing to diminish the infinite world within its own pages, a world waiting to be explored, explained, and explored again.

NOTES

1. For the pedagogical issues emerging from introducing counting to English departments, see Chapter 19 by Goldstone, "Teaching Quantitative Methods: What Makes It Hard (in Literary Studies)."

2. In the pages of Kuhn's *The Structure of Scientific Revolutions,* Margaret Masterman counts "not less than twenty-one different senses" of "paradigm," a tally that clearly "makes paradigm-elucidation genuinely difficult for the superficial reader" (61).

3. Ian Hacking notes that the incommensurability of paradigms is something that only "later critics . . . obsess about" (xviii). Kuhn, in the fifth section of a postscript to the 1969 edition of *Structure,* explains concretely that paradigms require at least some communication between themselves (197–203).

4. See Lincoln and Guba, and Guba and Lincoln, for examples of scholarship on early paradigm wars that already makes space for pragmatic mixing of quantitative and qualitative methods.

5. The importance of this integration is underscored throughout the more recent literature that aims to integrate methods, philosophy/paradigm, and methodology. See, for example, Fetters and Molina-Azorin.

6. These four fields make up 81.5% of the empirical articles that the *Journal of Mixed Methods Research* has published. The rest of the articles "most commonly focus on other disciplines, such as geography, management, communication, sport sciences, anthropology, criminology, agriculture, sustainability, and other topics" (Molina-Azorin and Fetters, 150).

7. In addition to the work cited already, for other introductions to and histories of mixed methods, see Tashakkori and Teddlie, especially 1–39, and Creswell. For critiques of its efficacy, see, for example, Giddings, who argues that "clothed in a semblance of inclusiveness, mixed methods could serve as a cover for the continuing hegemony of positivism, and maintain the marginalisation of non-positivist research methodologies" (195).

8. This mixing should not be understood, however, as merely doing both "distant" and "close" reading at the same time, whose similar ontological assumptions about the stability of a literary work Katherine Bode notes (91).

9. "GIS" stands for "geographic information systems/science." Deciding what the S stood for was its own battle in the wars. See Wright, Goodchild, and Proctor; and Pickles.

10. For a general introduction to the GIS wars, see Crampton.

11. For an extensive bibliography of critical GIS up to 2012, see Wilson, "Critical GIS Readling List." For a "history of the present" of critical GIS, see Wilson, *New Lines.*

12. Nadine Schuurman argues for the importance of practitioner-driven critique by writing, "Critique that is motivated by a genuine desire to create a better GIS, and suggests practical means of improvement, is more palatable that one that finds fault from afar" (99). This phenomenon exhibits some resonance with the digital humanities, as this volume and its predecessors reveal.

13. Knigge and Cope call this mixing "grounded visualization," and its focus on iteration, recursion, exploration, and uncertainty makes it an especially promising model for mixed digital humanities ("Grounded Visualization").

14. Marianna Pavlovskaya argues, in fact, that GIS is not, ipso facto, quantitative.

15. What follows is an updated and heavily truncated version of the method and argument I make in Sá Pereira (112–58). For details on the problems with constructing the dataset, which I did "by hand"—meaning with no machine reading or named entity recognition—see Sá Pereira (205–21).

16. By "site" here, I have in mind the specific flat ontological sense of site as described in Marston, Jones, and Woodward; and Woodward, Jones, and Marston. For "heteroglossia," see Bakhtin.

17. Some instances fit none of these three sites, because they appear in the few short passages that are other characters' interior monologues.

18. For more on average nearest neighbor analysis, see Clark and Evans.

BIBLIOGRAPHY

Bakhtin, Mikhail Mikhailovich. "Discourse in the Novel." In *The Dialogic Imagination: Four Essays,* edited by Michael Holquist, 259–422. Translated by Caryl Emerson and Michael Holquist. Austin: University of Texas Press, 1981.

Bode, Katherine. "The Equivalence of 'Close' and 'Distant' Reading; or, toward a New Object for Data-Rich Literary History." *Modern Language Quarterly* 78, no. 1 (2017): 77–106. doi:10.1215/00267929-3699787.

Clark, Philip J., and Francis C. Evans. "Distance to Nearest Neighbor as a Measure of Spatial Relationships in Populations." *Ecology* 35, no. 4 (1954): 445–53. doi: 10.2307/1931034.

Cope, Meghan, and Sarah Elwood. "Conclusion: For Qualitative GIS." In Cope and Elwood, *Qualitative GIS,* 171–77. doi:10.4135/9780857024541.n10.

Cope, Meghan, and Sarah Elwood, eds. *Qualitative GIS: A Mixed Methods Approach.* Los Angeles: SAGE, 2009. doi:10.4135/9780857024541.

Crampton, Jeremy W. "GIS after Critique: What Next?" In *Mapping: A Critical Introduction to Cartography and GIS,* 98–111. Chichester, UK: Wiley-Blackwell, 2009. doi:10.1002/9781444317411.ch8.

Creswell, John W. *Research Design: Qualitative, Quantitative, and Mixed Methods Approaches.* 3rd ed. Thousand Oaks, Calif.: SAGE, 2009.

English, James F. "Everywhere and Nowhere: The Sociology of Literature after 'the Sociology of Literature.'" *New Literary History* 41, no. 2 (2010): v–xxiii. doi: 10.1353/nlh.2010.0005.

Felski, Rita. "Introduction." *New Literary History* 47, no. 2 (2016): 215–29. doi: 10.1353 /nlh.2016.0010.

Fetters, Michael D., and José Molina-Azorin. "The *Journal of Mixed Methods Research* Starts a New Decade: The Mixed Methods Research Integration Trilogy and its Dimensions." *Journal of Mixed Methods Research* 11, no. 3 (2017): 291–307. doi:10.1177/1558689817714066.

Giddings, Lynne S. "Mixed-Methods Research: Positivism Dressed in Drag?" *Journal of Research in Nursing* 11, no. 3 (2006): 195–203. doi:10.1177/1744987106064635.

Goldstone, Andrew. "At DH 2014." July 2, 2017, http://andrewgoldstone.com/blog/2014/07/02 /dh2014/.

Goldstone, Andrew. "Social Science and Profanity at DH 2014." July 26, 2014, http:// andrewgoldstone.com/blog/2014/07/26/dh-soc/.

Guba, Egon G., and Lincoln, Yvonna S. *Effective Evaluation: Improving the Usefulness of Evaluation Results through Responsive and Naturalistic Approaches.* San Francisco: Jossey-Bass, 1981.

Hacking, Ian. "Introductory Essay." In Kuhn, *The Structure of Scientific Revolutions,* i–xxxvii.

Knigge, LaDona, and Meghan Cope. "Grounded Visualization: Integrating the Analysis of Qualitative and Quantitative Data through Grounded Theory and Visualization." *Environment and Planning A* 38, no. 11 (2006): 2021–37. doi:10.1068/a37327.

Knigge, LaDona, and Meghan Cope. "Grounded Visualization and Scale: A Recursive Analysis of Community Spaces." In Cope and Elwood, *Qualitative GIS,* 95–114. doi: 10.4135/9780857024541.n6.

Kuhn, Thomas S. *The Structure of Scientific Revolutions.* 4th ed. Chicago: University of Chicago Press, 2012.

Lincoln, Yvonna S., and Egon G. Guba. *Naturalistic Inquiry.* Newbury Park, CA: SAGE, 1985.

Long, Hoyt, and Richard Jean So. "Literary Pattern Recognition: Modernism between Close Reading and Machine Learning." *Critical Inquiry* 42, no. 2 (2016): 235–67. doi:10.1086/684353.

Marston, Sallie A., John Paul Jones III, and Keith Woodward. "Human Geography without Scale." *Transactions of the Institute of British Geographers* 30, no. 4 (2005): 416–32. doi:10.1111/j.1475- 5661.2005.00180.x.

Masterman, Margaret. "The Nature of a Paradigm." In *Criticism and the Growth of Knowledge,* edited by Imre Lakatos and Alan Musgrave, 59–90. Cambridge: Cambridge University Press, 1970. doi:10.1017/CBO9781139171434.008.

Molina-Azorin, José F., and Michael D. Fetters. "The *Journal of Mixed Methods Research* Starts a New Decade: The First 10 Years in Review." *Journal of Mixed Methods Research* 11, no. 11 (2017): 143–155. doi:10.1177/1558689817696365.

Moretti, Franco. "Conjectures on World Literature." *New Left Review,* no. 1 (2000): 54–68.

Morgan, David L. "Paradigms Lost and Pragmatism Regained." *Journal of Mixed Methods Research* 1, no. 1 (2007): 48–76. doi:10.1177/2345678906292462.

Pavlovskaya, Marianna. "Non-Quantitative GIS." In Cope and Elwood, *Qualitative GIS,* 13–39. doi:10.4135/9780857024541.n2.

Pickles, John. "Tool or Science? GIS, Technoscience, and the Theoretical Turn." *Annals of the Association of American Geographers* 87, no. 2 (1997): 363–72. doi: 10.1111/0004–5608.00058.

Rosen, Jeremy. "Combining Close and Distant, or, the Utility of Genre Analysis: A Response to Matthew Wilkens's 'Contemporary Fiction by the Numbers.'" *Post45* (2011), http://post45.research.yale.edu/2011/12/combining-close-and-distant-or -the-utility-of-genre-analysis-a-response-to-matthew-wilkenss-contemporary -fiction-by-the-numbers/#identifier_0_1805.

Sá Pereira, Moacir P. de. "The Site of the Novel: Objects in American Realism, 1930–1940." PhD diss., University of Chicago, 2014.

Schuurman, Nadine. "Critical GIS: Theorizing an Emerging Discipline." *Cartographica* 36, no. 4 (1999): 1–107.

Smith, Neil. "History and Philosophy of Geography: Real Wars, Theory Wars." *Progress in Human Geography* 16, no. 2 (1992): 257–71. doi:10.1177/030913259201600208.

Tashakkori, Abbas, and John W. Creswell. "The New Era of Mixed Methods." *Journal of Mixed Methods Research* 1, no. 1 (2007): 3–7. doi:10.1177/2345678906293042.

Tashakkori, Abbas, and Charles Teddlie. *Mixed Methodology: Combining Qualitative and Quantitative Approaches.* Thousand Oaks, CA: SAGE, 1998.

Wilson, Matthew W. "Critical GIS Reading List." Critical GIS.com. May 29, 2012, http:// criticalgis.blogspot.com/p/critical-gis-bibliography.html.

Wilson, Matthew W. *New Lines: Critical GIS and the Trouble of the Map.* Minneapolis: University of Minnesota Press, 2017.

Woodward, Keith, John Paul Jones III, and Sallie A. Marston. "Of Eagles and Flies: Orientations toward the Site." *Area* 42, no. 3 (2010): 271–80. doi:10.1111/j.1475–4762 .2009.00922.x.

Wright, Dawn J., Michael F. Goodchild, and James D. Proctor. "GIS: Tool or Science? Demystifying the Persistent Ambiguity of GIS as 'Tool' versus 'Science.'" *Annals of the Association of American Geographers* 87, no. 2 (1997): 346–62. doi: 10.1111/0004–5608.872057.

From Humanities to Scholarship: Librarians, Labor, and the Digital

BOBBY L. SMILEY

In the years since I became a professional librarian in 2013, my workplace identity has shifted three times. First hired as a "digital humanities librarian," I saw my title changed within less than a year to "digital scholarship librarian," with a subject specialty later appended (American History). Some three-plus years later at a different institution, I now find myself a digital-less "religion and theology librarian." At the same time, in this position, my experience and expertise in digital humanities (or "digital scholarship") are assumed, and any associated duties are already baked into the job description itself.

These title changes may seem like superficial rebranding, but it is important to pause and interrogate their plural meanings. At least for the immediate future, "digital humanities" is a term of some durability, almost as immediately intelligible to those inside the library as it is to the broader academic world. Anecdotally, the same cannot be said of "digital scholarship." This label might mean something to my fellow librarians, but it can leave other colleagues elsewhere blinking in confusion. Considered from this librarian's perspective, it is hard not to speculate that the "cash-value" (as William James might call it) of "digital humanities" might reserve it only for those working outside the library, while "digital scholarship" could reaffirm an implied division of labor, saddling librarians with more traditional notions of library service, such as collection development or research and reference assistance. The term "digital humanities" signals an enterprise associated with knowledge production and intellectual activity. But can the all-encompassing "digital scholarship," which is a term that librarians almost alone embrace, have similar meaning? Does "digital scholarship" necessarily point to knowledge production, while also fostering and supporting it? And what about a title that elides the "digital" altogether? Does that change suggest a direction where library work in digital humanities is increasingly rendered invisible or buried? Or, in this context, has "digital humanities" become a set of loosely defined duties that have simply been folded into the professional expectations for humanities librarians? Am I more "librarian" or "digital humanist" or both, even if the title on my business card only reflects one role, but not the other?

The positionality that librarians inhabit inflects these questions with greater complexity. I write as a research-university–based "professional" librarian, whose credentials include a graduate library science degree from a program accredited by the American Library Association (ALA), augmented by a research-based graduate degree in the humanities. Among my colleagues at other research institutions and small liberal arts colleges, this educational background is common for those engaged in DH library work. But in this same community, there are also librarians oriented toward information technology, metadata and digital curation librarians, archivists, library programmers exclusively trained in computer science, educational technologists, alt-acs with PhDs, and postdoctoral fellows, in addition to hybrid librarians with multiple appointments requiring both a PhD and an accredited library degree (and split, for instance, between the library and the English Department). Jonathan Senchyne has written about the need to reimagine library and information science graduate education and develop its capacity to recognize, accommodate, and help train future library-based digital humanists in both computational research methods and discipline-focused humanities content (368–76). However, less attention has been paid to tracking where these digital humanities and digital scholarship librarians come from, the consequences and opportunities that arise from sourcing librarians from multiple professional and educational stations, and the more ontological issues associated with the nature of their labor—that is, what is understood *as* work for the digital humanist in the library and what librarians could be doing.

In the abstract, the diverse educational backgrounds of DH librarians should make little overall difference. "The character of the digital humanities as a community," Geoffrey Rockwell stresses, "comes in part from the provision of a safe and inclusive space where having a faculty position (or not) made no difference" (250). Unfortunately, working against building that community are often university politics or structural inequalities between the library and other campus units that can routinely make that "safe and inclusive space" a little less of both. For instance, having PhD-holding librarians without a library degree working in DH centers alongside professionally trained librarians lacking doctoral degrees should seem, at first blush, unexceptional. But when libraries and digital humanities—arenas overly concerned with monitoring boundaries for who is in or who is out—are twinned professionally, what surfaces are deeply embedded and obliquely acknowledged tensions that do much to upset the generally irenic culture of digital humanities (Berry, 34).

In the past, the prevailing assumption was that professional librarians are only those with ALA-accredited library science degrees. But as Phillip J. Jones argues, "librarian" as a professional label has become more of a floating signifier than a fixed title, and the training required to claim that role is hardly a settled subject (437–38). In the first half the twentieth century, opinion among library directors and library school professors remained divided over whether academic librarians needed degrees beyond training in library science, especially discipline-specific PhDs. But in 1975, the Association of College and Research Libraries (ACRL), the principal professional association for university librarians, declared that the ALA-accredited master's degree in library science should be considered terminal. Conversation about further degrees and debates about credentials were halted. In the years since, university libraries have generally followed this accredited library degree mandate in their hiring practices (437). But the anxiety among nondoctorate-holding librarians has been amplified whenever the issue of revisiting alternative credentials has been raised, often clumsily by library administrators. This clumsiness is usually exhibited around discussions about salary, possibilities for professional advancement, and politically sensitive concerns about the role of librarians in the university. In the face of these concerns, many librarians react with a defensive horror that effectively ices out any further conversation (437).

Lisa Spiro, executive director of Digital Scholarship Services at Rice University's Fondren Library, writes of injured pride and frustration over the "institutional and cultural barriers" for digital humanists who choose to become librarians without a library science degree. "Sometimes I feel like an awkward pre-teen," Spiro relates, "like I don't quite fit in anywhere." This sentiment is echoed by other nonlibrary-degree–holding librarians, including many CLIR (Council on Library and Information Resources) Postdoctoral Fellows in Academic Libraries, who bristle at the perspective held by some librarians that fellows simply "couldn't cut it" on the academic market" or were out to poach the librarian positions. On the flip side, concerns about professional standing and possibilities for advancement, both in the library and across campus, stoke worry among librarians, who feel they will be crowded out by a population whom, under different circumstances, they would be serving. While concerns about job security, professional advancement, and opportunities for scholarship are genuine and sometimes justified, this anxiety can elicit from new, nontraditional librarians an opposite, defiant response that rejects the label "librarian."

These concerns become even more complicated when libraries become the locus of DH activity, as they are in many places. Already wary of colleagues who represent potential professional competition, many librarians believe that DH librarianship does not always fit their understanding of what a librarian does. Consequently, some argue about the qualities of "real librarians"; they are often a little too quick to decide that certain colleagues are not "real" librarians, but rather are "academics working in a library," as if this distinction would make the title holder any different from any other librarian with similar responsibilities. Such voices reify static notions about librarianship; the title "librarian"—historically determined and bureaucratically codified—speaks as much to a site as it does to a set of duties.

But, of course, that is not how the title is read. In this instance, "real librarian" simultaneously functions as a defensive badge of professional pride for some and as a term of disapprobation for others. Instead of focusing on sharing and trading digital skills and subject expertise, the digital humanist in the library confronts a shopworn and tiresome question: Who (or what) is in or out? With little time and attention given to thinking more expansively and democratically about what we mean by "librarian," the conversation far too frequently (often sub rosa and expressed indirectly over happy hour drinks, blog posts, and myriad listservs) highlights, as Marx described the predicament of labor, the "*estrangement of man* from *man* [emphasis in original]."

And what about that labor? As I personally discovered about DH librarianship, the nature of my work is saying "yes" to almost everything. Job descriptions for DH library positions reflect this stance and range from curating institutional repositories to drafting research data management plans and open-access policies, from collaborating with faculty on grant-based digital projects to managing a digitally pitched subject specialty or overseeing emerging technologies and maker spaces, among other activities. For a library just starting to build a DH program and campus presence, the freshly appointed DH or digital scholarship librarian arrives already freighted with unrealistic expectations and presumed mastery over all matters technology driven. Because of the elastic nature of the typical DH librarian job description, there is often a desire for the DH librarian to serve as a messianic unicorn: a person who singularly can immediately bring a library up to speed and insert it into campus DH initiatives and conversations. "Much of the discussion about building a DH-friendly library environment leans too hard on individual librarians," explains Miriam Posner (44). Beyond the responsibilities of DH library work, what enables and sustains its possibility? Should institutional support be directed more to cultivating people who build digital projects or to the products of their labor? As Posner says in a different context, we should "commit to DH People, not DH Projects."

But complicating a focus on people rather than projects are additional sensitive, political—even existential—questions that surface for librarians building DH capacity. What is their role in that work and the meaning of the work itself? If there are librarians doing DH work, asks Dot Porter, the curator for digital research services at the University of Pennsylvania, then "what the heck is a DH academic?" In high-level discussions of digital humanities in the library, there is often invoked an implied and problematic division between "librarians" and "DH scholars/academics," as well as an argument for understanding the role of "librarians as digital sherpas," separating out the work of the "DH skilled-librarians" from "DH academics" (Alexander et al.; Schaffner and Erway). Such a perspective is consonant with the traditional service orientation of library work, which emphasizes the role librarians play in providing critical support and guidance for DH projects. While acknowledging the importance of providing research support and technical assistance, I also recoil at the idea that my role is only to enable scholarship, but not to produce it. As Trevor Muñoz writes, "Digital humanities in libraries isn't a service," and the key is to encourage librarians to develop their own digital projects. In placing people over projects, libraries need to encourage and provide librarians with opportunities to

generate original scholarship and not limit their role to supporting projects initi-
ated elsewhere on campus. And by reimagining what Bethany Nowviske calls "an
organizational service mentality," librarians should embrace their role as scholars,
where our work and expertise establish us as "true intellectual partners" in any collaborative endeavor (58).

But, as CUNY Graduate Center librarian Roxanne Shirazi has asked, we need to
consider whether "librarians work *in service of scholarship* or are . . . *servile to* scholars
[emphasis in original]." The idea of "service" becomes doubly complicated for digital humanists in the library, especially when professional expectations and personal
research require work well outside the understood province of academic librarianship. Librarianship, long considered a "semi-profession" like nursing or social work,
has historically had a disproportionally female workforce, whose work was characterized as a form of affective labor ("labor that produces or manipulates affects") and
subject to the inequities directed at those jobs (Hardt and Negri, 108). Like the invisibility of certain types of digital labor, the affective labor of librarianship, in sociologist Arlie Russell Hochschild's description, gives "the appearance of working at a low
level of skills," while also, as Shirazi maintains, in a generative sense "reproduces the
academy" through "service." (84) That is, librarians help sustain the conditions that
enable scholarship and learning, such as teaching information literacy or developing
digital tools for citation management. Implicit here is an understanding that scholarship generated in the name of library service is not scholarship, rightly understood.
But instead of jettisoning "service," DH librarians are beginning to reimagine it in
an expanded field, as scholarly labor that encompasses instruction, consultation,
collaboration, and collections work. Cross-campus or institutional collaborations
including librarians and faculty as peers help problematize the top-down nature of
scholarly production, but there is also a need, as Shirazi underlines, for an "acknowl-
edgement of the fact that there are different power relations at play in these collaborative relationships." By naming that legacy of marginalization, DH librarians can
begin to discern those power relations and structural inequities in greater relief and
reposition themselves as collaborators and intellectual peers.

The charged valence of service can often serve to slot digital humanists working in the library into a category distinct from colleagues stationed elsewhere on
campus. "It doesn't make sense to measure the digital humanist-ness of someone,"
Porter argues, "based on their current post (especially as digital humanists tend to
be fairly fluid, moving between posts inside and outside of the library)." At Michigan State University, for instance, DH librarians helm a lab for digital research in
the social sciences, as well as help oversee and teach digital humanities for the College of Arts and Letters (Smiley). Despite not having "librarian" included in their
job titles, they self-identify as librarians and frequently collaborate with them, but
are sited outside the library. The idea of "deeply embedded subject librarians" speaks
not only to Porter's claim but also suggests the manifold roles DH librarians can play
in the broader university community.

Ultimately, it is the institutional location of DH librarians, however they got there or were trained, that informs their professional identity or the nature of their work. All the same, for many that job title still remains overburdened with meaning and an unclear range of presumed responsibilities. By unpacking the complicated positionality of the DH librarian, we can have more candid and fruitful conversations about our labor, our identity, and our locations. I opened this chapter by asking, among other questions, whether I am more "librarian" or "digital humanist." Like all good binaries that beg to be transgressed, the answer is both. I am perhaps best described as a digital humanist librarian, a formulation that more aptly captures the contours of my professional life and emphasizes the complementarity of the words in that description. In my experience, if there is any sense of communion in DH work, it derives from the organic sharing of knowledge, the trading of ideas, and the complementing and augmenting of strengths—all done in a spirit of generosity and scholarly inquiry that animates projects, encourages outreach, and engenders the comity that DHers so often like to invoke. What was, to me, originally a question about job rebranding became a deeper search for meaning. I am concerned, however, that while we make an ecumenical gesture to include all disciplines, we may lose the scholarly commitments implicit in digital humanities, ceding intellectual labor for only the handling of back-end considerations. That librarians have been—and continue to be—integral participants in digital humanities *as* digital humanists should not be forgotten, regardless of title, degree, or academic station.

BIBLIOGRAPHY

Alexander, Laurie, Beau Case, Karen Downing, Melissa Gomis, Melissa, and Eric Maslowski. "Librarians and Scholars: Partners in Digital Humanities." *Educause Review Online* (June 2014), http://er.educause.edu/articles/2014/6/librarians-and-scholars-partners-in-digital-humanities. Accessed January 2017.

Berry, John N. "But Don't Call 'em Librarians." *Library Journal* 128, no. 18 (November 2003): 34–36.

Hardt, Michael, and Antonio Negri. *Multitude: War and Democracy in the Age of Empire.* New York: Penguin, 2004.

Hochschild, Arlie Russell. *The Managed Heart: Commercialization of Human Feeling.* Berkeley: University of California Press, 1983.

Jones, Phillip J. "Academic Graduate Work in Academic Librarianship: Historicizing ACRL's Terminal Degree Statement." *Journal of Academic Librarianship* 24, no. 6 (November 1998): 437–48.

Marx, Karl. "Estranged Labor." *Economic and Political Manuscripts of 1844.* https://www.marxists.org/archive/marx/works/1844/manuscripts/labour.htm. Accessed January 2017.

Muñoz, Trevor. "Digital Humanities in the Library Isn't a Service." August 2012, https://gist.github.com/trevormunoz/3415438. Accessed January 2017.

Nowviskie, Bethany. "Skunks in the Library: A Path to Production for Scholarly R&D." *Journal of Library Administration* 53, no. 1 (2013): 58.

Porter, Dot. "What if We Do, in Fact, Know Best? A Response to the OCLC Report on DH and Research Libraries." dh + li. February 2014, http://acrl.ala.org/dh/2014/02/12 /what-if-we-do-in-fact-know-best-a-response-to-the-oclc-report-on-dh-and -research-libraries/. Accessed January 2017.

Posner, Miriam. "No Half Measures: Overcoming Common Challenges to Doing Digital Humanities in the Library" *Journal of Library Administration* 53, no. 1 (2013): 44.

Rockwell, Geoffrey. "Inclusion in the Digital Humanities." In *Defining Digital Humanities: A Reader,* edited by M. Terras, J. Nyhan, and E. Vanhoutte, 250. Surrey, UK: Ashgate, 2013.

Schaffner, Jennifer, and Ricky Erway. *Does Every Research Library Need a Digital Humanities Center.* 2014, http://www.oclc.org/content/dam/research/publications /library/2014/oclcresearch-digital-humanities-center-2014.pdf. Accessed January 2017.

Senchyne, Jonathan. "Between Knowledge and Metaknowledge: Shifting Disciplinary Borders in Digital Humanities and Library and Information Studies." In *Debates in Digital Humanities 2016*, edited by Matthew K. Gold, and Laurie F. Klein, 68–76. Minneapolis: University of Minnesota Press, 2016.

Shirazi, Roxanne. "Reproducing the Academy: Librarians and the Question of Service in the Digital Humanities." July 2014, http://roxanneshirazi.com/2014/07/15/repro ducing-the-academy-librarians-and-the-question-of-service-in-the-digital-humani ties/. Accessed January 2017.

Smiley, Bobby. "'Deeply Embedded Subject Librarians': An Interview with Brandon Locke and Kristen Mapes." *Scene Reports.* dh + lib. February 2016, http://acrl.ala.org /dh/2016/02/10/deeply-embedded-subject-librarians-an-interview-with-brandon -locke-and-kristen-mapes/. Accessed January 2017.

Spiro, Lisa. "What Is *She* Doing Here? Crafting a Professional Identity as a Digital Humanist/Librarian." #altacademy: a mediacommons project. May 2011, http://mediacom mons.futureofthebook.org/alt-ac/pieces/what-she-doing-here. Accessed January 2017.

PART V

FORUM: ETHICS, THEORIES, AND PRACTICES OF CARE

Forum Introduction

LAUREN F. KLEIN AND MATTHEW K. GOLD

In her plenary address at the 2014 *Digital Humanities* conference, Bethany Nowviskie, then director of the Scholars' Lab at the University of Virginia, introduced herself as "a builder and a caretaker of systems," emphasizing the equal weight that building and caring each play—or should play—in the field (i5). By characterizing activities such as the maintenance of digital platforms and the enhancement of metadata schemes as acts of care, Nowviskie sought to place the work of the digital humanities in the much broader frame of the Anthropocene—and from there to deep geological time. But one crucial change between the environment of 2014 and that of today is the climate brought about by the current U.S. president and his toxic governance, which has brought increased violence to people of color, to immigrant communities, to transgender people, and to women—to name only a few of the many targeted groups. In this context, the *longue durée* of geological time still assuredly matters. But so do the living, breathing bodies of the people and the communities that sustain us today.

In assembling this forum on ethics, theories, and practices of care, we seek to draw attention to the range of forms of care that currently sustain the digital humanities as well as to the range of people, in a range of roles, who are currently performing this work. We also seek to promote additional thinking about how care might be even more fully theorized, practiced, or otherwise applied in the field in the future. These contributions do not claim to represent the full scope of discussion on the subject of care in the digital humanities; scholars such as Susan Brown, Kari Kraus, Roopika Risam, and Jacqueline Wernimont, among others, are also doing important work in this area. But the pieces in this forum, both individually and collectively, gesture toward a future of the field in which the work of care is centered in our digital practices, made visible to our wide-ranging communities, and acknowledged each day in our research, teaching, and service.

Capacity through Care

BETHANY NOWVISKIE

The sobering environmental and social challenges of the twenty-first century, challenges that face (and link) little cultures and fragile creatures across the implacable Anthropocene, must be met by an academy made *capable*—in every sense of that open-handed word. It is vital that we take a more capacious view of our history and possible futures and that we organize ourselves to work effectively, simultaneously, and in deep empathy and interconnection with other fields and disciplines across multiple, varied scales. Happily, new datasets and technologies position scholars to discover, interpret, and build on an understanding that has been long desired in the liberal arts: the knowledge of relationships among the largest and smallest of things. But our perpetually erupting anxieties about data-driven research and inquiry "at scale" seem to betray a deep-seated—and ill-timed—discomfort with the very notion of *increased capacity* in the humanities.

There are obvious and valid reasons for humanities scholars to be skeptical of big data analysis, distant reading, or work in the longue durée: they include problems of surveillance and privacy; the political ends to which data mining can be put and the systems of consumption and control in which it is complicit; intractable and cascading structural inequities in access to information; and disparities in sampling and representation, which limit the visibility of historical and present-day communities in our datasets or filter them through a hostile lens. We can further understand and respect a discomfort with vastness in fields that have, most particularly over the past half-century, focused intently on the *little stuff*: working in bits and bobs and "small things forgotten."[1]

Humanities scholars make theoretical and practical advances—including advances in the cause of social justice—by forwarding carefully observed, exquisitely described jewel-box examples. Our *small data* add nuance and offer counternarratives to understandings of history and the arts that would otherwise fall along blunter lines. The finest contribution of the past several decades of humanities research has been to broaden, contextualize, and challenge canonical collections and privileged views. Scholars do this by elevating instances of neglected or alternate lived experience—singular human conditions, often revealed to reflect the mainstream.

The most compelling arguments against algorithmic visualization and analysis are not therefore fueled by nostalgic scholarly conservatism, but rather emerge across the political spectrum.[2] Yet they share a common fear. Will the use of digital methods lead to an erosion of our most unique facility in the humanities, the aptitude for fine-grained and careful interpretive observation? In seeking macroscopic or synthetic views of arts and culture, will we forget to look carefully and take—or teach—care?

I see the well-established feminist *ethic and praxis of care* itself as a framework through which the digital humanities might advance in a deeply intertwingled, globalized, data-saturated age. An ethic of care—as formalized in the 1970s and 1980s by Carol Gilligan, Nel Noddings, Joan Tronto, Virginia Held, and others—means to reorient its practitioners' understanding in two essential ways. The first is toward a humanistic appreciation of *context, interdependence, and vulnerability*—of fragile, earthly things and their interrelation. The second is away from the supposedly objective evaluation and judgment of the philosophical mainstream of ethics—that is, away from criticism—and toward personal, worldly *action and response*. After all, the chief contribution of the informing feminist ethics of the eighteenth and nineteenth centuries, in relation to earlier forms of moral philosophy, was to see the self as most complete when in connection with others. Kantian morality and utilitarianism had valorized an impartial stance and posited that, as a man grew in judgment and developed ethical understanding, he separated himself from others. The mark of a fully developed (implicitly masculine) self was its ability to stand apart from and reason outside of familial systems and social bonds.

A feminist ethic of care seeks instead to illuminate the relationships of small components, one to another, within great systems—just as many platforms for large-scale visualization and analysis and scholars' research agendas do. Noddings identifies the roots of this brand of care in what she calls *engrossment*: that close attention to and focus on the other that provoke a productive appreciation of the standpoint or position of the cared-for person or group—or (I would say) of the qualities and affordances of an artifact, document, collection, or system requiring study or curation. Humanities scholars hone and experience engrossment in archival research and close reading. We perform it in explicating subjectivity. We reward each other for going deep. Yet one concern in the literature of care has been whether engrossment can impede critical, objective disinterest by becoming *too* intense.[3] I believe the answer is the same for caregiving (nursing, teaching, tending, mothering) as it is for humanities scholarship: real experts are those who manifest deep empathy, while still maintaining the level of distance necessary to perceive systemic effects and avoid projection of the self onto the other. In other words, empathetic appreciation of the positional or situated goes hand in hand with an increase in effective observational capacity. A *care*-filled humanities is by nature a capacious one.

To me, this suggests that the primary design desideratum for anthropocenic DH and cultural heritage systems must be the *facilitation of humanistic engrossment* through digital reading (viewing, listening, sensing) and large-scale analysis.[4] Let us build platforms that promote an understanding of the temporal vulnerability of the individual person or object; that more beautifully express the relationships of parts, one to another and to many a greater whole; and that instill, by cultivating depth of feeling in their users, an ethic of care: active, outward-facing, interdisciplinary, and expansive, sufficient to our daunting futures and broadened scope.

NOTES

1. A phrase from a historical probate record that became the title of James Deetz's seminal book on early American material culture.

2. For an example of the former, see Kirsch and similar essays in the *New Republic*.

3. On engrossment, see Noddings (17, 69). The best capsule summaries of the critique are to be found in Sander-Staudt, and Tong and Williams.

4. I fully describe the concept of the Anthropocene and offer connections to DH themes and concerns in a *DH 2014* keynote talk, later reprinted in *Digital Scholarship in the Humanities*.

BIBLIOGRAPHY

Deetz, James. *In Small Things Forgotten: An Archaeology of Early American Life*. New York: Anchor Doubleday, 1996.

Held, Virginia. *The Ethics of Care: Personal, Political, and Global*. 2nd ed. New York: Oxford University Press, 2006.

Keller, Jean. "Autonomy, Relationality, and Feminist Ethics." *Hypatia* 12, no. 2 (1997): 152–64.

Kirsch, Adam. "Technology Is Taking over English Departments: The False Promise of the Digital Humanities." *New Republic*, 2014, newrepublic.com/article/117428 /limits-digital-humanities-adam-kirsch.

Noddings, Nel. *Caring: A Feminine Approach to Ethics and Moral Education*. Berkeley: University of California Press, 1984.

Nowviskie, Bethany. "Digital Humanities in the Anthropocene." *Digital Scholarship in the Humanities* 30, suppl. 1 (2015): 4–15, nowviskie.org/2014/anthropocene/.

Sander-Staudt, Maureen. "Care Ethics." *The Internet Encyclopedia of Philosophy*. 2016, http:// www.iep.utm.edu/care-eth/.

Tong, Rosemarie. and Nancy Williams. "Feminist Ethics." In *The Stanford Encyclopedia of Philosophy*, edited by Edward N. Zalta. 2014, plato.stanford.edu/archives/fall2014 /entries/feminism-ethics/.

Tronto, Joan C. (1993). *Moral Boundaries: A Political Argument for an Ethic of Care*. New York: Routledge.

Material Care

STEVEN J. JACKSON

What does it mean to care for things and not just people? This question has occupied a recent and growing subset of work in science and technology studies and in allied programs in the humanities. In the humanities and critical social sciences, the star of "care" has enjoyed a recent and deserved ascendance, casting new light on forms of work and value obscured by other ways of imagining human action and relationality. Building from theoretical but also highly practical concerns in feminist scholarship and politics, care has been deployed to account for possibilities of meaning and action denied under the instrumentalist logics by, to, and through which we all too often reduce and devalue human action in the world. Theorists of care have also called out practical forms of labor rendered invisible under such accounts, revealing the crucial but oft-neglected work through which human meaning and value are made, supported, and sustained.

As the uptake of these ideas underscores, it is easy to care for the human, at least at the conceptual level (although we also find so many ways *not* to, from the mundane to the creative to the abhorrent). It is also easy to care for things as a kind of second-order human effect, such as the nostalgia item that recalls a past human relation or the object that adds ease, functionality, or beauty to our lives. And it is easy to care for things that appear charismatic in human eyes—one of the reasons that ecological action and knowledge have long tipped toward the cuddly and the picturesque (think pandas vs. bacteria, national parks vs. Superfund sites).

But can we care for things *as* things, and not for the refracted glow of the human that we perceive in them? What would it mean to do so? And what might this mean for the digital humanities?

These questions have exercised recent strains of philosophical work from environmental and multispecies ethics to object-oriented ontology and speculative realism. It also forms the core ethical proposition (and for some, the sticking point) of recent science and technology studies (STS) approaches like actor-network theory. Critical humanities scholars themselves have had a long and complicated relationship to this question. On the one hand, things remain (for us as scholars as for everyone else) a chief modality of our work. Some fields, like archaeology and material anthropology, have been built substantially on and by the bones of things. Others rely on the great institutions of archive and document, library and memory. All of us live in great houses made of paper and, as the digital humanities usefully attest, also bits, silicon, and code.

On the other hand, we fall all too often into the error of discounting or disdaining things, treating them as passing or vulgar manifestations of a higher or spiritual real: this is an error traceable to Hegel or, if one prefers, all the way back to Plato. Alternately, we fall into the endless loop and echo of representationalism, in which the value and interest of things are made epiphenomenal to the human itself: stage furniture in the drama of human action.

But what if the road (back) to the human leads through things—and things *as* things, with all their messy materialities intact? What if we have been a stuff-y species, a thing-y people, all along?

This is where care (and specifically *material* care) comes in—as an ethical proposition, but most simply and powerfully as simple empirical observation. From subways (Denis and Pontille), to soils (de la Bellacassa, "Making Time for Soil," to Samsung Galaxies (Houston et al.; Ahmed and Jackson)—to cite just a few of the examples offered by recent scholars who have started to make this argument—we *do* care for the object worlds around us and in ways that cannot be fully attributed to instrumentalist, human-only, or human-first logics (see Figure 38.1). Care here has an affective dimension, speaking to forms of attachment (even love?) that people regularly enter into with the object worlds around them. Care also speaks to a certain ethical commitment, a sustained engagement with the well-being of things *as things* undertaken beyond and beneath the instrumentalist relations usually held to govern our interactions with objects. As the image of caring for a patient or a sick child attests, care also names a kind of patient attending, a slow and attentive *being with* by which the trajectory of others is secured and sustained through time. And as its roots in feminist political economy remind us, care may also speak to a distributive and practical politics, reminding us that if things need care, it may also be necessary to recognize, honor, and sometimes even *pay for* that work.

In light of this work, to neglect material care as a facet of human existence in the world is to ignore the evidence all around us and to stick to a two-world story of human exceptionalism that simply does not, in my view, hold up. (It also sounds rather lonely). From the perspective advocated here, being human is not what is left over after the haze and shadow of things are stripped away: it is what comes out at the end of the process, a state achieved in concert with the things around us. Acts of care and repair (whether performed on soils or subway signs) produce not only different objects but also different fixers. For this reason, human nature is best approached not naked but fully clothed, or as argued elsewhere, "we're made human by addition, not subtraction" (Jackson and Kang).

Figure 38.1. Participants at the New York Fixer's Collective working to restore an iPhone 5.

This position has value for the digital humanities, I believe. It can help us think differently about the things that surround and constitute DH work: hardware and maker spaces, for example, but also the curl of old paper, the faded edges of photographs, and the indescribable smell and feel of (some) archives. It can help us toward a different sense of time and temporality, locating digital forms and moments within longer and care-ful histories that *do not* run inevitably and relentlessly forward. It can lead us to imagine and recognize different forms of work and engagement, pointing away from preoccupations with novelty and design and back to the centrality and creativity of maintenance and repair. And it can speak to ethical ideals and aspirations that we may also want to advance and uphold through our work. Affective attachment, mutual responsibility, patient attending: these are also virtues of a digital humanities worthy of the name.

BIBLIOGRAPHY

Ahmed, Syed Ishtiaque, and Steven J. Jackson, "Learning to Fix: Knowledge, Collaboration, and Mobile Phone Repair in Dhaka, Bangladesh." *Proceedings of the 2015 Information and Communication Technologies for Development (ICTD) Conference,* Singapore, May 2015.

de la Bellacassa, Maria Puig. "Making Time for Soil: Technoscientific Futurity and the Pace of Care." *Social Studies of Science* 45, no. 5 (2015): 691–716.

de la Bellacassa, Maria Puig. "Matters of Care in Technoscience: Assembling Neglected Things." *Social Studies of Science* 41, no. 1 (2011): 85–106.

Denis, Jerome, and David Pontille. "Material Ordering and the Care of Things." *Science, Technology, and Human Values* 40, no. 3 (2015): 338–67.

Houston, Lara, Steven J. Jackson, Daniela Rosner, Syed Ishtiaque Ahmed, Meg Young, and Leo Kang. "Values in Repair." *Proceedings of the 2016 SIGCHI Conference on Human Factors in Computing,* San Jose, Calif., May 7–12, 2016.

Jackson, Steven J. "Rethinking Repair." In *Media Technologies: Essays on Communication, Materiality, and Society,* edited by T. Gillespie, P. Boczkowski, and K. Foot, 221–39. Cambridge Mass.: MIT Press, 2014.

Jackson, Steven J., and Leo Kang, "Breakdown, Obsolescence and Reuse: HCI and the Art of Repair." *Proceedings of the 2014 SIGCHI Conference on Human Factors in Computing,* Toronto, April 2014.

Caring Archives of Subalternity?

RADHIKA GAJJALA

A rchives of subaltern histories are being built across sectors in India. But the question that needs to be raised is whether in the process of digitizing archives, we are losing out on a close look at the people—the subalterns— whose voice and agency are being traced and mapped. With funding coming from corporate media and interest generated by popular culture, archives of subalternity are being produced by online philanthropic and charity organizations, state-sponsored governance projects, and even digital social justice projects. Though these groups may embark on these projects with good intentions, many of them do not investigate subaltern histories or accord necessary participation in the digitization process to the subalterns themselves. Is being consigned to a dataset doing justice to subaltern history? What of the subaltern citizens themselves?

Still, considering the difficulty of digitizing and organizing information, these popular, commercial, and NGO-based renderings of the digital subaltern should— and will likely—significantly affect projects ranging from digital history collections to cultural archives to big datasets. We must consider how the commercial/marketing and philanthropy platforms themselves navigate issues of subalternity. Add to this mix the range of digital social justice projects that employ gamification and other tech-adjacent techniques in the hopes of connecting the "haves" and "have-nots" through virtual giving and sharing. There are also the big datasets and archives that have emerged through state-sponsored governance projects, such as India's UID biometrics project, as well as through entrepreneurial and social justice movements (Arora). In this context, what does it mean to build a caring humanities archive of subaltern contemporary lives?

Indeed, we may also ask if we should even be raising the question of "the subaltern." Digital presence and configurations of access—framed in ways that privilege neoliberal individualization—compel us to revisit the question of subaltern representation, speech, and presence in ways more complex and nuanced than in the traditional writing of history through collection of subaltern archives—whether oral, textual, or material in other ways. The project of producing, maintaining, and curating (even sometimes gatekeeping) archives of digital subalternity poses many issues. The text/image work and code work we do in the digital humanities are very important indeed, but these efforts must be supplemented and enhanced with dialogic, collaborative, and ethnographic immersion. Such immersion would entail actual travel to subaltern spaces for extended periods of time and honest reporting of self-transformations that occur through such immersive experience. Frictions and contradictions must be worked with—not simplified and flattened. In building archives of subalternity, we need the strong presence of countertexts and counterarguments to prevent those archives from being engulfed by the market logic that aspires to mobilize the "bottom of the pyramid" as consumers. Our charge as humanities teachers and scholars is therefore to continually recover critique through engagement with the communities we seek to understand. For these communities, access to digital archives (and technologies more generally) in and of itself does not ensure access to decision making around the use of those archives and technologies. To care, then, would mean to intervene on behalf of those communities with multiple and countertexts.

Hands-on digital and scholarly/theoretical interventions must draw on continual and repeated (critical, feminist) ethnographic journeys. Dynamics of offline and contextual political economy of the everyday will bypass us if we stay in one place for too long, even while attempting to develop a critical engagement. For instance, looking at examples of online microfinance (e.g., Kiva.org, milaap.org) or the use of comics to empower women in the face of rape (e.g., the digital comic book, *Priya Shakti*) or games for change that interactively narrate empowerment such as the Facebook group "Half the Sky" (see Gajjala), a researcher might begin to feel really good about subaltern empowerment and social justice movements. But it is only when the researcher goes offline and spends extended periods of time in the environments in which such projects are intended to be received that she will see how westward-looking and devoid of community context some of these projects (and even critiques of these projects) truly are.

For instance, what use is a digital comic for empowerment, or an app that allows microborrowing, when social panics within local community contexts have led to the banning of the very mobile technologies required to employ them? Such was the case in 2016, when the local village heads restricted the use of cell phones by girls and women in the interest of their own protection (The Quint). Building apps, writing comics, setting up an online microfinance site, and "gaming for change" in and of themselves do not fix social evils. It is who the builders of the site and the funders of the startup invite into the process of change, and who they envision as needing to be changed, that are key in how such projects are designed and implemented (Gajjala). For digital technologies to work in concert with social justice movements—to build *caring* DH projects—much deeper groundwork is needed. Hactivist projects such as those described by micha cárdenas in her article, "Trans of Color Poetics: Stitching Bodies, Concepts, and Algorithms," show the need for a great deal of care and attention to how change might be mobilized through digital technologies—taking into account the materiality of life and death.

In a global economy where care, altruism, and philanthropy are simultaneously commodified and circulated—where the idea of "sharing" is often reduced to a "click"; where affects flow, scatter, and bounce around; where immaterial labor is extracted through the interface—only ethnography, done hermeneutically and self-reflectively, can allow us to see care as a situated notion. When we begin to recognize how knowledge production is itself framed by a political economy that mobilizes affect and care to extract unpaid and underpaid work from subaltern and feminized bodies worldwide, we will better understand the complexity of issues of care in digital global space. Questions about an ethics of care should be answered differently based on who and what this emerging field of digital humanities comes to include and "what disciplines . . . we practice and propagate" (Bianco, 99). Nowviskie, Klein, and others have already highlighted some issues around the ethic of care and the contradictions inherent in the labor of care in digital space and in pedagogic environments. These are valuable, but we need more DH work that builds theory while engaging the dynamic lived practices reflective of its global context.

BIBLIOGRAPHY

Arora, P. "Bottom of the Data Pyramid: Big Data and the Global South." *International Journal of Communication* 10 (2016): 1681–99, http://ijoc.org/index.php/ijoc/article /view/4297.

Bianco, J. "This Digital Humanities Which Is Not One." *Debates in the Digital Humanities,* edited by Matthew K. Gold, 96–112. Minneapolis: University of Minnesota Press, 2012.

cárdenas, m. (2016). "Trans of Color Poetics: Stitching Bodies, Concepts, and Algorithms." *Scholar & Feminist Online 13,* no. 3–14 ,no. 1 (2016), http://sfonline.barnard .edu/traversing-technologies/.

Gajjala, Radhika. *Online Philanthropy in the Global North and South: Connecting, Microfinancing, and Gaming for Change.* Lanham, Md.: Lexington Press, 2017.

Klein, Lauren. "The Carework and Codework of the Digital Humanities." June 8, 2015, http://lklein.com/2015/06/the-carework-and-codework-of-the-digital-humanities/.

Nowviskie, Bethany "On Capacity and Care." October 4, 2015, http://nowviskie.org/2015 /on-capacity-and-care/.

Prahalad, Coimbatore Krishnarao. *The Fortune at the Bottom of the Pyramid, Revised and Updated 5th Anniversary Edition: Eradicating Poverty through Profits.* 2009 [Kindle Edition version]. Retrieved from Amazon.com.

Quint, The. "Women Don't Need Mobile Phones: UP, Gujarat Village Heads." February 20, 2016, http://www.thequint.com/india/2016/02/20/women-dont-need-mobile-phones -up-gujarat-village-heads.

Shakti, Priya. *Priya's Shakti.* http://www.priyashakti.com.

A Pedagogical Search for Home and Care

MARTA EFFINGER-CRICHLOW

I teach at a college, New York City College of Technology, which sits at the foot of a colossal steel-and-granite structure called the Brooklyn Bridge, which opened in 1883. A less visible but no less colossal site, the African Burial Ground, also located in Lower Manhattan, serves as the first setting of inquiry for one of the courses I teach in my capacity as a professor of African American Studies. This national monument, this sacred ground, holds the remains of 419 Africans and their descendants. My students learn that it was the only burial site for approximately 15,000 African Americans and their African ancestors during the 1600s and 1700s. It was on the outskirts of town because people of African descent could not be buried with the rest of the population, and African funerals were illegal. When I teach about the burial ground, I emphasize that its location on the outskirts reflects the literal and figurative marginalization of people of African descent. This so-called final resting place signifies, moreover, that people of African descent were not welcome in the city and that their care, even in death, was not of paramount concern to New York's other inhabitants. Despite these oppressive structures, I stress to my students that these burials also illustrate to us today how African people cared for their own, maintained their system of beliefs, resisted being marginalized, and simultaneously articulated their desire for a place—a home.

Broadly interpreted, home is an intimate setting where we first encounter belonging and care. For instance, according to *The African Burial Ground: Unearthing the African Presence in Colonial New York,* artifacts placed atop the coffins, such as "shells may have symbolized the passage between the realm of the living and the dead, which many African groups associated with water" (U.S. General Services Administration, 100). We might also interpret the shells atop the coffins as a pronouncement about belonging and care. The act of remembering helps this collective to remain rooted in the diaspora. "During the time the African Burial Ground was in use, enslaved Africans probably held one or more ceremonies at graves months or years after burial, just as they had done in Africa" (29). The living consistently proclaim that the dead matter. Caring is ritualized and is central to the (re)creation of home, particularly for Africans stripped from their original homes. The African Burial Ground thus becomes a critical site for not only teaching but also knowing, because it helps the students in my *Black New York* class dissect the visible from the invisible: not only at the site of the burial ground but also in the conceptual space of city, past and present (Richards).

One student reflected, "This picture [of the bones] is so disturbing. When I saw it chills ran down my spine. This picture also makes me think [where are the unidentified bones] of the rest of black New York?" The student identified an absence that was filled with meaning. Without ever using the term "care," my students questioned the ways, both visible and invisible, in which their city treated African peoples in life and in death. My students reside in this same metropolis today and bring their current understandings of New York City into face-to-face and online discussions about their own feelings of belonging. In *Reimagining Equality: Stories of Gender, Race, and Finding Home,* law professor and scholar Anita Hill says home is "the greatest signifier of our belonging and independence" (40). Hill's text has inspired me to ask myself how might I use additional geographic or symbolic homes, including both physical sites and digitized spaces, to engage students in critiques about humanity and inhumanity, particularly as they relate to issues of belonging and care (Effinger-Crichlow). For instance, what does it mean to be invisible to others and to be denied a home, or to be denied care, in a physical versus a digital space? What does it mean to be visible in a home, of any form, and to use that home to control one's care, to (re)shape the discourse, to memorialize the culture or one's own narrative?

As I have seen in my classes, the African Burial Ground inspires students to act as caregivers of their own New York City neighborhoods and to reject others' stereotypes about their communities. For instance, when a student dared to call the Bronx a borough of decay, another student, reared in the Bronx, offered a verbal tour by describing the ornate architecture of the apartment buildings that line Grand Concourse, a main street. This student sought to protect and validate his home and, in so doing, exhibited an act of care.

Sites like the African Burial Ground fuel my desire to help students understand belonging and care. The earliest Africans in New York and their African American descendants resisted New York's attempt to leave them homeless and erase their existence. Instead, these people of African descent turned inward to reflect on, celebrate, and nurture their collective humanity. Centuries later, these daily acts of care serve as a guide for students as they study and navigate New York's complex landscape.

BIBLIOGRAPHY

Effinger-Crichlow, Marta. "Mapping Black New York: An Interdisciplinary Search for Home." Keynote address at the National Endowment for the Humanities' (NEH)

Advanced Topics in the Digital Humanities Summer Institute, Center for Meeting and Learning, Lane Community College, Eugene, Ore., July 15, 2015.

Hill, Anita. *Reimagining Equality: Stories of Gender, Race and Finding Home*. Boston: Beacon Press, 2011.

Richards, Sandra L. "Writing the Absent Potential: Drama, Performance and the Canon of African-American Literature." In *Performance and Performativity*, edited by Andrew Parker and Even Kosofsky Sedgwick, 64–88. New York: Routledge, 1995.

U.S. General Services Administration. *The New York African Burial Ground: Unearthing the African Presence in Colonial New York*. Washington, D.C.: Howard University Press, 2009.

DH Adjuncts: Social Justice and Care

KATHI INMAN BERENS

I t is not a question of whether or not adjuncts teach digital humanities, but whether adjuncts' DH pedagogy is infrastructurally visible. As digital humanities migrates from R-1s to small liberal arts colleges, regional comprehensive universities, community colleges, and precariously funded local private institutions, it is apt to be taught by adjunct faculty.[1] Adjuncts comprise the majority of the nontenure-track humanities professoriate in the United States: 75.5 percent of humanities faculty are tenure-ineligible. Digital humanities is thus taught and learned by the most vulnerable people in higher education.[2] A DH ethic of care should explicitly facilitate access and equity for them.

Laura Sanders adjuncted for seven years before jumping to an interim dean position at the community college where she had cobbled together several part-time teaching and grant-writing jobs quarter to quarter. "I believe that DH is a social justice practice," she declares. "DH has the potential to level the playing field by giving underrepresented communities a voice and the opportunity to offer their own narratives. As my students develop digital confidence as well as the ability to interrogate how knowledge itself is constructed, they also develop the tools they need to authorize themselves to be part of larger conversations" (qtd. in Berens and Sanders).

Such liberatory possibilities transpire under conditions of constraint. Because adjuncts cannot rely on students' access to computers, Sanders instructs students to do what she calls "cell phone scholarship." In small groups, students use their phones to look up themes, characters, or other aspects of the readings and then present their findings to the class. In this way, Sanders's students learn to leverage their phones as knowledge tools, re-inflecting this quotidian communication device as a purveyor of materials for knowledge work. In another assignment, Sanders teaches students how to use their phones to tag PDFs in publicly accessible data collections, such as the historical restaurant menus held by the New York Public Library or the nineteenth-century ship logs housed at oldweather.org.

Cell phone pedagogy is one strategy of care, a remedy to what Alex Gil articulates as the "barrier-to-participation" problem in DH: "How can one work with computers in the humanities when one is situated in a place where the hardware is more than a decade old, or where the Internet connection is unreliable, if it exists at all?" Global Outlook DH [GO::DH], a special interest group of the Alliance of Digital Humanities Organizations, offers minimal computing as a way "to maximize access, decrease obsolescence, and reduce e-waste."[3] Although focused on the global dimensions of DH work, GO::DH—with its emphasis on local conditions—also provides an important frame for understanding how adjuncts and their students in the United States practice digital humanities under constraint. An "architecture of necessity" grows out of the projects designed and enacted by adjuncts and their students, a practical bricolage of tools and problem solving akin to the process of "poaching" that Michel de Certeau describes in *The Practice of Everyday Life* (174).[4] In every class I taught as an adjunct, which I did for three years between full-time jobs, I taught students to "poach": to identify a problem, find the free tools and the time (students often pool their labor), and make the appropriate intervention.

Guerilla tactics such as poaching are the hallmark of adjunct DH work. As an adjunct, I did not have access to university servers beyond participation in course management systems. At one institution, my email address was not even listed in the university's faculty directory. Freemium platforms like YouTube, Twitter, and Google Maps gave me the servers and platforms to host student work. When my students chose to build a web app optimized for mobile (the app is called DigiToolSC, published in fall 2011), I hosted the app on my own server because my employment status at the university was unstable, and the administrators I consulted could not find server space to host the project.

In a position paper I presented at the 2015 Modern Language Association conference, I asserted that it is not enough to make digital tools and tutorials freely available: we need to pay adjuncts for the time it takes for them to learn those digital skills (Berens, "Want to Save the Humanities?"). Financial support for adjunct professional development is becoming increasingly available, but the systemic problem is that very little money is set aside for adjunct salaries. Adjuncts' experience of having to survive on a clutch of part-time gigs is one of the deleterious effects that stem from the modular, commercial logic of higher education funding priorities, where money can be found to train, but not sustain, faculty. An ethic of care oriented toward adjuncts would begin by resisting such modularity, demanding a stop to hiring practices that cap adjunct faculty labor at just below full-time employment. According to the U.S. Bureau of Labor, in 2014 the number of involuntarily part-time workers in retail had doubled since 2007.[5] It is hard to imagine that a similar trend is not happening in higher education, as tenure lines are replaced with fixed-term and adjunct faculty.

Rosemary Feal, the former executive director of the Modern Language Association, speculates that if college rankings were affected by having high ratios of adjunct to full-time faculty, university accreditors "could change this [adjuncting] game overnight" (qtd. in Segran). That is exactly what English professors Talia Schaffer, Carolyn Betensky, and Seth Kahn advocate in a letter urging *U.S. News and World Reports* (*USNWR*) to consider adjusting the "faculty resources" section of the America's Best Colleges rankings to more accurately reflect current academic realities. "Currently you allocate only 5% of this category to part-time vs full-time faculty, while you give 35% to faculty salaries," they write. "However, those faculty salary numbers do not reflect the majority of college instructors, who are contingent faculty: underpaid temporary workers."[6] The letter garnered more than 1,200 signatures, about 75 percent of which were from tenured or tenure-track faculty. Robert Morse, head of the *USNWR* ranking team, met with Schaffer, Betensky and Kahn. The three scholars have formed Tenure for the Common Good, an activist group that aims to "transform" tenure from being associated principally with "the professional achievements and privileges of the individual scholar into one that, in addition," promotes fair labor conditions for all faculty. The group exhorts "tenured allies" to talk publicly and privately about adjunct labor conditions as a "precondition" to "organized efforts" because "the exploitation of contingent faculty degrades us all."[7]

Whether it is an ethic of care or a fear of tarnished status that motivates institutional change, advocating for a pendulum swing away from adjuncting and back toward full-time employment would be one way to ensure that the faculty members charged with teaching digital humanities have the financial and interpersonal support to do so.

NOTES

1. Fall 2017, I saw a national job advertisement seeking a "DH adjunct" to teach the core courses of a nascent "Digital Humanities and New Media" major at Molloy College on Long Island, New York.

2. "Facts about Adjuncts" is published by the New Faculty Majority (NFM) Foundation drawing on a 2009 U.S. Department of Education report. The NFM's Coalition on Academic Workforce collected survey data disclosing that "over 80% of [20,000 survey respondents] reported teaching part-time for more than three years, and over half for more than six years."

3. Alex Gil and Jentery Sayers's abstract for a minimal computing workshop, proposed for the Digital Humanities 2016 conference, elaborates key principles. The workshop did not run because it did not attract enough participants.

4. "Architecture of Necessity presents a compelling example of digital curation, but [Ernesto Oroza's] most important contribution to our conversations about diversity, definition, and scope—and by extension barrier-to-entry—comes from his work as an impromptu ethnographer of Cuba's DIY culture," writes Gil in the introduction to his interview with Oroza.

5. "In 2007, about 685,000 of a total of 19.2 million workers in the retail sector were involuntarily employed part time, according to the Bureau of Labor Statistics. By 2014, the number of involuntary part-time retail workers had more than doubled, to 1.4 million, even as the total number of retail workers declined to 18.9 million" (Tabuchi).

6. The letter is viewable but is no longer accepting signatures: https://docs.google.com/document/d/1ILg0QaMrhzQLQvfPbOrE4BClsWfw_pLNPAUAB4yVR7w/edit.

7. See the Tenure for a Common Good pinned announcement on their Facebook page.

BIBLIOGRAPHY

American Association of University Professors. "The Annual Report on the Economic Status of the Profession, 2012–13." http://www.aaup.org/report/heres-news-annual-report-economic-status-profession-2012–13. Accessed July 20, 2015.

American Association of University Professors. "Background Facts on Contingent Faculty." https://www.aaup.org/issues/contingency/background-facts. Accessed August 11, 2016.

Anderson, Katrina, Lindsey Bannister, Janey Dodd, Deanna Fong, Michelle Levy, and Lindsey Seatter. "Student Labour and Training in Digital Humanities." *Digital Humanities Quarterly* 10, no. 1, http://www.digitalhumanities.org/dhq/vol/10/1/000233/000233.html. Accessed August 11, 2016.

Berens, Kathi Inman. "Is Digital Humanities Adjuncting Infrastructurally Significant?" Presented at *Digital Humanities 2018*, Mexico City, June 2018.

Berens, Kathi Inman. "Want to Save the Humanities? Pay Adjuncts to Learn Digital Tools." *Disrupting Digital Humanities*. http://www.disruptingdh.com/want-to-save-the-humanities-pay-adjuncts-to-learn-digital-tools/. Accessed August 11, 2016.

Berens, Kathi Inman, and Laura Sanders. "Adjuncts and DH: Putting the Human Back in the Humanities." In *Disrupting Digital Humanities,* edited by Dorothy Kim and Jesse Stommel, 249–66. Goleta, Calif.: Punctum Press, 2018.

Davis, Rebecca Frost, Matthew K. Gold, Katherine Harris, and Jentery Sayers, eds. *Digital Pedagogy in the Humanities*. New York: Modern Language Association, forthcoming. http://www.digitalpedagogy.commons.mla.org/.

De Certeau, Michel. *The Practice of Everyday Life*. Berkeley: University of California Press. 1984.

DigiToolSC. http://www.berens.org/digitoolsc/. Accessed January 8, 2018.

Fredrickson, Caroline. "There Is No Excuse for How Universities Treat Adjuncts." *The Atlantic Monthly*, September 15, 2015, http://www.theatlantic.com/business/archive/2015/09/higher-education-college-adjunct-professor-salary/404461/. Accessed August 11, 2016.

Gil, Alex. "Interview with Ernesto Oroza." In *Debates in the Digital Humanities 2016*, edited by Matthew K. Gold and Lauren F. Klein. http://dhdebates.gc.cuny.edu/debates/text/67. Accessed August 11, 2016.

GO:DH. Minimal Computing Working Group. http://go-dh.github.io/mincomp/. Accessed January 6, 2017.

Gold, Matthew K., and Lauren F. Klein, eds. *Debates in the Digital Humanities 2016*. Min-neapolis: University of Minnesota Press. 2016. http://dhdebates.gc.cuny.edu/.

Jacobs, Ken, Ian Perry, and Jenifer MacGillvary. "The High Public Cost of Low Wages." U.C. Berkeley Center for Labor Research and Education Report. April 2015, http://laborcenter.berkeley.edu/pdf/2015/the-high-public-cost-of-low-wages.pdf. Accessed August 11, 2016.

McGrail, Anne. "The 'Whole Game': Digital Humanities at Community Colleges." In *Debates in the Digital Humanities 2016*, edited by Matthew K. Gold and Lauren F. Klein. http://dhdebates.gc.cuny.edu/debates/text/53. Accessed August 11, 2016.

New Faculty Majority Foundation. "Facts about Adjuncts." http://www.newfacultymajority.info/facts-about-adjuncts/. Accessed January 6, 2018.

Oroza, Ernesto. "Architecture of Necessity/Aquitectura de la necesidad." http://architectureofnecessity.com/. Accessed August 11, 2016.

Sanders, Laura. "Syllabus for Writing 227." http://tinyurl.com/SandersWR227Fall2015. Accessed August 11, 2016.

Sayers, Jentery, and Alex Gil. "Minimal Computing: A Workshop." http://dh2016.adho.org/abstracts/304. Accessed January 6, 2018.

Segran, Elizabeth. "The Adjunct Revolt: How Poor Professors Are Fighting Back." *The Atlantic Monthly,* April 28, 2014, http://www.theatlantic.com/business/archive/2014/04/the-adjunct-professor-crisis/361336/. Accessed August 11, 2016.

Tabuchi, Hiroko. "Next Goal for Walmart Workers: More Hours." *New York Times*, February 25, 2015, https://www.nytimes.com/2015/02/26/business/next-goal-for-walmart-workers-more-hours.html?_r=0. Accessed January 8, 2018.

Tenure for the Common Good website. http://www.tenureforthecommongood.org. Accessed November 28, 2018.

Tenure for the Common Good Facebook page. Pinned announcement, September 3, 2017, https://www.facebook.com/groups/163317600885815/permalink/163433924207516/.

Self-Care Is Crunk

THE CRUNK FEMINIST COLLECTIVE

The Crunk Feminist Collective (CFC) has always been committed to an ethic of community accountability and care. To accommodate and negotiate our external caregiving practices, we concentrate on self-care as a preface to our activism. As women-of-color scholar-activists who are also mothers, professors, graduate students, homegirls, partners, caregivers, breadwinners, bloggers, and daughters, we understood early on that our shifting selves, over the years and in the midst of our various circumstances and social justice projects, would require that we emphasize and strategize self-care with the same fervor with which we care for others. We imagine crunk self-care to be an attitude, practice, and legacy of Black feminism that we must incorporate into our lives for survival and well-being. While our foremothers did not have access to the digital technology that we do, the lessons and warnings they issued—around doing too much, being too accessible, and prioritizing others above ourselves—inform how we choose to engage our work in the digital humanities.

As crunk feminists, we see Black feminist community-building, or creating what we want and need as a group, as one of the necessities of self-care. This means that in addition to our online presence, which has facilitated a feminist support network and helped usher in the Black feminist voices and representations of women of color that we now enjoy on the interwebs, we value our off-line relationships. We understand that technology gives us the opportunity to reach folk en masse, but for online communities to be sustainable—and this includes DH communities—they must be supported by offline relationships. Having an in-person support network is necessary when we need child care, emotional support, or someone to bring soup and tissues.

Crunk feminist self-care thus becomes a means of resisting and disrupting the individualism that causes much of the harm we experience in society. We care for ourselves by caring for each other. We reject the idea that we should do anything alone. Crunk feminist self-care resembles the way our mamas, aunties, and grandmas collectively cooked meals, raised babies, and mourned losses. As graduate students, we collectively resisted classroom spaces that refused to acknowledge the contributions of Black feminist theorists by taking over portions of the class to say their names. As professionals, we prepare for job talks, interviews, and tenure reviews with a delicate balance of gossip and wine. We hold space for one another and prioritize our friendships. We hold Google Hangout strategy sessions to design game plans for figuring out difficult work situations. We send each other handwritten notes, celebrate each other's success, and take trips together. As bloggers, we publicly show love and support for one another and our sisters and kinfolk, biological and chosen, because we understand the necessity of having each other's backs and covering each other's fronts. Our commitment to collectivism is as crunk as our feminism. We actively refuse to do anything alone, so we collectivize every part of our existence and find new applications for the communal self-care of our mothers.

We also recognize that self-care has limits. Asking women of color who often have limited financial, emotional, and spiritual resources to dig deep in the wells to care for self seems misguided and rooted in a neoliberal narrative about self-sufficient forms of individualism. The expectation that women of color who struggle due to their individual circumstances should "take care of themselves" without assistance is also contrary to the collaborative intentions of DH work and fails to account for intersectionality. We understand that sometimes we reach the limits of our individual capacity. This is why we believe in collectivity. Collectivity facilitates our ability to care for ourselves better by placing us in community with those who are mutually committed to sharing the load. Sometimes, we care for each other online by moderating the comment sections of especially contentious blog posts for each other. Other times, we start a text thread that simply says, #selfcareis, urging a response from each crunk feminist and adding suggestions if we feel that the self-care plan offered is insufficient. Occasionally, disengagement from digital space altogether is another form of care.

We also always prioritize people over product. This means that if we need to adjust the CFC blog schedule to accommodate life events, we do. In this way and others, we have created a structure that prioritizes care as a critical component of our notions of collectivity. But we recognize that we need to engage in an expanded cultural conversation. We must explore what structural care looks like in family-leave policies, habitable and hospitable workplace environments, and the creation of digital spaces that are not rife with harassment and discursive violence. We believe we can use technology to dream and create "care-fully" designed community networks where we might be able to live and thrive with long-term financial, personal, professional, spiritual, and sexual self-care. To broaden our understanding of how we best care for self and how we represent that care in digital spaces, our goal has been to recognize how our "whole self" feels: where she lives, what she does, and how she is loving.

Crunk feminist self-care is something that has to be demanded incessantly. Our feminist foremothers told us that the most difficult words for black women to say are "no" and "help." So we have sent up prayers, written in our journals, and called on our sisterfriends, all in the name of finding the courage to say these two words. When we are finally able to part our lips to say no or to ask for help, we are not always prepared for the possibility that our self-care efforts will be rejected. When people we love get angry at our newfound "no's" or when our pleas for "help" go unanswered, we are reminded that mastering these words does not only change us but also changes the nature of our relationships. To place limits on what we will no longer do, or to ask those people who rely on us to hold us up, strips away their image of us as superwomen. Like Audre Lorde, we see self-care as a necessary "act of political warfare." Our crunkness inspires us to care for ourselves and each other first and foremost.

The Black Box and Speculative Care

MARK SAMPLE

The legendary computer scientist Alan Kay once criticized *SimCity* as "pernicious . . . a black box" that "children can't look at, question, or change." The problem for Kay is that the game makes assumptions about the world—say, what causes crime—and obscures them within a closed container of compiled code. A commonly used concept in science and technology studies, a black box is a system we understand, as Langdon Winner puts it, "solely in terms of its inputs and outputs" (365). Its inner workings remain arcane and unknowable, what Apple might call "automagical." A great deal of work in the digital humanities and related fields such as media archaeology and platform studies has concentrated on opening computational black boxes, exposing previously hidden logic, transactions, and histories. Tara McPherson's excavation of race in the history of Unix, Lisa Nakamura's recovery of the labor of Navajo women in semiconductor factories, and my own dive into the algorithms of crime in *SimCity* come to mind (Sample, "Criminal Code").

There is a different kind of black box, of course, a real one: the flight recorder aboard every commercial aircraft that tracks the plane's location, altitude, velocity, and other flight data. These black boxes are visceral reminders of what Paul Virilio calls the "integral accident" (32). Every new technology makes possible a new kind of accident, he explains. The invention of planes, for example, made plane crashes possible. The "integral accident" describes a failure so devastating—the plane crash—that designers build the technology, the plane, with its eventual catastrophic failure in mind. The future accident is integral to the technology itself. As Paul Benzon observes in a media archaeological history of flight recorders, a flight recorder's "singular purpose is to record and retain information when all else around it is damaged or destroyed." Benzon expands on this paradox between presence and absence, between legibility and inaccessibility, noting that "the black box and its informational content only 'appear' in the case of dysfunction and destruction." We only remember the black box on a plane after a plane crash. We avoid thinking about it up until we cannot. And then it becomes something like a bloody finger-print at the scene of a crime, mere evidence to reconstruct past events.

What can the (actually, orange) black box of the flight recorder tell us about the (metaphorical) black box of complex technological systems, whether *SimCity* or Unix? And what does it matter to the digital humanities, where we tend to approach the black boxes of technology with what Matthew Kirschenbaum calls a "foren-sic imagination"—recovering the past through artifacts and inscriptions often too microscopic or encoded to be seen or deciphered with the unaided eye (251)? The black boxes of our studies are the aftermath of history.

But what if we took black boxes not as the endpoint of history, but as an incep-tion point? What if the digital humanities understood black boxes—both literal and metaphorical black boxes—as a site for future-looking inquiries instead of a way to reconstruct the past? This reversal is an implicit challenge of Steven Jackson's remarkable essay, "Rethinking Repair." In a meditation on what he calls "broken world thinking," Jackson asks what happens when we take "erosion, breakdown, and decay, rather than novelty, growth, and progress, as our starting points in thinking through the nature, use, and effects of information technology and new media" (221). Evoking examples as varied as the Bangladeshi shipbreaking industry and Apple's MacBook Pro, Jackson calls on us to prioritize care, repair, and main-tenance ahead of innovation and design. Broken world thinking shifts us from the question, "How did they make that?" to the more subtle question, "How do they keep it running?" Extending this broken world thinking to the realm of the digital humanities forces us to reckon with black boxes before they become the wreckage of the past.

Digital humanities as a community is already heeding Jackson's call. Describ-ing herself as a "caretaker of systems" (2), Bethany Nowviskie powerfully dem-onstrates in her "Digital Humanities in the Anthropocene" what is at stake on an existential level for the humanities—not to mention, humanity—with regard to care and empathy. More recently Lisa Marie Rhody poignantly critiques one strand of digital humanities that playfully privileges breaking, which she finds at odds with her own experience making "sure that nothing breaks" with public DH projects. To allow projects such as Zotero to break would violate the pub-lic's trust, a tragedy no less devastating than a brick-and-mortar library shutting its doors.

But I wonder whether there is some middle space between maintenance and breaking where the ethics of care can coexist with what I have described as the deformative humanities ("Notes"). This is what I mean by suggesting that black boxes can engender future-looking inquiries in addition to reconstructions of the past or revelations about the present. Imagine a twist on Jackson's broken world thinking. Call it speculative care. Like the plane designed with its eventual crash in mind, speculative care builds new digital work from the ground up, assuming that it will eventually fail. Technology will change. Funding will stop. User needs evolve.

It is ideal for DH projects to launch with sustainability strategies already in place; speculative care demands that there also be obsolescence strategies in place. Speculative care goes beyond what Bethany Nowviskie and Dot Porter call the "graceful degradation" of DH projects. Whereas graceful degradation focuses primarily on weathering the vagaries of personnel or funding—changes external to the work itself—speculative care embeds broken world thinking into the digital tool or project itself. In other words, what integral accident can we design into our work? Like Nick Shay in Don DeLillo's *Underworld*, a novel obsessed with hidden systems, who "saw products as garbage even when they sat gleaming on store shelves, yet unbought." (121), speculative care *expects* digital work to eventually break and imagines what breakdown will look like, what functions it can serve, and how digital scholarship and digital creativity can still be useful when broken. "We didn't say, What kind of casserole will that make," Nick recalls in *Underworld*. "We said, What kind of garbage will that make?" (121). *What kind of garbage will our digital work become?* That is the question of speculative care. Speculative care in this way joins Kari Kraus's typology of subjunctive practices: conjectural methods that let us explore and infer the unknown.

In this conjectural context, black boxes serve not merely as grist for our forensic imaginations, set on with clinical precision. Rather, they provide sustenance for a different kind of imagination—the compassionate imagination that seeks to understand and care for the future, *now,* before it is broken, busted, wrecked, or beyond repair. Designing a digital world with its integral accident in mind is the task that lies ahead for the digital humanities.

BIBLIOGRAPHY

Benzon, Paul. "Lost in the Clouds: A Media Theory of Flight Recorders." In *The Routledge Companion to Media Studies and Digital Humanities,* edited by Jentery Sayers, 310–17. New York: Routledge, 2016.

DeLillo, Don. *Underworld.* New York: Simon & Schuster, 2007.

Jackson, Steven J. "Rethinking Repair." In *Media Technologies: Essays on Communication, Materiality, and Society,* edited by Tarleton Gillespie et al., 221–240. Cambridge, Mass.: MIT Press, 2014.

Kay, Alan. *Email to Don Hopkins.* November 10, 2007, http://www.facebook.com/topic .php?uid=6321982708&topic=3486.

Kirschenbaum, Matthew. *Mechanisms: New Media and the Forensic Imagination.* Cambridge, Mass.: MIT Press, 2008.

Kraus, Kari M. *Family of Subjunctive Practices.* 2016, https://docs.google.com/document /d/1aKtMon5LE7tRMOLo41HNDKrfEThp2nFLduLAPJ5Vvy4/edit.

McPherson, Tara. "U.S. Operating Systems at Mid-Century: The Intertwining of Race and UNIX." In *Race after the Internet,* edited by Lisa Nakamura and Peter Chow-White, 21–37. New York: Routledge, 2012.

Nakamura, Lisa. "Indigenous Circuits: Navajo Women and the Racialization of Early Electronic Manufacture." *American Quarterly* 66, no. 4 (2014): 919–41.

Nowviskie, Bethany. "Digital Humanities in the Anthropocene." *Digital Scholarship in the Humanities* 30, suppl. 1 (December 1, 2015): i4–i15. doi:10.1093/llc/fqv015.

Nowviskie, Bethany, and Dot Porter. "The Graceful Degradation Survey: Managing Digital Humanities Projects through Times of Transition and Decline." 2010, http://dh2010 .cch.kcl.ac.uk/academic-programme/abstracts/papers/html/ab-722.html.

Rhody, Lisa Marie. "*Building Trust: Designing Digital Projects for the Public through Care and Repair.*" Paper presented at the Modern Language Association, Austin, Texas, 2016.

Sample, Mark. "Criminal Code: Procedural Logic and Rhetorical Excess in Videogames." *Digital Humanities Quarterly* 7, no. 1 (2013), http://digitalhumanities.org/dhq/vol/7/1 /000153/000153.html.

Sample, Mark. "Notes towards a Deformed Humanities." *Sample Reality*. May 2, 2012, http://www.samplereality.com/2012/05/02/notes-towards-a-deformed-humanities/.

Virilio, Paul. *Virilio Live: Selected Interviews*. Edited by John Armitage. London: SAGE, 2001.

Winner, Langdon. "Upon Opening the Black Box and Finding It Empty: Social Constructivism and the Philosophy of Technology." *Science, Technology, & Human Values* 18, no. 3 (July 1993): 362–78.

A Care Worthy of Its Time

JUSSI PARIKKA

How does one imagine care for a post-anthropocentric world? Care for your software like you would care about yourself? Love your infrastructure? Such questions amuse as tongue-in-cheek versions of posthuman ethics, but lead also to discussions of, for example, political economy and political ecologies of technology. Why would you want to care for infrastructures that are installed by global digital corporations? What sorts and forms of care are there that actually link up to current discussions in the digital humanities, as well as in critical posthumanities?

Bethany Nowviskie gives important clues and cues as to where to go when considering care in the digital humanities. As she argues, referring to Steven Jackson's work on repair and with a nod to feminist theory, there is a body of writing about care that needs careful revisiting. One direction relates to rethinking subjectivity, the seemingly most intimate center of agency that itself needs to be radically opened to account for more than the subject as an individual self. A second direction seems to point to scales relating to climate change and, when discussing technology, especially to distributed infrastructures.

What remains implicit in Nowviskie's account can be elaborated with some more detail about what feminist studies of care can bring to the discussion. In such developments, the important steps have moved care from being a feminized and essentialized "skill" or "attitude" or moral theory to a political theory (Braidotti, *Transpositions,* 120). Joan Tronto's definition from the early 1990s is a useful addition to the debate:

> We suggest that caring be viewed as a species activity that includes everything that we do to maintain, continue and repair our "world" so that we can live in it as well as possible. That world includes our bodies, our selves, and our environment, all of which we seek to interweave in a complex, life-sustaining web. Caring thus consists of the sum total of practices by which we take care of ourselves, others and the natural world. (103)

Reading Tronto through Rosi Braidotti, one ends up on a vector that leads to a radical rethinking of the subject of care not merely as an agent in control but also as part of a wider milieu—as part of a web of care that becomes a collective, posthuman, and post-anthropocentric network that does not merely fold back on the human. Instead of a human-centered perspective, Braidotti claims that "animals, machines and earth 'others' can be equal partners in an ethical exchange" (*Transpositions,* 121). Care detaches from being merely a relation among humans and becomes involved in a wider, more radical political ecology (and hence also involved in questions about what sorts of power relations are embedded in the situations of care that are unevenly distributed across the social field).

Hence, another line of inquiry emerges—one in conversation with Nowviskie: How does one develop practices of care that deal with technology, particularly in the political economy in which we are involved? Practices of repair, and perhaps also work with media archaeology understood as an interest in the relevancy of so-called old or obsolete media in digital culture, offer some ways of doing so. Indeed, many of the practices and theoretical developments associated with media archaeology explicitly detach from the glamor of the new and the corporate rhetorics of the digital. Instead of merely the new and the recent, one can attach to the longer durations of technology in the humanities; this is to remind us of the importance of the multiple time levels on which media cultural—digital, even—time moves: to think of the new through the old, abandoned, and forgotten and to find ways that work against "psychopathia medialis" (Zielinski), the drive toward standardized, preordered media reality. Drawing on Deleuze and others, Verena Andermatt Conley develops the idea of "care of the possible"—a care attached to a future that works as a speculative ethico-politics too. Conley's idea emphasizes care as a philosophical practice that interfaces with the context of posthuman theory. It develops through "responsibility, caution, attentiveness, concern, a willingness less to look after than to relate to and engage with" an account of the situated affects that goes far beyond an assumption of a contained humanist subject that often excluded many of the realities of race and gender from its core.

And there is more: we need to ask how the subject of care becomes concerned with more than isolated objects in contained settings; how to develop effective practices of care that scale up from tinkering with individual devices so as to address issues of infrastructure as they pertain to contemporary culture. These questions parallel some of the discussions in curating at the moment: *curare,* to care for the networks in which technology is an essential infrastructure, both for the increasing array of cultural/art artifacts and processes and as infrastructure for the cultural institutions themselves (see Krysa).

This is an issue of both scale and political economy; in other words, questions of infrastructure are strongly embedded in power structures of ownership, in the distribution of rights and responsibilities, and in the grim realities of digital economy as corporate culture. How much is this corporate infrastructuring the ground on and against which digital humanities must negotiate issues of care both as ethics and as political economy? Issues of infrastructural, distributed scale, and political economy indeed overlap. As Nowviskie hints as well, one has to reflect on what sort of subject will need to be involved in DH projects that are radically engaged with the wider global scope of planetary issues. Does digital humanities have things to say about, for example, postcolonial issues in digital culture and the strange planetary ties of digital infrastructures, whether those of satellite realities of visual culture, of supply chains of materials, of resource extraction, or of electronic waste as the residual level of dead media (see, for example, Bratton; Cubitt; Parikka; Parks and Starosielski)? And can DH develop its own contribution to the issues of nonhuman scale, non-anthropocentric modes of knowledge that are worthy of its time (see Braidotti, *Transpositions,* 18; Andermatt Conley)? One provisional response resides in the theoretical ideas and practical ties (including experimental practice in art and design) that the field might develop in conversation with the body of existing thought in postcolonial and race studies, environmental humanities, feminist and queer theories, and critical posthumanities (see Braidotti, "The Critical Posthumanities"). Care thus becomes a venture into methodological choices and radical thought.

BIBLIOGRAPHY

Andermatt Conley, Verena. "A Care of the Possible: A Creative Fabulation." *Cultural Politics* 12, no. 3 (November 2016): 339–54.

Braidotti, Rosi. "The Critical Posthumanities, or: Is 'Medianatures' to 'Naturecultures' as 'Zoe' Is to 'Bios'"? *Cultural Politics* 12, no. 3 (November 2016).

Braidotti, Rosi. *Transpositions. On Nomadic Ethics.* Cambridge: Polity, 2006.

Bratton, Benjamin. *The Stack.* Cambridge, Mass.: MIT Press, 2016.

Cubitt, Sean. *Finite Media.* Durham, N.C.: Duke University Press, 2016.

Krysa, Joasia. "The Politics of Contemporary Curating. A Network Perspective." In *The Routledge Companion to Art and Politics,* edited by Randy Martin, 114–21. London: Routledge, 2015.

Nowviskie, Bethany. "Digital Humanities in the Anthropocene." *Digital Scholarship in the Humanities* 30, suppl. 1 (2014), http://dsh.oxfordjournals.org/content/30/suppl_1/i4.

Parikka, Jussi. *A Geology of Media.* Minneapolis: University of Minnesota Press, 2015.

Parks, Lisa, and Starosielski, Nicole, eds. *Signal Traffic: Critical Studies of Media Infrastructures.* Champaign: University of Illinois Press, 2015.

Tronto, Joan. *Moral Boundaries: A Political Argument for an Ethic of Care.* New York: Routledge, 1993.

Zielinski, Siegfried. *Deep Time of the Media: Toward an Archaeology of Hearing and Seeing by Technical Means.* Translated by Gloria Custance. Cambridge, Mass.: MIT Press, 2006.

Acknowledgments

First and foremost, the editors would like to thank the authors whose work is included in *Debates in the Digital Humanities 2019* for their intellectual contributions to the volume, their generosity, and their time. From the initial peer-to-peer review, through the editorial process, and up to the prepublication phase, they responded to tight deadlines (and long pauses) with insight, industry, and care. We are grateful to them for entrusting us with their scholarship and for bearing with us through our many rounds of editorial feedback.

We would also like to thank our colleagues at the University of Minnesota Press for their continued support of the Debates in the Digital Humanities series. The editorial vision of Doug Armato, director of the Press, has been central to the development of the series since its inception. Danielle Kasprzak, humanities editor, has provided invaluable support and guidance over the course of the book's publication process, as she has for each volume in the DDH series. Susan Doerr, assistant director and digital publishing and operations manager, has been a valued partner in thinking through the Manifold digital platform on which the book will appear. Anne Carter, editorial assistant, has been a constant source of information and expertise. The efforts of Daniel Ochsner, Michael Stoffel, and Rachel Moeller in the production department, and Melody Negron, of Westchester Publishing Services, have allowed the book to transform from Word documents into the polished volume that you see.

As the print volume moves online (http://dhdebates.gc.cuny.edu), we remain grateful to Zach Davis and the team at Cast Iron Coding for transferring the existing DDH site over to a Manifold instance and for preserving existing reader highlights and annotations along the way, to Lael Tyler for his design work, and to Terence Smyre at the Press for his help in preparing the digital editions of the books in the series. We thank the Andrew W. Mellon Foundation for making the creation of the Manifold platform possible. We would also like to thank Emily Hamilton, Heather Skinner, and Maggie Sattler at the Press for helping us publicize the volume.

We thank our institutions, The Graduate Center, CUNY, and the Georgia Institute of Technology, for their continued support of this project. In particular, we wish to thank Chase Robinson, Joy Connolly, Louise Lennihan, Julia Wrigley, David Olan, Josh Brumberg, Jacqueline Jones Royster, Richard Utz, Brian Peterson, Julie Suk, Steve Brier, Janet Murray, George Otte, Luke Waltzer, Duncan Faherty, Elizabeth Macaulay-Lewis, Maura Smale, Cathy Davidson, Lev Manovich, Katina Rogers, and the GC Digital Initiatives staff for their collaboration, collegiality, and support. A particular note of thanks is owed to Travis Bartley and Anna Rider, doctoral candidates in English at the Graduate Center, for their exemplary work as our editorial assistants.

Finally, our deepest thanks go to our partners, Liza and Greg; our children, Felix, Oliver, Loie, and Aurora; and their grandparents and caregivers, who have given us the time to bring this project to completion. We dedicate this book to you.

Contributors

R. C. ALVARADO is program director of the Data Science Institute and cochair of the Center for the Study of Data and Knowledge at the University of Virginia. He is co-PI of the Multepal Project, which seeks to create a thematic and analytic research collection around core Meso-american texts.

TAYLOR ARNOLD is assistant professor of statistics at the University of Richmond. He is coauthor of *Humanities Data in R* and *A Computational Approach to Statistical Learning*.

JAMES BAKER is senior lecturer in digital history and archives at the University of Sussex and at the Sussex Humanities Lab. He is author of *The Business of Satirical Prints in Late-Georgian England*.

KATHI INMAN BERENS is assistant professor of digital humanities and book publishing at Portland State University.

DAVID M. BERRY is professor of digital humanities at the University of Sussex. He is author of *Digital Humanities: Knowledge and Critique in a Digital Age*, *Postdigital Aesthetics*, and *Critical Theory and the Digital*, among other books.

CLAIRE BISHOP is an art historian and critic. She is professor in the PhD program in art history at The Graduate Center, City University of New York.

JAMES COLTRAIN is assistant professor of history at the University of Nebraska-Lincoln.

THE CRUNK FEMINIST COLLECTIVE is a community of scholar-activists from varied professions that aims to articulate a crunk feminist consciousness for people of color. The Collective's first book is the *The Crunk Feminist Collection*.

JOHANNA DRUCKER is Breslauer Professor of Bibliographical Studies at UCLA in the Department of Information Studies. She has published widely on the history of the book, graphic design, experimental typography, visual forms of knowledge production, and digital humanities.

JENNIFER EDMOND is associate professor of digital humanities at Trinity College Dublin and the codirector of the Trinity Centre for Digital Humanities. She serves as president of the board of directors of the pan-European research infrastructure for the arts and humanities DARIAH-EU, which she represents on a number of European policy-making bodies.

MARTA EFFINGER-CRICHLOW is associate professor of African American studies at New York City College of Technology-CUNY. She is author of *Staging Migrations toward an American West: From Ida B. Wells to Rhodessa Jones*.

M. BEATRICE FAZI is research fellow in digital humanities and computational culture at the Sussex Humanities Lab and faculty member of the School of Media, Film and Music, University of Sussex. She is author of *Contingent Computation: Abstraction, Experience, and Indeterminacy in Computational Aesthetics.*

KEVIN L. FERGUSON is associate professor of English at Queens College, City University of New York. He is author of *Eighties People: New Lives in the American Imagination.*

CURTIS FLETCHER is associate director of the Ahmanson Lab at the Sidney Harman Academy for Polymathic Study, USC Libraries, University of Southern California.

NEIL FRAISTAT is professor of English at the University of Maryland. He is coeditor of *The Complete Poetry of Percy Bysshe Shelley* and *The Cambridge Companion to Textual Scholarship.*

RADHIKA GAJJALA is professor of media and communication and of American culture studies at Bowling Green State University. Her books include *Online Philanthropy: Connecting, Microfinancing, and Gaming for Change; Cyberculture and the Subaltern;* and *Cyberselves: Feminist Ethnographies of South Asian Women.* Coedited collections include *Cyberfeminism 2.0, Global Media, Culture, and Identity, South Asian Technospaces,* and *Webbing Cyberfeminist Practice.*

MICHAEL GAVIN is associate professor of English at the University of South Carolina. He is author of *The Invention of English Criticism, 1650–1760.*

MATTHEW K. GOLD is associate professor of English and digital humanities at The Graduate Center, CUNY, where he is director of the GC Digital Scholarship Lab and adviser to the provost for digital initiatives. He is editor of *Debates in the Digital Humanities* (Minnesota, 2012) and, with Lauren F. Klein, coeditor of *Debates in the Digital Humanities 2016* (Minnesota).

ANDREW GOLDSTONE is associate professor of English at Rutgers University, New Brunswick, New Jersey. He is author of *Fictions of Autonomy: Modernism from Wilde to de Man.*

ANDREW GOMEZ is assistant professor of history at the University of Puget Sound.

ELYSE GRAHAM is assistant professor of digital humanities at Stony Brook University. She is author of *The Republic of Games.*

BRIAN GREENSPAN is associate professor in the Department of English, the doctoral program in cultural mediations, and the MA programs in digital humanities and human–computer interaction at Carleton University.

JOHN HUNTER is professor of comparative and digital humanities at Bucknell University. He is editor of Blackwell's *Renaissance Poetry and Prose.*

STEVEN J. JACKSON is associate professor of information science and science and technology studies and chair of the Department of Information Science at Cornell University.

COLLIN JENNINGS is assistant professor of English at Miami University.

LAUREN KERSEY is a graduate of the MA program in English at Saint Louis University.

LAUREN F. KLEIN is associate professor in the School of Literature, Media, and Communication at the Georgia Institute of Technology, where she is director of the Digital Humanities Lab. She is coeditor, with Matthew K. Gold, of *Debates in the Digital Humanities 2016* (Minnesota).

KARI KRAUS is associate professor of English at the University of Maryland.

SETH LONG is assistant professor of English at the University of Nebraska, Kearney.

LAURA MANDELL is professor of English and digital humanities at Texas A&M University. She is author of *Misogynous Economies: The Business of Literature in the Digital Age* and *Breaking the Book: Print Humanities in the Digital Age.*

RACHEL MANN is a PhD candidate at the University of South Carolina, where she is specializing in late seventeenth- and early eighteenth-century British literature, the history of science, and digital humanities.

JASON MITTELL is professor of film and media culture at Middlebury College. He is author or editor of six books, including *Complex TV: The Poetics of Contemporary Television Storytelling*, *Television and American Culture*, and *Narrative Theory and ADAPTATION.*

LINCOLN MULLEN is assistant professor in the Department of History and Art History at George Mason University. He is author of *The Chance of Salvation: A History of Conversion in America.*

TREVOR MUÑOZ is interim director of the Maryland Institute for Technology in the Humanities (MITH), as well as assistant dean for digital humanities research at the University of Maryland Libraries.

SAFIYA UMOJA NOBLE is associate professor at the University of California, Los Angeles. She is author of *Algorithms of Oppression: How Search Engines Reinforce Racism* and coeditor of *The Intersectional Internet: Race, Sex, Culture, and Class Online* and *Emotions, Technology, and Design.*

DAVID "JACK" NORTON is on the faculty in history at Normandale Community College in Bloomington, Minnesota.

BETHANY NOWVISKIE is executive director of the Digital Library Federation (DLF) at the Council on Library and Information Resources and research associate professor of digital humanities in the Department of English at the University of Virginia.

ÉLIKA ORTEGA is assistant professor in the Department of Cultures, Societies, and Global Studies at Northeastern University. She is working on her first manuscript, *Binding Media: Print-Digital Literature, 1980s–2010s.*

MARISA PARHAM is professor of English at Amherst College. She is author of *Haunting and Displacement in African American Literature and Culture* and coeditor of *Theorizing Glissant: Sites and Citations.*

JUSSI PARIKKA is professor of technological culture and aesthetics at University of Southampton. He is author of *Insect Media* (Minnesota, 2010) and *A Geology of Media* (Minnesota, 2015).

KYLE PARRY is assistant professor of history of art and visual culture at the University of California, Santa Cruz.

BRAD PASANEK is associate professor of English at the University of Virginia. He is author of *Metaphors of Mind: An Eighteenth-Century Dictionary.*

STEPHEN RAMSAY is Susan J. Rosowski Associate Professor of English at the University of Nebraska-Lincoln. He is author of *Reading Machines: Toward an Algorithmic Criticism* and coauthor, with Patrick Juola, of *Six Septembers: Mathematics for the Humanist.*

MATT RATTO is associate professor in the Faculty of Information and the Bell Canada Chair in Human–Computer Interaction at the University of Toronto. He is coeditor, with Megan Boler, of *DIY Citizenship: Critical Making and Social Media.*

KATIE RAWSON is director of learning innovation at the University of Pennsylvania Libraries.

BEN ROBERTS is lecturer in digital humanities at the University of Sussex.

DAVID S. ROH is associate professor of English and director of the Digital Matters Lab at the University of Utah. He is author of *Illegal Literature* and coeditor of *Techno-Orientalism.*

MARK SAMPLE is associate professor of digital studies at Davidson College. He is coauthor of *10 PRINT CHR$(205.5+RND(1)); : GOTO 10.*

MOACIR P. DE SÁ PEREIRA is assistant professor and faculty fellow of English at New York University.

TIM SHERRATT is associate professor of digital heritage at the University of Canberra.

BOBBY L. SMILEY is associate director of the Divinity Library at Vanderbilt University.

LAUREN TILTON is assistant professor of digital humanities at the University of Richmond.

TED UNDERWOOD is professor of information sciences and English at the University of Illinois, Urbana-Champaign. He is author of *The Work of the Sun* and *Why Literary Periods Mattered.*

MEGAN WARD is assistant professor of English at Oregon State University. She is author of *Seeming Human: Artificial Intelligence and Victorian Realist Character* and codirector of *Livingstone Online.*

CLAIRE WARWICK is professor of digital humanities in the Department of English Studies, Durham University. She is coeditor of *Digital Humanities in Practice.*

ALBAN WEBB is lecturer in media and cultural studies at the University of Sussex.

ADRIAN S. WISNICKI is associate professor of English at the University of Nebraska-Lincoln. He directs the *Livingstone Online* and Livingstone Spectral Imaging Project initiatives and is author of *Conspiracy, Revolution, and Terrorism from Victorian Fiction to the Modern Novel* and *Fieldwork of Empire, 1840–1900: Intercultural Dynamics in the Production of British Colonial Literature.*